'Do not read this if you are looking for tips on running "happy organisations", nor simplistic models taught in executive away days. Witzel analyses the essence of leadership, and of "followership". In Iraq during the "Surge" we tried to understand "the elastic" of our strategic leverage over competing power brokers: we might have done better had we read this book. A thought-provoking serious study for thoughtful, serious leaders.'

— *Lieutenant General (Retd) Sir Paul Newton*

'This outstanding book is a must-read. Witzel draws on a huge range of historical examples to offer genuinely new insights into an issue of central and enduring relevance. He reveals the complexity of leadership as it actually practiced for good or ill in different contexts. This is a timely warning against the simplistic formulaic models of leadership that still abound.'

— *John Child, Professor of Commerce, University of Birmingham, UK and author of 'Hierarchy: A Key Idea for Business and Society'*

'It is all here: the history, culture, psychology, philosophy, politics and practice of leadership, set out in clear detail, with rich learning worn very lightly. Morgen Witzel has done us a service by showing how deep the roots of leadership are, even if we are sometimes too easily distracted by the noise and posturing of today's "leaders".'

— *Stefan Stern, Visiting Professor in Management Practice, Cass Business School, City, University of London, UK*

'*A History of Leadership* offers a unique perspective on the study of leadership. By looking at how leadership has been practiced in the past, Morgen Witzel cuts through much of the vagueness of leadership theory and looks at leadership in practice, warts and all. Some of the book is uncomfortable reading; all of it is fascinating.'

— *Dominic Barton, Global Managing Partner Emeritus, McKinsey & Company*

'Sometimes you come across a book that you wish you'd written: this is one of those – a critical, wide ranging and global survey of the history of leadership that I doubt will be bettered for many years to come.'

— *Keith Grint, Emeritus Professor, Warwick Business School*

A HISTORY OF LEADERSHIP

The evolution of leadership into a widely accepted concept occurred without any shared understanding and acceptance of its meaning and relevance in contemporary society. Why do some people become leaders? What is the source and legitimacy of leadership power? This book journeys into the heart of the relationship between leaders and followers, the social space and the arena where both contest and collaboration take place and leadership itself is played out.

In the book, Morgen Witzel moves beyond traditional traits and skills framing, offering a fresh, historical analysis that involves many different actors with different motives and needs. By analysing the evolution of power relationships, the book analyses the interactions around how power is used and control is bargained for to illuminate the centrepiece of leadership.

A wide-ranging history of a slippery subject, this book provides students, scholars and reflective practitioners with an empirical, historical base on which to test their own ideas and experiences.

Morgen Witzel is a Fellow of the Centre for Leadership Studies, University of Exeter, UK.

A HISTORY OF LEADERSHIP

Morgen Witzel

LONDON AND NEW YORK

First published 2020
by Routledge
2 Park Square, Milton Park, Abingdon, Oxon OX14 4RN

and by Routledge
52 Vanderbilt Avenue, New York, NY 10017

Routledge is an imprint of the Taylor & Francis Group, an informa business

© 2020 Morgen Witzel

British Library Cataloguing-in-Publication Data
A catalogue record for this book is available from the British Library

Library of Congress Cataloging-in-Publication Data
A catalog record for this book has been requested

ISBN: 978-1-138-06202-3 (hbk)
ISBN: 978-1-138-06206-1 (pbk)
ISBN: 978-1-315-16184-6 (ebk)

Typeset in Bembo
by Apex CoVantage, LLC

CONTENTS

1

INTRODUCTION

Why a history of leadership? It is a reasonable question, given that we have yet to get to grips with the problems and challenges of leadership in our own age; why waste time worrying about what happened in the past? The answer is that by studying the past, we can hope to gain some new perspectives on our own time and place. Given that we do still struggle to understand how leadership works, or even to define it, any perspective or lens that can help us gain new knowledge and insights should be pressed into service. Applied history is using the past to study the present, and that is what this book attempts to do.

A History of Leadership does not have all the answers. It does not attempt to define leadership itself, although it does offer some different views on how leadership works. It is not a book about leadership theory; I have made passing reference to some elements of leadership theory, particularly older theories such as the Great Man, but on the whole I have approached the subject as a historian, not a scholar of leadership. I have tried to capture some of what leaders actually did in the past, how leadership was really practiced and, occasionally, how people thought it should be practiced; there are references to Max Weber, Machiavelli, Han Fei and so on – and the natures of their relationships with their followers.

The approach is historioethnographical; I have studied hundreds of leaders across a wide range of fields – including business, government, the military, sport, music, religious institutions and others – reported what they did and how they practiced leadership, and tried to make sense of the results. Where I have resorted to theory, it is usually to make references to theorists in fields such as psychology, sociology, politics, religion and so on to help make sense of some of the dynamics I have observed.

This book is also not a biographical dictionary of leaders. I have not gone into the career of any leader in detail; the endnotes provide sources for those who wish to know more about particular cases. I have also tried to bring in a broad range of leaders, including some obscure ones, who illustrate particular points. Winston

Churchill, Napoleon, Gandhi and others are mentioned, but I do not go into great detail about them. Some readers will be disappointed that their favourite historical leaders are given scant or no attention. My apologies in advance, but that is not the purpose of this book. This is a work about leadership, not leaders.

I have said that I used a historian's perspective, but I have also shied away from theories of history. I have been particularly keen to avoid any teleological notion or the stadial approach of the Enlightenment. I do not know if leadership is 'better' or 'worse' now than it was in the past, and I do not think that is the question that needs answering. One historical theory I am prepared to admit in limited form is socio-cultural evolution; society and culture do change, and this does affect leadership, but I again want to avoid any sense of evolution leading us towards perfectibilism. The evolution of leadership is a journey, but we have no idea what its destination is. Looking at the world around us today, it is hard to state with confidence that leadership today is making the world 'better' or that we are 'better able' to lead now than we were in past times. Leadership has changed; whether it has changed for better or for worse is not a judgement I am prepared to make.

Leadership is also an omnipresent phenomenon. Forms of leadership ranging from highly concentrated to highly distributed can be observed across every society in recorded history, and most of those societies have had something to say about it. There is a danger when looking at the vast history of this subject that one might be tempted to focus on just one society or one period in time, salami-slicing off the piece of the past that interests us and then assuming all leadership is just like that. I have tried to avoid this by following Fernand Braudel's example; I have looked at the *longue durée*, gone back in time as far as possible and covered as many cultures as possible.[1] Inevitably the coverage is uneven; Europe and North America still get a disproportionate amount of attention, and so does the more recent past. This has much to do with my own linguistic abilities as anything else; my historical attention is limited by the records and accounts I can read. However, I have sought to demonstrate that many of the problems and challenges of leadership, how leaders emerge and how they interact with their followers are common across all societies, at all times.

The structure of the book is thematic rather than chronological. This will, I acknowledge, annoy some readers; so will the fact that leaders like Napoleon, John Lewis and Emmeline Pankhurst keep popping up in different chapters that cover different themes. That is intentional. Leadership is complex, and so are leaders. They exhibit different behaviours and have multiple sources of power and authority. Their relationships with their followers are equally complex because followers are not homogenous and have different needs and demands of their own.

Part I of the book sets out the key themes that run through it. Chapter 2 looks at power, particularly at power relationships between leaders and followers, and examines the sources of leadership authority that have existed in the past, ranging from conferred authority deriving from relationships to a supernatural force or deity – in some extreme cases, leaders have even declared themselves to be gods – to the power that derives from followers and is granted (sometimes unwillingly) by them to the leader. The nature of their authority gives legitimacy to leaders and determines whether followers will accept them.

Chapter 3 looks at the exercise of power, defining the concept of the *social space*, the interaction between leaders and followers. This is where leadership is exercised and made real. Two processes go on within the social space: contest, where leaders and followers strive to exert power over the other and defend their own power, and collaboration, where leaders and followers work together to achieve the purpose of the organisation. As the book makes clear, both these processes happen simultaneously, and both are part of the essence of leadership; without them, nothing gets done. The chapter also looks at the purpose of leadership, focusing on what followers want from leaders and why they are willing to surrender some of their own power and accept leaders in the first place. Chapter 4 carries on by discussing what makes leaders acceptable, what behaviours and characteristics help them establish themselves in the eyes of followers and what happens when followers turn against their leaders.

Part II, 'Servants of God', looks at otherworldly sources of authority, ranging from explicitly claimed divine connections to a more general sense of spirituality which can emanate from within the self. In these cases, the leader's authority derives in part from connection with a higher plane, or at least something beyond mundane. Faith and spirituality have historically played a large role in helping people understand the world and their place and role in society; in much of the world, they still do. For leaders, this connection can establish their authority more clearly, as long as their claim is seen to be authentic. Claims either of a divine connection or even of divinity itself are not sufficient; followers must accept these claims and believe in them. A leader is a god only if his or her followers agree that they are.

Part III, 'Servants of power', is a deeper examination of power and contest, beginning with absolutism and totalitarianism as philosophies that attempted to concentrate more power in the hands of the leader. The book examines how the power relationships works and why followers agree to hand over power. A key element is the creation of an enemy – the 'Other' – who threatens the organisation or the state. The leader then poses as the one person who can save the day by defeating the Other. Out of fear, followers agree to give the leader power. However, the book also examines why so many absolutist leaders, in every form of endeavour, end up as failures. There are limits, it seems, to the tolerance of followers; they still demand a share of power, and if they are denied it, they may rebel.

Part IV, 'Servants of the people', looks more closely at the role played by followers in leadership. After discussing the nature of followership, the book goes on to look in more detail at how leaders are chosen and why. A chapter on accidental leaders, people who did not seek positions of power but were compelled, often reluctantly, to accept them, discusses why particular people are seen by followers as being good leaders, even if they do not see it in themselves. We also look at the concept of leadership as service and how far the concept can be extended.

Part V, 'Servants of darkness', looks at leaders and followers who use their power for corrupt purposes and malignant ends. Chapters discuss organisations such as terrorist groups, criminal gangs and doomsday cults. What makes people join such organisations? How are leaders chosen, and what do followers expect from them? Why do people choose to follow and give power to leaders who may give orders that are harmful to others or even to themselves? Why, ultimately, does someone obey an order to commit suicide?

These final chapters may make for uncomfortable reading, but they are important. There is a tendency in leadership literature to assume that leadership is a positive force, something that does good in society. One could make a philosophical case that this is what leadership *should* do, but the historical facts clearly state that it does not, or, at least, not always. Leadership and leaders have done incalculable harm and are still doing such today. If we are serious about the study of leadership, we should not shy away from that.

What, ultimately, is the purpose of the book? Its aim is to bring a fresh perspective to a heavily discussed and highly important subject, with a view to understanding a little more about what leadership has been and is today. At the heart of the book is the relationship between leaders and followers: the social space, the arena where the contest collaboration takes place and leadership itself is played out. We too often see leadership as something inherent in leaders. The traits and skills of the leader are important, but the process of leadership is something different; it involves many different actors with different motives and needs. Each of them has power; how they use their power and how they bargain for control is the centrepiece of leadership.

Note

1 Fernand Braudel, *Civilization and Capitalism*, trans. Siân Reynolds, London: HarperCollins, 1982; J.H. Hexter, 'Fernand Braudel and the *Monde Braudelien*', *Journal of Modern History* 44 (1972): 480–539.

PART I
Leadership through the ages

2

POWER, AUTHORITY AND LEADERSHIP

As noted in the introduction, it is extremely difficult to capture the evolution of leadership in a linear and chronological fashion, thanks to the wide variety of ways that leadership has been described and practised. No society, as far as I am aware, has ever adhered completely to a single model of leadership. Multiple, competing views of what leadership is – and what it should be – exist and have always existed. Early China, for example, abounded in theories of leadership, from the hardcore authoritarianism of the Legalists, to the paternalistic, relational model posited by the Confucians, to the light-touch *laissez-faire* approach proposed by the Daoists, with many more schools of thought in between. Although a neo-Confucian model of leadership did come to dominate in China, the influence of the other approaches persisted then and persist today.[1]

The same is true in other parts of the world. No matter the dominant view of leadership, there were always competing schools of thought rooted in differing religious beliefs, cultural values and societal and personal expectations. However, despite this kaleidoscope of views, I feel it would be helpful to attempt to sketch out some of the ways in which leadership can be seen to have changed over time, if only to create a background for the discussions in the rest of this book. This sketch will focus on the *longue durée*, looking at deep-rooted generic changes, with a few examples to illustrate. Once again, though, we must avoid any attempt at teleology or perfectibilism. Our purpose here is not to attempt to discover some perfect form of leadership but to observe what has happened in the past to try to draw lessons from it.

Two trends in particular can be identified. First, in most societies, as power distance decreases – generally, it has decreased over time – leadership becomes somewhat less authoritarian and less ceremonial. This does not mean that authoritarianism and ceremony disappear, not by any means; but they are no longer the absolute bedrock on which leadership rests. Leaders in low-power distance societies who continue to try to rely on authority and ceremony are likely to struggle to make impact.

Second, and closely related to the first trend, the sources of the leader's authority have also changed over time. The notion that leadership is conferred on the leader by an external divine force or that certain individuals have a right to lead others is on the wane (although old habits are proving reluctant to die). Increasingly, leadership now emanates from the relationship between leaders and followers. This, too, is a consequence of changes in power distance, and it is to this concept that we should now turn our attention.

Power distance

Power distance refers to the unequal distribution of power within a society. The concept, first fully articulated by Geert Hofstede, suggests that different societies have different power structures depending on how power is concentrated or dispersed.[2] Although the ideas behind power distance had been discussed before, Hofstede's contribution was to create a method of measuring and quantifying power distance as part of a larger attempt to measure differences between cultures. According to Hofstede, in societies with a high power-distance score, power is strongly concentrated in the hands of a few. These societies tend to be very hierarchical and formal. People know their place in the hierarchy and conform to it. In contrast, societies with low power-distance scores tend to be less hierarchical, and relations between leaders and followers are less formal.

The theory further assumes that people in high power-distance cultures accept their situation and are happy to live with it and, indeed, that they are uncomfortable without a strong hierarchy to support them. Knowing their place makes people comfortable, whereas not knowing where they stand in the hierarchy can induce uncertainty and fear. That assumption, however, is easily challenged. Mauk Mulder's work on power distance shows that once power begins to weaken, those at the bottom of the hierarchy are quick to reject their position and attempt to seize more power for themselves and reduce the power distance. In response, privileged individuals who already have access to power will push back, attempting to protect what they hold and, if possible, increase their power at the expense of those less fortunate.[3]

We can see a good example of this tension in the history of China, which has one of the highest power-distance scores on Hofstede's index, indicating a strongly authoritarian, hierarchical society with power concentrated at the top. In the past it was often assumed that the Chinese people were somehow happy with this arrangement and content to accept their lot. Authoritarian government was seen as something that was essential to China, part of the natural law. Typical of this view was Max Weber's book *The Religion of China*, which painted a picture of a stagnant society, virtually immune to change and dominated by the dead hand of tradition.[4]

However, a quick glance at Chinese history shows how wrong this is. W. J.F. Jenner remarked not only that the history of imperial China is the history of tyranny but also that it is the history of rebellion.[5] The White Lotus Society, the Taipings, the Kuomintang and the Communist Party are just a few examples of very powerful rebel movements during the last three centuries. Although the first two were ultimately unsuccessful, they still shook Chinese state and society to their core.[6] Rebellion against authority is nothing new in China, and if surveys show that the Chinese people are more accepting of authority, we should probably question whether these surveys are wholly accurate.

Mulder's work suggests that power distance is a consequence of power itself; that is, if society is structured in such a way that power is concentrated in the hands of a few, the 'few' will make every effort to distance themselves from the 'many' in order to preserve their power. Conversely, if power is more widely distributed, the 'many' have a better chance of consolidating their own position and preventing the 'few' from acquiring more power and increasing power distance. Confirmation of this comes from the field of development economics, where the work of Debraj Ray and Amartya Sen, among others, shows how societies where power is concentrated in the hands of elites tend also to be societies with the highest levels of inequality. Breaking down that inequality nearly always involves dismantling the hierarchies of elites.[7]

Our few glimpses into prehistoric civilisations suggest that power distance was actually fairly low. During the Neolithic period, power in most societies was dispersed among kinship groups and clans rather than centralised at any higher level (although there were exceptions in parts of South America and Hawai'i, where larger polities evolved).[8] Modern anthropological studies of less developed societies tend to confirm this. Malinowski, in his early-twentieth-century study of the islanders of Melanesia, went as far as to claim that the people he studied had no concept of organisation, let alone leadership, and were incapable of imagining anything beyond individual self-motive; later, less paternalistic observers, such as Jared Diamond, depicted societies in which leadership is very light touch, with individuals already knowing what needs to be done and the leader there acting largely as wise councillor to adjudicate disputes.[9]

But by the time of the first great settled civilisations, in Mesopotamia, the Nile Delta and the valleys of the Ganges and the Yellow River, power distance was on the increase. As Diamond points out, the emergence of agriculture as the dominant form of food production – as opposed to the hunter-gatherer model of the Neolithic period – led to greater social stratification and inequality. Paradoxically, those who produced the food lost power to those who lived off the surpluses generated by agricultural labourers.[10] These societies became increasingly hierarchical, with a high degree of power distance. The technological revolutions of the Bronze Age and the Iron Age made societies still more complex. New agricultural tools expanded food production, and new weapons enabled warfare on a larger scale with more formal tactics.[11] Long-distance trade and exchanging surplus food for scarce metals led to the appearance of the first professional businessmen and women.[12] In Plato's *Republic*, he describes the new complexity of society, including such features as the division of labour and the emergence of markets.[13]

All this complexity needed guidance and direction, and the leaders who provided that direction – war leaders, priests, wealthy traders – were able to use their status as leaders to gather more power. Whether the marked increase in power distance that occurs around this time is due to the fact that the leaders needed power if they were to function effectively, as early works on statecraft, such as those of Kautilya and Han Fei, seem to indicate, or that the elites had the ability to seize power from the masses and hoard it, as modern Marxian analysis suggests, is a moot point.[14]

The elites now had, often literally, power of life and death over those who fell below them in the power structure. Despite this, they did not go unchallenged. Famously, in Athens, 399 BC, Socrates was put to death for questioning authority, and his acolyte Plato spent much of his career trying to create an ideal society where power derived from the people, not from some collection of remote deities on the heights of Olympus.[15] The Roman Republic also saw repeated challenges to its legitimacy, eventually collapsing into civil war and metamorphosing into the Roman Empire, which resulted in an even further increase in power distance.

During the Middle Ages in Western Europe, partly as a result of a medieval rediscovery of the philosophy of Plato, challenges to the hierarchy became more frequent and intense.[16] The revolts of Cola di Rienzo in Rome and Wat Tyler in England (fourteenth century) and Jan Hus in Bohemia and Girolamo Savonarola in Florence (fifteenth century) were not just protests by discontented peasants; each revolt had the deliberate aim of breaking the existing hierarchy, wresting power from existing civil and religious authorities and – ostensibly, at least – giving it to the people, thereby decreasing power distance.[17] These four men are examples of leaders who emerge from a particular state of social, political and religious turmoil derive their authority directly from the people they lead rather than existing formal power structures.

All failed, but they were straws in the wind. Beginning in the early sixteenth century, a succession of hammer blows broke down existing power structures – the Protestant Reformation, with its greater emphasis on personal responsibility for both prosperity and salvation; the eighteenth-century European Enlightenment, which rejected belief in favour of personal experience and pure faith in favour of pure reason; the Industrial Revolution, which challenged the old economic order (only to replace it with a new one); the French Revolution, with its assertion of the rights of man, and, equally importantly, the Suffragette Revolution, which further asserted the rights of women; and the further decline of faith in the twentieth century and the growing scepticism about the role of 'experts'. New structures rose to replace them, but the new order rarely managed to grab back the power that the old order had once possessed. Power-distance scores – and I accept the criticisms of Hofstede's theory and acknowledge that this is a crude (yet still useful) tool – are lower in Western societies (and lower still in largely Protestant societies) than in other parts of the world; thus, we can hypothesise that they are lower now than they would have been a hundred years ago – or a thousand years ago – had the tools to measure power distance existed.

South and East Asia, on the other hand, followed different historical trajectories. The British conquest of India increased power distance as the elites of first the East India Company and then the Raj deliberately placed barriers between themselves and the rest of the population and gathered more power to themselves. Only after India achieved independence did power distance begin, very slowly, to decline.[18]

In China, as noted, there is a long history of rebellion, but unlike the Reformation and the French Revolution, for many centuries the elites were strong enough to suppress the rebels and preserve their power. The 1911 revolution in China brought about a partial dismantling of the old structure, and the 1949 revolution saw a complete change at the helm; the old empire and republic elites were replaced with the new elites of the Communist Party.[19] Those elites still exist, but the economic reforms that began in 1979 have resulted in the creation of new elites emerging out of the worlds of finance and business. There is considerable overlap between these groups, but there is also occasional friction when their interests are not fully aligned. On the whole, power distance in China has declined, as Deng Xiaoping anticipated when he first set out the blueprint for economic reform, but once again the process has been slow, and it has not been without considerable push-back from the elites.[20]

Japan's trajectory has also been different. Faced with an assault on power not so much from the inside but from the outside, in the form of foreign traders and missionaries who were perceived as a threat to the status quo, the elites of the Tokugawa shogunate, in 1600 AD, sealed off the country from foreign influence and practised a form of barely diluted autocracy for more than three hundred years. The revolution, when it finally came, was driven not only by those who had been excluded from power by the Tokugawa regime – including the imperial family, which had ruled in name only, as power was concentrated in the hands of the *shogun* – but also by a faction within the elite party that recognised that the current system was unsustainable and agreed to give up part of its power in order to preserve itself.[21]

Yet again, new elites replaced old ones. By the end of the Russo-Japanese War Japan's burgeoning military-industrial complex had effectively usurped power and kept a tight hold on it until the final collapse.[22] Further change occurred during the American post-war occupation, with the military-industrial complex dismantled and a new, more democratic economic and political elite installed in its place. Yet Japan remains a strongly hierarchical society.[23] This is evident both in business and in politics and society, in the respect shown by junior managers to their seniors and the persistence of ceremonial aspects of leadership, such as company flags and company songs.[24]

To sum up, power distance is not static. As a concept, it is dynamic, fluid and often full of conflict and aggression. Nor is the victory of the masses inevitable, as Karl Marx had believed. The struggle for power is continuous, and the party that wins is the one best able to grab and keep power. As Machiavelli said, 'if we consider the objects of the nobles and the people. we must see that the first have a great desire to dominate, whilst the latter have only the desire not to be dominated, and consequently a greater desire to live in the enjoyment of liberty'.[25]

Paradoxically, how well they are able to do so, in turn, depends on leadership. The skill and ability of popular leaders like Savonarola, Oliver Cromwell, Maximilien Robespierre or Mao Zedong to claim power from the elites is one factor in the reduction of power distance, and that reduction in turn affects the nature of leadership, creating a circular process. Leaders who come from the elites tend to reinforce their position by relying on authority and ceremony; that is, 'I am the leader, and you will obey me, and the more often you obey me the more powerful I become'. Popular leaders who emerge when power distance is reduced are more informal and more openly dependent on the favour of their followers to stay in power (even if they do not always acknowledge or recognise this and even if they attempt to consolidate their hold on power by adopting authoritarian and ceremonial styles themselves; see chapter 12). In any society, the structures of power and the nature of the struggle have a significant effect on leadership.

Authority and legitimacy

The second trend, which is closely related, is a change in how people become leaders and how they maintain their position. Writing around a hundred years ago, Max Weber identified three sources of authority or *domination*: *charismatic*, derived from personal charisma but also family position and/or religion; *traditional*, inherited through patrimonial and feudal social systems; and *legal*, derived from law and the state (he later added a fourth source, which he refers to as *non-legitimate* domination).[26] A historical survey of the sources of authority and legitimacy suggests some modification of this scheme and reveals that sources of authority and legitimacy have, over the course of time, taken a number of different forms.

In early civilisations, the status of leader was often *conferred* by a higher power, often a divinity but sometimes a more general principle of natural law. As time passed, *inheritance*, often but not always through the male line, gradually came to dominate. In the eighteenth and nineteenth centuries, particularly in the West, the principle of inheritance was partly superseded by the belief that some people were destined to become leaders because of their *inherent* qualities and that these leaders would somehow emerge when fate called them. Others simply claimed leadership by virtue of their control of *power*, however it might be acquired. Finally, in the nineteenth and twentieth centuries we see a prevailing orthodoxy emerge, in which the leader's authority is derived by *consent* either from followers or from some other stakeholder group.

Established elites require authority and legitimacy to maintain their position and preserve power distance, but those who aspire to positions of leadership also require authority and legitimacy if their ambitions are to be taken seriously. This includes self-made leaders. Rebels against authority, founders of new organisations (such as new states, new religions or new sports teams), entrepreneurs who set up new businesses, all need to appear credible in the eyes of their supporters. They, too, will require a source of authority and legitimacy. Jeanne d'Arc (Joan of Arc), the fifteenth-century Burgundian peasant girl who rose from obscurity to became a war leader of France in the latter stages of the Hundred Years War, is a good example. As a woman and a peasant, Jeanne would never have been taken seriously had she not claimed divine inspiration, which gave her a source of authority.[27]

Conferred authority

Jeanne d'Arc is an example of what we can call conferred authority, that is, authority that has been vested in the leader by some supernatural power, either a deity or a metaphysical force such as *dao* or *dharma*. Divine leadership or, more commonly, divinely authorised and inspired leadership was common among the big settled civilisations that emerged in the late Neolithic era. In some cases, such as Egypt and the Phoenician city-states, the ruler was also the head of the religious hierarchy; in others, such as the various Chinese and Indian states, the ruler claimed to be favoured by the gods. As we shall see in chapter 4, rulers in some later polities, such as Imperial Rome, Japan and Aztec Mexico, claimed divine status for themselves.

Traces of conferred authority remain to this day. There is a strong religious element in the swearing in of newly elected democratic leaders, including the president of the United States; the monarch of the United Kingdom still lists *Defender of the Faith* prominently among her titles. Far from being mere ceremonial husks of an old and outdated view of leadership, these religious rites still mean something to many people.

Why did conferred authority emerge? Two issues stand out. The first is the greater complexity of society referred to earlier. Controlling and coordinating the activities of a technologically advanced city-state with complex markets and institutions – let alone the activities of an entire empire – required power. Divine authority and legitimacy gave leaders the power to get things done, including the power to lay down laws to govern society, such as the Hammurabic Code of Babylon, and the power to structure and order that society to ensure peace and prosperity, as described in the Egyptian *Duties of the Vizier*.[28] At the same time, these leaders were also creating institutions to help them cement their own control of power.

By and large, people accepted this. Religion in early civilisations was partly both a matter of faith and a way of explaining the world. Greek, Norse, Babylonian, Egyptian, Hindu and Chinese cosmologies helped people understand their environment, not only physical phenomena like the seasons, the movements of the sun and moon and stars, earthquakes, fires and floods but also metaphysical ideas such as life and death, light and darkness, time and space, love and hate.[29] People were less sceptical about religion because they could see what their gods were doing all around them, in the form of weather, harvests and crop yields, births and deaths, the passage of time itself. Early works of literature like *The Epic of Gilgamesh*, the *I Ching* and the *Iliad* show evidence of the reasoning: power comes from the gods, and as leaders have the power to get things done, it seems only natural to assume that leaders are in communion with the gods. Natural, too, was the further acceptance that the leader's divine power cascaded down through the various levels of hierarchy of administration. Hierarchy itself was seen as something that was divinely inspired, as is evident, again, in the *Duties of the Vizier*.[30]

Even where divinity is not directly invoked, leadership and hierarchy sometimes referred to natural law as sources of authority and legitimacy. Although Chinese scholars including Confucius, Laozi (Lao Tzu) and Han Fei all made reference to divinity, their idea of leadership was heavily grounded in the notion of *dao* (way), the natural order of things. Kautilya's *Arthashastra* makes similar references to natural law, as does Plato's *Republic*. Hierarchy exists, elites exist and leaders exist because that is the way things should be, and only Laozi in the *Daodejiing* ever questions the primacy and superiority of leaders, arguing that they should give up power to the people.[31]

The second issue is that the power conferred by deities or the natural law gave leaders a tool for suppressing dissent and, as noted, for consolidating their hold on power. Disobeying the leader's authority was not only treason but also sacrilege, and the leader was entitled to exact the maximum penalty, as Han Fei in particular makes clear.[32] Divine or divinely inspired leaders could use their status as leverage to increase power distance, something that notably occurs during the transition of Rome from a republic to an empire and the subsequent deification of the Julio-Claudian emperors. However, this deification did not entirely stifle dissent, as the emperors Caligula and Nero discovered to their cost.

One more point needs to be made about conferred leadership. Many pantheons of the ancient world had powerful goddesses: we can, for example, think of Hera/Juno and Artemis/Diana of the Greeks/Romans, Astarte in the ancient Near East, Isis in Egypt, Lakshmi and Parvati in India, Freyja in Norse mythology, Haumea in Hawai'i and Brighid of the Celts, and we might reasonably expect many women to claim positions of leadership directly through the patronage of these goddesses. Not so. Only in Scandinavia did women often succeed in claiming positions of leadership, including military leadership, on their own merit. The Danish chronicler Saxo Grammaticus records several women war leaders, including the Swedish shield-maiden Weborg, killed at the Battle of Brávallir in 750 AD, and the contemporary Norwegian queen Lagerda, or Lagertha, who was much admired for her fighting skills.[33] Elsewhere, with few exceptions, a woman could claim legitimate power only through inheritance.

Inherited authority

Leaders have always liked to choose their successors, and in most cases this has meant choosing a member of their own family. The power of conferred authority gave them the right do so; the leader could nominate his – or much more rarely – her own heir, and no one could challenge the decision. The divine power claimed by the leader was also then conferred upon the heir.

Dynastic rule was evident in Old Kingdom Egypt (*c.* 2700–2200 BC) and in Shang Dynasty China (certainly by c. 1600 BC, if not before). For several millennia, inheritance was the accepted way for power to be transferred, not only in the political sphere but also in many other fields of activity, including business. In medieval Florence, the Medici Bank, the most powerful business organisation in Europe and one of the first truly multinational enterprises, relied on tight control by the Medici family, including the transfer of power from father to son.[34] So did almost every other large business enterprise of the day; when the leader of the business lacked an heir, the business usually died with him, as was the case with the cloth manufacturer and trader Francesco Datini of Prato.[35]

There were other channels of inheritance beyond family, however. In *Foundations of Corporate Empire*, Karl Moore and David Lewis describe the career of Pasion, one of the most powerful and influential bankers in the city-state of Athens. A slave from Asia Minor, Pasion was purchased by two Athenian bankers, Antisthenes and Archistratus. He was employed at first as a menial servant, but his new owners found him to be honest and diligent and naturally gifted in accounting. He became so valuable to his owner-employers that they granted him his freedom and eventually deeded to him the inheritance of the bank after their deaths. Pasion went on to become highly successful, the richest banker and perhaps the most successful entrepreneur in ancient Greek history. In turn, he left the bank in his will to his own former slave and trusted advisor, Phormio, who sealed the deal by marrying Pasion's widow when he took over the bank.[36]

Other societies allowed leaders to choose heirs beyond their own immediate family. The disasters of the Julio-Claudian and Flavian dynasties turned Romans against the idea of heredity for a time, and beginning with Nerva in 96 AD, the standard practice was that the emperor would adopt an heir outside his own family. This lasted until 177 AD, when Marcus Aurelius proclaimed his son Commodus as heir, and thereafter Roman political history is scarred by a struggle for control between leaders who claimed the position through familial inheritance and the so-called 'barracks emperors' who attempted to seize power through military strength.[37]

Inheritance by reincarnation is a feature of leadership among Tibetan Buddhists. The best-known case of inherited leadership is the lineage of the Dalai Lamas, believed to be reincarnations of the bodhisattva Avlokitesvara. The fifteenth-century monk Gendun Drup was the first *tulku* (incarnated being) to bear the title; the current Dalai Lama is the fourteenth. Most Dalai Lamas came from humble origins, and many were recognised as reincarnations while they were still children. Other titles which are passed through reincarnation include the Panchen Lama and the Samding Dorje Phagmo, the female *tulku* who also serves as abbess of the Samding monastery.[38]

The notion of inherited authority solved some of the problems of conferred authority, where, as we saw, failure by the leader could be taken as a sign that divine favour had been withdrawn. But the principle of inheritance, especially once codified in law, made removing failed leaders more difficult; good or bad, the leader was still the leader, and anyone who did not accept this was stepping outside the law. In theory, inheritance also ended the uncertainty that surrounded a leader's death. This principle was perhaps best expressed in the French law of *la mort saisit la vif* (the dead seize the living), which declared that inheritance transferred at the moment of the previous leader's death. 'Le roi est mort; vive le roi!' declared the Duc d'Uzès in 1422, proclaiming Charles VII king of France immediately upon the death of his father, Charles VI. At a time of national crisis in France, with English armies occupying much of the country, the application of the law ensured there would be no power vacuum.[39]

One advantage of the system was that the new leader was already in place; he or she was a known quantity and in some cases had also received some training and experience of leadership to enable him or her to step up to the challenges of the position. In the fourteenth century King Edward III of England carefully groomed his son and heir, Edward of Woodstock, Prince of Wales, to succeed him by giving him various important posts, including army commander and governor of the province of Gascony, all with the purpose of giving him experience he would require as a king. Unfortunately, this effort was wasted; the prince fell ill and died in 1376, a year before his father.[40]

Laws of inheritance could also be tinkered with to exclude those deemed undesirable from positions of power. These included children born out of wedlock and, in many parts of the world, women. The most famous example is perhaps Salic Law, an ancient Frankish law code revived in France in 1328 to prevent the accession of Isabella, last surviving child of King Philippe IV, to the throne of France. This was partly political expediency; Isabella was married to Edward II of England, so her son would have inherited the thrones of both England and France. The French elites were understandably anxious to avoid being ruled by England, but there was a fair dash of misogyny in the decision too.[41] Most societies agreed that women were not fit to hold political power, and they were specifically excluded from inheriting the throne. Business and civil society followed the political world's lead.

There was one legal exception, however. Women could inherit power from their husbands, especially if there were no male children, or if those children were infants. The only two women to rule imperial China – Wu Zetian in the late seventh and early eighth centuries and Cixi (*de facto* as regent for the Guangxu Emperor) in the late nineteenth and early twentieth centuries – both came to power in this way. Wu was the wife of one deceased emperor; Cixi was the concubine of another.[42] Boudica, queen of the Iceni, who led a famous revolt against Rome in 60 AD, and Aethelflaed, the *Lady of the Mercians*, who successfully fought off several Viking invasions in the early tenth century AD, inherited power from their late husbands, as did Lili'uokulani, the last queen of independent Hawai'i, who was overthrown by an American-backed revolution.[43] Much more rarely, female leaders might inherit from a sibling. An example is Queen Nzinga of Ndongo, an African state in modern-day Angola, who staged a *coup d'état* after the death of her brother, the king, and ruled off and on for the next thirty years.[44]

In an era where it was extremely difficult for a woman to own private property, inheritance through widowhood was also one of the few ways that women could own and lead a business: for example, Marguerite Guerin was working as a waitress when she met and married an itinerant hat-seller named Aristide Boucicaut. Together, they founded a small drapery business which they later turned into the world's first department store, Au Bon Marché. Famous for the 'democratisation of luxury' and located in a purpose-built palace of glass and steel designed by Gustave Eiffel, Au Bon Marché became a Paris landmark in its own right. When Aristide died in 1877, ownership passed into the hands of Marguerite, who led the business until her own death ten years later.[45] Elizabeth Colt had been married to her husband, the firearms inventor and entrepreneur Colonel Sam Colt, for just four years when he died suddenly in 1862. Elizabeth inherited the business and transformed it, leading Colt Firearms through four decades of growth and establishing Colt as an iconic American brand.[46]

Finally, inheritance satisfied an innate human desire to pass on what one has created and see it in safe hands. If we cannot live forever, the reasoning goes, at least we can pass on our power to others who will make good use of it, and those who will make the best use of it will be our genetic descendants, whom we ourselves have created; for men in high places, the act of procreation itself is also often an expression of power, which is why in many cultures leaders were polygamous and kept concubines.[47] Whether this desire to leave legacy is a genuine psychological need or a learned behaviour is open to question, but we can see this phenomenon across history, right up to the present day, in business and politics, sport and science, and the arts. Also, children sometimes desire to follow in their parents' footsteps in order to gain approval. Finally, there continues to be a belief that inherited characteristics play a role and that the sons and daughters of successful leaders have the potential to be successful leaders themselves. One study, published in 2013, claims to have identified a leadership genome, but the jury is still out on whether this genome really does determine who will make a good leader and who will not.[48]

Regardless of the truth, the notion of inherited authority continues to carry a good deal of weight today. Political dynasties still exist, not only the European monarchies but also clans, such as the Kennedys and the Bushes in America. Some of the most famous global businesses – Tata, Cadbury, Lehman Brothers – were led by inherited leaders for four or five generations; indeed, the decline of Cadbury and Lehman Brothers arguably began when the inheritance connection was broken and appointed leaders from outside the family were brought in. Today, a third generation of the Murdoch family now controls the media empire.[49]

Inherent authority

As noted earlier, the Reformation and the Enlightenment in Europe both posed strong challenges to existing notions of legitimacy and authority. Such challenges had happened before: the Lollards and the Levellers in England and the Hussites in Bohemia rejected both conferred and inherited authority and argued that human beings were inherently free, in some cases even questioning whether leaders were needed at all.[50]

Jean-Jacques Rousseau, one of the central figures of the European Enlightenment, also posed that question. 'Man is born free, and everywhere he is in chains', Rousseau argued in his most famous work, *The Social Contract*. Freedom for Rousseau is consistent with the idea of natural law; authority is an artificial construct which is imposed on us, more often than not against our will, and Rousseau goes on to argue that such imposed authority is illegitimate and should be rejected.[51] The leaders of the American Revolution were strongly influenced by Rousseau, even before the war had ended in 1783 there was intense debate about what kind of leadership the newly independent United States should have. Many argued that it should have no central authority at all. Some of the more extreme ideologues of the French Revolution also believed that government as an institution was inherently oppressive and should be abolished, and their ideas were taken up later in the nineteenth century by the philosophical anarchists (see chapter 3).

However, this rejection of leadership never really caught on as a mainstream idea. Instead, the egalitarianism of the Enlightenment took a different turn. It should be pointed out, too, that this egalitarianism applied mainly to middle class white males. Women were excluded from power, and although the French Revolution extended the voting franchise to most adult males, the new revolutionary elites – who were largely drawn from the middle classes – strongly defended their power against outsiders, often using violence to do so. Olympe de Gouges, the leading French feminist and author of the *Declaration of the Rights of Woman and the Female Citizen*, and Jacques Hébert, the radical journalist and leader of the working class *sans-culotte* movement, were executed within a few months of each other for alleged crimes against the state.[52] In Europe and America, people of colour were also largely remained excluded from leadership (see chapter 3).

The new fashionable archetype of leadership was the Great Man (and again, the choice of gender is deliberate). Although the idea of great men goes back to Machiavelli (and further back still to Plutarch), the archpriest of the Great Man movement was Thomas Carlyle, whose book *On Heroes, Hero-Worship, and the Heroic in History* (1841), popularised the term 'great man' and introduced it as a subject for discussion.[53] In Carlyle's view, certain individuals had inherent qualities that made them 'great' leaders. These qualities included courage, intellect, imagination and passion, but there was also something more, a vital spark that attracted people to them and made them acceptable as leaders.

This quasi-mystical notion of leadership was strongly influenced by Romanticism, the new cultural current that swept through Europe in part as a result of the turmoil of the French Revolution. The poet and polymath Johann Wolfgang von Goethe argued that passion was an essential element of greatness; reason and intellect alone were not enough. Goethe also had sympathy for rebellious people who used their own innate genius to overturn the established order and create something fearless and new; this sympathy is typified, for example, in his famous poem 'Prometheus', about the Titan who dared defy Zeus.[54] Goethe was one of those who initially admired Napoleon Bonaparte, although he served in the Austrian army against France and later had his house in Weimar ransacked by French troops.

Another influential poet who evoked the mystical and passionate nature of leadership was Lord Byron. His heroes, such as the nobleman Manfred or the pirate leader Conrad, are brooding, smouldering figures, often with a tortured inner life, who nevertheless rise to greatness.[55] They are admired and despised in equal measure, and they care nothing for either admiration or hatred; they merely go their own way. Here is his portrayal of Conrad in 'The Corsair':

> Lone, wild, and strange, he stood alike exempt
> From all affection and from all contempt.[56]

Byron attempted to live up to his own ideal of leadership, courting controversy through much of his life before supporting the Greek independence movement against Ottoman Turkey and even putting himself forward as a candidate for king of Greece. He died of an illness contracted while fighting in Greece in 1824, an act which added him to the European pantheon of romantic hero-leaders. The Byronic hero was a very powerful influence throughout nineteenth-century Europe, and there are traces of this archetype in Friedrich Nietzsche's work and his concept of *übermensch*, or 'superman', the ultimate extension of the Great Man.[57]

Nietzsche also wrote about the will to power', which he believed to be one of the driving forces behind the *übermensch*. Great people, in Nietzsche's view are obsessed by power; they are ambitious, driven and passionate about success.[58] This will to power is that same vital spark that Carlyle identified; people are attracted to ambitious men and women and will attempt to follow their example.

The poetry of Byron and Goethe and the philosophy of Nietzsche matter because they reflect the spirit of the age. All three were both enormously popular and influential across Europe. The people who read their work looked around them for other archetypes and exemplars. Napoleon Bonaparte was one of the first heroes of the Great Man movement. His rise from relatively humble origins to the rank of general at the age of twenty-five and the spectacular success of his campaign in Italy – during which he won a series of battles against all odds and forced the powerful Austrian Empire to sue for peace – could not be explained by appeal to either conferred or inherent principles. Something innate to man, it was believed, must have been responsible for his success.[59]

Great Man theory also holds that Great Men emerge when the time is right; cometh the hour, cometh the Man. This was bad news for leaders who relied on conferred or inherited authority, as it effectively legitimated rebellion against them. 'One withstands the invasion of armies', wrote Victor Hugo in 1852, 'but one cannot resist an idea whose time has come'.[60] Given that he was writing about Napoleon III's recent *coup d'état* and assumption of power in France, Hugo was implying that one does not resist a Man whose time has come.

But there was another element to the inherent approach. Leaders were judged to be great if they were successful; conversely, leaders who were successful – or, more correctly, were seen to be successful – must therefore be great. The case of General James Wolfe is illustrative. Born in 1727, Wolfe was exactly the kind of ambitious yet melancholy hero whom Byron and Goethe depicted in their poetry. His public career during the Seven Years' War was brief but meteoric. In 1757 he took part in a failed raid on the French port of Rochefort; in 1758 he was second-in-command of the expedition against the fortress of Louisbourg in North America, where he was the first man to go ashore in the face of French fire; and in 1760 he led the expedition that captured the French fortress of Québec, which effectively ended French rule in Canada. Wolfe was mortally wounded in the moment of victory during the Battle of the Plains of Abraham.

Wolfe was a fairly popular hero in his own day, but the legend created after his death has prevailed. Nineteenth- and twentieth-century biographers portrayed him as a man of destiny, and his childhood home in Westerham, Kent, is still a place of pilgrimage for admirers.[61] In fact, his achievements were relatively modest. His victory at Québec was due to a stroke of luck – Wolfe had been on the verge of abandoning the siege and going home when the chance discovery of a path up the cliffs west of Québec came to his notice – and he owed his opportunity in the first place to another stroke of luck, the favour of his prime minister, William Pitt. Great Man theory, however, does not by and large admit luck. A leader's success is due to his or her own genius, supported in lesser measure by hard work and skill.

Great Man theory also led people to turn a blind eye to imperfections and immorality. American business during the Gilded Age, from the 1870s to the early 1900s, was dominated by powerful leaders sometimes known as the 'robber barons', such as J. P. Morgan, Daniel Guggenheim, Cornelius Vanderbilt and, above all, John D. Rockefeller. Many of them made their fortunes through dubious (to say the least) means. Rockefeller, who took Standard Oil from a small regional oil producer to the world's largest corporation, was particularly ruthless in his methods. Competitors who stood up to him were subject to blackmail, arson and violence. When summoned before a Congressional committee to answer for his behaviour, Rockefeller treated the congressmen with contempt and refused to answer their questions.[62] Initially, at least, none of this dented Rockefeller's reputation. His success was considered a mark of his greatness and perhaps even of divine approval, a perception that Rockefeller – a devout Baptist – was quick to reinforce.

One contemporary observer, the stock trader William Fowler, noted how the American stock market during this period was effectively a jungle, where any way of making a profit was considered legitimate. The big beasts of that jungle, such as Morgan and Rockefeller, exemplars of the Nietzschean *übermensch*, were widely admired. The fact that they succeeded through immoral means was not relevant; success itself was all that mattered. Another contemporary, the journalist Ida Tarbell, wrote that an entire generation had grown up seeing business as analogous to warfare; the ends justified the means.[63] It was Tarbell who eventually turned public opinion against Rockefeller. Her exposé on the Standard Oil empire and its corrupt practices – published first as a series of articles in *McClure's* magazine and then as a book – caused public outcry and led the US government to institute legal proceedings against Standard Oil and break up the company. But even after his misdeeds had been exposed, Rockefeller continued to have many admirers.[64]

Great Man theory assumed further that *great* leaders are born and not made. The Victorian statistician and protogeneticist Francis Galton argued in his book *Hereditary Genius* that innate genius could also be passed from father to son (he made no mention of mothers and daughters), thus blending the principles of inherent and inherited authority.[65] This notion was vigorously opposed by Herbert Spencer, one of the pioneers of evolutionary theory, but the belief that characteristics could be inherited has continued to persist (for more on the leadership genome, see this chapter, p. 27).[66]

Others believed that whereas some leadership characteristics are inherent, those characteristics can be improved. This view was particularly common in Japan, where the *samurai* caste, which provided most of Japanese society's leaders, took the notion of self-improvement very seriously. Works of *samurai* literature such as Miyamoto Musashi's *The Book of Five Rings*) or Yamamoto Tsunetomo's *In the Shadow of Leaves*, perhaps the ultimate expression of *samurai* philosophy from the early eighteenth century, discuss the issue of 'self-mastery' and 'self-leadership'. Both advance the implicit view that, in order to lead others effectively, one must first be able to lead oneself. Biographies of swordfighters from this period show how practice and self-development are seen as inseparable from leadership.[67] It might come as no surprise, then, to learn that Samuel Smiles's *Self-Help*, the popular Victorian self-improvement manual, was a best-seller in late nineteenth-century Japan.

The influence of the Great Man theory persists to this day. Its linear descendants, trait theory and competency theory, continue to be subjects of serious discussion. The idea of the Great Man has largely been debunked in academic leadership circles, but it remains embedded in popular culture, and some eminent historians continue to pay lip service to the concept – see, for example, Andrew Roberts's recent biography *Napoleon the Great*.[68] Winston Churchill is another who continues to be regarded as a Great Man in the works of authors such as Roberts and, more recently, Boris Johnson.[69] The latter's biography of Churchill devotes much space to trying to determine what made Churchill 'great'; by implication, of course, Johnson invites the reader to compare Churchill with his biographer and conclude that he, too, is destined to lead.

Authority by power

I will describe this source of authority and legitimacy only briefly because we will come back to it in much more detail later in this book. Some leaders are recognised as leaders because they control so much power that others feel compelled to follow them. This is different from inherent authority, when people follow the leader because of who he or she is; in the case of authority by power, people follow the leader because of what he or she controls. This is most frequently seen in cultures or organisations where power distance is very high. Examples include the military, dictatorships, and very autocratic organisations.

An element of authority by power is present in all forms of leadership, whether conferred, inherited or inherent; without the power to get things done, the leader is powerless. There are some cases, however, where people become leaders primarily because of their ability to control power. This typically happens when a leader either a) usurps power from an existing leader, acquiring what Max Weber refers to as non-legitimate domination, or b) creates a new source of power.

Usurper leaders are common in history. Many were regarded as Great Men: for example, Charles Martel, who pushed aside the moribund Merovingian dynasty and became *de facto* ruler of France, paving the way for his grandson Charlemagne to establish the Holy Roman Empire; Julius Caesar, who broke the power of the tottering Roman Republic and claimed power for himself; and Napoleon.[70] All three took steps to legitimate themselves after they had seized power, gathering support from the institutions of state or in some cases creating new institutions to consolidate support. Revolutionary leaders such as Oliver Cromwell, Robespierre and Mao Zedong also seized power and established themselves as leaders.[71] Capitalists who take over existing business and transform them can also be regarded as 'usurpers', although such takeovers are usually legitimate and sometimes even encouraged by governments. Men such as John D. Rockefeller and J. P. Morgan are also prime examples – in the late nineteenth century, these men formed and led powerful business monopolies called 'trusts'.[72]

Creating a new source of power means creating a new polity or state, sometimes as a breakaway from an existing state (South Sudan and East Timor are recent examples) or as a spinoff from an existing organisation – but more usually by starting an organisation from scratch. The most common type of leader who creates a new source of power is the entrepreneur, who uses capital to establish a new enterprise which he or she leads. The heyday of these entrepreneurs, known in the jargon of the time as 'business promoters', was the eighteenth and nineteenth centuries, when people like Richard Arkwright, Robert Owen, Alfred Krupp, the Boucicauts and John D. Rockefeller built powerful enterprises and made themselves wealthy. However, entrepreneurship can be found in other fields of endeavour than business. For example, Florence Nightingale and Mary Seacole disrupted the medical world and established themselves as leaders in nursing, and William Morris created a hybrid commercial-artistic endeavour based on socialist principles, using a combination of artistic and design skill and commercial acumen.[73]

Authority by power can be deceptive, however. Leaders often assume that because they are powerful, they have the right to lead. But implicit in the notion of authority by power – indeed in all the forms of authority and legitimacy mentioned so far – is the notion of consent. No leader, no matter how powerful they are, can govern for long without the consent of those being governed.

Authority by consent

Authority by consent means that the leader governs with the consent of the governed. Quite commonly the group chooses its leader, but even where this is not the case, the leader's authority and legitimacy are at least partially derived from the rest of the group. The leader can function as leader only if followers give their consent and agree to invest him or her with a measure of authority. There is a strong correlation between authority by consent and power distance; that is, lower levels of power distance often mean that more of the leader's authority is derived through consent.

Thus, there is a difference between this concept and that of inherent authority, in that inherent authority is to some extent imposed by the leader, whereas authority by consent implies that the move to choose the leader comes first from followers. There is, of course, considerable grey area between the two.

Neolithic societies, which had low levels of power distance, were largely governed by consent. Tribal groups chose their leaders and exercised considerable influence over how those leaders functioned.[74] In some parts of the world this practice lingered for a long time. Well into the Middle Ages, Viking leaders in Norway and Sweden governed in part through consultation with a *thing*, a popular assembly that convened at least once a year. In Anglo-Saxon England, the Witan, an assembly of nobles, claimed the right to choose the king, although in practice this 'choice' was more of a ratification of a new monarch's claiming the throne by right of inheritance.[75] The *Althing*, the parliament of Iceland, established around 930 AD, served as both a popular assembly and a court of law, although its right to have a say in governance was severely curtailed by Iceland's Norwegian overlords in the late fourteenth century.[76]

Authority derived from consent can also be seen in other parts of the world. Some of the early caliphs of Islam were elected, and the Ibadi, a Muslim sect in Oman, elected its own community leaders.[77] In India, 'republics' known as *gana-sang-has* appeared, mainly in marginal lands in the north and east. Their inhabitants were usually Buddhists or Jains rather than Hindus, and they rejected the Hindu caste system in favour of a less stratified society. Even so, access to power was restricted to the upper classes only, so these republics resemble the oligarchies of Athens or medieval Italy. The *raja* (leader) was answerable to the nobles and, in some cases, may have been chosen by ballot.[78] There is also some evidence that early kings in what is now Indonesia, especially on the islands of Bali and Java, were chosen by assemblies of nobles.[79]

In North America the *Kanien'kehaka* (Mohawk people), part of the Iroquois Confederacy, have a long tradition of choosing their chiefs. The *tekarihoga* (the principal chief) was chosen by the senior female member of the clan. In practice the system was part inheritance, as the matriarch tended to choose one of her own family; thus, following the death of Thayendanegea (Joseph Brant) in 1807, his wife, Adonwentishon, chose their son Ahyonwaeghs as his successor.[80] However, Mohawk families were rather fluid structures, and chiefs and matriarchs frequently adopted promising outsiders as family members, especially if they were seen to have leadership potential. For example, the former soldier John Norton, half-Scottish and half-Cherokee, was adopted by the Mohawks of the Grand River in Upper Canada and appointed their war chief in 1794.[81]

The democracies of ancient Greece may also have been survivors of an earlier tradition of authority by consent. Government in the Greek city-states took many forms, ranging from the dual monarchy of Sparta, where the actions of the two kings were overseen by a panel of elected officials known as *ephors*, to the oligarchy of Athens, where the *ecclesia* (assembly) chose the magistrates and other leaders of the city. Athens is often seen as the birthplace of democratic leadership, but it should be noted that the designer of the Athenian political system, Solon (*c.* 638–558 BC) was careful to preserve as much power distance as possible; women, slaves and the poor were excluded from democratic participation.[82]

Athens was the model for the Roman Republic, which in turn was the model for the early medieval city-republics of northern Italy, such as Milan, Florence and Venice, and the Dutch Republic established in the late sixteenth century when the Netherlands broke away from Spanish rule. Medieval Poland and England also developed traditions of authority by consent that ran side by side with more traditional notions of kingship based on inherited power. Parliament in England grew increasingly powerful in the early modern period, finally taking over executive power from the monarch, whereas the *Sejm* (Polish parliament) eclipsed the power of the king and even claimed the right to choose the monarch right up until the partitions of Poland and the disappearance of the Polish state in the late eighteenth century. All these systems were more or less oligarchical, with the franchise restricted to wealthy males.

A form of authority by consent also existed in many religious hierarchies. We have already noted that early caliphs of Islam were elected, although this changed with the rise to power of the Umayyad dynasty .[83] In the Christian church, the Byzantine emperor had the right to appoint the senior religious officers in his territory, including the patriarchs of Constantinople and Antioch, but following the collapse of the Western Roman Empire the papacy in Rome gradually moved to the present system of election by the college of cardinals. Somewhat paradoxically, the pope was chosen by his fellow cardinals but upon assumption of the papal throne became invested with divine, conferred authority, later codified as the doctrine of papal infallibility.[84]

The pope also had the right to appoint bishops and archbishops, but his authority did not extend over the monastic orders. Starting with the Benedictines and Cistercians, there were, by the end of the Middle Ages, many monastic and mendicant orders, nearly all with parallel male and female organisations. The abbots and abbesses of each convent were elected by the chapter, although local religious and secular authorities often tried to influence the election. The grand masters of the military-religious orders – such as the Knights Templar, the Order of Saint John and the Teutonic Order, hybrid organisations based on the monastic orders but armed and equipped for fighting – were also elected by the chapter of the order. Although abbots, abbesses and grand masters were in theory all-powerful, they could be deposed by their chapters through a vote of no confidence.[85]

As we saw earlier, the Enlightenment challenged the established sources of authority and insisted on a new primacy of authority by consent. Democracy or some form of it is now the established political system in most nations in the world, and in theory at least, authority by consent is widespread. It is worth reminding ourselves, however, that this is not true in every sphere of activity. The people vote for their political leaders, but they do not vote for their business leaders; very rarely do workers have a say in choosing who leads and manages them. Some sports teams choose their captains, but in many cases the captain is appointed, and so is the coach or manager, arguably a more powerful figure. There have been a few instances of military units electing their own officers; in the eighteenth and nineteenth centuries American militia units sometimes chose their officers by ballot, but this practice often resulted in officers who were popular with their men but incompetent; thus, it was discontinued.[86]

Three observations follow from this. First, authority by consent does not necessarily mean the consent of all followers. Put simply, it means the consent of those who control the most power, and if some followers do not have sufficient power to make their voices heard and influence their leaders, they remain largely shut out. Inequality of power among groups of followers is a continuing source of discontent in politics, business and other spheres of activity.

However, even in cases of high power distance, the lower orders are never entirely powerless, and they can and will find ways of making that discontent known. Military leaders have known for centuries that they will be more successful if their soldiers fight willingly and consent to being led. The Prussian army of the eighteenth century was one of the most disciplined the world has ever seen – conformity of manoeuvre and fire enforced with ruthless discipline – but its leaders knew that discipline and control were not enough. 'If a soldier, whether on foot or on horseback, is not animated with ambition', wrote Major General Emanuel von Warnery, 'if he has not that patriotic spirit, he cannot be depended upon on any occasion where it is not sufficient to act mechanically, but where personal bravery is likewise requisite'.[87]

Wise business leaders have always known the same. A number of speakers at the Rowntree management conferences, held in England in the 1920s and 1930s, made the point that capital and labour have a symbiotic relationship, and they called for greater recognition of this. The economist Sidney Webb, speaking in 1920, suggested that one of the key causes of labour unrest is not inequalities of wealth but inequalities of power; workers resent being given orders by autocratic owners and want a greater say in how the business that employs them is run.[88] Benjamin Seebohm Rowntree, one of the conference organisers, urged his audience in 1922 to join forces with their workers and create a partnership with them. 'Be captains of industry, not just employers', he told them. 'Be leaders whom your men trust and love, and be worthy of their loyalty'.[89]

Finally, there are the questions of why leaders are chosen and what is expected of them. The Enlightenment ideal was that the people chosen as leaders would be those who had experience or wisdom beyond the ordinary. They would function as guides or servants, lending their wisdom to the greater polity and enabling us all to prosper together. That view infused positivist philosophy, which in turn strongly influenced the early management movement; the writings of Frederick Winslow Taylor, Henri Fayol and Lyndall Urwick show how strongly knowledge and skill were considered valuable qualities in a leader.[90] Politicians, too, were elected in part for their experience in public service and public life.

Whereas logic dictates that leaders should be chosen on the basis of their fitness to lead, human beings are not always logical. In addition to authority based on experience and knowledge, there is something which, for want of a better term, I shall call *symbolic-charismatic authority*. Often, people have chosen leaders who appeal to them on emotional and charismatic rather than rational terms and who also symbolise something that the people themselves aspire or desire to achieve. French revolutionary leaders like Mirabeau and Camille Desmoulins rose to prominence as much because of their ability to move people's hearts as their ability to persuade.[91] The revolutionary orators appealed to emotion as much as they did to reason and tapped into the public's desire both for change and for a fair, free society.

Symbolic-charismatic leaders are often revolutionaries who seek to use their charisma to create change or acquire power. Often, they, too, come from outside the traditional elites. This does not necessarily mean they seek to reduce power distance; sometimes, they seek instead to tilt the balance of power towards themselves. The Iraqi Shi'a Muslim leader Muqtada al-Sadr and former UK Independence Party leader Nigel Farage are recent examples of an emergent leader who seeks to embody the aspirations of a particular group in society and help that group acquire more power.[92]

Summary

It is important to remember that when discussing how sources of authority and influence have changed over time, the process is not linear. There were certain eras when conferred authority seems to have been most common, but looking around the world, we can always find exceptions. The same is true of inherited and inherent authority; as already noted, whereas authority by consent seems dominant today, it is by no means universal.

It is also very difficult to find an example of a leader who relied on only one source of power and authority. In reality, there were nearly always other sources. The Mohawks may have chosen their leaders, but they often chose them from the same family line, usually the same line as that of the clan matriarch who was choosing. Monastic orders relied on a mixture of authority by choice, the election of the spiritual head, and conferred authority, the grace of God, which wrapped itself like a mantle around the successful candidate. Robert Owen, one of the most successful entrepreneurs of the Industrial Revolution, was running a business that employed three hundred people by the time he was nineteen. Highly intelligent, Owen seems to have had an instinctive ability to organise and lead, and we might put him in the inherent authority camp; but Owen himself was fully aware of the need to motivate his workers and win their trust so that they would follow him.[93]

This leads us back to the nature of power and authority. Leaders require authority, even if it is non-legitimate, in order to lead. Authority, in turn, derives from power; it is axiomatic that every study of leadership is also a study of power. Who controls power and how power is distributed therefore have a strong influence on the sources of legitimacy and authority. Low power distance gives people the opportunity to have some say in who their leaders will be; high power distance allows leaders to distance themselves from their followers, dictating not only how they lead but also who their successors will be.

That sounds simplistic, but the reality is much more complex. Power distance, distribution and control are dynamic. There is a near-constant struggle between those who have great power and desire to keep it and those who have comparatively little power but are ambitious to increase their share. For those in positions of leadership, there is a constant balancing act; how much power do they keep, and how much do they give away? The Daoists argued that leaders should surrender power to the people; this, they said, was in accordance with natural law, and once people were free to order their own affairs, society would become harmonious. In practice, this hardly ever happens. Greed, arrogance, ambition and – importantly – fear are barriers that leaders have always struggled to overcome.

Notes

1 Tim Ambler, Morgen Witzel and Chao Xi, *Doing Business in China*, 4th edn, London: Routledge, 2017.
2 Geert Hofstede, *Culture's Consequences: Comparing Values, Behaviors, Institution and Organizations Across Cultures*, 2nd edn, Thousand Oaks: Sage, 2001; Geert Hofstede and Geert Jan Hofstede, *Cultures and Organizations: Software of the Mind*, 2nd edn, New York: McGraw-Hill, 2005.
3 Mauk Mulder, *The Daily Power Game*, Leiden: Martinus Nijhoff, 1977.
4 Max Weber, *The Religion of China: Confucianism and Taoism*, New York: The Free Press, 1968.
5 W. J.F. Jenner, *The Tyranny of History: The Roots of China's Crisis*, London: Penguin, 1992.
6 Charles O. Hucker, *China to 1850: A Short History*, Stanford: Stanford University Press, 1977; Edwin E. Moise, *Modern China*, 3rd edn, London: Routledge, 2008; Jonathan Spence, *The Search for Modern China*, 3rd edn, New York: W.W. Norton, 2013; Spence, *God's Chinese Son: The Taiping Heavenly Kingdom of Hong Xiuquan*, New York: W.W. Norton, 1996; Edgar Snow, *Red Star Over China*, London: Victor Gollancz, 1937.
7 Debraj Ray, *Development Economics*, Princeton: Princeton University Press, 1997; Amartya Sen, *Poverty and Famines*, Oxford: Oxford University Press, 1983.
8 David Lewis-Williams and David Pearce, *Inside the Neolithic Mind: Consciousness, Cosmos and the Realm of the Gods*, London: Thames and Hudson, 2011; Robert J. Hommon, *The Ancient Hawaiian State: Origins of a Political Society*, Oxford: Oxford University Press, 2013.
9 Bronisław Malinowski, *Argonauts of the Western Pacific: An Account of Native Enterprise and Adventure in the Archipelagoes of Melanesian New Guinea*, London: Routledge and Kegan Paul, 1922; Jared Diamond, *Guns, Germs and Steel: The Fates of Human Society*, New York: W.W. Norton, 1997.
10 Jared Diamond, 'The Worst Mistake in the History of the Human Race', *Discover*, May 1987, http://discovermagazine.com/1987/may/02-the-worst-mistake-in-the-history-of-the-human-race.
11 The new complexity of agriculture is well described by the early Greek poet Hesiod (see Martin L. West (ed. and trans.), *Hesiod: Works and Days*, Oxford: Oxford University Press, 1978), while the new weapons and tactics can be seen in the works of Homer (*The Iliad*, trans. Herbert Jordan, Norman: University of Oklahoma Press, 2008; *The Odyssey*, trans. Robert Fitzgerald, New York: Farrar, Strauss and Giroux, 1998).
12 Karl Moore and David Lewis, *Foundations of Corporate Empire: Is History Repeating Itself*, London: Financial Times-Prentice Hall, 2000.

13 W.H.D. Rouse (trans.), *Great Dialogues of Plato*, New York: Mentor, 1956; Richard Kraut, *Cambridge Companion to Plato*, Cambridge: Cambridge University Press, 1992; Nickolas Pappas, *Plato and the Republic*, London: Routledge, 1995.

14 Umesh Kumar, *Kautilya's Thought on Public Administration*, New Delhi: National Book Organization, 1990; Burton Watson, *Han Fei Tzu: Basic Writings*, New York: Columbia University Press, 2003.

15 Donald Kagan, *The Fall of the Athenian Empire*, Ithaca: Cornell University Press, 1987.

16 Charles Homer Haskins, *The Renaissance of the Twelfth Century*, Harvard: Harvard University Press, 1927; Samuel K. Cohn, *Popular Protest in Late Medieval Europe*, Manchester: Manchester University Press, 2004.

17 Amanda L. Collins, *Greater Than Emperor: Cola di Rienzo and the World of Fourteenth-Century Rome*, Ann Arbor: University of Michigan Press, 2002; Rodney Hilton, *Bondmen Made Free: Medieval Peasant Movements and the English Rising of 1381*, London: Routledge, 1995; Thomas A. Fudge, *Jan Hus: Religious Reform and Social Revolution in Bohemia*, London: I.B. Tauris, 2010; Donald Weinstein, *Savonarola: The Rise and Fall of a Renaissance Prophet*, New Haven: Yale University Press, 2011.

18 Lawrence James, *Raj: The Making and Unmaking of British India*, London: Abacus, 1997.

19 Moise, *Modern China*; Harrison E. Salisbury, *The Last Emperors: China in the Era of Mao and Deng*, Boston: Little, Brown, 1992.

20 Richard Evans, *Deng Xiaoping and the Making of Modern China*, London: Hamish Hamilton, 1993.

21 Marius B. Jansen, *The Making of Modern Japan*, Cambridge, MA: Harvard University Press, 2000.

22 Richard Sims, *Japanese Political History Since the Meiji Renovation, 1869–2000*, New York: Palgrave Macmillan, 2001; Andrew Gordon, *A Modern History of Japan: From Tokugawa Times to the Present*, Oxford: Oxford University Press, 2003.

23 Takeo Doi, *The Anatomy of Dependence*, Tokyo: Kodansha, 2002.

24 Jon P. Alston and Isao Takei, *Japanese Business Culture and Practices: A Guide to Twenty-First Century Japanese Business*, Bloomington: iUniverse, 2005.

25 Niccolò Machiavelli, *The Discourses*, ed. B. Crick, trans. L.J. Walker, Harmondsworth: Penguin, 1970, pp. 121–2.

26 Max Weber, *Rationalism and Modern Society*, trans. Tony Waters and Dagmar Waters, New York: AIAA, 2015; Weber, *Economy and Society*, Berkeley: University of California Press, 2013.

27 Régine Pernoud, *Joan of Arc by Herself and Her Witnesses*, trans. Edward Hyams, New York: Scarborough House, 1982; Larissa Juliet Taylor, *The Virgin Warrior: The Life and Death of Joan of Arc*, New Haven: Yale University Press, 2009.

28 Daniel D. Luckenbill (trans.), *The Code of Hammurabi*, ed. Edward Chiera, in J.M.Powis Smith (ed.), *The Origin and History of Hebrew Law*, Chicago: University of Chicago Press, 1931; G.P.F. van den Boorn, *The Duties of the Vizier*, London: Kegan Paul International, 1988.

29 Diamond, *Guns, Germs and Steel*; Michael Shermer, *The Science of Good and Evil*, New York: Henry Holt, 2004; Heinrich Zimmer, *The Philosophies of India*, London: Routledge and Kegan Paul, 1952; Basil G. Mitchell, *The Justification of Religious Belief*, New York: Oxford University Press, 1981.

30 Van den Boorn, *Duties of the Vizier*; Kathryn A. Bard (ed.), *Encyclopedia of the Archaeology of Ancient Egypt*, London: Routledge, 1999.

31 John C.H. Wu (trans.), *Tao The Ching (Daodejing)*, Boston and London: Shambhala, 1990.

32 Watson, *Han Fei Tzu*.

33 Saxo Grammaticus, *Gesta Danorum*, ed. Hilda Ellis Davidson, trans. Peter Fisher, *The History of the Danes*, Woodbridge: D.S. Brewer, 1979.

34 Raymond de Roover, *The Rise and Decline of the Medici Bank*, Cambridge, MA: Harvard University Press, 1962.

35 Iris Origo, *The Merchant of Prato*, London: Jonathan Cape, 1957.

36 Moore and Lewis, *Foundations of Corporate Empire.*
37 Mary Beard, *SPQR: A History of Ancient Rome*, London: Profile Books, 2016; Chris Scarre, *Chronicle of the Roman Emperors*, London: Thames and Hudson, 2012.
38 Tsepon W.D. Shakapba, *One Hundred Thousand Moons: An Advanced Political History of Tibet*, Leiden: Brill, 2010; Peter Schwieger, *The Dalai Lama and the Emperor of China: A Political History of the Tibetan Institution of Reincarnation*, New York: Columbia University Press, 2014; Hildegard Diemberger, *When a Woman Becomes a Religious Dynasty: The Samding Dorje Phagmo of Tibet*, New York: Columbia University Press, 2007.
39 Malcolm Vale, *Charles VII*, Berkeley: University of California Press, 1974.
40 Richard Barber, *Edward, Prince of Wales and Aquitaine: A Biography of the Black Prince*, London: Allen Lane, 1978; Marilyn Livingstone and Morgen Witzel, *The Black Prince and the Capture of a King: Poitiers, 1356*, Oxford: Casemate, 2018.
41 Jonathan Sumption, *The Hundred Years War, Vol. 1, Trial by Battle*, London: Faber and Faber, 1990.
42 Marina Warner, *The Dragon Empress: Life and Times of Tz'u-Hsi, 1835–1908*, London: Weidenfeld and Nicolson, 1972; Jang Chung, *Empress Dowager Cixi: The Concubine Who Launched Modern China*, New York: Knopf, 2013.
43 Joseph E. Roesch, *Boudica, Queen of the Iceni*, London: Robert Hale, 2006; Pauline Stafford, 'Political Women in Mercia, Eighth to Early Tenth Centuries', in Michelle P. Brown and Carol A. Farr (eds), *Mercia: An Anglo-Saxon Kingdom in Europe*, Leicester: Leicester University Press, 2001; Lili'uokulani, *Hawaii's Story by Hawaii's Queen*, Boston: Lee and Shephard, 1898.
44 Hettie V. Williams, 'Queen Nzinga (Nijinga Mbande)', in Leslie M. Alexander and Walter D. Rucker (eds), *Encyclopedia of African-American History*, Santa Barbara, CA: ABC-CLIO, 2010.
45 Michael B. Miller, *The Bon Marché: Bourgeois Culture and the Department Store*, Princeton: Princeton University Press, 1994.
46 William Hosley, *Colt: The Making of an American Legend*, Amherst: University of Massachusetts Press, 1996.
47 Robert van Gulik, *Sexual Life in Ancient China*, Leiden: Brill, 2003; Laura Betzig, *Despotism and Differential Reproduction: A Darwinian View of History*, Piscataway: Transaction, 2008; Rita Banerji, *Sex and Power: Defining History, Shaping Societies*, London: Penguin, 2009.
48 Jan-Emmanuel De Neve, Slava Mikhalyov, Christopher T. Dawes, Nicholas A. Christakis and James H. Fowler, 'Born to Lead? A Twin Design and Genetic Association Study of Leadership Role Occupancy', *The Leadership Quarterly* 24 (1) (2013): 45–60.
49 Deborah Cadbury, *Chocolate Wars: The 150-Year Rivalry Between the World's Greatest Chocolate Makers*, London: HarperCollins, 2010; Peter Chapman, *The Last of the Imperious Rich*, London: Penguin, 2010; Morgen Witzel, *Tata: The Evolution of a Corporate Brand*, New Delhi: Penguin India, 2009.
50 Robert Lutton, *Lollardy and Orthodox Religion in Pre-Reformation England*, Woodbridge: Boydell and Brewer, 2006; Robert Rex, *The Lollards: Social History in Perspective*, New York: Palgrave Macmillan, 2002; Rachel Foxley, *The Levellers: Radical Political Thought in the English Revolution*, Oxford: Oxford University Press, 2013; Howard Kaminsky, *A History of the Hussite Revolution*, Berkeley: University of California Press, 1967; Thomas A. Fudge, *The Magnificent Ride: The First Revolution in Hussite Bohemia*, Aldershot: Ashgate, 1998; Fudge, *Jan Hus.*
51 Jean-Jacques Rousseau, *The Social Contract*, London: Wentworth, 1998.
52 Sophie Mousset, *Women's Rights and the French Revolution: A Biography of Olympe de Gouges*, London: Transaction, 2014; Sara E. Melzer and Leslie W. Rabine (eds), *Rebel Daughters: Women and the French Revolution*, Oxford: Oxford University Press, 1992; Annie Smart, *Citoyennes: Women and the Ideal of Citizenship in Eighteenth-Century France*, Wilmington: University of Delaware Press, 2011; William Doyle, *The Oxford History of the French Revolution*, Oxford: Clarendon, 1989; Simon Schama, *Citizens: A Chronicle of the French Revolution*, New York: Knopf, 1989.

53 Thomas Carlyle, *On Heroes, Hero-Worship and the Heroic in History*, London: James Fraser, 1841.

54 Johann Wolfgang von Goethe, 'Prometheus', in Nathan H. Dole (ed.), *The Works of J.W. von Goethe*, London: Francis Nicholls, 1839; Angus Nicholls, *Goethe's Concept of the Daemonic: After the Ancients*, London: Camden House, 2006.

55 Fiona McCarthy, *Byron: Life and Legend*, London: John Murray, 2002; Peter L. Thorslev, *The Byronic Hero: Types and Prototypes*, Minneapolis: University of Minnesota Press, 1962.

56 Lord Byron, *The Corsair*, London: John Murray, 1814.

57 Friedrich Nietzsche, *Thus Spoke Zarathustra*, trans. R.J. Hollingdale, London: Penguin, 1961.

58 Friedrich Nietzsche, *The Will to Power*, ed. and trans. Walter Kaufman, London: Vintage, 1968.

59 David Chandler, *Napoleon*, London: Leo Cooper, 2002; Frank McLynn, *Napoleon: A Biography*, London: Pimlico, 1998; Patrice Gueniffey, *Bonaparte, 1769–1802*, Cambridge, MA: Harvard University Press, 2015; Martin Boycott-Brown, *The Road to Rivoli: Napoleon's First Campaign*, London: Cassell, 2001.

60 Victor Hugo, *History of a Crime (The Testimony of an Eye-Witness)*, trans. T.H. Joyce and Arthur Lockyer, Paris: Mondial, 2005.

61 William Templeton Waugh, *James Wolfe, Man and Soldier*, Montréal: Carrier, 1928; William Wood, *The Winning of Canada*, Toronto: Glasgow, Brook, 1915; Robert Wright, *The Life of Major-General James Wolfe*, London: Chapman and Hall, 1864.

62 Henry Demarest Lloyd, *Wealth Against Commonwealth*, New York: Harper & Bros., 1894; Ida M. Tarbell, *The History of the Standard Oil Company*, New York: McClure's, 1904, 2 vols.

63 William W. Fowler, *Twenty Years of Inside Life in Wall Street*, Bristol: Thoemmes Press, 2001; Tarbell, *The History of the Standard Oil Company*.

64 Tarbell, *The History of the Standard Oil Company*; Ron Chernow, *Titan: The Life of John D. Rockefeller, Sr.*, New York: Random House, 1999.

65 Francis Galton, *Hereditary Genius*, London: Macmillan, 1869.

66 Herbert Spencer, *Principles of Psychology*, London: Arkose Press, 2015.

67 Miyamoto Musashi, *The Book of Five Rings: A Classic Text on the Japanese Way of the Sword*, trans. Thomas Cleary, Boston: Shambhala, 2005; Yamamoto Tsunetomo, *Hagakure: The Book of the Samurai*, trans. William Scott Wilson, Tokyo: Kodansha International, 1979; Sugawara Makoto, *Lives of Master Swordsmen*, Tokyo: The East Publications, 1985; John Stevens, *The Sword of No-Sword: Life of the Master Warrior Tesshu*, Boston: Shambhala, 1995.

68 Andrew Roberts, *Napoleon the Great*, London: Penguin, 2015.

69 Andrew Roberts, *Eminent Churchillians*, London: Weidenfeld & Nicolson, 1995; Boris Johnson, *The Churchill Factor: How One Man Made History*, London: Hodder, 2015.

70 Paul Fouracre, *The Age of Charles Martel*, London: Routledge, 2000; Luciano Canfora, *Julius Caesar: The People's Dictator*, Edinburgh: Edinburgh University Press, 2006; Beard, *SPQR*; Chandler, *Napoleon*; McLynn, *Napoleon*; Gueniffey, *Bonaparte*.

71 Peter Gaunt, *Oliver Cromwell*, Oxford: Blackwell, 1996; Peter McPhee, *Robespierre: A Revolutionary Life*, London: Yale University Press, 2012; Ross Terrill, *Mao: A Biography*, Stanford: Standford University Press, 1999.

72 Chernow, *Titan*; Jean Strouse, *Morgan: American Financier*, New York: Harper Perennial, 2000.

73 Mark Bostridge, *Florence Nightingale: The Woman and Her Legend*, London: Penguin, 2008; Jane Robinson, *Mary Seacole*, London: Constable, 2004; E.P. Thompson, *William Morris: Romantic to Revolutionary*, London: Lawrence & Wishart, 1955.

74 Marija Gimbutas, *The Civilization of the Goddess: The World of Old Europe*, New York: Harper & Row, 1991; Ian Kujit, *Life in Neolithic Farming Communities: Social Organization, Identity and Differentiation*, New York: Springer, 2000.

75 H.M. Chadwick, *Studies on Anglo-Saxon Institutions*, Cambridge: Cambridge University Press, 1905; Felix Liebermann, *The National Assembly in the Anglo-Saxon Period*, New York: Ulan Press, 2005.

76 Gunnar Karlsson, *A History of Iceland*, Minneapolis: University of Minnesota Press, 2000.

77 Valerie Jon Hoffman, *The Essentials of Ibadi Islam*, Syracuse: Syracuse University Press, 2012.

78 Romila Thapar, *The Penguin History of Early India from the Origins to* AD *1300*, London: Penguin, 2002.

79 Paul Michael Munoz, *Early Kingdoms of the Indonesian Archipelago and the Malay Peninsula*, Singapore: Editions Didier Millet, 2006.

80 Isabel Thompson Kelsay, *Joseph Brant, 1743–1807: Man of Two Worlds*, Syracuse: Syracuse University Press, 1984.

81 Carl Klinck and James J. Talman, *The Journal of Major John Norton, 1816*, Toronto: Champlain Society, 1970.

82 Martin Ostwald, *Oligarchia: The Development of a Constitutional Form in Ancient Greece*, Stuttgart: Steiner Verlag, 2000; Anton Powell, *Athens and Sparta: Constructing Greek Social and Political History from 478* BC, London: Routledge, 2001; Eric W. Robinson, *The First Democracies: Early Popular Government Outside Athens*, Stuttgart: Steiner Verlag, 2001.

83 Hugh N. Kennedy, *The Prophet and the Age of the Caliphates: The Islamic Near East from the 6th to the 11th Century*, Harlow: Pearson, 2004.

84 Roger Collins, *Keepers of the Keys: A History of the Papacy*, New York: Basic Books, 2000; Richard McBrien, *Lives of the Popes: The Pontiffs from St Peter to John Paul II*, New York: Harper & Bros, 1997.

85 C.H. Lawrence, *Medieval Monasticism*, Harlow: Pearson, 2001; Alan Forey, *The Military Orders From the Twelfth to the Early Fourteenth Centuries*, Basingstoke: Macmillan, 1992.

86 James B. Whisker, *The Rise and Decline of the American Militia System*, Selinsgrove, PA: Susquehanna University Press, 1999.

87 Emmanuel von Warnery, *Remarks on Cavalry*, London, 1798, repr. London: Constable, 1997.

88 Sidney Webb, 'The New Spirit in Industry', Rowntree Management Conference Paper, 16 April 1920.

89 Benjamin Seebohm Rowntree, 'Opening Address on the Increasing Claims Which Industrial Conditions Make Upon Administration', Rowntree Management Conference Paper, 21 September 1922.

90 Frederick Winslow Taylor, *The Principles of Scientific Management*, New York: Harper & Bros., 1911; Henri Fayol, *General and Industrial Management*, trans. Constance Storrs, London: Pitman, 1949; Lyndall Fownes Urwick, *The Golden Book of Management*, London: Newman Neame, 1956.

91 Barbara Luttrell, *Mirabeau*, Carbondale: Southern Illinois University Press, 1990; Violet Methley, *Camille Desmoulins: A Biography*, New York: E.P. Dutton, 1915; Schama, *Citizens*.

92 Patrick Cockburn, *Muqtada al-Sadr and the Battle for the Future of Iraq*, London: Simon & Schuster, 2008; 'The Nigel Farage Story', *BBC News*, 4 July 2016, www.bbc.co.uk/news/uk-politics-36701855.

93 Ian Donnachie, *Robert Owen: Social Visionary*, Edinburgh: John Donald, 2000.

3

THE SOCIAL SPACE
OF LEADERSHIP

As a species we tend towards optimism, even if there is no rational reason for us to be optimistic.[1] When we choose to follow leaders – assuming we have the ability to choose – we make our choice in the hope that the leader will act in our best interest. He or she will somehow make things better, both for us personally and for our society. But how do we make that choice? How do leaders persuade us that they can make a positive difference? And how – and more importantly, why – do we accept leaders when they are forced upon us and we apparently have little choice except to follow them?

Historically, we have sought for answers by first examining the characteristics and traits of the successful leader and then looking for 'recipes', combinations of traits that led to success. In his book on heroes, Thomas Carlyle argued that the study of heroic lives can help us unlock heroic traits that might be hidden in our own psyches and that might make us better people. Nineteenth-century and early-twentieth-century writers like Ralph Waldo Emerson and Frederick Adams Woods followed this same principle, producing their own catalogues of Great Men, complete with analysis of why and how they succeeded.[2]

As noted in the previous chapter, Great Man theory is a product of the modern era, but the idea that successful leaders can serve as role models for other leaders has ancient roots. Texts like the *Iliad*, the *Epic of Gilgamesh*, the *Bhagavad-Gita* and the Norse sagas give us examples of mythic heroes to study and learn from (although, in the *Iliad* and the sagas, we are invited to learn from both their mistakes and their successes).[3] From ancient Athens, Xenophon's *The Education of Cyrus*, purporting to explain how the Persian ruler Cyrus II enjoyed such overwhelming success, became an enduring classic. A little later, Thucydides, one of the first true historians, devoted much time to analysing the characters of the leaders of Athens and Sparta in his *History of the Peloponnesian War*.[4] During the Roman Empire, Arrian's study of Alexander the Great and the biography of the general Gnaeus Julius Agricola by the historian Tacitus (also his son-in-law) were both widely read, and Plutarch's *Lives*, written early in the second century AD, influenced many subsequent writers and thinkers, including Carlyle.[5]

But Xenophon and Thucydides in particular were also aware that leaders owe their success to the strength of the relationship they have with their followers. Xenophon begins his work by pointing out that most leaders failed because they could not persuade others to follow them, whereas Cyrus's 'greatness' lay in his ability to gain the trust of his people. Much later, Niccolò Machiavelli, in his two classic studies on power and leadership, *The Prince* and *Discourses on Livy*, made the point that leaders who are not certain of the loyalty of their followers will often fail.[6]

Modern leadership theory continues from this point, focusing heavily on the interaction between leaders and followers. Observers such as Richard Bolden and his colleagues in *Exploring Leadership* have talked about the 'social space' between leaders and others, that is, the arena in which this interaction takes place.[7] Rather than seeing leadership – and followership – as static principles inherent in people, we should consider them as dynamic principles taking place in that social space. How that social space has historically been defined and what happens within it is the subject of this chapter.

As a first observation, following from the previous chapter, we need to be aware that this arena is and has always been a place of both *collaboration* and *competition*. Leaders and followers work together, with varying degrees of willingness, to achieve their mutual aims; each relies on the other. Followers know or believe that leaders bring something to the table that they themselves do not already have, whereas leaders realise both that there is very little they can do on their own and that they need followers to help them get the job done.

At the same time, however, they are very often in competition with each other, each seeking to acquire power at the expense of the other. This competition can perhaps be seen most clearly in business organisations; the struggle for power between managers and workers. Although there are examples of businesses – mostly small entrepreneurial or family-owned businesses where a balance has been struck and there is genuine workplace harmony – in most cases there is constant tension between employers and employees.

What is more, this tension has been present since the dawn of recorded history. We can see this clearly at Setmaat (Place of Truth), today known as Deir el-Medina, where a community of workers built many of the Egyptian royal tombs in the Valley of the Kings between *c.* 1500 and 1100 BC. Thousands of papyrus and *ostraca* (pottery shards) records allow us to look at the working practices of this community in detail. Running throughout these records is a current of constant tension between the scribe, the pharaonic official in charge of the works, his foremen (on the one hand) and the excavators, plasterers, painters and assistants (on the other). This is the social space of the Place of Truth: a constant series of negotiations and bargains over pay, working conditions, the provision of tools and materials and time off for illness or other reasons; for example, one man begged for a day off because he needed to patch things up with his wife, with whom he had recently had an argument, whereas another claimed he needed to embalm his mother-in-law.[8]

Around 1170 BC, an official further up the line failed to deliver the workmen's wages to Setmaat, at which point the workers walked out in what may be history's first officially recorded strike. This incident shows the tensions in the social space, as the workers exercised their own power; while they were on strike, the work on the tomb could not proceed, and this was likely to bring the displeasure of the pharaoh down on the heads of the officials in charge. Here we glimpse the existence of another social space, the one between the scribe and his own leaders further up the hierarchy, as he negotiated with them to get the resources he needed to complete the job.[9] Leadership, it would seem, resides not in one social space but in many, even within the same organisation.

Collective bargaining for wages is one manifestation, but there are many others. Even the low-level negotiations between team members and team leaders over holidays and rest breaks are manifestations of this struggle for power. In part, as the American engineer and consultant Harrington Emerson once observed, leaders and followers are seldom aligned in terms of what they want and need. Workers are contributing their time and effort, Emerson said, but leaders are expecting output. Most workers will try, quite naturally, to reduce the energy they must expend on their jobs, whereas most leaders will, again quite naturally, wish to maximise productivity. The two goals are not always compatible.[10] Simultaneously, as a further distraction, leaders are often in competition with each other over who will get the resources their team needs, who will get the best projects, who will get promoted and so on. As Anthony Jay has pointed out in *Management and Machiavelli*, this, too, is a struggle for power.[11]

The same phenomena can be seen in other fields, although it often takes different forms. The military, outwardly regimented and disciplined, has always had its own share of internal power struggles. During the American Civil War, for example, regular army officers in the Union Army resented having militia officers promoted to positions of command above them and sometimes refused to obey their orders.[12] Sports teams also have their share of struggles. 'Rugby players are very good at doing what they want to do', said England rugby union head coach Eddie Jones in a television interview. 'My job is to get them to do what they don't want to do'. How combative that relationship between players and coach can become, with each pushing to expand his or her power over the other, is easily seen in the careers of many senior coaches, perhaps most notably Sir Alex Ferguson, the former manager of Manchester United.[13]

Rejecting leadership

As we saw in chapter 2, the struggle for power is heavily stacked in favour of the elites. As James Burnham argued in *The Managerial Revolution* in 1941, those who have control of power are more likely to be able to keep and consolidate it.[14] The result in some cases has been a rejection of the entire notion of leadership on the grounds that the moment we create leaders, we surrender power to them, and the more power they have, the more they will try to take from us.

It is worth pausing for a moment to reflect on the thinking of some of those who opposed the very idea of leadership – some of whom were themselves notable leaders in thought or in action – because this should tell us something about why leadership exists. The most common reason for rejection is the notion that leaders are effectively self-serving elites who have seized power illegitimately. In a world governed by natural order, there would be no leaders; everyone would be equal, with equal access to power. In the fourth century BC, the Daoist philosopher Zhuangzi (Chuang-Tzu) argued that social forces, rather than the actions of kings or priests, are what guide and shape society. Far from assisting in our development, the interference of leaders disrupts the natural order of things.[15] Zhuangzi also argued that people should live their lives spontaneously and that events should be allowed to happen naturally.

This notion of spontaneity is echoed in the writings of the early twentieth-century anarchist Rosa Luxemburg, who believed revolutionary change should come from below and denied the need for leaders or ideologues to shape and craft it.[16] Luxemburg was opposed to bourgeois capitalism, but she also fought a running battle with her fellow revolutionary leaders, whom she distrusted; she believed they were ambitious for power for their own ends, and there was a danger that the revolution they espoused would simply replace one set of elites with another. She was, of course, quite correct.

The same problem – how to avoid replacing one form of tyranny with another – plagued many revolutionary movements. For the Lollards, the heretical Christian sect that arose in England in the fourteenth century, the answer was to destroy not only the elites but also all notion of hierarchy. The Lollards rejected the authority of the established church and denied that priests had the right to hear confession, but they also attacked civil society: 'When Adam delved and Eve span', argued the Lollard preacher John Ball, 'which then was the gentleman? From the beginning all men were created equal by nature, and servitude has been introduced by the unjust and evil oppression of men, against the will of God'. Like many anti-authoritarian movements since, the Lollards looked back to primitive times, before the rise of high civilisation and the complex structures of modern society, and argued that true freedom was to be found in a simple society without hierarchy.[17] The Diggers, an English millenarian sect in the late 1640s, also rejected leadership and advocated communal living in which everyone took an equal share in governance.[18]

In *The Social Contract*, Rousseau argued not for a rejection of leadership *per se* but for a new relationship between leaders and followers, a recasting of the social space.[19] He had no objection in principle to monarchy, as long as the crown respected the rights of the people and recognised that it had obligations to them, and vice versa. As noted in chapter 2, Rousseau was a strong influence on the founders of the American republic, and some of the Founding Fathers saw independence from Britain as a chance to create an ideal form of government.[20] But others disagreed. They had just fought a long and divisive war to free themselves from one king and his repressive army; why should they subject themselves to another? Did they need a government at all?

One of the leading lights of this movement was Thomas Jefferson, who argued that accepting the authority of a leader and subordinating one's own thoughts and actions to another was 'the last degradation of a free and moral agent'.[21] (Perhaps ironically, Jefferson himself was a member of the political elite and later served as third president of the United States.) For several years after the end of the American Revolutionary War, there was no effective central government in the United States. The army, also feared as an instrument of oppression, was run down; at one point, in 1784, the US Army had been reduced to just eighty men.[22]

Shays' Rebellion, a revolt led by disgruntled former soldiers that threatened to overthrow the government of Massachusetts, finally forced all parties to agree – with varying degrees of reluctance – to the creation of a unified state and constitution.[23] Even so, George Washington, the first president of the new republic, faced a series of further rebellions. The most serious of these, the Whiskey Rebellion of 1791, ostensibly a protest about taxes, was in reality a challenge to authority by those who believed that no authority was necessary.[24]

The French Revolution also saw a rejection of authority from what we would now call the far-left-wing of the political spectrum. Among the leading figures in this movement were Anacharsis Cloots and Gracchus Babeuf, who declared that 'society must be made to operate in such a way that it eradicates once and for all the desire of a man to become richer, or wiser, or more powerful than others'.[25] Both men were guillotined by the revolutionary government, which habitually executed those who challenged its authority in order to disguise how weak its legitimacy really was, but their ideas went on to form the basis of the nineteenth-century philosophical anarchism of Pierre-Joseph Proudhon.

In *The General Idea of Revolution*, Proudhon described governments as instruments of terror and called for the formation of a society without authority, where people relied on each other for mutual support and assistance. Later anarchists, such as Prince Peter Kropotkin of Russia, echoed this view. Rather like Jefferson and the ancient Daoists, Kropotkin believed that people would flourish best when they were free, with no hand of authority placed over them. He advocated a society where people would voluntarily determine their own contributions and needs, working in harmony with their fellow citizens to achieve the best result for the common good.[26]

Some anarchists, like the individualists Émile Armand and Max Stirner, regarded all forms of authority as illegitimate: the legal authority of government and the police, capitalist domination of the economy, the spiritual domination exercised by organised religion, bourgeois morality, even the authority of the family – all should be swept away.[27] Defiance of authority, refusal to work, atheism, free love and vegetarianism were all considered legitimate acts of rebellion. Despite the passionate beliefs of many of its exponents, the anarchist rejection of authority never gained much traction.[28] Partly, this was due to living a life according to strict anarchist principles was not terribly practical (nor was it likely to be very comfortable). But as Plato had pointed out in his *Republic*, a complex civilisation requires organisation, and where there is large-scale organisation, there is likely to be leadership. People may not particularly like the idea of subordinating themselves to another, but most of us recognise that from time to time we need to do so, particularly when the only apparent alternative is chaos.

The purpose of the leader

The question then arises: why did people decide they needed leaders? What function did leaders fulfil in society? *Survival*, of course, is one of the most important reasons that leadership is needed; leaders can help us organise and fight to defend ourselves. Beyond that, leaders offer us a chance to fulfil our own *aspirations*, whether as *individuals* or as a *group*. We cannot always reach our goals unaided; sometimes, we need a leader to help us along the way.

Survival

The first and most primal reason why leaders were needed was survival. The Neolithic Revolution of *c.* 10,000 BC, which also saw the creation of the first settled, agricultural societies, saw an upsurge in warfare as those same societies competed for arable land and other scarce resources. The Bronze Age and then the Iron Age, which introduced new weapons and new tactics, brought about an increasing intensity of warfare. Military leadership requires a particular set of skills and a special mindset beyond the ability to fight; more importantly, it requires the ability to train and motivate other people to fight.[29]

Native American societies often appointed specialist war leaders to serve alongside traditional chieftains. Examples include John Norton of the Mohawks of the Grand River and, more famously, Thasunke Witko (Crazy Horse), the war leader of the Oglala Lakota who defeated the US Army on several occasions, most notably at the Battle of the Greasy Grass (Little Big Horn) in 1876.[30] Nearly all of these war leaders were men. Although native American women often fought on the battlefield – the Cheyenne even had a female warrior society – I have found only two examples of women who were recognised as war chiefs in their own right: Nonhelema (*c.* 1720–86), who led her clan from the Shawnee nation into war against the British during Pontiac's Rebellion, and Otaki (died *c.* 1878), a war leader of the Blackfeet people of Western Canada.[31] Mention should also be made of Xochitl, queen of the Toltec Empire, who organised a company of women warriors and led them alongside her husband's army into the battle of Tultitlán (916 AD), where she was killed.[32]

The mercenary commanders of the Italian Renaissance are another example of military leaders who were recruited to help communities survive. The period from *c.* 1350 to 1530 was one of political chaos, with four great powers – France, Spain, the Holy Roman Empire and the papacy – fighting a series of proxy wars in the Italian peninsula, forcing the Italian city-states to raise armies to defend themselves.

Despite Machiavelli's insistence that mercenaries were untrustworthy and that a well-trained militia was preferable both for loyalty and for fighting spirit, many city-states employed freelance soldiers known as *condottieri*.[33] Some of their captains came from humble backgrounds; for example, Sir John Hawkwood, the Englishman who became military commander of Florence in the late fourteenth century, started out as an ordinary archer. Others, like the Florentine Giovanni dalle Bande Nere in the early sixteenth century, came from rich and powerful families.[34] What united them was their ability to protect the city-states that hired them and to see off any rival army that approached.

Revolutionary movements required leaders with the requisite military skills to help the movements survive. In some cases these leaders were self-appointed, but if they could win a few victories and demonstrate competence, other people coalesced around them, believing that following this leader offered them the best chance of survival. Francisco Espoz y Mina, one of the most successful leaders of the Spanish *guerrillas* fighting against the occupying French army from 1808 to 1814, started out with just seven followers.[35] The more often he defeated the French, the more his strength grew, as men deserted other rebel bands to follow him.

In other cases, rebels deliberately search for leaders who can provide the skill they lack. When the Catholic counter-revolution broke out in the Vendée in Western France, the peasant rebels fighting the French revolutionary armies knew they lacked military skills. They approached a local nobleman and former navy officer, François de Charette, and invited him to lead them; when Charette demurred, the rebels threatened him at bayonet point to lead them.[36] Charette went on to become one of the movement's most successful leaders and one of the last to be captured and executed by the revolutionary government.

Survival requires more than military force, however. Sometimes, the leader must be a guide who can lead people to a place of safety; Moses, leading the Israelites out of Egypt, is an obvious example. Sometimes, political leadership is also required. After Neville Chamberlain resigned as prime minister of Great Britain in May 1940, there was a consensus across the political spectrum that Winston Churchill was the best candidate to replace him; he had the necessary qualities of determination and tenacity to lead the country against the threat it now faced.[37] Alexius I Comnenus, who ruled as emperor of Byzantium from 1081 to 1118, rescued his empire from decline and used his organisational skills and political nous to create alliances which would ward off looming threats from the Seljuq Turks in the east and the Normans in the west.[38] More recently, Aung San Suu Kyi continued to be the focal point around which the Burmese opposition coalesced, although she was under house arrest for many years. Without her symbolic authority, the opposition movement might well have collapsed.[39]

In the commercial world, we can see 'survival' leaders in the form of specialists being brought in to turn around failing enterprises and ensure they survive. Arthur Chamberlain, possibly the first person to be described as a 'company doctor', was a late Victorian entrepreneur who specialised in taking over moribund companies and breathing new life into them. His most spectacular success was at gunpowder-maker

George Kynoch and Co., which in 1888 was teetering on the brink of collapse. The shareholders dismissed the directors and brought in Chamberlain as chairman to reorganise the business. Under his direction, within eight years Kynoch had doubled its output and begun expanding and taking over other firms.[40] Similarly, when the 3M Corporation was facing bankruptcy, it appointed a twenty-nine-year-old executive, William McKnight, to the post of president, allegedly because he was the only person the board could persuade to take the job. McKnight provided the necessary leadership to stabilise 3M and turn it around.[41] In 1993, facing collapse, IBM turned to a tough-minded outsider with a track record of success, Lou Gerstner, and appointed him chairman and CEO. It took three years to effect a turnaround and culture change, but eventually IBM recovered its corporate health.[42]

Like the military leaders discussed earlier, these business leaders had something that no one else had, a combination of experience, skill, the determination to stand firm in the face of adversity and, above all, a clear view of what the organisation needed to do in order to survive. One notable thing about 'survival' leaders is that they have an ability to infuse some of their own determination into those around them and to persuade them that no matter how dark things are at the moment, they will make it through the ordeal. The explorer Ernest Shackleton also had this quality. Those who accompanied him on his Antarctic expeditions later described how Shackleton kept his men together and alive almost through sheer force of will. 'If I am in the devil of a hole and want to get out of it', wrote one fellow explorer, 'give me Shackleton every time'.[43]

Aspirations of the group

Beyond mere survival, however, leaders have fulfilled two other functions. Moving up the hierarchy of needs, we can see how they help us realise our aspirations as a group. We all belong to social organisations and entities, often to several at the same time, and each of those entities has a purpose and an aspiration.[44] When the entity succeeds, our sense of belongingness and our self-esteem increase. To put it simply, when the group prospers, we feel more secure and, therefore, happier.

When we enter the social space of leadership, therefore, we are saying to the leader 'We need you to help us achieve our aims'. To paraphrase Thomas North Whitehead in *Leadership in a Free Society*, leadership begins whenever we set out to do things together.[45] Of course, leadership is not always inherent in the single figure of a leader; it can be shared among the group. In music performance, small ensembles such as string quartets often function without a formal leader, and some larger orchestras also play without a conductor; the Orpheus Chamber Orchestra, founded in 1972, is perhaps the most famous example.[46]

In most larger orchestras, however, a conductor is regarded as essential. Originally, the role was simply that of a concert master, to ensure that all the performers in the orchestra were playing together. A large orchestra generates a great deal of noise, and performers cannot always hear what other members are doing or what notes they are playing; the concert master was there to direct them and keep them together. Over the course of the nineteenth century, the concert master's role evolved into that of the modern conductor, responsible for setting the tone and style of orchestral playing and determining how musical scores will be interpreted. Mark Wigglesworth, himself a noted conductor, refers to the conductor as the 'silent musician', pointing out the paradox that the conductor is central to the music-making process yet does not actually make a sound.[47]

Unsurprisingly, this social space between conductor and orchestra is contested. In *Crowds and Power*, Elias Canetti famously described the conductor as 'the living embodiment of law, both positive and negative. His hands decree and prohibit'.[48] Conductors often try to assert their dominance over orchestras; Arturo Toscanini and George Solti are examples of conductors who were known for their dictatorial manner, publicly rebuking musicians who failed to live up to their high standards.[49] But musicians are artists who have their own ideas about how music should be played, and they often push back against overly demanding conductors, both on and off stage. In 1944, when the London Philharmonic attempted to dictate terms to its conductor, Thomas Beecham, the latter walked out, going on to found his own rival orchestra a year or so later.[50] Riccardo Muti was forced to resign as director of the orchestra of the Teatro Alla Scala in Milan after a rebellion in the orchestra, and following his election as conductor of the Berlin Philharmonic, Simon Rattle had to win over disgruntled members of the orchestra who had preferred a different candidate.[51]

Sporting leadership is another space which can be contested, and tales of athletes at loggerheads with their captains or coaches and managers are too numerous to mention. In *The Art of Captaincy*, former England cricket captain Mike Brearley described the role of captain in a team sport as multifaceted, encompassing disciplinarian, planner, people manager, motivator and role model, among other things.[52] The one thing that sporting captains have always had to remember was that the sportsmen who follow their lead want their team to win; it is the captain's job to make sure it does. Selfish captains who put their own interests over those of the team tend to lose the backing of the team fairly quickly, and once that happens, the captain's tenure in post seldom lasts long.

That suggests the captain has the role of a facilitator or, in Greenleaf's phrase, a 'servant leader', something which may be somewhat at odds with our notion of sports captaincy.[53] Even more controversially, perhaps, Leo Tolstoy suggested that generals have exactly the same role. In *War and Peace*, Tolstoy contrasted the approaches of Napoleon, who believed firmly in his own greatness and that the army responded to his orders and did what he told it to do, and his Russian opponent Field-Marshal Kutuzov, who believed that his army would only fight when it was ready to fight and he himself could not force the issue.[54] In Tolstoy's words, 'Kutuzov waited until the army knew what it wanted to do', and then gave the orders to make it so.

Jamsetji Nusserwanji Tata in India and John Spedan Lewis in Britain are examples of business leaders who understood the same principle. Tata, who founded the Tata Group in 1868, believed his purpose was to help India grow strong and realise its aspirations, whereas Lewis, recuperating from a serious illness in the late 1920s, realised that the business had prospered in his absence and that the enthusiasm and dedication of his workers, not his own qualities as leader, were driving its success.[55] Both regarded their followers as the primary drivers of the organisation; their own purpose was to help the organisation – in Tata's case, his country – to fulfil its mission.

How the aspirations of followers reflect the kind of leader that emerges can clearly be seen in the women's suffrage movement in the United Kingdom in the years leading up to the First World War. In 1903 the movement split into two camps. The first, the National Union of Women's Suffrage Societies (NUWSS), insisted on campaigning for change through peaceful, democratic means, influencing opinion formers and political leaders in hopes of shifting public opinion in favour of votes for women. The second, the Women's Social and Political Union (WSPU), argued that women had already been campaigning for the vote for fifty years and had achieved nothing. Its members advocated direct action.[56]

The difference in tone – one group insisting on working for peaceful change inside the framework of the law, the other angry, demanding change now and willing to use almost any means to get it – resulted in two quite different leaders. Millicent Garrett Fawcett of the NUWSS was not exactly a pacifist, but she abhorred violence. She also participated in many campaigns to improve the health and education of women, and suffrage was only one of several strands to her work; her goal was to improve the lot of women more generally.[57] Emmeline Pankhurst was more focused and direct. Under her leadership the WSPU focused on a single goal – votes for women – and never deviated from this. Pankhurst also authorised acts of violence such as arson and breaking windows in order to draw attention to the movement. Pankhurst herself believed that the struggle for votes was a war, and like a good general she was ruthless in directing the efforts of her followers towards the chosen goal.[58] But it was the followers of both organisations that chose the goals, and when the split occurred, followers aligned themselves according to their own beliefs about how the struggle for suffrage should be conducted.

We have been talking thus far about the aspiration of organisations: an orchestra, a sports team, an army, a business, a political movement. Sometimes, though, leaders have to reflect the aspirations of an entire nation or even a group of nations, and here things become even more complicated. The leaders of the Latin American revolutionary movements, attempting to overthrow the colonial power of Spain in the early nineteenth century, are a good example of this. They had to deal with the aspirations of the big landowners, political and social conservatives who wanted to throw off Spanish authority but were not willing to give up any of their own power or concede any social reforms; the liberal intelligentsia who saw the chance to reform the entire political and social system based on revolutionary principles such as republicanism and democracy; the indigenous and *mestizo* (mixed race) peoples who saw the chance to slip out from under the yoke of Spanish domination and become free; and the desire of the revolutionary armies to win victories and glory.[59]

The competing and contradictory aspirations of these groups proved to be too much for any single leader to manage. The social space was simply too contested.

Simón Bolívar, the most famous of the South American revolutionary leaders, managed to establish new states in Bolivia and Venezuela, but he could not establish a stable balance of power. Ultimately he became a repressive figure, relying on the conservative elites and the army to establish himself as 'president for life' of a state that was a republic in name only and setting up a tradition of *caudillismo* (rule by strong men), which persists in the region to this day; Nicolás Maduro of Venezuela is arguably the latest manifestation.[60] In contrast, Bernardo O'Higgins, the liberator of Chile, won a series of battles against Spanish forces, but when he tried to introduce democratic social reforms in Chile, he was overthrown by the old nobility and forced into exile.[61]

Caught squarely in the middle were leaders like José de San Martín, a former Spanish general, and Juana Azurduy de Padilla, a *mestizo* guerrilla leader from Bolivia. Steeped in the ideals of the Enlightenment, San Martín dreamed of creating a series of free republics in South America, but like O'Higgins, he ran up against the intransigence of the elites. He realised, reluctantly, that Bolívar's dictatorship offered the best chance of success, but his conscience would not allow him to be part of it, and in 1822 he resigned his command and went into voluntary exile in Europe.[62] Azurduy, who by 1818 commanded an army of six thousand indigenous and mixed-race guerrillas, saw her ambitions for her people denied. There was no place for her in the new government of Bolivia, and she died in poverty.[63] Once again, leaders remain in place only as long as they can satisfy the aspirations of at least some of their stakeholder groups; usually, that means the most powerful ones.

Aspirations of the individual

'William James [the psychologist] tried to show us the relation between what he called the inmost nature of reality and our own powers', said the sociologist and political scientist Mary Parker Follett, speaking at a Rowntree management conference in 1928:

> He tried to show us that there is a significant correspondence here, that my capacities are related to the demands of the universe. I believe that the great leader can show me this correspondence, can arouse my latent possibilities, can reveal to me new powers in myself, can quicken and give direction to some force within me. There is energy, passion, unawakened life in us – those who call it forth are our leaders.[64]

Follett's view of leadership – which was highly influential in business and liberal political circles in the 1920s before the Great Depression and the age of autarky changed the leadership landscape – focused very strongly on the social space. In her best-known book, *Creative Experience*, she denied the existence of control and argued that what leaders think of as control is really a form of coordination – bringing people together so that they perform tasks as a group rather than as individuals.[65]

But individual aspiration, said Follett, is also important. Like General von War-nery, quoted in the Chapter 2, she argued that people will do their best for a cause they believe in, and in doing so, they will advance as individuals and fulfil their own destiny. This proves false the notion that people accept leaders because they *want to be led*. Follett suggested that, instead, people accept leaders because they think the leader can help them become a better person and meet their own personal needs for success, advancement, self-esteem and even self-actualisation. That sense of personal achievement and meeting their own aspirations is one of the things people seek when they go into the social space and look for leadership.

Why this is so, why most of us seem incapable of achieving our goals on our own, has been – and remains – a matter for speculation. Writing in the sixteenth century, Machiavelli refers to the defects of human nature; although conceding that few people are wholly good or wholly bad, he argues that the actions of a few bad people can disrupt a society and impoverish it. In order to achieve our personal goals, then, we need a leader who can protect us from the evil intentions of our neighbours.[66] Machiavelli, like Plato before him, comments that people achieve more when working together than when trying to do things on their own, a senti-ment embodied in the old Haitian proverb 'alone we are weak, together we are a river'.

In the late nineteenth century, Viennese psychologist Sigmund Freud thought that looking for a leader was a form of transference. We grow up under the author-ity of our parents and teachers, but when we grow up, we move out from their shadow. As we leave behind the leaders of our childhood and our youth, we seek unconsciously for another form of authority, a new leader whom we can follow.[67] Similar views can be found much earlier among the works of Confucius, who urged people to follow the wise leader, the sage.[68] A contemporary of Freud, Muhammad 'Abduh, an Egyptian theologian, advanced the idea that as human beings we are naturally inclined to work together. Comparing human society to a hive of bees, 'Abduh believed that the glue that held society together was love, not erotic love but the pleasure and satisfaction we get from the company of others of our species. We come together and work in groups or teams because that is where we find the greatest sense of self-fulfilment.[69]

It is likely, of course, that most or even all of these drivers – and others – will be present in the social space, depending on our own psychological make-up and needs. We seek leaders who will help us strengthen our own identity and give us the confidence to achieve. When Squadron Leader Douglas Bader took over as com-mander of No. 242 Squadron of the Royal Air Force during the Battle of Britain in 1940, he found his pilots were demoralised and had lost the will to fight. His response was first to remind them of who they were – professional fighter pilots fighting a desperate battle to save their homeland – and then to restore their pride in themselves and show them once more how to fight. Bader, who had lost both his legs in a flying accident before the war, faced an uphill struggle for acceptance at first, but once his men saw that he was authentic – not only an excellent pilot and a brave man but also a leader who cared about their welfare and was willing to stand up to authority in order to help them – they responded and followed his lead willingly.[70]

Individual aspirations and group aspirations often go hand in hand, and many leaders are able to meet both at the same time. As one of the leaders of the Indian independence movement, Mahatma Gandhi sought to help India achieve its aspirations for freedom, but many people also found him to be personally inspiring and followed his ideas and philosophy, especially the idea of *satyagraha* (holding fast to the truth) as a form of non-violent resistance to injustice.[71] The same is true of the American civil rights leader Martin Luther King and the anti-apartheid activist and former South African president Nelson Mandela, with the latter in particular continuing to serve as an inspiration even during his long imprisonment on Robben Island.[72] Like Aung San Suu Kyi, his leadership was largely symbolic during this period, but that did not make it any less powerful.

Religious leaders are perhaps the most obvious example of leaders helping people to achieve their personal aspirations. Strong religious leaders give people faith or strengthen their faith when it might be weak or wavering. St Paul the Apostle is a good example of this. In both his preaching and his writing, such as the letters to the Corinthians, Paul attempted to explain how faith made people stronger and enhanced the quality of their lives. Preaching in the Roman Empire in the turbulent fourth century AD, St John Chrysostom's gospel of truth and love was comforting to people living in dangerous times and gave them the inspiration they needed to carry on. At the beginning of the Reformation, Martin Luther's preaching helped people to change their understanding of themselves and their own purpose on Earth.[73]

In thirteenth-century Japan, the Buddhist preacher Nichiren likewise showed people how they could transform their lives, if they wished to do so. In the Middle East, Zaynab bint 'Ali, daughter of the Caliph 'Ali and one of the leaders of what later became known as the Shi'a branch of Islam, acted as a physical protector to her people, saving a number of lives after the defeat at the Battle of Karbala in 680 AD. She was also instrumental in keeping the Shi'a tradition alive after the death or capture of many of its leaders at Karbala, and she set a precedent for female participation in religious leadership within the Shi'a tradition; female leaders such as Nusrat Amin (1886–1983) and Zuhrah Sifati (1948–) are known as *mujtahidahs* and are equivalent in rank to male *ayatollahs*.[74]

Religious leaders have also helped people achieve their aspirations through teaching and educating. Aisha bint Abu Bakr, one of the wives of the Prophet Muhammad, is known in Islamic history as the 'mother of believers' for her role in laying down and interpreting Islamic scripture and law. She was also a noted preacher, and in 656 she led a rebel army against the forces of her cousin, the Caliph 'Ali, at the Battle of the Camel. Even after retiring from public life to her home in Madina, she continued to be regarded as a great scholar and teacher.[75] Tsongkhapa, fourteenth-century abbot of the Jakhyung Monastery and founder of the Gelung school of Tibetan Buddhism, was enormously influential in Buddhist circles because of his teaching and writing. Although some of his work was controversial, he was largely responsible for the development and spread of Madhyamaka Buddhism.[76]

Leaders of charities can also help people achieve their personal aspirations to make a contribution and create a better and fairer society. Mother Teresa of Calcutta began her career as a teacher in Kolkata, but the organisation she founded, the Missionaries of Charity, eventually numbered over five thousand nuns and priests and expanded outside India to operate in more than a hundred countries. In addition to providing health care and education that changed many lives, the Missionaries of Charity offered people the chance to participate in delivering these services to the poor, thus enriching their own lives.[77] In Victorian Britain, the Ragged School Union, which aimed to provide free schools to children in the London slums, struggled to gain visibility until Lord Shaftesbury, an eminent philanthropist and social reformer, became president of the union in 1844. Shaftesbury raised the profile of the union and attracted widespread support, financial and otherwise. Ragged schools remained one of the main providers of primary education until the end of the century, when they were gradually replaced by state schools.[78] The organisation attracted hundreds of volunteers who wanted to participate in the cause of spreading education and found personal fulfilment in doing so.

Sport is another field where personal aspiration is important, and it is clear that one of the roles of the captain or coach or manager is to enable athletes to excel in individual terms. Mike Brearley discussed this need for personal development in *The Art of Captaincy*, as did former Australian cricket captain Steve Waugh in his autobiography, *Out of My Comfort Zone*.[79] In addition to encouraging their development as cricketers, Waugh urged his team to get involved in activities outside sport, such as charity work, and when travelling overseas, to study and learn from the various cultures they visited. Francois Pienaar, the South African rugby captain, became a symbol for both national and personal aspirations, in part by leading the Springboks, the first multiracial sports team in modern South African history, to victory in the 1995 World Cup, in part through his close friendship with and mutual admiration of Nelson Mandela.[80]

Less cerebrally, Buck Sheldon, the captain of the New Zealand rugby union All Blacks in the late 1980s, became a symbol of endurance for his team after a match against France in 1987 when he continued to play even while badly injured. He also improved relationships between white and Maori communities in New Zealand by ensuring that his team performed the correct versions of the *haka*, the ceremonial dance performed before each All Blacks match.[81] In women's sport in England, Casey Stoney, captain of the football team, and Charlotte Edwards, the long-serving cricket captain, were both known for setting an example through professionalism and then challenging others to rise to their level.[82]

This notion of setting an example and leading from the front brings us back in the direction of Great Man theory again, but what we see clearly is that rather than following a leader because of his or her inherent characteristics, people follow leaders whom they trust and who they know will be with them, supporting them all the way. Emmeline Pankhurst not only preached civil disobedience but also took part in it; she was arrested numerous times, was imprisoned and led the first hunger strike in Holloway Prison. Her supporters in the WSPU followed her example.[83] At the Battle of Sorauren in 1813, the Duke of Wellington rode alone across country to a position where part of his British and Portuguese army was menaced by a much larger French force. The allied army, which had been wavering, quickly rallied when it recognised Wellington, the Portuguese soldiers setting up a chant of 'Douro! Douro!' in memory of the battle where he had first led them to victory several years before. Heartened, the allies stood firm and repulsed the French attack.[84]

Summary

In the previous chapter we saw how, historically, leadership has been enacted in part as a struggle for power, leaders striving to increase power distance and followers fighting to reduce it. In this chapter we saw how the social space is also a place of collaboration where leaders and followers attempt to work together in order to achieve their goals. However, one of the many paradoxes of leadership is that both conflict and collaboration take place at the same time. Leaders both work with their followers and push back against them, and followers do the same to leaders.

Of course, whether leaders can actually work with their followers to achieve anything useful depends entirely on whether the followers are willing to accept their leadership in the first place. Why and how they have done so is the subject of the next chapter.

Notes

1 Tali Sharot, *The Optimism Bias: A Tour of the Irrationally Positive Brain*, New York: Vintage, 2012.
2 Carlyle, *On Heroes*; Ralph Waldo Emerson, *Representative Men*, Boston: Phillips, Sampson, 1850; Frederick Adams Woods, *The Influence of Monarchs: Steps in a New Science of History*, New York: Macmillan, 1913.
3 Homer, *The Iliad*; S. Radhakrishnan, *The Bhagavad-Gita*, London: HarperCollins, 1993; *Epic of Gilgamesh*, trans. N.K. Sandars, Harmondsworth: Penguin, 1960; Örnólfur Thorsson, *The Sagas of the Icelanders*, London: Penguin, 2001.
4 Xenophon, *Cyropaedia: The Education of Cyrus*, ed. and trans. Walter Miller, London: William Heinemann, 1914; Thucydides, *History of the Peloponnesian War*, trans. Rex Warner; ed. M. I. Finley, Harmondsworth: Penguin, 1954.
5 Arrian, *The Campaigns of Alexander*, trans. Aubrey de Sélincourt, Harmondsworth: Penguin, 1971; Cornelius P. Tacitus, *The Agricola and the Germania*, trans. H. Mattingly, Harmondsworth: Penguin, 1970; Plutarch, *Lives of the Noble Greeks and Romans*, trans. Bernadotte Perrin, Loeb Classical Library 103, Cambridge, MA: Harvard University Press, 1926.
6 Niccolò Machiavelli, *The Prince*, trans. G. Bull, Harmondsworth: Penguin, 1961; Machiavelli, *The Discourses*.
7 Richard Bolden, Beverly Hawkins, Jonathan Gosling and Scott Taylor, *Exploring Leadership: Individual, Organizational and Societal Perspectives*, Oxford: Oxford University Press, 2011.
8 Leonard H. Lesko (ed.), *Pharaoh's Workers: The Villages of Deir El Medina*, Ithaca: Cornell University Press, 1994; M.L. Bierbrier, *The Tomb-Builders of the Pharaohs*, Cairo: American University in Cairo Press, 1989.
9 Ibid.

10 Harrington Emerson, *Efficiency as a Basis for Operations and Wages*, New York: John R. Dunlap, 1909.
11 Anthony Jay, *Management and Machiavelli*, London: Hodder & Stoughton, 1967.
12 Ezra J. Warner, *Generals in Blue: Lives of the Union Commanders*, Baton Rouge: Louisiana State University Press, 1964; Bruce Catton, *The Army of the Potomac*, New York: Doubleday, 1990.
13 Alex Ferguson and Michael Moritz, *Leading: Lessons in Leadership from the Legendary Manchester United Manager*, London: Hodder & Stoughton, 2016.
14 James Burnham, *The Managerial Revolution: Or, What Is Happening in the World Now*, London: Putnam, 1941.
15 Burton Watson, *The Complete Works of Chuang Tzu*, New York: Columbia University Press, 1968; A.C. Graham, *Chuang-tzu: The Seven Inner Chapters and Other Writings from the Book Chuang-tzu*, London: George Allen & Unwin, 1981.
16 Rosa Luxemburg, *Reform or Revolution and Other Writings*, Mineola: Dover, 2006; Jon Nixon, *Rosa Luxemburg and the Struggle for Democratic Renewal*, Chicago: University of Chicago Press, 2018.
17 Lutton, *Lollardy and Orthodox Religion in Pre-Reformation England*; Rex, *The Lollards*; Richard B. Dobson, *The Peasants Revolt of 1381*, London: Pitman, 1970.
18 Christopher Hill, *The World Turned Upside Down: Radical Political Thought in Seventeenth Century England*, London: Temple Smith, 1972; George Woodcock, *Anarchism: A History of Libertarian Ideas and Movements*, New York: World, 1962.
19 Rousseau, *The Social Contract*; Morgen Witzel, Richard Bolden and Nigel Linacre (eds), *Leadership Paradoxes*, London: Routledge, 2016.
20 Sidney M. Milkis and Michael Nelson, *The American Presidency: Origins and Development*, Washington, DC: CQ Press, 2008; Richard Morris, *The Forging of the Union, 1781–1789*, New York: HarperCollins, 1988; Roger H. Brown, *Redeeming the Republic: Federalists, Taxation and the Origins of the Constitution*, Baltimore: Johns Hopkins University Press, 1993.
21 Jefferson, Thomas (1989) Letter to Francis Hopkinson, 13 March 1789, full text at www.britannica.com/presidents/article-9116912.
22 Dave R. Palmer, *1794: America, Its Army and the Birth of a Nation*, Novato: Presidio, 1994.
23 David P. Szatmary, *Shays's Rebellion: The Making of an Agrarian Insurrection*, Boston: University of Massachusetts Press, 1980.
24 Steven R. Boyd (ed.), *The Whiskey Rebellion: Past and Present Perspectives*, Westport: Greenwood Press, 1985; Garry Wills, *A Necessary Evil: A History of American Distrust of Government*, New York: Simon & Schuster, 1999.
25 Gracchus Babeuf, *The Defence of Gracchus Babeuf Before the High Court of Vendôme*, ed. John Anthony Scott, Yale, CT: Gehenna Press, 1964, p. 57; see also R.B. Rose, *Gracchus Babeuf: The First Revolutionary Communist*, London: Routledge, 1978; Doyle, *The Oxford History of the French Revolution*.
26 Pierre-Joseph Proudhon, *The General Idea of the Revolution in the Nineteenth Century*, trans. John Beverley Robinson, London: Freedom Press, 1923; Peter Kropotkin, *The Conquest of Bread*, trans. David Priestland, London: Penguin, 2015.
27 Émile Armand, 'Anarchist Individualism as a Life and Activity', 1907, www.spaz.org/~dan/individualist-anarchist/library/emile-armand/life-activity.html; Saul Newman (ed.), *Max Stirner*, Basingstoke: Palgrave Macmillan, 2011; Woodcock, *Anarchism*.
28 Woodcock, *Anarchism*; Paul McLaughlin, *Anarchism and Authority: A Philosophical Introduction to Classical Anarchism*, Aldershot: Ashgate, 2007.
29 Sunzi (Sun Tzu), *The Art of War*, trans. L. Giles, ed. Samuel B. Griffiths, Oxford: Oxford University Press, 1963; Niccolò Machiavelli, *The Art of War*, trans. Ellis Farneworth, Cambridge, MA: Da Capo Press, 2001; S.L.A. Marshall, *Men Against Fire: The Problem of Battle Command*, Norman: University of Oklahoma Press, 2000.
30 Klick and Talman, *The Journal of Major John Norton*; Kingsley M. Bray, *Crazy Horse: A Lakota Life*, Norman: University of Oklahoma Press, 2008; Stephen E. Ambrose, *Crazy Horse and Custer: The Parallel Lives of Two American Warriors*, New York: American Library, 1975.

31 Gretchen M. Bataille (ed.), *Native American Women: A Biographical Dictionary*, New York: Garland, 1993; Bernard A. Cook (ed.), *Women and War: A Historical Encyclopedia from Antiquity to the Present*, Santa Barbara, CA: ABC-CLIO, 2006.

32 Elizabeth Salas, *Soldaderas in the Mexican Military: Myth and History*, Austin: University of Texas Press, 1990.

33 Machiavelli, *The Prince*; Michael Mallett, *Mercenaries and Their Masters: Warfare in Renaissance Italy*, New York: Rowman and Littlefield, 1974.

34 Francis Stonor Saunders, *Hawkwood: The Diabolical Englishman*, London: Faber and Faber, 2004; Christopher Hibbert, *The House of Medici: Its Rise and Fall*, New York: Morrow, 1975.

35 Francisco Espoz y Mina, *A Short Extract from the Life of General Mina*, London: Taylor & Hussey, 1925.

36 Anne Bernet, *Charette*, Paris: Perrin, 2005; Michael Ross, *Banners of the King: The War of the Vendée, 1793–4*, New York: Hippocrene Books, 1975.

37 Roberts, *Eminent Churchillians*; Martin Gilbert, *Finest Hour: Winston S. Churchill, 1939–1941*, London: William Heinemann, 1983; Roy Jenkins, *Churchill: A Biography*, London: Pan, 2002.

38 Anna Comnena, *The Alexiad*, trans. E.R.A. Sewter, Harmondsworth: Penguin, 1969; Peter Frankopan, *The First Crusade: The Call From the East*, London: The Bodley Head, 2011.

39 Peter Popham, *The Lady and the Generals: Aung Sang Suu Kyi and Burma's Struggle for Freedom*, London: Penguin, 2016.

40 'Arthur Chamberlain', *Grace's Guide to Industrial History*, www.gracesguide.co.uk/Arthur_Chamberlain.

41 Virginia Huck, *Brand of the Tartan: The 3M Story*, New York: Appleton-Century-Crofts, 1955; Susan Hamburger, 'McKnight, William Lester', in J.A. Garraty and M.C. Carnes (eds), *American National Biography*, New York: Oxford University Press, vol. 15, 1999, pp. 131–2.

42 Doug Garr, *IBM Redux: Lou Gerstner and the Business Turnaround of the Decade*, New York: Harper Business, 1999; Louis V. Gerstner, *Who Says Elephants Can't Dance?* New York: HarperCollins, 2002.

43 Apsley Cherry-Gerard, *The Worst Journey in the World*, London: Vintage, 2010; Roland Huntford, *Shackleton*, London: Hodder & Stoughton, 1985; Stephanie Barczewski, *Antarctic Destines: Scott, Shackleton and the Changing Face of Heroism*, London: Hambledon Continuum, 2007.

44 Charles Handy, *Understanding Organisations*, London: Penguin, 1976; Abraham Maslow, *Motivation and Personality*, New York: Harper & Bros., 1954.

45 Thomas North Whitehead, *Leadership in a Free Society: A Study in Human Relations Based on an Analysis of Present-Day Industrial Relations*, Cambridge, MA: Harvard University Press, 1936.

46 Orpheus Chamber Orchestra, 'History', http://orpheusnyc.org/about-orpheus/history/.

47 Michael Bowles, *The Art of Conducting*, New York: Doubleday, 1959; Mark Wigglesworth, *The Silent Musician: Why Conducting Matters*, London: Faber and Faber, 2018.

48 Elias Canetti, *Crowds and Power*, Harmondsworth: Penguin, 1973, p. 460.

49 Harvey Sachs, *Toscanini*, New York: Prima Press, 1995; Harvey Sachs and George Solti, *Solti on Solti*, London: Chatto and Windus, 1997.

50 Charles Reid, *Thomas Beecham: An Independent Biography*, London: Victor Gollancz, 1961.

51 'Muti quits Milan's legendary La Scala', 2005, www.upi.com/Muti-quits-Milans-legendary-La-Scala/70261112630428/; 'Rattle Set for Classic Music's Top Job', 1999, www.theguardian.com/uk/1999/jun/12/fiachragibbons.kateconnolly.

52 Mike Brearley, *The Art of Captaincy*, London: Pan Macmillan, 2001.

53 Ronald K. Greenleaf, *The Power of Servant Leadership*, San Francisco: Barrett-Koehler, 1998.

54 Leo Tolstoy, *War and Peace*, trans. Rosemary Edmonds, London: Penguin, 1957.

55 Witzel, *Tata*; John Spedan Lewis, *Fairer Shares*, London: Staples Press, 1954.

56 Leslie Parker Hume, *The National Union of Women's Suffrage Societies, 1897–1914*, London: Longman, 1982; Harold L. Smith, *The British Women's Suffrage Campaign, 1866–1928*,

London: Longman, 1998; Joyce Marlow (ed.), *Suffragettes: The Fight for Votes for Women*, London: Virago, 2015; Millicent Garrett Fawcett, *Women's Suffrage: A Short History of a Great Movement*, London: T.C. & E.C. Jack, 1911.

57 Fawcett, *Women's Suffrage*; Marysa Demoor, *Their Fare Share: Women, Power and Criticism in the Athenaeum, from Millicent Garrett Fawcett to Katherine Mansfield, 1870–1920*, London: Routledge, 2017.

58 Emmeline Pankhurst, *My Own Story*, London: Virago, 1989; Paula Bartley, *Emmeline Pankhurst*, London: Routledge, 2002; June Purvis, *Emmeline Pankhurst: A Biography*, London: Routledge, 2002.

59 Robert Harvey, *Liberators: South America's Savage Wars of Freedom, 1810–30*, London: Constable & Robinson, 2000.

60 Harvey, *Liberators*; John Lynch, *Simón Bolívar: A Life*, New Haven: Yale University Press, 2007; Marie Arana, *Bolívar: American Liberator*, New York: Simon & Schuster, 2013; Karl Marx, 'Bolivar y Ponte', in *The New American Cyclopedia*, New York: D. Appleon, 1858, www.marxists.org/archive/marx/works/1858/01/bolivar.htm; Hugh M. Hamill (ed.), *Caudillos: Dictators in Spanish America*, Norman: University of Oklahoma Press, 1992.

61 Harvey, *Liberators*; Stephen Clissold, *Bernardo O'Higgins and the Liberation of Chile*, London: Hart-Davis, 1968.

62 John Lynch, *San Martín: Argentine Soldier, American Hero*, New Haven: Yale University Press, 2009.

63 Pacho O'Donnell, *Juana Azurduy*, Madrid: Planeta, 1998; Jessica Amanda Salmonson, *The Encyclopedia of Amazons*, London: Paragon, 1991; Catherine Davies, Claire Brewster and Hilary Owen, *South American Independence: Gender, Politics, Text*, Liverpool: University of Liverpool Press, 2006.

64 Mary Parker Follett, 'Leadership', Rowntree Management Conference Paper, 28 September 1928.

65 Mary Parker Follett, *Creative Experience*, New York: Longmans, Green, 1924.

66 Machiavelli, *The Discourses*.

67 Carl Jung, *The Psychology of the Transference*, London: Ark, 1983; Michael Macoby, 'Why People Follow the Leader: The Power of Transference', *Harvard Business Review*, September 2004.

68 D.C. Lau, *Confucius: The Analects*, Harmondsworth: Penguin, 1979; Kwang-kuo Hwang, *Foundations of Chinese Psychology: Confucian Social Relations*, New York: Springer, 2011; Erin M. Cline, *Confucius, Rawls and the Sense of Justice*, New York: Fordham University Press, 2012.

69 Muhammad 'Abduh, *Risalat al-Tawhid*, trans. Ishaq Musa'ad and Kenneth Cragg, *The Theology of Unity*, London: George Allen & Unwin, 1966.

70 Michael Burns, *Bader: The Man and His Men*, London: Cassell, 1998; Paul Brickhill, *Reach for the Sky: The Story of Douglas Bader*, London: Odhams, 1954.

71 Rajmohan Gandhi, *Gandhi: The Man, His People and the Empire*, Berkeley: University of California Press, 2006; Raghavan N. Iyer, *The Moral and Political Writings of Gandhi*, Oxford: Oxford University Press, 1986–7; Richard L. Johnson, *Gandhi's Experiments With Truth: Essential Writings By and About Mahatma Gandhi*, New York: Lexington Books, 2006.

72 Michael G. Long, *Against Us, But for Us: Martin Luther King Jr and the State*, Macon, GA: Mercer University Press, 2002; Marshall Frady, *Martin Luther King Jr: A Life*, London: Penguin, 2002; Anthony Sampson, *Mandela: The Authorised Biography*, London: HarperCollins, 2011; Tom Lodge, *Mandela: A Critical Biography*, Oxford: Oxford University Press, 2006.

73 David G. Horrell, *An Introduction to the Study of Paul*, London: T&T Clark, 2006; Donald Attwater, *St John Chrysostom: The Voice of Gold*, London: Harvill, 1939; Derek Wilson, *Out of the Storm: The Life and Legacy of Martin Luther*, London: Hutchinson, 2007.

74 Daniel B. Montgomery, *Fire in the Lotus: The Dynamic Buddhism of Nichiren*, London: Dai Gohonzon, 1991; Muna Haeri Bilgrami, *The Victory of Truth: The Life of Zaynab bint 'Ali*, Karachi: Zahra Publications, 1986; Mirjam Künkler and Roja Fazaeli, 'The Lives of Two Mujtahidahs: Female Religious Authority in Twentieth-Century Iran', in Mirjam Künkler

and Devin Stewart (eds), *Female Religious Authority in Shi'I Islam: Past and Present*, Edinburgh: Edinburgh University Press, 2019.

75 Nadia Abbott, *Aisha, the Beloved of Muhammad*, Chicago: University of Chicago Press, 1942; Denise Spellberg, *Politics, Gender and the Islamic Past: The Legend of A'isha bint Abi Bakr*, New York: Columbia University Press, 1994.

76 Jinpa Thupten, *Self, Reality and Reason in Tibetan Philosophy: Tsongkhapa's Quest for the Middle Way*, London: Routledge, 2013.

77 Raghu Rai and Navin Chawla, *Faith and Compassion: The Life and Work of Mother Teresa*, Rockport, MA: Element Books, 1996; Anne Sebba, *Mother Teresa: Beyond the Image*, New York: Doubleday, 1997.

78 C.J. Montague, *Sixty Years in Waifdom, Or, the Ragged School Movement in English History*, London: Charles Murray, 1904.

79 Brearley, *The Art of Captaincy*; Steve Waugh, *Out of My Comfort Zone*, Melbourne: Penguin Australia, 2005.

80 John Carlin, *Playing the Enemy: Nelson Mandela and the Game That Made a Nation*, New York: Penguin, 2008.

81 Ron Palenski, *Rugby: A New Zealand History*, Auckland: Auckland University Press, 2015.

82 'England Captain Casey Stoney Is First Woman on PFA Committee', *BBC Sport*, 2013, www.bbc.co.uk/sport/football/24935248; 'England Cricketer of the Year Awards 2013–2014', *ECB*, 2014, www.ecb.co.uk/news/articles/england-cricketer-year-awards-2013-2014.

83 Pankhurst, *My Own Story*; Bartley, *Emmeline Pankhurst*; Purvis, *Emmeline Pankhurst*; Christabel Pankhurst, *Unshackled: The Story of How We Won the Vote*, London: Hutchinson, 1959.

84 Michael Glover, *Wellington as Military Commander*, London: B.T. Batsford, 1968; Jac Weller, *Wellington in the Peninsula, 1808–1814*, New York: Modern Literary Editions, 1962.

4

THE ACCEPTANCE
OF LEADERSHIP

Another feature of the social space of leadership is that very often we enter this space involuntarily. We are not always granted the luxury of choosing our leaders. In the military, in the church, in the workplace – to name but a few – the leader is chosen by a very small group of people who have the authority to make that choice. The rest of us are pretty much stuck with whatever leader is foisted upon us, and we must then make a choice about whether to follow that leader or not.

This, in my view, lies at the heart of Jefferson's complaint about submission to leadership being 'the last degradation of a free and moral agent'. According to the tenets of liberal democracy, no one should be forced to accept a leader they have not freely chosen, and any leader who attempts to force his or her authority on people who have not made a free choice is, to borrow Max Weber's phrase again, exercising non-legitimate domination. It might be expected that people would rebel against leaders whom they have not chosen, and indeed, sometimes they do, but not as often as one might think.

In general, people tend to accept the leaders they are given, with one important caveat: the leaders must make it clear that they are willing to collaborate and share at least a degree of power with followers. There are, of course, rebellions and mutinies, but they usually happen only when the balance between collaboration and competition in the social space is upset. If one party or the other refuses to collaborate, the conflict for power becomes open and often violent.

It is usually the leader who is responsible for upsetting that balance, either through neglect or incompetence or by deliberately challenging followers and attempting to gain more power at their expense. We saw in the last chapter how history's first strike happened when the Egyptian authorities failed to pay their workers on time, and that same sense of injustice has fuelled many strikes and labour disputes, including the Real del Monte strike by Mexican silver miners in 1766, the Homestead Strike in Pennsylvania, the Great Unrest among shipyard workers in the Clydeside region of Glasgow before the First World War and the walkout by women workers at Ford's Dagenham plant in 1968 to protest unfair working conditions.[1]

Rebels and mutineers

When we think of leadership without consent, one of the first examples that comes to mind is the military. There are generally three ways of raising military forces: hiring foreign mercenary units, calling on the local population to serve as volunteers (paid or unpaid), or raising forces through conscription – that is, drafting people into military service against their will. The latter has probably been the most common method of recruiting soldiers throughout history, from the feudal levies of medieval Europe and Japan to the conscript armies of the modern world.

We would expect there to be a steady stream of mutinies and insurrections among conscripted soldiers as they tried to gain their freedom, but in fact, instances of mutiny are surprisingly rare. To reinforce the point made earlier, they usually happen when the leaders fail to honour their side of the collaborative bargain.

Two examples will suffice to make the point. The British Royal Navy relied heavily on conscripted or *pressed* men to man its ships in the age of colonial revolutionary and Napoleonic wars, although as Roger Knight has pointed out, there were also plenty of volunteer sailors.[2] The navy was noted for its harsh discipline – punishments ranged from flogging to hanging – but there were also strict rules of discipline of which every sailor was aware; if sailors violated the rules, they most likely knew the penalty. Historian N.A.M. Rodger has pointed out that life on a ship required that everyone, officers and crew alike, work together both to keep themselves and the ship safe and to make it able to fight effectively. Accordingly, the sailors understood why derelictions of duty had to be punished, and they acquiesced in the discipline.[3] Other navies copied the Royal Navy by imposing similar systems of discipline; again, these systems were generally accepted without serious opposition.

Implicit within this system of discipline and punishment was an element of trust. Sailors trusted their officers to treat them fairly; they, too, had to obey the rules. But when captains began to cross the line, such as ordering arbitrary punishments or failing to provide proper rations, the men began to question the system. When they did so, the result was usually a swift and violent rejection of their leaders. Two famous examples of this phenomenon are Captain Pigot of HMS *Hermione* and Captain Golikov of the Russian battleship *Potemkin* – both Pigot and Golikov stepped beyond the bounds of what their crews considered acceptable, and both paid for this with their lives.[4]

During the Vietnam War, the US Army relied heavily on conscripted soldiers. At first, they fought loyally for their officers, but by 1969 a combination of high casualties and inept leadership had led to a decline in morale. Soldiers began openly defying their officers and refusing to fight. Desertion increased dramatically, as did drug use among those who remained. Using fragmentation grenades, or 'fragging' to kill unpopular officers increased to alarming levels; according to some estimates there were about one thousand fragging attacks which resulted in eighty to one hundred deaths and hundreds of injuries.[5] Once again, analysis suggests the soldiers who carried out the fragging attacks were not attempting to escape from the army. They merely wanted to get rid of leaders who either were incompetent or were perceived as bullies (or both). In units where soldiers trusted their officers, discipline was strong and fragging did not happen.

Apart from mutiny, another option open to soldiers and sailors who reject their leadership is desertion. This has been true of every army across time, and there are usually harsh penalties for deserting the ranks. Once again, though, we find desertion levels highest when the bonds of trust between officers and men wore or broke down. In both the Royal Navy and the US Army, men were more likely to desert if they did not trust their officers or believed the officers were no longer looking after their best interests.[6]

Perhaps the most extreme form of conscription was that of enslaved people. Examples include enslaved Mamluks, who, during the Middle Ages, were taken from the Caucasus and south Russia to fight across North Africa and the Middle East and as far as North India and Central Asia; and the Janissaries, non-Muslim men whom the Ottoman Empire conscripted as part of its *devşirme* (slave tax) system.[7]

These slave-soldiers could rebel against their master, and they often did. After the death of Sultan As-Salih Ayyub of Egypt in 1249, the last of the Saladin dynasty, Ayyub's wife, Shajar al-Durr, attempted to rule as regent for their infant son. Sensing a power vacuum, the Bahri Regiment of Mamluks took over the palace. Shajar al-Durr's slave women beat her to death with their wooden-soled shoes, and the Mamluk commander, Baibars Bunduqdari, installed himself, with the support of the army, as Sultan.[8] The Mamluks ruled Egypt until 1517, and the Egyptian army was still largely composed of Mamluks at the time of Napoleon's invasion.[9]

The Mamluks did not rebel in search of freedom from their oppressors; they rebelled in order to gain more power for themselves. Turkish history is similarly full of revolts and threats of revolts by the Janissaries; they deposed Sultans Osman II and Selim III and became kingmakers of the empire until they were disbanded by Mahmud II in 1826. Rather than escaping the tyrannical system and seeking freedom to return to their families, slave-soldiers like the Mamluks and the Janissaries gathered power at the expense of their erstwhile masters.

Slave-soldiers, rather like Pasion and the other educated slaves employed in clerical work in ancient Athens, were, paradoxically, both slaves and part of the elite. In most societies where slavery was prevalent, however, slaves were employed in large part to do manual labour. Slave revolts in these societies were common; the Spartacus revolt during the Roman Empire, Nat Turner's rebellion in Virginia or the slave mutiny on board the Spanish ship *La Amistad* are famous examples, but there were hundreds of others.[10] In many of these rebellions, the desire to be free was undoubtedly a powerful motive, but there was also a strong element of revenge against masters who have been particularly tyrannical or brutal. We shall come back to the psychology of slave rebellions in chapter 12, but for the moment we can observe that slave rebellions are also the product of interaction in the social space. Maltreatment of an individual slave was one of the most common sparks that ignited rebellions.

Imposed leaders

For the most part, then, soldiers and sailors in conscript armies and fleets accepted the leaders imposed arbitrarily upon them, as long as the leaders respected the rules and boundaries and treated their followers fairly (we must make an exception for most slaves, who did not acquiesce to their position and rarely had sufficient power to resist). The same is true of political leaders who came to power through non-legitimate means. Sometimes, those who attempted to stage coups were met with popular resistance. General Georges Boulanger's attempt to seize power in France in 1889 never got off the ground, because Boulanger realised that any attempt at a coup would be quickly defeated. Likewise, the revolt known as the Fronde, which paralysed France from 1648 to 1653, finally collapsed when the nobles who led the revolt against royal authority realised they had no support in the country at large.[11]

In other cases, however, the leaders of coups enjoyed popular support. Jerry Rawlings, who staged a *coup d'état* in Ghana (1979), handed back power to the civil authority and then led a second coup (1981). Rawlings had his opponents, but he generally enjoyed wide support, enough to allow him to resign as dictator, found his own political party and win the ensuing presidential election.[12] Gemal Abdel Nasser, the Egyptian army officer who led the overthrow of the monarchy and then seized the presidency, was very popular with the people of Egypt, if not always with the elites, and was a leader of considerable stature throughout most of the Middle East until his death.[13]

As noted earlier, employees of a business are usually given little say in who their leader is. The same is true among other institutions such as charities and the civil service. Appointing business and charity leaders is the prerogative of the board of directors; although today some boards consult with staff, this was extremely rare in the past. At English chocolate-maker Cadbury Brothers in the early twentieth century, works committees were sometimes consulted about particular appointments, but this is an exception that proves the rule.[14] When Cosimo de' Medici, head of the Medici Bank, the largest and wealthiest business enterprise in fifteenth-century Europe, took the unusual step of appointing an outsider, Giovanni d'Amerigo Benci, as general manager of the business, he consulted only a few close associates; even other members of his family were left out of the process.[15] In the final days of his life, without consulting anyone at all, General William Booth, the founder of the Salvation Army, wrote the name of his successor on a slip of paper and placed it in a sealed envelope. Unsurprisingly, when the envelope was opened after his death, it contained the name of his son, Bramwell Booth.[16]

The year of the four emperors

Whether we accept someone as a leader, then, does not always correlate to the legitimacy of that leader's authority. As we saw in chapter 2, legitimacy of power is important, but it is not always sufficient to ensure the leader's survival. Leaders who do come to power in non-legitimate ways nearly always rush to legitimate themselves, proclaiming themselves to be the true leader and either gathering support from established elites and legal institutions or creating new institutions to give them legitimacy. But that does not always work, as many ambitious would-be Roman emperors learned to their cost.

Following the assassination of Nero in 68 AD, the last of the Julio-Claudian dynasty, over the course of the next two years four men tried to seize the imperial throne: Galba, a Roman patrician who had recently been appointed governor of one of the Spanish provinces; Otho, an ambitious nobleman from Rome; Vitellius, the commander of the Roman army in Germany; and Vespesian, an army commander from a relatively humble background who at the time of Nero's death was engaged in suppressing a major revolt in Judea.[17] The first three failed and were killed, and only Vespesian managed to consolidate his hold on power. What made him different from the others? Why was he accepted as a leader, when Galba, Otho and Vitellius were not?

The answers shed some light on what happens in the social space between the leaders and the led. Elderly and unwell, Galba was a reluctant leader in the first place, and he hesitated for a long time before joining the rising tide of rebellion against Nero. Arriving in Rome after Nero's death, Galba was welcomed at first; the people thought that this dull, elderly patrician would be a safe pair of hands. However, Galba quickly alienated his supporters through a series of unpopular measures, including raising taxes, executing enemies without trial and openly disdaining the imperial ceremonies and rituals that were popular with the people.[18]

Galba also alienated the army units that had put him in power by refusing to reward them for their loyalty. In January 69 AD, two legions stationed on the Rhine frontier revolted and proclaimed their general, Vitellius, to be the new emperor. Other units in Germany and Gaul quickly joined the revolt, and Vitellius marched on Rome. Seeing Galba's regime crumbling, former supporters of Nero coalesced around a new leader, Otho, and on 15 January they murdered Galba and proclaimed Otho emperor. Otho quickly repealed the unpopular taxes and restored the ceremonies, gaining popularity with the people, but when Vitellius's rebels crossed the Alps into Italy, he panicked. His forces attacked Vitellius at once, without waiting for reinforcements, and were defeated. His army was still strong, but Otho suffered another loss of nerve. Believing all was lost, after a reign of just ninety-one days, he committed suicide.[19]

Like Galba, Vitellius was a reluctant leader, and seems to have been a puppet largely controlled by his generals. He had a reputation for gluttony and indolence, and although he did undertake some useful administrative reforms, he seems to have spent most of his time giving banquets. After his army was defeated by that of

Vespesian, he offered at once to abdicate, but was prevented from doing so by his own soldiers. He was executed at Vespesian's orders after the latter entered Rome.[20]

Vespesian, by contrast, was both ambitious and pragmatic. Seeing an opportunity in Nero's death, he began a campaign to gather support among Roman army units in the Balkans and Asia. Once he had sufficient assurances of support, he seized Egypt, which supplied most of the corn required to feed Rome. Control of Egypt gave him the power to starve the capital city, a fact which many in Rome understood very well; a number of patricians, believing Vespesian to have the upper hand, now joined his cause. Vespesian also made overtures to the surviving supporters of Otho, offering them rewards to join him. Finally, when he defeated Vitellius and seized power, Vespesian was careful to cultivate public opinion. Financial reforms and an improvement in army discipline went hand in hand with new building works, such as the Flavian Amphitheatre (now known as the Colosseum). Vespesian also abandoned the remote, godlike air of the Julio-Claudians and presented himself as a man of the people, never hiding his middle-class origins.[21] Most of all, Vespesian proved quickly that he could give Rome what it had hoped for from Galba; stability, peace, the rule of law and the opportunity for the economy to recover. Had he proved unable to deliver, Vespesian may well have gone the way of his immediate predecessors.

The social space of leadership, then, is a place of give and take, a market for promises and rewards and a place of judgement where followers assess what leaders have done or will do and decide whether to give or withhold their support. This is not a purely dyadic interaction. There were several players in the social space of Rome in 69 AD, including the Roman army and the Roman populace, and the competition between them for power became one of the defining features of Roman history, just as it was more recently in Burma during the long showdown between the generals and Aung San Suu Kyi.[22] The army versus the people is a standard trope in political power struggles, and would-be leaders often have to decide whom to ask for support.

Barriers to acceptance

The social space can also be a place of exclusion. Followers decide whom they will follow, but they also rule out those people whom they will *not* follow. Those excluded are not only individuals but also, in some cases, entire categories.

One group that often finds itself excluded is the lower classes. Barriers between classes have often been used by elites to preserve power for themselves and prevent others from gaining it. The rigid historiosocial stratifications of Japan and India are good examples of this; leadership was reserved for the *samurai* or the *kshatriyas*, and anyone trying to break into those classes faced strong barriers.

At other times and places the boundary was more porous. In theory, peasants were supposed to know their place, but people from quite lowly backgrounds could, if they engaged in trade and became wealthy, aspire to positions of power (especially if the elites were chronically short of money, which they often were). Sir John

Pulteney, Sir Richard Whittington and Sir William de la Pole were merchants and traders who came from fairly humble backgrounds and parleyed their wealth into positions of authority. Pulteney and Whittington both served as lords mayor of London on multiple occasions.[23] Monastic orders were another field where class was less important. In the medieval monasteries of Western Europe and East Asia, monks and nuns of noble birth often did receive preferment, but there are examples of people from modest backgrounds rising to positions of leadership. Nicholas Brakespear, who in 1154 became the only Englishman elected pope (becoming Pope Adrian IV), was the (possibly illegitimate) son of a clerk from St Albans, and Gregory VII, pope from 1073 to 1085, may have been the son of a blacksmith.[24]

Within a given society, different institutions might have quite different barriers. In the British Army, most officers purchased their commissions on the open market, ensuring that officers were men of wealth and high social class.[25] The British Army thus had a significant high power distance. The Royal Navy, on the other hand, was much more meritocratic. A look at Admiral Lord Nelson's famous 'band of brothers' during the revolutionary and Napoleonic wars reveals men from noble and bourgeois backgrounds, but there is also Captain George Westcott, the son of a baker from Devon. Two of the navy's most celebrated navigators, James Cook and William Bligh, started out as able seamen, ordinary sailors, before eventually advancing to the rank of captain; Bligh was the son of a customs officer, whereas Cook's father was a farm labourer.[26]

Class could be a strong barrier, but there were other, stronger ones. Historically, the two barriers most difficult to break have been gender and colour. As noted in the previous chapter, it was very difficult for women to achieve legitimate power, and most of the women whom we find in positions of power before the twentieth century and in the suffrage revolution inherited that power from a husband or a father.[27]

To nineteenth-century observers such as Olympe de Gouges, Mary Wollstonecraft, John Stuart Mill and Florence Nightingale, the reason why women were excluded from leadership was clear; those who already held power (i.e. men) were unwilling to share it or to see their own power reduced.[28] There is a fair amount of evidence to support this view. During his tenure as prime minister of Britain (1902–5), Arthur Balfour refused to grant women the vote in part because women were more likely to vote for the Liberal or Labour Parties, which would reduce the power of the ruling Conservatives. Paradoxically, one of his successors, the Liberal prime minister Herbert. Asquith, thought that granting votes to women would hand more power to the Conservatives at the expense of the Liberals; he, too, was opposed to women's suffrage.[29]

Even when women did come to power legitimately, they were often challenged. Wu Zetian, the only female empress of China, was overthrown shortly before her death, and Queen Nzinga of Ndongo fought off a series of rebellions by her male relatives, who attempted to seize her throne.[30] Marie de Medici, regent of France for her young son following the assassination of her husband, Henri IV, faced a series of challenges to her rule and was forced into exile more than once.[31] Other women were allowed to rule in name only, with real power in the hands of their husbands. The eleventh-century Byzantine empress Zoe was forced to marry and then name her husband as co-emperor, and after her death, her unmarried sister Theodora, the last of the Comneni dynasty, ruled, as a kind of caretaker, only for the last year of her life as the court decided who should succeed her.[32] Elizabeth I of England is a rare example of an unmarried woman who inherited and retained power until her death.

Generally, if women wanted to lead, they had to create a source of power and authority for themselves. In the fourteenth century, Christine de Pisan's *The Treasure of the City of Ladies* gently satirises male domination and suggests that the only way women could live in a free society was to create their own exclusive city, which must be free of men.[33] Certainly, there is evidence that many women joined Buddhist or Catholic monastic orders and entered convents not only for reasons of faith but also as a way of freeing themselves from male domination. In most monastic traditions, unlike the societies that surrounded them, men and women were regarded as equals.[34]

Entrepreneurship was another route open to women, and historians are beginning to realise that there were far more female entrepreneurs around than those who have been recognised. An example is Eleanor Coade, a talented sculptor who was the daughter of a wool merchant from Exeter. In 1769 Coade bought a struggling artificial stone business in London and turned it around, managing it until her death. Her customers included many of the eminent architects of the day, such as Robert Adam and John Nash, and in 1780 King George III commissioned her firm to do work at Windsor Castle. Although she used the title 'Mrs Coade' in public, Coade never married.[35]

Others found positions of leadership by stepping outside the social norms and rebelling. This could be dangerous; Olympe de Gouges was executed, and another leader of the French revolutionary feminist movement, Pauline Léon, was imprisoned, as was WSPU leader Emmeline Pankhurst.[36] German communist leader Rosa Luxemburg was murdered by counter-revolutionaries in Berlin in 1919.[37] Women could also go into crime, and many found surprising levels of acceptance in the underworld. Ching Shih, a nineteenth-century Chinese pirate leader, took over her husband's small operation after he died and turned it into a huge force, with over three hundred ships and twenty thousand men under her command. In the 1920s, during the era of Prohibition in America, Cleo Lythgoe set up a business as a wholesale supplier of whiskey to smugglers running alcohol into the United States and became one of the richest women in America. Around the same time, Stephanie 'Queenie' St Clair established a successful gambling and illegal moneylending operation in New York, fighting off rival (male) gangsters who tried to take over her operation. St Clair was an advocate for civil rights for black people and combined advocacy with her criminal operations.[38]

In Western Europe and America, people of colour remained all but excluded from leadership, largely because of prejudice. During the Enlightenment, we must remember, theories of race were first codified. In the mid-eighteenth century the

German anthropologist Johann Friedrich Blumenbach believed that certain 'races', particularly those originating in Africa and Asia, were somehow 'degenerate'.[39] Although Blumenbach also argued that 'degeneracy' did not make these other races incapable of greatness, others, such as the eighteenth-century historian Christoph Meiners, used Blumenbach's concepts to develop their own theories of scientific racism. Some prominent Enlightenment figures also held racist views: Voltaire, for example, opposed slavery as an institution but promoted the superiority of the white 'race', and the language he sometimes used to describe people of colour is too offensive to be repeated.[40]

The result was the formalised and – supposedly – scientifically legitimated exclusion of people of colour from mainstream Western society, which included positions of leadership. Black people could serve, but they could not lead. For example, when black residents of Upper Canada, many of them escaped slaves from the United States, banded together to form a militia unit to defend their homes against American invasion in the War of 1812, they were required to have white officers; the black man who raised the unit, Richard Pierpoint, could serve only as a private soldier.[41] In the early twentieth-century West Indies, cricket teams were captained by a white cricketer even if he was an inferior player to his black teammates; a black player, George Headley, captained the team for one match in 1927, but it was not until the 1960s that black captains began to be accepted.[42]

Once again, the best way to a position of leadership was to step outside the establishment and create one's own source of power and locus of authority. The few black leaders who came to prominence in the West prior to the late twentieth century were either entrepreneurs – such as Sarah Breedlove Walker and Annie Turnbo Malone, two successful African American businesswomen – or underground figures, such as Queenie St Clair.[43] The Haitian rebel leader Toussaint L'Ouverture attracted widespread sympathy and admiration in Europe and America; he, like Alexandre Dumas, openly espoused many Enlightenment ideals, including liberty and equality. Dumas became a respected and admired general in the French revolutionary army, but both his and L'Ouverture's careers ended with Napoleon's rise to power and ruthless crushing of revolutionary sentiment. Toussaint died in prison, and Dumas was forced out of the army.[44] A more successful example is Olaudah Equiano, a former slave who became one of the foremost advocates of abolition in Britain and a community leader among the black population of London until his death.[45]

What makes leaders acceptable

What, then, makes certain people acceptable as leaders, but not others? From the foregoing we can conclude that, throughout much of history, whiteness (in the West) and maleness (pretty much everywhere) have been requisite characteristics for acceptance. This has suited the ruling elites, as it allowed them to preserve their power and not share it with women or people of other races, with the result that, when it comes to finding leaders, the elites have arbitrarily and unnecessarily limited the pool of candidates. That aside, there would appear to be certain other things that influence our decision to follow a particular leader.

I should point out that we are not discussing the 'traits' of a successful leader here, or anything like it. We are discussing what we need from our leaders and what we seek when we go into the social space looking for leadership, not the things that are inherent to them. This issue of what we want from our leaders will be developed more fully throughout the book.

Credibility and visibility

In order to follow a leader willingly, we must believe that the leader is capable of leading. This belief depends on two things: the leader's actual ability to lead and whether the leader can communicate that ability to us in a believable manner. Galba was a capable administrator, but he had no real interest in people or in communicating to them. Vitellius lacked energy and commitment. In contrast, Vespesian had, by all accounts, an easy-going charm, and he was also a skilled communicator who took care to win people over to his cause before embarking on his campaign to seize the throne. Gnaeus Julius Agricola was also a superb communicator.[46]

There has been much discussion in leadership circles about the role played by charisma and personal magnetism. The idea of charismatic leadership goes back to Weber's and Carlyle's belief in inherent characteristics and suggests that charismatic people have some special quality that is denied to ordinary people and that makes others want to follow them.[47]

History offers plenty of examples of highly charismatic leaders, people who are able to communicate, both verbally and non-verbally, the messages their followers want to hear. Alexander the Great had the quality of almost otherworldly brilliance, and his attraction to his generals, mostly young men like himself, was magnetic and at times almost sexual. Elizabeth I of England had a similar ability to attract people to her and command the loyalty of powerful men like Walsingham, Cecil and Leicester. In the modern world, former General Electric chairman Jack Welch was famous for his charismatic presence, and at least one commentator ascribes much of GE's success to that presence. Apple co-founder Steve Jobs was another leader who attracted loyalty and brought people together.[48]

However, too much emphasis has been placed on charisma, with the result, other features of successful leadership have been overlooked. Alexander the Great and Elizabeth I were both shrewd tacticians in their various fields, and both benefitted from the advice of older and wiser advisors such as Parmenion and Sir Francis Walsingham. Elizabeth I's reign would not have been as long or as successful if Walsingham's highly effective spy service had protected her from persistent assassination attempts.[49] Steve Jobs may have been the magnet that held Apple together, but his success as a leader depended largely on the skill of his designers to create products that people wanted to buy. Charisma alone will not fill the social space, or at least, not for long.

Nor is every leader necessarily charismatic. Some of the most effective leaders are 'quiet' or 'soft'; they do not project their personality onto their followers but instead lead by example. William McKnight, the long-serving and highly successful chairman of the 3M Corporation, was soft-spoken and self-effacing, a leader who preferred to listen rather than talk; Jamsetji Nusserwanji Tata lived a simple and humble life, seldom giving speeches and preferring to talk to his staff and workers in small groups.[50]

The French cavalry officer Baron de Marbot paints an intriguing picture of his own leader, Marshal Gouvion St-Cyr, one of Napoleon's best and most dependable commanders. St-Cyr did not follow any of the fashionable principles, such as addressing his men before action and exhorting them to do their best for their country. Instead, as the battle was about to begin, he would take up a position on high ground or on top of a building, where all his men could see him, and simply stand and watch as they formed up for battle. When the fighting was over, he climbed down and went back into his tent without saying a word.[51] St-Cyr understood that followers like their leaders to be visible. This partly relates to the symbolic nature of leadership, which we shall discuss in more detail in the next chapter – we want to see our leaders leading so that we know we can rely on them. But St-Cyr also knew that once his men had the reassurance of his presence, they could be trusted to get on with things in their own way.

Modern-day popes travel constantly, preaching and holding communion with their followers around the world, because that is one of the ways they reinforce their authority. The phrase 'management by walking around' was coined at Hewlett-Packard in the 1970s, but the principle is far older.[52] At Bat'a Shoes in the 1920s, Czech entrepreneur Tomás Bat'a designed his new factory in the town of Zlín with a unique feature: his own office was in a lift. This enabled him to move up and down the five floors of the factory so that he could see and be seen. It also meant that if his workers wanted to see him, they did not have to come to his office; it would come to them.[53]

Fairness and equity

One of the reasons why Galba fell from power was the perceived inequity of his rule, the arrests, executions and arbitrary tax increases (to be fair, the taxes were probably necessary; Vespesian, too, increased taxes soon after his reign began).[54] When accepting leaders, we need to be able to trust them not to abuse their power.

Fairness does not necessarily mean mildness or a soft touch. Quite brutal regimes can be acceptable as long as the punishments are fair and justified. We saw how this was true in the Royal Navy, but it is also true in the workplace. The industrialist and entrepreneur Robert Owen, who was also a strict disciplinarian, stated in the early nineteenth century that fairness and equity were essential to leading and managing a workforce.[55] A century later, the Fabian socialist Sidney Webb voiced the same opinion, arguing that most workplace unrest was not about money or working conditions but about unfairness. Fair treatment and a fair day's wage for a fair day's work were foundational principles of scientific management.[56] In all walks of life, we expect our leaders to trust us, and if we feel we cannot, our commitment to them begins to wane and can result in our rejecting the leader.

Guidance and strategic direction

Writers on leadership in the late twentieth century, such as John Kotter and Warren Bennis, often claimed that one of the duties of the leader was to provide vision to establish the organisation's goals and then communicate those goals to followers.[57] However, a historical study of leadership provides very little evidence to back this up. As we saw earlier, followers usually have aspirations of their own. People volunteer for military service because they want to fight for their country; or if they are conscripts who were forced to join against their will, they will aspire to stay alive until it is time to go home again (as the experience of soldiers in the Vietnam War have shown). Doctors and nurses join health services or work for charities because they want to heal the sick; musicians join symphony orchestras because they want to make great music. All have their own goals, even if they are not always entirely clear about what they are.

Unfortunately, the goals of followers and those of the leaders don't always match. The leader of a corporate enterprise may establish goals such as achieving a certain market share or turnover target. However, the goals of cotton workers working at a mill during the Industrial Revolution would have been rather different. Their goals were to put food on the table, pay the rent, educate their children and perhaps put a little money aside for their old age. As Robert Owen recognised, they were not remotely interested in how much profit the firm made or whether the mill owner's business empire was larger or smaller than that of other mill owners. To cite Harrington Emerson once again, the workers were selling time, whereas the management was buying output.[58] That mismatch of interests has been and remains one of the chief problems in the social space of the workplace.

Followers also have group aspirations. Studies of employment going back to the Hawthorne experiments in the 1920s and 1930s show that people work more effectively if they believe their work has meaning and serves some social purpose.[59] In India, Jamsetji Tata was effective at harnessing both individual and group aspirations: your work creates wealth, he told his workforce, not only for you but also for your country. Tata was successful in part because his own aspirations were closely aligned with those of his workers.[60] In the early twentieth century, Tomás Bat'a did much the same at Bat'a Shoes, building a company which created value for both his workers and their country.[61]

Followers have vision, but they sometimes lack the skill and knowledge to realise it. They need a guide to help them towards it. The role of the leader in the past has been to first evoke a vision that brings people together and then to set out the path towards it. Napoleon liked to depict himself as a visionary, but even a cursory reading of his life will show that he was really just harnessing national aspirations to, from his perspective, make France great again. Later in his career, when the financial costs and the death tolls of his campaigns began to hit home, people became disillusioned, and resistance to his rule began to rise; as early as 1808, even some of his closest associates, such as Talleyrand, his imperial foreign minister, were plotting against him.[62] George Washington harnessed the aspiration of his followers to be independent of Britain and became their guide and strategist. Washington played an essential role in the American victory, but he did not create the vision, which had existed independent of him.[63]

The ability to get things done

Another criterion followers look for is whether the leader can do what he or she promises to do. For example, they may seek to follow people with particular skill sets. We saw this in the example of François de Charette, whom the Vendéen rebels chose to lead them because he had tactical skills and experience that they lacked.[64] In the late seventeenth and early eighteenth centuries, the Duke of Marlborough was an effective military leader who had the trust and confidence of both his army and his sovereign, Queen Anne, because he could be relied upon to outthink enemy commanders and win campaigns.[65] William McKnight was chosen by the directors of 3M Corporation to be president partly because they had no other choice but partly because they recognised that, despite his comparative youth, he had a talent for organisation and a flair for business. Bill Gates's reputation as leader of Microsoft was built on his extraordinary skill as a software programmer, which won him the respect of his followers; he was one of the top people in the field, and that made him attractive as a leader.[66]

In addition to technical skills, people look for leaders who can organise and coordinate, skills which will enable followers to combine their efforts and work together. Gates had this ability, and so did Dwight Eisenhower, the general who commanded Allied forces in Europe from 1943 to 1945. Eisenhower had no battlefield experience; when the Second World War began, he had never commanded an army. What he did have in abundance was skill as a diplomat, negotiator and planner, and he was able to bring his fractious American, British, French, Canadian and Polish generals together, smooth over their differences, sort out their arguments and generally get the best out of them. Strangely, during his post-WWII career, he showed little of the energy and drive he had displayed during the war, and his two terms as president of the United States had little impact.[67]

This ability to get things done is a highly attractive quality in a leader, and it sometimes leads people to overlook other flaws. Benito Mussolini, the Italian Fascist leader and dictator, projected an image of himself as a man of action and achievement; in the words of his admirers, 'he made the trains run on time'. John D. Rockefeller was admired for the size and wealth of his business empire, and not everyone felt that the illegal and immoral means by which he had gained his wealth were a problem; the ends, as Machiavelli said, justified the means. In *The Prince*, Machiavelli argued that it was sometimes necessary to lie and use violence in order to protect the people.[68]

Power

One of the many paradoxes of leadership is that although followers will contest the social space, seeking to increase their own power, they will reject leaders whom they see as powerless because those leaders cannot get things done. That ability to get things done depends in part on power, and access to power is one of the things that attract followers and lead to acceptance. If a leader has power, then they are more likely to deliver what followers want, which may persuade others, who were not originally inclined to follow this leader, to change their minds. When Vespesian took control of Egypt and, with it, Rome's food supplies, many Roman nobles who had been neutral or opposed to him accepted the inevitable and came over to his side.[69]

For the leader, then, there is a tough balance to be sought. If you acquire too much power, followers will feel threatened and may rebel against you; if you give up too much power, they will see you as ineffective and throw you overboard.

The nature and sources of power have been discussed many times before. In ancient China, Han Fei thought the primary 'levers' of power were reward and punishment; the leader rewards success and punishes failure. Machiavelli and Mao Zedong agreed that political power is to be found in force of arms, or as Russian dictator Josef Stalin once said of the pope, 'how many divisions does he have?' Carlyle and other Great Man theorists believed power came from innate qualities, whereas many medieval theologians believed that power emanated from God, who then granted it to men. French and Raven's famous typology of power combines all these views into a single framework: coercive power, reward power, legitimate power, referent power and expert power.[70]

Of these sources of power, there is little doubt that reward power plays an important role. Followers invest in their leaders emotionally, physically and, sometimes, financially – for example, through taxes and tithes or by giving up time which could have been spent more profitably in other occupations. They want to see something come back to them, usually in the form of an increase in their prosperity, their happiness or both. As noted, employees of a corporation go to work for money, but they also want to know that their work has meaning and purpose as this makes it more rewarding and increases their happiness.

At the optical lens and instrument maker Carl Zeiss Jena, the head of the firm, the physicist Ernst Abbé, gave his staff complete freedom to design and carry out their own research projects, knowing that this would not only lead to high-quality products – Zeiss was renowned as the finest maker of microscopes and telescopes in the world during the late nineteenth and early twentieth centuries – but also give them the chance to pursue projects that mattered to them personally. Similarly, at Polaroid a few decades later, the founder and chairman, Edwin Land, encouraged his research teams to pursue whatever opportunities they thought were most interesting and most valuable. If it took twenty years to produce a result, so be it.[71] Freedom to create was a reward that both Carl Zeiss and Polaroid scientists found attractive.

But as French and Raven point out, it is not simply a matter of separating one type of power from another. Most successful leaders rely on a combination of different types of power. More importantly, they derive a great deal of their power from their followers. In his classic work *On Guerrilla Warfare*, Mao Zedong repeatedly makes the point that power is also derived from the people; without popular support, no revolutionary movement can succeed. Business leaders – among whom Mao's work has in the past been popular – agree. John Spedan Lewis, the English department store owner, and Ricardo Semler, the Brazilian manufacturer, concluded independently that the workforce is the real source of power in the organisation and that without their willing support the business can do nothing.[72] They adjusted the balance of power accordingly, transferring more power to their supporters in an effort to create greater fairness in terms of power distribution.

This suggests that leaders who seek to excessively increase the power distance between themselves and their followers are deluded, because if followers are part of the source of the leader's power, increasing the distance between leader and followers will be counter-productive. In an attempt to exclude the lower classes from power, medieval European leaders conceived of a social stratification known as the three estates, the clergy, the nobility (including knights) and the peasantry. The clergy ensured society's well-being, the nobles and knights governed and safeguarded the realm and the peasants did menial work and grew food for the other two estates.[73] (That was the theory; in practice, the situation was usually much messier.) Unfortunately, some among the clergy and the knights thought that religious authority and force of arms gave them power over the peasantry, and they abused their power in a variety of ways, such as extortion, forced labour, excessive taxation, robbery, rape and murder.

When this happened, as with the naval mutinies described earlier, the peasantry realised the nobles and clergy had forfeited their trust, they and rebelled. In the minds of followers, the exercise of power is closely linked to fairness and equity. The Peasants' Revolt in England and the Jacquerie in France, both in the fourteenth century, were notable examples of revolutions sparked by perceived unfairness. Popular, often rural revolt continued in Europe into the twentieth century: in 1907, an agrarian revolt devastated parts of Romania and cost more than ten thousand lives.[74] Power, then, is something that must be shared, and the understanding that followers are not powerless and have strength of their own is something that wise leaders have always understood.

Once a leader loses control of power, his or her authority becomes compromised, and it is very hard to win it back. Byzantine Emperor Justinian II, who ascended the throne in 685 AD, decided to restore Byzantium to its former glory by picking a fight with the newly established Arab Empire in hopes of a military victory. Soundly defeated, Justinian took out his frustrations on his own people, raising unpopular taxes and provoking religious dissent. In 695, a popular rebellion forced Justinian to abdicate and go into exile. Unfortunately, his successor proved just as unpopular and incompetent, and in 705 Justinian returned to the capital, Constantinople, and seized power in a *coup d'état*. However, he had lost his authority, and he never really managed to get it back. His second spell on the throne was marked by almost constant rebellions and plots against him; finally, in 711, he was overthrown and killed by his own soldiers.[75]

Dharmavamsa, the ruler of the Isana kingdom of Java, expanded his kingdom at the expense of his neighbours, conquering Bali and part of southern Sumatra around 900 AD. His military successes made him popular, but Dharmavamsa over-reached, was badly defeated by a coalition of Sumatran princes and was forced to retreat. His aura of success was destroyed, and his own people began to turn against him. A few years later, rebels attacked a royal wedding and killed the king and most of his family.[76]

Luck

'Give me lucky generals', Napoleon is supposed to have said, although he himself never admitted to his own share of luck. As Tolstoy points out, Napoleon's greatest weakness was his refusal to admit that he was not in absolute control of every-thing. In his memoirs, written after his abdication, Napoleon continued to insist that everything he had achieved was due to his own genius.[77] But any leader with an ounce of humility will admit that luck plays a major role in his or her success. Allan Leighton, in his study of successful business leaders, referred to luck time and time again.[78] An accidental discovery of a new product, a serendipitous piece of market information, the illness or death of a key member of staff, an unexpected or unforeseen movement in the market, all can tip the balance of fortune for or against a business.

In *The Prince*, Machiavelli discusses two related phenomena, *fortuna* (luck) and *virtù* (the intelligence and mental strength required to see when luck has presented us with an opportunity and seize it with both hands). Their influence on successful leaders, Machiavelli estimated, was about fifty-fifty; that is, half of a leader's success is luck; half, skill. Ed Smith, the former cricket captain, picked up on this theme in his book *Luck*, reminding us that fortune plays a powerful role in the success of any leader. Even being born into the right family, which can provide one with a good education and a better chance in life, said Smith, is a matter of luck.[79]

Luck sometimes ensures that the right leader is in the right place at the right time, like Eisenhower in 1943, Churchill in 1940 and, arguably, Vespesian in 69 AD; sometimes, but not always. The notion of 'cometh the hour, cometh the man' is a seductive one, and we can point to plenty of other examples where it happen; con-versely, we can point to just as many examples where it did not. IBM Corporation was fortunate that Lou Gerstner was on hand to rescue it in 1993, and car-maker Chrysler was similarly fortunate that Lee Iacocca was able to take over in 1978 and pull the company back from the brink of collapse.[80] But there was no knight in shining armour ready to ride to the rescue of PanAm, one of the world's best-known airlines, when it collapsed in 1991; Stanley Motors, which was the world's most technologically advanced car manufacturer when it closed its doors in 1924; the South Sea Company, which collapsed in 1720 and nearly dragged the entire British economy down with it; the great and powerful Medici Bank, which foundered in 1499; or many others.[81] Similarly, there was no Eisenhower or Churchill ready to rescue the Aztec state as Cortéz's *conquistadors* closed in on Tenochtitlan in 1521, and no heroic leader was waiting in 1912 to rescue Robert Falcon Scott's doomed Antarctica expedition.[82]

Fortuna, said Machiavelli, is fickle, and no one should depend upon it. Nevertheless, the perception that some leaders are luckier than others has persisted. Leaders must at times take risks, and some have the knack of pulling off risky ventures and making them work, whereas others do not. Whether luck exists or not is immaterial – what matters is that people believe it does, and in the social space of leadership they make their choices about which leaders they will follow according to that perception.

Summary

Again, there is no one characteristic of a leader that decides whether he or she will be accepted. All of the issues discussed in this chapter come into play, along with many others; personal attractiveness is certainly a feature, as is health. Crippled by illness in 1922, Franklin D. Roosevelt spent much of his career confined to a wheelchair, but word of his disability was confined to only a few people for fear that the public would lose confidence if they knew the truth.[83]

The reasons why we accept leaders are complex, but the important lesson from this study is that acceptance is essential. People will not follow a leader they do not accept; if they do, they will not continue to follow for long, and they will fight back and attempt to seize power for themselves at the earliest opportunity. Once again, the social space of leadership is contested. If the leader is imposed upon unwilling followers by force, the contest very often will become more intense, even if the struggle is hidden from view.

Notes

1 Doris M. Ladd, *The Making of a Strike: Mexican Silver Workers' Struggles in the Real del Monte, 1766–1775*, Lincoln: University of Nebraska Press, 1988; David P. Demarest (ed.), *The River Ran Red: Homestead, 1892*, Pittsburgh: University of Pittsburgh Press, 1992; Iain McLean, *The Legend of Red Clydeside*, Edinburgh: John Donald, 2000; Sheila Cohen, *Notoriously Militant: The Story of a Union Branch at Ford Dagenham*, London: The Merlin Press, 2014.
2 Roger Knight, *Britain Against Napoleon: The Organization of Victory, 1793–1815*, London: Penguin, 2014.
3 N.A.M. Rodger, *The Wooden World: An Anatomy of the Georgian Navy*, New York: W.W. Norton, 1996; John D. Byrn, *Crime and Punishment in the Royal Navy: Discipline on the Leeward Islands Station, 1784–1812*, Brookfield, VT: Scolar Press, 1989.
4 Dudley Pope, *The Black Ship*, Barnsley: Pen & Sword, 2009; Neal Bascomb, *Red Mutiny: Eleven Fateful Days on the Battleship Potemkin*, Boston: Houghton Mifflin, 2007.
5 Richard A. Gabriel and Paul L. Savage, *Crisis in Command: Mismanagement in the Army*, New York: Hill & Wang, 1978; George Lepre, *Fragging: Why U.S. Soldiers Assaulted Their Officers in Vietnam*, Lubbock: Texas Tech University Press, 2011.

6 Knight, *Britain Against Napoleon*; Jack Todd, *Desertion: In the Time of Vietnam*, Boston: Houghton Mifflin, 2001.

7 Thomas Philipp and Ulrich Haarmann (eds), *The Mamluks in Egyptian Politics and Society*, Cambridge: Cambridge University Press, 1998; Rhoads Murphy, *Ottoman Warfare, 1500–1700*, London: Routledge, 1998; Halil Inalcik, *The Ottoman Empire, 1300–1600*, London: Weidenfeld & Nicolson, 2000.

8 Philipp and Haarmann, *The Mamluks*; W.B. Bartlett, *The Last Crusade: The Seventh Crusade and the Final Battle for the Holy Land*, London: The History Press, 2007.

9 Paul Strathern, *Napoleon in Egypt: The Greatest Glory*, London: Jonathan Cape, 2007.

10 Barry Strauss, *The Spartacus War*, London: Simon & Schuster, 2009; Kenneth S. Greenberg (ed.), *Nat Turner: A Slave Rebellion in History and Memory*, New York: Oxford University Press, 2003; Howard Jones, *Mutiny on the Amistad: The Saga of a Slave Revolt and Its Impact on American Abolition, Law and Diplomacy*, New York: Oxford University Press, 1987.

11 Frédéric Seager, *The Boulanger Affair*, Ithaca: Cornell University Press, 1969; Orest Ranum, *The Fronde: A French Revolution*, New York: W.W. Norton, 1993.

12 Paul Nugent, *Big Men, Small Boys and Politics in Ghana: Power, Ideology and the Burden of History, 1982–1994*, London: Pinter, 1996; Mohammed Bassiru Sillah, *African Coup d'Etat and the Revolutionary Mission of the Military: A Case Study of Jerry Rawlings in Ghanian Politics*, Lawrenceville, VA: Brunswick, 1984.

13 Said K. Aburish, *Nasser: The Last Arab*, New York: St Martin's, 2004; Richard Hrair Dekmejian, *Egypt Under Nasser: A Study in Political Dynamics*, Albany: State University of New York Press, 1971.

14 Edward Cadbury, *Experiments in Industrial Organization*, London: Longmans, Green, 1912.

15 de Roover, *The Rise and Decline of the Medici Bank*.

16 Roy Hattersley, *Blood and Fire: William and Catherine Booth of the Salvation Army*, New York: Little, Brown, 1999.

17 P. Cornelius Tacitus, *The Histories*, ed. Rhiannon Ash, trans. Kenneth Wellesley, London: Penguin, 2009; Gwyn Morgan, *69 AD: The Year of Four Emperors*, Oxford: Oxford University Press, 2005.

18 Ibid.; see also Cassius Dio, *Roman History*, trans. Earnest Cary, London: Loeb Classical Library, 1928, vol. 8; Suetonius, *The Twelve Caesars*, trans. Robert Graves, Harmondsworth: Penguin, 1957.

19 Ibid.

20 Ibid.

21 Ibid.

22 Beard, *SPQR*; Edward Gibbon, *The Decline and Fall of the Roman Empire*, London: Everyman, 2010; Popham, *The Lady and the Generals*; Nehginpao Kipgen, *Myanmar: A Political History*, New Delhi: Oxford University Press India, 2016.

23 Roger L. Axworthy, 'Pulteney, Sir John', in *Oxford Dictionary of National Biography*, Oxford: Oxford University Press, 2004; Anne Sutton, 'Whittington, Sir Richard', in *Oxford Dictionary of National Biography*, Oxford: Oxford University Press, 2004; E.B. Fryde, *William de la Pole: Merchant and King's Banker*, London: Hambledon, 1988.

24 Brenda Bolton and Anne J. Duggan (eds), *Adrian IV The English Pope (1154–9): Studies and Texts*, London: Routledge, 2003; H.E.J. Cowdray, *Pope Gregory VII, 1073–1085*, Oxford: Clarendon Press, 1998.

25 Knight, *Britain Against Napoleon*.

26 J.K. Laughton, 'Westcott, George Blagdon', in *Oxford Dictionary of National Biography*, Oxford: Oxford University Press, 2004; Anne Salmond, *Bligh: William Bligh in the South Seas*, Berkeley: University of California Press, 2011; Nigel Rigby and Pieter van der Merwe, *Captain Cook in the Pacific*, London: National Maritime Museum, 2002.

27 Georges Duby and Michelle Perrot (eds), *A History of Women in the West*, Cambridge, MA: Harvard University Press, 1992–4, 5 vols.

28 Mousset, *Women's Rights and the French Revolution*; Mary Wollstonecraft, *A Vindication of the Rights of Woman*, London: Vintage, 2015; John Stuart Mill, *The Subjection of Women*, ed. Susan M. Okin, London: Yale University Press, 1985; Florence Nightingale, *Suggestions for*

Thought to the Searchers After Truth Among the Artisans of England, New York: New York University Press, 1993.

29 R.J.Q. Adams, *Balfour: The Last Grandee*, London: John Murray, 2007; Roy Jenkins, *Asquith: Portait of a Man and His Era*, London: Collins, 1964.

30 Warner, *Dragon Empress*; Williams, 'Queen Nzinga'.

31 Michel Carmona, *Marie de Médicis*, Paris: Fayard, 1981.

32 Lynda Garland, *Byzantine Empresses: Women and Power in Byzantium, AD 527–1204*, London: Routledge, 1999; Michael Psellus, *Fourteen Byzantine Rulers: The Chronographia of Michael Sellus*, ed. and trans. E.R.A. Sewter, Harmondsworth: Penguin, 1979.

33 Christine de Pisan, *The Treasure of the City of Ladies*, trans. Sarah Lawson, Harmondsworth: Penguin, 1985.

34 Khandro Rinpoche, *Blossoms of the Dharma: Living as a Buddhist Nun*, Berkeley: North Atlantic Books, 1999; Karma Lekshe Tsomo, *Eminent Buddhist Women*, Albany: State University of New York Press, 2014; Eileen Power, *Medieval English Nunneries c. 1275–1525*, Cambridge: Cambridge University Press, 2010.

35 Alison Kelly, 'Coade, Elizabeth', in *Oxford Dictionary of National Biography*, Oxford: Oxford University Press, 2004.

36 Mousset, *Women's Rights and the French Revolution*; Melzer and Rabine, *Rebel Daughters*; Bartley, *Emmeline Pankhurst*; Purvis, *Emmeline Pankhurst*.

37 Nixon, *Rosa Luxemburg*; Elzbieta Ettinger, *Rosa Luxemburg: A Life*, Boston: Beacon, 1988.

38 Robert Antony, *Like Froth Floating on the Sea: The World of Pirates and Seafarers in Late Imperial South China*, Berkeley: University of California Press, 2003; Gertrude Lythgoe, *The Bahama Queen: The Autobiography of Gertrude 'Cleo' Lythgoe*, Mystic, CN: Flat Hammock Press, 2006; Shirley Stewart, *The World of Stephanie St Clair: An Entrepreneur, Race Woman and Outlaw in Early Twentieth Century Harlem*, New York: Peter Lange, 2014.

39 Raj Bhopal, 'The Beautiful Skull and Blumenbach's Errors: The Birth of the Scientific Concept of Race', *British Medical Journal* 335 (2007): 1308–9; Emmanuel Chukwudi Eze, *Race and the Enlightenment: A Reader*, Oxford: Blackwell, 1997.

40 Voltaire, 'The Different Races of Man', in *The Philosophy of History*, New York: Philosophical Library, 2007.

41 Steve Pitt, *To Stand and Fight Together: Richard Pierpoint and the Coloured Corps of Upper Canada*, Toronto: Dundurn Press, 2008.

42 Michael Manley, *A History of West Indies Cricket*, London: Andre Deutsch, 1988.

43 A'Lelia Perry Bundles, *Madam C.J. Walker: Entrepreneur*, New York: Chelsea House, 2008; Penny Colman, *Madam C.J. Walker: Building a Business Empire*, Brookfield, CT: Millbrook, 1994; J.N. Ingham and L.B. Feldman (eds), *African-American Business Leaders: A Biographical Dictionary*, Westport: Greenwood Press, 1994.

44 Madison Smartt Bell, *Toussaint l'Ouverture: A Biography*, New York: Pantheon, 2007; Tom Reiss, *The Black Count*, London: Vintage, 2013.

45 Olaudah Equiano, *The Life of Olaudah Equiano, or Gustavus Vassa, the African*, Mineola: Dover, 1999; Vincent Carretta, *Equiano, the African: Biography of a Self-Made Man*, Athens, GA: University of Georgia Press, 2005.

46 Barbara Levick, *Vespesian*, London: Routledge, 1999; Tacitus, *Agricola*.

47 Weber, *Rationalism and Modern Society*; Carlyle, *On Heroes*.

48 Arrian, *The Campaigns of Alexander*; Robin Lane Fox, *The Search for Alexander*, Boston: Little, Brown, 1980; Patrick Collinson, *Elizabeth I*, Oxford: Oxford University Press, 2007; Susan Doran and Thomas S. Freeman (eds), *The Myth of Elizabeth*, Basingstoke: Palgrave, 2003; Jack Welch, *Jack: Straight from the Gut*, New York: Warner Business Books, 2001; Bill Lane, *Jacked Up: The Inside Story of How Jack Welch Talked GE Into Becoming the World's Greatest Company*, New York: McGraw-Hill, 2008; Walter Isaacson, *Steve Jobs: The Exclusive Biography*, New York: Abacus, 2013.

49 Robert Hutchinson, *Elizabeth's Spy Master: Sir Francis Walsingham and the Secret War that Saved England*, London: Weidenfeld & Nicolson, 2007.

50 Huck, *Brand of the Tartan*; Witzel, *Tata*; R.M. Lala, *For the Love of India: The Life and Times of Jamsetji Tata*, New Delhi: Penguin India, 2004.

51 Jean-Baptiste de Marbot, *The Memoirs of Baron de Marbot*, trans. Arthur John Butler, London: Longmans, Green, 1892.

52 Mike Mears, *Leadership Elements: A Guide to Building Trust*, New York: iUniverse, 2009.

53 Tomás Bat'a, *Knowledge in Action: The Bata System of Management*, Amsterdam: IOS Press, 1992; Anthony Cekota, *Entrepreneur Extraordinary: The Biography of Tomas Bata*, Rome: Edizioni Internazionali Soziali, 1968.

54 Levick, *Vespesian*.

55 Robert Owen, *Some Observations on the Effect of the Manufacturing System*, London, 1815; Donnachie, *Robert Owen*.

56 Sidney Webb, *The Works Manager To-Day*, London: Longmans, Green, 1917; Taylor, *The Principles of Scientific Management*.

57 John P. Kotter, *A Force for Change: How Leadership Differs From Management*, New York: The Free Press, 1990; Warren G. Bennis and Burt Nanus, *Leaders: Five Strategies for Taking Charge*, New York: Harper & Row, 1985.

58 Emerson, *Efficiency as a Basis for Operations and Wages*.

59 Elton Mayo, *The Human Problems of an Industrial Civilization*, New York: Macmillan, 1933; Whitehead, *Leadership in a Free Society*.

60 Lala, *For the Love of India*.

61 Bat'a, *Knowledge in Action*.

62 McLynn, *Napoleon*; David Lawday, *Napoleon's Master: A Life of Prince Talleyrand*, London: Jonathan Cape, 2006.

63 Burke Davis, *George Washington and the American Revolution*, New York: Random House, 1975; John E. Ferling, *First of Men: A Life of George Washington*, New York: Oxford University Press, 2010.

64 Ross, *Banners of the King*.

65 Richard Holmes, *Marlborough: Britain's Greatest General*, London: HarperCollins, 2009.

66 Huck, *Brand of the Tartan*; Michael Becraft, *Bill Gates: A Biography*, Westport: Greenwood, 2014.

67 Stephen E. Ambrose, *Eisenhower*, New York: Simon & Schuster, 1983–4, 2 vols; Jean Edward Smith, *Eisenhower in War and Peace*, New York: Random House, 2012.

68 Peter Neville, *Mussolini*, London: Routledge, 2014; Richard Bosworth, *Mussolini*, London: Hodder & Stoughton, 2002; Chernow, *Titan*; Machiavelli, *The Prince*.

69 Morgan, *69 AD*; Levick, *Vespesian*.

70 Mao Zedong, *On Guerrilla Warfare*, trans. Samuel B. Griffiths, New York: Dover, 2005; John R.P. French and Bertram Raven, 'The Bases of Social Power', in Dorwen Cartwright (ed.), *Studies in Social Power*, Ann Arbor: University of Michigan, 1959; Watson, *Han Fei Tzu*; Machiavelli, *The Prince*; Carlyle, *On Heroes*.

71 Felix Auerbach, *The Zeiss Works and the Carl-Zeiss Stiftung in Jena*, trans. S.F. Paul and F.J. Cheshire, London: Marshall, Brookes and Chalkley, 1904; Victor K. McElheny, *Insisting on the Impossible: The Life of Edwin Land*, New York: Perseus, 1998.

72 Mao, *On Guerrilla Warfare*; Lewis, *Fairer Shares*; Ricardo Semler, *Maverick! The Success Story Behind the World's Most Unusual Workplace*, New York: Random House, 2001.

73 Marc Bloch, *Feudal Society*, trans. L.A. Manyon, Chicago: University of Chicago Press, 1961; Susan Reynolds, *Fiefs and Vassals: The Medieval Evidence Reinterpreted*, Oxford: Oxford University Press, 1994.

74 Cohn, *Popular Protest in Late Medieval Europe*; Philip Gabriel Eidelberg, *The Great Rumanian Peasant Revolt of 1907: Origins of a Modern Jacquerie*, Leiden: Brill, 1974.

75 Constance Head, *Justinian II of Byzantium*, Madison: University of Wisconsin Press, 1972; J.B. Bury, *A History of the Later Roman Empire*, London: Macmillan, 1889, vol. 2.

76 Munoz, *Early Kingdoms of the Indonesian Archipelago*.

77 Tolstoy, *War and Peace*; Louis Antoine Bourrienne, *The Memoirs of Napoleon Bonaparte*, ed. R.W. Phipps, London: Richard Bentley, 1885.

78 Allan Leighton, *On Leadership*, London: Random House, 2008.

79 Ed Smith, *Luck: What It Means and Why It Matters*, London: Bloomsbury, 2012.

80 Garr, *IBM Redux*; Gerstner, *Who Says Elephants Can't Dance?*; Lee Iacocca and William Novak, *Iacocca: An Autobiography*, New York: Bantam, 1986; Charles K. Hyde, *Riding the Roller Coaster: A History of the Chrysler Corporation*, Chicago: Wayne State University Press, 2003.
81 Robert L. Gandt, *Skygods: The Fall of Pan Am*, New York: Morrow, 1995; Karen H. Dacey, *The Stanleys of Newton: Yankee Tinkerers in the Gilded Age*, Kingfield, ME: Stanley Museum, 2009; Charles Mackay, *Extraordinary Popular Delusions and the Madness of Crowds*, London: Richard Bentley, 1841; de Roover, *The Rise and Fall of the Medici Bank*.
82 Bernal Diaz, *The Conquest of New Spain*, trans. John Cohen, Harmondsworth: Penguin, 1973; David Crane, *Scott of the Antarctic: A Life of Courage, and Tragedy in the Extreme South*, London: HarperCollins, 2005; Cherry-Gerard, *The Worst Journey in the World*.
83 James MacGregor Burns, *Roosevelt: The Lion and the Fox*, Norwalk, CN: Easton Press, 1956; Jean Edward Smith, *FDR*, New York: Random House, 2008.

PART II
Servants of God

5

LEADERSHIP AND DIVINE CONNECTIONS

As we have seen in previous chapters, people are often willing to accept leaders imposed upon them without choice, provided those leaders can give followers what they want: safety, security and a chance to realise their own aspirations for themselves and their communities. To be accepted, leaders have to demonstrate qualities that followers expect in a leader: credibility and visibility, fairness and equity, guidance and strategic direction, power and the ability to get things done, and a fair slice of luck.

One way in which leaders of early civilisations tried to establish legitimacy was that of conferred leadership, the principle that authority has been vested in the leader by a supernatural power, either a deity or group of deities or some principle of natural law. In more extreme cases, the leader claimed to be a deity or, alternatively, to be descended from deities and therefore personally imbued with supernatural force. In other cases, the leaders, although not divine themselves, were nevertheless believed to have a direct connection with the godhead, whether through reincarnation (some Tibetan lamas) or divinely conferred grace (for example, the popes of the Roman Catholic Church).

Two points need to be made about these imperial deities and priest-kings: first, whereas this particular form of conferred leadership was once relatively common (though by no means universal), it had, by the end of the twentieth century, all but disappeared, apart from a few isolated examples, such as those mentioned in the previous paragraph. Understanding why this happened sheds light on the changing needs of followers and their relationship with and expectation of their leaders. Second, this type of leadership was manifested within a fairly narrow sphere of political-military-religious states and organisations. I have found no examples of business leaders making any serious or believable claims to be gods; as we shall see later in this book, there are plenty of business leaders – and those in sport, the arts, charities and so on – who claim religious inspiration, but that is not quite the same thing. So why did leaders of political, military and/or religious organisations and their followers feel that a direct connection with divinity was important?

Several other questions must also be answered: first, what was the nature of the power relationship between these leaders and their followers, and what happened in the social space between them? What social function did the religious element of leadership fulfil? Second, what did followers expect of their leaders? Why were some leaders with divine authority accepted, and what happened to others who were not? Finally, why did conferred leadership decline in popularity? What led to its supersession by other forms of legitimacy and authority?

Divine leaders

We sometimes talk about rulers in ancient societies being treated as gods, but in fact the number of cases where rulers were regarded as actual divinities in their own lifetime is comparatively small. There were a few instances of this in ancient Mesopotamia, such as Naram-Sin, ruler of Akkad, who reigned from 2254 to 2218 BC, and Shulgi, priest-king of Ur, who ruled from *c.* 2029 to 1982 BC and declared himself a deity in the twenty-third year of his reign. Although some contemporaries attacked Shulgi for what they saw as his impiety, he seems to have been a successful and popular ruler.[1] Naram-Sin was less fortunate: he faced widespread rebellion towards the end of his reign, and the kingdom of Akkad collapsed not long after his death.

Other isolated examples can be found in Java and Cambodia, where the concept of *devaraja* (god-king) developed and was practiced, most notably by Jayavarman II, founder of the Khmer Empire. The devaraja was considered to be an incarnation of one of the principal Hindu gods, often Shiva but sometimes Vishnu. Jayavarman was declared to be a devaraja after a special religious ceremony performed by the high priest of the kingdom, and his successors continued the practice, ostensibly deriving their authority as rulers directly from the godhead. But this 'divine' authority, did not always protect them, just as it failed to protect Naram-Sin. The fourth Khmer king, Yasovarmin I, succeeded to the throne only after a lengthy struggle with his brothers; the eighth king, Harshavarman II, was overthrown and died in exile. These examples remind us that declaring oneself to be a god does not necessarily mean that one's divinity will be accepted by one's followers.[2]

One ruler who discovered this the hard way was Roman Emperor Caligula, the third of the Julio-Claudian dynasty, who declared himself to be a god in 40 CE and ordered temples to be built for his worship. He was murdered less than a year later. Caligula's successor, Claudius, refused a proposal to erect a temple in his name, declaring that only gods can choose gods. However, it thereafter became customary for Roman emperors to be declared gods by the Roman Senate after their death.[3] The same was common in other parts of the ancient Near East: Kubaba, the only woman to rule the state of Sumer (*c.* 2400 BC), was also declared a goddess by her successors, and in the third century BC, King Pharnavaz of Kartli (modern-day Georgia in the Caucasus) was deified after his death, probably by nobles influenced by the Roman example.[4] Generally, the honour of deification was reserved for rulers who were particularly well regarded or had achieved some important success. The Roman practice of deifying rulers as a blanket policy was unusual and it lasted until the early sixth century, well after the adoption of Christianity as the official religion of the empire.[5]

More commonly, instead of claiming to *be* gods, the ruling lineage, sometimes the entire elite class, declared themselves to be *descended* from gods. The sun god or goddess was a common choice of ancestor. The pharaohs of Egypt claimed descent from the god Horus, the sky god who governed the sun and the moon; the emperors of Japan traced their lineage back to Emperor Nimmu, who was said to be descended from the sun goddess Amaterasu; and the Sapa Inca, the ruler of the Inca Empire, claimed descent from the sun god Inti.[6] The *ali'i*, the hereditary nobility of the kingdom of Hawai'i, claimed divine descent, and the *ghanas* (kings) of Wagadu in West Africa may have done the same.[7]

Not all leaders felt the need for a formal connection with a particular deity or group of deities. Especially in less-structured societies, where hierarchies were flatter and power distance was lower, leaders might claim a connection with the supernatural more generally, with the world of spirits, the natural forces of the earth or a combination of both. Veleda, priestess and spiritual leader of the Bructeri Germanic tribe in the first century AD, claimed the power of prophecy; according to the Roman historian Tacitus, she was regarded by her people as a living goddess, but this is probably an exaggeration.[8] It is more likely that she was seen as a human being who had been imbued with certain divine powers. The same is true of the Skomantas (or Skomond), who was both the political and the religious leader of the Jatwingians, a Prussian tribe who in the fourteenth century fought a long resistance against the Teutonic Order, a German military-religious order. A variety of supernatural powers were attributed to Skomantas, including shapeshifting and flight.[9] Changamire Dombo, founder of the Rozvi state (modern-day Zimbabwe) in the late seventeenth century, was also reputed to have magical powers.[10]

Others claimed to have the power to act as intermediaries between the real world and the world of the spirits. Examples include the *böö* and *udgan*, male and female spirit leaders of the Mongols up to the time of Genghis Khan, who served as the Mongolian tribes' connection with their ancestors. A similar function was performed by the 'medicine men' of the Lakota people in North America, including Thathanka Iyotake (Sitting Bull), one of the architects of the victory over the US Army at Greasy Grass, and Hehaka Sapa (Black Elk), who left a vivid account of the role of the medicine man and his spiritual experiences.[11]

The examples of Veleda, Skomantas, Changamire Dombo, Thathanka Iyotake and Hehaka Sapa raise an interesting point, namely that in low power distance societies, religion is less hierarchically structured. Individual deities are less important than the spiritual world. However, with increasing power distance comes more hierarchy, not only in terms of priests and temples but also in terms of the heavens, with gods and goddesses assigned distinct roles within a pecking order. A more complex world demands more order and structure in matters of faith and, indeed, in leadership.

Theocrats

Theocracy is a governance system in which priests rule in the name of a god or gods, with authority conferred directly by those deities. (Modern-day Iran, often described as a theocracy, is technically speaking a *theonomy*, a state ruled in accordance with divine law; the distinction is subtle but important.) In cases such as pharaonic Egypt or the Rozvi state founded by Changamire Dombo, the secular ruler is also considered to be a high priest. In the case of the Phoenician city-states of Tyre and Sidon, as they transitioned from the Bronze Age to the Iron Age, the priests took over secular rule. As Karl Moore and David Lewis describe in detail, a cabal of high priests formed the government of these city-states, and lower ranking priest-administrators controlled every aspect of social and political life: religion, the army and navy, business and commerce, and administration, taxation and justice.[12] In pre-Christian Iceland, each community was led by a *gothi*, who combined the functions of priest, judge and administrator and may also have been a war leader.[13]

The collapse of the Roman Empire saw the rise of many theocratic states in Western Europe. In Eastern Europe and Asia, for example, the Byzantine Empire continued to anoint its rulers as gods after death, but following the reign of Anastasius I (491–518), the practice was discontinued because of its incompatibility with Christian monotheism. In the West, however, Roman and Byzantine power had been largely eroded by the end of the sixth century AD. Spotting a power vacuum, the Roman Catholic papacy declared itself independent of temporal authority and assumed the civil administration of Rome.

As time passed, the papacy became more ambitious. The crowning of Charlemagne as Holy Roman Emperor by Pope Leo III was an adroit act intended in part to enlist Charlemagne's support against the pope's rebellious subjects and in part to establish the primacy of spiritual authority over the state.[14] Around the same time, the papacy began to assert direct political control over a large swathe of central Italy, in part by referring to a forged document known as the Donation of Constantine, which purported to grant fiefdom over these lands and cities to the papacy. Charlemagne himself was largely content to work with the papacy and share power, but by the tenth century an open power struggle had broken out between popes and emperors. This lasted for several centuries; finally, in 1527, Emperor Charles V effectively broke the temporal power of the papacy by sending his mercenaries to sack Rome and loot the Vatican. The papacy continued to rule Rome and a portion of central Italy, but even this was lost when the nineteenth-century Risorgimento unified Italy under a secular power.[15]

Other Christian religious leaders followed the papal example. By 1500 there were many independent states led by prelates, most of them in the German and Austrian regions of the Holy Roman Empire. Others were scattered around Europe, such as Andorra, which was ruled solely by the bishops of Urgell from 988 to 1278 and, thereafter, jointly by the bishops and the counts of Foix; another example is the bishopric of Durham, which, although it was in England, existed semi-independently of the English Crown until 1836. The largest and most powerful of these political-religious leaders, the archbishops of Mainz, Trier and Köln, ruled lands the size of a kingdom and participated in the election of the Holy Roman Emperors.

European Christianity also created other theocratic institutions. The first European monastic order, the Benedictines, were founded by St Benedict of Nursia in 529 and thereafter spread rapidly across Europe. Other orders followed, most notably the Cistercian, which was founded in 1098 and grew to rival the Benedictines in power. Both orders also had female branches, allowing female leaders a rare chance to emerge. The religious orders were highly decentralised; there was an abbot-general who in theory held sway over each order, but in practice power was devolved to individual monasteries. Some of these monasteries were very large; at the height of their power they comprised hundreds of monks or nuns, controlled vast resources and tens of thousands of acres of land and were virtually independent of the civil authority around them: that is, states within a state.[16] The influence of abbots and abbesses such as Anselm of Bec, Bernard of Clairvaux, Heloise of Argenteuil and Hildegard of Bingen spread beyond their orders and into civil society.[17]

An offshoot of the monastic orders were the military orders. The three largest of these were the Knights Templar, the Knights Hospitaller and the Teutonic Knights, and their ostensible purpose was to carry out crusades against purported enemies of Christianity. They, too, owned vast amounts of land across Europe, and although they were subordinate to the papacy in theory, in practice their grand masters were entirely independent.[18] 'The sword is our pope', snarled one commander of the Teutonic Order when an aggrieved Livonian official threatened to appeal to the papacy. His statement was indicative of the Order's general world-view; it recognised no authority but God and no power but its own. The Order continued to defy papal authority until 1525, when their grand master, Albrecht of Brandenburg, converted to Lutheranism and abolished the entire order.[19]

There are plenty of other historical examples of theocracy that we could discuss. The early Islamic Empire, established by the successors of the Prophet Muhammad, hovered between theocracy and theonomy. The Tibetan Buddhist monasteries, like those of the west, existed as states within a state and gave rise to theocratic rule in most of the country, the Ganden Phodrang regime, which was led by the Dalai Lamas and which lasted from 1642 to 1950. There were a few short-lived theocracies in Europe in the aftermath of the Reformation, notably Geneva under the unofficial rule of John Calvin. Even more short-lived was Deseret, the theocratic state established by the Mormon leader Brigham Young in 1849, which lasted just two years until it was absorbed into the new Utah Territory. Young continued to rule Utah as a theocracy until the territory was occupied by the United States Army in 1858 and Young was forced to resign.[20]

Divine power in the social space

It would be easy to assume that these religious leaders declared themselves either to be gods or to have direct connection with the gods in order to gather more power to themselves and control their followers. But as the work of van Henten and ter

Borg demonstrates, that assumption may be too simplistic. There is a close relationship between religion and power, but that does not necessarily imply dominance; religion can also be used as a base from which to challenge existing power structures, as Martin Luther demonstrated to great effect during the Protestant Reformation.[21]

And as psychologists of religion have pointed out, people use religion for a variety of purposes, one of which is to create greater cohesion within society. Religion offers a set of values and beliefs around which people can come together and coalesce into a larger society, and that society, in turn, provides reassurance, trust and safety to its members.[22] As we saw in chapter 2, religion offered explanations for things both worldly and otherworldly, including natural phenomena, such as the sun, moon and stars, and the mysteries of birth, life and death. In a world of apparent confusion and chaos, in which people had only a limited degree of scientific understanding, faith offered reassurance. Mostly, the gods were remote and invisible, but the priest-kings and god-emperors were real and visible, daily reminders of that faith and reassurance and the values and beliefs that the people themselves held dear.

If we accept that people choose religion rather than having it foisted upon them by their leaders, it will follow that one of the reasons why they choose religion is to achieve this sense of social cohesion. Leadership structures then emerge which foster cohesion and create a sense of identity, which leads to another paradox: we can easily identify elements of coercion in many forms of leadership, with institutions such as religious courts – most famously, perhaps, the Inquisition of the Catholic Church – convened to enforce conformity to a canon of accepted belief.[23] At the same time, there is a strong element of voluntary acceptance of that canon. Far from being purely an institution of repression, the Inquisition enjoyed broad popular support.

However, when people stop believing or begin to believe in a different creed, the old faith dies, and often it dies quickly. Islam's rapid undermining of Zoroastrianism in Persia was not simply a matter of military conquest. Many Persians found the new faith more expedient and, indeed, more attractive. It is interesting to note that although there was some Zoroastrian resistance, most of the population converted peacefully to Islam. At the same time, though, the Persians emphatically and successfully rejected attempts by their conquerors to force Arabic language and culture on them, preserving their own identity.[24] These people were not devoid of free will.

Very well, one may argue: but why, then, invest the rulers with holy status and then voluntarily subjugate to them? The answer may lie in sociologist Émile Durkheim's concept of 'collective effervescence', whereby people coalesce, without any deliberate programme or even conscious thought, around a symbol or *totem* that they see as an emblem of their own beliefs and desires. Collective effervescence was particularly common in early societies, Durkheim believed, because they were intellectually less sophisticated and more likely to react to stimuli of faith and instinct rather than reason.[25]

The symbols at the centre of collective effervescence took many forms. Temples and sacred buildings such as the pyramids of Egypt are the most obvious, but the leaders themselves were also important symbols. Their trappings of office – palaces, elaborate costumes, masks and regalia; gilded chariots, the leaders' servants, slaves and concubines – all were intended as highly visible symbols of power. Shulgi of Ur, in the poem known as the 'Self-Praise of Shulgi', was careful to praise all his lavish possessions, even the royal barge, which was decorated with 'holy horns' and stars to make it resemble the sky. The Mormon leader Brigham Young instituted a programme of temple building in Utah and is also reputed to have had fifty-five wives. Did he need this many wives? No one knows. But we do know they were an important symbol of his power to the rest of the Mormon community.[26]

Indeed, it could be argued that the symbolic function of these priest-kings and god-emperors was the most important aspect of their power. The symbolic power conferred by the deities led others to coalesce around them, and the more followers the leader had, the greater his or her power became. The people were willing to trade a share of their own power in exchange for greater physical and psychological security and a sense of social cohesiveness. The presence of these divine or semi-divine leaders filled a greater social and spiritual need in society, and a high degree of power distance was considered a price worth paying.

It should also be pointed out that not every society went down this route. Ancient Greece had a complex panoply of deities, as did the Norse and Slavic peoples, but none of these societies ever felt the need to declare their rulers divine or hand over direct rule to priests (the *gothi* of Iceland are an exception). Religion played a major role in these societies, and priests were respected figures, but the temporal power was supreme, and religion played a carefully defined and often limited role in society.

What made the difference? We can only speculate. On the one hand, Greek, Norse and Slavic societies, such as the Mongolians and Lakota, had a lower power distance; kings and other leaders were sometimes elected, and there was a degree of popular representation in government. But there were also differences in the nature of religious faith in these societies. The works of early Greek writers such as Homer and Hesiod make it clear that the gods themselves were far less remote than those in high power distance societies, such as Egypt or Imperial Rome; there was interaction, even interbreeding, between gods and mortals. Nor were the gods themselves considered to be perfect. Writing in the fifth century BC, pre-Socratic philosopher Xenophanes of Colophon was prepared to criticise the gods for their weaknesses and failings.[27] The Slavs and Balts, on the other hand, regarded their gods as spirits that inhabited the landscape and other natural phenomena, such as Perkunas, the Baltic god of thunder, and Mesyats, the Slavic god of the moon. Although the gods were respected, they were also part of everyday life, coexisting with the people.[28]

Rejection and failure

Even in high power distance societies where the leaders were worshipped as gods, there were still boundaries around their power, and if they overstepped those boundaries, they paid the price. Mention has already been made of Caligula, murdered after declaring himself to be a god. Subsequently, the Roman Senate took the precaution of not declaring emperors to be deities until after they were dead, but in the third century AD, another emperor, Elagabalus, declared the supremacy of a new cult, Sol Invictus (Unconquered Sun), with himself as its high priest and supreme religious and civil authority. The Roman people, normally tolerant of new gods and new faiths, rejected Elagabalus; he was overthrown and murdered by a cabal of nobles led by his own grandmother, the formidable kingmaker Julia Maesa.[29]

Akhenaten, the Egyptian pharaoh of the 18th Dynasty, also attempted religious revisionism, replacing worship of the old Egyptian pantheon with that of a single deity, Aten. There seems to have been no open resistance until after Akhenaten's death, but under the rule of his son and successor, Tutankhamun, the religious reforms were swept away, and the old order was restored. There followed a deliberate campaign to erase Akhenaten from history, nearly every trace of him was rubbed out from inscriptions and documents. When Tutankhamun died heirless, his chief minister, Ay, seized the throne for himself, and his heirs were, in turn, usurped by the army commander, Horemheb.[30] Japanese history is likewise full of revolts against the god-emperors, such as the Hōgen rebellion (1155–6), when Go-Shirakawa fought off several rival emperors to seize the throne; and the Sengoku era, a series of civil wars lasting from 1457 to 1600, ending with the establishment of the Tokugawa shogunate, which stripped virtually all civil power from the emperors. Although still considered to be divine beings, the emperors exercised little authority; real power now rested with the *shoguns*.[31]

The theocrats fared no better. Despite their claims to have a direct connection to the deity, the medieval popes were roughly treated by their followers. More than one pope was forced to flee Rome to escape the wrath of the people. In 799 AD, Pope Leo III was attacked in the street and knocked unconscious by an armed gang which then tried to tear out his tongue and eyes; his offer of the crown of the Holy Roman Empire to Charlemagne the following year was as much as anything an attempt to secure armed protection for himself.[32] In the tenth century, Gregory VII and Urban II survived repeated attacks and assassination attempts, and in 1527, Rome was overrun by an imperial army, one of whose commanders was Pompeo Colonna, a senior cardinal at the papal court and member of a powerful Roman family bitterly opposed to Pope Clement VII.[33]

In all these cases, the leader or leaders failed to manage the social space. Collaboration turned into conflict, and divine connection or no, the leaders were nowhere near as powerful as they thought they were. Akhenaten and Elagabalus both attempted to interfere with the established order and gather more power to themselves; both paid the price, even if the campaign against Akhenaten did not start until after his death. The medieval popes were engaged in power struggles with the various political factions in Rome and with the Holy Roman Emperors, over whom they had claimed authority. In both cases the papacy was attempting to increase its own power by taking power away from its followers and rivals.

Ironically, by taking part in these overtly political struggles the papacy lost much of its symbolic authority. In the early sixteenth century, popes such as Alexander VI, who made no secret of his mistresses and promoted his son Cesare Borgia – Machiavelli's patron and friend – to positions of high office, and Julius II, a warrior-pope who liked to site his own artillery, turned the papacy into just another temporal state; its symbolic authority was largely lost.[34] Rival claims to the papal throne further weakened the institution, as did crude money-making schemes like jubilees (whereby one could travel to Rome to have his or her sins absolved for a fee) or the selling of indulgences (pieces of paper which absolved its owner of *all* sins, past, present and future). Anti-papal feeling was already running high even before the Reformation; in parts of southern Germany, anticlericalism had reached such a pitch that, especially in the countryside, many clergy had been driven out, and their churches stood empty.[35] The papacy had been robbed of much of its legitimate authority, and people in many parts of Europe turned away from it, searching for other institutions that could offer the necessary reassurance and cohesion. The door was open, waiting for Martin Luther to walk through.

Divine status did not provide leaders with as much protection as one might assume. Not even the gods themselves were entirely invulnerable. The ancient Greeks, with their lower power distance society, had a long tradition of rebelling against the gods. The Titan Prometheus defied the gods in order to give the gift of fire to humanity; although the gods punished him for doing so, the usual interpretation of the myth is that Prometheus was doing the right thing.[36] As we have seen, even in high power distance societies, no leader could transgress against his or her followers for long. As long as leaders carried out their own duties and provided symbolic authority, followers accepted them. But once they broke the implicit contract between the leaders and the led, either by exploiting their authority for personal gain or by changing the status quo in a manner followers were not prepared to accept, even the mostly godlike leaders were in danger.

The decline of the divine

As time went on, the notion of a divine leader became increasingly obsolete. The spread of two major monotheistic religions, Christianity and Islam, destroyed the notion of god-emperors; as we have seen, the practice had died out in Christian countries by the sixth century. In some parts of the world the concept lingered: the Humanity Declaration, imposed during the American military occupation of Japan, finally ended the semi-divine status of Japanese rulers, but in truth the emperors had bargained away most of their power already, first to the *shoguns* of the Tokugawa dynasty and then to the military-political elites that emerged in the later nineteenth century.[37] Theocracies also declined. The papacy survived as an institution, but it lost most of its temporal powers during the political upheavals surrounding the Reformation and made a conscious decision to refocus itself as a primarily religious institution.

Why did civilisations no longer need this type of conferred, symbolic leadership? Perhaps, this is due to the fact that the symbols that gave meaning to our lives had begun to change. The philosopher and theologian Paul Tillich has argued that the meanings we attach to symbols evolve and change as our culture evolves and changes. Some symbols lose their meaning entirely, in which case, says Tillich, they become *dead* symbols; they still exist, perhaps, but are devoid of meaning. As our culture changes, we also change. We move on, looking for different symbols to give us new meaning.[38]

There is not enough space here to go into detail about the reasons for the change in attitude to religious symbols, but a few possibilities can be advanced. First, the Protestant Reformation led to a more individualist age, epitomised (in the early stages, at least) by a supreme egoist, Henry VIII of England, who made his own kingship into the living, breathing symbol of an England that was shedding free the papal yoke.[39] Second, this individualism, coupled with greater personal freedom of thought and expression, made religious scepticism and its offshoots, atheism and agnosticism, increasingly more acceptable. Social cohesion no longer required religious symbols; people developed and expressed their identities in other ways. Third, as already discussed, the gradual lessening of power distance in most societies meant that the idea of remote, all-powerful beings governing our lives was no longer acceptable. As people, we began to take more responsibility for governing ourselves, and our expectations of our leaders changed accordingly.

Summary

The social space created between god-emperors and priest-kings and their followers was full of symbols, and the authority of these leaders rested largely on their ability to serve as symbols that reflected their followers' aspirations. Sacred beings or no, they still required the acceptance of their followers if they were to function as leaders, and that meant being all the things we discussed in the previous chapter; they had to be fair and equitable, they had to have wisdom and the ability to give guidance, they had to be able to get things done because not doing so was usually seen as a sign that divine status had been withdrawn and, most of all, they had to be credible and visible. People need to see either their symbols or, at least, visible signs of their existence; hence, the importance of temples and pyramids and royal barges decorated with sacred horns.

Conferred, symbolic leadership of the type described in this chapter provided a necessary element in the structure of society, like a centre post holding up the roof, around which all else revolved. Early societies needed that structure and reassurance, especially in times of turmoil and chaos, when existence was threatened. This, perhaps, answers the question posed at the start of the chapter: why was divine leadership so prominent in political, military and religious organisations but not in others, such as business? The answer is that these were the key institutions that held society together; they were the largest in scale and scope at a time when most businesses were still quite small. It was here that symbolic authority was most needed.

Looking at the social space of leadership in these societies, one is struck by how collaborative this space was and at the same time by how contested it was. A superficial glance at ancient Egypt or the Roman Empire or the medieval papacy might show a picture of a tyrannical ruler governing a populace who gave unquestioning obedience, but when we look in more detail at these societies, we can see clearly how the leaders depended utterly on their followers. As long as followers accepted the symbols leaders provided and found meaning in them, society functioned in a fairly harmonious way.

But when the symbols lost their meaning, either through the passage of time, as Paul Tillich indicates, or through the ineptness and arrogance of the leaders themselves, the balance of power was upset. The contests that ensued were won by the party that could best capture and wield power, and divine status or no, the winner was not always the leader. The case of Elagabalus is particularly instructive here. His rise to power came amid the chaos following the murder of his cousin, Emperor Caracalla, and he came to the throne with the backing of a powerful group of nobles led by his grandmother Julia Maesa. Three years later, when she had decided that Elagabalus had outlived his usefulness, Maesa ordered his assassination; his headless body was dragged through Rome and then dumped in the Tiber. His status did not protect him. To paraphrase an old saying, power eats status for breakfast.

Notes

1 Samuel Noah Kramer, *The Sumerians: Their History, Culture and Character*, Chicago: University of Chicago Press, 1971; Harriet Crawford, *Ur: City of the Moon God*, London: Bloomsbury, 2015.
2 Munoz, *Early Kingdoms of the Indonesian Archipelago and Malay Peninsula*; George Coedès, *The Indianized States of South-East Asia*, trans. Susan Brown Cowing, Honolulu: University of Hawaii Press, 1968; Charles Higham, *The Civilization of Angkor*, Berkeley: University of California Press, 2001.
3 Anthony A. Barrett, *Caligula: The Corruption of Power*, London: B.T. Batsford, 1989; Josiah Osgood, *Claudius Caesar: Image and Power in the Early Roman Empire*, Cambridge: Cambridge University Press, 2010; Barbara Levick, *Claudius*, New Haven: Yale University Press, 1990; Suetonius, *The Twelve Caesars*; Cassius Dio, *Roman History*; Beard, *SPQR*.
4 Ronald Grigor Suny, *The Making of the Georgian Nation*, Bloomington: Indiana University Press, 1994; Maarten J. Vermaseren, *Cybele and Attis: The Myth and the Cult*, trans. A.M.H. Lemmers, London: Thames and Hudson, 1970.
5 S.R.F. Price, *Rituals and Power: The Roman Imperial Cult in Asia Minor*, Cambridge: Cambridge University Press, 1986.
6 Bard, *Encyclopedia*; Ian Shaw, *The Oxford History of Ancient Egypt*, Oxford: Oxford University Press, 2003; William M. Tsutsui, *A Companion to Japanese History*, New York: John Wiley, 2009; Gordon McEwan, *The Incas: New Perspectives*, New York: W.W. Norton, 2006.
7 Hommon, *The Ancient Hawai'ian State*; Nehemia Levitzion, *Ancient Ghana and Mali*, London: Methuen, 1973.
8 Tacitus, *The Agricola and the Germania*.
9 Stephen C. Rowell, *Lithuania Ascending: A Pagan Empire Within Eastern Europe, 1295–1345*, Cambridge: Cambridge University Press, 1994.
10 Elizabeth Allo Isichei, *A History of African Societies to 1870*, Cambridge: Cambridge University Press, 1997.
11 Walter Heissig, *The Religions of Mongolia*, London: Routledge, 2000; Robert M. Utley, *The Lance and the Shield: The Life and Times of Sitting Bull*, New York: Henry Holt, 1993; Ambrose, *Crazy Horse and Custer*; Hehaka Sapa, *Black Elk Speaks: Being the Life Story of a Holy Man of the Oglala Sioux*, Lincoln: University of Nebraska Press, 1932.
12 Moore and Lewis, *Foundations of Corporate Empire*.
13 Jon Hnefill Adelsteinsson, *A Piece of Horse Liver: Myth, Ritual and Folklore in Old Icelandic Sources*, trans. Terry Gunnell and Joan Turville-Petre, Reykjavik: Iceland University Press, 1998.

14 Roger Collins, *Charlemagne*, Toronto: University of Toronto Press, 1998; Einhard, *Life of Charlemagne*, trans. Lewis Thorpe, *Two Lives of Charlemagne*, Harmondsworth: Penguin, 1969.

15 Brian Tierney, *The Crisis of Church and State 1050–1300*, Toronto: University of Toronto Press, 1964; Matthew Harris, *The Notion of Papal Monarchy in the Twelfth Century*, Lewiston: Edwin Mellen, 2010; E.R. Chamberlin, *The Sack of Rome*, New York: Dorset, 1979; Lucy Riall, *Risorgimento: The History of Italy from Napoleon to Nation-State*, Basingstoke: Palgrave Macmillan, 2009.

16 Charles Cary-Elwes, *St Benedict and His Rule*, London: Catholic Truth Society, 1988; G.R. Evans, *Bernard of Clairvaux*, Oxford: Oxford University Press, 2000.

17 Richard W. Southern, *St Anselm: A Portrait in a Landscape*, Cambridge: Cambridge University Press, 1990; Evans, *Bernard of Clairvaux*; Constant J. Mews, *Abelard and Heloise*, Oxford: Oxford University Press, 2005; Sabina Flanagan, *Hildegard of Bingen, 1098–1179: A Visionary Life*, London: Routledge, 1989.

18 Helen Nicholson, *The Knights Templar: A New History*, Stroud: Sutton, 2001; Jonathan Riley-Smith, *Hospitallers: The History of the Order of St John*, Oxford: Hambledon, 1999; Erik Christiansen, *The Northern Crusades*, London: Penguin, 1997.

19 Richard Fletcher, *The Conversion of Europe: From Paganism to Christianity, 371–1386 AD*, London: HarperCollins, 1987.

20 Patricia Crone, *God's Caliph: Religious Authority in the First Centuries of Islam*, Cambridge: Cambridge University Press, 1986; Schwieger, *The Dalai Lama*; Shakabpa, *One Hundred Thousand Moons*; Andy Veraegen, *The Dalai Lamas: The Institution and Its History*, New Delhi: DK Printworld; Bruce Gordon, *Calvin*, New Haven: Yale University Press, 2009; Leonard J. Arrington, *Brigham Young: American Moses*, Chicago: University of Illinois Press, 1985; Richard Lymon Bushman, *Mormonism: A Very Short Introduction*, New York: Oxford University Press, 2008.

21 Wilson, *Out of the Storm*; Michael A. Mullett, *Martin Luther*, London: Routledge, 2004.

22 Jan Willem van Henten and Meerten T. ter Borg (eds), *Power: Religion as a Social and Spiritual Force*, New York: Fordham University Press, 2010; Wilson, *Out of the Storm*; Richard Sosis and Candace Alcorta, 'Signaling, Solidarity and the Sacred: The Evolution of Religious Behavior', *Evolutionary Anthropology* 12 (6) (2003): 264–74.

23 James B. Givins, *Inquisition and Medieval Society*, Ithaca: Cornell University Press, 2001; Edward Peters, *Inquisition*, New York: The Free Press, 1988.

24 Richard Foltz, *Religions of Iran: From Prehistory to the Present*, London: Oneworld, 2013.

25 Émile Durkheim, *The Elementary Forms of the Religious Life*, trans. Joseph Swain, New York: The Free Press, 1965.

26 Crawford, *Ur*; Arrington, *Brigham Young*.

27 Homer, *The Iliad*, *The Odyssey*; West, *Hesiod*; James H. Lesher, *Xenophanes of Colophon: Fragments, a Text and Translation with a Commentary*, Toronto: University of Toronto Press, 2001.

28 Marija Gimbutas, *The Slavs*, New York: Praeger, 1971; Linda J. Ivanits, *Russian Folk Belief*, Armonk: M.E. Sharpe, 1989; Rowell, *Lithuania Ascending*.

29 Cassius Dio, *Roman History*; Martin Icks, *The Crimes of Elagabalus: The Life and Legacy of Rome's Decadent Boy Emperor*, London: I.B. Tauris, 2011; Jasper Burns, *Great Women of Imperial Rome: Mothers and Wives of the Caesars*, London: Routledge, 2006.

30 Cyril Aldred, *Akhenaten: King of Egypt*, London: Thames and Hudson, 1991; Donald B. Redford, *Akhenaten: The Heretic King*, Princeton: Princeton University Press, 1984.

31 Paul H. Varley, *Jinno Shotoki: A Chronicle of Gods and Sovereigns*, New York: Columbia University Press, 1980; Michael James Lorimer, *Sengokujidai: Autonomy, Division and Unity in Later Medieval Japan*, London: Olympia, 2008; Chie Nakane and Shinzaburou Oishi, *Tokugawa Japan: The Social and Economic Antecedents of Modern Japan*, Tokyo: University of Tokyo Press, 1990.

32 Collins, *Charlemagne*; Einhard, *Life of Charlemagne*.

33 Cowdray, *Pope Gregory VII*; Chris Wickham, *Medieval Rome: Stability and Crisis of a City, 900–1150*, Oxford: Oxford University Press, 2015; Chamberlin, *The Sack of Rome*.

34 Ludwig von Pastor, *The History of the Popes*, London: Kegan Paul, 1902, vol. 7; Christpher Hibbert, *The Borgias and Their Enemies*, New York: Harcourt, 2008; Christine Shaw, *Julius II: The Warrior Pope*, Oxford: Blackwell, 1996.
35 R.W. Scribner, *Popular Movements and Popular Culture in Reformation Germany*, London: Continuum, 1987; Pastor, *The History of the Popes*.
36 Carol Dougherty, *Prometheus*, London: Taylor and Francis, 2006; Goethe, *Prometheus*.
37 Peter Wetzler, *Hirohito and War*, Honolulu, University of Hawaii Press, 1998.
38 Paul Tillich, *Theology of Culture*, Oxford: Oxford University Press, 1964; William L. Rowe, *Religious Symbols and God: A Philosophical Study of Paul Tillich's Theology*, Chicago: University of Chicago Press, 1968.
39 David Starkey, *The Reign of Henry VIII: Personalities and Politics*, New York: Random House, 2002; John Bowle, *Henry VIII: A Study of Power in Action*, New York: Little, Brown, 1964.

6
THE DIVINE RIGHT TO LEAD

As we saw in the previous chapter, instances of leaders declaring themselves to *be* gods were comparatively rare, but establishing some sort of divine connection *with* the gods was more common. The concept of political authority being conferred through a direct connection with the divine could be found in many societies around the world. In theory, this strengthened the power of leaders and rendered any challenge to their authority illegitimate and impious, although as we saw, divine status ultimately provided little protection if people were dissatisfied with their leader.

As noted, though, the era of authority conferred directly by the gods came largely to an end, with only a few surviving outposts of the old order remaining. The rise of monotheism was largely responsible for this. Christianity finally put an end to the Roman practice of deifying emperors in the early sixth century, and Islam, spreading across Asia and parts of Africa in the seventh century, also eliminated polytheistic practices. Both religions also had a well-organised cosmological structure with strict divides between the divine and the human; there was no longer room for leaders to claim dynastic descent, as the Egyptian and Inca rulers did. Hong Xiuquan, leader of the Taiping Rebellion in nineteenth-century China, identified himself as the son of God and younger brother of Jesus, but he is a fairly rare exception.[1]

However, the idea of a connection with leadership and the godhead remained a highly attractive one. In the West, polytheism was on the retreat, but religion itself was still a powerful force in society (exactly how powerful depended on the time and place), and people still needed symbols to coalesce around, especially in times of danger or stress. Western societies therefore set about reinventing the notion of divinely conferred authority, inventing the concept of 'divine right', sometimes also known as the 'divine right of kings'.

The mandate of heaven

This principle of divinely conferred authority had already been developed in China. The very earliest Chinese rulers, the semi-mythical Three Sovereigns and Five Emperors, were considered to be divine beings; later, the Chinese historian Sima Qian singled out Huangdi, the Yellow Emperor, who was believed to be the ancestor of the Chinese people and who was – and remains – a symbol of Chinese nationalism.[2]

But the connection with these early divine leaders was broken through repeated rebellions and the accession of new dynasties of leaders. Whereas the Egyptian pharaohs always managed to finesse these breaks between dynasties – often by marrying members of previous dynasties to maintain the divine link – around 1120 BC the leaders of a new incoming dynasty in China, the Zhou, decided to dispense with the connection to divinity; instead, they invented a new concept, the 'mandate of heaven'. Emperors of China continued to rule by the mandate of heaven until the overthrow of the empire thirty centuries later.[3]

The mandate of heaven did not confer divine status, although the adoption of titles such as *Tianzi* (son of heaven) led some foreign observers to conclude that it did. Instead, the mandate of heaven indicated that the leader was divinely favoured and ruled with the consent of heaven; again, a fine but crucial distinction. Of particular importance is the concept that favour and consent could be withdrawn by the will of the gods. But how did followers know favour had been withdrawn? Certain signs were considered indicative. Failures by the leader such as a military defeat or a popular insurrection could be considered signals, but so could events such as earthquakes, extreme weather or failed harvests. Never mind that the leader had no control over these; the events themselves were symbols of divine displeasure and, in effect, a sign that rebellion against the leader was now divinely sanctioned.[4]

The Zhou dynasty ultimately perished during the Warring States period (*c.* 475–221 BC) and was replaced by the Qin dynasty, which in turn was replaced by the Han dynasty in 206 BC. The first Han emperor, Liu Bang, who took the throne as Emperor Gaozu, was not of imperial blood; he was the son of a minor law-enforcement official (although later Han dynasty publicists created a back story which included descent from the Yao Emperor, another mythical figure from ancient China). The mandate of heaven did not depend on birth or nobility; instead, it depended on competency to rule, and anyone of any background who demonstrated such competency could claim the mandate. When the ruler was no longer considered competent, the mandate was deemed to have been withdrawn.[5]

The mandate of heaven was imitated by several other East Asian states within China's orbit. In particular, it was adopted wholesale by the rulers of Vietnam, along with other Chinese imports, including Confucianism and state bureaucracy, especially by the Nguyen dynasty, which came to power in the early nineteenth century.[6] The mandate of heaven was also taken up by the rulers of Korea, although with some interesting limitations. Under the Joseon dynasty (1392–1897 AD), the authority of the mandate of heaven was also tempered by a body of laws and traditions known as the *gyeongguk daejon* (Grand Code for State Administration), by which rulers were expected to abide. Royal officials had the right to remonstrate with the king if they thought he was deviating from the gyeongguk daejon. Disasters both civil and natural also required the king to present himself to his people, accept their criticisms of him and make an apology if required, and failure to do so could result in the mandate of heaven being withdrawn. In Korea, it seemed, the celestial powers required the leader to be accountable to his followers.[7]

Divine right

In Europe, the notion of the divine right of kings was first codified in the sixteenth and seventeenth centuries, although there are plenty of earlier precedents. Proponents of divine right pointed to the example of Saul and David, Israelite kings from the Old Testament, both of whom enjoyed divine favour, and to that of St Paul's Epistle to the Romans, where the writer declares that 'the powers that be are ordained of God; therefore, whosoever resisteth the power, resisteth the ordinance of God'. The early Christian emperors of Rome, especially Constantine I (312–324 AD), who supported the Christian faith (even if he probably became a Christian himself only on his deathbed) and Theodosius I (379–395 AD), who outlawed the old Roman gods and made Christianity the state religion of the empire, were also examples of leaders who claimed to enjoy divine favour.

Constantine, Theodosius and their successors had inherited the old Roman tradition of autocracy. Now they proceeded to co-opt the Christian church to further support and strengthen their authority. Unlike the popes and prince-bishops of Western Europe, who ruled over theocratic states, the Byzantine emperors (as later historians have called them; they considered themselves to be emperors of Rome right up until the fall of Constantinople in 1453) considered themselves to be the supreme religious and civilian authority. In this system of Caesaropapism, as it later came to be called, Constantine, Theodosius and many of their successors appointed bishops, convened church councils and dictated – or at least attempted to dictate – both administrative policy and theology to the church hierarchy.[8]

As with the mandate of heaven in China, there was no absolute requirement for the leader to be part of the elites. Most were, but there were exceptions. Justin I, who reigned 518–27, was the son of a peasant farmer who rose through the ranks of the army to become commander of the palace guard before his election as emperor; his wife, Lupicina, was a former slave.[9] Phocas, Michael II and Romanus I were soldiers who also came from humble backgrounds, and Basil I was a peasant from Macedonia who rose through the ranks of the imperial civil service.[10]

At the heart of Caesaropapism lay a philosophical concept known as *katechon* (holding back or restraining).[11] Rome was seen as the centre of the world, and the emperor of Rome (or Byzantium) was its most powerful figure. He was given the task of defending the civilised order against chaos, specifically, the coming of the Antichrist, who would destroy the world and everyone in it. The Last Judgement would come at some unknown point in the future; until that time came, the emperor was the first line of defence for civilisation, and everyone else, including church leaders, was under orders to serve him (or very rarely, as noted earlier, her).

It is easy to see why this concept caught on and was accepted. When Constantine came to the throne, the Roman Empire was under extreme stress, and that stress continued intermittently until the empire's final collapse. Between c. 300 and 700 AD, the empire was repeatedly attacked by tribal groups migrating from the east, including the Goths, Franks, Vandals, Lombards and Huns.[12] In 378 AD, Theodosius's predecessor, Emperor Valens, was killed fighting a Gothic army at the Battle of Adrianople. As the centuries passed, other waves of attackers followed: Sassanian Persians, Arabs, Vikings, Turks and European crusaders. Given the turbulence of the times, there was a natural desire for security and safety, and people chose to put their faith in leaders who not only were strong but also had God's favour and, through that favour, sufficient power to hold back chaos. Following the collapse of the Byzantine Empire in 1453, the mantle of protector of the civilised world against the barbarians – along with the divine right to rule – was inherited by the tsars of Russia, whose policies and attitudes towards power and authority were already strongly influenced by the Byzantine example.[13]

The ancient Persian concept of *khvarenah* (royal glory) may have been influenced by *katechon* and is thought to be the grace conferred by Ahura-Mazdah on the kings of the Sassanid dynasty.[14] After the collapse of the Sassanid kingdom following the Arab invasions in the seventh century, the tradition of a mingled political and religious framework of authority persisted – it persists today in the government of Iran. That tradition also influenced the Abbasid caliphs of the Islamic Empire, who, after establishing their capital at Baghdad, brought in many Persian bureaucrats to help order the empire and set up an efficient administration. The Barmakids, a hereditary family of bureaucrats, served several Abbasid caliphs in the eighth and ninth centuries and helped establish a Caesaropapist system whereby the caliph, the leader of the faithful, was not only the chief administrator and war leader but also the final arbiter on religious matters.[15]

Although it is not certain if there was a direct influence, Henry VIII of England was certainly harking back to the Caesaropapist tradition when, following the break with Rome and at the beginning of the English Reformation, he appointed himself as head of the new Church of England.[16] (Conveniently, he also retained the title *Defender of the Faith*, awarded to him by Pope Leo X in 1521 as thanks for Henry's early opposition to Protestantism. This title was also co-opted into Henry's Caesaropapist ideology; the only difference was that now he was defending a different faith.) Whereas previously in Western Europe, the papacy had claimed sole right to consecrate monarchs – the coronation ceremony was always presided over by a bishop or a cardinal, echoing Pope Leo III's crowning of Charlemagne – now Henry was claiming a direct link to God. Thereafter, although monarchs continued to be crowned by archbishops of the Church of England, everyone present was aware that the monarch was also head of that church and in effect the archbishop's superior officer, which connoted an entirely different symbolic meaning.[17]

One of the first formal codifications of the notion of divine right was set out by King James VI in Scotland, particularly in his 1597 work, *The True Law of Free Monarchies.*[18] Although a Protestant himself, James drew heavily on earlier Catholic works, notably the *Policraticus* of John of Salisbury and the *De regno* (On Kingship) of Thomas Aquinas.[19] Following Salisbury in particular, James argued that the king is the head of the kingdom and controls it in the same way that the head and brain control the body. Unless the rest of the body obeys the commands of the brain, chaos will ensue. Influenced by Aquinas, James further claimed that this state of affairs embodied natural law and could therefore be said to be divinely ordained; in other words, to obey the king is to obey the will of God. As we shall see shortly, James was quoting selectively from both these sources.

Once again, we can see why James wrote as he did. He had been crowned king when he was just over a year old, following the forced abdication and imprisonment of his mother, Mary, Queen of Scots. Scotland had been ripped apart by a particularly vicious religious and civil war, and the Catholic bishops had been driven out and replaced by hardline Calvinist Protestants.[20] Establishing the independence of the crown from papal control was certain to please the anti-Catholic element. At the same time, however, James was sending a signal to a country that was tired of conflict and wished to heal at least some of the wounds of war and unite, and in *The True Law of Free Monarchies*, James pitched himself as the leader who could do exactly that. Finally, following the execution of his mother and with the ageing and unmarried Elizabeth I of England unlikely to produce an heir, James was the heir apparent to the throne of England. His book reassured the English Protestants that he shared their views and would be a trustworthy leader. *The True Law of Free Monarchies* thus satisfied the safety and aspirational needs of several groups of followers at once, and although James VI of Scotland (now also James I of England) did not exactly have a trouble-free reign in either country, on the whole he enjoyed broad popular support.

The extent of this support can be seen in the work of the conservative English writer Sir Robert Filmer. A strong supporter of King James after his assumption of the English throne, Filmer argued in his *Patriarcha* that the king is a father to his people. Just as children owe their parents unquestioning obedience, so, too, should the king command the unwavering loyalty of his subjects. The argument is based on religious principles and cites numerous examples from the Old Testament in particular.[21] However, despite the arguments of Filmer and others, the concept of divine right did not last long in England and Scotland, at least, not in practice – the English Civil War, which ended with the execution of James's son Charles I, meant that thereafter the concept of divine right existed in name only. When Charles's son James II attempted to reinstate divine right, he, too, was overthrown and forced into exile.[22]

Despite the events in England (and Scotland), the concept of divine right continued to flourish in continental Europe. The idea of divine right certainly found favour in the Holy Roman Empire, whose emperors, although never quite reaching the heights of Byzantine Caesaropapism to which they aspired, had won their power struggle with the papacy and achieved independence. The princely prelates, the archbishops of Köln, Mainz and Trier, who helped elect the emperor, were now clients of the Habsburg family, from whom emperors were chosen on the basis of heredity.[23] Elsewhere in Europe, absolutist monarchs found that the principle of divine right fit well with their own centralising projects, breaking the power of the old nobility and concentrating it in the hands of the crown. The master of this particular art was Louis XIV of France, who famously summed up his views in one sentence: 'L'état c'est moi' (I am the state).

Divine right in the social space

Is it correct to see concepts such as the mandate of heaven, Caesaropapism and the divine right of kings as further expressions of Durkheim's collective effervescence? Did divine right serve as a symbol that people could rally around? Certainly, that was what leaders hoped would happen. Chinese and Byzantine emperors deliberately cultivated the notion of imperial protection through a host of other symbols: grand, ornate residences that were part palace and part temple or church, brilliant regalia laden with religious symbolism, presence at key religious festivals and so on. Byzantine emperors were often depicted with halos, as if they were saints (see, for example, the mosaics of Emperor Justinian I, successor to Justin I, and his wife, Empress Theodora, at the church of San Vitale in Ravenna).[24] Liutprand of Cremona, a papal ambassador who visited the Byzantine court in 968 CE, described the imperial throne room:

> Before the emperor's seat stood a tree, made of bronze gilded over, whose branches were filled with birds, also made of gilded bronze, which uttered different cries, each according to its varying species. The throne itself was so marvellous fashioned that at one moment it seemed a low structure, and at another it rose high into the air. It was of immense size and was guarded by lions, made either of bronze or of wood covered over with gold, who beat the ground with their tails and gave a dreadful roar with opening mouth and quivering tongue.[25]

The symbols – the mastery over nature and the ability to reproduce it, the automated animals and birds and, most of all, the throne that could ascend towards heaven – were there to remind onlookers of the power of the emperor. Henry VIII of England was another master of symbols; even before the break with Rome, his summit meeting with François I of France near Calais was marked with lavish displays of wealth, including canvas pavilions faced with gold cloth in such quantities that the meeting later became known as the Field of the Cloth of Gold. In the seventeenth century Charles I of England commissioned elaborate and hugely expensive entertainments known as masques, featuring music, singing and dancing, often around Biblical themes, in which the monarch himself often performed.[26]

Just as we did in the previous chapter, we need to ask whether these symbols were simply an attempt by the leader to bolster his or her power, or whether followers also needed – even demanded – such symbols for their own purposes. That they do need these symbols is an argument that has been made many times. The philosophical concept of immanence – that the divine world somehow connects with and interpenetrates the human world and that we all have a need to partake of the divine essence – is a concept that goes back as far as ancient Greece and early Buddhism. The nineteenth-century Russian philosopher Pyotr Chaadaev argued that immanence bound all people together and was the chief driving force behind the creation of society, a sentiment echoed by the Egyptian Muslim scholar Muhammad 'Abduh in his *Risalat al-Tawhid* (The Theology of Unity). The German sociologist Ferdinand Tönnies argued for a distinction between community, where people interact directly and personally with each other, and society, where interactions are more indirect and impersonal. Symbols are particularly important in society, as they represent the values around which people coalesce, taking us back again to collective effervescence.[27]

But what are followers seeking to find in these symbols? They need safety and protection, and the era of divine right and the mandate of heaven was also, as we saw particularly in the Byzantine Empire, a time when danger were often clear and present. Followers also needed to partake more personally of the divine essence described in the concept of immanence. Proximity to people who apparently ruled by divine right allowed people to believe that they, too, were closer to divinity. Personal touch was important; French and English kings and queens were believed to be able to cure certain illnesses, such as scrofula, merely by touching the afflicted person.[28] To put it in modern terms, leaders who ruled by divine right had star quality, and other people wanted to be around them in hopes that some of the stardust would fleck off and fall on them.

In the modern, individualist Western world, this may seem odd (although the experience of social media shows that, for many, the desire to adhere to some sort of group remains very strong). But in times of greater danger, when societies face extreme levels of risk – as many early societies did from natural phenomena such as disease, fire, flood and wild animals and from their own aggressive neighbours as they competed for control of resources, such as agricultural land or minerals – cohesion becomes vitally important. Importantly, too, symbols serve not only as rallying points but also as means of exclusion. Those who reject the symbol or the totem are shut out. There can be no tolerance for dissent, for dissent threatens the security of the state, society and life itself. Conformity (or at least compliance) was seen as essential; when it failed, chaos ensued.[29] The religious civil war in Scotland that preceded the reign of James VI was fought by two groups demanding control of that society, each threatening the total exclusion of the other if it were victorious.

Paradoxically, this example also shows one of the flaws in the concept of divine right, namely that if society accepts a level of inherency (that is, if anyone who has the skill and character to become a successful leader can receive divine favour), leadership itself quickly becomes a gladiatorial contest between rival leaders and their groups of followers, each side seeking to grab its share of power. The religious and quasi-religious civil wars of the sixteenth and seventeenth centuries – the Scottish civil conflict, the French Wars of Religion, the Thirty Years War in Europe, the English Civil War – are examples of struggles for control in which each side claimed divine right.

The same is true of the Taiping Rebellion in nineteenth-century China. After failing his civil service entrance examinations, Hong Xiuquan fell under the influence of Christian missionaries and developed his own indigenous brand of Christianity. Claiming divine support, he called upon the Chinese authorities to instigate economic and social reforms. The young Xianfang Emperor, guided by his mother, the Dowager Empress Cixi, felt he had to defend the mandate of heaven against the encroachments of Christianity. With neither side willing to back down, the result was an eleven-year civil war costing as many as thirty million lives.[30]

The trade-off between followers and leaders in this social space was that followers would accept the concept of divine right and allow leaders to exercise power over them as long as those leaders were successful and helped followers achieve their aspirations (including aspirations for dominance over dissenting members of their own society). They watched keenly for any signs that divine favour had been withdrawn, and when they believed it had, they were very quick to throw their former totems overboard and seek out new ones. In the reign of Charles I of England, people contrasted the expensive ceremonies and court masques, symbols of his power, with the increasing poverty and hunger in the country. Many concluded that the ceremonies were now just empty gestures and turned against him. This was by no means the only cause of the English Civil War and the overthrow and execution of Charles I – historical causation is rarely that simple – but it was certainly a contributing factor.[31]

Most societies settled for execution or exile of leaders who had lost divine support, but the Byzantine Empire had a different approach. Rather than being killed outright, deposed leaders were kept alive, but they were mutilated, usually facially, to mark them as failures. God is perfection; therefore, rulers who received divine favour were required to be perfect, and mutilation was a clear symbol that favour had been withdrawn. It also ensured that, in theory at least, the leader could not reclaim divine favour and make a new bid for power. The first form of mutilation practised was rhinkopia, the cutting of the nose (there is some debate among scholars whether this meant amputating the entire nose or splitting it open to disfigure it). Justinian II, deposed in 695 AD and exiled, got around the problem by having a false nose made out of solid gold that hid his mutilation. Thus equipped, he made another bid for power and returned to the throne in 705.[32]

After Justinian II's final overthrow, the policy changed, and failed leaders were blinded. For example, Romanos IV became emperor in 1068 with widespread support from the aristocracy and the military, which expected him to drive back the invading Turks and restore Byzantine power. After initial successes, he was defeated by the Turks at the Battle of Manzikert in 1071. The defeat was a clear signal; God had turned his back on Romanos, and the former favourite was quickly deposed and blinded.[33]

Divine right represented a confusing muddle of different types of power. Was it truly, as proponents like Thomas Aquinas or James I claimed, consistent with natural law, or was it just a concept made up by people desperate to cling to power? Was it inherited, i.e. did divine favour flow through the bloodline, or was it inherent, as cases like Justin I and Basil I seemed to indicate? And most of all, was the claim to divine right alone enough to justify their claim to power over their followers? The answer most of the time was yes, so long as the leaders delivered what the followers wanted in terms of safety, security and aspirations. When they failed to do so, the answer could easily become a brutal, violent and bloody 'no'; or even worse, civil strife between two or more groups all claiming the same mandate.

Intellectual attacks on divine right

The weaknesses of the concept of divine right were apparent from the beginning, and critical thinkers were not slow to remark upon them. In China, the concept of the mandate of heaven invented by the Zhou dynasty never drew much intellectual support. The most dogmatic of Chinese schools of philosophy, the Legalists led by Han Fei, argued that the leader had a duty to uphold the *dao* – the nearest Chinese equivalent to natural law – but there is no indication that the leader receives any divine favour or protection for doing so.[34] Confucius, with his passion for order and structure, believed in hierarchy and felt that in the natural order of things subordinates had a duty of obedience to their leader, but agreed that the leader was subordinate to the *dao* without necessarily partaking of it. Xunzi, one of Confucius's most prominent disciples, suggested that order, structure and symbols are themselves part of natural law; this view could, if taken to extreme, be an argument for the mandate of heaven, but Xunzi never quite commits to this position.[35]

At the same time another follower of Confucius, Mencius, came out in direct opposition to the mandate of heaven. According to him, the Confucian system was one of mutual rights and obligations. Mencius supported the Zhou dynasty concept of the right to rebel against unjust leaders, but he also argued that there is no basis in natural law for leaders to claim the right to rule. It is true that in the Confucian world order, subordinates owe a duty to their leader, but that obligation is a two-way street; leaders must also respect the views of their supporters and work in their best interests. For Mencius, it is the support of followers that keeps a leader in power, not any concept of divine right to lead or rule.[36]

The view that the leader is there to uphold the natural law but cannot claim to be divinely ordained is also implicit in the work of the great Indian political philosopher Kautilya in the second century BC. His *Arthashastra* was enormously influential in India for centuries to come and challenged earlier Hindu concepts of divine of semi-divine rulers.[37] The concept of duty was implicit in Manicheism, the dualistic faith that emerged in the third century BC, and in later Roman cults such as Sol Invictus and Mithras.[38] Early Islamic leaders such as the Caliph 'Ali also stressed that leaders were subordinate to Allah and had a religious duty to uphold the law, but this did not necessarily imply divine sanction.[39]

Along with these traditions of doubt about the authenticity of divine law, in the Graeco-Roman world there also developed an intellectual concept known as tyrannicide, the just killing of an unjust ruler. Aristotle had discussed the notion in his *Politics*, but perhaps the most vigorous exponent of the principle was the Roman senator Marcus Tullius Cicero, who defended the Roman republic during its final days and sympathised with (though he did not participate in) the plot to assassinate Julius Caesar in 44 BC. Cicero was eventually murdered on the orders of Mark Antony, another would-be tyrant whom Cicero had repeatedly criticised.[40]

Drawing on these earlier examples, and especially on Aristotle, medieval writers developed theories of justification of armed conflict, including rebellion. As noted earlier, both John of Salisbury and Thomas Aquinas indicated support for the principle of divine right but, perhaps paradoxically, both also supported tyrannicide. John of Salisbury was perhaps a little more reserved, arguing that tyrannicide could only be countenanced in extreme circumstances, but Aquinas was more enthusiastic. In both *De regno* and his earlier commentary on the *Sentences* of Peter Lombard, Aquinas argued that killing tyrants is a Christian duty, and that those who assassinate them deserve praise and reward.[41]

By the end of the sixteenth century, when James VI of Scotland was writing *The True Law of Free Monarchies*, the concept of divine right was coming under sustained attack from both sides of the new European religious divide. The Jesuits, flag-bearers for the revival and reform of the Catholic Church, were particularly sceptical. The influential Cardinal Robert Bellarmine scorned the idea of divine right, a view which brought him into dispute with the papacy, which was unsurprisingly rather more conflicted on the issue. Another Jesuit, Juan de Mariana, argued that the idea of monarchs having a particular personal relationship with God was a fiction – kings ruled not through divine grace, he said, but through a pact with their own subjects. We see here again the notion of a two-way street in which leader and followers have mutual responsibilities: if the leader fails in those responsibilities, said Mariana, followers have the right to remove him. His 1598 treatise *De rege et regis institutione* (On the King and the Royal Institution) was widely read and highly influential across the political and religious spectra.[42]

On the Protestant side, early movements such as the fourteenth-century Lollards and fifteenth-century Hussites had expressed doubt about divinely sanctioned rule. The Reformation's founders were divided on the issue; Martin Luther expressed qualified support for divine rule, but John Calvin had doubts. Certainly, said Calvin, if rulers behaved in a way which was contrary to God's law, their subjects had not only the right but also the duty to rise up and overthrow them.[43] Calvin's views were taken much further by François Hotman, one of the leaders of the Monarchomachs, a group of Protestant anti-monarchists that formed in France in the aftermath of the St Bartholomew's Day Massacre, when thousands of Protestants were killed by Catholic mobs, allegedly at the instigation of the Catholic queen, Catherine de Medici. Hotman's book *Franco-Gallia* denied the existence of divine right and called for the monarch to be elected directly by the people. Other Monarchomachs made open calls for kings to be assassinated.[44]

Ultimately, these disparate views coalesced into a single political philosophy calling for a rejection of divine right and the placing of human and social limitations on rulers. The two most influential figures in this movement were probably the Englishman John Locke and the Frenchman Jean-Jacques Rousseau. Following the execution of Charles I, England and Scotland were governed by Oliver Cromwell, Lord Protector of the Commonwealth of England, until the restoration of the Stuart monarchy in 1660. The new king, Charles II, was willing to bargain with his subjects and allow them to place limits on his authority, but his brother and successor, James II, was not. James attempted to restore the divine right to rule but encountered fierce opposition and was overthrown just three years after his coronation.[45] Locke's *Two Treatises of Government*, written partly in response to these events and partly as a rebuttal of Filmer's *Patriarcha*, were in effect an endorsement of the rebels who ended the Stuart dynasty, and following earlier writers, he argued that when confronted with tyranny, revolution is not only a right but also an obligation.[46]

Although the *Two Treatises of Government* were little regarded in Locke's lifetime, they exercised a profound influence on the American revolutionaries. The Constitution of the United States contains several paraphrases of Locke's ideas. Some influence of Locke can also be detected in the work of Rousseau, especially in his *The Social Contract* (1762). Rousseau argued that what we call society, far from being a divinely ordained order of things, is in effect a network of social contracts established to create order and security and allow complex societies to function. Instead of divine right, Rousseau established the notion of the *general will*, the objectives that society sets for itself, the values it holds and the direction in which it wishes to travel. The leader then becomes a kind of executive officer whose task is to help society achieve its goals, a concept which re-emerged in some twentieth-century schools of leadership thought, such as Greenleaf's 'servant leadership'.[47] Rousseau was famously one of the intellectual inspirations behind the French Revolution, along with Cicero and the tyrannicides of the classical world.

The end of divine right?

The French Revolution and the execution of King Louis XVI dealt a shattering blow to the concept of divine right in Europe. The restoration of the Bourbon monarchy saw an attempt to restore divine right, but that attempt, too, met with powerful resistance, including further revolutions in 1830 and 1848. The latter revolt was part of a Europe-wide series of popular revolutions which, although seldom resulting in regime change, forced many countries, including Austria and the German states, into reforms that limited the power of the monarchy.[48]

A form of Caesaropapism continued to hold sway in tsarist Russia, but from the 1860s onwards the tsars, too, came under increasing assault from a range of ideological foes, including social democrats, who desired to reform society; Marxists, who wanted to restructure it; and anarchists, who wanted to abolish the existing social order altogether. The rise of philosophical anarchism represented the challenge to divine right taken to its extreme. Mikhail Bakunin, for example, argued that authority is not fixed in one person: each of us has a form of authority that is inherent in our own personal knowledge and expertise. The exercise of authority is a voluntary form of exchange, authority traded for subordination, but that trade lasts only as long as the exchange itself. When we no longer have need of a particular form of authority, we discard it and move on. The most extreme form of this came from Sergey Nechayev, who argued that the authority of church and state was inherently immoral, no matter how wisely or justly it might be exercised, and every human being had the right to shake off that authority and fight back.[49] After repeated revolts and assassinations, the tsarist government was finally overthrown in 1917.

Anarchism also played a role in bringing about the end of the mandate of heaven in China. Sun Yat-sen, founder of the Kuomintang political party, espoused a philosophy akin to Christian socialism (he was baptised in 1884), but in 1905 he formed a coalition with a broad range of other anti-imperial groups, including Han nationalists and anarchists, forming a federation known as the Tongmenghui (Chinese Revolutionary Alliance). French-educated Chinese anarchists joined the Tongmenghui and supported Sun, including the scholar and entrepreneur Zhang Renjie and the journalist Lin Zongsu, founder of the first women's suffrage society in China. The Xinhai Revolution in 1911 broke the emperor's hold on power in China; the last emperor, Puyi, abdicated the following year and brought the mandate of heaven to an end.[50]

So, has divine right been consigned to the history books? Not entirely. Symbols remain, and sometimes they are quite powerful. The sovereign of the United Kingdom still bears the title Defender of the Faith and is still head of the Church of England, a residual ghost, perhaps, of Caesaropapism. Presidents of the United States are sworn in during a ceremony which is redolent with religious symbolism and which has some features in common with a coronation. Although religious observance has declined dramatically in Europe and North America, we have not lost our need for symbols. Religious symbols still exist, although they are now competing with many other, different types of symbol for attention.

But religious observance comes in cycles. The fifteenth and eighteenth centuries were also times when religious observance declined sharply in many Western countries, but each period was succeeded by a strong religious revival, during the Reformation and again during the Victorian age. When we look outside our Western bubble, we can see many parts of the world where religious observance continues and is even strengthening and where religious symbols play a strong role in unifying society. Only the boldest of prophets would dare predict that the age of divine right will never come again.

Notes

1 Spence, *God's Chinese Son*.
2 K.C. Chang, *Art, Myth, and Ritual: The Path to Political Authority in Ancient China*, Cambridge, MA: Harvard University Press, 1983; Burton Watson, *Ssu-ma Ch'ien: Grand Historian of China*, New York: Columbia University Press, 1958.
3 Elizabeth Perry, *Challenging the Mandate of Heaven: Social Protest and State Power in China*, Armonk: M.E. Sharpe, 2002.
4 Ibid.
5 Ibid.; Watson, *Ssu-ma Ch'ien*; Hucker, *China to 1850*; Ban Gu, *The Book of Han*, trans. Homer H. Dubs, *The History of the Former Han Dynasty*, Baltimore: Waverley, 1938.
6 Nguyen Khac Vien, *Vietnam: A Long History*, Hanoi: The Gioi, 1999; Ben Kernan, *Viet Nam: A History From Earliest Times to the Present*, Oxford: Oxford University Press, 2017; Alexander Woodside, *Vietnam and the Chinese Model: A Comparative Study of Vietnamese and Chinese Government in the First Half of the Nineteenth Century*, Cambridge, MA: Harvard University Press, 1971.
7 Peter H. Lee and William Theodore de Bary (eds), *Sources of Korean Tradition*, vol. 1, New York: Columbia University Press, 1997; Martina Deuchler, *The Confucian Transformation of Korea: A Study of Society and Ideology*, Boston: Harvard University Asia Center, 1992.
8 Timothy D. Barnes, *Constantine and Eusebius*, Cambridge, MA: Harvard University Press, 1981; Stephen Williams and Gerard Friell, *Theodosius: The Empire at Bay*, London: Yale University Press, 1995; John Meyendorff, *Byzantine Theology: Historical Trends and Doctrinal Themes*, New York: Fordham University Press, 1983.
9 Procopius, *The Secret History*, trans. G.A. Williamson, Harmondsworth: Penguin, 1966; A.A. Vasiliev, *Justin the First*, Cambridge, MA: Harvard University Press, 1950.
10 Romilly Jenkins, *Byzantium: The Imperial Centuries, AD 610–1271*, Toronto: University of Toronto Press, 1987; Norman Tobias, *Basil I, Founder of the Macedonian Dynasty: A Study of the Political and Military History of the Byzantine Empire in the Ninth Century*, Lewiston: Edwin Mellen, 2007.
11 Dennis Eugene Engleman, *Ultimate Things: An Orthodox Christian Perspective on End Times*, Chesterton, IN: Conciliar Press, 1995.
12 Guy Halsall, *Barbarian Migrations and the Roman West, 376–568*, Cambridge: Cambridge University Press, 2008; J.M. Wallace-Hadrill, *The Barbarian West, 400–1000*, Oxford: Blackwell, 1996.
13 John Meyendorff, *Byzantium and the Rise of Russia: A Study of Byzantino-Russian Relations in the Fourteenth Century*, New York: St Vladimir's Seminary Press, 1997.
14 Mary Boyce, *A History of Zoroastrianism*, Leiden: Brill, 1975.
15 André Clot, *Harun al-Rashid and the World of a Thousand and One Nights*, trans. John Howe, Lanham, MD: Rowman and Littlefield, 1989.
16 Bowle, *Henry VIII*; Starkey, *The Reign of Henry VIII*.
17 A.G. Dickens, *The English Reformation*, University Park: Penn State University Press, 2005.
18 David Harris Willson, *King James VI and I*, London: Jonathan Cape, 1963.
19 John of Salisbury, *Policraticus*, trans. J. Dickinson as *Policraticus: The Statesman's Book*, New York: Knopf, 1927; St Thomas Aquinas, *De Regno*, trans. Gerald B. Phelan, Toronto: Pontifical Institute of Medieval Studies, 1949; Thomas Gilby, *The Political Thought of Thomas Aquinas*, Chicago: University of Chicago Press, 1958.
20 Willson, *King James VI and I*; Jane Dawson, *John Knox*, London: Yale University Press, 2015.
21 Robert Filmer, *Patriarcha and Other Writings*, ed. Johann P. Sommerville, Cambridge: Cambridge University Press, 1991.
22 Richard Cust, *Charles I: A Political Life*, Harlow: Pearson Education, 2005; Steven Pincus, *1688: The First Modern Revolution*, London: Yale University Press, 2009.
23 Joachim Whaley, *Germany and the Holy Roman Empire*, Oxford: Oxford University Press, 2012; Robert Evans, *The Making of the Habsburg Monarchy, 1500–1700*, Oxford: Clarendon, 1979.

24 Otto G. von Simson, *Sacred Fortress: Byzantine Art and Statecraft in Ravenna*, Princeton: Princeton University Press, 1987; James Hall, *A History of Ideas and Images in Italian Art*, London: John Murray, 1983.

25 Liutprand of Cremona, *Relation de Legatione Constantinopolitana*, trans. F.A. Wright, New York: E.P. Dutton, 1930.

26 Glenn Richardson, *The Field of the Cloth of Gold*, London: Yale University Press, 2014; Barbara Ravelhofer, *The Early Stuart Masque: Dance, Costume and Music*, Oxford: Oxford University Press, 2006.

27 Andrzej Walicki, 'Pëtr Iakovlevich Chaadaev', in Edward Craig (ed.), *Routledge Encyclopedia of Philosophy*, London: Routledge, 1998, vol. 2, pp. 270–4; 'Abduh, *Risalat al-Tawhid*; Ferdinand Tönnies, *Community and Civil Society*, trans. José Harris, Cambridge: Cambridge University Press, 2006; Durkheim, *The Elementary Forms of the Religious Life*.

28 Marc Bloch, *The Royal Touch: Sacred Monarchy and Scrofula in England and France*, trans. J.E. Anderson, London: Routledge & Kegan Paul, 1973.

29 D.R. Forsyth, *Group Dynamics*, New York: Wadsworth, 2013.

30 Spence, *God's Chinese Son*; Stephen R. Platt, *Autumn in the Heavenly Kingdom: China, the West and the Epic Story of the Taiping Civil War*, New York: Knopf, 2012.

31 Cust, *Charles I*; Diane Purkiss, *The English Civil War: A People's History*, London: Harper-Collins, 2007.

32 Head, *Justinian II*.

33 Psellus, *Chronographia*.

34 Watson, *Han Fei Tzu*; Morgen Witzel, 'The Leadership Philosophy of Han Fei', *Asia Pacific Business Review* 18 (4) (2012): 1–15.

35 Hwang, *Foundations of Chinese Psychology*; Lau, *The Analects*; John Knoblock, *Xunzi: A Translation and Study of the Complete Works*, Stanford: Stanford University Press, 1988.

36 Philip J. Ivanhoe, *Ethics in the Confucian Tradition: The Thought of Mencius and Wang Yangming*, Indianapolis: Hackett, 2002.

37 Kumar, *Kautilya's Thought on Public Administration*.

38 Samuel Lieu, *Manicheism in the Later Roman Empire and Medieval China*, Tübingen: Mohr, 1992; Manfred Clauss, *The Roman Cult of Mithras: The God and His Mysteries*, London: Routledge, 2001.

39 'Ali ibn Abi Talib, *Nahjul Balagha* (Peak of Eloquence), trans. S.A. Reza, Elmhurst: Tahrike Tarsile Qu'ran, 1978.

40 Anthony Everitt, *Cicero: A Turbulent Life*, London: John Murray, 2001.

41 John of Salisbury, *Policraticus*; Aquinas, *De regno*; Dino Bigongiari (ed.), *The Political Ideas of St Thomas Aquinas*, New York: Hafner, 1953; Cary J. Nederman, 'A Duty to Kill: John of Salisbury's Theory of Tyrannicide', *The Review of Politics* 50 (3) (1988): 365–89.

42 Richard J. Blackwell, *Galileo, Bellarmine and the Bible*, Notre Dame: University of Notre Dame Press, 1991; Harald Braun, *Juan de Mariana and Early Modern Spanish Political Thought*, Aldershot: Ashgate, 2007.

43 Mullett, *Martin Luther*; Wilson, *Out of the Storm*; John Balserak, *Calvin as Sixteenth-Century Prophet*, Oxford: Oxford University Press, 2014.

44 Barbara B. Diefendorf, *The St Bartholomew's Day Massacre: A Brief History with Documents*, New York: St Martin's, 2008; Donald R. Kelly, *François Hotman: A Revolutionary's Ideal*, Princeton: Princeton University Press, 1973; Paul-Alexis Mellet, *Et de sa bouche sortait une glaive; les Monarchomachs au XVIème siècle*, Geneva: Droz, 2006.

45 Eveline Cruickshanks, *The Glorious Revolution*, Basingstoke: Palgrave Macmillan, 2000.

46 Richard Ashcraft, *Locke's Two Treatises of Government*, Boston: Unwin Hyman, 1987; Michael P. Zuckert, *Launching Liberalism: On Lockean Political Philosophy*, Lawrence: University Press of Kansas, 2002.

47 Rousseau, *The Social Contract*; Robert K. Greenleaf, *The Power of Servant Leadership*, San Francisco: Barrett-Koehler, 1988.

48 Schama, *Citizens*; Priscilla Robertson, *The Revolutions of 1848: A Social History*, New York: Harper, 1952.

49 Mikhail Bakunin, 'What Is Authority?', 1871, www.marxists.org/reference/archive/
bakunin/works/various/authrty.htm; Paul Avrich, *Bakunin and Nechayev*, New York:
Freedom Press, 1974.

50 Tijo Kayloe, *The Unfinished Revolution: Sun Yat-sen and the Struggle for Modern China*, Singapore: Marshall Cavendish, 2017; Lyon Sharman, *Sun Yat-sen: His Life and Its Meaning*,
Stanford: Stanford University Press, 2007; Arif Dirlik, *Anarchsim in the Chinese Revolution*,
Berkeley: University of California Press, 1991; Ma Yuxin, *Women Journalists and Feminism
in China, 1898–1937*, Amherst: Cambria Press, 2010.

7

GOD IS MY CO-PILOT

Leaders with God on their side

The title of this chapter is taken from a best-selling memoir of American fighter pilot Col. Robert L. Scott Jr.[1] Deemed too old for frontline duties at the start of the Second World War, Scott instead joined a group of freelance pilots known as the American Volunteer Group, colloquially known as the Flying Tigers, fighting in support of the Chinese against the invading Japanese. When the Flying Tigers were incorporated into the US Army Air Forces in 1942, Scott took over command of the 23rd Fighter Group.

In *God Is My Co-Pilot*, Scott recalls that he came up with the title while lying on an operating table to have shrapnel extracted from his back, having been wounded in a dogfight with the Japanese. One member of the medical staff expressed astonishment that Scott could fly his single-seat aircraft and shoot at enemies all on his own. Before the pilot could reply, the doctor who was operating on him intervened:

> No, son – you're not up there alone – not with all the things you come through. You have the greatest co-pilot in the world even if there is room for just one in that fighter ship – no, you're not alone.[2]

Reflecting on this, Scott decided the doctor was right: 'I believe when this war is over that we will be closer to God than at any time in the past', he wrote. 'I believe this because I have seen instances of real faith on several fronts in this war, and have heard of them on all fronts'. He recounted another case of a badly damaged aircraft landing on its home airfield. As the wounded pilot was carried away, someone asked him, 'How in the world did you bring this ship in?' 'I don't know', replied the pilot. 'Ask the Man upstairs'.[3]

Divinely favoured rulers

It is understandable that, in times of extreme stress, such as combat, people attribute their apparently miraculous survival to divine intervention. But in *God Is My*

Co-Pilot, Scott was doing something more. The book was written in 1943, while the war was at its height and its outcome was still in doubt. Scott was urging his fellow countrymen to believe that God was watching over them and that their cause was a just one. Rather than divine right, which offers a theoretical mandate to the leader and commanded obedience from followers, the concept of divine protection suggests that the leader is 'watched over'. 'Even though I walk through the valley of the shadow of death', says the 23rd Psalm, 'I will fear no evil, for thou art with me, and thy rod and they staff comfort me'. Texts from other major religions express a similar sentiment: those who have sufficient faith can claim divine protection.

Divine protection is also closely linked to the notion of the just cause. Both Confucius and Aristotle considered whether warfare can ever be justified, and they concluded that, if war is necessary to protect the innocent and root out evil, it is justified. The *Mahabharata*, the ancient Hindu philosophical-religious epic, concluded the same thing, and in the West, St Thomas Aquinas and the political philosopher Marsilius of Padua developed frameworks for considering when and where warfare may be considered justifiable and concluded that, paradoxically, war is sometimes necessary to defend the peace.[4]

For a leader to benefit from divine protection, therefore, he or she must be fighting for something that is good and righteous. Of course, how goodness and righteousness are defined depends entirely on the definer, and there are plenty of examples where soldiers on both sides believed their cause was just. During the Third Crusade, both Richard I, the Christian king, and Salah ad-Din Yusuf (Saladin), the Muslim sultan, believed their cause had divine approval and used religious imagery on their banners and armour.[5] In the opening days of the First World War, British army chaplains encouraged the troops by telling them that God was watching over them. It came as an unpleasant surprise to find that the German soldiers they opposed had the phrase *Gott mit uns* (God is with us) imprinted on their belt buckles.

As these examples demonstrate, divine protection extended beyond the leader. Those who followed the leader also benefitted from the same protection: if they were killed in battle, either they were assured of a place in paradise or, at the least, they would be remembered as heroes who died for a just cause. The officers who served under Jeanne d'Arc during the Hundred Years War believed that they benefitted from her aura, although one of them, Gilles de Rais, was later accused of witchcraft and satanism.[6]

The principle of divine guidance and protection played and continues to play a major role in many societies. In the Greco-Roman world, leaders called upon the gods for assistance as a matter of course; traders made sacrifices to the gods before setting out on voyages, and generals did likewise before embarking on campaign. Their reference points were the epics of their own past, Homer's *Iliad* and *Odyssey* and Virgil's *Aeneid*, in which the gods and goddesses intermingled and even interbred with mortal men and women, and every successful leader had to have at least one god as a supporter, if only to watch his back and fend off other, hostile gods.[7]

In Hindu, Jain and Buddhist societies the concept of the *chakravarti*, the ruler who 'turns the wheel' of the *dharma*, was widely discussed and practiced. One of the great exemplars was the Mauryan king Ashoka, who supported the Buddhist faith by founding many monasteries and temples throughout his domains (there is some debate as to whether Ashoka himself was ever a practising Buddhist). In return, Ashoka enjoyed a long and largely peaceful reign, and he continues to be regarded throughout Southeastern Asia as an exemplary ruler. The *chakravarti*'s most important characteristic is merit, which he or she must demonstrate through merit-making acts such as prayers, donations to the poor and, of course, support for the faith. According to the *Vessantara Jataka*, the legend of one of the Buddha's past lives, the ruler should seek to be the most meritorious person in the kingdom.[8] The *Vessantara Jataka* has been particularly influential in Thailand, many of whose kings have striven to become ideal Buddhist rulers.

The caliphs of Islam believed that faith was both a form of protection and a source of divine inspiration, and Caliph 'Ali, in his letters and sermons, reminded his people that the caliph ruled by God's law but was also answerable to God; to obtain divine favour and protection, one first had to have faith. Christian rulers adhered to similar principles. The *doges* of Venice (the independent city-state's rulers) conducted elaborate ceremonies such as the famous *sposalizio del mare* (marriage of the sea), which not only symbolised Venice's maritime supremacy in the Mediterranean but also indicated that this supremacy was the result of divine favour.

Generally, though, symbolism was less important in demonstrating divine protection. Banners, armour and engraved belt buckles existed, of course, but they were there primarily as reminders. Deeds, not words, were what counted. King Louis IX of France, later canonised as St Louis, became the ideal Christian monarch, rather as Ashoka became the ideal Buddhist king. According to his friend and biographer Jean de Joinville, Louis was the servant both of God and of his people. Piety and justice were the hallmarks of his reign. Louis was particularly concerned with justice and fairness – at least among his Christian subjects – and constantly showed marks of his piety. He spent long hours in prayer, and sometimes wore a hair shirt as a mark of penance. He collected holy relics, most notably the Crown of Thorns, for which he built the remarkable Sainte-Chapelle in Paris, and he endowed many religious houses, including hospitals and orphanages. His own kitchen fed more than a hundred paupers, and St Louis would sometimes invite beggars and lepers to dine at his own table while he washed their feet (an imitation of Christ washing the feet of the poor).[9] In return, Louis could claim to enjoy divine protection. On one occasion, says Joinville, the ship in which he was travelling was hit by a sudden storm. The sailors were terrified, but the king simply lay down on the deck with his arms outstretched like a figure on a cross. The storm abated, and the ship sailed peacefully on.[10]

Louis's piety had a dark side. Believing that he was following God's law, he outlawed usury – the lending of money at interest – and confiscated and burned Jewish books, including works of scripture. The rebellion of the Cathar heretics in southern France had largely been suppressed, but Louis established the Inquisition to stamp out the last pockets of religious non-conformism. The Inquisition used torture and the death penalty to punish not only heretics but also those suspected of supporting them; it was responsible for a notable massacre at Montségur in 1244.[11] Louis famously led the Seventh Crusade against Muslim Egypt, which ended in the annihilation of his army and his own capture by the Egyptian Mamluks.[12] Undeterred, Louis tried again, launching the Eighth Crusade against the North African port of Tunis. This, too, ended in disaster, and Louis himself was among the dead.[13]

Regarding this dismal tale from the comfort of the modern world, we might be tempted to say that this makes a mockery of the concept of divine protection. God did not protect Louis or his followers, quite the contrary. The medieval mind, however, did not see it that way. To his contemporaries, Louis was a faithful servant of God who died as a martyr to his faith. Anyone who perished while on crusade, whether in battle or of natural causes, was guaranteed eternal salvation: that much had been promised by Pope Urban II when he ordered the First Crusade.[14] For Louis to die while on crusade, after a life of exemplary piety, might be considered an almost perfect ending.

As with divine right, whether you felt divine protection and favour were accorded depended on perspective. Mary I of England, a devout Catholic, was one of the most pious monarchs in English history. As a young girl, she continued to profess her mother's Catholic faith despite the threats and rages of her father, Henry VIII; having reaching the throne herself, she was determined to roll back the Protestant Reformation and restore Catholic rule. Understandably, this met with the approval of Catholics everywhere, including the pope, and Mary was considered by her fellow Catholics to be divinely guided. Equally understandably, Protestants had a different view, especially after Mary had ordered the execution of nearly three hundred protestants, many of whom were burned alive.[15] To Protestants, she was a figure of evil; they nicknamed her Bloody Mary, and that epithet persisted long after her death.

Some rulers claimed piety and divine favour in public, but in private they behaved rather differently. In the thirteenth century, under pressure from two crusading orders of knights – 'the Teutonic Knights and the Livonian Order' (based in modern-day Latvia) – Grand Duke Mindaugas of Lithuania, a pagan, agreed to be baptised as Christian and crowned king of Lithuania. Once these ceremonies were completed, the crusaders no longer had a pretext to attack Lithuania and instead devoted their attention to other pagan states in the region. Mindaugas continued his Christian observance in public, but it seems likely that he also continued to practice his pagan faith in private. In 1260, after both crusading orders had suffered disastrous military defeats, Mindaugas reckoned he was now strong enough to hold them off. He renounced his Christian faith and restarted the war. Late-fourteenth-century Lithuanian leader Jogaila, also a pagan, converted to Christianity in order to secure a strategic alliance with Poland against the Teutonic Order, but his brother Vytautas remained a pagan, partly to secure the continued support of the country's overwhelmingly pagan population.[16]

Finally, we should remember the people who felt a real connection with the divine and used the inspiration they drew from this to lead their people. In chapter 5, I mentioned several examples, including Veleda, a priestess of the Bructeri who led the resistance against Rome, and Hehaka Sapa (Black Elk), the Lakota medicine man. Hehaka Sapa had repeated visions, the first of which he experienced at the age of nine, when he communed with spirits known as the Grandfathers, heavenly beings who told him the destiny of his people. Using the knowledge gained from his visions, Hehaka Sapa counselled the leaders of the Lakota and played a significant role in resisting American encroachment. At Wounded Knee, when American troops had opened fire on a largely defenceless Lakota encampment, Black Elk rode out towards the American guns, drawing their fire and allowing many other Lakota to escape. He was grazed by a bullet but otherwise unharmed. Although Hehaka Sapa later converted to Catholicism, he continued to believe that divine spirits had protected him at Wounded Knee.[17]

Justification and support

Although leaders within elite groups have often used the notion of divine protection and favour to secure support, the concept has also helped emergent leaders from outside the elites establish themselves and win acceptance. The case of Jeanne d'Arc is instructive. As a prospective leader, she faced three significant barriers: a) she had no military experience, b) she was a peasant in an era when military leadership was supposed to be the exclusive province of the knightly classes and c) she was a woman. Despite this, she became the principal military leader of France for a brief period, with tough military professionals such as Gilles de Rais, La Hire and Arthur de Richemont, the constable of France, accepting her orders and working under her command.[18]

Why was Jeanne successful? First, although male historians over the past centuries have found this difficult to accept, Jeanne was an inherently skilful tactician. When she arrived at the Siege of Orléans, she spotted the weaknesses of the English position almost at once, and her gamble to take the dauphin to Rheims where he could be formally crowned king was very possibly the tipping point of the war. She opposed the king's plan to attack English-held Paris, and she was right – the French were defeated, and Jeanne herself was wounded. Second, she was clearly a charismatic figure. She was able to quickly win over the dauphin and his senior commanders and was popular with the common soldiers, who regarded her as their totem and charm. Finally, while working in the garden in her home village of Domrémy, she had a vision in which three saints including the warrior Saint Michael, appeared and told her it was her task to drive the English out of France. Jeanne stuck to this vision, insisting it was true despite the best efforts of various inquisitors to disprove her story; what is more, she convinced others it was true. La Hire, a hard-bitten Gascon captain with a reputation for drinking and profanity, believed in her utterly.[19]

The vision acted as a persuader: it convinced the dauphin and others to give her a hearing. But visionaries were common in the later Middle Ages, and most of them had little impact on their contemporaries.[20] Although the vision opened the door, what ultimately gained Jeanne acceptance was her undoubted inherent competence. Her men followed her because she was not only a visionary but also a skilful leader. In a very different time and place, Victorian England, former pawnbroker William Booth also had a religious mission, but he was able to succeed in establishing the Salvation Army only because he was a skilled communicator and a very good organiser. Starting small in the East End of London, Booth had spread the Salvation Army movement to fifty-eight countries by the time of his death.[21] People came to hear him preach his message of faith and salvation, but they stayed with him because of his inherent skills and ability to guide and control his organisation.

Many leaders have found inspiration in religion and tried to build a religious message and purpose into their work. In 1943, Father José Maria Arizmendiarrieta, the local priest of the Basque town of Mondragón, established a technical college to train young people. The programme of education was a combination of Catholic socialism, strongly grounded in both faith and community values, and technical education in fields such as engineering. Arizmendiarrieta's hope was that graduates of the college could establish their own businesses and help improve the economic prospects of the Basque region, which was impoverished after the Spanish Civil War. In 1956, he encouraged some of his graduates to set up a small co-operative, Ulgor, which went on to become the Mondragón Cooperative Corporation, which today employs around seventy-five thousand people. Although Mondragón is very much a commercial enterprise, Arizmendiarietta's religious faith was one of its founding and guiding principles. Others managed the growth of the business, but Arizmendiarietta was its spiritual leader until his death.[22]

Some religious groups are noted for blending faith and entrepreneurial spirit, including the Quakers and the Parsis. English Quakers are famous for their ability to build businesses based strongly on religious principles. Three chocolate dynasties, Cadbury, Fry and Rowntree's, are perhaps the best-known examples of Quaker success, but there are many more, such as gunsmith Samuel Galton, steel-maker Benjamin Huntsman, banker John Freame, co-founder of the firm that later became Barclays, and biscuit-maker George Palmer, partner in the firm Huntley & Palmer.[23] These firms, except for Galton's (he was attacked by fellow Quakers for selling arms when their faith forbid the shedding of blood), were strongly imbued with Quaker principles. George Cadbury was a pioneer in providing benefits such as housing and education to employees, and he built the model village Bourneville on the outskirts of Birmingham. Joseph Rowntree and his son Benjamin Seebohm Rowntree were very active social reformers. Elizabeth Fry, who married the chocolate-maker John Fry and whose parents came from Quaker banking families, was heavily involved in social reform, especially in prisons.[24]

India's Parsi community – Zoroastrians who emigrated from Persia and settled in India in the seventeenth and eighteenth centuries in part to escape religious persecution – produced a number of notable business dynasties. One of the first Parsi entrepreneurs was Lovji Nusserwanji Wadia, who founded the first shipyard in Mumbai and built ships for the East India Company. His descendants expanded into shipping and transport, and the Wadia Group continues to flourish today.[25]

The Tata group, founded by Jamsetji Nusserwanji Tata, emerged at the end of the nineteenth century and played a prominent role in the economic development of India before and after independence. Other dynasties include the Godrej, Mody and Mehta families, and again, with few exceptions, most have historically harked back to their Parsi roots and run their businesses in ways that are strongly imbued with religious and social values. Sir Homi Mehta was a leading philanthropist who also served as India's representative to the League of Nations and the International Labor Organization; Sir Hormusjee Mody was one of the co-founders of the University of Hong Kong.[26]

Individual business leaders and entrepreneurs also turned to religion for inspiration. Yoshio Maruta, the charismatic chairman of Japanese chemicals corporation Kao from 1971 to 1990, was fascinated by ancient Buddhist thought. One of his intellectual heroes was Queen Srimala of the Satavahana dynasty in Andhra, Eastern India, who flourished in the third century AD. She is the presumed author of *Srimaladevi Simhanada Sutra* (Lion's Roar), a devotional work emphasising the need for human beings to seek perfection by putting an end to all suffering. Srimala advocated the quality of mercy, not only pitying but 'seeking also' to understand and accept the views of others. Maruta urged his executives to embrace the same spirit, to treat customers with respect, to listen to them and to understand their point of view.[27]

The entrepreneur Ma Ying-piao adopted Christian values of service when founding Sincere, Hong Kong's first department store. Like George Cadbury, Ma believed in education for his workers and their children and taught Sunday school every week. He trained his staff to put the customer first and remember that they were there to serve. 'Ma also faced' public outrage by hiring female clerks and paying them the same wage as that of his male employees.[28]

Henry Ford was a devout Episcopalian who appointed his own pastor, Samuel S. Marquis, to head the sociology department at Ford Motors. The sociology department itself was a pioneering experiment in applying sociological theory to business organisations, with a view to making the workforce not only more efficient but also happier and more fulfilled. In the early days, at least, Ford believed that business had both a social and an economic purpose, and he channelled his religious faith into turning Ford Motors into a model employer.[29] The oil tycoon John D. Rockefeller was a member of a Northern Baptist congregation from an early age; he read the Bible daily and attended church faithfully. As a boy of sixteen he began donating a portion of his wages to charity, and he later claimed that his life plan was founded on advice given to him by his pastor: make as much money as possible and then give away as much as possible.[30]

But Ford and Rockefeller had their dark sides. In 1910, Ford was one of the most admired business leaders in the world. The Ford Model T had revolutionised not only the car industry but also American society; cheap motoring gave people, especially women, freedom of movement they had not enjoyed before. Ford's plant at

Highland Park was a marvel of engineering organisation, and other business leaders from around the world came to study it. He paid his workers five times the going rate and earned their loyalty and trust.

Ten years later, a different picture had emerged. Fuelled by his hardline religious beliefs, Ford had metamorphosed into a vicious anti-Semite who even purchased his own newspaper to spread anti-Jewish propaganda. A hypocritical side had also emerged; Ford would not tolerate sexual immorality among his executives and workers, but he himself kept a mistress for many years. Somewhat worryingly, both Lenin and Hitler admired him and gave orders that his works should be translated and distributed in their own countries. Ford became an autocrat who brooked no opposition. He drove out most of his senior managers and turned from an enlightened employer to a despot who enforced rigid discipline that was sometimes backed with violence.[31]

Rockefeller was convinced that his business success had been ordained by God and that because of God's favour he was untouchable. He, too, drove away many of his loyal supporters within Standard Oil; as a result, several of them were willing to talk to the journalist Ida Tarbell, giving her the information she needed to expose Standard Oil's corrupt practices. Even after Tarbell's book was published, Rockefeller refused to change his ways, still believing that he was right and that God would watch over him.[32]

A mighty fortress

In his introduction to *God Is My Co-Pilot*, Col. Robert Scott encouraged his readers to use religious faith as a kind of rallying point from which to carry on the struggle against the enemy. We will win, he said, because God is protecting us. Perhaps, but in reading the book – and the works of other people who knew him, such as his commanding officer at the Flying Tigers, Gen. Claire Chennault – it becomes apparent that Scott was also a leader of remarkable skill and courage who shot down thirteen enemy aircraft and was several times decorated for valour.[33]

In chapter 5, I briefly discussed the ways in which people use religious faith and symbols as a unifying device in much the manner that Scott advocated. Martin Luther's famous hymn 'Ein feste Burg ist unser Gott' (A Mighty Fortress Is Our God) expresses the sentiment; especially in times of strife and conflict, some people turn to religion for security in the belief that faith offers some kind of certainty in an otherwise uncertain and dangerous world. There are of course different kinds of faith; in Christianity, the word *faith* has connotations of trust, whereas in Buddhism the concept of *pali* is more aligned with ideas such as commitment and dedication.[34] Generally, however, we can observe that faith can serve as a useful basis for a society, a community or an organisation, identifying the values of the group and helping members to proceed towards common goals.

These groups search for leaders to help them do what they cannot do themselves. Soldiers, sailors and combat pilots look for people who have extraordinary courage and an array of skills. Colonel Scott was one example of such a leader; 'Jeanne d'Arc was another'. Businesses seek leaders who can see the bigger picture, help the organisation coalesce around its chosen strategy and goals and so on. This remains true whether people are seeking security and safety, the fulfilment of aspirations or some combination of both.

We look for leaders whom we know to be inherently skilful and who have the power to get things done. But when choosing which leaders we will follow, there is always an element of uncertainty. Can they deliver on what they have promised? Is it possible that there is better leader out there whom we should be following if we want to get things done? As a result, we seek extra assurance, something more than just competence, which tells us we have made the right choice and are following the right person. In the midst of change and uncertainty, we want the calm, strength and protection of the fortress.

Divine protection and favour offered that assurance. As noted, divine favour alone was rarely if ever enough to get someone accepted as a leader, especially an emergent leader coming in from outside the established elites. Had the English commanders Lord Talbot and Sir William Glasdale defeated the French at Orléans, Jeanne d'Arc would be little more than a footnote to history. But it was clear right away that she had both talent and courage. She made mistakes; for example, during the fighting on 5 May 1429, she attacked too soon and her troops were routed, but she quickly rallied them and carried on fighting even after she had been wounded twice. Her personal courage, like that of Col. Scott, served as an example to others, and her men fought for her willingly because they knew she took the same risks as they did. Her vision of Archangel Michael, which she experienced in her garden at Domrémy, opened doors; it persuaded men of power to listen to her. The rest was all down to Jeanne herself.

In addition to competence, the elements of trust and fairness are implicit both in the Christian idea of faith and in that of some other religious groups. In some societies, notably Norse and Greco-Roman, the gods did not always play fair when dealing with humans or with each other. Loki was a trickster who delighted in creating mischief for others; Zeus adopted disguises in order to seduce mortal girls and boys. But in the monotheistic religions and in Buddhism, there is an understanding that divinity plays fair. 'Is not Allah the best of judges?' asks the Qur'an. Allah dispenses justice to all, according to what they deserve, and the faithful can always expect fair treatment. Those to whom divine favour or protection is granted will necessarily be fair; if they fail to be just and equitable towards their followers, it follows logically that divine favour will be withdrawn.

There is no doubt that strong faith can offer inspiration, even if that inspiration is not always directed to ends that we would today consider acceptable. The anti-Semitism of Louis IX and Henry Ford was, we must remember, partly rooted in faith; but so too was the social welfare and reform work of the Rowntrees and Elizabeth Fry. Yoshio Maruta found in Buddhism the inspiration he needed to drive his business forward, and Father José Maria Arizmendiarietta drew on his Christian faith to set up a college and then a business to help his people.

In terms of authority, then, we are looking here at a blend of inherent and conferred authority, with the inherent element as the core but the conferred element adding something extra, a little touch of stardust that makes people follow these leaders more willingly with greater belief that they will succeed and greater assurance that they will treat their followers and subordinates fairly, punishing their crimes and rewarding their successes. Knowing that God or the gods were looking after their leader gave followers a little more confidence that they would succeed.

There is of course an element of hindsight to all this. It was easy to claim divine grace; many people did, some fraudulently, some in genuine belief. For every visionary war leader or wise mystic, there were many others who were simply ignored. In August 1356, another peasant from Eastern France, a man this time, approached King Jean with a message which he too said had been relayed to him in a divine vision; if the king went to battle with the English that summer, disaster would ensue. The king ignored the peasant and carried on with his preparations for war. Two months later the French army was routed at the Battle of Poitiers, and Jean himself was taken prisoner.[35] Similarly, not every devout Quaker or Parsi who founded a business went on to enjoy national or international success. Human beings do not like uncertainty, and especially in the West, imbued as they are in the Cartesian tradition of causality, they like clear explanations as to why things happen. Why were some people more successful than others? How did individuals from humble backgrounds emerge as accepted leaders? It was tempting, in an age of faith, to look back at such cases and see the hand of God at work.

A combination of faith, inspiration and skill has always been an attractive package in a leader. Faith does not need to be linked to a particular set of religious beliefs; in modern Europe, many contemporary leaders describe themselves as 'having faith' without necessarily adhering to a single religious doctrine. Knowing that our leaders believe in something other than themselves tends to make them more credible and acceptable.

Notes

1 Robert L. Scott, *God Is My Co-Pilot*, New York: Ballantine, 1943.
2 Ibid., p. i.
3 Ibid., p. i.
4 Michael Walzer, *Arguing About War*, London: Yale University Press, 2004; Nicholas Fotion, *War and Ethics*, London: Continuum, 2007; Marsilius of Padua, *Defensor Pacis*, trans. Annabel Brett, Cambridge: Cambridge University Press, 2005.
5 Malcolm Cameron Lyons and D.E.P. Jackson, *Saladin: The Politics of Holy War*, Cambridge: Cambridge University Press, 1982; John Gillingham, *Richard I*, New Haven: Yale University Press, 1999.
6 Matei Cazacu, *Gilles de Rais*, Paris: Tallandier, 2007.
7 Homer, *Iliad*; Homer, *Odyssey*; Virgil, *The Aeneid*, trans. Robert Fagles, London: Penguin, 2010.
8 Patrick Jory, *Thailand's Theory of Monarchy: The Vessantara Jataka and the Idea of the Perfect Man*, Albany: State University of New York Press, 1998; D.C. Ahir, *Ashoka the Great*, New Delhi: B.R. Publishing, 1995.

9 Jean de Joinville, *The Life of St Louis*, trans. Margaret R.B. Shaw in *Joinville and Villehard-ouin: Chronicles of the Crusades*, Harmondsworth: Penguin, 1963; Cecilia M. Gaposchkin, *The Making of Saint Louis: Kingship, Sanctity and Crusade in the Later Middle Ages*, Ithaca: Cornell University Press, 2008; Jacques Le Goff, *Saint Louis*, trans. Gareth Gollrad, Notre Dame: University of Notre Dame Press, 2009.

10 Joinville, *Life of St Louis*.

11 Jonathan Sumption, *The Albigensian Crusade*, London: Faber and Faber, 1978.

12 Joinville, *Life of St Louis*; Christopher Tyerman, *God's War: A New History of the Crusades*, London: Allen Lane, 2006.

13 Tyerman, *God's War*; Le Goff, *Saint Louis*.

14 Tyerman, *God's War*.

15 Susan Doran and Thomas Freedman (eds), *Mary Tudor: Old and New Perspectives*, Basing-stoke: Palgrave Macmillan, 2011; Eamon Duffy, *Fires of Faith: Catholic England Under Mary Tudor*, London: Yale University Press, 2009.

16 Rowell, *Lithuania Ascending*; Christiansen, *The Northern Crusades*.

17 Hehaka Sapa, *Black Elk Speaks*.

18 Taylor, *The Virgin Warrior*; Pernoud, *Joan of Arc*; Françoise Meltzer, *For Fear of the Fire: Joan of Arc and the Limits of Subjectivity*, Chicago: University of Chicago Press, 2001; Anton Kaiser, *Joan of Arc: A Study in Charismatic Women's Leadership*, Black Hills: Black Hills Books, 2017.

19 Ibid.

20 Elizabeth Alvida Petroff, *Body and Soul: Essays on Medieval Women and Mysticism*, Oxford: Oxford University Press, 1994.

21 Hattersley, *Blood and Fire*; George Scott Railton, *The Authoritative Life of General William Booth*, London: George H. Doran, 1912.

22 William Foote Whyte and Kathleen King Whyte, *Making Mondragon: The Growth and Dynamics of the Worker Cooperative Complex*, Ithaca: ILR Press, 1989; Keith Bradley and Alan Gelb, *Co-operation at Work: The Mondragón Experience*, London: Heinemann, 1983.

23 Cadbury, *Chocolate Wars*; Jenny Uglow, *The Lunar Men: The Friends Who Made the Future*, London: Faber and Faber, 2002; Gordon Goodwin, 'Huntsman, Benjamin', in *Oxford Dictionary of National Biography*, Oxford: Oxford University Press, 2004; Margaret Ackrill and Leslie Hannah, *Barclays: The Business of Banking, 1690–1996*, Cambridge: Cambridge University Press, 2001; T.A.B. Corley, 'Palmer, George', in *Oxford Dictionary of National Biography*, Oxford: Oxford University Press, 2004.

24 Cadbury, *Experiments in Industrial Organisation*; A.G. Gardiner, *Life of George Cadbury*, London: Cassell, 1923; Robert Fitzgerald, *Rowntree and the Marketing Revolution*, Cambridge: Cambridge University Press, 2007; June Rose, *Elizabeth Fry*, Basingstoke: Macmillan, 1980.

25 Zoroastrian Educational Institute, 'The Wadias of India: Then and Now', n.d., www.zoroastrian.org.uk/vohuman/Article/The%20Wadias%20of%20India.htm.

26 Lala, *For the Love of India*; Witzel, *Tata*; Zoroastrian Educational Institute, 'The Life and Times of Sir Hormusjee Naorojee Mody, the Napoleon of the Rialto', n.d., www.zoroastrian.org.uk/vohuman/Article/Hormusjee%20Naorojee%20Mody.htm; Burjor Kurshedji Karanjia, *Vijitatma: Pioneer-Founder Ardeshir Godrej*, Bombay: Penguin, 2004; Bakhtiar K. Dadabhoy, *Barons of Banking: Glimpse of Indian Banking History*, New Delhi: Random House India, 2013.

27 Alex Wayman and Hideko Wayman, *The Lion's Roar of Queen Srimala*, New York: Columbia University Press, 1990; Anthony W. Barber, *Buddhism in the Krishna River Valley of Andhra*, Albany: State University of New York Press, 2009; Otto Kalthoff, Ikujiro Nonaka and Pedro Nueno, *The Light and the Shadow: How Breakthrough Innovation Is Shaping European Business*, Oxford: Capstone, 1997.

28 Wellingon K.K. Chan, 'The Organizational Structure of the Traditional Chinese Firm and Its Modern Reform', *Business History Review* 56 (2) (1982): 218–35; repr. in R. Ampalavanar Brown (ed.), *Chinese Business Enterprise: Critical Perspectives on Business and Management*, London: Routledge, 1982, vol. 1, pp. 216–30.

29 Steven Watts, *The People's Tycoon: Henry Ford and the American Century*, New York: Alfred A. Knopf, 2005; Allan Nevins, *Ford: The Man, The Times, The Company*, New York: Scribners, 1954; Morgen Witzel, *Managing for Success*, London: Bloomsbury, 2015.

30 Chernow, *Titan*; Burton W. Folsom, *The Myth of the Robber Barons*, New York: Young America, 2003; Allan Nevins, *Study in Power: John D. Rockefeller, Industrialist and Philanthropist*, New York: Charles Scribner's Sons, 1953.

31 Watts, *The People's Tycoon*; Witzel, *Managing for Success*.

32 Chernow, *Titan*; Ida M. Tarbell, *All in the Day's Work: An Autobiography*, Champaign: University of Illinois Press, 2003.

33 Scott, *God Is My Co-Pilot*; Claire Chennault, *Way of a Fighter*, New York: Putnam's, 1949.

34 Paul Tillich, *The Dynamics of Faith*, New York: Harper & Row, 1957; Tillich, *Theology of Culture*; Bertrand Russell, *Human Society in Ethics and Politics*, London: Routledge, 2009; Steven M. Emmanuel (ed.), *A Companion to Buddhist Philosophy*, Chichester: Wiley-Blackwell, 2013.

35 Livingstone and Witzel, *The Black Prince*.

8

THE DIVINE SPARK

Spiritual inspiration in leadership

'The spirit of self-help is the root of all genuine growth in the individual', wrote the journalist and political campaigner Samuel Smiles in 1859, 'and, exhibited in the lives of the many, it constitutes the true source of national vigour and growth'.[1] His book *Self-Help* sold twenty thousand copies in its first year of publication, and by the time of the author's death, it had been translated into twenty languages and sold more than 250,000 copies worldwide. *Self-Help* was especially popular in Japan following the Meiji Restoration, when a new class of self-made administrators and entrepreneurs rose to prominence; Sakichi Toyoda, founder of the Toyota group, was one of many young people who drew inspiration from the book.[2]

Smiles's argument was simple: we all have it within us to achieve great things, but we must not expect these things to be handed to us on a plate. Rising to the summit of one's profession, be it business, law, politics, the military or the arts, requires us to work hard; study hard; cultivate habits such as thrift, patience and perseverance; value knowledge for its own sake; and, above all, reach inside ourselves for the resources we need. Do not rely on others to help you, Smiles warned. To succeed, you must learn to stand on your own two feet. 'Help from without is often enfeebling in its effects', he wrote. 'Whatever is done *for* men or classes, to a certain extent takes away the stimulus and necessity of doing for themselves, and where men are subjected to over-guidance and over-government, the inevitable tendency is to render them comparatively helpless'.[3]

Smiles claimed his intention was to encourage young people to better themselves and live more rewarding and fulfilling lives through personal learning and growth. There is an element of Darwinism here, and Charles Darwin is said to have been a fan of the book. However, there is also a subtext. A campaigner on issues such as political reform, free trade and women's suffrage (though women are barely mentioned in *Self-Help*), Smiles had a strong dislike of the establishment. He was critical of the Great Man theory espoused by Thomas Carlyle and others; he referred to it as

'Ceasarism' and describes it as 'human idolatry in its worst form – a worship of mere power, as degrading in its effects as the worship of mere wealth would be'.[4] At times he appeared to reject the concept of leadership itself. 'Even the best institutions can give a man no active help', he wrote. 'Perhaps the most they can do is leave him free to develop himself and improve his individual condition'.[5] Voting for members of parliament was an activity which he described as largely irrelevant.

Ironically, perhaps, having decried the tradition of the Great Man, Smiles then stuffed his book full of examples of people (with which this present book is likewise stuffed) who achieved greatness through self-discipline and self-improvement. One of his heroes was Robert Owen, who died the year before *Self-Help* was published. A non-conformist and an outsider, Owen was an example of the principles Smiles espoused. Born in Wales in 1771, Owen walked to London when he was ten years old to take a job with his brother. Later, while serving an apprenticeship with a draper, he taught himself to read and write and gave himself a short but intensive education. At sixteen he moved to Manchester, where he set up his first business making spinning machines; at nineteen he was appointed works manager at Peter Drinkwater's cotton mill, running a factory that employed five hundred people. In 1795, he set up his own factory, the Chorlton Twist Mill and became a member of the Literary and Philosophical Society of Manchester, to which he presented several papers.[6]

In 1800, Owen bought the cotton mill at New Lanark on the Clyde and turned it into a model of enlightened capitalism. His purpose, as he later said, was not only to run a cotton mill but also to improve the quality of life for the people who worked there.[7] To this end he introduced many reforms, including shortening the working day, abolishing child labour and providing free education to his workers and their children. A lifelong atheist, Owen also abolished religious education and instead, as he put it, provided education that would strengthen the mind and character and make people more self-reliant. 'Owen believed in the power of education, rightly directed, to turn the world's affairs into a prosperous course', wrote a later biographer.[8]

Self-made men and women

It could be argued that Smiles and Owen were both fortunate to have lived when they did. The eighteenth and nineteenth centuries in Britain were a time and place when it was relatively easy for people of humble origins to emerge as leaders, especially in business. Several factors conspired to make this so. The Protestant Reformation had engendered a new spirit of self-reliance and self-determination, generally known today as the 'Protestant work ethic'.[9] Hard work was seen as a virtue, and those who worked hard enough would be rewarded with riches in this life and salvation in the next. Personal salvation could no longer be achieved through ritual and prayer: work, not faith, was the key to the kingdom of Heaven. The Enlightenment – itself influenced by the Reformation and Counter-Reformation that followed – encouraged a more individualistic approach to the world.[10]

Finally, the scientific and engineering breakthroughs of the Industrial Revolution offered scope for clever and ambitious young men and women to build businesses based on new inventions.[11] The Industrial Revolution was the great age of the inventor-entrepreneur turned business leader. Eleanor Coade did not invent artificial stone *per se*, but she perfected an already existing process, producing a durable, weatherproof product which is still known today as Coade stone. She led and managed her business based on this product for more than fifty years. Richard Arkwright turned a basic invention, the spinning frame, into an entire system of factory production; he was owner or partner in thirteen cotton mills and sold manufacturing machinery to other factory owners. A penniless refugee fleeing the French Revolution, Marc Brunel invented a machine for making pulley blocks, an indispensable part of the rigging of ships. By 1808, his factory was making 130,000 blocks a year and supplying the whole Royal Navy. Capitalising on the new interest in classical art and architecture, the potter Josiah Wedgwood designed a range of products that captured the public imagination across Europe and won him the patronage of royalty at home and abroad. A wealthy self-made man, Wedgwood spent much of his fortune funding scientific investigations and campaigning against slavery.[12]

A similar meritocracy developed in Japan in the aftermath of the Meiji Restoration, when Western ideas about economy and society – including, as we saw, *Self-Help* – were introduced by the reforming government. The idea of self-development and the cultivation of personal virtue has a long history in Japan and is present in both Japanese Buddhism and the Shinto faith. The *Hagakure*, the primary codification of the philosophy of the *samurai* class, emphasises virtue and self-mastery, and the same principles can be seen in biographies of swordfighters, most famously Miyamoto Musashi's *The Book of Five Rings*; many aspiring Japanese read both Miyamoto and Samuel Smiles.[13] Sakichi Toyoda was one of a wave of entrepreneurs who emerged during this period; others included Iwasaki Yataro, a farmer's son turned ship-owner who founded the Mitsubishi Corporation; Hirose Saihi, who started his working life as a clerk before going on to revive the moribund mining company Sumitomo and turn it into a powerful corporation; and another farmer's son, Shibusawa Eiichi, who founded the Daiichi Bank.[14]

There were other fields where hard work and dedication could sometimes be enough to help people advance to positions of leadership. Science was one such area; Sir Isaac Newton, the son of a farmer, went on to be president of the Royal Society, whereas Michael Faraday, the son of a blacksmith, became one of the most prominent figures at the Royal Institution.[15] Religious orders also allowed advancement on merit; Thomas Wolsey, reputed to be the son of a butcher, rose through the ranks of the Catholic church to become a cardinal who was one of the most powerful people in England during the early years of the reign of Henry VIII.[16]

As noted in chapter 4, unlike the British army (where until 1871 most officers purchased their commissions and advancement was restricted to the wealthy), the Royal Navy made promotions based on a mixture of merit and patronage, and young men from humble backgrounds sometimes rose to high ranks. Sir John Norris was born in Ireland to parents unknown and entered the navy as a captain's servant; eight years later he was commissioned as a lieutenant and thereafter advanced through the ranks, and in 1734, he was appointed admiral of the fleet, the highest rank in the navy.[17] Two of the Royal Navy's most celebrated navigators and explorers, James Cook and William Bligh, also worked their way up from the bottom. Cook, the son of a farm labourer, served for many years as a merchant sailor before joining the Royal Navy as an able seaman. He had already developed a reputation as a navigator even before receiving his first commission at the age of thirty-nine. Bligh's father was a customs officer; he, too, joined the navy as an able seaman and served under Cook's command, acting as sailing master of HMS *Resolution* during Cook's third and final voyage to the Pacific, which ended with the latter's death in Hawai'i. Bligh finally received his first commission at the age of twenty-seven.[18]

Bligh's case contrasts with that of his sometime friend Fletcher Christian. Ten years younger than Bligh, Christian came from a good if impoverished family and was made a midshipman, the lowest commissioned rank, at the age of nineteen. Ironically, he owed much of his fortune in the navy to Bligh, under whose command he served for several years; it was Bligh who secured him an officer's position on HMS *Bounty* during its fateful voyage to the South Pacific. On 28 April 1789, Christian led a mutiny against Bligh, seizing control of the *Bounty* and depositing the captain and eighteen loyal members of the crew in an open boat. However, Christian did not enjoy his success for long. Hunted by the Royal Navy, he and his crew escaped to remote Pitcairn Island, where he died four years later, possibly killed by one of his own men. Bligh, on the other hand, sailed his tiny boat across twelve hundred miles of uncharted ocean to reach safety in Indonesia, a voyage that still ranks as one of the great feats of navigation in history; he went on to enjoy a celebrated naval career and rise to the rank of vice-admiral.[19]

Kicking down walls

Whereas a society which encourages hard work and promotion by merit doubtless helps some leaders rise to maturity, there is also evidence that having something to kick against is also helpful. Hardship can be a useful spur. Li Ka-shing arrived in Hong Kong as a twelve-year-old refugee without a penny to his name. Orphaned at fifteen, he survived the Japanese occupation of Hong Kong; after the war he got a job as a store clerk in order to make ends meet. In 1950, he started a small business, Cheung Kong, making and selling plastic flowers. After a slow start, the business diversified into property and banking, and by the time of his retirement in 2018, Li was one of the richest men in the world.[20] Ghanshyam Das Birla and one of his brothers walked from Rajasthan to Calcutta in 1910, where they lived together in a single room while starting their business. At the time, the only substantial Indian-owned business in British-ruled India was the Tata group; much of the rest of the economy was controlled by British firms. Nevertheless, by 1919, Birla Brothers was the thirteenth-largest business in India, and the Aditya Birla Group today continues to occupy a prominent place in the Indian economy.[21]

Other leaders managed to overcome physical issues. At five feet, seven inches tall, Yogi Berra was considered too small to be a successful baseball player, but he made up for his short stature with determination and skill. Few players have been more dedicated to the craft of the game than Berra. He became one of the great players of his time, playing with the New York Yankees from 1947 to 1963, winning the World Series ten times, before going on to become a highly successful baseball manager.[22] Franklin D. Roosevelt had already established his political career when, in 1921, he fell ill and lost the use of both legs through paralysis. This should have finished his career – the social climate of the time would never have accepted a disabled man in a position of high office – but Roosevelt believed he was destined for great things and refused to give in. He taught himself to stand and walk for short periods of time and managed his image carefully so that the public never saw the wheelchair he normally used. Twelve years later he was elected president of the United States for the first time.[23]

Historically, leaders who have had to work hardest to gain acceptance have been women and, in the West, people of colour. For the latter, the only position of leadership many were able to occupy was as leaders of revolts, like Toussaint L'Ouverture. Windows did occasionally open, such as the early years of the French Revolution, when Joseph Bologne, the Chevalier de St-Georges, and Alexandre Dumas, attained high rank in the army: Dumas became a general and for a time commanded the French Army of the Alps. Otherwise one is left with rare examples, such as Olaudah Equiano, a former slave who became a leading light in the British abolitionist movement and a community leader among the black population of Georgian London; he was prominent in both black organisations, such as the Sons of Africa, and broader political groups, such as the London Corresponding Society. Equiano might well have gone on to still more positions of authority had he not died suddenly in 1797.[24]

Mary Pickford is a fairly rare example of a female leader who commanded respect almost from the beginning. Born in Canada, she became a stage actress at the age of seven and made her first film with the director D. W. Griffith at seventeen, demanding – and receiving – twice the usual fee for her role. Within a few years she was producing her own films, and in 1919 she co-founded the United Artists studio with Griffiths and Douglas Fairbanks. Still not yet thirty, she was one of the most powerful people in Hollywood. Her success seems in part to have been due to sheer charisma: it was said that people instinctively rose to their feet the moment she entered a room.[25]

The pioneering scientist Mary Somerville, on the other hand, had to overcome the opposition of her family and her first husband, none of whom were in favour of educating women; as a result she was forced to study and read in her own time, sometimes in secret. Taking over the family steel business in Pennsylvania after the death of her husband, Rebecca Lukens had to deal with the prejudices of the community, her competitors and her own employees as she strove to turn the failing company around. Despite her vast knowledge of the Arab tribes and ability to speak Arabic fluently and although she held a commission as a captain in the British

Army, Gertrude Bell – the first woman to serve as an officer – struggled to get her male counterparts in British intelligence to take her seriously, and her reports and advice were often ignored.[26]

To be a woman *and* black took the difficulties to an entirely new level. Born in Illinois, the child of former slaves, Annie Turnbo Malone was orphaned as a young girl and reared by her elder sister. She became interested in hair and hair care and realised that there were few products on the market that suited the needs of black women; she resolved to fill this gap. In 1902 she established her first business in St. Louis, Missouri, opening shops and selling door to door. She found her niche in the market and the business expanded rapidly; by the 1920s, she was a multimillionaire and one of the richest women in America. Much of the profit for the business was ploughed into social initiatives such as a training college for young black women, other educational institutions and an orphanage. However, in 1927 her husband sued her for divorce and claimed half the business, arguing that he had been instrumental to its success. Turnbo Malone's company, Poro, never fully recovered from that loss. Her main business rival, Sarah Breedlove Walker (who traded as Madam C. J. Walker) enjoyed similar commercial success before her early death from overwork in 1919.[27] Both Turnbo Malone and Walker did manage to break through and establish successful businesses, but the barriers they faced were daunting.

Mirrors for princes

Samuel Smiles was by no means the first to urge people to cultivate virtue if they wished to attain greatness. In the *Analects*, Confucius had made a very similar moral argument, as did Aristotle in the *Nicomachean Ethics*, and the Chinese strategist Sunzi (Sun Tzu) argued that commanders needed to know their own capabilities, strengths and weaknesses if they wished to be successful. Machiavelli made much the same argument in *The Prince*.[28]

Books of advice for leaders and would-be leaders have a very long history. One of the earliest is an ancient Egyptian *instructional text* known as *Maxims of Ptahhotep*, composed around 2400 BC. Other Egyptian works include the *Instructions of Kagemni*, composed as early as 2600 BC but likely at a later date, and the *Instructions of Amenemope*, probably written between 1300 and 1100 BC, all of which offer guidance as to how leaders should conduct themselves and maintain relationships with subordinates.[29]

The *Arthashastra* of Kautilya, mentioned earlier, fulfilled much the same function in India, not only giving advice on how to structure an administrative organisation but also offering moral guidance to leaders. So influential was this work that nearly every other Indian work on administration for the next thousand years referenced it, some copying out entire passages. The Greco-Roman world offers examples of guidance literature, too, notably *The Education of Cyrus* by Xenophon and the *De Clementia* of the Roman philosopher Seneca, written for the young Emperor Nero. Seneca advised leaders to understand the human failings and foibles of their followers and to cultivate virtues such as clemency and mercy. Although widely read, the book had little impact on Nero himself, who forced Seneca to commit suicide ten years later.[30]

The tenth-century Muslim philosopher al-Farabi also offered advice to rulers in works such as *Aphorisms of a Statesman* and *The Virtuous City*, as did the Andalusian Muslim scholar and jurist al-Turtushi in his book *The Lamp of Kings*.[31] Both stressed the difference between virtuous and vicious rulers and described the characteristics a virtuous ruler should cultivate. The same theme runs through Persian advice literature, most notably *The Book of Government*, written by the Persian bureaucrat Nizam al-Mulk, and the *Mirror for Princes*, by Kai Kaus ibn Iskandar, Prince of Gurgan.[32] Like the *Arthashastra*, whose influence is apparent in both books, they are a mixture of administrative detail and moral guidance: the Nizam al-Mulk, for example, warns leaders not to make decisions when they are drunk.

The genre of literature known as *specula principium* (mirrors for princes) reached its full flowering during the European Middle Ages and Renaissance. In the ninth century, Hincmar, archbishop of Rheims, produced his *De regis persona*, a book of advice for the Frankish kings.[33] Like Seneca's *De Clementia*, it seems to have been largely ignored by its intended audience but was widely read elsewhere. I have already mentioned the two most important mirrors for princes from the Middle Ages – John of Salisbury's *Policraticus* and Thomas Aquinas's *De Regno* – but there were scores of other such works, including the *De Regimine Principum* by Giles of Rome, written for King Louis IX's son Philip the Fair, and the *Livre de la paix* by Christine de Pisan, one of the few such books to be written by a woman.[34]

The Renaissance brought probably the most complete mirror for princes, *The Book of the Courtier* by Baldesar Castiglione. Very much like Samuel Smiles, Castiglione argued that to get ahead in life, one should be well-educated and presentable, have good manners and behave as a gentleman.[35] Machiavelli's *The Prince* takes a different view; both books were widely read, although Machiavelli's work was proscribed by the Catholic Church as immoral, and it circulated only in clandestine editions. An even more cynical work is *Treatise on the Court* by Eustache de Refuge. This rather bleak book is a kind of survival guide to life at court and gives advice on subjects such as how to avoid getting attached to the wrong party in a dispute, how to come out on the winning side in a conflict, how to curry favour with the monarch and, importantly, how to recognise that one's career has peaked and that it is time to make a graceful exit.[36]

What all these mirrors for princes and similar works had in common was that they offered recipes for success. With some exceptions, like *The Prince* and *Treatise on the Court*, the recipe is much the same in each case: work hard, live simply, pray often and cultivate frugal habits of one's own but be generous towards followers, respect other people and so on. In the vast majority of these books, there is an equation between moral virtue and success. To some extent this is understandable. There is a strong argument in favour of moral virtue on the part of leaders; followers are more likely to trust leaders who will treat them fairly and equitably and who will reward them generously.[37] One of the traits expected of a leader in the European

Middle Ages, whether they be war leaders or merchant princes, was largesse – the generous giving of gifts in the form of money, jewels, property or patronage. Louis IX and Edward of Woodstock, the Black Prince, were very different characters, but both understood the power of largesse, and they used it to bind followers to them more closely.[38]

The principle of self-help is that anyone can achieve greatness if he or she tries hard enough. But is that necessarily so? History is full of examples of men and women who did all the things we have listed and, for one reason or another, fell short. Sometimes, as Eustache de Refuge suggested, they made friends with the wrong people or were on the wrong side politically. Sometimes they were simply unlucky; sometimes they failed to capture the attention of their followers, who rejected their authority. In October 1812, an American army attempting to invade Canada was defeated at Queenston Heights, Ontario, by a British and Canadian force commanded, initially, by General Isaac Brock. While leading a counter-attack against the Americans early in the battle, Brock was shot and killed. Command then shifted to the next senior officer, General Roger Sheaffe, who renewed the attack and forced the Americans to surrender.[39]

Brock's contribution to the battle had been minimal; the tactical plan that sealed the victory had been devised by Sheaffe. Nevertheless, Canadian public opinion decided that Queenston Heights had been Brock's victory, and it downplayed Sheaffe's role. In the months after the battle the Canadians campaigned ceaselessly to have him recalled from his post, and after the British defeat at York the following April, the Canadian militia made it clear they would not serve under his command. Although he was not to blame for the loss of York, Sheaffe was nevertheless recalled, and he never saw active service again.[40]

The difference lay in the character of the two men. Both were competent soldiers, although both made their share of mistakes. But Brock was a charismatic figure who was admired by many Canadians. Sheaffe was more reclusive and suffered from ill health, and the Canadians always perceived a distance between themselves and him, whereas Brock was a man of the people. Put simply, they liked Brock and were willing to follow him, whereas they were never certain if they could trust Sheaffe.

At the same time, however, there are also plenty of examples of leaders who did *not* adhere to the programme of virtuous behaviour and works set out by Smiles and the authors of the mirrors for princes but who yet managed to succeed. Charles-Maurice de Talleyrand-Périgord, the French nobleman who abandoned a career in the Catholic church to join the French revolutionaries and went on to serve in the governments of Napoleon I, Louis XVIII and Louis-Philippe, was regarded even by his friends and colleagues as a slippery, self-serving, treacherous and financially corrupt sexual predator. Napoleon once referred to him as 'shit in a silk stocking'.[41] None of this seems to have made any difference to his long career, and he died in 1838 a wealthy and successful man.[42] Basil Zaharoff started off as a small-time smuggler in the eastern Mediterranean but parlayed his expertise in deal-making into a position as sales agent for various arms companies, including Nordenfeldt,

Maxim and Vickers, becoming co-owner of the latter. He often secured contracts by paying bribes and in the run-up to the First World War sold large volumes of weapons and munitions to both France and Germany, thus contributing materially to the arms race that has been identified as one of the causes of the war. Although he was knighted by King George V for his contributions to weapons production, the British press vilified him after the war, blaming him for the carnage and loss of life. Undeterred, Zaharoff moved to Monte Carlo, where he bought the famous casino, married a duchess and died peacefully in his sleep at the age of eighty-seven.[43]

The divine spark

What makes the difference between success and failure? One theory held that successful leaders have an innate force within them, something variously referred to as the 'vital force', 'animal magnetism' or the 'divine spark'. The concept was much discussed by biologists and chemists in the eighteenth and nineteenth centuries; not everyone agreed with its existence, but there was a solid body of opinion that some sort of animating life force was present in all living beings.[44] Further, this force is stronger in some people than in others, and those who have the strongest vital force tend to exercise an attraction for others around them. It is this attraction that makes others want to follow them. Add a dose of Protestant pre-destination – those who have the strong life force were in some way 'chosen' or marked out as potential leaders – and we have the recipe for Thomas Carlyle's Great Man.

The theory of vital force has been comprehensively disproven, so what was it that contemporaries could see or thought they could see? A study of historical examples suggests it was probably a combination of several attributes, including energy, charisma and luck. The early career of Napoleon Bonaparte demonstrates all three. Contemporaries wrote of his furious energy and how he seemed to be everywhere at once, and a compelling charisma endeared him to his men and frightened his otherwise fractious generals into obedience; as for luck, he was often in the thick of the fighting but suffered only one serious wound, at the siege of Toulon in 1793.[45]

Horatio Nelson, the Royal Navy's most famous admiral, is another example. The son of a poor clergyman, he joined the navy at age thirteen but was almost immediately spotted by his superiors as having potential. He received his first command of a ship at the age of twenty-three and was knighted and made an admiral at thirty-nine. Nelson, too, was famous for both his energy and his charisma, and he had a near-total disregard for danger.[46] As noted, Jeanne d'Arc had both energy and charisma, and her vision of Archangel Michael might reasonably be considered a matter of luck: why was she chosen to receive it, not one of the thousands of other young peasant women in France at the time?

In business, Henry Ford; Honda Sochiro, the founder of the Honda Group; and Jack Welch, the former chairman of GE, are examples of leaders with strong charisma and huge reserves of energy, and Mary Pickford was a highly charismatic force who also benefitted from luck at several points, not the least in securing the patronage of the influential director D. W. Griffiths. Annie Turnbo Malone and her rival, Madam C. J. Walker, were both charismatic and influential figures who worked tirelessly. To throw in one more example, the dancer Loie Fuller, arguably the most influential figure in the world of dance before the First World War, likewise had a formidable blend of energy and charisma. Her ideas, not only in choreography but also in lighting and other forms of technology, were pioneering, and she was also a highly influential teacher; Isadora Duncan, later her rival, was one of her pupils. A chance meeting with Princess Marie of Romania gave Fuller the support she needed to set up her own dance schools and stage her own productions.[47]

Charisma, or the divine spark, helps us understand that not all leaders were created equal. Some, thanks to circumstances and force of personality, were always going to have an advantage when it came to success. Of course, plenty of things could happen along the way. A stray bullet, a bad business decision, the loss of a key patron or assistant, a natural disaster, all could derail a career at any time. General Barthélemy Joubert was one of the most talented young French generals of the 1790s; Napoleon Bonaparte had declared that he was marked for greatness, and Talleyrand and other senior figures in the French government were preparing to offer him the post of dictator (in part to forestall the ambitions of Napoleon), until he was killed at the Battle of Novi.[48] Francesco Datini's flourishing business was nearly wiped out in 1400 when an outbreak of plague killed many of his workers and managers; he himself survived, but his business never fully recovered.[49]

Whether the divine spark really exists is probably irrelevant. What mattered was that people thought it existed, and following the theory of Freudian transference, they attached themselves to leaders they believed would be lucky, had strong charisma, could get things done, or a combination or all of the three. Was there still a lingering religious element to all this? Very possibly. The Gnostics, an early Christian mystic movement, believed that every human being possesses a little of the essence of God inside them and that our human mission is to find that vital spark and release it into the world.[50] If people could not discover the divine inside themselves, it made perfect sense for them to coalesce around others who had apparently done so; and perhaps by following people in whom the flame burned brightly, they could then kindle the spark within themselves.[51] The social space of leadership, then, was a space where people came looking for that spark.

Does this still happen? Of course it does. Football manager José Mourinho has described himself as 'the special one' and 'the only one', and Bernie Ebbers, the entrepreneurial founder of WorldCom, reportedly claimed that he had been chosen by God (Ebbers is currently serving a twenty-five-year prison sentence for conspiracy and fraud).[52] We may read and approve of Samuel Smiles's doctrine that our destiny lies within us and that hard work and perseverance will receive their reward, but in our hearts we doubt whether this is actually true. So, we seek out others who – we hope – will help us achieve our aspirations. Sometimes they do. But sometimes, they turn out to be idols with feet of clay. That has been true throughout history and will probably go on being true for a long time to come.

Notes

1 Samuel Smiles, *Self-Help: With Illustrations of Character and Conduct*, London, 1859; repr. Oxford: Oxford University Press, 2002, p. 1.
2 Sasaki Tsuneo, 'Toyoda Sakichi', in Morgen Witzel (ed.), *Biographical Dictionary of Management*, Bristol: Thoemmes Press, 2002.
3 Smiles, *Self-Help*, p. 1.
4 Ibid., p. 3.
5 Ibid., p. 1.
6 Donnachie, *Robert Owen*; G.D.H. Cole, *The Life of Robert Owen*, London: Macmillan, 1930.
7 Lyndall Fownes Urwick and E.F.L. Brech, *The Making of Scientific Management*, London: Management Publications Trust, 1949.
8 Cole, *The Life of Robert Owen*, p. 126.
9 Max Weber, *The Protestant Ethic and the Spirit of Capitalism*, New York: Dover, 2003.
10 Roy Porter, *The Enlightenment*, Basingstoke: Palgrave Macmillan, 2001; Jonathan Israel, *Democratic Enlightenment: Philosophy, Revolution and Human Rights, 1750–1790*, Oxford: Oxford University Press, 2011.
11 Uglow, *The Lunar Men*; Margaret C. Jacob, *Scientific Culture and the Making of the Industrial West*, Oxford: Oxford University Press, 1997.
12 Kelly, 'Coade'; Richard S. Fitton, *The Arkwrights: Spinners of Fortune*, Manchester: Manchester University Press, 1999; Sidney Pollard, *The Genesis of Modern Management*, London: Edward Arnold, 1965; Knight, *Britain Against Napoleon*; Jonathan Coad, *The Portsmouth Block Mills: Bentham, Brunel and the Start of the Royal Navy's Industrial Revolution*, Aldershot: Ashgate, 2005; Uglow, *The Lunar Men*; Neil McKendrick, John Brewer and J.H. Plumb, *The Birth of a Consumer Society: The Commercialization of Eighteenth-Century England*, London: Europa, 1982.
13 Yamamoto, *Hagakure*; Miyamoto, *The Book of Five Rings*.
14 Mark Weston, *Giants of Japan: The Lives of Japan's Greatest Men and Women*, Tokyo: Kodansha International, 1999; Johannes Hirschmeier, *Origins of Entrepreneurship in Meiji Japan*, Cambridge, MA: Harvard University Press, 1964.
15 Gale Christianson, *Isaac Newton and the Scientific Revolution*, Oxford: Oxford University Press, 1996; James Hamilton, *Faraday: The Life*, London: HarperCollins, 2002.
16 Jasper Ridley, *Statesman and Saint: Cardinal Wolsey, Sir Thomas More and the Politics of Henry VIII*, London: Viking, 1983.
17 J.K. Laughton, 'Norris, Sir John', in *Oxford Dictionary of National Biography*, Oxford: Oxford University Press, 2004.
18 Richard Hough, *Captain James Cook*, London: Hodder & Stoughton, 1994; Rob Mundle, *Bligh: Master Mariner*, Melbourne: Hachette, 2010.
19 Mundle, *Bligh*; William Bligh, *Mutiny on Board the HMS Bounty*, New York: Pendulum, 1979; Richard Hough, *Captain Bligh and Mister Christian: The Men and the Mutiny*, New York: E.P. Dutton, 1973.
20 A.B. Chan, *Li Ka-shing: Hong Kong's Elusive Billionaire*, Hong Kong: Oxford University Press, 1996.
21 Gita Piramal, *Business Legends*, New Delhi: Penguin India, 1998.
22 Allen Barra, *Yogi Berra: Eternal Yankee*, New York: W.W. Norton, 2009.
23 Smith, *FDR*.
24 Bell, *Toussaint l'Ouverture*; Gabriel Banat, *The Chevalier de Saint-Georges: Virtuoso of the Sword and the Bow*, Hillsdale: Pendragon Press, 2006; Pierre Bardin, *Joseph de Saint-Georges, le Chevalier Noir*, Paris: Guénégaud, 2006; Reiss, *The Black Count*; Equiano, *The Life of Olaudah Equiano*; Caretta, *Equiano, the African*.
25 Eileen Whitfield, *Pickford: The Woman Who Made Hollywood*, Lexington: University Press of Kentucky, 1997.
26 Kathryn A. Neeley, *Mary Somerville: Science, Illumination and the Human Mind*, Cambridge: Cambridge University Press, 2001; Jill Jepson, *Women's Concerns: Twelve Women Entrepreneurs*

of the Eighteenth and Nineteenth Centuries, New York: Peter Lang, 2009; Georgina Howell, *Daughter of the Desert: The Remarkable Life of Gertrude Bell*, London: Macmillan, 2006.

27 Ingham and Feldman, *African-American Business Leaders*; Bundles, *Madam C.J. Walker*; Colman, *Madam C.J. Walker*.

28 Lau, *Confucius*; Aristotle, *Nicomachean Ethics*, trans. Robert C. Bartlett and Susan D. Collins, Chicago: University of Chicago Press, 2011; Sunzi, *The Art of War*; Machiavelli, *The Prince*.

29 R.B. Parkinson, *Poetry and Culture in Middle Kingdom Egypt: A Dark Side to Perfection*, London: Continuum, 2002. Stephen E. Thompson, 'Textual Sources, Old Kingdom', in Kathryn A. Bard (ed.), *Encyclopedia of the Archaeology of Ancient Egypt*, London: Routledge, 1999, pp. 801–2.

30 John M. Cooper and J.F. Procope, *Seneca: Moral and Political Essays*, Cambridge: Cambridge University Press, 1995.

31 Miriam Galston, *Politics and Excellence: The Political Philosophy of al-Farabi*, Princeton: Princeton University Press, 2002; 'Abu Bakr al-Turtushi's *Siraj al-Muluk: A Masterpiece of Andalusi Political Philosophy*', https://ballandalus.wordpress.com/2014/12/08/abu-bakr-al-turtushis-siraj-al-muluk-a-masterpiece-of-andalusi-political-philosophy-2/.

32 Nizam al-Mulk, *The Book of Government or Rules for Kings*, trans. Hubert Darke, London: Routledge and Kegan Paul, 1960; Kai Kaus, *A Mirror for Princes*, trans. Reuben Levy, London: The Cresset Press, 1951.

33 Rachel Stone and Charles West (eds), *Hincmar of Rheims: Life and Work*, Manchester: Manchester University Press, 2015.

34 Charles F. Briggs, *Giles of Rome's De Regimine Principum: Reading and Writing Politics at Court and University*, Cambridge: Cambridge University Press, 2009; Christine de Pisan, *The Book of Peace*, University: Pennsylvania State University Press, 2008.

35 Baldesar Castiglione, *The Book of the Courtier*, trans. Charles S. Singleton, New York: Anchor, 1959.

36 Eustache de Refuge, *Treatise on the Court*, trans. J. Chris Cooper, Boca Raton: Orgpax, 2008.

37 Morgen Witzel, *The Ethical Leader*, London: Bloomsbury, 2018.

38 Joinville, *Life of St Louis*; Barber, *Edward, Prince of Wales and Aquitaine*.

39 Robert Malcomson, *A Very Brilliant Affair: The Battle of Queenston Heights, 1812*, Toronto: Robin Brass Studio, 2003.

40 Ibid.; Robert Malcomson, *Capital in Flames: The American Attack on York, 1813*, Toronto: Robin Brass Studio, 2008.

41 Lawday, *Napoleon's Master*.

42 Ibid.; J.F. Bernard, *Talleyrand: A Biography*, New York: Putnam, 1973.

43 Donald McCormick, *Peddler of Death: The Life and Times of Sir Basil Zaharoff*, New York: Holt, Rinehart and Winston, 1965; Anthony Allfrey, *Man of Arms: The Life and Legend of Sir Basil Zaharoff*, London: Weidenfeld & Nicolson, 1989.

44 Sebastian Normandin and Charles T. Wolfe (eds), *Vitalism and the Scientific Image in Post-Enlightenment Life Science, 1800–2010*, New York: Springer, 2013.

45 Bourriene, *The Memoirs of Napoleon Bonaparte*; Boycott-Brown, *The Road to Rivoli*; Chandler, *Napoleon*; McLynn, *Napoleon*; Strathern, *Napoleon in Egypt*.

46 John Sugden, *Nelson: A Dream of Glory*, London: Jonathan Cape, 2004; Stephanie Jones and Jonathan Gosling, *Nelson's Way: Leadership Lessons From the Great Commander*, London: Nicholas Brealey, 2005.

47 Richard Nelson Current and Marcia Ewing Current, *Loie Fuller: Goddess of Light*, Boston: Northeastern University Press, 1997; Rhonda K. Garlick, *Electric Salome: Loie Fuller's Performance of Modernism*, Princeton: Princeton University Press, 2009.

48 Boycott-Brown, *The Road to Rivoli*; Chandler, *Napoleon*.

49 Origo, *The Merchant of Prato*.

50 David Brakke, *The Gnostics: Myth, Ritual and Diversity in Early Christianity*, Cambridge, MA: Harvard University Press, 2010.
51 Ronald E. Biggio, Ira Chaleff and Jean Lipman-Blumen (eds), *The Art of Followership: How Great Followers Create Great Leaders and Organizations*, New York: Wiley, 2008.
52 www.mirror.co.uk/sport/football/news/real-madrid-boss-jose-mourinho-1260409; Jamie Oliver and Tony Goodwin, *How They Blew It: The CEOs and Entrepreneurs Behind Some of the World's Most Catastrophic Business Failures*, London: Kogan Page, 2010.

PART III
Servants of power

9

AUTHORITARIANISM AND TOTALITARIANISM

In April 2019, the Hansard Society published the results of an opinion poll on British attitudes to domestic politics. Asked whether 'Britain needs a strong ruler willing to break the rules', 54 per cent agreed and only 23 per cent disagreed. In response to a further question, 42 per cent believed that government would be more effective if it could ignore or bypass the elected House of Commons.[1] Commentators have pointed to similar opinion polls and electoral results elsewhere in Europe and in North and South America and have suggested that support for authoritarian leadership is on the rise. This is generally seen as a retrograde step, an erosion of democracy and a return to the politics of the past.

But authoritarianism takes many forms. Authoritarian political leaders are not necessarily extremists; in the past, some have adopted extreme views, but some have also been centrists and liberals, and some have even come from the left wing. Some have come to power through democratic elections. The purpose of this chapter is to look at some of the forms authoritarianism takes and to attempt to shed a little light on how authoritarian leaders maintain power and how they acquire power in the first place.

Authoritarian leaders often rise to power in the first place for one of two reasons. First, there may be a crisis – real or manufactured – which needs to be dealt with. Often this crisis takes the form of a threat – either a foreign entity that threatens the security of the organisation or the state or an internal body which can be painted as potentially disruptive and/or threatening to seize control. The German political philosopher Carl Schmitt argued that there is a division between 'friends' and 'enemies', the latter being an alien force which poses a threat to the existence of the state or the organisation. Strong centralised leadership is necessary to tackle this threat.[2] Second, the organisation may be newly established or changing its mission and purpose and sailing into uncharted waters. A strong leader who can get things done quickly is essential to overcoming resistance to change and ensuring the organisation reaches its goals. Followers are willing to hand over substantial amounts of power to leader in exchange for the promise to get things done.

As long as leaders are seen to be meeting the threat and/or getting things done, they can usually count on the support of enough followers to maintain power. Problems for the leader begin when the crisis is over or the job is done, and followers – understandably – want some of their power back. The social space of leadership can then sometimes become the scene of an intense power struggle, and it very often ends with the leader being expelled; as the pre-Socratic Greek philosopher Thales once remarked, it is rare to see an old tyrant.[3]

To avoid this fate, leaders have several options. First, they can attempt to renew the crisis or start a new one, identifying or creating new enemies or new threats that must be confronted, as Mao Zedong attempted to do during the Cultural Revolution in China in the 1960s.[4] Second, they can accept that they no longer have sufficient authority to keep them in power and attempt to negotiate a dignified exit on their own terms, as Jerry Rawlings did when handing over power to a civilian administration in Ghana. Third, they can attempt to form alliances with other power groups to try to keep themselves in power. Sometimes this works, and the leaders are able to pass on their authority and power to their heirs, founding a dynasty.

However, attempts at founding dynasties are not always successful. The chief reason for this seems to be that the authority of the newly risen authoritarian leader is closely tied to the leader's personality and character. Authoritarian leaders have a strong level of symbolic–charismatic authority, which comes in part from within them but also in part from their followers' willingness to accept them (see chapter 2). When the leader dies or is replaced, that symbolic–charismatic authority does not transfer at once to the next in line. Oliver Cromwell commanded the loyalty of the army during his years as Lord Protector of the Commonwealth of England, in part because he had been a highly successful military commander in his own right: the army knew and trusted him. His son Richard, who took over after Cromwell died, had no such connection to the army. His reign lasted for just eight months before the army overthrew him and invited Charles II to take the throne.[5] The sultan Baibars, the first Mamluk ruler of Egypt, instructed that power go to his son Solamish after his death, nominating his friend and fellow general al-Mansur Qalawun as guardian of the kingdom, but two years later Qalawun pushed Solamish to one side and took the throne himself.[6] The *caudillos*, the strongmen who ruled many Latin American states in the nineteenth and twentieth centuries, seldom established dynasties.

Authoritarian thinking: legalism

One of the earliest traditions of authoritarianism, legalism, emerged in China in the fourth century BC, during a time of chaos known to later historians as the Warring States Period. Following the collapse of the Zhou dynasty, rival kings fought each other for control of the country, with devastating results. As much as half the population of

China may have perished from war, famine or disease. There was a perceived need for strong leadership to restore the country and bring about the return of peace.

The first legalist thinker and writer was probably Shang Yang (390–338 BC), prime minister of the embattled state of Qin. Shang Yang rejected the Confucian and Daoist idea that rulers should govern benevolently and with a light hand. He argued that the people must never become more powerful than the state; if they did, confusion, disorder and corruption would prevail. The horrors of the Warring States Period were the result of such misguided benevolence. Shang attempted to put his principles into practice under Duke Xiao of Qin, creating a highly central-ised and efficient state with an effective civil service, but he was executed by Duke Xiao's successor after a personal disagreement.[7]

Shang Yang's ideas were taken up by Han Fei, a prince from the royal house of the state of Han, who in the years before 233 BC wrote a series of essays on govern-ment, administration and leadership that today are collectively known as the *Han Feizi*.[8] He began by painting a bleak picture of the times in which he lived: corrupt courtiers and officials appropriating tax money for their own use, rapacious land-lords exploiting the peasants, widespread corruption among the merchant classes, private armies of swordsmen roaming the land and plundering at will and weak rulers unable or unwilling to stop any of this.

Opposing Confucius, who urged leaders to be wise, benevolent and tolerant, Han Fei insisted that benevolence and tolerance were signs of weakness. To survive – and more importantly, for their people to survive – rulers must be ruthless and strong. He also rejected the Confucian and Daoist notion that most men tend towards the good and can be relied upon to behave ethically through a social system which exerts pressure on people to conform. To Han Fei, the only way to achieve conformity was the application of the rule of law.

Han Fei's system of thought was based on three important principles: the first was *fa* (roughly, 'prescriptive standards', with connotations of law and punishment). People should comply with *fa* so that their behaviour conformed with the public good; they should be punished if they failed to do so. The second was *shi* (authority or power). The exercise of *shi* is necessary to ensure compliance with *fa*; it is the authority to punish people if they do not behave correctly. The third was *shu*, the technique of controlling the bureaucracy by comparing 'word' with 'deed' (more generally, potential performance with the actuality).

The task of the leader, said Han Fei, was to set the prescribed standards for behav-iour and action and then wait to see how well people lived up to those standards. He refers to the 'two handles' of government, the means by which leaders can enforce their will: reward and punishment. Legalist government was a brutally simple matter of carrot and stick. Succeed and you will be rewarded; fail and you will punished savagely. Repeatedly, the *Han Feizi* urged leaders to judge their subordinates by how well they had performed their duties and to deliver on the promises they had made. Judgement was made by matching people's words to their actions (that is, *shu*). Did people achieve what they said they would? Did they carry out the functions of their offices as required? If so, reward them; if not, punish them.

The recipe for dealing with chaos, then, is a rigid system of government where everyone knows what is expected and everyone his or her their place and does not depart from it. The harshest punishments in the legalist system were reserved for officials who overstepped the bounds of their position, even if their intentions were good.

Like Machiavelli – whose ideas were in some ways remarkably similar – Han Fei has been accused of immorality, but in his view, this system of state control is entirely moral because the state has the power to protect people from all the evils described earlier. A well-run, well-regulated state is essential if people are to survive and prosper. Machiavelli would have agreed, and in *The Prince* in particular he similarly argued that the leader must be ruthless, have a single-minded purpose and strong will and be unafraid to punish those who transgress against the state; again, this is all for the good of the state. Neither Machiavelli nor Han Fei had any time for self-aggrandising leaders, and Han Fei reminds us again and again that the leader is the servant of the law, not its master. The law itself is the ultimate sovereign.[9]

The new duke of Qin, Shi Huangdi, read Han Fei's writings with approval and adopted many of his ideas. In 221 BC, taking advantage of the weakness of his rivals and a general desire for an end to war and the need for unity and peace, Shi Huangdi reunited China and proclaimed himself emperor. On many levels, his reign was a success. He imposed order on China and brought about peace, building the Great Wall to keep out foreign raiders and improving the economy. But he was also a brutal tyrant who killed tens of thousands of his own people, often by simply working them to death on his massive public works projects. There is plenty of evidence of punishment during Shi Huangdi's reign, and not much evidence of reward. When his dynasty was overthrown, the incoming Han dynasty – ironically, members of Han Fei's family – ostensibly threw out legalism and adopted Confucianism as the state creed. However, the influence of legalism persisted, especially in the state bureaucracy where the principles of *fa*, *shi* and *shu* were still observed. Legalism continued to underpin Chinese absolutism until the fall of the empire and, arguably, even after that.

Authoritarian thinking: tyranny and *caudillismo*

Whereas legalism was based on conformity to law and hierarchy, the ancient Greek system of tyranny was a legitimate system of rebellion against authority. Peisistratos, who ruled Athens from 561 to 527 BC, came to power as leader of a popular revolt against the elites who dominated Athenian political life. He was twice ousted from power by the elites, but each time returned to the city on the back of a wave of popular support. Later commentators wrote of his reign with approval, noting that he respected the laws and ruled fairly and justly without enriching himself.[10] The same was true of some other tyrants of the time, notably the rulers of the Sicilian city-state of Syracuse. Hiero, who reigned from 478 to 467 BC, was regarded by Xenophon as a model ruler.[11]

Other tyrants were bad rulers: Dionysos I of Syracuse was a strong ruler but a cruel man, resembling Qin Shi Huangdi in some ways, and his son Dionysos II was twice forced into exile after having been unseated by popular rebellions. Having acquired a taste for power, tyrants were often reluctant to let go of it, and this turned their formerly sympathetic followers against them.[12] The same was true in republican Rome where the general Gaius Marius, having been appointed consul as a popular ruler at a time of political crisis, then clung to power long after he had lost popular support. He was finally unseated by another general, Lucius Cornelius Sulla, who led a *coup d'état* against him. Both men seized power illegally, but at the end it was Sulla who had the most support from his followers. Prudently, Sulla retired after having restored peace to the city and did not attempt to take power again.[13] Machiavelli refers several times to the examples of Marius and Sulla and commends the latter for putting the needs of the people before his own ambitions.[14]

This tradition of strong men taking power in a time of crisis can be seen during the Italian renaissance, when mercenary soldiers like Sir John Hawkwood were promoted to positions of power with popular consent in order to safeguard the state. Like Sulla, Hawkwood retired when Florence no longer had need of his services, but other *condottieri* like Francesco Sforza in Milan and Federico di Montefeltro in Urbino remained in power. Some of these rulers enjoyed widespread popular support and evolved from military strongmen to what people at the time considered model rulers; Montefeltro, for example, was a famous patron of the arts and supported artists such as Raphael.[15]

As noted in Chapter 3, the Latin American revolutionary Simón Bolívar started off as a republican, but realising he could never build a stable coalition to govern the territories he had liberated in Spain, he instead established himself as a dictator with the collaboration and support of the elites, the large landowners and merchants and the Catholic church. Bolívar was the first of the *caudillos* (leaders or chiefs), the strongmen who by the middle of the nineteenth century ruled most of Latin America save for Brazil, and continued to do so until well into the twentieth century.[16] Brazil had constituted itself into an independent empire, but the empire was overthrown by a republican movement with the support of the army in 1889; the republic lasted until 1930 when it, too, was overthrown by Getúlio Vargas, who ruled as a *caudillo* until 1945.[17]

Caudillos came in many forms and were rather like the Greek tyrants in that their approach to leadership varied widely. At one end of the spectrum were the true dictators, men whose only interest was in acquiring and keeping power: for example, Rafael Trujillo in the Dominican Republic (1930–61), Alfredo Stroessner in Paraguay (1954–89) and Anastasio Somoza García in Nicaragua (1937–56). All three used force to seize and retain power and brutally suppressed opposition movements; Trujillo and Somoza also presided over a kleptocracy that saw much of the national wealth end up in the hands of their families and supporters.[18] Others such as Antonio López de Santa Anna in Mexico (1833–54, with interruptions), Juan Manuel de Rosas in Argentina (1829–52) and Augusto Pinochet in Chile (1973–88) were army officers who made common cause with social and political conservatives to exclude populists and keep power concentrated in the hands of the elites.[19] Rosas also used his power to enrich himself, and a judicial inquiry has been set up in Chile to establish whether Pinochet did the same.

Others took a different approach. Porfirio Díaz, who ruled Mexico from 1876 to 1911, was a political liberal who formed a broad coalition of support after he seized power. He launched a programme of economic development that made him popular initially with both the elites and middle classes, but his government became increasingly centralising and conservative as time went on. Regardless of his political views, he started much of the economic development of modern Mexico. In Argentina, Juan Péron (1943–55 and 1973–4) built a broad coalition of both elites and left-wing groups, including trades unions, and his wife, Eva Péron, delivered support from women's organisations; as a result, Péron was able to assume power relatively peacefully. However, the early promise of his unity fell apart; Péron became increasingly authoritarian, an admirer of Fascism and a protector of Nazi refugees post-1945. Unlike Díaz, he was not able to manage the economy and Argentina slipped into economic chaos. Fidel Castro was a Marxist who turned to the disenfranchised lower classes and built a power base among them, from which he launched repeated attempts to overthrow the previous *caudillo* of Cuba, Fulgencio Batista. Ultimately successful, Castro led Cuba from 1959 to 2008.[20]

As these examples show, there were *caudillos* across the political spectrum, from hard right to hard left. But why did this system flourish for so long? Two factors were in play. First, there was the presence of ambitious men who were not always scrupulous about how they attained or retained power. For many, power was a goal in its own right. Second, and much more importantly, there was a belief on the part of followers that strong leadership equated to stable leadership. In turbulent times, people naturally sought safety and security, and the *caudillos* promised this; indeed, the idea that strength equated to safety is one of the central principles of *caudillismo*. Diego Portales, himself briefly dictator of Chile in the early nineteenth century, summed up the prevailing view when he said that both democracy and monarchy were to be distrusted. Democracy was pointless if the people did not know what they wanted, whereas monarchy promoted the weak into positions of power regardless of their merit. The interests of the republic would be best guarded by a strong leader in whom power was concentrated.[21]

In hindsight, the idea that a strong leader would necessarily bring peace and security seems laughable. Porfirio Díaz did manage to bring about a measure of stability in Mexico, but the reigns of most *caudillos* were marked by internal instability and external threats. In part this was deliberate: by insisting that the state was in a constant state of danger, even the most violent and kleptocratic of dictators could portray themselves either as defenders and saviours of the nation or, at least, as better than any known alternative. In the Dominican Republic, Trujillo picked a series of fights with neighbouring nations, especially Haiti, for exactly this reason, and in Chile, Pinochet constantly warned of the communist threat posed by supporters of former president Salvador Allende, whose regime Pinochet had overthrown.

Of the *caudillos* mentioned we have discussed, Pinochet, Trujillo, Stroessner, Castro and Porfirio Díaz all came to power through *coups d'état* or revolutions, and Somoza seized power through rigged elections. Santa Anna was initially elected, although with a limited franchise but later seized power by force. Juan Péron won several elections, although there were doubts about the legitimacy of the vote. The regimes of the *caudillos* also tended to end violently. Trujillo and Somoza were assassinated, and Stroessner, Santa Anna and Díaz were forced from power by further *coups d'état* and revolutions; Pinochet ceded power voluntarily in Chile but may well have faced a revolution had he not done so. Juan Péron and Fidel Castro are rare exceptions: the former died in office; the latter handed over power peacefully to his brother and retired.

Díaz and, to a limited extent, Pinochet are also rare in that their states flourished under their rule. The Dominican Republic under Trujillo and Paraguay under Stroessner sank deep into poverty. Even worse was the example of a previous Paraguayan *caudillo*, Francisco Solano López. Coming to power in 1862, López almost immediately plunged his tiny country into war with its powerful neighbours, Brazil, Argentina and Uruguay. By the time the conflict ended in 1870, the country had been devastated and occupied and half the population were either casualties or refugees; López himself was one of the casualties.[22]

The example of the *caudillo* is interesting for the light it sheds on the social space of leadership. The *caudillos* were ambitious men who desired power, but they were also products of their time. They were created by societies characterised by two things: the desire for security, and a high degree of internal fracture with different groups – landowning elites, entrepreneurs, the Catholic Church, the peasantry, indigenous peoples – all competing for power. Often, as Roger Haigh shows in his study of an early Argentine *caudillo*, Martín Güemes, the *caudillos* were the product of this rivalry: each group put forward its own strong leader, and in the ensuing competition, the strongest leader won.[23] The other groups, however, seldom took defeat lying down, and as soon as they could, they found new leaders and carried on the struggle. In the end, the leader with the most powerful followers was the one who won the day.

What is interesting is that, despite the failure of *caudillismo* to deliver peace and stability, people nevertheless persisted in putting their faith in the system. Followers, it seems, are not always entirely realistic or logical when it comes to choosing which leader to follow. Furthermore, *caudillismo* shows us how the social space of leadership can be a very crowded place. The struggle for power is not a dialectic between leaders and followers; the social space encompasses many groups of followers, usually each with its own leader. This is an altogether too common phenomenon in the corporate world, as Anthony Jay describes in *Management and Machiavelli*.[24] In another corporate example, Coca-Cola was ruled by a *caudillo*, Robert Woodruff, from the 1920s until 1984. Known as the Boss, Woodruff stepped down as president in 1954, but he remained on the board, and within the corporation his word was considered to be law. In the late 1970s Woodruff deliberately stirred up rivalry between his senior executives, in effect establishing a gladiatorial contest whereby the strongest and most politically adroit would take over the company. The winner of this competition was Roberto Goizueta, who became the new *caudillo* until his death in 1997.[25]

Authoritarian thinking: totalitarianism

One of the main weaknesses of *caudillismo* was its highly personal nature. Leaders were chosen in large part because of their symbolic-charismatic authority, which in turn determined how successful they were at attracting followers, but the door was open for anyone who felt *they* had sufficient authority to gather their own followers and have a go at seizing power. Twentieth-century thinkers on power tried to get around this problem by eliminating the element of the individual and concentrating power in the state itself. The result was totalitarianism, the total sublimation of every member of the state into the greater polity and the near-complete centralisation of power.

Attempts had been made at creating highly controlled centralised states before, notably in France under the Bourbon monarchs in the seventeenth and eighteenth centuries. Faced with pressure from hostile states such as Spain and the Holy Roman Empire and needing to put behind it the chaos of the sixteenth-century religious civil war that nearly tore the nation apart, France opted for a strong and centralised monarchy. Some progress was made towards this goal, notably under Louis XIV, who used a mixture of potent symbolism, such as the building of the new royal palace at Versailles, the promotion of a new administrative elite loyal to himself as a counterweight to the old nobility and military campaigns designed to enhance France's prestige by drawing power around the throne. His efforts met with only partial success. Strong limits on royal power remained, and the old nobility retained much of its power and influence. Louis's expression 'L'état, c'est moi' was never much more than wishful thinking.[26]

Following the French Revolution, the trend in Europe ran away from absolutism and authoritarianism and towards republics or constitutional monarchy; since most of the rest of the planet was now dominated by Europe, that meant the world followed suit. Following the Meiji Restoration, Japan moved towards a mixture of constitutional monarch and oligarchy, although this eroded after the Russo-Japanese War in 1904–5, when the army became increasingly dominant.[27] China, Persia and Ottoman Turkey all clung to forms of authoritarian government, but internal divisions and foreign pressure saw government authority progressively crumble, and all three countries experienced violent revolution in the twentieth century. In the cases of China and Turkey, this brought about complete regime change.[28]

Following the First World War, however, the currents of political thinking began to drift back towards authoritarianism. Giovanni Gentile, who served as minister of education in Benito Mussolini's government, drew on neo-Hegelian thought to argue that the state was the ultimate conception of society. He rejected the Marxist notion of a dialectic between capital and labour; to Gentile, both capital and labour were part of the larger state and owed the state their loyalty.[29] This also applied to every other human institution; taking his argument to extremes, Gentile even insisted that criminal organisations were part of the state and should be subservient to it, which rather misses the point of why many criminal organisations exist in the first place (see Chapter 19). A follower of Gentile, Ugo Spirito, developed a theory of corporatism whereby all economic institutions, including corporations and trades unions, were brought together under government supervision and, essentially, instructed to work together to fulfil government policy.[30] Spirito favoured concentrating ownership in the hands of workers rather than capitalists, a view which led other fascists to accuse him of Bolshevism.

In Germany, Carl Schmitt harked back to both European absolutist monarchs and the tyrants of the classical world, holding them up as political examples to admire and describing the European monarchies as the supreme example of European political achievement. Regarding the Weimar Republic, the weak and often chaotic government of Germany in the decade after the First World War, Schmitt argued that democracies were slow and inefficient; in order to get things done, government required an element of dictatorship. Strong leadership, he felt, was necessary to restore order in Germany. Schmitt also conjured up an 'Other' in the form of the Jews, whom he regarded as enemies of the state. He was far from the only anti-Semite in Germany in the 1920s, but his arguments gave anti-Semitism a form of spurious intellectual legitimacy.[31] Despite not always favouring the Nazi establishment, Schmitt was a member of the Nazi Party and enjoyed the patronage of Hermann Göring.

The Soviet Union followed a different intellectual trajectory, although it arrived at more or less the same destination. Following Marxist thought, Lenin envisioned a 'dictatorship of the proletariat', whereby the people would nominate their leaders, who would then work in the interests of the people. The purpose of this dictatorship of the proletariat was to protect the state from capitalist and bourgeois elements that would seek to overthrow it. This idea bears considerable resemblance to the ancient Greek idea of tyranny, but Lenin had a deeper purpose in mind. The purpose of the dictatorship of the proletariat was not only to defend the state but also to challenge and defeat the capitalists and bourgeois, wherever they might be found. When the world was rid of enemies, the state itself would naturally wither away, and there would no longer be a need for leaders (a state of affairs for which Kropotkin and the philosophical anarchists had been arguing for some time).[32] Under Stalin, once it became clear that the defeat of capitalism would not be accomplished quickly, the prevailing political philosophy reverted to conventional authoritarian tropes: the need to defend the state from enemies within (the peasants, Jews, ethnic minorities, intellectuals) and without (capitalism and fascism), the sense of crisis and the need to get things done (economic advancement, collectivisation).

Despite the bloody failures of Italian and German fascism and the later collapse of the Soviet Union, there were many who admired the totalitarian ideal. In China, Mao Zedong borrowed elements of totalitarian authority, in particular the notion of unity and indivisibility of interests between the state and the people (advocated by Stalin).[33] In Argentina, as we have seen, Juan Péron attempted to draw on fascist examples, and in Spain, following the end of the Spanish Civil War, Francisco

Franco also adopted a totalitarian approach, at the same time consciously styling himself after the South Americans *caudillos*.[34] The Burmese military dictatorship of Ne Win and the Khmer Rouge state established by Pol Pot in Cambodia also embraced totalitarian ideals.[35]

Unlike most totalitarian leaders, Adolf Hitler came to power through the democratic process after the elections of 1932, forming a coalition of several smaller parties to achieve a majority in the Reichstag, the German parliament, and secure for himself the position of chancellor. The reasons why people voted for him have often been discussed, but they can be summed up broadly as the desire for stability after the economic chaos of the Weimar government and the Great Depression and the fear of the Other. This Other took two broad forms. The first, initially the most important, was the fear of communism: most Germans still remembered the communist revolutions of 1919 that had come very near to success, and the Nazis played on popular fears of that chaotic time. The second, of course, was the fear of the Jews, who were seen as part of an international conspiracy (very often linked to the communists) that threatened Germany.[36]

Fear was one of the major reasons why people were persuaded to vote for Hitler in 1932. Similarly, the passage of the Enabling Act by the Reichstag in effect gave Hitler the powers of a dictator, and it was also broadly supported. Once in power, Hitler and the Nazis maintained themselves by continuing to pose as the only force that could create stability and repel the Other. As a result, even when people disagreed with the regime's policies, they still continued to support the regime itself. The fear that the collapse of the Nazis might lead to chaos and the triumph of the Other outweighed any feelings of distaste they might have had for the party and its leader. As time passed, the state of crisis became the new normal; people who might once have questioned the leader's authority accepted it as necessary.[37]

Much the same pattern can be seen in other totalitarian states, where a political or an economic crisis is kept alive through the conjuring up of limitless armies of bogeymen determined to destroy the state. Communists, capitalists, Jews, Chinese and Muslims, among others, have all made convenient scapegoats who can be eliminated, thus reassuring the rest of the populace that the state is being successfully defended. Force, to paraphrase Max Weber, is the state monopoly on violence and a defining characteristic of totalitarian regimes, who use violence to eliminate those who might pose a threat to the defining ideology. In this way the state is kept pure, maintaining the fiction set out by Gentile, Schmitt and Lenin that the state itself is united and whole. In reality, this is never true, and totalitarian regimes are forced to use more and more violence, eliminating more and more enemies.

However – and this, too, is important point to note – totalitarian leaders eliminate their enemies with the consent of their followers, however tacitly or reluctantly that consent may be given. During the rise of Hitler to power and his consolidation of that power during the 1930s, there were numerous opportunities to stop him, had his followers in Germany wished to do so.[38] They failed to do so because, once again, sufficient numbers of Germans either agreed with his ideology or believed he was the least bad alternative – it is impossible to say how many fell into each camp;

thus, he was able to fend off attempts to thwart or overthrow him and remain in power.

The final observation to make about totalitarianism is that, ultimately, the ideology itself is flawed. The totalitarianism of Gentile and Schmitt sought to subvert the individual and place all under the will of the state. But, as George Orwell observed so acutely in *Nineteen Eighty-Four*, it is necessary for someone to give guidance and direction to the state.[39] Lenin's idea of the disappearance of the state is utopian: there is always a need for Big Brother, and if he does not yet exist, the people will turn to a strong figure of authority in order to try to invent him. Most totalitarian states in the end become states ruled by *caudillos*: Hitler, Stalin, Mao, Franco, Pol Pot, Ne Win, *et al*; then, once the person becomes identified with the state, the loyalty of followers transfers from the state to the person. We saw how quickly the authority of the English Commonwealth evaporated after the death of Cromwell. Hitler's state did not long survive him; admittedly, Nazi Germany was overrun by the Allied powers, but the democratic state of the Federal Republic of Germany was created with the overwhelming support of the German public in the west of the country, as new leaders offered a new type of contract with their followers.[40] The deaths of Franco, Stalin and Mao were followed by progressive dismantling of the totalitarian state; even if in Stalin's case, the dismantling took a long time, culminating in 1991.[41]

Conclusion

And therein lies the problem. The relationship between leaders and followers is personal, not institutional. This is not to say that people will not also follow an idea or an ideology; patriotism and religion are two examples of cases where they do.[42] But history shows they are more likely to follow that ideal if there is a strong leader involved. The leader who has or appears to have access to power will usually command a larger following; paradoxically, much of that power comes from followers themselves, who enable the authoritarian leader to seize control in the first place. Followership and power become a self-reinforcing mix. Leaders who can introduce power into the social space and use it to guide, shape and regulate the thoughts and actions of followers will often succeed, no matter what political colours they wear.

On the other hand, when the strong leader fails, unless there is another strong leader available, the entire edifice of power will begin to crack. New leaders with new ideologies will enter the social space, winning over followers with fresh promises. People who have been ready to accept authoritarian rule for years can suddenly change their minds almost overnight. As Edvard Beneš, the former president of Czechoslovakia, once observed, every imperial state looks invincible until five minutes before its collapse.[43]

The irrationality of human behaviour is the rock on which authoritarian regimes tend to founder. Han Fei, the chief ideologue of Chinese legalism, recognised this when he commented that it is easier for an artist to paint ghosts and monsters than real people. Ghosts and monsters are creatures of the imagination, and the painter has free rein to depict them however he or she wishes. People, on the other hand, can be observed only from the outside, and the artist can only guess at what goes on inside their minds.[44] Despite all his attempts to constrain human action and force conformity, Han Fei accepted that people are – at least in the realms of the mind – individual and unique. The paradox between individualism and conformity was never fully resolved in his work, and of course, it still perplexes leaders today.

In his *Foundation* trilogy, published in the 1950s, science fiction writer Isaac Asimov made the point that societies cannot be regulated by systems; no matter how perfect the system might seem, the irrational human element will eventually throw a spanner in the works.[45] The trap that many authoritarian leaders fall into is the belief that they are mightier than their followers and that the edifices they build will last even beyond their lifetimes. Ultimately, followers have the last word. Their power endures, even after the leader has gone.

Notes

1 Peter Walker, 'UK Poised to Embrace Authoritarianism, Warns Hansard Society', *The Guardian*, 8 April 2019, www.theguardian.com/politics/2019/apr/08/uk-more-willing-embrace-authoritarianism-warn-hansard-audit-political-engagement.
2 Carl Schmitt, *The Concept of the Political*, trans. George D. Schwab, Chicago: University of Chicago Press, 1996.
3 Richard D. McKirahan, *Philosophy Before Socrates*, Indianapolis: Hackett, 1994.
4 Roderick McFarquhar and Michael Schoenhals, *Mao's Last Revolution*, Cambridge, MA: Harvard University Press, 2006; Moise, *Modern China*; Terrill, *Mao*; Salisbury, *The Last Emperors*.
5 Gaunt, *Oliver Cromwell*; Ronald Hutton, *The Restoration: A Political and Religious History of England and Wales, 1658–1667*, Oxford: Clarendon, 1985.
6 Philipp and Haarmann, *The Mamluks*; Linda S. Northrup, *From Slave to Sultan: The Career of al-Mansur Qalawun and the Consolidation of Mamluk Rule in Egypt and Syria*, Stuttgart: Franz Steiner Verlag, 1998.
7 Li Yu-ning, *Shang Yang's Reforms*, Armonk: M.E. Sharpe, 1977.
8 Watson, *Han Fei Tzu*; Witzel, 'The Leadership Philosophy of Han Fei'.
9 Ibid.; Machiavelli, *The Prince*.
10 Herodotus, *The Histories*, trans. Aubrey de Selincourt, London: Penguin, 2003.
11 Xenophon, *Hiero the Tyrant and Other Treatises*, trans. Robin A.H. Waterfield, London: Penguin, 2006.
12 Lionel J. Sanders, *Dionysos I of Syracuse and Greek Tyranny*, London: Croom Helm, 1987.
13 Plutarch, *Lives*; Marc Hyden, *Gaius Marius: The Rise and Fall of Rome's Saviour*, London: Pen & Sword, 2017; Arthur Keaveney, *Sulla: The Last Republican*, London: Routledge, 2005.
14 Machiavelli, *The Discourses*.
15 Mallett, *Mercenaries and Their Masters*.
16 John Lynch, *Caudillos in Spanish America, 1800–1850*, Oxford: Oxford University Press, 1992; Lynch, *Simón Bolívar*; Hamill, *Caudillos*; R.A. Humphreys, *Tradition and Revolt in Latin America*, New York: Columbia University Press, 1969.
17 Richard Bourne, *Getulio Vargas of Brazil: Sphinx of the Pampas*, London: Knight, 1974.
18 Hamill, *Caudillos*; Howard J. Wiarda, *Dictatorship and Development: Methods of Control in Trujillo's Dominican Republic*, Gainesville: University Press of Florida, 1968; Robert D. Crassweller, *Trujillo: The Life and Times of a Caribbean Dictator*, New York: Macmillan, 1966; Carlos R. Miranda, *The Stroessner Era: Authoritarian Rule in Paraguay*, Boulder: Westview Press, 1990; Michael D. Gambonne, *Eisenhower, Somoza and the Cold War in Nicaragua, 1953–1961*, New York: Praeger, 1997.

19 Hamill, *Caudillos*; Lynch, *Caudillos in Spanish America*; Will Fowler, *Santa Anna of Mexico*, Lincoln: University of Nebraska Press, 2007; Pamela Constable and Arturo Valenzuela, *A Nation of Enemies: Chile Under Pinochet*, New York: W.W. Norton, 1993; John Lynch, *Argentine Dictator: Juan Manuel de Rosas, 1829–1852*, Oxford: Oxford University Press, 1981.

20 Hamill, *Caudillos*; Paul Garner, *Porfirio Díaz*, Harlow: Pearson, 2001; Laurens B. Perry, *Juárez and Díaz: Machine Politics in Mexico*, DeKalb: Northern Illinois University Press, 1978; Joseph Page, *Perón: A Biography*, New York: Random House, 1983; Nicolas Fraser and Marysa Navarro, *Evita: The Real Life of Eva Perón*, New York: W.W. Norton, 1980; Robert E. Quirk, *Fidel Castro*, New York: W.W. Norton, 1993; Fidel Castro, *My Life*, New York: Charles Scribner, 2009.

21 Simon Collier, *Ideas and Politics of Chilean Independence, 1808–1833*, Cambridge: Cambridge University Press, 1967.

22 Chris Leuchars, *To the Bitter End: Paraguay and the War of the Triple Alliance*, Westport: Greenwood Press, 2002.

23 Roger M. Haigh, *Martin Güemes: Tyrant or Tool? A Study of the Sources of Power of an Argentine Caudillo*, Fort Worth: Texas Christian University Press, 1968.

24 Jay, *Management and Machiavelli*.

25 Mark Pendergrast, *For God, Country and Coca-Cola*, New York: Basic Books, 2000; David Greising, *I'd Like to Buy the World a Coke: The Life and Leadership of Roberto Goizueta*, New York: Wiley, 1998.

26 John B. Wolf, *Louis XIV*, New York: W.W. Norton, 1968; Richard Wilkinson, *Louis XIV*, London: Routledge, 2017.

27 Sims, *Japanese Political History*; William G. Beasley, *The Rise of Modern Japan: Political, Economic and Social Change Since 1850*, New York: St Martin's, 1995.

28 Kayloe, *The Unfinished Revolution*; Moise, *Modern China*; Mangol Bayat, *Iran's First Revolution: Sh'ism and the Constitutional Revolution of 1905–1909*, Oxford: Oxford University Press, 1991; M. Sukru Hanioglu, *The Young Turks: Preparation for a Revolution, 1902–1908*, Oxford: Oxford University Press, 2001.

29 Stanley G. Payne, *A History of Fascism*, London: Routledge, 1995; James A. Gregor, *Giovanni Gentile: Philosopher of Fascism*, Piscatawa: Transaction, 2001.

30 Payne, *A History of Fascism*; Roger Griffin, *Fascism*, Oxford: Oxford University Press, 1995.

31 Jens Meierhenrich and Oliver Simons (eds), *The Oxford Handbook of Carl Schmitt*, Oxford: Oxford University Press, 2017; John P. McCormick, *Carl Schmitt's Critique of Liberalism*, Cambridge: Cambridge University Press, 1999.

32 Robert Service, *Lenin: A Biography*, London: Macmillan, 2000; Kropotkin, *The Conquest of Bread*.

33 Maurice Meisner, *Mao's China and After*, New York: Free Press, 1999; Terrill, *Mao*; McFarquhar and Schoenhals, *Mao's Last Revolution*.

34 Stanley G. Payne, *Fascism in Spain, 1923–1977*, Madison: University of Wisconsin Press, 1999; Paul Preston, *Franco: A Biography*, London: HarperCollins, 1993.

35 Vincent Boudreau, *Resisting Dictatorship: Repression and Protest in Southeast Asia*, Cambridge: Cambridge University Press, 2004; Philip Short, *Pol Pot: The History of a Nightmare*, London: John Murray, 2004; Popham, *The Lady and the Generals*.

36 Samuel Halperin, *Germany Tried Democracy: A Political History of the Reich From 1918 to 1933*, New York: W.W. Norton, 1965.

37 Ibid.; Ian Kershaw, *Hitler: A Biography*, New York: W.W. Norton, 2008; William L. Shirer, *The Rise and Fall of the Third Reich*, New York: Simon & Schuster, 1960; John Michael Steiner, *Power Politics and Social Change in National Socialist Germany: A Process of Escalation Into Mass Destruction*, The Hague: Mouton, 1976; Anton Gill, *An Honourable Defeat: A History of the German Resistance to Hitler*, London: Heinemann, 1994.

38 Gill, *An Honourable Defeat*.

39 George Orwell, *Nineteen Eighty-Four*, London: Penguin, 2004.

40 Charles Williams, *Konrad Adenauer: The Father of the New Germany*, Chichester: Wiley, 2001.

41 Ronald Grigor Suny, *Revenge of the Past: Nationalism, Revolution and the Collapse of the Soviet Union*, Stanford: Stanford University Press, 1993; Serhii Plokhy, *The Last Empire: The Final Days of the Soviet Union*, New York: Oneworld, 2014.
42 Van Henten and ter Borg, *Power*; Eric Hobsbawm, *Nations and Nationalism Since 1780: Programme, Myth, Reality*, Cambridge: Cambridge University Press, 1992.
43 Zeman Zbyněk, *The Life of Edvard Beneš*, Oxford: Clarendon, 1997.
44 Watson, *Han Fei Tzu*.
45 Isaac Asimov, *Foundation*, New York: HarperCollins, 2016.

10

AUTOCRATIC LEADERS

Whereas the previous chapter focused on authoritarianism, this one will discuss the closely related concept of autocracy, the concentration of power in the hands of a single individual. There is of course considerable overlap between these ideas; many authoritarian regimes have autocratic leaders, and many autocrats are also authoritarians. As noted, even when authoritarian regimes are ruled by an oligarchy, such as Burma under the generals or Argentina under the military *junta* of the 1970s, individual leaders like Ne Win, Jorge Videla and Leopoldo Galtieri tended to emerge as *primus inter pares*.[1]

Despite this, examples of true autocracy, where power really is concentrated in the hands of a single person, are quite hard to find. Criminal gangs and terrorist groups, as will be discussed in Part V of this book, sometimes obey the will of a single leader, but even they are likely to comprise factions competing for power. In reality, even the most autocratic leaders depend on a cadre of others in order to make their wishes known and enforce their will.[2] History is full of examples of people who *believed* they were autocrats and behaved accordingly, but quite often power slipped through their grasp; largely because, although they continued to believe in their own autocracy, the people around them had other ideas about who really held power.

In this chapter, I want to concentrate on a particular form of autocracy, that which is linked to ownership. The people who own organisations – and 'own' is a contested word in this context – often behave as if they could bend those organisations to their will. I will examine two particular areas where people 'owned' organisations, the armed forces and business, and look at the issues of power, authority and conflict that surround this style of leadership. Finally, I want to look at another form of autocracy, often found in areas such as sport and the arts, where authority is derived not through ownership but through factors such as expertise, reputation and skill.

The same point needs to be made here as it was in previous chapters: namely people did willingly accept the authority of autocratic leaders, but only if it suited them and their needs. This means that the very idea of autocracy is open to challenge. Did the people who owned military units or companies really control them, or were they labouring under a delusion? As discussed in Chapter 3, the political scientist Mary Parker Follett believed the latter to be the case. Control, she declared in her book *Creative Experience*, was largely a myth.[3] It is impossible for any leader to directly control more than a small number of subordinates, a view which was given further weight by the calculations of the Lithuanian engineer V. A. Graicunas, who argued that managers should have no more than four or five subordinates because this was the maximum number of people they could directly control. He agreed with Follett that most of what we think of as *control* in organisations is largely a matter of *coordination*.[4]

There is, therefore, often a mismatch between what leaders think is happening and what is really happening. This chapter will explore some of the issues around that mismatch and try to gain a clearer picture of the nature of autocratic leadership.

The monopoly of violence

Max Weber observed that the state monopoly of violence – that is, the state reserving for itself the right to used armed force – is one of the hallmarks of a nation-state.[5] However, that has not always been the case. The Chinese Empire and the Roman Empire had large standing armies, and the Aztecs had professional warrior societies such as the Jaguars and the Eagles, which correspond roughly to our modern idea of military regiments, but depending on social structure and economic power, not every state could afford to – or desired to – maintain a standing army.[6]

Governments relied on other agencies to supply them with military force. Athens and many other Greek city-states relied on citizen volunteers who were called up for military service in time of need.[7] In Japan, the feudal system required the *samurai* class in particular to turn out for military service when required by their overlord, and the feudal states of Northern Europe could also command military service.[8] However, depending on the terms of the social contract between the lords and their subjects, that service could be quite limited; the period of military service could be quite short, or subjects might have the right to refuse service outside their home country.

In fourteenth-century England, a new system had evolved. Experienced commanders, usually knights and nobleman, entered into an individual contract known as an indenture with the crown. The terms of each indenture were different, but each specified the number of men the indenture holder would recruit, along with their equipment and length and terms of service. Although the indenture holder was required to obey the orders of the crown and its chief officers, the primary loyalty of the men he recruited was to himself, and indenture holders could and did intervene to give their followers preferred positions or protect them from punishment.[9]

In practice, the commanders tended to treat the companies they raised through indenture as their own property, subject to their own will, and this tendency increased as time went on. In peacetime, indentured companies were supposed to be disbanded, but enterprising commanders saw no reason to do so. One of the common bonds that united the commanders with the men they recruited was the desire for wealth: in addition to good wages, the men who joined up were promised the chance to acquire wealth through looting the private property of enemy civilians. When the fighting stopped, the looting often continued. Following the Battle of Poitiers in 1356, which resulted in a temporary cessation of hostilities between England and France, many English companies essentially became bandits, plundering their way across France.[10] They were completely outside the control of the English crown, which had employed them in the first place, and the damage they did worked against English interests.

Navies were similarly made up of hired ships on contracts, and their captains and admirals likewise tended to put their own interests first; once again, whereas the crown might have a political agenda, the men who served at sea were primarily interested in profit. It was not uncommon for ships to function as warships, merchant ships and pirates all on the same voyage; the Genoese admiral Benedetto Zaccaria also dabbled in diplomacy and espionage on his own account, ignoring his orders as it suited him.[11] One historian, John Guilmartin, has suggested that terms such as war, piracy and commerce could be abolished and replaced with a single catch-all, 'armed violence at sea'.[12]

The other method of raising troops was to recruit foreign mercenaries, which became big business in the later Middle Ages. In the fourteenth century the trade was dominated by two Italian family firms, the Dorias, based in Genoa, and the Grimaldis, also Genoese, who seized the castle of Monaco around 1300 and set up a base there, recruiting mercenary soldiers from all over Italy for service mainly in France.[13] Many other mercenary companies served in Italy, notably the White Company commanded by Sir John Hawkwood.[14] Although wealthy cities such as Florence and Venice could have afforded to raise standing armies, for largely political reasons they continued to employ mercenaries, despite the words of Machiavelli, who warned that mercenaries would always put their own interests first and could not be relied upon to defend the state.[15]

Aware of the problems of losing the monopoly on violence, states began attempting to establish more control. The result was a licensing system which saw armed forces take on a corporate form, similar to the chartered companies, such as the East India Company, which were evolving at the same time.[16] Trusted individuals were licensed to raise regiments for military service. The rank of colonel originally denoted someone who had been given a license to raise his own regiment. The wars of the sixteenth century, including the Thirty Years War and the English Civil War, were fought by regiments raised by military entrepreneurs under license from the crown. The most prominent of these entrepreneurs was Albrecht von Wallenstein, who by 1630 had recruited more than fifty thousand men for service in the armies of the Holy Roman Empire and who also owned the agricultural land, textile mills, foundries and other services that supported them in the field.[17] In the Empire, the system whereby regiments were owned by their proprietors, or Inhabers, persisted until the nineteenth century.[18] Only then did most European governments succeed in bringing their armed forces under direct control, with 'ownership' of military units passing into the hands of the state, finally achieving Weber's state monopoly of violence.

But trust was a limited commodity, and even those close to the crown, such as Wallenstein, could not always be trusted. Forced into retirement once doubts were raised about his loyalty, Wallenstein was recalled to active service and took command of his military empire once more, but he became increasingly independent of imperial authority. He made his own decisions about strategy, and on one occasion he apparently entered into negotiations with the enemy without telling his government. Given the size of his army, if Wallenstein had decided to change sides, this would have been a real danger to the state; accordingly, the authorities ordered his assassination.[19]

There are two problems with military entrepreneurships, and Wallenstein's case highlights one of them; the problem of the over-mighty subordinate. As we saw earlier in this book, one of the reasons why societies came together and why people put their trust in leaders was defence; the leaders of the state were tasked with ensuring the survival and prosperity of their followers. However, if the troops charged with their defence turned against the state and the people, the leaders were deemed to have failed in their duty. In Renaissance Italy, it was not unknown for the population to go over to the side of the mercenaries and expel their existing leaders, promoting mercenary captains to the vacant leadership roles.[20] As Samuel P. Huntington later pointed out, the only way to ensure the loyalty of the military was to professionalise them and make them part of the apparatus of the state, but as the history of *coups d'état* shows, even this does not always work.[21]

The second problem is that the military entrepreneurs themselves, although they claimed to own their free companies and their regiments, rarely had complete control over them. The colonel or the *Inhaber* might well provide his soldiers with pay, uniforms, rations and all the means of subsistence, but that did not always mean that he had their full loyalty.

Ownership of the means of force

What exactly did the colonel or the *Inhaber* own? He (very occasionally, she) owned the license to raise a retinue or a company or a regiment – in Wallenstein's case, an army – and he owned the equipment and weapons issued to the men, but he did not own the men themselves. He owned the means of force, but not the people who carried it out. Only in very rare instances, such as the slave-armies of the Mamluks, could the soldiers be said to be property. Although the colonels tried to enforce their authority through contract and military laws, their ability to do so was often limited.

War was a business, and men joined regiments or served on warships for the same reasons they do today; for comradeship and a sense of belonging, for the chance to fight for a cause and for pay. In addition to daily wages, there were opportunities for bonuses in the form of loot and prize money, and these were a considerable incentive. During the Napoleonic Wars, Royal Navy recruiting parties would loudly proclaim how many enemy ships their captain had taken and how much prize money each man had earned on the last cruise. There is evidence to suggest that men were readier to join ships whose crews earned higher levels of prize money than those whose crews earned little or nothing.[22] The successful colonel or ship's captain was the one who could give his men what they wanted. Those colonels who could not do so risked seeing their men desert to join other regiments; captains who had been unsuccessful at taking prizes were liable to set sail with understrength crews.

The nature of the contract between commanders and soldiers also meant that discipline was problematic. Soldiers regarded loot as a right, and commanders who attempted to stop their men from looting could and did meet with resistance to the point of mutiny. A prudent commander might think it better to allow his men to carry on robbing – even when in friendly territory – than to try to stop them and then watch them desert. Losses in battle during the Thirty Years War were nothing compared to the devastation caused by marching armies, who tended to strip the land bare like locusts.[23] Thus, whereas the colonel or *Inhaber* or ship's captain might claim to *own* his regiment or his ship and control it, in reality he had a contract with his men; they would obey his orders as long as he gave them what they wanted in order to fulfil their reasons for joining the service in the first place.

Entrepreneurs

The notion that businesses are owned by their shareholders has deep historical roots and persists to this day. As early as 1905, the lawyer John Davis argued that corporations have an independent legal standing and are owned by no one, but as Robert Eccles and Tim Youmans (among others) have noted, the view that shareholders own companies remains highly influential in management theory and practice.[24] In fact, the legal position is quite clear: in limited companies and corporations, shareholders own the capital invested in the business and, sometimes, the land or machinery used by the business, but they do not own the business itself. Furthermore, just as in private military units – except in extreme cases, such as slavery – they do not own the people who work for them.

But the myth of ownership is a powerful one. Economists such as Milton Friedman refer explicitly to shareholders as owners of the corporation, and the godmother of neo-liberalism, Ayn Rand, created a series of business leaders in her novels *Atlas Shrugged* and *The Fountainhead*, exalting them as heroic owners and masters of corporations.[25] Consciously or unconsciously, Rand was following the Great Man tradition, which saw business leaders as exceptional people who had triumphed because of their own innate abilities; in other words, their own greatness.

Of course, shareholders and business leaders are not necessarily the same thing. In large corporations in the UK and the US, the separation of ownership and control (more on that in a moment) means that although business leaders often own shares, they rarely have a controlling interest. Elsewhere in the world, however, businesses are often run by individuals or families who also own a substantial portion of the firm's capital and are able to control its destiny. The separation of ownership and control is a relatively new concept: until the mid-twentieth century, it was axiomatic that the people who owned the share capital in a company should also take a direct interest in its management. There were exceptions; sometimes people inherited capital but were debarred by infirmity or simply had no interest in running a business. Sometimes, too, certain classes were excluded from participating in management; in the Roman Republic and under the Roman Empire, patricians were forbidden to engage directly in commerce, which meant their business investments had to be handled by managers (and sometimes, by slaves).[26]

Business leaders were not particularly prominent in most early societies, in part because businesses were usually quite small and in part because of the social stigma often attached to commerce and banking. Early Christian thinkers regarded business, especially the concept of profit, as inherently sinful, and it was not until the thirteenth century that a new wave of theologians, led by St Thomas Aquinas, began looking at the issue again and conceded that business had a valuable role to play in society.[27]

Fourteenth-century Europe saw the rise of large-scale capitalism and the emergence of bankers and traders like Sir John Pulteney, Sir William de la Pole and Sir Richard Whittington, all of whom were bankers at one time or another to the English Crown; Jacques Coeur fulfilled a similar function in France.[28] The first business leaders of international stature, Cosimo de' Medici in Florence and Jakob Fugger in Augsburg, rose to prominence in the fifteenth century.[29]

The Medici and Fugger banks were family businesses, but they also engaged extensively in partnerships, developing trading networks across Europe and beyond. Like most businesses of the time, they were highly diversified: in addition to banking, the Medici engaged in mining, cloth manufacturing and general trade, and this diversification was largely achieved through a broad range of partnerships with local businesses and specialists. That meant giving away part of the ownership of the firm and thus a good deal of control. Cosimo de' Medici gave his partners a good deal of freedom to engage in whatever business activities they chose, provided they were profitable. He was enormously respected and influential throughout the business, and when he made his wishes known, they were generally obeyed; the same was true in the city of Florence – although he never held any official post, he was the dominant figure in city politics for several decades.[30] But the notion of partnership figured large in Cosimo's leadership style, and he always preferred collaboration to competition. In no sense would he have claimed to *own* the Medici Bank; he was the dominant shareholder, but there were plenty of others engaged with the firm. The same was true of Fugger and of banking enterprises in other parts of the world, such as the house of Chand in India, whose leaders bore the title Jagat Sheth (Bankers to the World), and the Ningbo banking guild that emerged in China around the twelfth century, probably as an offshoot of the treasury bureau of the Zhou dynasty.[31] All of these enterprises relied heavily on networks of distributed power.

More concentrated forms of enterprise began to appear during the Industrial Revolution. Cloth manufacturing had formerly used a putting out system whereby processes such as spinning, weaving, dyeing and so on were contracted out to individual providers, a process which is similar to modern outsourcing. Contractors provided their own tools and worked from their own premises, usually their homes, and were largely able to work on their own with limited direction from the entrepreneur. With the development of new technologies, entrepreneurs such as Richard Arkwright, Robert Owen and Samuel Oldknow in England and Joseph Jacquard in France were able to concentrate labour on a single site, where they now owned both premises and means of production, and workers received a wage in exchange for their labour.[32] Within a few decades the new production system had spread to other manufacturing industries, and the principles of industrial organisation were being tried out in sectors as diverse as mining and retailing.[33]

At the same time, the concept of property was receiving attention from philosophers and economists. The intellectual notion of private property had been only vaguely sketched out before the beginning of the European Enlightenment, and much land in England and Scotland was held in common, owned by communities rather than individuals.[34] Starting in the late Tudor period, however, there was a growing movement to enclose common land and transfer ownership to individual landowners. Justification came from writers such as Thomas Hobbes and John Locke, both of whom argued that those who worked the land and made it productive had the right to own it.[35] Although this could have been construed as support for popular ownership – and many writers, including Adam Smith, argued for limits on the amount of land any individual was allowed to own – the concept was instead co-opted by the capitalist class and used to justify their ownership and control of factories. It was their ideas, their genius, their capital and their technology that made the factories productive; it stood to reason that they owned the businesses they had created.

As a result, many of them behaved like dictators, demanding hard work and obedience from their employees. Employees at Arkwright's first mill at Cromford, including children as young as seven, worked thirteen-hour days. Those who arrived late for their shift were turned away and lost a day's pay. Arkwright was unusual in allowing his employees one week's holiday every year; others, like Samuel Oldknow, allowed no holidays.

Even more enlightened employers used strict controls. Robert Owen famously cut the working day at New Lanark from fourteen hours to ten and a half, forbade child labour and provided free housing and education to his workers. But his mill superintendents enforced strict discipline, including a 'silent monitor' system of coloured symbols placed over each worker's station in the mill to connote the quality of their conduct and performance from the previous day. Excellent conduct resulted in a white symbol and good conduct a yellow one, while a blue symbol meant indifferent conduct and black, the mark of shame, meant the worker was being publicly humiliated for what the superintendents believed was poor performance.[36] William Lever, who also provided many benefits to his employees, including education and housing, built his original factory at Port Sunlight in the form of a panopticon so that from his office he could see every work station and watch what his workers were doing.[37] Marguerite Bouicaut, who co-founded the department store Au Bon Marché in Paris and ran it after her husband's death, required her young female shop workers to live in-house and attempted to regulate virtually every aspect of their lives.[38] All these people considered themselves to be the owners of the businesses they had founded and managed and led; ownership gave them the right to expect unquestioning obedience.

The Gilded Age

The entrepreneurs of America's Gilded Age had similar views on capital and ownership, some of which were often more strongly held. The divide between wealthy owners of capital and the workers who served them was sharply etched; to use Hofstede's term, power distance was very high. Social Darwinism was very influential in America in the 1880s and 1890s, and the labouring poor were considered to be almost another species, put on Earth primarily to serve the wealthy.[39] Workers were considered to have few if any rights, and punishments and wage cuts were handed out arbitrarily. When workers dare to show dissent, business leaders reacted harshly, calling on the military to suppress them as in the cases of the Homestead strike or the Pullman strike in 1894 that resulted in thirty workers being shot dead by the army. Alternatively they brought in armed private security forces such as the Pinkerton Agency, who were also used to quash the strike at Homestead; Daniel Guggenheim would later use the Pinkerton Agency to break attempted strikes at his mining corporation, ASARCO.[40]

One of the foremost social Darwinists was William Graham Sumner, a professor of sociology at Yale University and a strong supporter of big business interests. Sumner saw society as a matter of 'them' and 'us'; warfare, he said, was a natural condition in civilised society – that is, it was part of the process of competition between states. That same process of competition went on within societies. In his essay 'What Social Classes Owe to Each Other' (1883), Sumner supported the notion that the classes could not exist without each other, but he is clear what the duty of each is; the business owner and leader commands, and the worker 'obeys without question'.[41] A more nuanced view of the same argument was given by one of Sumner's colleagues at Yale, Arthur Twining Hadley, who argued that the power of capital enabled it to make labour more 'efficient' but warned that simply driving down wages was short-sighted and would not produce positive results. Business leaders ignored the latter point and drove down wages whenever they wished; during the economic depression that followed the Panic of 1893, many firms cut wages unilaterally by as much as 50 per cent.[42] Again, they justified their actions by claiming ownership; it is my firm, and I can do whatever I want.

The position of capital versus labour in America from the 1880s to the outbreak of the First World War is a clear illustration of how the Marxian dialectic functions in practice. In order to strengthen their power, business leaders developed the concept of combinations, or trusts, that brought together every major business in a particular sector into a single entity. Famous examples include U.S. Steel, Standard Oil, the Beef Trust, the Whiskey Trust and many others.[43] From the perspective of this book, this was a daring attempt by leaders to seize near-total control from their followers, increasing power distance to the limits and taking command of the social space.

Why did they attempt to do so? The obvious answer is that increasing their own power meant increasing their wealth, but fear was also an important factor. With very few exceptions, the business leaders who emerged in late nineteenth-century America were of British or Western European origin, whereas the great mass of immigrants who formed the bulk of the workforce were from Eastern or Southern Europe or from other hinterlands, such as Ireland and China.[44] Faced with this tidal wave of inward migration by the Other and fearing that they might pose a challenge to their own way of life, the elites resolved to put the newcomers firmly in their place.[45] This raises another more general question about leadership; to what extent is oppression a symptom of fear among the leadership group? It is not hard to see similar symptoms of fear in the repressive control systems in totalitarian states, organised programmes of religious persecution or even more mundane relationships between workers and employers.

Resistance

Seeing their own power increasingly alienated, to borrow another Marxian term, the workers resisted. Despite attempts to stop them, trade and craft unions emerged, followed by broader umbrella movements that tried to bring all workers together. The first of these, the Knights of Labor, collapsed in 1886 after the Haymarket Square protest in Chicago, where workers gathered to demand an eight-hour day, ended in violence.[46] The later 1880s saw the emergence of the American Federation of Labor, led by the charismatic Samuel Gompers. He had the wisdom to stay clear of politics and not develop links with socialist or anarchist movements, which would have invited state repression, concentrating instead on improving conditions for workers. Faced with multiple threats, including other much more radical movements like the Industrial Workers of the World, which did have links to anarchism and syndicalism, business leaders saw in Gompers someone they could trust and do business with. By conceding a little power to Gompers, they could avoid losing power altogether in the event of a violent revolution.[47]

Resistance could take other forms. The techniques of scientific management – the atomisation of working processes through methods such as time-and-motion studies and rewards contingent upon productivity – were introduced in the late 1890s at Bethlehem Steel in Pennsylvania. The founders of scientific management – Frederick Winslow Taylor, Henry Gantt, Frank Gilbreth and his wife, the psychologist Lillian Gilbreth – intended it to be a means of rewarding workers more fairly for their efforts, but workers saw correctly that, in many cases, employers were using scientific management to sweat more labour out of their workforce without increasing wages. As a result, consultants carrying out time-and-motion studies met with a variety of obstructions, ranging from men deliberately slowing their rate of work to generate false data, to threats of and actual violence against the consultants.[48]

American workers were also able to call on outside help from a political spectrum ranging from liberal journalists like Ida Tarbell, whose spectacular assault in print on the Rockefellers and Standard Oil resulted in the company's prosecution and legal break-up by the American authorities, to socialists and anarchists preaching revolution, peaceful or otherwise. In response to the violent suppression of the Homestead strike, anarchist Alexander Berkman attempted to kill a senior steel company executive, Henry Clay Frick, in his own office. Frick was badly wounded but survived. Less fortunate was the pro-business American president William McKinley, shot and mortally wounded by an anarchist in 1901. The banker J. P. Morgan Jr survived several assassination attempts.[49]

Despite this, the culture of confrontation continued and to some extent still continues in the American workplace social space. In Europe, business leaders took the threat more seriously and began ceding more power to workers. Many efforts centred around pay, and hundreds of firms introduced profit-sharing schemes or even co-ownership, where workers received shares in the business and were paid dividends. Some of these schemes worked well, like that at John Lewis, but others struggled, and even enlightened employers were uneasy about the merits of co-ownership. The ship-owner Christopher Furness called for a new partnership between capital and labour and introduced a co-ownership scheme at his firm, Furness Withy, but it was abandoned after less than a year.[50] Benjamin Seebohm Rowntree wrote in favour of co-partnership but admitted he had never been able to work out how to introduce an effective scheme in his own firm.[51] As John Lewis pointed out, workers could not truly reap the benefits of ownership unless they also had control, and ceding control was not something that many entrepreneurs could countenance. They were still trapped in the paradigm of ownership; the business belonged to them, and only they knew what was best for it.

The separation of ownership and control

Lewis had hit upon a fundamental issue that cuts to the heart of the issue of property: if, for a moment, we accept the argument that entrepreneurs own their businesses, is it necessarily incumbent upon them to also control those businesses?

The seizure of power by unscrupulous entrepreneurs and especially the rise of the big monopolistic combinations, the trusts, convinced many that entrepreneurs were not to be trusted. Both Ida Tarbell and Henry Lloyd argued that the trusts were fundamentally undemocratic, as they concentrated power in the hands of a few. Increasingly, economists like Jeremiah Jenks and John Bates Clark were coming around to their point of view.[52] One of the leading promoters of the trust movement, Charles Flint, argued that trusts were in fact a force in favour of democracy as they diffused ownership among many different shareholders, rather than concentrating it in the hands of a family or a single person, but his argument fell on deaf ears. The problem in the minds of many was not ownership but control.[53]

Shortly after the First World War, Walther Rathenau, the German industrialist who served briefly as foreign minister in the Weimar Republic until his assassination, argued that ownership and control should be separate. The owners of capital were too likely to surrender to their own selfish impulses and too focused on maintaining their own power. For the sake of their enterprises and for the sake of society as a whole, they should step back and hand over control to professional, impartial managers who would run the company in the best interests of its stakeholders.[54] This was an attractive idea, and it caught on quickly in America, although as Mark Roe points out, there was also a political agenda: the American government had belatedly realised the threat to its own power posed by big business and saw the separation of ownership and control as a means of weakening the power of the big industrial barons.[55]

But did this really solve the problem? Some leading economists were doubtful, and one, Harvard professor William Ripley, argued that by surrendering control to managers, the owners of capital were abrogating their responsibilities. James Burnham, the Trotskyite turned libertarian philosopher, poured scorn on the separation of ownership and control and argued that over time control becomes *de facto* ownership; those who have control of an asset will behave as if they owned it. The separation of ownership control merely means exchanging one set of elites for another.[56]

There are plenty of examples to suggest Burnham was right; I will offer just one here, but it is highly illustrative. In the 1890s, the most successful team of hotel managers in the world was undoubtedly César Ritz and his partner, the renowned chef Auguste Escoffier. After running a number of high-end hotels together, they were invited to London by the owner of the Savoy Hotel, Richard D'Oyly Carte, and offered the chance to run it. As part of the agreement, Carte stepped back from management and left everything to Ritz and Escoffier, his professional managers. They proceeded to run the hotel very much as if they owned it, including taking bribes to provide special services to guests and helping themselves to the hotel's food and wine stocks to hold banquets for private clients. Escoffier later accepted that he had stolen more than £8,000 from the hotel. When both men were fired, there was a near riot among the staff, who were loyal to Escoffier and Ritz, and the police had to be summoned to remove them forcibly from the hotel premises.[57]

The alternative, as proposed by economists such as Seebohm Rowntree, Sidney Webb and many others at the Rowntree conferences in the 1930s, was to move from a confrontational approach to a more collaborative one. In their view, leaders and followers needed to come together in the social space and learn to work together. A particularly poignant plea was made by the entrepreneur Eric Gordon England, who believed that the purpose of business was to seek out truth. What holds people back from the truth is the twin sirens of revolution and conservatism, each of which warps our thinking so that we can no longer see the truth: 'revolutionary thought represents the cry of hate, whereas conservative thought represents the cry of fear.

Between these two there should intervene the thought of goodwill and the thought of courage'.[58] The quest for truth absolutely depended on partnership and goodwill between all those involved in business – the owners of capital, the managers and the workers.[59]

But there is little evidence that business leaders listened to England and others like him; if they did listen, they did not take action. In the twenty-first century we once again hear similar arguments; will things be different this time? Can the actors in the dysfunctional social space of business put aside at least some of their differences and work together? Of course, they do to an extent; otherwise, nothing in business would ever get done. But the impulse to confront, built on a foundation of greed, mistrust, fear and historical example, is still very strong. As long as it persists, opportunities will continue to be wasted and value will continue to be lost.

Creative autocracy

The social space has many facets, and the collaboration and the confrontation that take place there can come in many forms. In business, leaders and followers struggle for control because they believe it will help them achieve their goals: prosperity, wealth, personal satisfaction and fulfilment. In other fields, the need for collaboration is more obvious and visible, and it is more widely recognised that nothing happens without collaboration on several dimensions, between followers and leaders and between the followers themselves.

We have looked so far at autocracy as a driving force behind conflict over power, but autocrats can also be a useful tool for overcoming conflict and pushing collaboration up the agenda. In sport, part of the role of the coach or manager is to ensure that there is no conflict and that the team functions in a harmonious fashion in order to achieve its goals. Mention has been made earlier of some autocratic leaders, such as the football coach Sir Alex Ferguson and the baseball coach Yogi Berra, but perhaps the best example of an autocrat who generated positive results was Vince Lombardi, coach of the Green Bay Packers American football team, who is widely regarded as one of the greatest coaches of all time.[60]

Lombardi was regarded by others as being cold and aloof. He made few close friends, and his marriage was often troubled. However, he was able in a short space of time to turn the Packers, formerly one of the worst teams in American football, into champions. His players went in awe of him, but they respected his formidable ability, and they knew he could give them what they wanted; the organisation and the training to be the best team in their sport and to win championship titles. Over the course of time, they also came to respect him for his principled stance on matters of race and sexuality. Lombardi increased the number of black players on his team from one to thirteen and came down hard on any signs of racial abuse within the team; at a time when much of America was still racially segregated, Lombardi made it clear that his team would patronise only those hotels and restaurants where black and white people were treated equally. Although homosexuality was still a criminal offense in many parts of America,

Lombardi encouraged gay players and coaching staff to join his team and made it clear that he would fire anyone who abused them or objected to their presence.[61] Lombardi laid down rules without consultation and expected people to follow them; they did so because his goals were also their goals.

Music has traditionally been full of autocratic leaders and conductors who know exactly what they want and will stop at nothing to get it; mention has already been made of Georg Solti and Arturo Toscanini. Herbert von Karajan, the long-serving conductor of the Berlin Philharmonic, was an autocrat and eccentric full of odd prejudices. Follically challenged members of the orchestra were instructed to wear wigs so Karajan did not have to look at their bald heads, and he once quarrelled with principal flautist James Galway when the latter grew a beard. Like Lombardi, Karajan made his own rules and expected others to follow his leadership without question. They did not always do so; his relationship with the orchestra was sometimes tempestuous, but on the whole the orchestra members accepted his authority because they knew he was making them into the premier classical orchestra in Europe, if not the world.[62] Frank Zappa was perceived by members of his band, the Mothers of Invention, to be an autocrat who prioritised musical perfection over human feelings and emotions. He controlled almost every aspect of the band's music and performances, including touring schedules, and when times were hard, he sometimes paid them out of his own pocket. In the end, he disbanded the Mothers of Invention because he felt some members were insufficiently committed. Although his musicians were often angry and found Zappa frustrating to work with, they accepted that his high standards enabled them to make music they could be proud of.[63]

Jean-Baptiste Lully, court composer and choreographer at the court of Louis XIV, was an autocrat who expelled from court any other musician or dancer who challenged his authority. The dancer Isadora Duncan, a protégé of Loie Fuller, controlled her own career to the last detail, including choreographing her own dances and designing her own costumes. She also controlled the lives of her dance pupils to such an extent that many adopted her surname as their own.[64] In education, two of the most influential educators of all time, Dr Thomas Arnold, a headmaster at Rugby School, and Charles Eliot, a president of Harvard University, exhibited autocratic tendencies. Arnold remodelled the curriculum and ethos of Rugby, ensuring that its value conformed to his own, with harsh punishments for both staff and students who transgressed; Eliot oversaw every aspect of the university's operations, attempting to control and regulate what was taught and what sports were played; he once attempted to ban football, believing its competitive nature was not consistent with the university's ethos. Both men had loyal followers because they recognised that Arnold and Eliot were genuinely improving the quality of education.[65]

We could go on, but the point has been made. Autocrats seek power, but how well they are accepted and the level of opposition they meet depend on their motives for doing so. If they seek power for its own sake or to repress and put down their followers, opposition will likely continue. If, on the other hand, they seek power in order to help followers meet their goals, there will be a greater chance of acceptance. In such cases, the emphasis shifts from conflict to collaboration as followers more or less willingly give up power in the expectation that they will reap benefits in the form of satisfaction, growth, the chance to excel and to improve their own skills and achieve their dreams. To paraphrase Franklin D. Roosevelt, our leader may be an autocrat, but he is *our* autocrat.

Notes

1 Popham, *The Lady and the Generals*; Anthony Pereira, *Political Injustice: Authoritarianism and the Rule of Law in Brazil, Chile and Argentina*, Pittsburgh: University of Pittsburgh Press, 2005.
2 Douglass C. North, John Joseph Wallis and Barry R. Weingast, 'Violence and the Rise of Open Access Orders', *Journal of Democracy* 20 (1) (1998): 56–68.
3 Follett, *Creative Experience*.
4 V.A. Graicunas, 'The Span of Control', in Luther Gulick and Lyndall Fownes Urwick (eds), *Papers on the Science of Administration*, New York: Institute of Public Administration, 1937.
5 Weber, *Rationalism and Modern Society*.
6 Ross Hassig, *Aztec Warfare: Imperial Expansion and Political Control*, Norman: University of Oklahoma Press, 1998.
7 Jason Crowley, *The Psychology of the Athenian Hoplite: The Culture of Combat in Classical Athens*, Cambridge: Cambridge University Press, 2012.
8 Lorimer, *Sengokujidai*; Nakane and Oishi, *Tokugawa Japan*; William Wayne Ferris, *Heavenly Warriors: The Evolution of Japan's Warriors*, Cambridge, MA: Harvard University Press, 1995; Bloch, *Feudal Society*; Reynolds, *Fiefs and Vassals*; Philippe Contamine, *War in the Middle Ages*, trans. Michael Jones, Oxford: Blackwell, 1984.
9 Contamine, *War in the Middle Ages*; Marilyn Livingstone and Morgen Witzel, *The Road to Crécy: The English Invasion of France, 1346*, Harlow: Longman, 2005; Andrew Ayton, 'English Armies in the Fourteenth Century', in Anne Curry and Michael Hughes (eds), *Arms, Armies and Fortifications in the Hundred Years War*, Woodbridge: Boydell, 1994.
10 Contamine, *War in the Middle Ages*; Anne Curry, *The Hundred Years War*, Basingstoke: Macmillan, 1993.
11 Roberto Lopez, *Zaccaria: Genova Marinara nel Duecento*, Milan: Messina, 1933.
12 John Guilmartin, *Gunpowder and Galleys*, Cambridge: Cambridge University Press, 1976.
13 Livingstone and Witzel, *The Road to Crécy*; Anne Edwards, *The Grimaldis of Monaco*, New York: William Morrow, 1992.
14 Saunders, *Hawkwood*; Mallett, *Mercenaries and Their Masters*.
15 Machiavelli, *The Prince*; Machiavelli, *The Discourses*.
16 John Davis, *Corporations*, New York: G.P. Putnam's Sons, 1905.
17 Geoff Mortimer, *Wallenstein: The Enigma of the Thirty Years War*, New York: Springer, 2010; C.V. Wedgewood, *The Thirty Years War*, London: Jonathan Cape, 1963; Peter Gaunt, *The English Civil War: A Military History*, London: I.B. Tauris, 2014.
18 Boycott-Brown, *The Road to Rivoli*.
19 Mortimer, *Wallenstein*.
20 Mallett, *Mercenaries and Their Masters*.
21 Samuel P. Huntington, *The Soldier and the State: The Theory and Politics of Civil-Military Relations*, Cambridge, MA: Belknap Press, 1957; Samuel E. Finer, *The Man on Horseback: The Role of the Military in Politics*, London: Routledge, 2002.
22 Knight, *Britain Against Napoleon*.
23 Wedgewood, *The Thirty Years War*.
24 Davis, *Corporations*; Robert G. Eccles and Tim Youmans, 'Materiality in Corporate Governance: The Statement of Significant Audiences and Materiality', Harvard Business School working paper, 2015.
25 Milton Friedman, 'The Social Responsibility of a Business Is to Increase Its Profits', *New York Times Magazine*, 13 September 1970; Ayn Rand, *Atlas Shrugged*, New York: New

American Library, 1957; Ayn Rand, *The Fountainhead*, New York: New American Library, 1971.

26 Moore and Lewis, *Foundations of Corporate Empire*.

27 Raymond de Roover, 'Scholastic Economics: Survival and Lasting Influence from the Sixteenth Century to Adam Smith', *Quarterly Journal of Economics* 69 (2) (1955): 161–90.

28 Axworthy, 'Pulteney, Sir John'; Fryde, *William de la Pole*; Sutton, 'Whittington, Sir Richard'; Kathryn L. Reyerson, *Jacques Coeur: Entrepreneur and King's Bursar*, London: Pearson, 2004.

29 de Roover, *The Rise and Decline of the Medici Bank*; Hibbert, *The House of Medici*; Richard Ehrenberg, *Capital and Finance in the Age of the Renaissance: A Study of the Fuggers and Their Connections*, trans. H.M. Lucas, London: Jonathan Cape, 1928.

30 de Roover, *The Rise and Decline of the Medici Bank*; Hibbert, *The House of Medici*.

31 Ehrenberg, *Capital and Finance in the Age of the Renaissance*; L.C. Jain, *Indigenous Banking in India*, London: Macmillan, 1929; Andrea McElderry, *Shanghai Old-Style Banks (Ch'ien-chuang) 1800–1935*, Ann Arbor: Centre for Chinese Studies, University of Michigan, 1976.

32 Pollard, *The Genesis of Modern Management*; Sidney Pollard, *Peaceful Conquest: The Industrialization of Europe, 1760–1960*, Oxford: Oxford University Press, 1981; Joel Mokyr, *The Industrial Revolution: An Economic Perspective*, Boulder: Westview, 1999; Fitton, *The Arkwrights*; Donnachie, *Robert Owen*; George Unwin, *Samuel Oldknow and the Arkwrights: The Industrial Revolution at Stockport and Marple*, Manchester: Manchester Univerity Press, 1967; Janet Delve, 'Joseph Marie Jacquard: Inventor of the Jacquard Loom', *Annals of the History of Computing* 29 (4) (2007): 98–102.

33 Pollard, *The Genesis of Modern Management*; Urwick and Brech, *The Making of Scientific Management*.

34 Christopher Hill, *Liberty Against the Law: Some Seventeenth-Century Controversies*, London: Allen Lane, 1996.

35 Ashcraft, *Locke's Two Treatises on Government*; Ross Harrison, *Hobbes, Locke and Confusion's Empire: An Examination of Seventeenth-Century Political Philosophy*, Cambridge: Cambridge University Press, 2003.

36 Donnachie, *Robert Owen*.

37 Charles Wilson, *The History of Unilever: A Study in Economic Growth and Social Change*, London: Cassell, 1954; W.P. Jolly, *Lord Leverhulme: A Biography*, London: Constable, 1976.

38 Miller, *The Bon Marché*.

39 Mark Wahlgren Summers, *The Gilded Age, Or the Hazards of New Functions*, London: Pearson, 1997.

40 Demarest, *The River Ran Red*; Almont Lindsay, *The Pullman Strike: The Story of a Unique Experiment and a Great Labour Upheaval*, Chicago: University of Chicago Press, 1943; Edwin Palmer Hoyt, *The Guggenheims and the American Dream*, New York: Funk and Wagnalls, 1967; Matthew Josephson, *The Robber Barons*, New York: Harcourt Brace Jovanovich, 1990; Folsom, *The Myth of the Robber Barons*.

41 William Graham Sumner, *What Social Classes Owe to Each Other*, New York: Harper & Bros, 1883; Mike Hawkins, *Social Darwinism in European and American Thought, 1860–1945*, Cambridge: Cambridge University Press, 1997.

42 Arthur Twining Hadley, *Economics: An Account of the Relations Between Private Property and Public Welfare*, New York: Harper & Bros, 1896; Barbara Tuchman, *The Proud Tower*, New York: Macmillan, 1966; Douglas Steeples and David O. Whitten, *Democracy in Desperation: The Depression of 1893*, Westport: Greenwood, 1998.

43 Hadley, *Economics*; Lloyd, *Wealth Against Commonwealth*; Richard T. Ely, *Monopolies and Trusts*, New York: Macmillan, 1900; William Z. Ripley (ed.), *Trusts, Pools and Corporations*, Boston: Ginn & Co, 1905.

44 Thomas Archdeacon, *Becoming American: An Ethnic History*, New York: The Free Press, 1984.

45 Thorstein Veblen, *The Theory of the Leisure Class: An Economic Study in the Evolution of Institutions*, New York: Macmillan, 1899.

46 Craig Phelan, *Grand Master Workman: Terence Powderly and the Knights of Labor*, Westport: Greenwich, 2000; Paul Avrich, *The Haymarket Tragedy*, Princeton: Princeton University Press, 1984.

47 Bernard Mandel, *Samuel Gompers: A Biography*, New York: Penguin, 1963; Julie Greene, *Pure and Simple Politics: The American Federation of Labor and Political Activism, 1881–1917*, New York: Cambridge University Press, 1998; Melvyn Dubofsky, *We Shall Be All: A History of the Industrial Workers of the World*, New York: Quadrangle, 1973.

48 Taylor, *The Principles of Scientific Management*; Horace B. Drury, *Scientific Management*, New York: Longmans Green, 1915; Robert F. Hoxie, *Scientific Management and Labor*, New York: D. Appleton, 1915; Frank Watts, *An Introduction to the Psychological Problems of Industry*, London: George Allen & Unwin, 1921.

49 Beverly Gage, *The Day Wall Street Exploded: The Story of America in Its First Age of Terror*, New York: Oxford University Press, 2009; Woodcock, *Anarchism*; Candace Falk, *Love, Anarchy and Emma Goldman*, New Brunswick: Rutgers University Press, 1990; Ron Chernow, *The House of Morgan: An American Banking Dynasty and the Rise of Modern Finance*, New York: Atlantic Monthly Press, 1990.

50 Christopher Furness, *Industrial Peace and Industrial Efficiency*, West Hartlepool: Alexander Salton, 1908.

51 Benjamin Seebohm Rowntree, *The Human Factor in Business: Experiments in Industrial Democracy*, London: Longmans Green, 1921.

52 Lloyd, *Wealth Against Commonwealth*; Tarbell, *A History of the Standard Oil Company*; Jeremiah Jenks, *The Trust Problem*, New York: Macmillan, 1900; John Bates Clark, *The Control of the Trusts*, New York: Macmillan, 1901.

53 Charles R. Flint, *The Trust, Its Book: Being a Presentation of Several Aspects of the Latest Forms of Industrial Evolution*, New York: Doubleday Page, 2002.

54 Walther Rathenau, *The New Society*, London: Williams & Norgate, 1921.

55 Mark J. Roe, *Strong Managers, Weak Owners: The Political Roots of American Corporate Finance*, Princeton: Princeton University Press, 1994.

56 Adolph A. Berle and Gardiner C. Means, *The Modern Corporation and Private Property*, New York: Macmillan, 1932; William Z. Ripley, *From Main Street to Wall Street*, New York: Harper & Bros, 1926; Burnham, *The Managerial Revolution*.

57 Luke Barr, *Ritz and Escoffier: The Hotelier, the Chef and the Rise of the Leisure Class*, New York: Clarkson Potter, 2018.

58 Eric Gordon England, 'The Eternal Quest', Rowntree Management Conference Paper, 30 September 1928.

59 Ibid.

60 Donald T. Phillips, *Run to Win: Vince Lombardi on Coaching and Leadership*, New York: St Martin's, 2001; David Maraniss, *When Pride Still Mattered: A Life of Vince Lombardi*, New York: Simon & Schuster, 1999; John Eisenberg, *That First Season: How Vince Lombardi Took the Worst Team in the NFL and Set It on the Path to Glory*, New York: Houghton Mifflin, 2009.

61 Ibid.

62 Richard Osborne, *Herbert von Karajan: A Life in Music*, Boston: Northeastern University Press, 2000; Raymond Holden, *The Virtuoso Conductors*, London: Yale University Press, 2005.

63 Barry Miles, *Frank Zappa*, London: Atlantic Books, 2004.

64 R.H.F. Scott, *Jean-Baptiste Lully*, London: Peter Owen, 1972; Peter Kurth, *Isadora Duncan: A Sensational Life*, Boston: Little Brown, 2001.

65 Michael McCrum, *Thomas Arnold, Headmaster*, Oxford: Oxford University Press, 1989; Hugh Hawkins, *Between Harvard and America: The Educational Leadership of Charles W. Eliot*, New York: Oxford University Press, 1972.

11

LEADERSHIP BY CONQUEST

In the previous two chapters we discussed how leaders attempt to control power without making much distinction as to how they acquired that power. In this chapter and the next we will focus on leaders who obtain, in Max Weber's words, non-legitimate domination; that is, they seize power by force. These can be roughly divided into two categories: revolutions, where the intention is to dismantle the existing elites and their structures of power and replace them with a new ideology or faith; and takeovers, where the power structure remains the same and all that happens is one set of elites is replaced by another.

In the next chapter we will look at revolutionary leaders and how they acquire and maintain power, but in this chapter we will look at cases where elites are replaced by other elites. How do they persuade followers to transfer their loyalty from one leader to another? And why do followers agree to do so?

The two arenas where this supplanting of elites by other elites is most common are political regime changes and business takeovers. The latter are not (usually) non-legitimate in Weber's definition – they take place through established legal frameworks, often with the consent of all the elites involved. However, they usually happen without the consent of followers, who, as in the case of regime changes, are required to accept new leaders without having much say in the process. Ironically, illegal *coups d'état* usually have a degree of popular support, whereas legitimate business takeovers may have little or no support from followers.

Politics and power, hearts and minds

'Political power grows out of the barrel of a gun', Mao Zedong once told his followers, and he was not the only leader to believe that a non-legitimate transfer of power can be more efficient and effective than waiting for legitimate systems to do their work, especially if the elites already in power are using non-legitimate means to maintain their position.[1] Typically, non-legitimate transfers of power take place through one of three means: *coups d'état*, rebellion or civil war, or invasion and conquest by another state.

Not all of these transfers of power are successful, and many coups and invasions are defeated. One question, therefore, is what makes the difference? Does leadership play a role in the success or failure of these movements? As we saw in Chapter 6, the success or failure of any attempted coup was often used to pass retrospective judgement on the leaders; if they succeeded, clearly they were destined to do so; if they failed, that failure was due to some weakness on their part. But the picture is more complex than that, and success or failure depends in large part on the dynamics between the rival leaders and their followers. Each group of elites is trying to expand or defend its own power and has its own set of interests; how many followers who share those interests can it recruit?

There is another open question as to what leaders actually control during these movements. How much of what happens during an uprising is actually driven by the leaders, and how much is a product of what Rosa Luxemburg called spontaneity? Are the leaders of coups the moving force behind events, or are they the product of larger forces that make the coup possible in the first place? The answer would seem to be a mixture of both, and as we shall see again in the next chapter, the ability of leaders to shape events and take advantage of fortune does play an important role; however, there can be no leadership without opportunity. Events, circumstances and the demands of followers all come together to make a coup or an uprising possible, and only once they have done so do leaders emerge.

Coups d'état

The term *coup d'état* (stroke against the state) entered common use in the early nineteenth century, but the notion of regime change by force has been around since the beginning of civilisation. We have seen a number of examples already in this book, notably the successive coups in Rome that brought Galba, Otho, Vitellius and Vespasian to power respectively. The events of that year could also be classified as a civil war, and the two concepts overlap to a degree; failed *coups d'état* often lead to a longer internal conflict; for example, a failed military *coup d'état* in Spain was the opening act of the Spanish Civil War.[2] Somewhat arbitrarily, I have defined a coup as an attempt at regime change enacted over a relatively short period of time, not necessarily involving violence, whereas a civil conflict or an uprising is a longer and more complex series of events. I accept that there is considerable grey area between them.

Coups in the classical world were often supported by citizens if the coup leader promised to defend their city or their state. Mancur Olson described the problem as one of 'roving bandits' versus 'stationary bandits'. During times of anarchy and disorder, roving bandits plunder the countryside with no other motives than destruction and enrichment. To defend themselves from roving bandits, citizens hire other bandits to protect them. These stationary bandits will try to align their motives with those of the population, creating a bond whereby the population gives willing support in exchange for protection.[3]

But coups take place for other reasons. Sometimes the elites in power are seen as corrupt and self-serving, no longer meeting the needs of the people. When strong factions within the populace believe their state has been weakened or let down or have ambitions for 'greatness' in the form of economic power or territorial expansion, the conditions will be ripe for a coup, assuming a suitable leader can be found.

Exactly these conditions propelled Benito Mussolini to power in Italy in 1922. Taking advantage of a weak liberal government and an economy that had stalled in the aftermath of the First World War, Mussolini, a former socialist, harked back to traditional conservative values and a desire by many Italians to recreate the glory days when their nation had been the dominant power in the Mediterranean.[4] He also played on conservative Italian fears about the threat posed by socialism and employed a private army known as the *squadristi* to intimidate and assault left-wing politicians and trades union leaders. Mussolini also had a rival, Gabriele d'Annunzio, who had become a public hero after seizing the disputed city of Fiume, which many Italians regarded as rightly theirs, and holding it for over a year before being forced to surrender. More popular than Mussolini and with a large following of his own, d'Annunzio seemed like a leader in waiting.[5]

To forestall d'Annunzio as much as anything else, Mussolini gathered his *squadristi* and marched on Rome. When the prime minister, Luigi Facta, attempted to use military force to stop them, he was overruled by King Victor Emmanuel III, who forced Facta to resign and invited Mussolini to form a national government in coalition with several conservative factions. This was followed by an election where the Fascists and their allies won a large majority, which Mussolini used to cement his control of Italy until his overthrow.[6]

D'Annunzio was popular, a poet and war hero, but Mussolini had a strong programme to restore the Italian economy, recover its lost overseas possessions and make Italy great again. That appealed to the elites, who threw their support behind him. Why his opponents failed to respond and allowed him to tighten his grip on power is a mystery. Mussolini himself confessed that there were moments early in his regime when a determined opposition could have overthrown him, but no one emerged to lead it.[7]

Technically, Mussolini's assumption of power – like Hitler's – was legitimate; the king had the right to dismiss his prime minister and appoint a new one, and the result was confirmed by a democratic election (there were accusations of irregularities, but it is not clear whether these affected the overall result). The same could not be said of Napoleon Bonaparte's seizure of power in France in the coup of 18 Brumaire (9 November 1799). The events of Brumaire were the latest in a series of coups which had overthrown various revolutionary governments, beginning with the coup of Thermidor in 1794, which had seen the downfall of Robespierre and the Jacobin faction. The most recent strongman to arise, Emmanuel Sièyes, was a colourless technocrat, an intellectual who had engineered the downfall of most of his rivals but who lacked broad support. Faced with challenges to his authority, he invited Bonaparte, a highly successful and popular general, to stage a coup that would strengthen Sièyes's grip on power. Instead, Bonaparte double-crossed him and assumed power himself. Like Mussolini, Bonaparte identified with popular aspirations, to reverse recent military defeats and make France strong and prosperous once more; his coup attracted widespread public support.[8]

The craving for a strong leader who will serve national ambitions, usually by meeting the paradoxical goals of peace and prosperity on the one hand and military strength on the other, has played a key role in many successful coups, as coup leaders ride a wave of popular support. In Napoleon's case, the previous government had become fatally weakened by infighting, thus providing further opportunities for a coup.

The same is true of the coup of Yuan Shikai, the Chinese general who seized power after the fall of the empire. Yuan interposed himself between the empire, represented by child-Emperor Puyi, and the revolutionary Kuomintang movement, led by Sun Yat-sen, which had popular support in urban areas but lacked the military force to topple the empire. Yuan played both ends against the middle, negotiating with the Kuomintang while simultaneously compelling the abdication of Puyi and his own appointment as prime minister of China. Once in power, he used the army and support from conservative, pro-imperial elites to displace the Kuomintang and force Sun Yat-sen into exile. In 1915, Yuan declared himself emperor of China, but continued Kuomintang opposition meant he was not able to consolidate his hold on power before he died. Yuan was able to use his authority as general to keep control of the central institutions of the empire, but unlike Napoleon, he was unable to expand his power and create a broad power base. The Kuomintang, which had popular support, could not win over enough of the elites. Both Yuan and Sun failed, and China descended into chaos.[9]

Weak and complacent governments invite coups, and all that is needed is a combination of an ambitious leader and a group of followers who share the leader's ideology and are strong enough to place him or her in power. The classic example of an elite group apparently sitting idly by and doing nothing while their power eroded is the Merovingian dynasty, which ruled France from the mid-fifth century to the mid-eighth. Over the course of time the Merovingian monarchs delegated more and more of their power to their senior officials, the mayors of the palace, to the point where the mayors had more power than the kings. Following the death of King Theuderic III in 737, the mayor, Charles Martel, continued to rule without a king until his own death four years later. A new king, Childeric III, was crowned but deposed two years later in a bloodless coup by Martel's son Pepin the Short, who had the full support of the Frankish nobles, who agreed with Pepin's assertion that whoever controlled power should be entitled to it.[10]

Although Napoleon and Mussolini enjoyed popular support, some coups take place behind closed doors with little involvement by the populace. In these cases, the coup leaders often draw their support from foreign powers. In 1880s Hawai'i, opposition to the monarchy was led by the Hawaiian Patriotic League, a group which, despite its name, was mostly composed of foreign residents, including a number of wealthy American sugar plantation owners. The group received tacit encouragement from the government of the United States, which had long been interested in acquiring the islands as a strategic base in the Pacific. In 1888 the League seized control of the palace and forced King Kalakaua to sign the Bayonet Constitution, which handed over many of his powers to an elected assembly composed mostly of members of the League. Following the king's death 1891, his sister and successor, Queen Lili'uokulani, attempted to repeal the Bayonet Constitution and sought support among the old Hawai'ian nobility. The League's response was a second coup, using its superior weapons to overthrow the queen and turn Hawai'i into a republic. The islands were annexed by the United States in 1898.[11]

The Hawai'i example shows the importance of the power of followers. A successful coup depends not so much on how many followers you have but on what power they control. Two attempted coups against the Weimar government in Germany, the Kapp-Luttwitz Putsch and the Beer Hall Putsch, were quickly defeated when it quickly became apparent that neither the populace nor the elites were prepared to support the coup leaders. The Kapp-Luttwitz Putsch collapsed with opponents mounted a general strike; Hitler's Beer Hall Putsch ended almost before it began when the army and the police refused to support it and instead dispersed his followers with gunfire. It was the failure of this event that caused Hitler to realise he needed to build a broad coalition of support to try to take power by peaceful means.[12] A rather narrower defeat was experienced by French royalists who attempted to overthrow the revolutionary government in the coup of 13 Vendémiaire in 1795. Although the royalists had built a strong coalition of support among people discontented with the government, the bulk of the population and most of the army continued at that time to support the government; loyal troops led by Napoleon Bonaparte defeated the insurgents and broke the power of the royalists.[13]

Civil conflicts

Like coups, civil wars and other internal conflicts often begin when one group of elites is dissatisfied with the status quo and believes it and its followers have sufficient power to either overthrow the existing government or break away and create a new state. Sometimes one follows the other. The Zulu chieftain Mzilikazi rebelled against his king, Shaka, but lacked sufficient force to overthrow him. Changing his strategy, Mzilikazi led his followers out of Zululand, first into the Transvaal and then, under increasing pressure from Boer migrants, north into present-day Zimbabwe, where he founded a new state with its capital at Bulawayo. Mzilikazi also persuaded many other tribal groups to join his federation and, perhaps impressed by his military force, they agreed to do so.[14]

The American Civil War was the opposite case. The leaders of the southern states, feeling that their power was being eroded by the dominant north, chose to secede from the Union and set up their own polity, the Confederate States of America.[15] However, unlike Mzilikazi, they were unable to migrate, and as a result they were forced into an unequal war for dominance which, lacking the population and resources of the North, they were unable to win. Jefferson Davis, the president of the CSA, and his generals enjoyed a high degree of popular support, but they lacked the men and the guns to enforce their will.[16] More fortunate were the rebels in Texas, who revolted against the Mexican regime of the *caudillo* Antonio de Santa Anna. When Santa Anna invaded Texas, he found most of the population united against him and was defeated at the Battle of San Jacinto by the Texan leader Sam Houston. The Texan republic survived for ten years as an independent state, largely because, like the Hawai'ian rebels later in the century, Houston was able to call on American support. Even so, the Texan state was not fully viable, and the United States annexed it ten years later.[17]

Most civil wars, however, follow the principle of 'last man standing', with victory going to the leader who is able to gather enough power to see off all rivals. Generally, this is done by absorbing other smaller factions, building coalitions of followers who may be united by little else than loyalty to the most powerful leader. Followers, in turn, are seeking to impose their will on rival groups and pick the leader who they believe will be strongest and best able to help them achieve their goal. During the *Sengoku-jidai* (Age of the Country at War) in sixteenth-century Japan, the number of factions slowly dwindled to just two. One, based in eastern Japan, was led by Tokugawa Ieyasu; the other was a coalition of his opponents led by Mori Terumoto. After Mori's defeat at the battle of Sekigahara, which left Tokugawa in undisputed power, Mori's own followers turned against him and forced him to retire from public life.[18] The so-called Age of the Sturlungs, a period of prolonged conflict in Iceland, likewise saw rival chieftains vying for support. They were eliminated one by one, and eventually the people appealed to the king of Norway to intervene. The conflicted ended with the formerly independent Commonwealth of Iceland dissolving itself, accepting the Norwegian king as Iceland's ruler.[19]

The *Sengoku-jidai* and the Age of the Sturlungs are unusual in that they pitted multiple leaders heading multiple factions against each other, with factions dropping out because their leaders were killed or because followers had lost confidence in them. More commonly, such as in the American Civil War, civil wars are a dyadic struggle with two rival factions competing for power. The Fronde, a series of conflicts between the nobility and leading generals on the one hand and the supporters of the young King Louis XIV on the other flickered fitfully through the mid-seventeenth century; neither side was able to gain a decisive advantage, but ultimately, public support swung to the king. The nobles, leaders of the opposition, were unable to unite and often quarrelled among themselves, whereas the king's supporters remained cohesive and had a clear ideology – loyalty to the crown – which people could understand and appreciate.[20]

The Carlist civil wars in nineteenth-century Spain were likewise fought between supporters of Queen Isabella II and her cousin and rival for the throne, Carlos de

Bourbon. The Carlist rebels were, for a long period, unable to seize the throne, but the queen's supporters were not strong enough to put them down; eventually she was forced to abdicate. The Carlists, having won the throne, could not keep it, and in 1876 Isabella's son Alfonso XII seized power.[21] In both the Fronde and the Carlist cases, the appeal to inherited authority, with the legitimacy and tradition that accompanied it, was strong; the sovereign was able to draw on this source of power, whereas his or her rivals were not.

As with *coup d'états*, whether factions prospered in civil wars depended not so much on the qualities of the leaders as on the power of their followers. This does not mean that quality was unimportant; the perception of a leader's strength and ability was a major factor in determining whether followers were willing to follow. If Prince Charles Edward Stuart had been a more intelligent leader and followed the advice of his talented military commander, Lord George Murray, he might well have succeeded in occupying Scotland in 1745 and defending it against the British Crown. Instead, his rash decision to march on London with only a tiny army doomed the Jacobite rising to failure. Once Charles was forced to retreat, his support began to ebb; at the final battle at Culloden there were more Scots in the government ranks than there were in the Jacobite army.[22] Hugh O'Neill, Earl of Tyrone, commanded widespread support in Ireland at the end of the sixteenth century, and on multiple occasions during the ten-year conflict known as Tyrone's Rebellion, he had opportunities to defeat the English army and wrest control of Ireland from English hands. But he failed to recognise these opportunities or take advantage of them, and after each defeat the English forces were able to regroup and continue to fight. In 1603, Tyrone was forced to abandon the fight and go into exile.[23]

Invasions

A successful invasion of a country requires more than just military occupation. In Ireland, the English built fortresses and planted towns with migrants from England and Scotland, but through the centuries they never succeeded in fully quelling opposition and resistance. Heavy repression, such as happened in the reigns of Henry VIII, Elizabeth, Oliver Cromwell and William III, created more bitterness and sowed the seeds for future rebellion. In the nineteenth century, the failure to grant home rule radicalised the Irish populace and created greater support for full independence, especially after the Easter Rising.[24]

Successful invaders are generally have something to offer the followers of a defeated leader. Before launching the invasion, they are clear what that offering will be. Often, the invader senses discontent among followers in the target country before launching the invasion. In two successful invasions of England in the eleventh century, the invading leader was aware of discontent inside the country and believed that at least some of the people would come over to his side and support him. When Cnut of Denmark landed in England, the English king Aethelred the Unready had already been driven from his throne and had only just returned. Apart from Edmund Ironside, the king's son, few offered any resistance. After Edmund was defeated, Cnut made a point of co-opting the leading Anglo-Saxon notables and elites into his regime, with the result that his two-decade rule over England was largely peaceful.[25]

William the Conqueror, arriving in 1066, was likewise aware that there was discontent with the ruling house of Godwin and that King Harald Godwinson had quarrelled with his brother and forced him into exile. In fact, resistance was stronger than William expected, and it took some hard fighting before the Anglo-Saxon nobility finally recognised *force majeure*. He too co-opted the remaining nobles, arranging marriages to leading Norman families and subsuming them into the Norman-French aristocracy.[26] The Arab invasion of Spain similarly took advantage of the weaknesses of the Visigoth kingdom and its people and won over many of them peacefully by promising good government and the restoration of law and order. In the early seventeenth century, the Manchus took advantage of the weakness and instability of the Ming dynasty in China, encouraging soldiers and officials to defect to them. So many did so that the Manchu army that marched into Beijing numbered more ethnic Chinese than Manchus.[27]

Napoleon Bonaparte's French empire also relied on co-opting local elites and bringing them into power. In Italy, Bonaparte initially relied on Italian revolutionaries who believed in the ideals of the French Revolution and intended to set up revolutionary states of their own. When Napoleon proclaimed himself emperor and annexed most of the peninsula to his empire as the Kingdom of Italy – the remainder, the Kingdom of Sicily, was ruled by his sister Caroline and her husband, Marshal Joachim Murat – most of the former radicals deserted him; in their place, Napoleon co-opted the old conservative elites, the nobility and the merchant classes.[28] In the Netherlands, likewise, the revolutionary movement which had forced the House of Orange from power was co-opted into a new republic and later into a kingdom. In the western German states, the French capitalised on local fears of domination by Prussia or Austria, the two main Germanic powers, and offered the states a form of limited independence, albeit under fairly strict French control.[29]

Failure to co-opt local elites or gain broader popular support makes invasion a costly and risky business. Following the Spanish-American War, Filipino independence fighters declared the creation of the First Republic of the Philippines. The United States, which had taken possession of the islands under the terms of the Treaty of Paris, did not recognise the new state and occupied the islands with military force. The result was an extremely bloody war which cost around five thousand American and at least 250,000 Filipino lives. Guerrilla resistance continued even after the main power of the Filipino army was broken. Appalled by the casualties, the American government changed tack and withdrew much of its army, creating civilian institutions, including a democratic government, and gradually handing these over to local control.[30]

The Prussian invasion of France in 1870 was successful in the first instance, with the main French field army destroyed and Emperor Napoleon III captured – all

within six weeks. But Paris refused to capitulate; whereas the Prussian army con‐
centrated on laying siege to the city, resistance movements and volunteer armies
sprang up all over France. Alarmed by the growing resistance, the Prussians signed a
peace treaty and withdrew.[31] By bringing the war to a swift end, the Prussians may
have avoided the fate of Java and its king, Dharmavamsa, who attempted to conquer
the state of Srivijaya in Sumatra. Landing with overwhelming force, Dharmavamsa
quickly overran much of the state but failed to capture its maharaja, Culamanivar‐
madeva. The latter organised a resistance movement among his vassals and called
for assistance from China. His counter‐stroke shattered Dharmavamsa's army and
forced him to retreat to Java. His own reputation destroyed, Dharmavamsa was
overthrown by his nobles soon after.[32]

Acceptance and control

It is one thing to acquire power; it is another to keep it. During conflict, followers
choose leaders who have the power to get things done; either they have the skills
and the knowledge, such as Sam Houston or Tokugawa Ieyasu did, or they have
symbolic‐charismatic authority, such as Mussolini did. Preferably, they have both,
such as Napoleon Bonaparte did. But as the rival Roman emperors found out, once
they had power, they needed to adjust their stance in order to keep it. The naked
display of power and aggression was no longer enough. Followers wanted some‐
thing more.

They want, of course, the things we discussed in Chapter 4: credibility, fairness
and guidance. Cnut provided these in England, although his successors failed to
do so; thus, his empire did not survive for long after he died. Napoleon also pro‐
vided these, at least in the first instance, enacting a wide range of social and legal
reforms, ranging from improvements to education to the writing of a new legal
code to the introduction of the metric system. That he did these things with the
primary purpose of making France more fit to wage war was not noticed by his
followers; at least, not at first.[33] In medieval Spain, although there were excep‐
tions and sporadic persecutions of other religions, on the whole the Arab rulers
treated their conquered subjects with respect and dignity, even promoting them
to high posts in government. The Norman conquerors of Sicily at the end of
the eleventh century did likewise. Under Roger II, the Sicilian court was a place
where Christians, Jews and Muslims mingled as equals, all treated with tolerance
and respect.[34]

Norman Sicily is a rare case in which leaders managed to pull the great majority
of their followers together and rule a unified polity. More commonly, leaders who
have just assumed power will continue to look to their original follower group, while
at the same time trying to broaden their power base by attracting other followers
(in part, as a means of diluting the power of the original followers and winning
more control). Napoleon Bonaparte was adept at doing this; while continuing to
rely on the army for the backbone of his support, he reached out to other groups
that had suffered under the corrupt revolutionary government, including judges,

administrators and merchants. His nephew Napoleon III, who was elected president of France in 1848 and then seized permanent power in a coup in 1852, followed his uncle's example and tried to appeal to a broad range of follower groups to help him establish his authority but still relied heavily on the army and the conservative bourgeoisie.[35]

On the other side of the coin, newly established leaders will continue to repress those who oppose them. Indeed, there is evidence to suggest that repression usually increases following a successful coup.[36] In the months after he seized power in France, Napoleon III ordered the arrest of more than twenty thousand of his opponents, most of them republicans who objected to his re-establishment of the French Empire. Thousands were exiled from France; some were sent to the penal colony at Devil's Island, many without trial or due process of law.[37] Soon after Hitler's rise to power in Germany, five thousand communists were arrested and sent to the newly opened Dachau concentration camp; in the end, more than three million Germans were arrested for political offences, in addition to those arrested because of ethnicity, religion or sexual orientation.[38]

Reaching out to other follower groups sometimes means looking for sources of authority beyond simple access to power and the consent of followers. Symbolic forms of authority can become particularly important. Some leaders revived previous symbols. Napoleon re-established monarchies and made himself emperor in a conscious imitation of Charlemagne; he also created a new class of nobles, turning his military commanders into counts, dukes and princes. Yuan Shikai attempted to re-establish the Chinese Empire, and Mussolini harked back to the Roman Empire; the symbol of his rule, the *fasces*, was based on the axes carried by some high Roman officials as a token of authority. Hitler shrugged off most of the old royal symbolism of Prussia and created new symbols to reinforce his vision of a thousand-year Reich, such as the grandiose architecture of Albert Speer; the symbolism and heraldry of military units, such as the SS, which was derived in part from Norse mythology; and the co-opted music of Richard Wagner, which spoke of high drama with historical roots.[39] Seldomly, a new leader consciously rejects symbolism; unlike other military coup leaders, who often promote themselves to high rank, Jerry Rawlings in Ghana retained his original rank of flight lieutenant and continued to drive his own car from his residence to his office.[40] Such a rejection of symbols is itself, of course, a highly symbolic act.

As well as symbolic authority, new leaders often try to create dynasties or, at least, control who will succeed them. There may have been valid reasons for this: according to Andrej Kokkonen and Anders Sundell, dynasties based on inheritance by primogeniture were inherently more stable, perhaps because people knew who the new leader would be, thus removing a good deal of uncertainty.[41] That said, inheritance also gave people time to size up the new leader and determine whether or not they would follow him or her. Again, the failure of Richard Cromwell to succeed his father comes to mind.

Corporate takeovers

Corporate takeovers are similar to *coups d'état*, although as noted, nearly all take place within legal frameworks (although coercion and force have sometimes been used to gain consent). Some take the form of boardroom battles for control. In 1985, the CEO of Apple Computers, John Sculley, organised a coup against the executive chairman, Steve Jobs. Sculley's plan was to restructure the company such that power would be concentrated around himself, rather than Jobs. When Jobs attempted to fire Sculley, he realised he did not have enough support on the board; his authority had been eroded by poor financial results and increasing competition from Microsoft and IBM. Seeing his own power disappearing, Jobs ceded control to Sculley and resigned.[42]

These kinds of internal coups are common to other types of organisations; they take place when followers lose confidence in the original leader. Once that has happened, the leader is doomed to lose power unless he or she can build a new coalition of followers, but that rarely happens. More commonly, followers settle on a new leader who has the kind of authority they desire and who they believe will serve their ends. In 1975, opposition within the UK Conservative Party to its leader, Edward Heath, coalesced around the figure of Margaret Thatcher, the former secretary of state for education. Although Thatcher had not been previously seen as a leadership contender, she was the choice of the right wing of the party, which had become disenchanted with the more centrist position of Heath. Thatcher also represented the rising middle class within the party, rather than the old-style Tory grandees like Heath or William Whitelaw. As a result of this coalition of support from factions seeking change in the party, Thatcher defeated both Heath and Whitelaw in a leadership contest and went on to become leader of the Conservative Party and, four years later, prime minister. In 1991, after several years of declining popularity within the party, her colleagues staged another coup, in which she was replaced by John Major.[43]

A different and arguably more disruptive type of change comes when businesses are taken over by outside agencies, either other businesses or the state. Takeovers of businesses as a going concern, as opposed to the rescue of those on the edge of bankruptcy, are a relatively new phenomenon, although as noted, businesses often did come together through voluntary partnerships. In these cases, the individual businesses kept their own identity and could easily de-merge, meaning the effect of these mergers on followers was relatively limited.[44]

The first large-scale takeovers began during the Industrial Revolution. Robert Owen, during his career as an industrialist, experienced two takeovers, one as a young man when Peter Drinkwater's mill in Manchester, which he had been managing, was sold to Samuel Oldknow, and one when he himself took over David Dale's mill at New Lanark. Frustratingly, Owen tells us very little about the takeover in Manchester, but it is clear he did not like Oldknow and refused the offer to stay on as manager even at a greatly increased salary. At New Lanark, he took over from

Dale an established business with a workforce and management already in place. By Owen's own testimony, working conditions under Dale had been harsh, and he moved swiftly to mitigate the situation and make life for his workers more bearable. We can only assume that, in this case, the takeover was regarded as a positive move by Owen's followers.[45]

Less positive were the views of workers employed by the big industrial combinations, the trusts, in America's Gilded Age. Again, we know frustratingly little about their views, in large part because many of the workers were semi-literate, at best; they had to rely on others – social welfare campaigners, journalists, anarchists and labour leaders – to give them a voice. It is thanks to the journalist Ida Tarbell, for example, that we know that one method used by John D. Rockefeller to compel smaller oil businesses to merge was campaigns of violence and intimidation against their workers. Tarbell had seen some of this at first hand – her father had been in the oil industry – and one of Rockefeller's former executives, Henry Flagler, had given her more detail of the arson, beatings and shootings that were used to put pressure on workers of rival firms, who in turn put pressure on their owners.[46]

The mergers went ahead, but it is doubtful if anyone was happy, workers or managers. Flagler was just one of many Standard Oil executives who regretted joining forces with Rockefeller. In other trusts, some actively rebelled against their masters. Richard Reynolds reluctantly agreed to merge his family-owned chewing tobacco firm into the Tobacco Trust after coming under severe coercive pressure. In 1907, angry at the mismanagement and inefficiency of the trust, defying its leaders to stop him, Reynolds launched a bid to break away. The campaign took four years, but ultimately R. J. Reynolds became independent once more.[47]

Some business leaders were coerced into joining the trusts, but others merged their firms because they believed this was in their own best interests; their firms would prosper, and they would make more money. Few if any consulted their workers before making the decision to merge; that would have gone against the prevailing ethos of 'ownership', in which the business was seen as the entrepreneur's personal property, to be disposed of as they saw fit. In fact, as Reynolds was quick to realise, few of these entrepreneurs made much money by joining the trusts. Huge and monolithic, the trusts struggled to achieve economies of scale and became increasingly inefficient and costly to run.

When leaders responded by cutting costs, the workers went on strike. Striking, it seemed, was the only way they could express themselves and the only way of winning back power. Although cause and effect are hard to determine, it would seem to be no coincidence that the level of labour unrest and violence in America increased at almost exactly the same time that the monopolistic trusts were being formed and many small firms were losing their independence or, indeed, that the unrest and violence reached their greatest levels among workers at the trusts. As already noted, the level of violence at Guggenheim's mining combination, ASARCO, reached the point of pitched battles between armed miners and Pinkerton agents. Guggenheim, who initially favoured repression, had a change of heart and backed down; by the early 1910s, he was writing articles in favour of tolerance and better labour relations.[48] In 1914 a serious strike at a Standard Oil subsidiary, Colorado Iron and Fuel, led Rockefeller's son John D. Rockefeller Jr to call in the noted Canadian labour lawyer William Lyon Mackenzie King to work out a peace plan. Among King's recommendations were greater consultation between employers and workers and the treatment of the latter like partners in enterprise.[49]

The early twentieth century saw an increase in interest in worker consultation, but this interest was by no means universal. The trusts were replaced by the large conglomerates, such as Alfred Mond's Imperial Chemical Industries in Britain and, later, Harold Geneen's ITT in America Once again, smaller firms were bought up and absorbed into these larger entities.[50] There is little evidence that workers were consulted, yet again, the larger entities were riven by strikes. It is instructive to note what happened at nationalised industries in Britain. During the First World War, when the ship-building industry was taken under state control, the Clydeside area of Glasgow, already restive, became a centre for labour revolt. Some labour leaders were arrested and exiled from Glasgow, but after the war ended, new leaders, such as William Gallacher and Emanuel Shinwell, emerged.[51]

Some of these leaders, like Gallacher, had links to the communist movement, and this, too, created an interesting dynamic. It seems clear that workers regarded nationalisation – even when carried out under a left-wing government – not as a move towards a socialist workers' paradise but as a concentration of power in the hands of the state at the workers' expense.

The waves of nationalisation in the early 1950s and the 1960s were accompanied by a similar rise in activism. Automobile-maker British Leyland experienced a series of crippling labour disputes and strikes. Blame was laid at the door of the chief union organiser, Derek Robinson, known popularly as Red Robbo. A member of the Communist Party, Robinson was seen as an arch-agitator who stirred up the workers against the company. In fact, many of the strikes at British Leyland were spontaneous 'wildcat' strikes organised by workers themselves, and there is probably truth to the view that Robinson was more often a moderating force, holding back his more radical followers.[52] Discontent in the coal-mining industry coalesced around Arthur Scargill, who rose to become leader of the National Union of Mineworkers and led it through a long-running strike. Like Robinson, Scargill was seen as the architect of the strike, urging his fellow miners on; in reality, at the beginning he enjoyed widespread support among the miners and represented the views of many of them. However, as time went on, his own increasingly radical views alienated his more moderate followers, and this lack of solidarity within the NUM was one of the reasons for the ultimate failure of the miners' strike.[53]

Whatever their other virtues and vices, trades unions have historically been about the only way for workers to have their voices heard on the issues of takeovers and changes of ownership. The belief by owners that they can do whatever they wish with 'their' businesses, including disposing of them, has not been widely shared by followers. When they object, and their objections are not heard, they tend to vote with their feet and, sometimes, with their fists.

Notes

1 Mao Zedong, *Quotations From Chairman Mao Tse-Tung*, Beijing: Foreign Languages Press, 1972.

2 Hugh Thomas, *The Spanish Civil War*, London: Penguin, 2003; Stanley G. Payne, *The Spanish Civil War*, Cambridge: Cambridge University Press, 2012; Payne, *Fascism in Spain*.

3 Mancur Olson, *Power and Prosperity: Outgrowing Communist and Capitalist Dictatorships*, Oxford: Oxford University Press, 2000.

4 Bosworth, *Mussolini*; Neville, *Mussolini*; Adrian Lyttleton, *The Seizure of Power: Fascism in Italy, 1919–1929*, London: Routledge, 2009.

5 Michael Ledeen, *D'Annunzio: The First Duce*, London: Routledge, 2001; Lucy Hughes-Hallett, *Gabriele d'Annunzio: Poet, Seducer and Preacher of War*, New York: Knopf, 2014.

6 Ibid.

7 Robert Paxton, *The Anatomy of Fascism*, New York: Knopf, 2004.

8 Doyle, *The Oxford History of the French Revolution*; Chandler, *Napoleon*; McLynn, *Napoleon*; Georges Lefebvre and Albert Soboul, *The Directory*, London: Routledge and Kegan Paul, 1962.

9 Sharman, *Sun Yat-sen*; Kayloe, *The Unfinished Revolution*; Ernest P. Young, *The Presidency of Yuan Shih-K'ai: Liberalism and Dictatorship in Early Republican China*, Ann Arbor: University of Michigan Press, 1977.

10 Fouracre, *The Age of Charles Martel*; Rosamond McKitterick, *The Frankish Kingdoms Under the Carolingians*, London: Longman, 1999; Burnham, *The Managerial Revolution*.

11 Lili'uokulani, *Hawaii's Story by Hawaii's Queen*; Ralph Simpson Kuykendall, *The Hawaiian Kingdom, 1784–1893*, Honolulu: University of Hawaii Press, 1967.

12 Kershaw, *Hitler*; Anthony McElligott, *Weimar Germany*, Oxford: Oxford University Press, 2009; John Dornberg, *Munich 1923: The Story of Hitler's First Grab for Power*, New York: Harper & Row, 1982.

13 Chandler, *Napoleon*; McLynn, *Napoleon*.

14 R. Kent Rasmussen, *Mzilikazi of Ndbele*, London: Heinemann, 1977; Peter Becker, *Path of Blood: The Rise and Conquests of Mzilikazi, Founder of the Matabele Tribe of Southern Africa*, London: Penguin, 1979; E.A. Ritter, *Shaka Zulu*, London: Penguin, 1978.

15 Edward L. Ayers, *What Caused the Civil War? Reflections on the South and Southern History*, New York: W.W. Norton, 2005; Emory M. Thomas, *The Confederate Nation, 1861–1865*, New York: Harper & Row, 1979.

16 Catton, *Army of the Potomac*; Allen C. Guelzo, *Fateful Lightning: A New History of the Civil War and Reconstruction*, New York: Oxford University Press, 2012.

17 Sam W. Haynes and Gerald D. Saxon (eds), *Contested Empire: Rethinking the Texas Revolution*, College Station: Texas A&M University Press, 2015; James L. Haley, *Sam Houston*, Norman: University of Oklahoma Press, 2002.

18 Jansen, *The Making of Modern Japan*; Tsutsui, *A Companion to Japanese History*; Michael James Lorimer, *Sengokujidai: Autonomy, Decision and Unity in Later Medieval Japan*, London: Olympia, 2009.

19 Adelsteinsson, *A Piece of Horse Liver*; Karlsson, *A History of Iceland*; Thorsson, *The Sagas of the Icelanders*.

20 Orest Ranum, *The Fronde: A French Revolution, 1648–1652*, New York: W.W. Norton, 1993.

21 Edgar Holt, *The Carlist Wars in Spain*, New York: Putnam, 1967.

22 Frank McLynn, *Charles Edward Stuart: A Tragedy in Many Acts*, London: Routledge, 1988; John Prebble, *Culloden*, London: Athenaeum, 1962.

23 James O'Neill, *The Nine Years War, 1593–1603: O'Neill, Mountjoy and the Military Revolution*, Dublin: Four Courts Press, 2018.

24 S.J. Connolly (ed.), *The Oxford Companion to Irish History*, Oxford: Oxford University Press, 1998; Charles Townshend, *Easter 1916: The Irish Rebellion*, London: Penguin, 1996.

25 Timothy Bolton, *Cnut the Great*, London: Yale University Press, 2017.

26 David C. Douglas, *William the Conqueror: The Norman Impact Upon England*, Berkeley: University of California Press, 1964.

27 Roger Collins, *The Arab Conquest of Spain, 710–797*, Oxford: Blackwell, 1989; Hucker, *China to 1850*; Frederic Wakeman, *The Great Enterprise: The Manchu Reconstruction of Imperial Order in Seventeenth-Century China*, Berkeley: University of California Press, 1985; John King Fairbank and Merle Goldman, *China: A New History*, Cambridge, MA: Belknap, 2006.

28 Owen Connolly, *Napoleon's Satellite Kingdoms*, New York: The Free Press, 1966; Desmond Gregory, *Napoleon's Italy*, New York: AUP, 2001.

29 Connolly, *Napoleon's Satellite Kingdoms*.

30 A.B. Feuer, *America at War: The Philippines, 1898–1913*, Santa Barbara: Greenwood, 2002; Stuart Creighton Miller, *Benevolent Assimilation: The American Conquest of the Philippines, 1899–1903*, New Haven: Yale University Press, 1982.

31 Michael Howard, *The Franco-Prussian War: The German Invasion of France, 1870–1871*, London: Rupert Hart-Davis, 1961; Alistair Horne, *The Fall of Paris: The Siege and the Commune, 1870–71*, London: Macmillan, 1965.

32 Munoz, *Early Kingdoms*.

33 Chandler, *Napoleon*; McLynn, *Napoleon*; Roberts, *Napoleon the Great*.

34 Hubert Houben, *Roger II of Sicily: Ruler Between East and West*, Cambridge: Cambridge University Press, 2002; John Julius Norwich, *The Kingdom in the Sun, 1130–1194*, London: Longman, 1970.

35 James F. McMillan, *Napoleon III*, London: Routledge, 1991; Roger Price, *The French Second Empire: An Anatomy of Political Power*, Cambridge: Cambridge University Press, 2007.

36 George Derpanopoulos, Erica Frantz, Barbara Geddes and Joseph Wright, 'Are Coups Good For Democracy?', *Research and Politics* 3 (1), 2016.

37 McMillan, *Napoleon III*; Price, *The French Second Empire*.

38 Gill, *An Honorable Defeat*; David Clay Large (ed.), *Contending With Hitler: Varieties of German Resistance in the Third Reich*, Cambridge: Cambridge University Press, 2013.

39 Kershaw, *Hitler*; Shirer, *The Rise and Fall of the Third Reich*; Richard Grunberger, *The Twelve-Year Reich: A Social History of Nazi Germany, 1933–1945*, New York: Holt, Rinehart and Winston, 1971.

40 Sillah, *African Coup d'Etat*.

41 Andrej Kokkonen and Anders Sundell, 'Delivering Stability: Primogeniture and Autocratic Survival in European monarchies, 1000–1800', QoG Working Paper, University of Gothenburg, 2012.

42 Isaacson, *Steve Jobs*; Jeffrey S. Young, *Steve Jobs: The Journey Is the Reward*, Glenview: Scott Foresman, 1987.

43 John Campbell, *Margaret Thatcher: The Iron Lady*, London: Pimilico, 2003.

44 de Roover, *The Rise and Decline of the Medici Bank*; Origo, *The Merchant of Prato*.

45 Donnachie, *Robert Owen*.

46 Tarbell, *The History of Standard Oil Company*; Tarbell, *All in the Day's Work*.

47 Nannie M. Tilley, *The R.J. Reynolds Tobacco Company*, Chapel Hill: University of North Carolina Press, 1985.

48 Hoyt, *The Guggenheims*.

49 Daphne Taras, 'The North American Workplace: From Employee Representation to Employee Involvement', in Bruce E. Kaufman *et al.* (eds), *Industrial Relations to Human Resources and Beyond: The Evolving Process of Employee Relations Management*, Armonk: M.E. Sharpe, 2003; William Lyon Mackenzie King, *Industry and Humanity*, Toronto: University of Toronto Press, 1918.

50 Hector Bolitho, *Alfred Mond, First Lord Melchett*, London: Martin Secker, 1932; Anthony Sampson, *The Sovereign State of ITT*, Greenwich: Fawcett Publications, 1974; Robert J. Schoenberg, *Geneen*, New York: W.W. Norton, 1985.

51 McLean, *The Legend of Red Clydeside*; Peter Slowe, *Manny Shinwell*, London: Pluto Press, 1983.

52 Otto Jacobi *et al.* (eds), *Technological Change, Rationalisation and Industrial Relations*, London: Routledge, 1986.

53 Peter Wilsher, Donald McIntyre and Michael Jones (eds), *Strike: Thatcher, Scargill and the Miners*, London: Andre Deutsch, 1985; Michael Crick, *Scargill and the Miners*, London: Penguin, 1985; Jonathan Winterton and Ruth Winterton, *Coal, Crisis and Conflict: The 1984–85 Miners' Strike in Yorkshire*, Manchester: Manchester University Press, 1989.

12

LEADERSHIP IN REVOLUTIONS

If *coups d'état*, civil wars and invasions take place with a view to replacing one set of elites with another very similar set of elites, revolutions have the aim of replacing the old power structure entirely.[1] Typically, they feature an attempt by followers to pull down the leaders and take control themselves. In reality, this almost never happens: the new revolutionary leaders may start off as representatives of the people, but all too often they simply turn into the new elite. As Crane Brinton put it in his study of revolutions, 'All are begun in hope and moderation, all reach a crisis in a reign of terror, and all end in something like a dictatorship'.[2]

A distinction between coups and revolutions might thus seem to be a false one: both very often end up in the same place. However, there are differences in terms of power, authority and the nature of the social space, enough to make the subject of revolutionary leadership worthy of separate treatment. As Brinton also points out, revolutionary groups begin outside the existing structures of power, or as we might put it, beyond the legitimate social space.[3] The leaders of the Confederate States during the American Civil War, or Napoleon Bonaparte and his nephew emerged from within the existing power structures; revolutionary movements, on the other hand, have to create a new social space, often outside existing law, and then gradually persuade followers to switch from one to the other. A classic example is the women's suffrage movement, which, particularly in Britain and America, created its own parallel social space with leaders and followers, from which it launched its struggle against the existing authorities.

Brinton argues that a 'revolution by consent' is not really a revolution: to him, revolutions are something that one group, often a minority, imposes on the rest of society.[4] In *Crowds and Power*, Elias Canetti argues the opposite: a revolution succeeds when enough people are ready to follow it and fails when it is unable to gather enough followers with enough power to enforce its will.[5] There are also internal power struggles, revolutions within revolutions. In his study of the French

Revolution, Simon Schama describes how the early revolutionary leaders, such as the Marquis de Lafayette, were pushed aside by more radical figures, such as Danton and Robespierre. The latter group succeeded because they could mobilise more followers who had, through force of numbers, more power; they could turn out the Paris mobs, whereas Lafayette could only count on the doubtful loyalty of a few army and national guard units. Even these, as time passed, sensed which way the wind was blowing and began defecting to the popular movement.[6] On the other hand, following the English Civil War, Oliver Cromwell was able to see off the challenge of the radical movements, the Diggers and the Levellers, because he enjoyed a broad range of support among the army, the merchant classes and some of the more liberal gentry and nobles.[7]

The examples of Lafayette and Cromwell remind us of one of the paradoxes of revolution: whereas many revolutionary movements are made or at least taken over by followers at the lowest end of the social scale, their leaders very often come from the middle class or even from the elites. Schama has pointed out that many early leaders of the French Revolution, including Lafayette and Mirabeau, came from the nobility; those who edged them out, such as Danton, Desmoulins and Robespierre, were from the middle classes. Robespierre and Desmoulins were both lawyers by profession.[8] The same is true of other revolutionary leaders: Oliver Cromwell was a landowner from the gentry classes, Mao Zedong was the son of a landowner and later worked as a librarian and Ho Chi Minh's father was a magistrate; Ho himself allegedly worked as a pastry chef in London, an occupation which in his home country of colonial Viet Nam might well have been considered rather bourgeois.[9]

Thomas Rainsborough, one of the leaders of the Levellers, was a navy officer and former diplomat; Giuseppe Mazzini, one of the leading Italian revolutionaries of the nineteenth century, was the son of a university professor; and Rafael Guillén, who, under the names Subcomandante Marcos and Delegate Zero, was one of the leaders of the Zapatista movement in Mexico in the 1990s, was a self-professed member of the middle classes, the son of a businessman who owned a chain of furniture stores.[10] The list could go on for some time. There are of course examples to the contrary; Wat Tyler, the principal leader of the Peasants Revolt in England, was a working man, and in late-fourteenth-century China, an impoverished beggar named Zhu Yuanzhang, most of whose family had starved to death in a recent famine, rose to lead the Red Turban Revolt and then become the first emperor of the Ming Dynasty.[11] Carlos Fonseca, one of the founders of the Sandinista Liberation Front in Nicaragua, was the illegitimate son of a peasant woman (his co-founder, Ernesto Cardenal, came from a wealthy family).[12] There are other examples, but it is still remarkable how often the middle classes manage to take control of revolutionary movements.

But do they seize control by force, as Crane Brinton suggests? Or are they invited to do so, as Canetti implies? There are several questions we must ask about revolutionary leaderships: how are leaders chosen? How do they emerge, and why? What qualities do followers ask of them? We also need to look at their sources of authority: what makes them acceptable as leaders? Finally, why do some revolutionary movements succeed, whereas others fail? Asymmetries of force are clearly one reason, but does leadership also contribute to success or failure? if so, how?

The rise of revolutionary leaders

Crane Brinton argues that all revolutions have broadly similar features, but paradoxically, each is also unique in that it reflects the circumstances of its time, the desires of the revolutionary leaders and the nature of the opposition they face. The Italian Risorgimento is a case in point. The basic idea of a unified Italy was itself rejected by many different groups: the Austrian Empire, which ruled about two-thirds of the Italian peninsula, and the Kingdom of the Two Sicilies, which controlled the southern third; the papacy, which feared the loss of its control over the city of Rome; and the conservative landowners and other elites who were apprehensive about the loss of their own power and privileges. The coalition that overcame them and eventually brought about reunification was equally diverse; its leaders included Giuseppe Garibaldi, a merchant navy captain, mercenary and adventurer whose Red Shirt Army provided much of the revolution's military force, Giuseppe Mazzini, the journalist and philosopher who was the revolution's chief ideologue and who won much support for the Italian cause elsewhere in Europe, and Camillo Benso, Conti di Cavour, prime minister of the independent kingdom of Sardinia-Piedmont, who masterminded the political coalition that finally achieved reunification.[13]

In a complicated situation which sometimes seemed like a revolution, sometimes a civil war and sometimes a *coup d'état*, these three leaders depended on each other. Cavour the aristocratic politician, Mazzini the intellectual and Garibaldi the man of action depended on one another; none of them could have succeeded on their own. They brought together not only a coalition of their followers but also a combination of skills and experience that were needed to achieve the complex project of reunification.

Spontaneous revolts

Other revolutions are simpler, or at least they appear to be. Looking at examples of revolutions throughout history, it is notable that some appear to be almost entirely spontaneous. This was the sort of revolution of which Rosa Luxemburg approved; unplanned, emergent, with leaders coming to the fore when needed. The Peasants Revolt was in part the result of grievances going back decades, but the flashpoint came when royal officials tried to arrest people in Essex for non-payment of taxes. The people fought back, and several officials were killed. The revolt then spread quickly as word of mouth travelled across southeastern England; Wat Tyler, the principal leader of the revolt, emerged about a week after the fighting began, and there is no record of his having been involved in protests before this time.[14] The Prayer Book Rebellion, which erupted in Devon and Cornwall in 1549, began when the people of the village of Sampford Courtenay in Devon refused to allow their parish priest to use the newly introduced Book of Common Prayer; the rebellion then spread rapidly across both counties. The leader who emerged, a Cornish landowner named Humphrey Arundell, had no previous involvement in radical causes.[15]

Earlier in the fourteenth century the peasant revolt known as the Jacquerie erupted in northern France when a group of peasants, protesting the failure of the French government to protect them in the time of chaos after the Battle of Poitiers, attacked and killed a knight. A local landowner named Guillaume Cale, who had connections with another rebel movement in Paris, offered his services, and the rebels, aware that they lacked the skills to organise a proper revolt, appointed Cale their leader.[16] More recently, the Velvet Revolution that overthrew the communist government of Czechoslovakia began as an isolated student protest; then, when it became clear that the authorities did not intend to crack down, it spread rapidly and without apparent organisation. Although Václav Havel, the human rights activist and future president, was prominent amid the demonstrations, it was only after the fall of the communists that he emerged as an important leader in his own right; before that, he was merely a respected symbol of opposition.[17]

Mention has already been made of François de Charette, the – initially, at least – unwilling leader of the counter-revolutionaries in the Vendée, itself a spontaneous revolt that erupted following the revolutionary government's suppression of the Catholic Church. The 1848 revolution in Vienna began with a group of students presenting a petition to the government demanding greater freedoms, including freedom of the press. A passer-by, a young doctor named Adolf Fischhof, stopped to see what the disturbance was and began talking to the some of the students, urging them to protest more strongly and insist their demands be met. The students raised him up on their shoulders and called on the crowd to listen to him. A few days later, once the government had fallen and the students had taken control of Vienna, Fischhof was appointed chairman of the Committee of Safety, the body that now governed the city.[18]

Naval and military mutinies are a (usually) limited and localised form of revolution. These, too, usually begin spontaneously. The mutiny on the Russian battleship *Potemkin* began when the crew were served rotten meat for their rations; when they protested, an officer drew his revolver and shot one of the sailors dead. In the ensuing mutiny, most of the officers, including the captain, were killed, and the sailors took over the ship. A revolutionary committee of sailors was then appointed to decide what to do next. Although he was never formally appointed captain, the leader who emerged was Afanasy Matushenko, the ship's quartermaster and a non-commissioned officer (not one of the lower deck sailors). Matushenko's position as leader was largely unspoken; he had a clear head and knew what to do in a crisis, and the rest of the crew came quickly to look to him for guidance.[19]

In April 1797, a mutiny broke out on more than a dozen Royal Navy ships at Spithead, an anchorage near Portsmouth. This mutiny more nearly resembled a strike: the mutineers were protesting over pay and working conditions, and after an initial stand-off, Admiral Lord Howe agreed to meet the mutineers, and he acceded to some of their demands. Meanwhile, however, a much more serious mutiny had erupted in the Nore, the navy's main base, located on the Thames Estuary. Richard

Parker, a former officer who had been court-martialled for insubordination and reduced to the ranks, played no part in the initial mutiny, but he was invited to join the mutineers for much the same reason as Charette; the mutineers needed someone with knowledge of organisation, and as an ex-officer Parker fit the bill. He was appointed president of the mutineers' council, the Delegates of the Fleet; according to him, the appointment was made without his knowledge. When the mutiny collapsed, he was arrested and hanged.[20]

Programmistic revolts

Other revolts, although they perhaps have a spontaneous element, are actually the fruits of a long-nourished programme of change whereby a particular group intends to destroy the existing elites and replace them with new ones. In these cases, leaders often have already been chosen and are waiting to take power. The revolution of 1848 in France began when the government tried to suppress the democratic movement, which had been seeking to bring down the Bourbon monarchy through peaceful protests. The democrats already had an organised programme, and once the monarchy fell, the government of the Second Republic, led by the poet Alphonse Lamartine, settled fairly smoothly into power.[21] There was of course a hidden actor in all this, Louis-Napoleon Bonaparte, who lent his support to the revolutionaries as part of his own programme of gaining power; as we saw in the last chapter, he later staged a coup against the Second Republic and became Emperor Napoleon III.

The Chinese Communist Party was nearly annihilated by Chiang Kai-Shek's nationalists in 1925. Taking over the survivors, Mao Zedong and his colleagues gave the party a new strategy and a new direction, concentrating on rallying the rural peasantry rather than the urban proletariat and developing a complex programme of revolution which they ultimately spread across China.[22] Although the American Revolution began with a single flashpoint, the action at Lexington on 19 April 1775, the Sons of Liberty, the leading revolutionary organisation, had, in fact, been campaigning for independence for years.[23] Mahatma Gandhi's revolutionary programme of non-violence, *satyagraha*, was first put into effect in 1919 and carried on for decades until India finally achieved independence. Satyagraha itself was a product of Gandhi's earlier ideas, outlined in his book *Hind Swaraj* (1909), in which he pointed out that the British occupied India only because of the cooperation of Indians and that all that was needed to compel the British to leave was the withdrawal of this cooperation.[24]

Other revolts demonstrate a mixture of programme and spontaneity. Although the storming of the Bastille was a spontaneous event, as surprising to the revolutionaries as to the monarchy, it was in part the outcome of a long campaign of pressure by liberals and radicals, including Lafayette and Mirabeau, to put pressure on the government to enact reforms. Lafayette and Mirabeau were both allies and rivals, would-be leaders waiting in the wings.[25] The Indian Mutiny ostensibly began at Meerut, when ninety-five soldiers in the Indian Army were court-martialled for disobedience; their comrades mutinied in order to free them. But there had been unrest before this point, and there is considerable evidence that the mutiny had been organised on a wide scale before the violence broke out. Unlike the *Potemkin* and Spithead-Nore mutinies, although conditions of service were one of the soldiers' grievances, there were also complex political forces at work, and several Indian princely states joined the rebellion. As a result, the leadership of the revolt was a mixture of Indian non-commissioned officers, such as Subedar Bakht Khan, and princes, such as the Nana Sahib and Lakshmibai, the Rani of Jhansi.[26] The Bohemian revolt known as the Defenestration of Prague, when several Catholic nobles were thrown from the windows of the palace by Protestant rebels in 1619, was likewise a spontaneous act, but the Protestants had already laid their plans for overthrowing their Catholic king and chosen their own leader, the Protestant noble Count Thurn.[27]

Authority and acceptability

Sometimes leaders emerge spontaneously, and sometimes they have already been chosen. But from where did they derive their authority, and what made them acceptable?

One interesting point that should be noted is that revolutionary activity, because it happened outside formal, existing social spaces in a created space of its own, gave opportunities for those traditionally denied access to positions of power. In particular, revolutionary women could find positions of power either through leading other women, as in the French Revolution or the suffrage movement, or, in some cases, through leading movements of mixed gender. The latter tended to occur in other marginal or non-legitimate social spaces, such as revolutionary socialism and anarchism, where leaders such as Rosa Luxemburg and Emma Goldman were able to gain a certain amount of authority and power.[28] During the Paris Commune uprising, anarchist women, including Louise Michel, Nathalie Lemel and Maria Pantazi, achieved positions of leadership. In Chinese anarchist circles, journalist Lin Zongsu was recognised as a leading figure.[29]

That said, women were met with substantial opposition. The Society of Revolutionary Women, founded in Paris, was ordered to shut down by the authorities after little more than a year; in 1793, the National Convention banned *all* women's organisations on the grounds that they were hotbeds of sedition. Olympe de Gouges, author of the *Declaration of the Rights of Women and the Female Citizen*, was executed, as was Jeanne Roland, who was not a member of the society but who was a leading political figure in her own right. Théroigne de Méricourt was beaten and later confined to an asylum for the insane; Pauline Léon and Claire Lacombe, the founders of the society, were both arrested, and they barely escaped execution.[30]

Going back to the beginning of this chapter, if we follow Crane Brinton, we would expect that the authority of revolutionary leaders be derived from access to power and force, whereas Elias Canetti would argue that it be derived from the consent of followers. Looking at examples of historical leaders, we can see that both are true, but there are other types of authority and legitimacy. The nature of the leader's authority and the source of their power are heavily dependent on circumstances, including what the context of the revolution is and what the goals of followers might be. The big defining factor is whether the revolutionary leader can identify those goals and help gather the support of followers.

Consent

Spontaneous revolts are sometimes launched by people who have a burning cause they wish to follow; other times, revolts are launched by people who are simply desperate but lack the experience and skills to organise and lead a revolution. They then deliberately choose leaders who they believe can help them. An example can be found in the women's suffrage movement in the UK. A number of local suffrage societies had gradually been brought together as the National Union of Women's Suffrage Societies (NUWSS) by the scientist and suffrage leader Lydia Becker, but the movement still lacked impetus. Becker's elected successor, Millicent Garrett Fawcett, was a skilled organiser and campaigner who raised the organisation's profile and increased its membership to more than fifty thousand. In addition to women's suffrage, Fawcett campaigned on a number of issues, including Irish home rule, education, poverty and more general women's rights. At the NUWSS, she gave the organisation a structure and the means to campaign much more effectively around a set of defined issues.[31]

Afanasy Matushenko, the quartermaster of the battleship *Potemkin*, was chosen as the leader of the mutineers because he had the skills to command and guide the ship; among other things, he was one of the few of the relatively unskilled crew who knew how to steer it. Fletcher Christian was likewise chosen as the leader of the mutineers on HMS *Bounty* because he knew how to manage and sail the ship, the rest of the crew not trusting their own ability to do so.[32] Both men's authority derived from their skills as seamen, which was essential to give these spontaneous revolts focus and direction. In addition, Matushenko had a political agenda: he had connections with the social revolutionaries in Russia, and as the *Potemkin* mutiny coincided with the 1905 revolution against the rule of the tsars, some of his fellow crew members hoped he would lead them to intervene on the side of the revolutionaries.

We have already discussed the role played by Charette in the Vendée revolt; his authority and legitimacy derived from his military skills. The same is true of other rebel leaders, including Henri de la Rochejacquelein and Jean-Nicolas Stofflet, both former army officers; during the Vendée rebellion, the only leader of note not to have extensive military experience was Georges Cadoudal, leader of the Chouan rebels in Brittany. Cadoudal was a physically imposing man who made no secret of his willingness to die for the royalist cause (which he ultimately did). Although he was a capable commander, his authority was more symbolic-charismatic in nature.[33] Throughout the Vendée period, the rebels claimed the right to choose their leaders, usually by acclamation rather than election, and they deserted those who they did not think were leading well.[34] Spartacus, the leader of the slave revolt against Rome, was likewise chosen by his companions as leader on the basis of his skills and experience. Gladiators were trained to fight individually, but they had no experience of organisation; Spartacus had been a mercenary soldier and then a legionary in the Roman army, so he had the skills his followers lacked.[35]

Another example is the woman known to history as Nanny of the Maroons. Born in West Africa, she was enslaved and sent to a plantation in Jamaica, from which she escaped, possibly as part of a larger slave revolt. Leading other escaped slaves into the Blue Mountains, she founded a community of Maroons (the colloquial name for escaped slaves and their descendants living in free communities), known in her honour as Nanny Town. She led her people in successfully resisting the British Army during the First Maroon War in 1728–39; following a peace treaty, she led her followers to found a new settlement on land granted by the government. Nanny may have been chosen partly because her followers believed her to have supernatural powers; on the other hand, their ascribing of such powers to her may have come about as a result of her own extraordinary skills and abilities. For whatever reason, her followers chose her as their leader, and the mountain communities of Jamaica still remember her name today.[36]

As noted in Chapter 2, many symbolic-charismatic leaders emerge as leaders of revolutionary movements, and from the examples discussed here we can hypothesise that in many cases – but by no means in all – symbolic-charismatic leaders emerge in more programmatic movements, where the purpose of the movement is understood and an organisation of sorts is already in place. Symbolic-charismatic leaders are chosen because they are living symbols. Their charisma attracts people, but there is also something about them that is emblematic of their cause. Sometimes, like Nanny of the Maroons, these leaders emerge spontaneously out of particular circumstances – in her case, out of a slave revolt – but sometimes they are chosen, often for reasons that are instinctive and emotional rather than rational and that speak to our need for symbols. Leaders do more than just give direction: they are a banner that others can rally around.[37]

The women's suffrage agenda in the UK was already well established by the time Emmeline Pankhurst broke away from the NUWSS and founded the Women's Social and Political Union. Without in any way denying Pankhurst's own formidable organisational skills, her chief role and that of her daughters, Sylvia and Christabel, was to serve as a rallying point for that element of the suffrage movement that demanded more urgent action. Compared to the NUWSS, the WSPU was small, only about two thousand members at its height, but it was carefully focused and organised around a single goal. Women chose to follow Pankhurst because they believed that her militancy was the best way to achieve that goal, and even when she was in prison or on hunger strike, they continued to regard her as their leader.[38]

Rafael Guillén, the poet and intellectual who became Subcomandante Marcos, had the charisma to project the Zapatista message to a wider audience. At times, Guillén's leadership seems to resemble a piece of performance art; he once went on a tour around Mexico, this time under the pseudonym Delegate Zero, giving talks and readings to interested and slightly bemused audiences. For Frederick Douglass, the escaped slave and abolitionist leader in *antebellum* America, the medium of expression was photography; he used the camera to document the horrors of slavery to great effect and won much sympathy for the abolitionist cause. He was also an effective public speaker and writer.[39]

The French Revolution was full of symbolic-charismatic leaders. Some early leaders, such as Mirabeau and the journalist and fiery orator Camille Desmoulins, whose speeches provoked the uprising of 1789 and the storming of the Bastille, were necessary to catalyse the revolution, but by 1791 various groups were emerging, each with their own programmes and each in search of leaders. They found them: Mirabeau, until his death, and Lafayette to represent the old liberal nobility and the bourgeoisie; Danton, Desmoulins and Jean-Paul Marat to represent the radical republicans; Jacques Hébert and Anacharsis Cloots to lead the *sans-culottes* (working poor); Charles Dumouriez, Lazare Hoche and Jean-Charles Pichegru to lead the aspirations of the army, which demanded its own share in the game; all flamboyant characters, able speakers and writers with a good deal of personal magnetism.[40]

There were other, less colourful leaders, and it is interesting to note that they, too, were successful. Maximilien Robespierre was in no way a charismatic figure; he had a weak speaking voice, often struggled to make his speeches heard, suffered from poor eyesight and was chronically nervous, but such was his mastery of intrigue that he became dictator of France for nearly a year. Lazare Carnot, engineer, scientist and army officer, was a colourless and uninteresting technocrat, but his abilities as a military organiser and 'architect of victories' kept him in positions of leadership for several years.[41] But the prominence of symbolic-charismatic leaders in revolutionary France suggested that various groups of followers – royalists, republicans, Girondins, Jacobins, *sans-culottes* – had their own programmes and were looking for leaders to rally around. The revolution ultimately failed because these groups could not or would not stop fighting each other until they were all finally suppressed or co-opted by Napoleon.

Revolutionary faith

The consent of followers plays an enormous role in determining whether revolutionary movements succeed or fail. There is no formal contract between leaders and followers; because these social spaces are outside the usual legitimate space, even devices such as oaths of loyalty cannot ensure that followers will never desert. Followers can and do move from faction to faction or even give up on the revolutionary movement entirely, and when this happens, the leader can be left high and dry. This happened to Danton and Desmoulins during the French Revolution when their faction decided to throw their weight behind Robespierre instead, and not even Desmoulins's childhood friendship with Robespierre could save him from the guillotine.

In order to tie followers more closely to them, leaders will sometimes attempt to gain access to other sources of authority and legitimacy. One possibility was to appeal to the religious faith of followers. One of the causes of the Vendée revolt was the French revolutionary government's repressive policies towards the Catholic Church, and the leaders of the revolt used religious imagery and symbolism, including styling themselves the Catholic and Royal Army and flying banners bearing an image of a sacred heart. Hong Xiuquan, the leader of the Taiping Rebellion in nineteenth-century China, preached his own brand of Christianity to his followers, although probably with limited effect outside his immediate circle.[42] During the Arab revolt against Turkey in 1916, the leader of the revolt, Sharif Ali, argued that the Young Turks who controlled the Ottoman government had violated their faith, and he called on true Muslims to rise up against them. The government countered that the sultan, who was still nominally on his throne, was also caliph and leader of the faithful, and therefore it was Ali and his followers who were guilty of impiety.[43]

The *ikko-ikki*, a rebel movement in fifteenth- and sixteenth-century Japan, were a broad coalition of small landowners, peasants and even some of the nobility, but at their heart they were Buddhist warrior-monks, followers of the branch of Japanese Buddhism known as Jodo Shinshu. The *ikko-ikki* rebels were inspired by the head of the sect, a charismatic monk named Rennyo who advocated self-defence, urged his followers to band together for protection but did not approve of revolution. Despite this, the Buddhist-inspired rebels were a major political force in Japan during the Age of the Country at War. On the other hand Gandhi, rather than inspiring people to war, urged his followers towards peace. The concept of *satyagraha*, the guiding ideal of Gandhi's revolution, is grounded in principles of Hindu faith.[44]

In addition to religious faith, leaders could also appeal to shared secular ideals. Following the principles of spontaneity, Rosa Luxemburg did not as much guide her followers as offer them encouragement by referring constantly to the principles of freedom and equality that she and her comrades espoused. She was so effective a communicator during the German revolution that after her arrest, her enemies paid her the compliment of murdering her rather than just locking her up, as they did with most revolutionary women.[45]

But killing a revolutionary leader could backfire, creating new sources of symbolism and faith. The Sandinistas in Nicaragua took their name from Augusto César Sandino, a guerrilla leader who fought from 1927 to 1933 against the American troops who occupied the country and was later assassinated on the orders of the dictator Anastasio Somoza García. When revolt broke out against the regime of Somoza's son, it was only natural to hark back to the ideals of Sandino. Similarly, the Zapatista movement took its name from another murdered revolutionary hero, Emiliano Zapata, who led the rebels of southern Mexico during the Mexican revolution; his followers styled themselves Zapatistas.[46] Faith and belief in leaders who are still alive but imprisoned can also serve as powerful symbols; as noted earlier, Nelson Mandela and Aung Sang Suu Kyi are useful examples of this.

Inherited leadership

Examples of inherited leadership of revolutionary movements are rare. Napoleon III and Prince Charles Stuart both claimed leadership through inheritance, the former through his uncle Napoleon I and the latter through his grandfather King James II of England, who was overthrown in 1688. As described in the previous chapter, these are more properly coups or civil wars, in which the aim was regime change, not complete revolution. Mention could also be made of revolutions led by people who falsely claimed to be descended from previous leaders, such as Yemelyan Pugachev, who claimed to be the deposed Tsar Peter III of Russia, or Perkin Warbeck, who posed as one of the sons the dead King Richard III of England, but both of these should also be catalogued as civil wars or coups rather than revolutions.[47]

Why are inherited revolutionary leaders so rare? In large part, this is due to the fact that most revolutions did not last very long and that most revolutionary leaders died young. Even in Ireland, where there was a long tradition of rebellion against English rule, there is surprisingly little in the way of inherited leadership. Michael Collins, a prominent figure during the Easter Rising and head of the provisional government of Ireland after the First World War, came from a family with a history of involvement in rebel movements, but none of his ancestors had held positions of leadership.[48]

Inherent leadership

Followers may look for a leader who has the skills and experience they need; but in a revolutionary moment, someone senses the opportunity and knows they have what it takes to lead. The leader steps forward and imposes control. There is then the potential for conflict: followers can attempt to reject the leader's offer, or if they believe the leader really *does* have what it takes to lead them where they want to go, they can fall in line.

Chief among the necessary inherent characteristics in these cases is a degree of ruthlessness. 'A revolution is not a dinner party, or writing an essay, or painting a picture, or doing embroidery', Mao Zedong warned. 'It cannot be so refined, so leisurely and gentle, so temperate, kind, courteous, restrained and magnanimous. A revolution is an insurrection, an act of violence by which one class overthrows another'.[49] As a leader, Mao often demonstrated that sort of ruthlessness. Taking over the wreckage of the Communist Party of China, he rebuilt its organisation and then led it on the legendary Long March to establish a new base beyond the reach of either Chiang Kai-Shek's Republican armies or the invading Japanese. He also knew how to play the long game, allying with Chiang to hold back the Japanese and then turning against his former ally once the first struggle was done. That ruthlessness and strong will were what the party needed in order to survive.[50]

Giuseppe Garibaldi was another leader who imposed himself on the scene. When his small army of Red Shirts first arrived in Italy, people were hesitant to support him. Garibaldi proved himself as a military commander and won admiration for his courage; his refusal to back down meant that, rather like George Washington in the American Revolutionary War, he won nearly as many admirers and followers in defeat as he did in victory.[51] Toussaint L'Ouverture began the Haitian revolution as a relatively minor commander, but he won respect for his skills as both a soldier and a diplomat. After the French government agreed to the abolition of slavery in 1794, the new nation of Haiti came under attack from both Britain and Spain. Taking command, Toussaint used his makeshift army to hold off both and preserve Haitian independence. Although Toussaint was later betrayed by some of his former allies and died in a French prison, the state he created survived all attempts to conquer it.[52]

Returning to England after a period in exile, the Anglo-Saxon nobleman Hereward the Wake found his country had been conquered by the Normans under William I. With only a few followers, he raised the standard of revolt in the East Anglian fens, around the Isle of Ely. His early successes gave heart to others, and he was joined by men from all over England, including Morcar, the dispossessed former Earl of Northumbria.[53] Stenka Razin, the Cossack rebel leader of seventeenth-century Russia, also saw the potential for rebellion and stepped up to take action. The Cossacks were a marginalised people inhabiting the steppes of southern Russia, an uneasy no-man's land between the rival powers of Russia, Ottoman Turkey and Poland. Razin was originally a bandit leader who defied Russian attempts to suppress him. His independence inspired many to join him, including opponents of the tsar's regime, peasants fleeing brutal overlords and disaffected ethnic minorities such as the Kalmyks. Seeing how unpopular the tsar was and how many followers he himself had, Razin launched an open revolt, marching on Moscow. At first, other districts in southern Russia rose up and joined him. However, after his forces were defeated by the tsar's army, his authority quickly collapsed. His supporters lost faith in his ability lead and deserted him.[54]

To repeat the point made earlier, the relationship between leaders and followers in the revolutionary social space is fragile, and there is no formal contract between them, at least, not one that is enforceable. Followers go their own way, depending on what their needs are and what they perceive the risks to be. Successful leaders need to appeal to something other than just the consent of followers.

It is worth noting that of all the leaders of the French Revolution we mentioned earlier, Lafayette, Dumouriez, Pichegru and Carnot were forced into exile; Hoche may have died of natural causes (although poison has not entirely been ruled out); Marat was assassinated; and Danton, Desmoulins, Robespierre, Hébert and Cloots all went to the guillotine, along with the majority of the rest of the early revolutionary leadership. Their followers did not save them; in the end, their followers handed them over to their enemies. Something else, some broader sense of authority and legitimacy, was needed.

Success and failure

But could the leaders of the French Revolution, or any revolution, be said to have failed? For one thing, in this social space, what do success and failure look like? The Easter Rising was crushed by British troops in the streets of Dublin, but it paved the way for the Irish War of Independence, which led to the establishment of the Irish Free State, the first time most of Ireland had been free of English or British control for eight centuries. So, did the Easter Rising fail?[55]

Going back to Chapter 3, when we look into the social space, we see that followers engage with leaders in order to reach their own goals, survival or realisation of aspirations. If they failure to realise their aspirations, or fail to survive, or both, then it would seem clear that the revolution has failed. Of course, this measure has to be a general one; it is inevitable that some revolutionaries will be casualties and that some will survive who are not satisfied. But taken in aggregate, we can see that the suffragist movement was a successful revolution, and both Pankhurst and Fawcett can be described as successful leaders. So could Gandhi, although he did not live to see Indian independence; and Nanny of the Maroons; and Garibaldi, Mazzini and Cavour, who achieved the reunification of Italy; and Mao Zedong. Carlos Fonseca did not live to see the Sandinistas, under a new generation of leaders, overthrow the Somoza regime, but Ernesto Cardenal did; Toussaint died, but his country, Haiti, survived. The Arab revolt was a limited success in that its leaders managed to establish semi-independent states in Jordan and Iraq.

Others were not so fortunate. The Vendée revolt was crushed, and its leaders were killed in battle or executed. The fate of Spartacus is well known. The Taiping rebels were crushed, and the *ikko-ikki* were virtually exterminated, many choosing to die rather than surrender. Stenka Razin was captured and executed, and Hereward the Wake's revolt was eventually crushed. He disappeared into the fens, his fate unknown.

What makes the difference? As mentioned, asymmetries of force certainly play a role; it is hard for any revolutionary movement to overcome the armed might of the state. There is also the quality of the resistance the state offers. In *The Discourses*, Machiavelli makes the point that the fear of losing power can be just as powerful a spur to action as the desire to gain it, and faced with the loss of power, the elites will fight back.[56] How well they fight depends on the quality of *their* leadership and how likely they think they are to win. Convincing them that they will lose is one of the tasks of a revolutionary leader; one of the first signs of imminent success is that elites start changing sides and joining the revolutionaries.

That brings us to one of the things that make revolutionary leaders successful; their ability to attract support and connect with followers. That is not as straightforward as it might seem. The followers must actively work for the cause, not just connect with it, and they must even be prepared to sacrifice themselves for it. As Mancur Olson puts it in *The Theory of Collective Action*, a large and diffuse follower base will always include 'free riders', people who have joined and are going along with the cause because they hope to benefit from the exertions of others without doing any work themselves.[57] This was the logic followed by Emmeline Pankhurst in keeping the WSPU small and tightly focused; a smaller group of truly dedicated revolutionaries, willing to put their lives on the line, would make more of an impact.

At the same time, two thousand suffragists ('suffragettes', as the WSPU preferred to call themselves) could hardly overturn the balance of power. What the WSPU did instead was to win sympathy from the broader public. They smashed windows and committed acts of arson to gain attention; when the state responded with arrests and hunger strikes, they received more attention. With attention came sympathy.

People not involved in the movement admired their courage and took an interest in their cause. When Liberty's and other London department stores where people of fashion shopped began dressing their windows in the white, purple and green colours of the suffrage movement, the battle was half won.

Like Pankhurst, Mao Zedong favoured elite cadres to take action but recognised that broad popular support was essential. Perhaps the single-most significant factor in the history of the Communist Party of China was Mao's decision to set aside the Marxist-Leninist position that the revolution should be led by the proletariat; he instead devised a new theory of revolution that focused on China's agricultural labourers. Gaining their support was crucial to the Chinese revolution.

The mutineers on the *Potemkin*, on the other hand, failed because they could not build support, either inside their own crew or more broadly. Matushenko and some of the crew had connections with the social democrats and other revolutionaries, and they favoured taking the *Potemkin* to the city of Odessa, then in the throes of revolt, and joining in on the side of the rebels. Once the rest of the crew found out what was planned, they objected; if the battleship's big guns opened fire on the city in support of the rebels, the authorities would show them no mercy. They opted instead for a negotiated surrender. Matushenko and the men around them tried to persuade the crew, but to no avail; meanwhile, the rebels of Odessa, who expected the *Potemkin* to open fire, began to withdraw their support. Eventually, the *Potemkin* sailed to neutral waters in Romania and surrendered. Returning to Russia several years later, Matushenko was arrested and executed.[58]

Coalition building, then, is an essential part of what revolutionary leaders must do. The Risorgimento, the Vietnamese revolution under Ho Chi Minh, the Velvet Revolution in Czechoslovakia all succeeded because the initial revolutionary group built a broad base of support. This, in turn, convinced the elites in power that they could not win. Sometimes they fought to the end anyway; in most cases, they either removed themselves from the scene or accepted *realpolitik* and joined the rebels. On the other hand, failure to build those coalitions meant failure of the revolution. In China, Sun Yat-sen relied on far too narrow a base of followers, and when Yuan Shikai turned against him, he had nowhere to go except exile.

In 1918, a coalition of left-wing parties, including socialists, communists and anarchists, seized power in Munich and declared a republic. Their leader was the socialist journalist and politician Kurt Eisner, a charismatic man who was described as the symbol of the Bavarian republic; Max Weber even mentioned him as an example of charismatic authority.[59] But despite early sympathy from the population – one official made a promise of free money to the public – the new government proved incapable of organising even basic services. The factions fell to fighting among themselves, with the communists eventually driving out their rivals. When the army and elements of the right-wing mercenary *Freikorps* attacked, the city could not defend itself. The republic was crushed with the loss of several hundred lives.[60] A highly skilled and charismatic leader, even if they have the consent of the immediate followers, needs to broaden that support base, and that nearly always means appeals to other sources of authority and legitimacy.

Notes

1 Charles Tilly, *European Revolutions, 1492–1992*, Oxford: Blackwell, 1995.
2 Crane Brinton, *The Anatomy of Revolution*, New York: Vintage, 1965, p. 24.
3 Ibid.
4 Ibid., p. 4.
5 Canetti, *Crowds and Power*.
6 Schama, *Citizens*; Olivier Bernier, *Lafayette*, New York: E.P. Dutton, 1983; Marc Leepson, *Lafayette: Lessons in Leadership From the Idealist General*, Basingstoke: Palgrave Macmillan, 2011.
7 Gaunt, *Oliver Cromwell*; Gaunt, *Tne English Civil War*; Purkiss, *The English Civil War*; Foxley, *The Levellers*.
8 Schama, *Citizens*; McPhee, *Robespierre*.
9 Gaunt, *Oliver Cromwell*; Terrill, *Mao*; Jung Chang and Jon Halliday, *Mao: The Unknown Story*, London: Jonathan Cape, 2005; Jean Lacouture, *Ho Chi Minh: A Political Biography*, New York: Random House, 1968.
10 Foxley, *The Levellers*; Whitney R.D. Jones, *Thomas Rainborowe (c.1610–1648): Civil War Seaman, Siegemaster and Radical*, Woodbridge: Boydell, 2005; Denis Mack Smith, *Mazzini*, London: Yale University Press, 1996; Nick Henck, *Subcomandate Marcos: The Man and the Mask*, Durham: Duke University Press, 2007.
11 Hilton, *Bondmen Made Free*; Dobson, *The Peasants Revolt of 1381*; Edward L. Farmer, *Zhu Yuanzhang and Early Ming Legislation: The Reordering of Chinese Society Following the Era of Mongol Rule*, Leiden: Brill, 1995.
12 Matilde Zimmermann, *Sandinista: Carlos Fonseca and the Nicaraguan Revolution*, Durham: Duke University Press, 2000.
13 Riall, *Risorgimento*; Martin Clark, *The Italian Risorgimento*, London: Routledge, 2009; Lucy Riall, *Garibaldi: Invention of a Hero*, London: Yale University Press, 2008; Jasper Ridley, *Garibaldi*, New York: Viking, 1976; Denis Mack Smith, *Mazzini*, New Haven: Yale University Press, 1996; Denis Mack Smith, *Victor Emanuel, Cavour and the Risorgimento*, Oxford: Oxford University Press, 1971.
14 Dobson, *The Peasants Revolt of 1381*; Hilton, *Bondsmen Made Free*.
15 Julian Cornwall, *The Revolt of the Peasantry, 1549*, London: Routledge & Kegan Paul, 1977.
16 Cohn, *Popular Protest in Late Medieval Europe*.
17 Michael Andrew Kukral, *Prague 1989: Theatre of Revolution*, New York: Columbia University Press, 1997; James F. Pontuso, *Václav Havel: Civic Responsibility in the Postmodern Age*, New York: Rowman & Littlefield, 2004.
18 Priscilla Robertson, *Revolutions of 1848: A Social History*, New York: Harper & Row, 1960.
19 Bascomb, *Red Mutiny*.
20 Knight, *Britain Against Napoleon*; Conrad Gill, *The Naval Mutinies of 1797*, Manchester: Manchester University Press, 1913.
21 Robertson, *Revolutions of 1848*.
22 Terrill, *Mao*; Chang and Halliday, *Mao*; Snow, *Red Star Over China*; Ed Jocelyn and Andrew McEwen, *The Long March: The True Story Behind the Legendary Journey That Made Mao's China*, London: Constable and Robinson, 2006; Barbara Barnouin and Yu Changgen, *Zhou Enlai: A Political Life*, Hong Kong: Chinese University of Hong Kong, 2006.
23 Pauline Maier, *From Resistance to Revolution: Colonial Radicals and the Development of Opposition to Britain, 1765–1776*, New York: W.W. Norton, 1972; Harlow Unger, *John Hancock: Merchant King and American Patriot*, Edison: Castle Books, 2000.
24 Gandhi, *Gandhi*; Iyer, *The Moral and Political Writings of Gandhi*; Johnson, *Gandhi's Experiments With Truth*; Dennis Dalton, *Mahatma Gandhi: Nonviolent Power in Action*, New York: Columbia University Press, 1993.
25 Schama, *Citizens*; Bernier, *Lafayette*; Luttrell, *Mirabeau*.
26 Christopher Hibbert, *The Great Mutiny: India 1857*, London: Allen Lane, 1980; Sekhar Bandyopadhyay (ed.), *1857: Essays from Economic and Political Weekly*, Hyderabad: Orient Longman, 2008; David Saul, *The Indian Mutiny*, London: Penguin, 2003; Petr Mikhailovich

Shastitko and Savitri Shahani, *Nana Sahib: An Account of the People's Revolt in India, 1857–1859*; New Delhi: Shubhada-Saraswat, 2006; Harleen Singh, *The Rani of Jhansi: Gender, History and Fable in India*, Cambridge: Cambridge University Press, 2014.

27 Wedgewood, *The Thirty Years War*.

28 Ettinger, *Rosa Luxemburg*; Nixon, *Rosa Luxemburg*; Falk, *Love, Anarchy and Emma Goldman*.

29 Louise Michel, *The Red Virgin: Memoirs of Louise Michel*, trans. Bullitt Lowry and Elizabeth Ellington Gunter, Tuscaloosa: University of Alabama Press, 1981; Dirlik, *Anarchism in the Chinese Revolution*.

30 Smart, *Citoyennes*; Melzer and Rabine, *Rebel Daughters*; Dominique Goudineau and Katherine Streip, *The Women of Paris and Their French Revolution*, Berkeley: University of California Press, 1998; Frank Hamel, *A Woman of the Revolution: Théroigne de Méricourt*, New York: Brentano, 1911; Ida M. Tarbell, *Madame Roland: A Biographical Study*, New York: Charles Scribner's Sons, 1896.

31 Fawcett, *Women's Suffrage*; Marlow, *Suffragettes*; Smith, *The British Women's Suffrage Campaign*.

32 Bascomb, *Red Mutiny*; Bligh, *Mutiny on Board the HMS Bounty*.

33 G. Lenotre, *Georges Cadoudal*, Paris: Editions Transition, 1918.

34 Ross, *Banners of the King*; Anne Rolland-Boulestreau, *Les Colonnes Infernales: Violences et Guerres Civiles en Vendée Militaire (1794–1795)*, Paris: Fayard, 2015.

35 Strauss, *The Spartacus War*; M. J. Trow, *Spartacus: The Man and the Myth*, Stroud: Sutton, 2006.

36 Karla Lewis Gottlieb, *The Mother of Us All: A History of Queen Nanny, Leader of the Windward Jamaican Maroons*, Trenton: Africa World Press, 2000; Mavis Christine Campbell, *The Maroons of Jamaica, 1655–1796: A History of Resistance, Collaboration and Betrayal*, Trenton: Africa World Press, 1990.

37 Rowe, *Religious Symbols and God*; Victor Turner, *Dramas, Fields and Metaphors: Symbolic Action in Human Societies*, Ithaca: Cornell University Press, 1975; Tim Marshall, *Worth Dying For: The Power and Politics of Flags*, London: Elliott and Thompson, 2017.

38 Pankhurst, *My Story*; Bartley, *Emmline Pankhurst*; Purvis, *Emmeline Pankhurst*; Pankhurst, *How We Won the Vote*.

39 David W. Blight, *Frederick Douglass: Prophet of Freedom*, New York: Simon & Schuster, 2018.

40 Luttrell, *Mirabeau*; Bernier, *Lafayette*; Schama, *Citizens*; Doyle, *The Oxford History of the French Revolution*; Violet Methley, *Camille Desmoulins: A Biography*, New York: E.P. Dutton, 1915; David Lawday, *Danton: The Giant of the French Revolution*, London: Jonathan Cape, 2009; Clifford D. Connor, *Marat: Tribune of the French Revolution*, New York: Pluto, 2012; Roland Mortier, *Anacharsis Cloots ou L'utopie foudroyée*, Paris: Stock, 1995; Charles J. Esdaile, *The Wars of the French Revolution*, London: Routledge, 2018.

41 McPhee, *Robespierre*; Charles C. Gillespie, *Lazare Carnot*, Princeton: Princeton University Press, 1971.

42 Ross, *Banners of the King*; Spence, *God's Chinese Son*.

43 Rashid Khalidi, *The Origins of Arab Nationalism*, New York: Columbia University Press, 1991; T.E. Lawrence, *Revolt in the Desert*, London: Wordsworth, 1997.

44 Carol Richmond Tsang, *War and Faith: Ikko Ikki in Late Muromachi Japan*, Cambridge, MA: Harvard University Press, 2007; Neil McMullin, *Buddhism and the State in Sixteenth-Century Japan*, Princeton: Princeton University Press, 1984; Dalton, *Mahatma Gandhi*; Iyer, *The Moral and Political Writings of Gandhi*.

45 Ettinger, *Rosa Luxemburg*; Nixon, *Rosa Luxemburg*.

46 Sergio Ramírez, *Sandino: The Testimony of a Nicaraguan Patriot, 1921–34*, trans. Robert E. Conrad, Princeton: Princeton University Press, 1990; John Womack, *Zapata and the Mexican Revolution*, New York: Vintage, 1968.

47 John T. Alexander, *Autocratic Politics in a National Crisis: The Imperial Russian Government and Pugachev's Revolt*, Bloomington: Indiana University Press, 1969; Ann Wroe, *Perkin: A Story of Deception*, London: Vintage, 2004.

48 Tim Pat Coogan, *Michael Collins: The Man Who Made Ireland*, Basingstoke: Palgrave Macmillan, 2002.

49 Mao, *On Guerrilla Warfare*, p. 84.

50 Jocelyn and McEwen, *The Long March*; Snow, *Red Star Over China*.

51 Riall, *Garibaldi*; Ridley, *Garibaldi*.

52 Bell, *Toussaint l'Ouverture*.

53 Peter Rex, *The English Resistance: The Underground War Against the Normans*, Stroud: Amberley, 2014.

54 Cecil Field, *The Great Cossack: The Rebellion of Stenka Razin Against Alexis Michaelovitch, Tsar of All the Russias*, London: H. Jenkins, 1947; Paul Avrich, *Russian Rebels 1600–1800*, New York: Schocken, 1976.

55 Michael T. Foy and Brian Barton, *The Easter Rising*, Stroud: The History Press, 2011.

56 Machiavelli, *The Discourses*, p. 124.

57 Mancur Olson, *The Logic of Collective Action: Public Goods and the Theory of Groups*, Cambridge, MA: Harvard University Press, 1971.

58 Bascomb, *Red Mutiny*.

59 Weber, *Rationalism and Modern Society*.

60 Allan Mitchell, *Revolution in Bavaria, 1918–1919: The Eisner Regime and the Soviet Republic*, Princeton: Princeton University Press, 1965.

PART IV

Servants of the people

13
FOLLOWERSHIP

Leaders may be imposed on people through a variety of means: divine grace, inheritance, conquest or revolution, appointment by a higher authority, such as a board of directors, and so on. However, once they have taken up the reins of authority, they maintain themselves in power only through the consent of their followers.[1] That consent may be tacit or explicit; it may be given grudgingly or even out of fear, but it is essential if the leader is to survive. It is therefore time to take a look at followers, specifically how – and why – they choose whom they will follow and express their consent.

It is tempting to think that consent is the only legitimate source of authority and that view has been argued many times.[2] However, as Alexis de Tocqueville pointed out in his study of democracy in America, consent can easily turn into a form of tyranny, as the majority – or even a significant minority – who choose to follow a leader can use their power to oppress those who do not.[3] We will come back to this point in the next chapter.

For the moment, we shall concentrate on followers themselves. Thus far we have spoken of followers as a homogeneous body, united and coalesced around a single purpose, but in practice this rarely happens. Because followers are not united and are often formed into factions, leaders need other sources of authority who are also important in helping leaders to establish themselves and become accepted.

What do followers demand of leadership? What are they looking for? Having discussed this, we will then look at situations where followers have the power to choose their own leaders and some of the ways in which they do, the purpose being to shed further light on follower expectations. From there we will go on to look at the nature of the contract between leaders and followers. Even when followers do not directly choose their leaders, they still have a choice as to whether to serve that leader, and we will examine how that choice is made.

Followership

The idea that followers are not a homogenous body with a single mind and will is hardly new, although it is surprising how often we discuss them as if they were. Writing in *Harvard Business Review*, Robert Kelley classified followers along two dimensions, their level of independence and their level of activity. He came up with classifications such as 'sheep' (low independence, passive), who need constantly to be encouraged and motivated; the 'alienated' (high independence, passive), whose views of leadership are largely negative and who are unlikely to follow the leader willingly; the 'star followers' (high independence, active), who will judge leaders on their own merits but who are strong supporters of the leader they decide to follow; and the 'pragmatics' (average independence, average activity), who tend to go along with whatever the majority decides to do.[4]

Barbara Kellerman also classified followers by their level of engagement, with a spectrum ranging from 'isolates', who know little and care even less about who their leaders are and who certainly do not follow them willingly to 'bystanders', 'participants', 'activists' and, finally, 'diehards', who are devoted to their leader or cause and will, figuratively and sometimes literally, be prepared to die for them.[5]

Boas Shamir, on the other hand, looked at the interaction between leaders and followers and found several different theoretical models, including:

- Followers as recipients of leadership, a model which sees followers as largely passive, receiving and obeying directions from leaders but not part of the leadership process;
- Followers as moderators of leadership impact, where the effectiveness of the leader depends in large part on the response of the followers;
- Followers as constructors of leadership, where the idea of leadership is constructed by followers, i.e. followers create the leaders they need;
- Followers as leaders, a form of shared leadership in which leaders and followers evolve out of each other and the distinction between them becomes blurred.[6]

Shamir's scheme is useful because it shows how many different ideas there are about the ideal distribution of power. In the first model, power is heavily concentrated in the hands of leaders, which is probably one of the reasons why so many leaders have been attracted to it. The other models accept a lesser or greater distribution of power and recognise the collaborative and contested nature of the social space.

But what none of these concepts of followership do is to show the internal dynamics of followers themselves. Followers do not remain conveniently in their boxes, nor do they fit neatly into Shamir's categories; or at least, not throughout their entire career as followers. They change their minds; their expectations and hopes evolve; their views of their leader will change as they become more familiar with that leader and learn more about them.

There are, apparently, passive followers who take directions and follow orders without comment or complaint; until suddenly they turn against their masters, like the slaves on *La Amistad* or in Toussaint L'Ouverture's Haiti. There are also dynamic, highly engaged followers who will suddenly switch off and become disengaged, particularly if there is a change in leadership. The New Model Army served Oliver Cromwell faithfully, suppressing challenges to his leadership by both royalists and radicals, such as the Levellers and Fifth Monarchists, but after his death they became disengaged and made no move to prevent the restoration of the monarchy; some regiments actively supported King Charles II.[7] Sir Alex Ferguson was an inspirational coach at Manchester United football club, but his successor, David Moyes, coaching the same players, struggled to make impact and lost his job after just ten months.[8] Steve Jobs was revered by many of his employees at Apple, but those same employees failed to give the same devotion to his successor, John Sculley.[9]

What divides followers, and what causes them to change their behaviour? Historically, many of the divisions between follower groups were – and to a large extent still are – determined by birth. Social class, education, wealth and gender coloured views of leadership and led not only to differing expectations but also to inequalities in power distribution within the broader society. To these we can add other personal and psychological barriers, such as information asymmetries, fear, lack of trust, lack of experience, lack of cognitive ability and other issues, that mean people perceive the world around them in very different ways. Conflicts between groups with different expectations and perceptions often led to the rise of leaders who would represent them and lead them in the struggle. Although expectations differed, the one common theme was that people followed leaders who would take them were they wanted to go.

Historical views of followership

Historical writings on leadership and followership shed a little light on the motivation of followers. They also show the relationship between followership and power. In Shamir's scheme, the concept of followers as recipients of leadership can be linked to a high power distance and a concentration of power in the hands of leaders. The ancient Egyptian text known as the *Duties of the Vizier* defined a society and administrative structure with power strongly concentrated at the top; the task of followers was to obey without questioning. In ancient China, the legalist scholar Han Fei held much the same view.[10] It should be added that in both societies, followers were far from powerless, as the long history of revolts and palace *coups d'état* clearly attests.

More realistically, in the sixteenth century both Machiavelli and his near-contemporary Baldesar Castiglione argued that followers choose their leaders; accordingly, they recognised that followers have power.[11] Both also discussed the motivation of followers. Machiavelli made a distinction between mercenaries and citizens, the former group serving out of self-interest and the latter out of a duty to their city and their people; Castiglione urged his readers to consider carefully which leader to serve and to accept only one who would help them further their own careers. The Japanese writer Yamamoto Tsunetomo believed in a duty of service, but he too held to a theory of choice; a *samurai* should find a master who will allow him to discharge that duty in an honourable manner.[12]

The European Enlightenment brought about a new consideration of the roles of follower and leader. Rousseau's concept of a social contract was predicated on reciprocity; leaders and followers both have power, which they agree to combine in order to achieve a common end. Tocqueville believed that a constitutional monarchy was the best system for regulating the distribution of power, with the sovereign and the people keeping each other in check. The notion of distributed power is also present in the works of some early writers on business and management, including Lillian Gilbreth, author of *The Psychology of Management*, Henri Fayol's *General and Industrial Management* and Walther Rathenau's *The New Society*, all written in the first quarter of the twentieth century.[13]

Mary Parker Follett argued that power was distributed still more broadly and that real power lay in the hands of followers; it was they who decided through their collective actions what course a society or an organisation should take and who would lead them. In her view, successful leadership was very much contingent on the demands of followers, and like later writers such as Boaz Shamir and Ronald Greenleaf, she blurred the boundaries between follower and leader, arguing that *control* is a myth and that true leadership is a matter of effective *coordination*.[14] Followers, in turn, were motivated by a desire to create a fair and just society and thus would naturally work together to reach this goal.

Finally, of course, Karl Marx and his followers argued for a complete redistribution of power away from the elites to the mass of people, the so-called 'dictatorship of the proletariat'. Followers of Marx interpreted this idea in several ways. Lenin advanced the idea of a one-party state where the proletariat delegated power to a new set of leaders who would be responsible to the people. Rosa Luxemburg believed, correctly, that this would simply turn into another form of authoritarianism and, as we have seen, argued for spontaneity, with leaders being created as needed by the people. Taking this view to the ultimate extreme, Kropotkin and other anarchist writers rejected the notion of leadership entirely.[15] Without leaders, of course, there could also be no followers.

But proponents of distributed power, including Marx, Luxemburg and Kropotkin, ran up against the same problem; followers are not homogenous, and they want different things. As we saw in Chapter 3, they share common goals – the need for survival and the desire to fulfil personal and group aspirations – but they define those aspirations in different ways.

Often, the fulfilment of one's own aspirations is achieved at the expense of the aspirations of others. The executives who followed John D. Rockefeller and helped him build his business empire, Standard Oil, achieved their aspirations to create a large and powerful company, but they did so by crushing rival firms and throwing their employees out of work, condemning them to poverty. The London merchant John Baillie became rich through his ownership of the Roehampton Estate, a sugar plantation near Montego Bay in Jamaica, but the slaves who worked his estate lived in misery and fear. Eventually, that fear gave them power; during the Baptist War in 1831, they rebelled and burned Roehampton to the ground.[16]

We will come back to the problem of conflict between follower groups later in this chapter, but first we need to consider the nature of followership. This typically expresses itself in two ways: choosing the leader and choosing whether to follow the leader. Not everyone has the power to choose his or her own leader, but as the Roehampton example shows, even the most oppressed have the choice of whether to serve.

Choosing leaders

The power to choose leaders is a very important kind of power, and those who have it tend to guard it jealously. The extreme reluctance with which various governments granted the right to vote to women – Switzerland only granted full female suffrage in 1971, and in many former colonies women only gained the franchise after separation from the colonial power – shows how elites tend to try to reserve the power of choice to themselves. Of course, this refers only to formal choice, which is recognised by law; in practice, women responded to their exclusion from power by choosing leaders of their own. Ethnic minorities, members of the lower classes and other excluded groups did the same, competing with elites within the social space or setting up new independent spaces outside the established power system.

The power to choose leaders has traditionally been seen as the prerogative of a small group of elites (oligarchy) or a broader spectrum of the population (democracy).[17] In practice, it can be hard to tell the difference between the two concepts. Ancient Athens veered for a time between oligarchy and democracy before settling on the latter, but the democratic franchise was extended only to landowning men, thereby excluding women, servants, slaves and the poor.[18] Democracy, yes, but democracy for the few.

Oligarchies

Until early modern times, leaders who were chosen directly were nearly always selected by oligarchies. The Roman Republic, for example, was closely modelled on Athens. A rare exception is the Althing, the parliament of medieval Iceland, which could be attended by any free man (once again, women and slaves were excluded). This system lasted until 1262, when Iceland submitted to the Norwegian Crown and became a monarchy; the Althing continued to exist but was now more of an advisory body, similar to the English parliament. The Althing recovered its full sovereign function in 1940, when Iceland declared independence.[19]

The Italian republics of the Middle Ages originally elected their leaders, although many fell under the control of military dictators; Florence continued to elect its leaders until 1532, when it came under the direct control of the Medici family, and the Republic of Venice survived until 1796, when the city was conquered by Napoleon.[20] The Veche, the assembly of nobles in the Russian city of Novgorod, held effective power in the city and elected its *de facto* leaders, the *posadnik* (mayor), *tysyatsky* (commander of militia) and the city's archbishop. The Veche also invited princes such as Alexander Nevsky to become titular leaders, but often the prince was an absentee, represented in the Veche by his lieutenant, the *namestnik*.[21]

In the fifteenth century, the Sejm, the assembly of nobles of Poland, began to acquire more power at the expense of the king, and from 1573 to the partition of Poland, the Sejm also elected the king, doing away with the concept of monarchy by inheritance.[22] Elected kingship was also a feature of Igbo society in what is now Nigeria. In the kingdom of Nri, one of the major Igbo polities, the *eze* (king) was elected by the priestly class and was himself a priest. Another kingdom, Osomari, had a dual monarchy with separately elected kings and queens, the king looking after 'male' affairs and the queen dealing with 'female' business, including trade and commerce. Omu Okwei, elected queen in 1935, was elected by her fellow traders after a very successful business career.[23] From the thirteenth century onwards, Holy Roman Emperors were, technically speaking, elected, but they were chosen by an elite group of just seven electors, three archbishops and four princes or kings. By the sixteenth century the Habsburg dynasty had become so dominant that the title became *de facto* hereditary, with the electors automatically choosing the heir of the last emperor.[24]

What kind of leader were these oligarchs looking for? In the case of Novgorod, the Veche was very often looking for a war leader. Aleksandr Nevsky had been invited to be prince of Novgorod in the expectation that he would remain a figure-head, but in a time of crisis he turned out to be quite a good military commander, defeating a Swedish invasion at the Battle of the Neva. He then returned to his home in Vladimir, but when Novgorod was threatened with a new attack, this time by the Teutonic Order, the Veche sent for Aleksandr once more. Returning to the city, he defeated the Order at the Battle of Lake Peipus. He later proved to be an effective diplomat, negotiating a peace treaty with Sweden.[25]

The Polish Sejm also looked for war leaders and diplomats, sometimes choosing non-Poles as kings if they were felt to have good international connections. Henri, duke of Anjou and a younger son of Henri II of France, was elected king for this reason, although he did not prove to be an overwhelming success. Some *doges* (dukes) of Venice were also war leaders, but on the whole doges were chosen for their skill as diplomats and administrators, able to govern not only Venice itself but also its widely dispersed empire in the eastern Mediterranean. The remarkable Enrico Dandolo, elected doge when he was in his mid-eighties and blind, strengthened Venetian control over the Dalmatian coast and then masterminded the coalition of Venetian and crusader forces that seized Constantinople in 1204, giving Venice control of most of the Byzantine Empire for the next sixty years.[26]

Elites also chose leaders who would protect their own interests, primarily by preserving the oligarchy. One of Henri of Anjou's first acts as king of Poland was to sign into law a number of privileges for the nobility, including formalising their right to elect their kings. Early in his reign as doge of Venice, Enrico Dandolo issued an edict expelling foreign merchants from the city, thus protecting the interests of the native Venetian merchants who had elected him. Although the signing of the Magna Carta at Runnymede is often hailed as the beginning of English democracy, a close examination of the charter's clause shows a number of measures designed to protect the interests of the barons who forced King John to sign.[27] The College of Cardinals, the oligarchical group that chose the pope – usually selecting a candidate from their own number – tended to choose popes who would first and foremost be sympathetic to the interests of the cardinals themselves or their patrons. Clement V was elected pope thanks to the votes of French cardinals, themselves acting on instruction from the French king, Philippe IV, who sought to control the papacy for his own political purposes.[28]

Even where the elites had no power to choose the leader, they nonetheless created institutions through which they could express their views and attempt to influence decisions in their favour. The Diet of the Holy Roman Empire, the Estates-General of France, the Cortes of León in Spain and the Parliament of England are examples of institutions, initially of nobles only, which sought to take back a measure of power from the monarchy. In the case of England, this led several times to open conflict between the elites and their leader, notably in the Barons' Wars and the English Civil War.[29] The Estates-General and the English (and later the Scottish) Parliament expanded to allow representation from other groups, notably the clergy and the wealthy middle classes, in effect admitting them to the elites.

Transition

Some very early societies chose their leaders democratically, and some still do. Psychologists and anthropologists such as Steve Taylor and Margaret Power have shown how some hunter-gatherer groups choose leaders spontaneously, replacing them as needed, and team up to prevent power-hungry leaders from gaining control by ostracising or expelling those individuals before they can take power.[30] However, as we saw earlier in this book, the increasing complexity of civilisation led to the emergence of elites and higher levels of power distance across most societies. Although those follower groups that were excluded from power made sporadic attempts to reclaim it, they rarely succeeded; when they did succeed, they established themselves as a new elite, perpetuating the power distance.[31]

In politics, however, things did begin to change. Particularly in Europe, different states evolved very different trajectories. Around 1300, England, France and the Holy Roman Empire were governed along broadly similar lines by inherited monarchies with assemblies either of nobles or at least dominated by nobles representing the interests of followers. However, all three states then evolved in different ways.

In England there was a gradual move towards constitutional monarchy and parliamentary democracy. Particularly in the aftermath of the Second Barons' War, the monarchy began to evolve a closer relationship with parliament, expanding it to include representation from the minor gentry and the towns.[32] The crown conceded still more power to parliament over the years, to the extent that when Charles I attempted to curb the power of parliament, parliament's response was to rise in revolt, leading to the English Civil War. Further concessions were made during the restoration of the monarchy and after the accession of William III and Mary in 1689.[33] In the nineteenth century, reform movements such as the Chartists called for still broader access to power by widening the franchise and allowing more people to take part in elections. By 1884 the Representation of the People Act allowed around 60 per cent of adult males to vote, although the poorest men – and women, of course – remained excluded until the full franchise was finally granted.[34]

In France, by contrast, democracy retreated from the already low threshold it had reached in the Middle Ages. The Estates-General met in 1614, but during the period of absolutist rule that followed they were not summoned again until 1789. When the Estates-General did meet, it shrugged off royal control and transformed itself into a revolutionary movement, evolving into a series of short-lived democratic institutions, the National Assembly, the National Constituent Assembly and the National Convention. Napoleon, and then later the restored Bourbon monarchy, rolled back these democratic reforms. There was another brief flirtation with representative government after the monarchy was overthrown again, but it was not until the foundation of the Third Republic that the path towards democracy was resumed.[35] In the Holy Roman Empire and its successor, the Austrian Empire, the diet became a cipher with no real power. The revolutions of 1848 created pressure for more representative government, and the elites gave a little ground, reluctantly, but it was not until the collapse of the empire that anything like democracy emerged.[36]

Why did these countries evolve in such different ways? Anglo-Saxon England had its own representative assembly, the Witan, and the early parliaments may have been harking back to this model.[37] Even more importantly, the political and economic structures of medieval England made it virtually impossible for the king to rule without consent of parliament because parliament, especially the House of Commons, where the membership consisted mostly of wealthy gentry and merchants, had access to money, and the king very often did not. Gaining control of the king's ability to levy taxes was a key moment; from then on, parliament had power the king could not ignore, and it used its position to steadily gather more power to itself. In France, the king was able to keep control of tax-gathering powers, but abuse of that power to overtax the poorest members of society and an inability to manage public finances finally led to an explosion and the downfall of the monarchy. In Austria, the same problems existed, but the state managed to maintain its monopoly of violence and crushed dissent whenever it arose.

Of course, the shift in power in Britain was just that, a transfer of power from the monarchy to an elite group of nobles and the middle classes. This group used their power very effectively to exclude other members of society for several centuries. What ultimately forced them to give ground was the threat of revolt, first in the guise of Chartism, later in the form of socialism, anarchism and other radical movements, and finally in the women's suffrage movement.[38] Unlike many other countries, the British elites were wise enough to give ground to the radical movements before real violence erupted. In the case of women's suffrage, however, they refused to budge, and ultimately part of the women's movement did turn to violence in order to achieve its end.

Resistance to change was partly a matter of the elites protecting their own interests, but even those who had an ideological interest in changing society had doubts about whether democracy was the best way forward. Edmund Burke, the leading British conservative thinker of the late eighteenth century, believed that the common people lacked the necessary knowledge and education to exercise the vote responsibly; left to their own devices, they would fall prey to orators and demagogues. The 'will of the people' or 'will of the nation', can lead to a despotism every bit as cruel as a dictatorship. The liberal supporters of the Risorgimento in Italy in the nineteenth century were similarly dubious, unsure whether the people could be trusted to vote in a responsible manner, and a later Italian writer, Vilifredo Pareto, argued that democracy would simply lead to the creation of new elites. James Madison, who went on to become fourth president of the United States, thought that democratic government would be unstable and turbulent and, like Burke, lead to the tyranny of the majority and the oppression of minorities. It would be better, Madison said, to have a stable republican government controlled and guided by elites.[39]

And many states and polities still did not offer followers a choice of leader at all. Nor, outside of politics, did many other institutions. Popes were elected, and members of the military-monastic orders, the Knights Templar, the Knights Hospitaller and the Teutonic Order, were chosen by the senior officers of the order, but other church leaders were appointed. As we saw earlier, formal military units almost never chose their leaders, which were instead imposed upon them through the chain of command. Mutineers, who have defied authority and rejected the chain of command, will often choose their leaders, like Fletcher Christian on the HMS *Bounty* or Richard Parker, the emergent leader of the Nore mutiny, but they are a special case. There is evidence that the crews of some pirate ships in the seventeenth century elected their captains, but these were not formal military organisations.[40]

It was also extremely rare for businesses to allow their employees a say in who their managers and bosses were. In large part this is due to the view that entrepreneurs 'owned' their businesses, and the only duty of employees was to obey orders. Entrepreneurs and their managers feared that sharing or delegating power would lead to loss of control. Many businesses only appointed family members to top positions, on the grounds that only family could be fully trusted; at the Medici Bank, Cosimo de' Medici made certain that every accountant and manager with responsibility for finances was a member of his extended family, although he did make one exception; Giovanni d'Amerigo Benci, a talented young accountant, was promoted to the senior executive team and eventually became Cosimo's deputy.[41]

The exception was cooperatively owned businesses. Although there are earlier examples, the growth of cooperatives began during the Industrial Revolution, in part as a response to the overwhelming power of the factory-owning entrepreneurs. Robert Owen, one of the first promoters of the movement, aimed to create entire communities that were self-sufficient and self-governing.[42] His attempts to do so, notably at New Harmony in the United States, were not successful, but Owen's ideas were picked up by others, notably by William King, who founded a newspaper to disseminate information about cooperatives. By the end of the nineteenth century, there were hundreds of cooperatively owned businesses in Britain, including the Rochdale Pioneers and the Co-operative Wholesale Society. There were also cooperatively owned financial institutions, variously known as building societies, friendly societies or credit unions. The idea also spread to Europe, perhaps most famously to Spain, where the Mondragón cooperative grew into a major business. Some cooperatives, like the Rochdale Pioneers, seem to have managed without formal leaders at all, at least in the first instance; decisions were made collectively. Many others elected their leaders from among their membership or chose managers from outside their ranks. But they remained and remain a small minority of business enterprises.[43]

Democracies

By the end of the First World War, pressure from increasingly articulate, well-educated and confident people who were no longer prepared to accept their exclusion from power and who were armed with new and powerful ideologies, liberalism, socialism and anarchism eroded the power of the elites.[44] In some cases, such as Britain, France, America and the Scandinavian countries, they gave way voluntarily, ceding power to their followers and granting near universal suffrage to both men and women. In others, such as Russia, Austria and Germany, the old order collapsed, and those who had been followers moved in to fill the power vacuum, seizing the right to vote in their own leaders. In all three countries, this situation did not last for long; democracy was too fragile to withstand the forces of autarky and totalitarianism. But when the totalitarian regimes also collapsed, democracy in one form or another returned.

What changed? There seems little doubt that social expectations and aspirations had changed. Enlightenment notions of personal liberty coupled with the impact of rising prosperity had created new ambitions.[45] The middle classes were already enjoying the fruits of that prosperity in forms such as department stores and mass tourism.[46] Now, the rest of the populace also wanted these material things, and they knew that they needed power in order to get and keep them. Coupled with this was a desire for personal freedom. Mere survival was no longer enough. In *Self-Help*, Samuel Smiles had set out a gospel for self-improvement and progress, whereas other writers, such as Émile Zola in France and Theodore Dreiser and Upton Sinclair in America, used fiction to win the sympathy of the middle classes and cause some of them, at least, to lend their own power to the workers.[47] The Fabian Society in Britain is just one example of an ultimately middle-class institution set up to change society and tilt the balance of power more towards followers of all ranks.[48] Meanwhile in the background, Marx, Engels and their followers were promising to upend the social order, sweep away the old elites and put the proletariat firmly in charge.

Change duly came and the universal franchise was introduced in most democracies. But the 'universal' franchise was not really universal. Once the proletariat had been admitted to the franchise, like the bourgeoisie before them, they closed the gate behind them and turned the key. As John Stuart Mill pointed out in *On Liberty*, democracies have a habit of denying the vote to those who are not deemed worthy of it for one reason or another: for example, Roman Catholics in Britain were denied the vote until 1829, purely on the grounds of their religion. In *The Subjection of Women* Mill again takes the new order to task for excluding women on the spurious grounds that they were not deemed to have the mental capacity to exercise the vote; a decision made entirely by men, one that could only be justified by men's unwillingness to share power.[49] And even once the franchise had been extended, as Michel Foucault has pointed out more recently, society still excludes those who are deemed 'unfit', such as convicts, the mentally ill and children; again, it is society that decided, often arbitrarily, what these unfit categories are and why they should be denied representation.[50] Non-citizens are also excluded, although the actions of government could have severe consequences for them.

In addition to demanding the franchise in order to exert power and make changes in society more generally, followers now also began to demand more power in the workplace. Some, like John Spedan Lewis, the department store owner, handed over control willingly, convinced that giving workers ownership and control of the business was the fair and responsible thing to do. Others experimented with co-partnerships schemes, giving workers a share of the business without ceding control; in fairness, even John Lewis did not give his workers the right to appoint their own bosses. Others like Benjamin Seebohm Rowntree and Christopher Furness struggled honestly to see how such a scheme could work in practice.[51] In the case of Furness, at least, we can see a desire to do the right thing conflicting with an almost instinctive fear of giving up control.

And, of course, the vast majority of owners refused to even contemplate ceding control to workers. As a result, the workers turned to their own parallel structures, forming their own institutions and choosing their own leaders. Facing this new challenge, the elites fought back. In many countries, trades unions were initially illegal, and membership of a union could be a criminal offence. In tsarist Russia, union organisers were imprisoned or exiled to Siberia, and in 1905 a demonstration by workers in St Petersburg was broken up by Cossacks, with more than a hundred people killed. The Peterloo Massacre in Britain and the Pullman and Homestead strikes in America are similar examples of repression, with the lower death toll being the only difference.[52]

The response by the workers and their newly chosen leaders was twofold. Some, like Samuel Gompers in the US, encouraged their followers towards moderation, stressing that they could get what they wanted through peaceful negotiation. Others, like the Industrial Workers of the World, turned towards radical politics and made alliances with socialists and anarchists. Russian trade unions became closely connected with the social revolutionary movement, and from 1905 onwards were increasingly involved in violence; many senior Bolsheviks, such as Felix Dzherzinsky, the future head of the Soviet secret police, started off as trades union organisers.[53] In Spain the Confederación Nacional del Trabajo was founded with the deliberate aim of fomenting revolution and overthrowing the state, in opposition to older established unions, which preferred to engage in collective bargaining. The CNT was the principal organisation of the Spanish anarcho-syndicalist movement.[54]

In the end, the radicals faded away, and the middle ground, the leaders like Gompers who favoured sharing power with the elites rather than seizing it by force won the day. The term 'industrial democracy' had been coined by the anarchist philosopher Pierre-Joseph Proudhon, who took it to mean the workers running the workplace themselves and choosing their managers from among their own number. But in the work of the Fabian socialists Beatrice and Sidney Webb, industrial democracy came to mean something else: management and workers existing together on terms of equality, negotiating away their disputes and recognising a mutual harmony of ends. Prosperity requires workers and managers to work together, the Webbs said, and to share power. Theirs is perhaps the ultimate expression of the principle of collaboration in the workplace social space.[55]

The social contract

That brings us to the final point of this chapter, namely that even when followers cannot choose their leaders directly, what they can do is choose to serve the leaders that are imposed upon them. That choice can be constrained and sometimes dangerous, but in theory at least, some degree of choice is often possible.

Whether followers decide to follow depends on their own motivation – in particular, what levels of risk they are willing to run – and their relationship to their leaders. As the classifications of leaders we have described make clear, there will always be some who identify with their leaders and are prepared to follow them to the bitter end, just as there will always be some who reject the leader and refuse their authority, offering passive or even active resistance.

When making that choice, followers look at the social contract that is on offer and make a calculation based on three principles. First, what benefits are on offer? Will I, as a follower, be able to achieve my own aspirations? Second, can this leader deliver? Can I, the follower, trust them to keep their promises to me? And do they have the power to make good on those promises? And third, if I choose to reject this contract, what risks do I run? Will the consequences of rejection be greater or less than the potential rewards of accepting the contract and toeing the line?

Leaders are not passive observers of the choice process. They can and do intervene in order to try to influence various follower groups, and the nature of that intervention will depend on the degree of engagement followers already have. Alexis de Tocqueville may have been the first theorist to comment on the role of the media – in his case, newspapers – and more generally, leaders have long been aware that communications channels of any kind, from personal appearance and speeches to social media, are vitally important in influencing followers.[56] Communications channels are particularly useful for influencing *middle-ground* groups identified at the start of this chapter, the pragmatics and bystanders, and persuading them to commit to the leader.

In the end, though, it is the offer contained within the social contract that matters most. To illustrate, let us take two examples of leaders who came to power in difficult circumstances: Konrad Adenauer, the first chancellor of the Federal Republic of Germany, and Yoshida Shigeru, the first prime minister of postwar Japan.[57] Adenauer, a former mayor of the city of Köln, helped found the Christian Democratic Union in 1946, with a promise to unite German society in the aftermath of the Second World War. As someone who had been imprisoned several times by the Nazis – and as an avowed anti-communist at a time when the Cold War was beginning – he was acceptable to the Allied powers, who still held Germany under military occupation; at the same time, he had stood up to the Allied generals on several occasions and was not seen as an Allied puppet. Most importantly, he rejected demands to concentrate on de-nazification, rooting out Nazi sympathisers and punishing them, and focused instead on rebuilding the ruined economy. Adenauer recognised that the German people, exhausted by the war and on the verge of starvation by its end, wanted peace and prosperity most of all, and he made that his promise to them. He was elected chancellor and served for another fourteen years.

Much the same is true of Yoshida, a former diplomat who had also been imprisoned briefly by the Japanese military government near the end of the war; he joined the newly founded Liberal Party in 1945. He became prime minister and won three successive elections on a promise of economic growth and prosperity. Yoshida and Adenauer are both sometimes described as visionaries who created a future for their ruined countries and persuaded others to follow them. An alternative view is that both correctly assessed the needs of their followers and offered them a social contract, one where the benefit to followers was the peace and prosperity they desperately wanted.

Sources of power

Consent, based on either knowledge and skill or symbolic-charismatic authority – sometimes, on both – is vitally important, but it does not fully explain the choice processes. When choosing which leader to follow, followers look for reasons to trust this leader or believe this is the person who will give them what they want. In doing so, they look beyond the social space and examine the character and nature of leaders or potential leaders. In particular, they look at what other sources of power the leader might offer.

Historically, conferred authority, be it claims to divine status or just a general sense of spirituality, has been an important source of authority. Even in recent, more secular times, that sense of spirituality offers an assurance of trust. People of faith, it is argued – often erroneously – must also be good people. Followers who also have faith, however vaguely held, will tend to gravitate towards leaders of a similar disposition, but even followers of a different faith or no faith at all can be persuaded to follow a leader who promises generosity, justice and fairness based on religious principles. George Cadbury, the Quaker leader of chocolate-maker

Cadbury Brothers, won the loyalty of his workforce, most of whom were not Quakers, both by making it clear that he was interested in their welfare and wanted to make their lives better and by treating them almost as partners in the business rather than cogs in a machine. The same is true of Ma Ying-piao, the Christian Chinese entrepreneur who founded Sincere department store in Hong Kong. Ma's combination of Confucian paternalism and Christian values, which he lived and exemplified in his own life and work, made him the model of a trustworthy employee. Jamsetji Tata's Zoroastrian faith and values helped him establish himself as a leader respected and admired by his Hindu, Muslim, Sikh and Christian workforce.[58]

Inheritance can also play a role in acceptance. In the past, the view that power could and perhaps even should be inherited was stronger than it is today, but there are logical reasons for this view. Inheritance meant the leader was probably – hopefully – already trained to do the things followers wanted them to do: lead armies into battle, administer justice, govern companies so that they would prosper and so on. When the leader was manifestly not able to do these things, followers became uneasy. The death of a leader while their heir was still a child and unable to govern was often a time of instability and unrest. Similar uncertainties prevailed when the leader died without a direct heir and a new dynasty needed to be founded. The death of Elizabeth I of England was a matter of deep concern; her nearest heir was the Scottish king James VI, and England had been at war with Scotland for much of the last four centuries. Could the new king be trusted? The same uncertainties bubbled up when the last Stuart monarch, Queen Anne, died and was replaced by the elector of Hanover, George I.[59]

The importance of inherent authority would seem to be obvious, as is the importance of access to power and the ability to use it effectively. To reiterate a point made several times already, we choose leaders who we know can get things done and help us achieve our goals. Conversely, if we think the leader cannot get things done and/ or is not trustworthy, we will turn away from them. Much depends on how well the leader projects their own character, abilities and values; that is, the impression they create in the minds of followers. Creating this impression is much easier said than done, especially given the diversity among followers that we saw at the start of this chapter. How they go about doing so is the subject of the next one.

Notes

1 Riggio *et al.*, *The Art of Followership*; Barbara Kellerman, *Followership: How Followers Are Creating Change and Changing Leaders*, Boston: Harvard Business Review Press, 2008; Barbara Kellerman, *The End of Leadership*, New York: HarperCollins, 2012; Marc Hurwitz and Samantha Hurwitz, *Leadership Is Half the Story: A Fresh Look at Followership, Leadership and Collaboration*, Toronto: University of Toronto Press, 2017; Boas Shamir, Rajnandini Pillai, Michelle C. Bligh and Mary Uhl-Bien (eds), *Follower-Centered Perspectives on Leadership*, Greenwich: Information Age Publishing, 2007.

2 Robert A. Dahl, *On Democracy*, London: Yale University Press, 2000; Dennis Thompson, *The Democratic Citizen: Social Science and Democratic Theory in the Twentieth Century*, Cambridge: Cambridge University Press, 1970; Edmund Morgan, *Inventing the People: The Rise of Popular Sovereignty in England and America*, New York: W. W. Norton, 1989.

3 Alexis de Tocqueville, *Democracy in America*, ed. Andrew Hacker, trans. Henry Reeve, New York: Washington Square Press, 1964.

4 Robert E. Kelley, 'In Praise of Followers', *Harvard Business Review*, November 1988, pp. 142–8.

5 Kellerman, *Followership*.

6 Shamir *et al.*, *Follower-Centered Perspectives on Leadership*.

7 Ian Gentles, *The New Model Army in England, Ireland and Scotland, 1645–1653*, Oxford: Blackwell, 1998; Gaunt, *Oliver Cromwell*.

8 Ferguson and Moritz, *Leading*.

9 Isaacson, *Steve Jobs*; Young, *Steve Jobs*.

10 van den Boorn, *The Duties of the Vizier*; Watson, *Han Fei Tzu*.

11 Machiavelli, *The Prince*; Castiglione, *The Book of the Courtier*.

12 Yamamoto, *Hagakure*.

13 Lillian E. Gilbreth, *The Psychology of Management*, London: Sir Isaac Pitman, 1914; Fayol, *General and Industrial Management*, trans. Constance Storrs, London: Pitman, 1949; Rathenau, *The New Society*.

14 Follett, *Creative Experience*; Shamir *et al.*, *Follower-Centered Perspectives on Leadership*; Greenleaf, *The Power of Servant Leadership*.

15 Karl Marx and Friedrich Engels, *The Communist Manifesto*, London: Penguin, 2015; Luxemburg, *Reform or Revolution*; Kropotkin, *The Conquest of Bread*; McLaughlin, *Anarchism and Authority*.

16 Tarbell, *A History of Standard Oil*; Mary Turner, *Slaves and Missionaries: The Disintegration of Jamaican Slave Society, 1787–1834*, Chiago: University of Illinois Press, 1982.

17 Dahl, *On Democracy*; Morgan, *Inventing the People*; Ben Isakhan and Stephen Stockwell (eds), *The Secret History of Democracy*, Basingstoke: Palgrave Macmillan, 2011; Jeffrey A. Winters, *Oligarchy*, Cambridge: Cambridge University Press, 2011.

18 Mogens Herman Hansen, *Athenian Democracy in the Age of Demosthenes*, Oxford: Blackwell, 1991.

19 Karlsson, *A History of Iceland*.

20 Hibbert, *The House of Medici*; Maurizio Viroli, *As If God Existed: Religion and Liberty in the History of Italy*, Princeton: Princeton University Press, 2012.

21 *The Chronicle of Novgorod*, trans. Robert Mitchell and Nevill Forbes, London: Camden Society, 1914.

22 Norman Davies, *God's Playground: A History of Poland*, New York: Columbia University Press, 2005; Oskar Halecki, *A History of Poland*, New York: Roy, 1961.

23 Isichei, *A History of African Societies to 1870*; Karin Loewen Loewen, 'Okwei of Osomari', in Anne Commire (ed.), *Women in World History: A Biographical Encyclopedia*, New York: Gale, 2002.

24 Whaley, *Germany and the Holy Roman Empire*.

25 *The Chronicle of Novgorod*; Mari Isoaho, *The Image of Aleksandr Nevsky in Medieval Russia: Warrior and Saint*, Leiden: Brill, 2006.

26 Roger Crowley, *City of Fortune: How Venice Won and Lost a Naval Empire*, London: Faber & Faber, 2011; Thomas F. Madden, *Enrico Dandolo and the Rise of Venice*, Baltimore: Johns Hopkins University Press, 2003.

27 James C. Holt, *Magna Carta*, Cambridge: Cambridge University Press, 2015; Stephen D. Church, *King John: England, Magna Carta and the Making of a Tyrant*, London: Macmillan, 2015.

28 Collins, *Keepers of the Keys*; Joseph Strayer, *The Reign of Philip the Fair*, Princeton: Princeton University Press, 1980.

29 Joseph F. O'Callaghan, *A History of Medieval Spain*, Ithaca: Cornell University Press, 1975; Schama, *Citizens*; John Maddicott, *The Origins of the English Parliament, 924–1327*, Oxford: Oxford University Press, 2010.

30 Steve Taylor, *The Fall: The Insanity of the Ego in Human History and the Dawning of a New Era*, London: Iff, 2018; Margaret Power, *The Egalitarians, Human and Chimpanzee: An Anthropological View of Social Organization*, Cambridge: Cambridge University Press, 2008.

31 Brinton, *The Anatomy of Revolution*; Canetti, *Crowds and Power*.

32 Maddicott, *The Origins of the English Parliament*; John Maddicott, *Simon de Montfort*, Cambridge: Cambridge University Press, 1996; Margaret Wade Labarge, *Simon de Montfort*, London: Eyre & Spottiswood, 1962.

33 Purkiss, *The English Civil War*; Cruickshanks, *The Glorious Revolution*.

34 Derek Heater, *Citizenship in Britain: A History*, Edinburgh: Edinburgh University Press, 2006.

35 Schama, *Citizens*; Doyle, *The Oxford History of the French Revolution*; Robertson, *Revolutions of 1848*; Maurice Agulhon, *The Republican Experiment, 1848–1852*, Cambridge: Cambridge University Press, 1983; Jean-Marie Mayeur and Madeleine Rebirioux, *The Third Republic from Its Origins to the Great War, 1871–1914*, Cambridge: Cambridge University Press, 1988.

36 Pieter M. Judson, *The Habsburg Empire: A New History*, Cambridge, MA: Harvard University Press, 2016; Robin Okey, *The Habsburg Monarchy, c. 1765–1918: From Enlightenment to Eclipse*, Basingstoke: Palgrave Macmillan, 2002.

37 Maddicott, *The Origins of the English Parliament*; Patrick Wormald, *The Making of English Law: King Alfred to the Twelfth Century*, Oxford: Blackwell, 1999.

38 Dorothy Thompson, *The Chartists: Popular Politics in the Industrial Revolution*, Aldershot: Ashgate, 1986.

39 David Bromwich, *The Intellectual Life of Edmund Burke: From the Sublime and the Beautiful to American Independence*, Cambridge, MA: Belknap, 2014; Hannah F. Pitkin, *The Concept of Representation*, Berkeley: University of California Press, 1972; Riall, *Risorgimento*; Joseph Femia, *Against the Masses: Varieties of Anti-Democratic Thought Since the French Revolution*, Oxford: Oxford University Press, 2001; Alexander Hamilton, James Madison and John Jay, *The Federalist*, ed. Goldwin Smith, New York: The Colonial Press, 1901; David F. Epstein, *The Political Theory of the Federalist*, Chicago: University of Chicago Press, 1984.

40 David Cordingly, *Under the Black Flag: The Romance and the Reality of Life Among the Pirates*, London: Random House, 2006.

41 de Roover, *The Rise and Decline of the Medici Bank*.

42 Donnachie, *Robert Owen*.

43 David J. Thompson, *Weavers of Dreams: The Origins of the Modern Cooperative Movement*, Berkeley: University of California Press, 1994; George Jacob Holyoake, *The History of the Rochdale Pioneers*, London: Swan Sonnenschein, 1893; Johnston Birchall, *The International Co-operative Movement*, Manchester: Manchester University Press, 1997; Whyte and Whyte, *Making Mondragon*.

44 E.P. Thompson, *The Making of the English Working Class*, London: Penguin, 2013.

45 John Benson, *The Working Class in Britain, 1850–1939*, London: I.B. Tauris, 2003; Jonathan Rose, *The Intellectual Life of the British Working Classes*, London: Yale University Press, 2010.

46 Miller, *The Bon Marché*; Piers Brendon, *Thomas Cook: 150 Years of Popular Tourism*, London: Secker & Warburg, 1991.

47 Smiles, *Self-Help*; Émile Zola, *Germinal*, trans. Roger Pearson, London: Penguin, 2004; Theodore Dreiser, *An American Tragedy*, New York: Signet, 2010; Upton Sinclair, *The Jungle*, London: Penguin, 2002.

48 A.M. McBriar, *Fabian Socialism and English Politics, 1884–1918*, Cambridge: Cambridge University Press, 1962; Lisanne Radice, *Beatrice and Sidney Webb: Fabian Socialists*, London: Macmillan, 1984; George Bernard Shaw (ed.), *Essays in Fabian Socialism*, London: Fabian Society, 1931.

49 John Stuart Mill, *On Liberty, Utilitarianism and Other Essays*, Oxford: Oxford University Press, 2015; Mill, *The Subjection of Women*.

50 Michel Foucault, *Discipline and Punish: The Birth of the Prison*, trans. Alan Sheridan, London: Penguin, 1991.

51 Lewis, *Fairer Shares*; Rowntree, *The Human Factor in Business*; Furness, *Industrial Peace and Industrial Efficiency*.

52 Walter Sablinsky, *The Road to Bloody Sunday: Father Gapon and the St Petersburg Massacre of 1905*, Princeton: Princeton University Press, 1976; Robert Reid, *The Peterloo Massacre*, London: William Heinemann, 1989; Demarest, *The River Ran Red*; Lindsay, *The Pullman Strike*.

53 Sheila Fitzpatrick, *The Russian Revolution*, Oxford: Oxford University Press, 2017; Robert Service, *The Russian Revolution, 1900–1927*, Basingstoke: Palgrave Macmillan, 2009.

54 Dick Geary, *Labour and Socialist Movements in Europe Before 1914*, Oxford: Berg, 1989.

55 Pierre-Joseph Proudhon, *What Is Property? An Inquiry Into the Principle of Right and Government*, Cambridge: Cambridge University Press, 1994; Beatrice Webb and Sidney Webb, *Industrial Democracy*, London: Longmans, Green, 1897.

56 Tocqueville, *Democracy in America*.

57 Williams, *Konrad Adenauer*; J.W. Dower, *Empire and Aftermath: Yoshida Shigeru and the Japanese Experience, 1878–1954*, Cambridge, MA: Harvard University Press, 1988.

58 Gardner, *George Cadbury*; Chan, 'The Organizational Structure of the Traditional Chinese Firm'; Lala, *For the Love of India*.

59 Collinson, *Elizabeth I*; Hannah Smith, *Georgian Monarchy: Politics and Culture, 1714–1760*, Cambridge: Cambridge University Press, 2006.

14
CONNECTING LEADERS WITH FOLLOWERS

'There go my people', quipped the French socialist politician Alexandre Ledru-Rollin. 'I must go after them, for I am their leader'. In another version the quote finishes, 'I must go after them, so I can find out where they want me to lead them'. The quote may be apocryphal, but it nevertheless sums up a problem faced by many leaders: where do followers want to go?

Ledru-Rollin himself never worked it out. During the revolution of 1848 he first advocated the socialist cause, but then inexplicably changed his mind and backed the liberal republican Alphonse de Lamartine. The liberals never fully trusted him because he was a socialist, and the socialists never forgave him for backing the liberals; his power dwindled and he spent twenty years in exile in England. Nor is he unique. Not long before this book was written, the imam of a mosque in the Sudan was confronted by a crowd of angry worshippers insisting he lead them in protests against the government of the dictator Omar al-Bashir. 'Get up and lead us!' one man shouted at him.[1]

Although leadership theory often insists it is the responsibility of the leader to develop the organisation's vision and then encourage followers to share it, some writers have argued that followers also have a role in creating vision. In *War and Peace*, Leo Tolstoy contrasts Napoleon, the autocrat who believed mistakenly that events moved according to his direction and that he was in control of his own destiny, with his opponent the Russian Field-Marshal Kutuzov who, as Tolstoy puts it, waited until the army knew what it wanted to do, and then gave the appropriate orders. *War and Peace* is of course a novel, but Tolstoy drew heavily on the experience of his uncle, Aleksandr Ostermann-Tolstoy, who had been one of Kutuzov's senior commanders, and there is good reason to believe that the picture he paints is accurate.[2] Similar sentiments were expressed in the twentieth century by Mary Parker Follett, who argued that citizens working together in communities of mutual interest should determine what is best for them, rather than having a strategy forced on them from the outside.[3]

Nevertheless, many leaders find it tempting to impose their own authority and insist the organisation conforms to *their* vision, not that of anyone else. Sometimes, as we saw in Chapter 10, this works. Frank Zappa, Herbert von Karajan and Vince Lombardi imposed their own vision on their organisations and were highly successful. The key factor is whether this vision is shared by enough follower groups. Where followers disagree with the vision or feel that their own interests are threatened by it, conflict is likely to ensue.

Because followers are fragmented into different groups, there will always be some who do not engage with the leader, and this means that some element of conflict is always likely to exist. At the same time, there will always be some people prepared to go along with the leader. How the leader secures the loyalty of the latter groups and imposes his or her will on the former is one of the key challenges of leadership.

A second challenge concerns the conflicts that emerge between these disparate follower groups. Internal conflict, fragmentation, loss of cohesion and direction can all threaten an organisation's stability, be it civil conflict within a society or disagreement among members of a sporting club. How well leaders manage these inevitable clashes of interest and conflicts is another important test of their leadership, especially when these different follower groups create leaders of their own. With multiple leaders and multiple follower groups in play, the social space of leadership can become very crowded indeed.

Contest and collaboration

As noted, two types of interaction between leaders and followers (and between leaders and leaders, and followers and followers) take place in the social space: contest, and collaboration. The contest for power between leaders and followers, each attempting to claim power from the other, has already been well documented in this book. At the same time, leaders and followers are forced to collaborate with each other in order to achieve their ends and get things done.

Leadership is only effective when the correct balance between these two forces has been achieved. In the past some leaders have been tempted to try to eliminate one or the other; that is, to achieve a social space that is either a) entirely collaborative and free from conflict, or b) purely adversarial without any hint of collaboration or compromise with the other parties. Rarely has any attempt to do either of these things been successful.

Attempts to eliminate conflict have taken two forms: peaceful negotiation to end conflict, and a short-term limited use of force to eliminate dissidents, so that peace and unity will prevail in the long run. Both have a long track record of failure. The attempts by the papacy to peacefully negotiate an end to the split between two branches of the Franciscan order of friars, the Observants and the Conventuals, ended in failure. The dispute was not a violent or dangerous one, concerning as it did two different interpretations of the rule of the order laid down by St Francis of Assisi, but it proved intractable. The Conventuals simply ignored attempts by successive popes to negotiate with them, knowing that the popes had very little bargaining power. The Conventuals knew where they wanted to go, and it was not where the popes wanted them to go. Nor could the popes use force against a movement that was distinguished by its piety and Christian observance and therefore could claim a great deal of moral authority.[4]

Forswearing violence and force, Gandhi attempted to unite the Indian independence movement by peaceful means. He was largely successful, but his authority was challenged by several groups, including Hindu nationalists who favoured armed insurrection, such as Subhas Chandra Bose, and more importantly the All-India Muslim League led by Muhammad Ali Jinnah. The latter was prepared to work with Gandhi on some levels, but he disliked the notion of *satyagraha*, fearing it would lead to chaos and the breakdown of order. The failure of Gandhi and Jinnah to work effectively together led to the partition of India.[5]

The other, paradoxical strategy of achieving peace by obliterating one's enemies, fared little better. We have already seen examples such as Stalin's purges and Mao's fomenting of the Cultural Revolution, both of which had the ostensible aim of eliminating 'enemies of the people'; both were still busy purging fresh groups of enemies when they died in office. Maximilien Robespierre was another who systematically eliminated enemies of the French Republic, proclaiming that only by doing so could the Republic find peace and unity. Fear that he was planning a fresh round of arrests and executions of members of his own faction, the Jacobins, led some of his intended victims to plot against him, staging the coup of Thermidor and removing him from power.[6] Diocletian's attempts to eliminate the dissenting Christian faith from the Roman Empire and impose religious conformity led to the deaths of several thousand Christians, but failed in its objective; many of his own officials disobeyed the order to arrest and execute Christians, and just thirteen years after Diocletian's death, Christianity received official recognition.[7]

Attempts to avoid collaboration or cooperation with followers and rule solely by force, whether force of law or military force, have been similarly unsuccessful. As we saw in Chapter 9, totalitarianism posited an ideal whereby all citizens obeyed the state, but in practice that never happened; the alienated and the isolates always existed, and resistance continued. Plots against Adolf Hitler continued throughout his regime, and in July 1944 a plot led by men at the heart of the German army and government came very close to killing him.[8]

Very often, violence only increases resistance. Captain Hugh Pigot of the Royal Navy believed in keeping his men in line through violent punishment; during his command of the frigate HMS *Success* he ordered regular floggings, despite two members of the crew dying of injuries. On his next command, HMS *Hermione* he continued to flog his crew, including one of his own officers, and ordered the bodies of several men who had died in accidents to be thrown overboard without a funeral. His punishments backfired when the crew mutinied and killed him.[9] In 1910 black sailors in the Brazilian navy complained about the brutal punishments being meted out by their white officers, often for no apparent reason. When their commanders ignored them, the sailors mutinied and took over several battleships. Opposition politicians took up the mutineers' cause, and the government was forced to engage in what it saw as a humiliating set of negotiations and offer an amnesty.[10]

Sometimes lack of collaboration is a consequence of neglect rather than deliberate force. In 1920, members of a British army unit raised in Ireland, the Connaught Rangers, protested when they heard that British-backed paramilitaries, the Black and Tans, were committing atrocities against Irish civilians. The initial protest was peaceful, the soldiers demanding something be done to check the abuses of the Black and Tans but received no response. Angry at being ignored, they staged an armed revolt. The mutiny was quickly put down and its ringleader, James Casey, was executed, but the entire affair could have been avoided by more sensitive handling.[11]

Collaborative space

What constitutes collaboration in the social space? What do leaders do in order to collaborate with followers? First of all, they understand and anticipate follower needs and aspirations. Importantly, as the previous chapter showed, these needs and aspirations are not homogenous; they fill a spectrum, and often quite a broad one, from the isolates and bystanders through participants, activists and diehards.

Two contrasting examples of leaders who realised this are the religious leader St Benedict of Nursia and the atheist entrepreneur Robert Owen. Born around 480 AD, Benedict opted for religious life and spent several years as a hermit before being to become abbot of a rather lax community of monks near Rome. Lacking experience as a leader, Benedict imposed his own ideas of discipline on the community, but this did not suit the monks, who resented his attempt to control them and tried to poison him. Surviving this experience, Benedict founded a new community at Monte Cassino. This time he was careful to set expectations for his followers, writing a combination of mission statement and procedures manual which became known as the Rule of St Benedict. This statement of intent was attractive to monks who wanted a clear understanding of their obligations to the monastery and what the monastery would give them in turn. Monte Cassino grew rapidly and the Rule of St Benedict was disseminated to other monastic communities around Europe. At New Lanark, Robert Owen was likewise aware that not all of his workers were motivated in the same way. He attempted to deal with this by catering to a broad range of needs, providing employment but also housing, education and other services to help his workers and their families meet their aspirations, whereas in the workplace the 'silent monitor' was designed to encourage those who were less engaged.[12]

Collaboration also involves negotiating with other actors in the social space. In particular it involves integrative negotiation whereby all parties share information and seek outcomes that benefit everyone.[13] Inevitably this involves giving up at least a small amount of power, trading power for some other benefit; or perhaps even for reciprocal power. The history of business is full of conflict between bosses and workers, but there are also examples of leaders bargaining with their employees to achieve a result that benefits all parties. The Czech manufacturer Tomás Bat'a introduced a profit-sharing plan for all employees, whom he called 'associates', and made dialogue with the associates part of his own management style. At his new factory in Zlín, Bat'a installed his office in a lift, so that when employees wanted to see the boss they did not come to him; his office came to them. In 1922 during an economic downturn, Bat'a offered his workers a choice of keeping everyone employed with lower wages until the economy improved again or making redundancies. In a show of solidarity, the workers chose the former; the workforce at Bat'a was very cohesive, and the workers were loyal to each other and to the firm. To make up the difference in lost wages Bat'a then paid local stores to give discounts on food and other goods until full wages could be restored.[14]

Like Bat'a, Pierrepont Noyes believed in partnership with his workers. Taking over the troubled tableware-maker Oneida, he introduced a number of measures to improve worker welfare, including higher wages. He once remarked that employers should 'make no welfare moves from fear, but always and only because you believe that company success should add to the comfort and happiness of every member of the working group'.[15] During the recession of 1921, Noyes called his workers together and gave them a frank picture of the economic situation of the company. He then asked if they would be willing to take a pay cut in exchange for a share of the profits, should there be any. The workers agreed and gave Noyes a standing ovation.[16]

The notion that leaders and followers are partners in an organisation has been long discussed. Benjamin Seebohm Rowntree, the Quaker chocolate-maker, was in favour of this principle, and he, Sidney Webb and other speakers made this point repeatedly in papers presented to the Rowntree conferences at Oxford in the 1920s and 1930s.[17] Harrington Emerson, the American railway engineer and management philosopher, borrowed from the military experience and encouraged organisations to use a 'line and staff' model, likening the 'line' to the hands and feet of an organisation that performed the actual work and the 'staff' to the brain that guided and controlled them.[18]

Emerson's model was crude; it allowed for no reciprocity, any suggestion that the workers on the 'line' might have brains of their own and be feeding back to the 'staff'. More sophisticated was the biological model of organisation first posited by Plato and described in more detail by the philosopher John of Salisbury in the twelfth century. According to Salisbury, the prince can be described quite literally as the 'head' of the state; the senate is its heart, the peasants and soldiers are equivalent to its limbs and so on. Crucially, Salisbury said that all these elements are linked together and depend on each other: the head cannot exist alone; it needs the heart and hands.[19] (Although it would be another five hundred years before William Harvey showed in detail how blood circulates through the body, physicians had been aware since classical times of the circulatory system and the role it played.)[20] This metaphor was also picked up and expanded on by many writers on business management including Andrew Ure in the 1830s, Charles Knoeppel in the early twentieth century and Gareth Morgan in the 1980s, who included the organisation as a biological organism as one of his eight metaphors for organisation.[21]

The idea of partnership offered a natural route to the sharing of power and control, which in practice meant leaders handing over power and control to followers. In *Utopia*, Thomas More suggested that the perfect society would have an elected prince responsible and accountable to the people (it should be added that More's perfect society also had slaves, usually convicted criminals, manacled with chains of gold).[22] Other utopian and millenarian groups, such as the Levellers and Diggers in England, the Beghards of medieval Germany and the Adamites, who appeared in the Middle East in the third and fourth centuries AD and then resurfaced in Bohemia in the fourteenth century, had either elected leaders or no leaders at all. Some of the influence of these movements can be detected in the writings of anarchists such as Proudhon and Kropotkin.[23] As already noted, Mary Parker Follett advocated communal decision-making, and the French socialist Charles Fourier laid down a structure for intentional communities known as *phalansteries*, where people would live and work communally and share power and control.[24]

But sharing power and control does not come easily to most leaders, who often become leaders in the first place because they are attracted to power and control; sharing these things, once achieved, does not fit with their mental models. Nevertheless, a surprising number of leaders have handed over power and control to their followers, and business again provides some outstanding examples. John Lewis gave both control and share ownership to his employees, arguing that only ownership could give authentic and lasting power to make decisions. Robert Owen experimented with intentional communities built around places of work, and more recently control of the architectural and engineering firm Arup was handed over to a series of trusts that spread profits among past and present employees. The firm's founder, Sir Ove Arup, has always been motivated by a desire to create a workplace where people can express their own creativity, and getting rid of control from the top was his way of freeing people to make their own decisions.[25] Sharing power and control do not have to be formal institutions; Ernst Abbé at Carl Zeiss and Edwin Land at Polaroid both gave their employees free reign and encouraged them to take control of and responsibility for their own work, believing this greater creative freedom would be good for both their people and their business.[26]

Contested space

It is a curious feature of leadership that most leaders seem to feel more at home in contested space than in collaborative space, despite the fact that contested space is considerably riskier. The British politician Enoch Powell once remarked that all political careers end in failure – his own would turn out to be no exception to the rule – but the same can be said of leaders in many fields of activity.[27] The captains and managers of sports teams stay in post until their team members and fans lose confidence in them and force them to depart; captains of industry wait until the corporation hits a crisis and the board of directors compel them to resign; generals and admirals may have glittering careers but eventually their powers begin to wane. Following the Battle of Austerlitz, Napoleon remarked that generals have a limited span of effectiveness before they burn out, adding that he gave himself five more years. He was proved right; by the time of the 1809 campaign in Austria his powers were on the wane, and in 1812 he led the disastrous invasion of Russia.[28]

Those leaders who have engaged successfully in contests with their followers and their rivals – who sometimes are the same people – share certain attributes. One of these is strength of purpose, the will and the courage to continue to fight a cause to the bitter end. Napoleon had this, as do many successful generals and business leaders; they also have an ability to recover from defeat and to carry on in the face of adversity. Emmeline Pankhurst's iron will carried her through repeated imprisonments and hunger strikes, and through conflicts with some of her own followers including one of her daughters.[29]

They also understand the inner workings of power, the sources of power and authority, and how to acquire it, and how to use power without abusing it. The line between use and abuse is often a fine one, and many leaders step over it. Robespierre's power derived in part from his moral authority – Thomas Carlyle called him the 'sea-green incorruptible' – but he overstepped the bounds of legitimate power and so was brought down.[30] Other attributes of the successful leader are patience, the willingness to make alliances and delegate power where necessary – an element of collaboration being required even in the midst of the most bitter contest – and ruthlessness, eliminating or driving out those followers who do not support you. These are all attributes that leaders fondly imagine they have. In reality, only a few leaders possess the full range of powers necessary to lead successfully over time. For the rest, short spasms of success are followed by inevitable decline.

Leaders who do possess all these attributes include Emmeline Pankhurst and Louis Gerstner, the former McKinsey consultant who turned IBM around from the brink of bankruptcy in the 1980s is one example. Patience and a strong will were needed force reforms through, but Gerstner also understood the power structure of IBM and what levers he needed to pull in order to exercise it. He was also ruthless in forcing out executives who could not or would not join his reform project. Other examples include Ratan Tata, the former chairman of the Tata Group in India, who took over a business riven by factions and lacking strategic direction and, through patience and determination, united the business once more turned it into a global leader. In Italy during the Renaissance, Francesco Gonzaga, Marquis of Mantua and his brother-in-law Alfonso d'Este, Duke of Ferrara, both managed to keep their states intact despite pressure from far larger powers including France, Spain, the papacy and the republic of Venice using a combination of skilful diplomacy and armed force. Both survived several attempts to kill them or force them out of office.[31]

Leaders who fail are often ones who get caught in the middle, either squeezed between rival groups of followers or unable to compete with more skilful leaders who lure their followers away. Unable to match the radical demands of his followers, Derek Robinson, the union leader at British Leyland, lost support, and eventually the firm's managers felt his power had weakened sufficiently to enable them to fire him. Alexander Kerensky successfully led the February Revolution in Russia in 1917, but he could not unite the various political factions that swirled around him, nor could he win the trust and support of the military. Through the summer of 1917 he progressively lost his grip on power and was overthrown by Lenin in October. Leon Trotksy, one of Lenin's lieutenants, rose to prominence as commander of the Red Army during the ensuing civil war, but following the war he failed to hold onto his power, which was progressively eroded by the new Soviet bureaucracy controlled by his rival Stalin. Trotsky was forced into exile and later murdered.[32] Lafayette similarly failed to hold onto power, despite the high hopes entertained of him when he first became leader of the National Guard in Paris, and Girolamo Savonarola, welcomed as a saviour by the people of Florence when he first seized power, alienated the people who had put him in power with his refusal to compromise and meet their demands. His followers abandoned him and he was overthrown, arrested and burned at the stake.[33]

Conflicts between followers

Followers have different aspirations and different demands, and where those aspirations and demands clash – or are perceived to clash – with those of other followers, conflict is likely to ensue. This can be dangerous for leaders, whose task is usually perceived to be the ending of conflict, either by suppression or by negotiation, to restore unity to the polity or institution. In authoritarian or totalitarian regimes, the leader will have a variety of repressive means to hand in order to end conflict; banning, arrest, imprisonment, exile or execution.

Those means still exist in democracies, but there are check and balances that limit their use. Ironically, those checks and balances were usually put there by followers, who fear that otherwise the same instruments of repression might be used against themselves. The classic example of this is the constitution and government structure established in the US after independence. Specifically, the army and navy were reduced to almost nothing thanks to fears that the government of the new country might use them against the populace. Instead of a standing army, people were given the right to defend themselves, including against the state; as the Second Amendment to the United States Constitution famously says, 'a well-regulated militia being necessary to the security of the state, the right of the people to keep and bear arms shall not be infringed'.[34]

As well as the danger of repression from the state, however, there is also the danger of what de Tocqueville described as the 'tyranny of the majority'. He was particularly critical of the US in this regard. 'I know of no country in which there is so little independence of mind and real freedom of discussion as in America', he wrote.[35] The majority in America, he maintained, set strong barriers to freedom of thought; within those barriers people were free to say and write what they thought, but those who went beyond those barriers were pilloried. His views are not unfounded. The War of 1812 between the US and Britain had opened up divisions in American society between the majority who favoured the war and the minority who did not, and newspaper editors who espoused the minority position were physically attacked and their homes and offices were ransacked.[36]

The problem for democratic leaders has been, and continues to be, the impossibility of reconciling the competing demands of followers. The majority can claim, with justification, that they are the majority; their views should prevail on utilitarian grounds, in that what they want will result in the greatest good for the greatest number. This has resulted in what Chantal Mouffe refers to as the paradox of democracy. Democracies claim to abide by liberal principles: liberty, the rule of law, respect for human rights. But what happens when the democratic principle of majority rule conflicts with this? What if the majority demands an end to the rule of law, or the abrogation of human rights?[37]

In the view of Alexis de Tocqueville, the task of leaders in a democratic society or organisation is to manage that paradox by reconciling democratic rights with liberal principles. It can be done. For more than a century the Conservative Party in Britain followed a philosophy of 'one-nationism', arguing that it had a duty to represent and govern all the populace, not just those people who voted for them. Since 1919 the Church of England has similarly tried to reconcile various competing views within the synod on issues such as human rights and sexuality. But the one-nation consensus within the Conservative Party collapsed in the 1980s under pressure from its more right-wing members who brought Margaret Thatcher to power, and the Church of England is under increasing strain from pressure groups promoting their own ideology.[38]

What choices do leaders have when confronted by conflicted between follower groups? Historically, they have had three: a) remain neutral and take action to suppress the conflict by force, b) attempt to negotiate and bring the partners together or c) take sides with one of the faction and help it defeat its rivals, thus increasing one's own power at the same time.

The first option requires the leader to have access to a considerable amount of power and the courage and confidence to use it. Tito, the postwar leader of Yugoslavia until 1980, is an example of a leader who had both. Yugoslavia was a patchwork of often conflicting nationalities and ethnic groups include Serbs, Croats, Bosniaks, Slovenes and Albanians. Tito's policy was to give the same rights to all ethnic groups, but to crack down hard on any who demanded more; he imprisoned a number of Albanian nationalists, and ruthless suppressed the 'Croatian Spring' movement in 1971, arresting more than two thousand people. As a result, Yugoslavia held together during his lifetime. His successors, unable to wield the same amount of power, were unable to prevent its breakup.[39] John Loudon, CEO of Royal Dutch Shell from 1952–65 also suppressed factionalism within his company, particularly between British, American and Dutch executives. His forceful methods led some to describe him as the 'iron fist in the iron glove'.[40]

The second option, bringing the parties together and negotiating a solution requires the leader to be a skilled negotiator and to also have a certain amount of moral authority derived from conferred or inherent sources to ensure they are taken seriously. Gandhi's humble demeanour and lifestyle won him respect and, later in life, an aura of sanctity which enabled him to command the respect of many of the competing factions demanding Indian independence and bring them together; Konrad Adenauer's record of opposition to the Nazis and his courage in standing up to the Allied military commanders in occupied Germany similar gave him a moral force which encouraged Germans to coalesce around his leadership.[41] Nelson Mandela's immense moral authority enabled him to bring white and black South Africans together, although healing the division between his African National Congress and the Inkatha Freedom Party took longer.[42] Elbert Gary, the first head of United States Steel, used his legal skills to negotiate a union between the Carnegie Steel Company and several other companies, forging them into a single entity.[43] In seventeenth-century Lebanon, the patriarch of the Maronite church, Istifan al-Duwayhi, drew together various faction in the church including those who favoured closer union with Rome and those who wished to preserve the church's independence, revitalising the church and strengthening its unity.[44]

Taking sides in the conflict is often the only option of a leader who wishes to unite the organisation or polity but lacks the power to do so. Uniting their own power with the power of the follower faction, on the other hand, will give them sufficient leverage to suppress or drive out other factions and restore unity. Alternatively, leaders sometimes ally with factions quite cynically to serve their own interest. During the merger between car manufacturers Daimler-Benz and Chrysler the chairman, Jürgen Schrempp, continued to favour executives from his own firm, Daimler-Benz, rather than those from Chrysler. Lacking the authority to impose his wishes on Chrysler unaided, he allied himself with the Daimler faction to take control. This was not the only reason for Schrempp's resignation and the failure of the merger, but it was certainly one of them.[45]

Simon de Montfort, Earl of Leicester, was the brother-in-law of King Henry III and the most powerful man in England. During Henry's conflict with his barons, Montfort could have chosen to support the king; had he done so, the rebellion would probably have failed. But Montfort had a fractious relationship with the king and in any case, saw an opportunity for himself. Taking command of the rebel army, he defeated and captured the king at the Battle of Lewes in 1264 and took control of the kingdom. However, his faction soon grew tired of his autocratic ways and many defected to the royalists. Less than a year later Montfort was defeated and killed.[46] The Marquis de Lafayette was a little more fortunate during the French Revolution. Allying himself with a faction that favoured reform of the monarchy but not its opposition, he took command of the National Guard and attempted to impose his authority on both the hardline royalists and the radicals led by Marat, Danton and Robespierre. Unfortunately, his faction did not have sufficient power to overcome the others, and Lafayette fled France; after a spell in an Austrian prison, he went into exile.[47]

Projecting leadership

Contest and collaboration both require active leadership; that is, the leader must attempt – and be seen to be attempting – to influence what is going on around them. Historically, passivity and inaction, especially in a time of crisis, is one of the worst sins a leader can commit. King Henry III of England was a pious man who won admiration for his good works in much the same way that his contemporary Louis IX of France did, but there the similarity ends. From our modern vantage point we might deplore Louis's objectives, but there is no doubt that he was an active leader who projected his authority, contesting against his opponents and collaborating with his allies. Henry, on the other hand, was a largely passive monarch who made only weak attempts to engage with his supporters and was not very good at handling conflict. The rebellion of the Second Barons' War was partly a consequence of his perceived weaknesses.[48]

How leaders project their authority is dependent on a number of things. One, of course, is the nature of their followers and how many different follower groups they have. Another is the nature of their own authority; conferred, inherited and inherent authority, authority by power and authority by consent can all be expressed in different ways. Conferred authority, for example, is more reliant on symbols and forms, whereas inherent authority is more a matter of personal expression. Byzantine emperors were not required to be 'authentic' in the modern sense; instead, they needed to play the game, perform the ceremonies and rituals of their role and behave in accordance with their semi-divine status. Napoleon's generals, on the other hand, had risen to their ranks based on personal ability and merit; their authenticity was one of the things their followers admired about them.[49]

Communication

How did leaders project their authority? As already discussed, they did so first of all through communicating with their follower groups. This meant not only finding the right channels of communication but also ensuring that the message was one that the followers wanted to hear. Conductors of symphony orchestras, those often-cited metaphors of leadership, succeed or fail based on how well they communicate with their orchestras, how well they deliver their own message and how carefully they listen to the messages the orchestra sends back.[50] All have their own styles of communication; some like Toscanini and Karajan were autocrats, but others were more collaborative.

Even at the height of his fame, the composer and conductor Joseph Haydn remained a modest and humble man, known for his honesty and gentle humour. To the musicians of his orchestras he was a father figure, who looked after their welfare and cared about them as people; the players called him 'Papa'.[51] In the early twentieth century, Pierre Monteux guided his orchestra through the opening performance of Stravinsky's *The Rite of Spring*, remaining calm and keeping the worried orchestra together despite a riot breaking out in the theatre behind him. Later he rebuilt the battered Boston Symphony Orchestra, which had been riven by strike action, infighting and resignations, but calmly and patiently reminding his players why they were there and what their purpose was.[52] Serge Koussevitzky, who succeeded Monteux in Boston, enjoyed a long career with the orchestra based on a close partnership with his musicians; working together, they made the BSO one of the leading orchestras in America partly through Koussevitzky's programme of mentoring young musicians and helping them establish their careers.[53]

Communicating the message is particularly important if there are barriers to the leader's acceptance that must be overcome. Revolutionary leaders who succeed, at least in the short term, are likely also to be leaders who can communicate well. During the French Revolution, Camille Desmoulins was an orator who could command the attention of crowds, and he and Jean-Paul Marat were also skilled journalists who attracted followers through their writing. Lenin also had a gift with words, spoken and written, and Emma Goldman the American anarchist was a prolific writer. Emmeline Pankhurst was also a persuasive speaker; recordings of her speeches reveal a radical message being delivered in a calm and measured manner, and all the more powerful for it.[54]

Symbols

I referred earlier to the importance of symbols and knowing how to use symbols to reinforce conferred or inherent authority is also an important way of projecting leadership. Symbols – icons, flags, coats of arms, trademarks and brand names – carry associations which can influence people's perceptions, but the importance and value of symbols changes over time and between cultures. It is important to know what symbols to use and when. Akhenaten, the heretic pharaoh of Egypt who attempted to replace the Egyptian pantheon with worship of a single deity, Aten, was probably motivated by personal belief, but his actions outraged his subjects who were deeply attached to their old gods and the panoply that surrounded them. After Akhenaten's death, records his reign was expunged from public monuments and histories.[55]

Akhenaten failed, but the Roman emperor Constantine I succeeded in introducing a new symbol and using it to draw his followers closer to him. Marching against Rome, Constantine saw a vision in the sky, possibly a solar halo or 'sun dog', which he perceived to be the *chi-rho* symbol often used by the Christian faith. It is possible that Constantine, who favoured the cult of Sol Invictus – although his mother was a Christian – did not fully understand the meaning of the symbol and merely took this vision as a sign from heaven; alternatively, he may have felt that this symbol would appeal to his soldiers, at least some of whom were secretly Christians. At all events, he emblazoned the *chi-rho* symbol on the banners of the army and went on to defeat his rival Maxentius at the Battle of Milvian Bridge and take control of the empire.[56]

Sports teams have also used symbols including logos, emblems, uniforms, mascots and cheerleaders to promote cohesion among followers. The practice of followers of fans wearing the colours of their team dates back to the Roman Empire and the bitter rivalry between chariot racing teams, the Greens and Blues. In 532 AD the Nika riots between followers of the two teams wrecked much of central Constantinople.[57] Music can also be a powerful symbol around which people coalesce; examples include military marches, religious hymns and the company songs that employees of Japanese firms would sing every morning in order to share in the *shafu* (company spirit).[58]

Individuals can even serve as symbols in their own right. Most offices of the Tata Group contains a portrait of its inspirational founder, Jamsetji Tata, in the foyer, and during his long tenure as chairman of General Electric, Jack Welch became a personal symbol of the company and its ambitions.[59] The image of Winston Churchill smoking a cigar became synonymous with the spirit of resistance in London during the Blitz, and the controversial American general George Patton, nicknamed 'Blood and Guts' by his troops, won the loyalty of his followers – through not his superior officers – through his flamboyant personality and language; a very different personality, Jeanne d'Arc, similarly became a symbol for the French people through her courage and piety.[60]

Values

Having a strong sense of the values that followers expect – including the characteristics discussed in Chapter 4, such as fairness, justice, generosity and humility – can be a strong factor in creating greater unity among followers and persuading them to follow willingly. We do not need to agree with these values, but we should recognise the conviction with which they were held. Trust in the leader is another important issue, and followers will often make their decision to follow based on whether the leader will live up to their promises. This often means living and enacting those values in daily life, or in modern parlance, 'walking the walk'.

Several of the business leaders already mentioned in this book could serve as examples. Jamsetji Tata, again, embodied his own values of service and responsibility to the community, and built business enterprises whose purpose was to serve the people. Tomás Bat'a believed in free enterprise as a means of spreading wealth among the people, and Robert Owen's commitment to social justice was embodied in many of his workplace and social reforms.[61] Other examples include Josiah Wedgwood, the English potter and entrepreneur who also supported causes including the advancement of science, social reform and the abolition of slavery. A prominent backer of the radical politician John Wilkes, Wedgwood also paid his employees well and treated them with respect, all in accordance with his own Unitarian religious values.[62]

Owen was an atheist, but other leaders draw their strong values from religious faith. Florence Nightingale felt a calling, not to faith itself, but to do something that would help others in society, including the less fortunate; it was this sense of calling that led her to take an interest in nursing several years before the Crimean War began.[63] Experience of war and imprisonment may have been one of the factors that turned Francis of Assisi towards a more spiritual life and awakened a sense of calling that led to the foundation of the Franciscan order.[64] In both cases, those strongly held values and the courage to live them attracted other people to join them.

Leading by example

Closely related is the notion of leading by example, or at the very least, being present alongside followers especially in times of crisis. Followers like their leaders to be visible. They also like to know that their leaders are running the same risks as themselves and not merely sending the followers out to the dirty work while they sit in their offices in comfort. One of the main complaints by front-line troops during the First World War – not always justified – was that while they endured the mud and danger of the trenches, their general lived in comfort far behind the lines. During the so-called Nivelle Offensive, French troops marching to the front lines began making 'baa' noises like sheep whenever they saw a senior officer, indicating that they knew they were being marched to the slaughter. A few days later widespread mutinies broke out, forcing the French commanders to cancel the offensive.[65]

In contrast, Frederick II of Prussia made a point of sticking with his men no matter how dangerous the situation was. At the Battle of Torgau, both Frederick and the commander of the opposing Austrian army, Field-Marshal Daun, were wounded, although neither was serious. The battle at this point was going in favour of the Austrians and Daun, assuming he had won, left the field to have his wounded dressed. Frederick, in contrast, stayed with his men despite his pain, rallied the army for another effort, and won.[66]

In sport, too, captains who set an example to their team tend to command greater loyalty. Douglas Jardine, the English cricket captain who led his team through the 'bodyline' tour of Australia in 1932–3, took full responsibility for his team's tactics, bowling straight at opposing batsmen in a manner which many thought was unsportsmanlike, and shielded his players from criticism. Later, when other teams began inevitably to use the same tactics against England, Jardine led from the front, facing the opposition's fast bowlers despite the obvious physical risks and blunting their attack. A complex character, Jardine was not always personally liked by his team members, but all the players respected and followed him.[67]

Making alliances

Given the element of collaboration involved in leadership, the ability to make alliances is a powerful way of extending and projecting leadership to other follower groups, not just one's own. During his short career as secretary-general of the United Nations, Dag Hammarskjöld showed considerable skill at pulling disparate, often quarrelling groups together and bringing them to see his point of view. His only major failure was to overcome the opposition of the Soviet leader Nikita Khrushchev, who was attempting to control the United Nations for his own political ends.[68]

An earlier politician, William Pitt the Younger, prime minister of Britain from 1783 to 1801 and again from 1804 to 1806, governed at a time when the political scene was highly fragmented; the two main factions, Tories and Whigs, were split into sub-factions that at times had more in common with the opposing party than each other. Pitt was able to unite enough of these factions to form a remarkably long-lasting and effective government at a time of crisis in the country. His successor, Lord Grenville, attempted to replicate Pitt's methods in the so-called Ministry of All the Talents, but lacking Pitt's diplomatic skills his government fell apart after little more than a year.[69]

Getting results

Followers like winners, and they gravitate towards leaders who can get things done because they know these leaders offer them the best chance of meeting their own aspirations. Alexander of Macedon inspired loyalty in his troops because he had a habit of winning; although he did not win all of his battles, he won enough that people remembered the victories and forgot about the rest.[70] Sports team managers such as Vince Lombardi and Alex Ferguson would always receive support from their players, so long as they continued to win matches and trophies.[71]

Getting results is, of course, easier said than done, partly because what good results look like varies so widely from field to field, from sport, religion and the arts and music to commerce, politics and war. For leaders who want to succeed, the lesson seems to be that both contest and collaboration are necessary elements of leadership, and the good leader is someone who can turn their hand to both in equal measure.

Leaders can of course be trained to take on both these roles. One of the purposes of hereditary or inherited leadership is to allow leaders to be trained by their prede-cessors. Succession planning lies at the heart of the hereditary principle, and always has done. Monarchs and business tycoons who trained their successor well and were lucky enough to pre-decease them could die secure in the knowledge that what they had built would endure, and they had passed on the baton. Followers too had the comfort of knowing that the incoming leader had experience and knew more or less what they were doing.

But history does not come in neat packages and not every inheritance of power worked as planned. Many leaders stumbled into power by accident, or certainly had never been expected to occupy positions of leadership. How did they cope with the challenges? How did they manage to acquire power and assert authority? The answer to these questions is the subject of the next chapter.

Notes

1 Robertson, *Revolutions of 1848*; J.B. Halsted, *Alphonse de Lamartine: History of the Revolu-tion of 1848*, Basingstoke: Palgrave Macmillan, 1969; 'Sudan worshippers turn on imam over protests against President Bashir', 11 January 2019, www.bbc.co.uk/news/world-africa-46846612.

2 Tolstoy, *War and Peace*.

3 Follett, *Creative Experience*.

4 John Moorman, *A History of the Franciscan Order From Its Origins to the Year 1517*, Oxford: Oxford University Press, 1968.

5 Dalton, *Mahatma Gandhi*; Gandhi, *Gandhi*; Johnson, *Gandhi's Experiments With Truth*; Ayesha Jalal, *The Sole Spokesman: Jinnah, the Muslim League and the Demand for Pakistan*, Cambridge: Cambridge University Press, 1994; Yasmin Khan, *The Great Partition: The Making of India and Pakistan*, London: Yale University Press, 2008.

6 Schama, *Citizens*; Doyle, *The Oxford History of the French Revolution*; McPhee, *Robespierre*; Ruth Schurr, *Fatal Purity: Robespierre and the French Revolution*, London: Metropolitan Books, 2006.

7 Timothy D. Barnes, *The New Empire of Diocletian and Constantine*, Cambridge, MA: Har-vard University Press, 1982; Barnes, *Constantine and Eusebius*.

8 Philipp von Boeselager, *Valkyrie: The Plot to Kill Hitler*, London: Weidenfeld & Nicolson, 2009; Peter Hoffman, *German Resistance to Hitler*, Cambridge, MA: Harvard University Press, 1988; Gill, *An Honorable Defeat*; Large, *Contending With Hitler*.

9 Pope, *The Black Ship*.

10 Joseph L. Love, *The Revolt of the Whip*, Stanford: Stanford University Press, 2012; Zachary R. Morgan, *Legacy and the Lash: Race and Corporal Punishment in the Brazilian Navy and the Atlantic World*, Bloomington: Indiana University Press, 2014.

11 Anthony Babington, *The Devil to Pay: The Mutiny of the Connaught Rangers, India, July, 1920*, London: Pen & Sword, 1991.

12 Justin McCann, *Saint Benedict*, London: Sheed & Ward, 1937; Donnachie, *Robert Owen*.

13 Leigh L. Thompson, *The Mind and Heart of the Negotiator*, New York: Pearson, 2008.

14 Bat'a, *Knowledge in Action*; Cekota, *Entrepreneur Extraordinary*.

15 Walter D. Edmonds, *The First Hundred Years, 1848–1948*, Oneida: Oneida Ltd, 1948, p. 8.

16 Edmonds, *The First Hundred Years*; Esther Lowenthal, 'The Labour Policy of the Oneida Community Ltd', *Journal of Political Economy* 35 (1927): 114–26.

17 Rowntree, *The Human Factor in Business*; Urwick and Brech, *The Making of Scientific Management*.

18 Emerson, *Efficiency*.

19 Salisbury, *Policraticus*.

20 Andrew Gregory, *Harvey's Heart: The Discovery of Blood Circulation*, Cambridge: Icon, 2001; Charles Singer, *A History of Biology*, London: Abelard, 1959.

21 Andrew Ure, *Philosophy of Manufactures*, London: H.G. Bohn, 1835; Charles Knoeppel, *Organization and Administration*, New York: McGraw-Hill, 1918; Gareth Morgan, *Images of Organization*, Newbury Park: Sage, 1986.

22 Thomas More, *Utopia*, trans. Dominic Baker-Smith, London: Penguin, 2012.

23 Foxley, *The Levellers*; Jones, *Thomas Rainborowe*; Cohn, *Popular Protest*; Proudhon, *What Is Property?*; Kropotkin, *The Conquest of Bread*.

24 Jonathan Beecher and Richard Bienvenu (eds), *The Utopian Vision of Charles Fourier: Selected Texts on Work, Love and Passionate Attraction*, Boston: Beacon, 1971.

25 Lewis, *Fairer Shares*; Donnachie, *Robert Owen*; Peter Jones, *Ove Arup: Master Builder of the Twentieth Century*, London: Yale University Press, 2006.

26 Auerbach, *The Zeiss Works*; McElheny, *Insisting on the Impossible*.

27 Enoch Powell, *Joseph Chamberlain*, London: Thames & Hudson, 1977.

28 Alastair Horne, *How Far from Austerlitz? Napoleon 1805–1815*, London: Macmillan, 1997; McLynn, *Napoleon*; Chandler, *Napoleon*.

29 Bartley, *Emmeline Pankhurst*; Purvis, *Emmeline Pankhurst*.

30 Thomas Carlyle, *The French Revolution: A History*, Oxford: Oxford University Press, 2019.

31 Garr, *IBM Redux*; Witzel, *Tata*; Sarah D.P. Cockram, *Isabella d'Este and Francesco Gonzaga: Power Sharing at the Italian Renaissance Court*, London: Routledge, 2013; Sarah Bradford, *Lucrezia Borgia: Life, Love and Death in Renaissance Italy*, London: Viking, 2004.

32 Jacobi, *Technological Change*; Richard Abraham, *Kerensky: First Love of the Revolution*, New York: Columbia University Press, 1987; Joshua Rubenstein, *Leon Trotsky: A Revolutionary's Life*, London: Yale University Press, 2011.

33 Bernier, *Lafayette*; Leepson, *Lafayette*; Weinstein, *Savonarola*.

34 David H. Williams, *The Mythic Meanings of the Second Amendment: Taming Political Violence in a Constitutional Republic*, New Haven: Yale University Press, 2003.

35 Tocqueville, *Democracy in America*, p. 96.

36 Alan Taylor, *The Civil War of 1812: American Citizens, British Subjects, Irish Rebels, Indian Allies*, New York: Vintage, 2011.

37 Chantal Mouffe, *The Democratic Paradox*, New York: Verso, 2000.

38 Andrew Vincent, *Modern Political Ideologies*, Chichester: John Wiley, 2009; Stephen Neil, *Anglicanism*, Harmondsworth: Penguin, 1960.

39 Jasper Ridley, *Tito: A Biography*, London: Constable, 1994; Fitzroy Maclean, *Heretic: The Life and Times of Josip Broz-Tito*, New York: Harper & Bros, 1957; Carole Rogel, *The Breakup of Yugoslavia and the War in Bosnia*, Westport: Greenwood, 1998.

40 George David Smith, John T. Seaman and Morgen Witzel, *A History of the Firm*, New York: McKinsey, 2011.

41 Dalton, *Gandhi*; Gandhi, *Gandhi*; Williams, *Konrad Adenauer*.

42 Lodge, *Mandela*; Sampson, *Mandela*; David Birmingham, *The Decolonization of Africa*, London: Routledge, 1995; Daphna Golan, *Inventing Shaka: Using History in the Construction of Zulu Nationalism*, Boulder: Lynne Riener, 1994.

43 Edward S. Meade, 'The Genesis of the United States Steel Corporation', *Quarterly Journal of Economics* 15 (4) (1901): 517–50; Kenneth Warren, *Big Steel: The First Century of the United States Steel Corporation, 1901–2001*, Pittsburgh: University of Pittsburgh Press, 2001.

44 Matti Moosa, *The Maronites in History*, Piscataway: Gorgias, 2005; R.J. Mouwad, *Les Maronites: Chrétiens du Liban*, Turnhout: Brepols, 2009.

45 Bill Vlasic and Bradley A. Stertz, *Taken for a Ride: How Daimler-Benz Drove Off With Chrysler*, New York: John Wiley, 2000; Svenja Stellmann, *The Impact of Cultural Differences on the Daimler Chrysler Merger*, Munich: Grin Verlag, 2013.

46 Labarge, *Simon de Montfort*; Maddicott, *Simon de Montfort*.

47 Bernier, *Lafayette*; Leepson, *Lafayette*; Schama, *Citizens*.

48 David Carpenter, *The Reign of Henry III*, London: Hambledon, 1996; Labarge, *Simon de Montfort*; Maddicott, *Simon de Montfort*; Gaposchkin, *The Making of Saint Louis*; Le Goff, *Saint Louis*.

49 Jenkins, *Byzantium*; Simson, *Sacred Fortress*; David Chandler (ed.) *Napoleon's Marshals*, London: Weidenfeld & Nicolson, 1987.

50 Bowes, *The Art of Conducting*; Holden, *The Virtuoso Conductors*; Wigglesworth, *The Silent Musician*.

51 David Wyn Jones, *The Life of Haydn*, Oxford: Oxford University Press, 2009; Robbins H.C. Landon and David Wyn Jones, *Haydn: His Life and Music*, Bloomington: Indiana University Press, 1988.

52 John Canarina, *Pierre Monteux, Maître*, New York: Rowman & Littlefield, 2003.

53 Arthur Lourie, *Serge Koussevitzky and His Epoch*, New York: Andesite Press, 2016.

54 Methley, *Camille Desmoulins*; Connor, *Marat*; Service, *Lenin*; Falk, *Love, Anarchy and Emma Goldman*; Bartley, *Emmeline Pankhurst*; Purvis, *Emmeline Pankhurst*.

55 Aldred, *Akhenaten*; Redford, *Akhenaten*.

56 Barnes, *Constantine and Eusebius*; Barnes, *The New Empire*; Ross Cowen, *Milvian Bridge AD 312: Constantine's Battle for Empire and Faith*, Oxford: Osprey, 2016.

57 Beard, *SPQR*; Procopius, *The Secret History*.

58 Alston and Takei, *Japanese Business Culture*.

59 Witzel, *Tata*; Lane, *Jacked Up*.

60 Gilbert, *Finest Hour*; Jenkins, *Churchill*; Martin Blumenson, *Patton: The Man Behind the Legend*, New York: William Morrow, 1985; Alan Axelrod, *Patton: A Biography*, New York: Palgrave Macmillan, 2006; Pernoud, *Joan of Arc*; Taylor, *The Virgin Warrior*.

61 Lala, *For the Love of India*; Cekota, *Entrepreneur Extraordinary*; Donnachie, *Robert Owen*.

62 Brian Dolan, *Josiah Wedgwood: Entrepreneur to the Enlightenment*, New York: Harper, 2004; Joel Mokyr, *The Enlightened Economy: Britain and the Industrial Revolution, 1700–1850*, London: Penguin, 2011.

63 Bostridge, *Florence Nightingale*; Siobhan Nelson and Anne-Marie Rafferty (eds), *Notes on Nightingale: The Influence and Legacy of a Nursing Icon*, Ithaca: Cornell University Press, 2010.

64 John Moorman, *A History of the Franciscan Order*; Augustine Thompson, *Francis of Assisi: A New Biography*, Ithaca: Cornell University Press, 2012.

65 Alastair Horne, *The Price of Glory: Verdun, 1916*, New York: St Martin's Press, 1963; Guy Pedroncini, *Les mutineries de 1917*, Paris: Presse Universitaires de France, 1983.

66 Christopher Duffy, *The Military Life of Frederick the Great*, New York: Athenaeum, 1986.

67 Christopher Douglas, *Douglas Jardine: Spartan Cricketer*, London: Methuen, 2002.

68 Roger Lipsey, *Hammarskjöld: A Life*, Ann Arbor: University of Michigan Press, 2016.

69 William Hague, *William Pitt the Younger*, London: HarperCollins, 2005; Michael Turner, *Pitt the Younger: A Life*, London: Continuum, 2002; Peter Jupp, *Lord Grenville*, Oxford: Oxford University Press, 1985.
70 Arrian, *The Campaigns of Alexander*; Lane Fox, *The Search for Alexander*.
71 Eisenberg, *That First Season*; Maraniss, *When Pride Still Mattered*; Ferguson and Moritz, *Leading*.

15

RELUCTANT LEADERS

The accidental servants are leaders who did not intend to become leaders, but who are thrust into positions of leadership nonetheless. Some fail. Andrew Johnson was picked as a figurehead running mate for Abraham Lincoln in the 1864 US presidential election, during the closing months of the American Civil War. As a senator from the southern states who had argued in favour of union and opposed the Confederacy, he was seen as a useful symbol in Lincoln's bid to re-unite the country.

The Lincoln-Johnson ticket won, and Johnson became vice-president but it was never expected by him or anyone around him that he would ever hold power. On 14 April 1865, Lincoln was assassinated and Johnson suddenly became president. His subsequent career was a disaster, he was impeached by the House of Representatives and failed to win nomination in the next election. Historians regard him as one of America's worst presidents.[1]

Types of accidental servant

The failure of Johnson and others like him will come as no surprise. The deck is stacked against the accidental servants, who receive little or no training or preparation for leadership. Many are reluctant to take on the role, and do not really regard themselves as leaders. And yet, paradoxically, that reluctance seems to be one of the things that makes them good leaders. They are not ambitious for themselves, at least not initially. They do regard themselves as servants, and sometimes when they see that their work is done, they lay down the burdens of leadership and retire. Aethelred, who became King of Mercia in England during the late seventh century AD, did not expect to inherit the throne and only became king after the sudden death of his brother Wulfhere. He ruled competently and defended his kingdom against various invasion attempts and then, once Mercia was secure, he abdicated and retired to a monastery, exchanging the crown and authority for the robes of a humble monk.[2]

Unexpected inheritance

Some accidental servants like Aethelred inherit power unexpectedly, generally when the person who was expected to inherit dies suddenly without an heir. When Caligula was assassinated, his cousin Claudius feared for his own life. According to one report, the Praetorian Guards found him hiding behind a curtain, and dragged him out forcibly and proclaimed him as emperor. After some disagreement, the Roman senate accepted him and Claudius became Rome's most reluctant emperor. Despite the circumstances of his accession, however, he was largely successful, overseeing imperial expansion and improvements in trade and the economy during a largely peaceful reign.[3]

As the daughter of the disgraced Anne Boleyn, Elizabeth Tudor spent much of her life in captivity with the threat of execution hanging over her. Only in early 1558 did Queen Mary I, her half-sister, accept that she would not have a child and name Elizabeth as her heir. Mary died later that year, giving Elizabeth only a few months to prepare for her unexpected task.[4] Prince Albert of England, the second son of King George V, never expected to become king himself; a shy and quiet man with a speech impediment, he assumed like everyone else that his older brother the Prince of Wales would become king. But a few months after George V died, Edward VIII abdicated so he could marry his mistress, Wallis Simpson. Upon receiving news that he was about to be king, by his own admission Prince Albert 'broke down and sobbed like a child'.[5] But as George VI he went on to become a conscientious monarch, insisting that he and his family would remain in London during the Blitz to share the same risks as his subjects.

Unexpected inheritance happens in family businesses too. Born in 1904, J.R.D. Tata was only distantly connected to the Tata business group; his father, Ratanji Tata, was first cousin to the group's founder, Jamsetji Tata. Ratanji's own business was in Paris, where he lived with his French wife, and as a small boy Tata stood on the shore of the English Channel and watched Louis Blériot make the first flight from France to England. Thereafter his sole ambition was to be a pilot. He received the first commercial pilot's licence to be granted in India and went on to found Tata Aviation Service, the forerunner to Air India. He had no ambitions to lead the Tata group, but when it became clear that there was no other successor to the current chairman, Nowroji Saklatwala, he reluctantly agreed to take the job out of duty to his family. In 1938, just thirty-four years old, Tata became chairman of the Tata Group and led it for the next fifty-three years and overseeing its growth into India's largest business group.[6]

Stepping up, stepping in

Sometimes too, a leader goes missing or is deemed incompetent and there is no planned successor. In 1804 Quashquame, one of the leaders of the Sauk people along the upper reaches of the Mississippi river, signed a treaty with the American military authorities guaranteeing peace and handing over a large tract of Sauk territory to white settlers. Consensual decision-making was part of Sauk culture, and Quashquame's followers were upset that he had done so without their permission. His power with his people collapsed, but there was no obvious successor. Eventually a young man named Makattai-meshekiakiak, more generally known as Black Hawk, emerged as the new leader. He was a surprising choice, as he was the son of the tribe's spiritual healer, or medicine man, and had expected to carry on in that role himself. However, within a few years he was also the tribe's new war leader and led the Sauk into action on the British side during the War of 1812.[7]

William McKnight had only just become vice-president of the ailing 3M Corporation when the president, Edgar Ober, fell ill and had to be replaced. McKnight was just twenty-nine years old, a cost accountant with no commercial experience, and there were other more experienced executives who could have taken over the company. However, knowing that the company was on the verge of collapsing and seeing the post as a poisoned chalice, all of them declined. With no other choice, the board invited McKnight to take over the company. He went on to run 3M for another fifty years, turning it into a global corporation.[8] Less successful in the long run was Götz von Berlichingen, a mercenary captain who found himself caught up in the German Peasants War. By his own account, he joined the peasant rebels for much the same reasons as François de Charette joined the French Catholic rebels in the Vendée; if he had not joined, they would have killed him. He took service under a peasant leader named Jack Rohrbach, but after Rohrbach ordered the brutal massacre of prisoners near the town of Weinsberg, his followers deposed him and appointed Berlichingen their leader instead. Berlichingen managed to survive the suppression of the revolt, and after a spell in prison resumed his career as a mercenary.[9]

The right place at the right time

Accidental leaders sometimes emerge by chance; they happen to be present at a moment when leadership is needed, and followers turn to them. Wat Tyler, leader of the Peasants Revolt in England and Fischhof, one of the leaders of the revolt in Vienna are examples; it will be recalled the Fischhof was merely passing by a demonstration and stopped to engage one of the protestors in conversation, whereupon he was hoisted in someone' shoulders and told to make a speech to the crowd. Returning home from service with the imperial army, Hans Müller was caught up in the Peasants War and seized upon a group of peasants who elected him their captain.[10]

Tyler, Fischhof and Müller were all captured and executed, but others were more fortunate. Parachuting into occupied France during the Second World War, Pearl Witherington worked as a courier for Special Operations Executive (SOE) network, but after the network's leaders were arrested by the German army, she stepped in and took over. By the end of the war she was leading more than fifteen hundred *maquis* resistance fighters and played an important role in tying down German forces before the D-Day landings.[11] Even more accidental was the career of the

Australian socialite Nancy Wake. She was living in luxury in Marseille when the Second World War began, but joined the French resistance after the fall of France and became one of its celebrated members. The Gestapo called her the 'White Mouse', naming her the most dangerous woman in France and putting a price on her head. By 1944 Wake commanded a force of over seven thousand maquis, who fought off repeated attacks by the Germany army. It has been estimated that around 70 per cent of German casualties sustained in the war against the resistance movement were inflicted by Wake's brigade.[12]

Sometimes quite small actions catapult people into positions of leadership. When, in 1955, Rosa Parkes refused to give up her seat on a bus in Montgomery, Alabama to a white passenger, she had no idea that this simple act of rebellion would catapult her into a position of leadership. She became an icon of the civil rights movement, travelling and speaking across the US and working with figures such as John Conyers, Malcolm X and Martin Luther King.[13] When Ignacy Paderewski, the renowned concert pianist and one of the few living Poles with an international reputation, met the new Polish head of state, Marshal Pilsudski, in 1918, Pilsudski became convinced that Paderewski was the best man to represent Poland abroad. He appointed Paderewski to the posts of prime minister and minister of foreign affairs and sent him to France as Poland's lead representative during the negotiations before the Treaty of Versailles. After helping to establish Polish independence, Paderewski returned to Poland and oversaw the rebuilding of the country and then, believing his work was done, he resigned and returned to his career as a pianist.[14]

Possession of a particular skill can push an individual towards leadership, especially in a time of crisis. The surgeon and homeopath Dr Joseph Kidd volunteered to assist victims of the Irish potato famine in the countryside around Bantry, and found himself directing medical efforts as he was the only qualified physician in the district.[15] Mary Seacole, the daughter of a British army officer and a Jamaican traditional healer, already has considerable medical experience by the time of the outbreak of the Crimean War. She applied several times to join the nursing staff going to the Crimea but was rebuffed, possibly on account of race. Using her own resources she travelled to the Crimea and built a convalescent hospital out of driftwood and packing cases, and set about giving medical care to the sick and wounded. Seacole had come to England at the start of the war to offer her serviced prepared to be a follower; because no leader would accept her, she became a leader herself.[16]

Reluctant leaders

We have mentioned some reluctant leaders already, Charette in the Vendée and Fischhof in the Viennese revolution. Rennyo, the head of the Jodo Shinshu Buddhist sect in fifteenth-century Japan, was regarded also as the spiritual head of the *ikko-ikki* warrior monks who rebelled against the government. In fact Rennyo was a pacifist who believed violence was only allowable in self-defence, but the *ikko-ikki* continued to regard him as their leader long beyond his lifetime.[17] George

Washington was willing to serve as war leader during the American Revolution, but he was much more hesitant about taking up leadership in peacetime. Washington only reluctantly joined the Virginia delegation to the Constitutional Convention, where he played a major role in defining the shape of the new government of the US. Upon being elected he planned to serve for only one term, and had to be persuaded to run again for a second.[18] The Byzantine empress Zoe Porphyrogenita had been dethroned and banished to a nunnery by her nephew, Michael V, and had no desire to return to political life. When a popular rebellion overthrew Michael and demanded for Zoe to be reinstated, she hid in the convent chapel and had to be dragged out by force and carried back to Constantinople.[19]

Few political leaders were more reluctant than Elisabeth of Wied, who married King Carol I of Romania in an arranged marriage. As Queen Elisabeth, she devoted herself to charitable work and championed the cause of women in higher education, in addition to leading the nursing service that cared for sick and wounded soldiers during wartime. She also campaigned for the left-wing social democrats, spoke in favour of class equality, and called for the abolition of the monarchy and the founding for a republic. Archduchess Elisabeth of Austria, granddaughter of Emperor Franz Josef, also joined the Austrian Social Democratic party and campaigned for socialist causes.[20]

Religious organisations have a long tradition of reluctant leaders. After spending a decade in the cutthroat world of Byzantine politics as papal ambassador to the court in Constantinople, Gregorius the monk returned to his monastery in Rome, determined to spend the rest of his life there. In 590, following the death of Pope Pelagius, Gregory was elected pope by acclamation, without ever having sought or campaigned for the office. He spent the first year of his papacy writing letters in which he lamented the peace and seclusion of his monastery and wished he could lay down his burdens and return there. But he was a conscientious and strong leader, and he is remembered today as St Gregory the Great, one of the best-known and most effective popes in history. Pope Pius X, elected in 1903, tried at first to decline the nomination on the grounds that he was not worthy of the office. His fellow cardinals eventually persuaded him to accept.[21]

What makes these leaders so reluctant to serve? In some cases, like Pius X, there is a genuine belief that the individual does not have what it takes to be a good leader. In others, like Gregory I and George Washington, there is a reluctance to take up the burdens of office, often coupled with a personal desire for peace and tranquillity. In still others, like Elisabeth of Wied and Rennyo – and Charette, whose reluctance to serve was based in part on a belief that the Vendée revolt would fail – there is a fundamental disconnect with the cause that followers have espoused. Leader and followers do not share the same beliefs. If followers learn the leader's true feelings, they will often lose confidence and the result will be a failure of leadership. Elisabeth's case is particularly fascinating because she made no secret of her socialist views, but she also performed the duties of monarch faithfully and well. As a result, her followers respected her both for her authenticity and her devotion to themselves and their needs.

Why do accidental leaders succeed?

To answer this question, we need to examine several issues. First, there is the question of how and why accidental leaders are chosen in the first place. What makes them acceptable as leaders, especially when, like Fischhof, they have no prior leadership experience? Second, there is the question of power. Where do accidental leaders derive their power? What maintains them in positions of leadership once the initial acceptance stage has passed? And finally, is there any merit to the concept of accidental leadership? Should we stop planning for leadership, and simply wait and let leaders emerge?

Leaders emerging

Many accidental leaders emerge out of a crisis. Rosa Parkes became a leadership figure during the era of civil right protests, a time of upheaval in American society. William McKnight stepped up as leader of 3M when the company was on the verge of bankruptcy and no one else could be found to run it. Mary Seacole came forward and began providing nursing care when there was a desperate lack of a care and the void had to be filled. The two popes, Gregory I and Pius X, were both elected at a time of crisis in the Catholic church, the former at a time when the split between Rome and Constantinople was widening, the latter when Emperor Franz Josef attempted to intervene in the papal election, causing a split between the Austrian cardinals and their colleagues in the conclave. Rennyo emerged out of the violence of war-torn Japan, Nancy Wake joined the Resistance after the fall of France, and so on.

Sometimes the leader emerges because he or she has the courage to do what no one else has dared to do, and it is that courage that marks them out from the crowd. People gravitate towards them initially because courage is one of the virtues that are admired in a leader. Rosa Parkes falls into this category, and so too does Black Hawk the Sauk leader; despite being a 'medicine man' or healer, he had shown his courage in battle on previous occasions. Another spiritual leader, Hehaka Sapa (Black Elk) also emerged as a leader after demonstrating his courage at the Wounded Knee massacre.[22] The D-Day landings in Normandy produced many example of low-level leadership emerging out of the crisis of combat, people stepping forward to take on leadership roles even if only for a few hours, or a few minutes, to get the job done, the most famous example perhaps being the attack by American paratroopers led by Lieutenant Richard Winters on a German artillery battery at Brécourt.[23]

The other, more common feature of accidental leaders is that they have a skill that followers do not have, but very much need if they are to reach their own goals. Particularly when a new organisation is being established, followers look for leaders who have what they lack, and leaders emerge to fill the void.[24] That does not necessarily mean leadership skills. Charette, Götz von Berlichingen, Hans Müller, Pearl Witherington and Nancy Wake all had military skills; McKnight and J.R.D. Tata were capable organisers; Fischhof was a communicator; Paderewski was a natural diplomat who had international connections unavailable to most people in divided and occupied Poland; Mary Seacole and Joseph Kidd had medical skills, all of which were badly needed at the time. Leadership in these situations is not a skill possessed by the leader; rather, it is something that evolves out of the interplay between leaders and followers over time.

Finally, the symbolic–charismatic element of leadership can sometimes come into play. Claudius, Elizabeth I and George VI all came to power through inheritance, being next in line to the throne after the expected monarch died or abdicated. At the time it was widely expected that the first two would be figureheads only, controlled by a clique of their followers, but they confounded expectations by taking more power for themselves, in part because they appealed to the broader population. Although partially disabled and possessed of a speech impediment, Claudius was fond of sports and games and this endeared him to the people.[25] Rosa Parkes was and remains a highly important symbol for African-American aspirations, and much of George Washington's success as a leader was due to his symbolic authority as the victorious general during the American Revolution.

Sources of authority

Accidental leaders tap into the same sources of authority as other leaders, but they do so *ad hoc*. Nancy Wake and Pearl Witherington both started off as couriers with the resistance movement, a relatively lowly position. However, their mobility gave them access to knowledge, of the locations of various maquis units and their commanders and of German outposts and bases, places of safety and points of danger. This tactical knowledge became invaluable when they stepped up into positions of leadership after their male predecessors had been killed or captured. Elizabeth I may not have been prepared to rule as queen, but she had been given a very good education by her tutor, the scholar and educational theorist Roger Ascham.[26] Mary Seacole had learned the profession of nursing from her mother and her own subsequent practice, particularly during a cholera epidemic in Panama.[27] Inherent ability and knowledge is one of the key sources of power for any leader, but the possession of by these accidental leaders depended heavily on their prior experience and education. In other words, not everyone would have been able to step up; the right person at the right time is needed.

Inheritance could sometimes be a useful source of power, as in the cases of Elizabeth and Claudius who inherited in uncertain times and faced plots against their rule. Inheritance gave a sense of legitimacy which could persuade some 'bystander' followers to get off the fence and rally around them. However, the great majority of accidental leaders do not inherit power. Similarly, conferred authority was useful in helping the reluctant popes to overcome any reservations followers might have about them – and their own reservations too; Pius X reportedly spent several hours in prayer before finally agreeing to accept his nomination as pope – but these too are special cases.[28] Inherent ability and the consent of followers are the two key attributes that help accidental leaders into power.

They are also the attributes that help to keep them in power once they have arrived. As noted, not every accidental leader is successful, and followers are often very quick to recognise whether a newly emerged leader has the qualities that will enable them to succeed; and success, of course, means helping followers to realise their own goals. If the leader is fulfilling this function, then he or she will stay in power; if not, they will quickly be disposed of, like Andrew Johnson.

Important too, however, is the emergent leader's ability to build coalitions and attract other groups of followers. Elizabeth I was highly skilled at this, drawing on groups from all walks of life and all corners of society, even tolerating secret Roman Catholics, such as the court composers Thomas Tallis and William Byrd, and being willing to countenance an alliance with Catholic France against her main enemy, Catholic Spain.[29] Mary Seacole could not have carried out her work alone; she built good relationships with the British military authorities in the Crimea, especially the medical officers. J.R.D. Tata and Paderewski were both accomplished diplomats and consensus-builders. François de Charette, on the other hand, had a reputation for being cold and aloof, and refused to work with fellow rebel leaders such as Stofflet or la Rochejacquelein. His failure to collaborate with them was a major factor in the failure of the Vendée rebellion.[30] The ability to build sustainable coalitions immediately after coming to power often makes the difference between success and failure for accidental leaders.

Succession

Thus far, though, we have seen no major differences between leaders who become leaders by accident, and those who are carefully trained and prepared for leadership positions. Examples of success and of failure are easy to find in both groups. I know of no research that attempts to compare rates of success and failure between accidental and 'prepared' leaders, and this might be an interesting subject for future investigation, although of course we need to be careful to ensure we know what constitutes 'success' and 'failure'.

But all this begs a question. If accident and circumstance can produce good leaders, and if those who take power reluctantly are just as effective as their more ambitious colleagues, is there any point in spending vast sums and large amounts of time to train leaders? Would it not be cheaper and just as effective to sit back and let leaders emerge? The problem with that position is that, as Chapters 9 and 12 in particular have shown, we then have no control over what kind of leader or leaders might emerge. Leaving leadership to chance opens the door to a drift towards forms of leadership such as totalitarianism. Setting aside all moral issues for the moment, the main problem with these forms of leadership is that they don't tend to work very well, and when they do fail they are accompanied by a great deal of destruction. Followers, no matter what faction they belong to, rarely achieve their goals in the long run.

So, there is a need for some sort of guidance, planning and structure if we are to get the best leaders we want. (That of course begs the question of who 'we' are and which follower group we represent.) But the starting point for this process should be the goals we share as followers; in other words, first set the goals; then choose the leaders. However, we should not entirely dismiss the accidental leaders. Especially in times of crisis, we need to leave the door open for them to emerge and be ready to share power with them when they do. Charles VII of France opened the door to Jeanne d'Arc, and the result was the defeat of the invading English and the salvation of his own throne and dynasty. By sharing power with this unexpected leader, his own power was ultimately greatly increased.

What made Jeanne effective was her selflessness and her determination to sacrifice herself for her leader and her own followers. The concept of the leader as the good servant, who works for the good of others and not themselves, is the subject of the next chapter.

Notes

1 David O. Stewart, *Impeached: The Trial of Andrew Johnson and the Fight for Lincoln's Legacy*, New York: Simon & Schuster, 2009.
2 Barbara Yorke, 'The Origins of Mercia', in Brown and Farr (eds), *Mercia*.
3 Levick, *Claudius*; Osgood, *Claudius Caesar*.
4 Collinson, *Elizabeth I*; Doran and Freeman, *The Myth of Elizabeth*.
5 Sir John Wheeler-Bennett, *King George VI: His Life and Reign*, London: Secker & Warburg, 1958, p. 286.
6 R.M. Lala, *Beyond the Last Blue Mountain: A Life of J.R.D. Tata*, New Delhi: Penguin, 1992; Piramal, *Business Legends*; Anant Pai, *J.R.D. Tata: The Quiet Conqueror*, Mumbai: India Book House, 2004.
7 Black Hawk, *Life of Black Hawk*, ed. Milo M. Quaife, Chicago: Lakeside Press, 1916; Kerry A. Trask, *Black Hawk: The Battle for the Heart of America*, New York: Holt, 2006.
8 Huck, *Brand of the Tartan*; Hamburger, 'McKnight'.
9 Peter Blickle, *The German Peasants War of 1525 From a New Perspective*, trans. Thomas A. Brady and H.C. Midelfort, Baltimore: Johns Hopkins University Press, 1981; Douglas Miller, *Armies of the German Peasants War 1524–1526*, Oxford: Osprey, 2003.
10 Ibid.; Dobson, *The Peasants Revolt of 1381*; Robertson, *Revolutions of 1848*.
11 Pearl Witherington Cornioley, *Codename Pauline: Memoirs of a World War II Special Agent*, ed. Kathryn J. Attwood, Chicago: Chicago Review Press, 2015.
12 Nancy Wake, *Autobiography of the Woman the Gestapo Called the White Mouse*, Melbourne: Macmillan, 1985; Russell Braddon, *Woman in Arms: The Story of Nancy Wake*, London: Collins, 1963.
13 Rosa Parkes and James Haskins, *Rosa Parkes: My Story*, New York: Scholastic Books, 1992; Douglas Brinkley, *Rosa Parkes: A Life*, New York: Penguin, 2005.
14 Mary Lawton (ed.) *The Paderewski Memoirs*, London: Collins, 1939; Davies, *God's Playground*; Margaret Macmillan, *Peacemakers: Six Months That Changed the World*, London: John Murray, 2003.
15 Francis Treuherz, *Homeopathy in the Irish Potato Famine*, London: Samuel Press, 1995.
16 Robinson, *Mary Seacole*; Helen Rappaport, *No Place for Ladies: The Untold Story of Women in the Crimean War*, London: Aurum, 2008.
17 Tsang, *War and Faith*; James C. Dobbins, *Jodo Shinshu: Shin Buddhism in Medieval Japan*, Bloomington: Indiana University Press, 1989.
18 Davis, *George Washington and the American Revolution*; Ferling, *First of Men*; John R. Alden, *George Washington: A Biography*, Baton Rouge: Louisiana State University Press, 1996.
19 Psellus, *Fourteen Byzantine Rulers*; Garland, *Byzantine Empresses*.

20 Eugen Wolbe, *Carmen Sylva: der Lebensweg einer einsamin Königin*, Leipzig: Kochler & Amelang, 1933; Friedrich Weissensteiner, *Elisabeth, die rote Erzerhogini*, Vienna: Piper Verlag, 2007.

21 Carole E. Straw, *Gregory the Great: Perfection in Imperfection*, Berkeley: University of California Press, 1988; John Cavadini (ed.), *Gregory the Great: A Symposium*, Notre Dame: University of Notre Dame Press, 1995; Owen Chadwick, *A History of the Popes, 1830– 1914*, Oxford: Oxford University Press, 2003.

22 Hehaka Sapa, *Black Elk Speaks*.

23 Michael David Pierce, *The Overlord Effect: Emergent Leadership Style at the D-Day Invasion*, London: AuthorHouseUK, 2013; Stephen E. Ambrose, *Band of Brothers*, New York: Simon & Schuster, 1997.

24 Riggio *et al.*, *The Art of Followership*.

25 Levick, *Claudius*; Osgood, *Claudius Caesar*.

26 Collinson, *Elizabeth I*; Doran and Freeman, *The Myth of Elizabeth*; L.V. Ryan, *Roger Ascham*, Stanford: Stanford University Press, 1963.

27 Robinson, *Mary Seacole*.

28 Chadwick, *A History of the Popes*.

29 Collinson, *Elizabeth I*.

30 Ross, *Banners of the King*.

16

SERVANT LEADERS

The notion of the leader as servant of the organisation is an old one. Implicit in many early religious writings on leadership is the notion that even the highest leaders are themselves also servants of God, and they should use their conferred authority and power for the good of the people; the Caliph 'Ali, for example, warned his successors that their deeds on Earth would be judged by Allah when they reached heaven.[1] Enlightenment political thinkers, notably John Locke and Jean-Jacques Rousseau, discussed the responsibility leaders have to followers, and Mary Parker Follett believed that the role of the leader was to help followers reach their highest point of development, individually and collectively.[2] In the late twentieth century Greenleaf codified the concept of 'servant leadership', which remains widely discussed today.

One of the most popular metaphors of servant leadership is the shepherd and his flock.[3] Although at first sight – so the metaphor goes – the shepherd is in charge of the flock and the sheep follow his or her direction, the reality is that the sheep generally know where they want to go, searching out the best grazing and sources of water. The shepherd's task is to guide the sheep to and from the fields and watch over them and protect them from predators. The shepherd is humble and knows that the flock is more important than themselves, for it is the flock that sustains the shepherd's life.

An examination of what shepherds actually do pours a bit of cold water on this idea. In *The Shepherd's Life*, British shepherd James Rebanks describes the work in detail, including practices such as selective interbreeding in order to get the best stock, and castrating young rams by tying elastic bands around their testicles until they drop off.[4] Although leaders have in the past done very similar things to their followers, it is hard to think that these leaders would be described as 'servants'. Nevertheless, Rebanks makes the point that there is a partnership between shepherds and sheep, and shepherds have a strong moral and economic duty to their flocks, not only for the well-being of the sheep but also for the good of the environment itself.

Sheep don't always do what a shepherd wants or needs them to do, and sometimes their behaviour puts them into danger. When that happens, the shepherd must step in and attempt to assert control. Although the servant leadership model looks highly collaborative and, therefore, very attractive to those leaders and followers who value collaboration and dislike conflict, there is also an element of conflict here.

To repeat a point made several times already, followers are not homogenous; they have varying levels of engagement, and it is almost inevitable that some will be hostile to the leader, no matter how noble and selfless the leader's motives and actions may be. Some followers will not be interested in the same goals as the rest of the organisation; some may wish to take over the organisation and make it serve their own ends; some may be angry and working to actively sabotage the organisation. It may be possible to engage with these followers and try to persuade them drop their resistance, or it may not. If it is not, then conflict will ensue. Collaboration and contest still exist in this social space, although the balance between them may change.

One of the purported advantages of the servant model of leadership is that it may be more authentic. Considering the needs of followers first, rather than one's own needs as a leader, should lead to a more honest and transparent relationship where followers feel they can trust the leader.[5] Of course authenticity comes in many forms, and historically there has been no shortage of narcissistic, sociopathic and psychopathic leaders who do *not* put their followers' interests first; but again, these would not usually be described as servant leaders. In this chapter, therefore, we are looking at a subset of leaders – how narrow or how broad that subset might be is a matter for conjecture – who can be said to genuinely have the interests of their followers at heart, and priorities followers' needs over their own; most of the time.

Some servant leaders have been more effective than others; some died while serving their followers, sometimes while trying to defend them. Some, like Rebanks's shepherd, were not always gentle with their followers. Mother Teresa, according to some reports, was a leader of strong will who expected her followers to do their duty and was not backward about expressing herself when they did not. Abraham Lincoln was often scathing about some of his followers, including to their faces, and Malcolm X did not shy away from conflict.[6] But they won respect from most of their followers – enough to sustain them in power – to repeat a point made earlier, it was recognised that they were working not only for their interests but also for those of their followers. In some cases, serving the needs of followers resulted in leaders making considerable personal sacrifice.

Defence and survival

As we saw in Chapter 3, followers attach themselves to leaders for three basic reasons: survival, the fulfilment of individual aspirations, and the fulfilment of group aspirations. In terms of the first, survival, the selfless leader is the one who will do anything and go to any lengths to ensure their followers survive and are protected.

Ernest Shackleton, the Antarctic explorer, is a good example. His concern for his men and their welfare during the 1914–6 expedition was demonstrated over and over again; on one occasion he gave his only pair of mittens to a man who had lost his, and later suffered frostbite on his fingers. After the expedition's ship was lost and the crew was left stranded on remote Elephant Island, it became necessary to send for help to the nearest inhabited island, South Georgia, 720 miles away. Rather than delegate this dangerous journey to his men, Shackleton led it himself. Although the expedition failed in its objective, Shackleton brought his entire crew safely home.[7]

Mary Seacole not only managed her nursing establishment in the Crimea but also treated sick and wounded men herself, and she joined in with chores such as cooking meals and washing dishes. A contemporary, Florence Nightingale, shared the hardships of her nursing corps in the hospital at Scutari and worked long hours beside them in appalling conditions; the exhaustion she suffered from may have contributed to her illnesses in later life. Nightingale's dedication to her work and her patients carried over into the training programmes for nurses she established after the war. Personally, she could be somewhat distant and had few close friends, but everyone who knew her respected her dedication.[8] Much the same could be said of Mother Teresa of Calcutta, who founded and ran the Missionaries of Charity. In the 1980s, after suffering a heart attack, she offered to resign her post, but the nursing sisters begged her to stay on. She continued to serve until shortly before her death.[9]

Serving followers by defending them physically has been a feature of many cultures and societies over time. A distinction needs to be made between people who serve for pay and who, although they risk their lives, also have an element of self-interest, and those who step forward voluntarily take up the reins of leadership with little thought of personal reward. We have already seen several examples from North America, including Black Hawk of the Sauk, Thathanka Iyotake and Hehaka Sapa of the Lakota, the former leading his people through the war with the US, the latter interposing himself between American soldiers and helpless civilians at Wounded Knee. Another good example is Tecumseh, the Shaawanwaki (Shawnee) war leader who resisted American expansion in the early nineteenth century. Recognising that his own tribe was too weak to defend itself alone, Tecumseh tried to create a confederacy of tribes and form a nation of their own that would be capable of standing up to the Americans. Although he succeeded in bringing many tribes together, even with British support they still could hold back the tide. Tecumseh was killed in 1813, resisting to the end.[10]

In the first century AD, two Vietnamese sisters, Trung Trac and Trung Nhi, emerged as leaders of popular resistance against the invading Chinese armies of the Han dynasty. They held off the Chinese for three years until they were killed in battle.[11] Lady Xian, a hereditary chieftain of the Li people in southern China in the sixth century AD, was a powerful figure who suppressed banditry, abolished slavery and defeated an invasion, all in order to protect her people. The turmoil surrounding the collapse of the Ming dynasty and the invasion and conquest of China by the Manchus in the seventeenth century saw a number of defenders of the people emerge, each struggling to protect their own people. Qin Liangyu, who took over as magistrate in a small district in Sichuan after her husband was imprisoned, defeated both rebels against the Ming dynasty and Manchu invaders, and later helped refugees from the fighting elsewhere settle in her district. Her contemporary Shen Yunying took over her father's regiment after he was killed and fought the Yellow Tiger rebels who were slaughtering people in Sichuan. She later became a general in her own right and continued the resistance against the Manchus in southern China. On the opposite side, at least at first, was Gao Guiying, who trained and led troops of female rebels in the army of Li Zicheng that briefly overthrew the Ming dynasty. Li was killed the following year by the Manchus, and Gao changed sides and joined the remnants of the Ming army. Like Shen, she became a leader of the anti-Manchu resistance in south China.[12]

Sometimes the service of the people requires leaders to make the ultimate sacrifice. The Trung sisters were killed in battle, and so probably was Gao Guiying, who died in 1647. Although we may disagree today with what they did, there is no escaping the fact that many of the *kamikaze* pilots who flew suicide missions against American warships in the Second World War were motivated by a desire to defend their people, even at the cost of their own lives. The commander of the *kamikazes*, Admiral Ugaki Matomi, himself flew a final suicide mission the day Japan surrendered. The *kamikazes* have had their equivalents in other cultures; the German air force, the Luftwaffe, also formed a unit known as Sonderkommando Elbe, whose pilots volunteered to ram attacking American bombers. As far as we know, only one attack was ever carried out.[13]

Selfless service of other people, either physically defending them or healing them to make them well, is something that captures our imaginations. Shackleton is regarded as an exemplary leader, and despite their very different personalities and styles both Mary Seacole and Florence Nightingale are regarded as heroes. Temples were erected to Lady Xian and she was venerated as a minor deity, and the Trung sisters were venerated as national heroines after Vietnam gained independence in the 1960s. In all these cases, skill was allied to some form of altruistic behaviour, and it seems clear that it is the combination of the two, rather than one or the other, that distinguishes leaders.

Serving the faith

Religious faith has been and continues to be important for both individuals and societies, and religious organisations require leadership just like any other. Given the fallibility of human beings, it comes as no surprise that positions of leadership have often been occupied by venal and corrupt individuals like the Borgia pope, Alexander VI, or Charles de Talleyrand, who later abandoned the church to become Napoleon's foreign minister; or those driven by personal ambition, like Pope Innocent III or Thomas Becket, although the latter experienced a conversion around the time he became Archbishop of Canterbury, putting away his ambitions and becoming a much more dedicated servant of the church. This conversion later cost him his life.[14]

When choosing a religious leader, followers look for faith and piety, but they also look for humility and a devotion to the ideal of service. Hildegard of Bingen, philosopher, theologian composer of music, scientist and visionary, embodied that ideal in many ways. Her convent at Disibodenberg in Germany was subordinate to a male Benedictine monastery, but Hildegard was determined that the nuns should have more independence and be able to govern their own affairs. After her unanimous election as *magistra* of the community, Hildegard campaigned tirelessly for separation from the monastery. Her wish was ultimately granted, and she became prioress of a new community at St Rupertsberg, later founding a second nunnery nearby. From her youth until her death, Hildegard worked in the service of her faith and her community.[15]

Similarly, the Buddhist nun An Lingshou played an important role in the spread of Buddhism in parts of Shandong province of China during the fourth century AD, and set an example through her own piety and good works. A century later the nun Baoxian became leader of a nunnery in Henan province, having been recognised as leader for both her organisational skills and her knowledge of Buddhist theology and devout belief.[16] In the twentieth century another nun, Dharmachari Guruma, played an important role in the revival of Buddhism in Nepal, despite religious repression from the government; Dharmachari herself was arrested and exiled. Returning to Nepal in later years she founded a nunnery and became one of the country's spiritual leaders.[17]

Other leaders founded new movements to meet the needs of followers who wished to express their faith in different ways. Recovering from injuries sustained in battle, the soldier Ignatius Loyola experienced a religious conversion and went on to found the Jesuit order, a radical Catholic movement that revived the Catholic faith and restored it to its spiritual roots. The Jesuits were also defenders of the poor and the helpless, a position that sometimes led them to clash with the civil authorities, especially in the Spanish colonies in the Americas where they tried to defend the oppressed indigenous population.[18]

In nineteenth-century India, growing restive under British rule, the monk Swami Vivekananda and the aristocratic landowner and businessman Debendranath Tagore both founded new movements aimed at preserving and reviving spiritual faith in India. Tagore was a founder of the Brahmo Samaj movement, which attempted to modernise Hinduism by moving away from rituals and avatars towards a more personal connection with God; his writings spread rapidly throughout India. Influenced by Brahmo Samaj, Vivekananda founded the Ramakrishna mission which spread the faith not only in India but also overseas, and played a role in bringing about greater understanding of Indian faith and culture.[19] Leonard Howell did not claim to lead the Rastafarian faith, but as a dedicated preacher he played a major role in its spread, and came to be seen by many as a leader thanks to his apostolic and missionary work. His arrest and persecution by the British authorities in colonial Jamaica only added to his standing and reputation.[20]

Prosperity and status

The general perception of entrepreneurs and company bosses is that they are in business to make money for themselves, and any survey of business history will struggle to disprove this theory. Nevertheless, there are exceptions to the rule, and it is no coincidence that those leaders who are genuinely behave responsibly towards their followers – and towards society at large – are rewarded with greater loyalty and trust. That loyalty in turn transmits into several things. First, good people are attracted by the reputation of the business and want to work for it; second, those people are more creative and innovative and deliver superior value to customers and clients; and third, customers and clients are more loyal and tend to stay with the firm for longer, generating more revenue and more profits.[21]

That was the business model employed by Jamsetji Tata when setting up the Tata Group, and by John Lewis when handing over his company to employee ownership and control. When he established the first cooperatives of the Mondragón group in Spain, Father José Maria Arizmendiarrieta's purpose was to revive the economy of the Basque region, which had suffered severe repression in the aftermath of the Spanish Civil War, and give its people hope and prosperity. Tata, similarly, had as one of his goals the building of a strong Indian economy in advance of hoped-for independence.[22]

Sometimes entrepreneurs were ambitious for themselves *and* their followers. Ma Ying-piao, the founder of the Sincere department store in Hong Kong, was an ambitious businessman but he also believe that one of the purposes of business was to contribute to society by creating jobs and spreading prosperity. The French husband-and-wife team who founded Au Bon Marché, Aristide and Marguerite Boucicaut, came from poor backgrounds and desire prosperity, but they also knew their department store had an important social role, making goods available to the rising middle classes and helping them achieve their own aspirations. The principle became known as the 'democratisation of luxury'. At the same time, the Boucicauts paid their staff well and looked after them, earning the reluctant admiration of that most scathing of social critics, Émile Zola.[23]

Just as the Boucicauts helped middle-class French households improve their standard of living and their social status, two American entrepreneurs helped black women at a time when black Americans were striving for great recognition. The beauty industry has plenty of critics, but rightly or wrongly personal appearance plays an important part in self-esteem.[24] In the late nineteenth century there were no hair care products suitable for black women's hair. Annie Turnbo Malone, the poor child of slave parents, saw the need and addressed it, using her own largely self-taught knowledge of chemistry to develop a range of products and market them. One of her employees, Sarah Breedlove Walker, branched out and started her own business. Although Malone and Walker were in competition, the market was more than large enough for both of them to flourish, and both used their wealth to make large donations to civil liberties organisations and black educational institutions.[25]

There are other examples, and we have already seen some of them such as the Quaker and Unitarian business leaders who emerged out of the Industrial Revolution in Britain, Josiah Wedgwood and the Cadburys and Rowntrees. What they all have in common is the simple fact that they were perceived as doing 'good', putting the interests of their employees and the community before themselves. Goodness itself is not enough; entrepreneurs need other sources of power, including inherent skills and abilities, and the consent of followers. But is interesting how many of the cases we have discusserd have an element of conferred authority, a spiritual element that has nothing to do with commerce or trade or industry and much to do with the person and their beliefs.

Political aspirations

Politicians, like entrepreneurs, are a group of leaders who have traditionally been treated with distrust. The modern-day disenchantment with the political classes is nothing new; one has only to look at the cartoons of James Gillray and Thomas Rowlandson in the Georgian era, or listen to the broadside ballads of the seventeenth and eighteenth centuries, or go further back and read the *Satires* of the Roman author Juvenal or the plays of Aristophanes, to see this.[26]

However, there are political leaders who have won respect for their firm adherence to their own values and their obvious dedication to making a difference to the world around them, rather than satisfying their own ambitions. Their appointed to task is to help their followers achieve their political aspirations. In American mythology, George Washington and Abraham Lincoln are two such leaders, and an examination of their careers largely bears this out. Washington seems to have been remarkably devoid of personal ambition; from his early service as a militia officer during the Seven Years War to his command of the Continental Army during the American Revolution to his two terms of president, he was motivated by a sense of duty. He longed for his home, Mount Vernon, and talked often of retiring there, but that sense of duty continued to call him away. As a young lawyer Lincoln saw at first hand the hardship and misery of the poor and developed a commitment to social justice, and he was also a committed abolitionist. During the early days of the Civil War, when the Union army crumbled and the Confederacy won victory after victory, Lincoln's steadfastness made him into a symbol of the Union.[27]

Washington was a leader of rebels, Lincoln was an outside, and this raises an interesting point; when we look at servant leaders in politics, the vast majority seem to be rebels and outsiders. This is perhaps a little unfair. Robert Gascoyne-Cecil, third Marquis of Salisbury and long-serving prime minister and foreign minister in late Victorian Britain, was motivated by a sense of duty, and believed it an honour and a privilege to serve the empire.[28] He had enough support from fellow imperialists to maintain him in power, but whose interests was he really serving? By any disinterested standard, Salisbury was serving a very small group of privileged white males, whereas the rest of society and the empire was left outside in the cold.

Salisbury may have believed in service, but to call him a servant leader would be to stretch the definition to the breaking point.

Those who conform most closely to the definition of servant leaders, putting their own ambition aside and genuinely serving the people, include cases such as Gandhi, the leader of Indian independence, and Paderewski, who gave up his musical career to serve as the first prime minister of Poland. Other examples include Subcomandante Marcos and his fellow Zapatista leaders in Mexico and Emiliano Zapata, the guerilla leader who was not only the movement's inspiration, the Mexican guerrilla leader, who championed the poor and defended them from the oligarchy led by Porfirio Díaz, Mexico's president. Augusto César Sandino, the upright defender of Nicaragua in the 1930s, similarly won admiration for his stand; his murder by the Somoza regime made him a martyr, and the later Sandinista guerrilla movement took its name from him. In Czechoslovakia in the 1970s and 1980s, the playwright Václav Havel won respect for his peaceful opposition to the communist regime in his country. After the regime's fall, the new democratic Federal Assembly chose Havel as president by unanimous vote.[29] Rosa Luxembourg was widely admired for her passion and honesty even by some of her political opponents, but we should also remember more obscure figures like Sakine Cansiz, one of the founders of the Kurdistan Workers Party (PKK), a leading Kurdish independence movement, or Adele Balasingham, the Australian-born nurse who became leader of the women's wing of the Liberation Tigers of Tamil Eelam in Sri Lanka.[30]

Life is not always easy for these leaders. Havel and Cansiz spent lengthy spells in prison and Cansiz was tortured; she was later assassinated while in exile in Paris. Mahatma Gandhi, Luxembourg, Zapata and Sandino were also killed. Yet it is the risks they run that gives these leaders more authority. Their courage and willingness to lay their lives on the line gives them power, sometimes more power than establishment figures can command. There is danger for these outsiders, but there is also opportunity too.

The struggle for freedom

Like political aspirations, social aspirations often require struggle and for leaders to have courage and selflessness. Established elites try to collect political power at the expense of their followers, as in the case of Lord Salisbury, but they also maintain the social status quo, often refusing to concede power or privilege to followers unless forced to do so.

Breaking the control of these elites usually requires building coalitions among followers. Organisations like the Langham Place Group in London and the Ladies' Dining Society in Cambridge were major forces in the opening up of education, especially higher education, to women in late nineteenth-century Britain. After decades of appealing to the male-dominated colleges to admit women, these societies and others simply raised money from wealthy sympathisers and started their own colleges. Girton College, founded in 1869 by Emily Davies, received strong support from the Langham Place Group through Davies' friend the artist Barbara Bodichon. Newnham College, founded by Anne Clough, played a central role in the Ladies Dining Society; Eleanor Sidgwick, one of its leading members, also held a teaching post at Newnham.[31]

Many of this group, especially Emily Davies and Barbara Bodichon, were also deeply involved with the women's suffrage movement, regarding education and the vote as two aspects of the broader issue of women's rights. The emergent leader of the largest female suffrage organisation, the NUWSS, was Millicent Garrett Fawcett, who also took a strong interest in education; her sister, Elizabeth Garrett Anderson, was the first woman to be dean of a medical school in Britain and the first woman to serve on a school board. Unlike Emmeline Pankhurst, who focused solely on suffrage, Fawcett campaigned for a broad range of women's rights. She was a very good communicator, possessed of a clear speaking voice and a natural talent for writing, and it was this that led to her initial prominence, but she became a leader because she embodied the aspirations of thousands of women and liberal men who supported the same causes as herself. She had clear and strong principles and she was utterly dedicated to those causes, without a hint of personal ambition, and this made her very attractive to followers.

Selflessness and high principles distinguish some of the civil rights campaigners in the twentieth century America. We have already mentioned Rosa Parkes, the accidental leader who devoted the rest of her life to civil rights and died in poverty. Martin Luther King's private life was not free of incident, but his unswerving devotion to the cause of civil rights made him a hero to his followers who saw him as a symbol. Breaking away from the Nation of Islam, Malcolm X founded the Organization of Afro-American Unity to provide a rallying point for activists in favour of racial integration. Both men continued their work in the face of considerable danger; both ultimately were assassinated, Malcolm X in 1965 and King three years later.[32]

Eighteenth and nineteenth-century abolitionist leaders such as Olaudah Equiano and Frederick Douglass, themselves both former slaves, faced less personal danger but were tireless activists. Equiano was also a community leader for black residents of London, looking after their welfare and pleading their cause with the authorities. In 1790s England, black people had few advocates and few people they could turn to for help. Equiano filled that void, and in the process became a leader. Active in America in the 1840s and 1850s, Douglass toured the northern states giving speeches and rallying support for the abolitionist cause, and after the Civil War continued to work to support black people and their aspirations for a better life until his death in 1895.[33]

Servant leaders

What can these examples tell us about servant leadership? The first lesson seems to be that servant leaders are successful because they provide followers with what they want. But that raises another question: if followers know what they want, why do they need leaders? Why don't they simply take it for themselves, taking over the social space entirely as Marx and Kropotkin imagined, and dispensing with leadership altogether?

The answer is that servant leaders are more than just proxies for followers. They provide things that followers do not have. First, as already discussed, they often provide specialist skills and knowledge, not only technical skills but also the ability to communicate and spread a vision and message. Second, they often have networks and access to sources of power that followers do not have; they have the necessary contacts to build coalitions and increase the strength of the follower group. Third, and related to this, they have uniting and coordinating abilities to bring followers together and help them focus on their destination, perhaps winning over some of the more reluctant followers in the process. They do this partly through communicating, but also through the symbolic element; successful leaders are sometimes emblems or totems in and of themselves, signifying the cause and rallying people are around it.

Finally, they have the singleness of purpose and the will to get things done. In the case of servant leaders, they will continue to work for the cause even if it puts themselves at hazard. This requires attributes such as confidence and courage, things which are partly inherent but are partly the product of environment and education. There may be some truth to the saying attributed, probably wrongly, to the Duke of Wellington that 'the battle of Waterloo was won on the playing fields of Eton'. The ingrained sense of superiority engrained into boys at English public schools in the eighteenth and nineteenth century may have been one of the factors that gave Wellington's officers the confidence to lead, and to win. Another paradox of leadership, then, is ambition and humility; servant leaders need to be strong and ambitious on behalf of their followers, even as they try to be humble themselves.

We also might need to think again about the issue of authenticity. Theorising around authenticity suggests that the leader should be themselves and not try to pretend to be something they are not. But will that always meet the expectations of followers? The paradox of ambition and humility means that followers often want both. They want leaders who understand them; but they also want leaders who will symbolise their own ambitions and lead them towards their goals. It turns out that the notion of conferred authority is not so dead as we thought it was. Faith, either religious faith or general spirituality, can be a powerful lodestar. So can the ability to find and create symbols that will give people a spiritual and psychological point around which they can coalesce.

And this has its dangers, because that process can be corrupted. Servant leadership rests on the notion that followers know where they want to do and what they want to do, but that is not always the case. Many things can happen to cloud the judgement of followers and prevent them from making decisions about what is best for them, and in the contest social space of leadership, some leaders are ready to take advantage of this. How and why they do so is the subject of the next chapter.

Notes

1 'Ali, *Nahjul Balagha*.

2 Ashcraft, *Locke's Two Treatises of Government*; Zuckert, *Launching Liberalism*; Rousseau, *The Social Contract*; Follett, *Creative Experience*; Follett, 'Leadership'.

3 Blaine McCormick and David Davenport, *Shepherd Leadership: Wisdom for Leaders From Psalm 23*, San Francisco: Jossey-Bass, 2003; Larry Osborne, *Lead Like a Shepherd: The Secret to Leading Well*, Nashville: Thomas Nelson, 2018.

4 James Rebanks, *The Shepherd's Life*, London: Penguin, 2016.

5 Rob Goffee and Gareth Jones, *Why Should Anyone Be Led By You? What it Takes to be an Authentic Leader*, Boston: Harvard Business School Press, 2015; Herminia Ibarra, *Act Like a Leader, Think Like a Leader*, Boston: Harvard Business Review Press, 2015.

6 Sebba, *Mother Teresa*; David H. Donald, *Lincoln*, New York: Simon & Schuster, 1996; Doris Kearns Goodwin, *Teams of Rivals: The Political Genius of Abraham Lincoln*, New York: Penguin, 2009; Malcolm X, *Autobiography of Malcolm X*, New York: Penguin, 2007.

7 Barczewski, *Antarctic Destinies*; Huntford, *Shackleton*.

8 Robinson, *Mary Seacole*; Bostridge, *Florence Nightingale*.

9 Rai and Chawla, *Faith and Compassion*; Sebba, *Mother Teresa*.

10 John Sugden, *Tecumseh: A Life*, New York: Henry Holt, 1998; Gregory Evans Dowd, *A Spirited Resistance: The North American Indian Struggle for Unity, 1745–1815*, Baltimore: Johns Hopkins University Press, 1992.

11 Keith Weller Taylor, *The Birth of Vietnam*, Berkeley: University of California Press, 1983; Hue-Tam Ho Tai, *The Country of Memory: Remaking the Past in Late Socialist Vietnam*, Berkeley: University of California Press, 2001.

12 Reina Pennington, *Amazons to Fighter Pilots: A Biographical Dictionary of Military Women*, Westport: Greenwood, 2003; Barbara Bennett Peterson, *Notable Women of China: Shang Dynasty to the Early Twentieth Century*, Armonk: M.E. Sharpe, 2000; Willard J. Peterson (ed.), *The Cambridge History of China*, vol. 9, Cambridge: Cambridge University Press, 2018.

13 Edwin Hoyt, *The Last Kamikaze: The Story of Matome Ugaki*, Westport: Greenwood, 1993; Alfred Price, *The Last Year of the Luftwaffe*, London: Greenhill, 2015.

14 Hibbert, *The Borgias and Their Enemies*; Bernard, *Talleyrand*; Lawday, *Napoleon's Master*; Helene Tillman, *Pope Innocent III*, New York: Elsevier, 1980; Michael Staunton, *Thomas Becket and His Biographers*, Woodbridge: Boydell, 2006.

15 Flanagan, *Hildegard of Bingen*; Fiona Maddocks, *Hildegard of Bingen: The Woman of Her Age*, New York: Doubleday, 2001.

16 Lily Xiao Hong Lee and A.D. Stefanowska (eds), *Biographical Dictionary of Chinese Women*, vol. 1, Armonk: M.E. Sharpe, 2007.

17 Sarah LeVine and David N. Gellner, *Rebuilding Buddhism: The Theravada Movement in Twentieth-Century Nepal*, Cambridge, MA: Harvard University Press, 2006.

18 Philip Caraman, *Ignatius Loyola: A Biography of the Founder of the Jesuits*, New York: HarperCollins, 1990; John W. O'Malley, *The First Jesuits*, Cambridge, MA: Harvard University Press, 1995.

19 David Kopf, *The Brahmo Samaj and the Shaping of the Modern Indian Mind*, Princeton: Princeton University Press, 2015; Narayan Chaudhuri, *Maharshi Debendranath Tagore*, New Delhi: Sahitya, 2010; Amiya P. Sen, *Swami Vivekananda*, New Delhi: Oxford University Press, 2013.

20 Clinton A. Hutton *et al.* (eds), *Leonard Percival Howell and the Genesis of Rastafari*, Kingston: University of the West Indies Press, 2013; Anthony Bogues, *Black Heretics, Black Prophets: Radical Political Intellectuals*, London: Routledge, 2003.

21 Witzel, *Tata*; Witzel, *Managing for Success*.

22 Whyte and Whyte, *Making Mondragon*: Lala, *For the Love of India*.

23 Miller, *The Bon Marché*; Émile Zola, *Au Bonheur des Dames (The Ladies' Delight)*, London: Penguin, 2001.

24 Naomi Wolf, *The Beauty Myth: How Images of Beauty are Used Against Women*, London: Vintage, 1991.

25 Ingham and Feldman, *African American Business Leaders*; Bundles, *Madam C.J. Walker*; Colman, *Madam C.J. Walker*.

26 Matthew Hodgart, *Satire: Origins and Principles*, Piscataway: Transaction, 2009.

27 Alden, *George Washington*; Ferling, *First of Men*; Donald, *Lincoln*; Goodwin, *Teams of Rivals*.

28 A.L. Kennedy, *Salisbury, 1830–1903: Portrait of a Statesman*, London: John Murray, 1953; Tuchman, *The Proud Tower*.

29 Womack, *Zapata*; Ramírez, *Sandino*; Pontuso, *Václav Havel*.

30 Sakine Cansiz, *Sara: My Whole Life Was a Struggle*, London: Pluto, 2015; Adele Balasingham, *The Will to Freedom: An Inside View of Tamil Resistance*, London: Fairmax, 2003.

31 Jane Robinson, *Bluestockings: The Remarkable Story of the First Women to Fight for Education*, London: Penguin, 2010. Daphne Bennett, *Emily Davies and the Liberation of Women*, London: Andre Deutsch, 1990; Pamela Hirsch, *Barbara Leigh Smith Bodichon: Feminist, Artist and Rebel*, London: Chatto & Windus, 1998; Gillian Sutherland, 'Clough, Anne Jemima', in *Oxford Dictionary of National Biography*, Oxford: Oxford University Press, 2004.

32 Brinkley, *Rosa Parkes*; Parkes and Haskins, *Rosa Parkes*; Frady, *Martin Luther King*; Long, *Against Us, But For Us*; Malcolm X, *Autobiography of Malcolm X*.

33 Carretta, *Equiano*; Blight, *Frederick Douglass*.

PART V

Servants of darkness

17
DARK FOLLOWERS

The phenomenon of dark leadership has long been recognised, even if there is no clear agreement as to what it is. Generally, it is regarded as leadership of a malign nature, in terms of oppressing and bullying followers, being a destructive force in society, or both.[1] Most attention to date has been concentrated on the psycho-social personalities of dark leaders, with in some cases a suggestion that they can be *cured* by overcoming their dark personality traits. This may well be correct in some cases, but it ignores a historical truth, namely that some leaders choose the paths of darkness not only because it is to their advantage and they can gain more power but also because they have followers who are willing to follow them down those dark roads.

Even the worst tyrants, those most guilty of corruption, violence and murder, have followers who support them; indeed, they could hardly maintain themselves in power without them. The open question is, why do people choose to follow leaders who are doing wrong and harmful things? Various explanations have been advanced; that they are deluded and lied to by propaganda, and follow dark leaders without realising they are dark; that they follow unwillingly, aware of the consequences for themselves if they disobey; and that they are victims of the herd instinct and simply go along with the crowd because it is human nature to do so.[2]

Propaganda certainly plays a role in persuading followers to follow, and we will come back to this later in the chapter. Coercion also plays a role, but that role is limited. The best coercion can usually do is ensure passive followership and prevent active opposition; it is hard to persuade someone to act willingly at the point of a bayonet. Passive followership on behalf of the majority is sometimes sufficient, so long as there is a core of active and committed followers to work with the leader, although this combination seldom makes for a high-functioning organisation. In kleptocracies, for example, where the leader is in power only to enrich themselves by plundering the organisation – Mobutu Sese Seku in Zaire and Bernie Madoff at Madoff Investment Securities being examples – this is good enough.[3] Generally, though, leaders will seek to ensure that they have a large number of actively engaged followers, for they are an important source of power.

The herd instinct is more problematic. In the 1840s, in *Extraordinary Popular Delusions and the Madness of Crowds*, Charles Mackay described a number of instances of the phenomenon, including tulipmania, the South Sea Bubble, the persecution of witches and medical fads such as 'magnetising', without really attempting to analyse the herd mentality itself. In the late 1890s Gustave le Bon discussed the nature of the 'collective unconscious' and the emergence of the 'group mind', in which individual members of the group sublimate their own values, needs and desires to those of the larger crowd. Twenty years later Wilfred Trotter discussed these concepts in even more pessimistic terms, suggesting that the herd instinct robs people of judgement and undermines civilisation itself, taking the 'war fever' in the years before the First World War as an example.[4]

The question is whether people can be coerced into joining the herd, or whether they do so willingly. The Milgram experiments, carried out at Yale University in the early 1960s, reported that if ordered to do so, people would give painful electric shocks to other people. The people giving the shocks seemed clearly distress and upset about the pain they were causing, but they still followed orders. However, the results have been questioned, with one reviewer suggesting that many participants were aware that that the giving of shocks was a pretence and no actual pain was being caused.[5]

This raises the possibility not only that people go along with the herd because they feel pressure to do so but do not really believe in their hearts in the cause the herd has espoused but also that there are limits to behaviour and there will come a time when the herd has had enough and will revolt. The extreme cruelty with which Jack Rohrbach executed prisoners at Weinsberg during the German Peasants' War turned his followers against him; Rohrbach was killed and replaced by Götz von Berlichingen.[6] Even fanatics like the Waffen SS, the elite units of the armies of Nazi Germany who were devoted to Hitler, rebelled once they became disillusioned; large numbers of men deserted from the Thirteenth SS Division in Yugoslavia, some joining the anti-German partisans, and in the same year two battalions stationed in France mutinied, killed their officers and went over *en masse* to the *maquis*, the French resistance.[7]

Shared ideology

Followers, especially the committed ones, follow for a reason, and so we come back to the question of why they follow dark leaders. The herd instinct does play a role, but so does genuine shared belief, what social scientists refer to as 'sacred values', people's ideals and aspirations for their own society.[8] Leaders will attempt to persuade followers to stop simply being part of the herd and commit, but the core of followers who believe in the cause already existed before the leader came to power. These are the activists and die-hards, the followers for whom the cause is their primary motive.

Benito Mussolini did not found the fascist movement in Italy; many of the movement's primary tenets including anti-communism and nationalism had already been established by earlier leaders like D'Annunzio. Mussolini emerged as the leader who best symbolised the aspiration of Fascism.[9] Stalin added very little that was new to Marxist-Leninist ideology; if anything that ideology became more conservative and less prone to change and adaptation during his regime in the Soviet Union; much of his effort was directed at eliminating other, more ideological rivals to his power, such as Sergey Kirov and Nikolai Bukharin.[10] Pol Pot was just one of many young Cambodian students in Paris in the late 1940s who embraced communism, and he worked with other members of the Communist Party of Cambodia for many years before finally emerging as leader of the Khmer Rouge. Like Mussolini and Stalin, he emerged as leader of an existing movement with a strong and committed following.[11]

In the US in the nineteenth century, the ideology of 'manifest destiny', the view that America was naturally destined to control the North American continent and even the entire new world mingled with a belief in racial superiority. The Native American peoples were seen as inferior, a barrier to civilisation and progress. General William T. Sherman, the commander-in-chief of the US Army, argued for the complete extermination of the native Americans, and Colonel William Chivington, who led volunteer troops during the Sand Creek massacre in which more than a hundred Cheyenne women and children were killed, stated that killing 'Indians' was ordained by God and he was justified in using any means to kill them.[12] Elwell Otis, an American army officer who fought in the wars against the western American tribes, argued that the Indians could never be civilised, and therefore should be annihilated as an impediment to Christian civilisation; later, as military governor of the Philippines, he encouraged his troops to commit atrocities against the Filipino civilian population who were also regarded as inferior.[13]

The point about these men was not that they held their views, but that they represented many others who felt the same. Sherman, and especially Chivington, were to a large extent reflecting the views of settlers and prospectors on the frontier, who wanted the native American lands for themselves and justified their position by claiming racial superiority. Not everyone agreed with them; the American president Ulysses S. Grant tried to remove Sherman from power, and Otis was eventually recalled from the Philippines after protests about the brutality of his men. But the men they led, and especially the soldiers under their command, were willing to carry out their orders. Racial superiority was also ingrained in the government of British India, where many argued that the British had a duty to *civilise* India and any Indian who stood in their way deserved to be crushed; thus atrocities like the Amritsar massacre were justified as necessary to preserve peace and the natural order of British superiority.[14] The sense of racial superiority ingrained in the Japanese army in China led to the massacre at Nanjing, in which as many as 300,000 civilians were killed; in this case, the massacre happened without orders and the Japanese commander General Matsui Iwane was reportedly horrified by what had happened.[15]

Ignorance

On the opposite end of the scale is ignorance. Lacking any ideology or belief system of their own, followers are easily influenced by leaders who offer them a programme, particularly if there is also an explicit threat to their own interests. *The Protocols of the Elders of Zion*, a forgery purporting to contain a master plan for Jewish world domination, was widely circulated; the industrialist Henry Ford paid for 500,000 copies of an English translation to be distributed in the US.[16] Despite its being fairly obviously a forgery, with entire passages being plagiarised from modern novels, people who knew nothing about Judaism were prepared to believe it. In the early 1920s Hitler frequently referenced the *Protocols*, linking the Jews and communists as a united threat, although as senior Nazis later admitted, they knew the Jewish people had neither an intention to dominate the world nor the organisation to do so. They played on popular gullibility.[17]

So too did ambitious politicians and religious leaders during the witch-hunting craze in the sixteenth and seventeenth centuries. Witchcraft had been a part of popular folklore since medieval times, and sorcery was one of the charges levelled against the Knights Templar when the organisation was forcibly broken up in the fourteenth century; in fact this was a charge trumped up by King Philippe IV, who not only felt the Templars were too powerful but also coveted their lands and wealth.[18]

In the late sixteenth century, there was an explosion of popular hysteria about witches, especially in Protestant countries where the new faith was still insecure. Intent on creating an Other, some Protestant leaders made an association between satanism and Catholicism. Catholics were burned at the stake in England and other countries, and now innocent people suspected of being witches began to suffer the same fate. The advent of the printing press played an important role in spreading fear among the ignorant, and books such as the *Malleus Maleficarum*, by Heinrich Kramer, and the *Daemonologie*, by King James VI of Scotland, received wide circulation. James reportedly feared that witches were trying to kill him, but there was a political reason for his encouraging the fear of witches; they were the Other, a threat to his unstable kingdom, and if he could pose as defender of the faithful he would win more followers. Matthew Hopkins, the self-proclaimed Witchfinder General, also used popular fear of witches to create a following for himself.[19]

Fear

People are often frightened by what they do not understand.[20] Fear played a considerable role in the witchcraft hysteria in part because witches represented something unfamiliar and unknown. In Spain, the Dominican friar Tómas de Torquemada rose to be the head of the Spanish Inquisition by playing on popular fears of two groups, the marranos and the moriscos, Spanish Jews and Muslims who had converted to Catholicism.[21] In those portions of Spain which had been under Muslim rule, Jews and Muslims had been economically dominant, and after the reconquest of much of

Spain by the Catholic powers of the north, it was feared that these converts would attempt to regain their old powers. Torquemada and his inquisitors used torture and execution to root out supposed 'heretics' who, they claimed, only pretended to be Catholics and in reality continued to practice their old religion. Eventually the moriscos and many of the marranos were rounded up and expelled from Spain. All of these measures had broad support from the Catholic population of Spain.

Fear also motivated the Teutonic Order during their brutal suppression of the indigenous Prussians. The Prussians, who were Slavs and pagans, made an ideal Other for the Order, which exterminated or assimilated the Prussians and handed over their lands to German migrants from the west.[22] Fear also played a role in the savage suppression of slave revolts in the West Indies and Southern American states, as the white masters were well aware that their slaves outnumbered them, often by a considerable margin. By 1830 there were an estimated 300,000 slaves on the island of Jamaica, outnumbering the white population by around twenty to one. The slave revolt known as the Baptist War was harshly repressed, with more than five hundred slaves killed. Apart from missionaries, who tried to defend the slaves, the white population was solidly behind the punishments and demanded more. Paradoxically, the reason the authorities stopped the executions was fear that more bloodshed would cause the slaves to rise up again.[23]

Fear was – and is – also an element in anti-Semitism.[24] There are of course many aspects of anti-Semitism, including religious resentment, cultural differences and fear of the Jewish people's perceived economic clout, but it was the perception of Jews as a different 'race' that has probably provoked the most fear in recent times. The notion that the Jewish Diaspora was somehow an underground movement poised to rise up and take control of Europe is explicit in the writings of members of the populist *völkisch* movement in Germany in the first two decades of the twentieth century, and *völkisch* organisations such as the Thule Society, founded in 1918, disseminated anti-Semitic propaganda in much the same way that Henry Ford did in America. Their ideas were taken up the Nazis; Hitler makes explicit references to *völkisch* theories in *Mein Kampf*.[25]

Anger and revenge

Fear can be manipulated, and clever leaders will use it to motivate followers. Instead of fleeing from their fears, followers are urged to confront the source of those fears and to fight. Ironically, this involves giving people power, in this case, the power and authority to punish, to wound and even to kill. Not everyone wants this power, at least not in every circumstance. After the fall of the city of Cawnpore to Indian sepoys and rebels led by the Nana Sahib, around 120 women and children were captured and held as hostages. Learning that British troops were about to assault the city, Nana ordered his followers to kill the prisoners. They refused, raising their rifles to fire in the air rather than at the women and children, and Nana had to call for volunteers from the city to carry out the killings. He found people who hated the British sufficiently to do so, and the women and children were killed and their bodies thrown down a well. When British troops took the city and discovered the well, their own anger led them to commit a number of brutal atrocities against Indian prisoners.[26]

Anger and the desire to punish played a role in massacres committed by both sides during the crusades. In the worst of these, the crusaders who captured Jerusalem from its Muslim garrison indulged in an orgy of unplanned violence in which as many as six thousand people died.[27] In twentieth-century China, Sun Yat-sen urged his followers to see the ruling Manchus as foreign invaders. Some of his followers were only too ready to do so and there were massacres of Manchus in Nanjing and Xi'an; as many as twenty thousand people may have died in the latter city, with the survivors enslaved.[28] Some of the early massacres of Armenians instigated by the Young Turks in the Ottoman Empire were revenge attacks for Armenians having apparently supported the government against the Young Turk Revolution, and the slaughter of more than six thousand mainly Muslim Bosniaks at Srebrenica by Serb soldiers was an expression of religious and racial hatred; although senior Serb military commanders were later convicted of war crimes, the killings appear to have begun spontaneously after the town fell to the Serbian army.[29]

The kind of anger that makes men willing to kill without being ordered to do so is a very useful tool for dark leaders, who recruit such men in order to channel their aggression and anger towards intended targets. The SS, the elite force of the German army during the Second World War, contained plenty of men whose sense of racial superiority and race hatred made them ideal tools. The Einsatzgruppen were units of volunteers tasked with killing Jews, men who had been educated and trained to think of Jews as sub-human and deserving to die. They were responsible for many mass killings including most infamously the massacre at Babi Yar near Kiev, when around thirty-three thousand Jews were killed and their bodies thrown into a ravine.[30] Christian militiamen from the Lebanese Forces militia wore helmets with SS marks scratched on painted on them during their attack on the Palestinian refugee camp in the Beirut suburb of Karantina in 1976, during which around fifteen hundred Palestinian civilians, many of whom were Christian, were shot and mutilated. The anger of the Lebanese Forces men was in part sparked by the actions of the Palestinian Liberation Organisation, which the Lebanese government could no longer control; in parts of the country the PLO had taken *de facto* control. But there was also a general hatred of Palestinian refugees who were seen as interlopers, and attacks like Qarantina were designed to drive them out of the country. In revenge, Palestinians attacked the Christian town of Damour two days later, killing nearly five hundred people.[31]

Greed

Greed is also a force in followers that leaders can use to their advantage. Greed has also played a role in anti-Semitism, where the belief that Jews were wealthy played a role in encouraging attacks on them. In 1096, German troops marching to take part in the First Crusade extorted money from Jewish communities in the Rhineland, and later attacked and looted Jewish homes and synagogues in Worms and Mainz.[32] In England before the Third Crusade and again during the Second Barons' War, noblemen who owed money to Jewish bankers incited their followers to attack the homes of the bankers and destroy records of their loans.[33] The promise of plunder was often held out to followers as an incitement; the crusaders who attacked Constantinople in 1204 and the mercenaries who invaded Rome in 1527 were both promised the chance to loot a powerful city and make themselves rich.[34]

Greed, the promise of a share of the spoils, sometimes persuades followers to become part of corruption in businesses, although generally speaking business corruption is confined to quite small groups within the larger organisation. However, corrupt leaders tend to attract corrupt followers, and the culture of greed and winning at all costs established by John D. Rockefeller at Standard Oil pervaded the entire organisation; there is no reason to believe that the Rockefeller employees who attacked and burned the premises of rival firms did so unwillingly.[35] Scandals in sport and politics similarly tend to be quite enclosed affairs with small numbers of participants. Examples could include the Black Sox scandal, when members of the Chicago White Sox baseball team conspired to lose games in return for payment from a gambling syndicate organised by the gangster Arnold Rothstein; the Teapot Dome scandal, when members of President Warren Harding's administration took bribes from companies; or the Watergate affair, when a team around President Richard Nixon organised illegal break-ins and wiretapping of Democratic party headquarters. Again, there were people greedy for money and power, or both, who were willing to step forward and take part.[36] Finally, of course, as we shall see further in Chapter 19, criminal organisations attract people for whom greed is a major motivating force.

Dark leadership

In the social space of dark leadership, leaders look first for followers who share their own interests and ideology. In order to expand their power they then appeal to the greed of other groups of followers, or exploit their ignorance, or both.

The appeal to greed is usually a simple matter of either offering a reward or giving followers permission to take something that belongs to someone else. In the former case, followers are free to make their own calculation of reward versus risk. In the latter, the leader will often direct followers to attack a group who have already been identified as the Other, like the Manchus in China, the Palestinians in Lebanon or the Jews in Europe; seizing the property of the Other goes hand in hand with an already established ideology of hatred, and greed is merely an additional spur.

Exploiting ignorance is more subtle and can take more time. To do this, leaders need to call on other sources of power and authority. Conferred authority might give the leader a kind of moral force which can be communicated to followers; for example, referring to religious texts as revealed truth and insisting that followers have a religious duty, as Pope Urban II did when he preached the crusade at Clermont.[37] Inherent authority makes the leader more believable. People listened to Henry Ford when he distributed anti-Semitic propaganda because he had already achieved a reputation as a business genius, and therefore a man who should be listened to. Army officers who give orders to commit atrocities are obeyed because of their rank.

Once the sources of authority are established, leaders need to tell followers and potential followers a story, a narrative that explains the world around them and persuades others to follow them. We have already seen how the creation of a threatening Other can both exploit people's fears and arouse anger and a determination to fight back. In creating the Other, leaders explicitly position themselves as the one force that can fight back and keep followers safe and strong. Mobutu Sese Seko championed African culture and tried to expunge all traces of colonialism, changing the name of his country from Congo to Zaire, the old name of the Congo river, and forbidding people from using Western names or adoption Western styles of dress. Mobutu also posed as the champion of the people; his name means 'the all-powerful warrior'. Ironically, at the same time as he was opposing Western influence, Mobutu was allegedly receiving large sums from the US in exchange for opposing Soviet and Chinese influence in Africa.[38]

The caudillos in Latin America, whom we examined in Chapter 9, also used the cult of personality to maintain themselves in power, becoming living symbols of their own ideology. The same is also true of Henry Ford. An engineering genius who revolutionised the automobile industry and made cheap motoring available to the population of America and then the world, he was regarded as a towering figure. Capitalising on this reputation, Ford wrote books and gave speeches in which he posed as a wise figure who knew what was best for society. During the First World War he chartered a 'peace ship' and sailed to Europe in the belief that he could single-handedly negotiate an end to the First World War.

From the 1920s onwards, his company, Ford Motors, was increasingly run as an autocracy. Talented managers who might have become rivals for power like James Couzens and William Knudsen were driven out of the firm. The culture of Ford became one of discipline and control; and the industrial psychology department, originally set up to improve working conditions, became the primary instrument of repression. Workplace discipline was handed over to a former Chicago gangster, who had no hesitation in assaulting and beating up workers who stepped out of line. But Ford remained in power until almost the bitter end thanks to his personal prestige.[39]

The Nazi regime in Germany is perhaps the most powerful example symbolism as both a weapon and a refuge, persuading otherwise reluctant people that the regime was there to defend them against the Other, first communists and Jews, and then later Slavs and other people deemed to be inferior. The regime then interposed itself between their followers and the Other, transforming the Nazi party into a symbolic wall that kept the Other out. The declaration of a 'thousand-year Reich' signalled permanence; the Other would be defeated, the Reich would prevail. The notion of racial superiority built around Aryan identity was used as 'proof' of German superiority. A wide variety of symbols were deployed to reinforce this newly created myth, ranging from the music of Richard Wagner, which was redefined by Nazi propagandists to demonstrate the triumph of the Aryan people, to visual symbols such as the swastika, taken to be an ancient Aryan symbol. Taken together, these symbols told a potent story that played on the psychology of undecided or wavering followers and convinced them to join in the narrative and become part of the story themselves.[40]

The Nazis dreamed on a grand scale, but the whipping up of fear and anger can also be done on a smaller scale. During the Vietnam War, American soldiers were encouraged to see the enemy, especially the Viet Cong guerrillas, as the Other, members of an inferior race and inferior ideology (communism) who wanted to destroy the American way of life. Many soldiers were conscripts, and this depiction of the Other was meant to stimulate their desire to fight. On 16 March 1968, Charlie Company of the 1st Battalion, 20th Infantry Regiment, was deployed to clear Viet Cong insurgents out of the village of Son My. The company commander, Captain Ernest Medina, told his men that all civilians had left the area and that the only people left in Son My were Viet Cong; therefore, they should kill anyone they found.

In fact, there were no Viet Cong in Son My; three weapons were later found in the village, but none were used against the Americans. When Charlie Company arrived in the hamlets of My Lai and My Khe, part of Son My, they found the streets and roads crowded with people getting ready for market day. It was clear that there were no armed enemies present; it was equally clear that many of the people were women and children, nonetheless, the men of Charlie Company began to kill everyone they saw. Some people were ordered to lie down in a ditch and then sprayed with automatic rifle fire; others were shot as they ran away, and some women were raped before being killed. Between 350 and 500 civilians died. When a helicopter pilot, Warrant Officer Hugh Thompson, landed his aircraft and begged to at least be allowed to take the wounded away, he was told by a soldier that there would be no wounded. Thompson later received a medal for attempting to stop the massacre. He threw it away.[41]

The question posed during the subsequent investigation, and never fully answered, was why the men of Charlie Company obeyed Captain Medina's order to kill, even when it was clear that there was no resistance. The answer is that their fear and anger, already roused to fever pitch by earlier fighting and casualties Charlie Company had suffered, meant that they were ready to kill, and once they started killing, those emotions could no longer be checked. The U.S. Army's leaders had attempted to dehumanise the Vietnamese in order to persuade their conscript soldiers to fight, but the attempt backfired. The My Lai massacre shocked American public opinion and played an important role in turning sentiment against the Vietnam War. The madness of crowds can be terrible, but it can also be dangerous to those who attempt to control it.

There is yet another paradox in the leader-follower relationship. For followers to have dreams and aspirations, and for followers to choose leaders to help them meet those aspirations, is one thing. But what about when the aspirations of followers include dominating, exploiting and murdering others? Does there not come a point when the aspirations of followers should be checked? Logic and morality both would suggest there does come such a point, and further, that it is the duty of leaders to control followers so they do not run amok, rather than encouraging them to do so. Therein lies one of the key differences between dark leadership and, as Gay Haskins and her colleagues put it, leadership with kindness.[42]

But making the distinction between these two kinds of leadership is not easy, and indeed there is probably an argument against making the distinction at all; there may well be an element of darkness in every leader. One area where the distinction can be very hard to discern is terrorism, where *darkness* depends on one's moral standpoint, and it is to this subject that we turn in the next chapter.

Notes

1 Gary L. McIntosh and Samuel D. Rima, *Overcoming the Dark Side of Leadership: The Paradox of Personal Dysfunction*, Ada: Baker Books, 1998; Dennis Tourish, *The Dark Side of Transformational Leadership: A Critical Perspective*, London: Routledge, 2013; Bekir Emre Kurtulmuş, *The Dark Side of Leadership: An Institutional Perspective*, Basingstoke: Palgrave Macmillan, 2018.
2 John J. Mearsheimer, *Why Leaders Lie: The Truth About Lying in International Politics*, Oxford: Oxford University Press, 2013; Edward Bernays, *Propaganda*, London: Routledge, 1928; Timothy Snyder, *On Tyranny: Twenty Lessons from the Twentieth Century*, New York: Tim Duggan, 2017; Wilfred Trotter, *Instincts of the Herd in Peace and War*, New York: Macmillan, 1919; Mackay, *Extraordinary Popular Delusions*; Gustave le Bon, *The Crowd: A Study of the Popular Mind*, New York: Dover, 2002.
3 Sean Kelly, *America's Tyrant: The CIA and Mobutu of Zaire*, Washington: American Universities Press, 1993; Harry Markopolos, *No One Would Listen: A True Financial Thriller, the Madoff Whistleblower*, New York: Wiley, 2010.
4 Mackay, *Extraordinary Popular Delusions*; le Bon, *The Crowd*; Trotter, *Instincts of the Herd*.
5 Arthur G. Miller, *The Obedience Experiments: A Case Study of Controversy in Social Science*, New York: Praeger, 1986; Gina Perry, *Behind the Shock Machine: The Untold Story of the Notorious Milgram Psychology Experiments*, New York: The New Press, 2013.
6 Blickle, *The German Peasants War*.
7 John Keegan, *Waffen SS: The Asphalt Soldiers*, London: Pan, 1970.
8 Nafees Hamid and Clara Pretus, 'The Neuroscience of Terrorism: How We Convinced a Group of Radicals to Let Us Scan Their Brains', *The Conversation*, 12 June 2019.
9 Lyttleton, *The Seizure of Power*; Paxton, *The Anatomy of Fascism*; Payne, *A History of Fascism*.
10 Service, *The Russian Revolution*; Robert Service, *Stalin: A Biography*, London: Macmillan, 2004; Oleg V. Khlevniuk, *Stalin: New Biography of a Dictator*, trans. Nora Seligman Favorov, London: Yale University Press, 2015; Robert W. Thurston, *Life and Terror in Stalin's Russia, 1934–41*, London: Yale University Press, 1998.
11 Short, *Pol Pot*; Ben Kiernan, *How Pol Pot Came to Power: Colonialism, Nationalism and Communism in Cambodia, 1930–1975*, New Haven: Yale University Press, 2004.
12 Robert G. Athearn, *William Tecumseh Sherman and the Settlement of the West*, Norman: University of Oklahoma Press, 1956; Dee Brown, *Bury My Heart At Wounded Knee*, New York: Bantam, 1972.

13 Elwell Otis, *The Indian Question*, New York: Sheldon, 1878; Miller, *Benevolent Assimilation*.

14 James, *Raj*; Nigel Collett, *The Butcher of Amritsar: General Reginald Dwyer*, London: Continuum, 2006.

15 Iris Chang, *The Rape of Nanking: The Forgotten Holocaust of World War II*, New York: Basic, 2012.

16 Watts, *The People's Tycoon*.

17 Norman Cohn, *Warrant for Genocide: The Myth of the Jewish World Conspiracy and the Protocols of the Elders of Zion*, London: Eyre & Spottiswood, 1967; Joel E. Dimsdale, *Survivors, Victims and Perpetrators: Essays on the Nazi Holocaust*, London: Taylor & Francis, 1980.

18 Nicholson, *The Knights Templar*; Malcolm Barber, *The Trial of the Templars*, Cambridge: Cambridge University Press, 2012.

19 Gary F. Jensen, *The Path of the Devil: Early Modern Witch Hunts*, New York: Rowman & Littlefield, 2006; Craig Cabell, *Witchfinder General: The Biography of Matthew Hopkins*, New York: Sutton, 2006.

20 Joanna Bourke, *Fear: A Cultural History*, London: Virago, 2005.

21 Henry Kamen, *The Spanish Inquisition: A Historical Revision*, London: Yale University Press, 1999.

22 Christiansen, *The Northern Crusades*; William Urban, *The Prussian Crusade*, Chicago: Lithuanian Research and Studies Center, 2000.

23 Turner, *Slaves and Missionaries*; Michael Craton, *Testing the Chains: Resistance to Slavery in the British West Indies*, Ithaca: Cornell University Press, 1983.

24 Avner Falk, *Anti-Semitism: A History and Psychoanalysis of Contemporary Hatred*, Westport: Praeger, 2008.

25 Fritz Stern, *The Politics of Cultural Despair: A Study in the Rise of German Ideology*, Berkeley: University of California Press, 1961; George L. Mosse, *The Crisis of German Ideology: Intellectual Origins of the Third Reich*, New York: Grosset & Dunlap, 1964.

26 Shastitko and Shahani, *Nana Sahib*; Saul, *The Indian Mutiny*.

27 Frankopan, *The First Crusade*; Tyerman, *God's War*.

28 Edward J.M. Rhoads, *Manchu and Han: Ethnic Relations and Political Power in Late Qing and Early Republican China, 1861–1928*, Seattle: University of Washington Press, 2000.

29 Donald Bloxham, *The Great Game of Genocide: Imperialism, Nationalism and the Destruction of the Ottoman Armenians*, Oxford: Oxford University Press, 2005; Lara J. Nettlefield and Sarah E. Wagner, *Srebenica in the Aftermath of Genocide*, Cambridge: Cambridge University Press, 2014.

30 Martin Gilbert, *The Holocaust: The Human Tragedy*, London: HarperCollins, 1989.

31 Jonathan C. Randal, *The Tragedy of Lebanon: Christian Warlords, Israeli Adventurers and American Bunglers*, London: Chatto & Windus, 1983.

32 Frankopan, *The First Crusade*; Tyerman, *God's War*; Robert Chazan, *European Jewry and the First Crusade*, Berkeley: University of California Press, 1987.

33 Tyerman, *God's War*; Maddicott, *Simon de Montfort*.

34 Tyerman, *God's War*; Chamberlin, *The Sack of Rome*.

35 Oliver and Goodwin, *How They Blew It*; Tarbell, *The History of the Standard Oil Company*.

36 David Pietrusza, *Rothstein: The Life, Times and Murder of the Criminal Genius Who Fixed the 1919 World Series*, New York: Basic Books, 2011; Leonard J. Bates, *The Origins of Teapot Dome*, Urbana: University of Illinois Press, 1963; Theodore H. White, *Breach of Faith: The Fall of Richard Nixon*, New York: Atheneum, 1975.

37 Frankopan, *The First Crusade*; Tyerman, *God's War*.

38 Kelly, *America's Tyrant*; Kevin C. Dunn, *Imagining the Congo: The International Relations of Identity*, Basingstoke: Palgrave Macmillan, 2003.

39 Nevins, *Ford*; Watts, *The People's Tycoon*.

40 Shirer, *The Rise and Fall of the Third Reich*; Grunberger, *The Twelve-Year Reich*; Mosse, *The Crisis of German Ideology*; Turner, *Dramas, Fields and Metaphors*; Malcolm Quinn, *The Swastika: Constructing the Symbol*, London: Routledge, 2005; Leon Poliakov, *The Aryan Myth: A History of Racist and Nationalistic Idea in Europe*, New York: Barnes & Noble, 1996.

41 Michael R. Belknap, *The Vietnam War on Trial: The My Lai Massacre and the Court Martial of Lieutenant Calley*, Lawrence: University Press of Kansas, 2002; William Peers, *The My Lai Inquiry*, New York: W.W. Norton, 1979; Trent Angers, *The Forgotten Hero of My Lai: The Hugh Thompson Story*, Lafayette: Arcadian House, 1999; Stanton, *The Rise and Fall of an American Army*; Ward and Burns, *The Vietnam War*.
42 Gay Haskins, Mike Thomas and Lalit Johri (eds), *Kindness in Leadership*, London: Routledge, 2018.

18
TERRORIST LEADERS

An examination of leadership in terrorist organisations provides a useful lens through which to examine dark leadership and the relationship between leadership and force more generally. The response of the state to terrorism has usually been to try to kill or capture terrorist leaders, on the grounds that terrorist leadership is highly personal and terrorists depend strongly on their leaders. Decapitating terrorist organisations should cause them to disintegrate, making the problem go away.[1]

History suggests that this does not work very well. Terrorist leadership is indeed highly personal with very loose and fluid organisational structures, but removing the leader often merely results in their replacement by another leader and a return to business as usual. The assassination of al-Qaeda leader Osama bin Laden by American special forces troops made very little difference to the strength of al-Qaeda; competition from other Islamic terrorist groups has been arguably a greater threat.[2] Even when the organisation does disintegrate, followers usually just migrate to another similar organisation, or create a new one.

Terrorist leaders and followers are adaptable. Russian anarchists who fled the country to avoid arrest in the 1890s arrived in Macedonia and Bulgaria, where they helped set up organisations such as the Macedonian Secret Revolutionary Committee and the Boatmen of Salonika and launching attacks against Ottoman Turkey.[3] Ilich Ramírez Sánchez, better known as Carlos the Jackal, was a member of the Venezuelan Communist Party and then served for several years with the Palestinian group the Popular Front for the Liberation of Palestine (PFLP) before setting up as a freelance, suspecting of having links to Armenian terrorist groups and several state intelligence agencies. The Bonnot Gang, an anarchist group active in northern France in 1911, straddled the boundary between terrorism and crime during a series of bank robberies, and in tsarist Russia anarchists and social revolutionaries both financed their activities by robbing banks and post offices. As a young man, Stalin participated in a bank robbery in the Georgian capital, Tblisi, in which forty people were killed.[4] Terrorist define their own causes; they also define how and when they will serve those causes, in ways that are sometimes unexpected.

There is of course an open question as to what terrorism actually is. The United Nations defines terrorism as acts intended to kill or cause harm with the purpose of intimidating people and governments, but this description could also apply to many acts carried out by military forces of the state. This chapter will ignore state terrorism, although it is an important subject in its own right and concentrate instead on what might be called 'revolutionary' terrorism where leaders and followers are opposed to the state. Even here there are difficulties. As has often been observed, one person's terrorist is another person's freedom fighter. The *sicarii*, the Jewish assassins who murdered Roman officials and collaborators between 60 and 73 CE, were regarded as heroes by the population of occupied Judea, and during the Second World War the *maquis* in occupied France used terrorist tactics including bombings and assassinations. So, too, did the Women's Social and Political Union, which engaged in arson and destruction of public property and plotted assassinations, although they were never carried out. The WSPU were not treated as terrorists at the time – possibly because they had high degree of support in wider society – but according to current British anti-terrorist legislation it would probably be classified as such today.[5]

Although there are older organisations such as the sicarii and the Assassins of Persia that used methods similar to today's terrorists, the concept of terrorism has its origins in state repression. Speaking to the National Convention in France in 1794, Maximilien Robespierre stated that 'the basis of popular government in a time of revolution is both virtue and terror; virtue without which terror is murderous, terror without which virtue is powerless'. He went on to equate terror with justice. Rejecting this ideology, conservatives like Edmund Burke in Britain labelled Robespierre and others like him as 'terrorists'.[6]

Some anarchist writers in the nineteenth century, including Mikhail Bakunin, Sergey Nechayev and the Italian Carlo Piscane, revived Robespierre's ideas in different forms. They argued that peaceful protest would never achieve reform and advocated 'propaganda of the deed', the use of violent acts to draw attention to injustice and bring about a revolution.[7] This idea was taken up particularly in Russia and an organisation dedicated to propaganda of the deed, Narodnaya Volna (Will of the People) was created with the particular aim of killing Tsar Alexander II, a goal it achieved in 1881. Other anarchist groups such as the Black Banners kept the tradition alive in Russia right up until the 1917 Revolution. In France there was a wave of anarchist attacks in the 1880s and 1890s, and sporadic attacks elsewhere claimed the lives of Empress Elizabeth of Austria, President Carnot of France, King Umberto of Italy, Prime Minister Canova of Spain and President McKinley of the US, among others.[8]

As with Robespierre, the anarchist writers emphasised the importance of virtue; to them, violence was a form of justice. It should be added that the vast majority of anarchists, including Kropotkin, abhorred the notion of propaganda of the deed, but for those who supported it there was a merciless logic to the idea and an almost spiritual notion that they were fighting for a just cause, to defend the people from oppression. Most terrorists are not only fighting against an enemy but also fighting *for* something, for a cause, for land, for their own people. The anarchists launched their attacks in the belief that they could overturn an unjust social order and create freedom and equality; the Palestinian terrorists of the 1960s and 1970s were fighting for a homeland for their people; the al-Qaeda terrorists of the 1990s and 2000s believed they were protecting their fellow Muslims from oppression and injustice.[9]

Many launched their attacks knowing they themselves were about to die. Ignacy Hriniewiecki threw the bomb that killed Tsar Alexander knowing it would probably kill him; Gavrilo Princip, the Bosnian Serb terrorist who killed Archduke Franz Ferdinand and his wife in Sarajevo in 1914, attempted to shoot himself after the event in order to avoid capture.[10] Princip was not an anarchist, but nationalist organisations like Young Bosnia used many of the same methods and shared some of their ideology. So do modern terrorist groups including al-Qaeda and Islamic State. We have come to associate suicide attacks with Islamic terrorism, but terrorists of many persuasions plan their attacks in full expectation that they will not survive.

That willingness to die, even the expectation of death, gives followers a certain amount of power. There is the moral authority that comes with courage, but there is also a pragmatic issue; if someone knows their death is imminent, they know also that there are no effective sanctions for disobedience. No one can punish you once you are dead. As a result, leadership in terrorist organisations has tended to be light touch, with individual members given a great deal of latitude. There are exceptions; for example, Narodnaya Volna was structured into cells and led by an executive committee which included both men and women. Sophia Perovskaya and Vera Figner were executive committee members who played leading roles in planning the assassination of Alexander II. Perovskaya was later hanged, and Figner spent twenty years in prison.[11]

The Palestine Liberation Organisation was created by Yasir Arafat and his allies to give the Palestinian movement a political structure, but relations between PLO high command and the terrorist groups under its umbrella, such as the PFLP and the Democratic Front for the Liberation of Palestine (DFLP) were fragile; the leaders of the latter resented Arafat's attempts to control him and tried several times to kill him.[12] The Provisional IRA structured itself like a military unit with regional commands and brigades, but in practice many of these brigades were self-governing and had only limited connection with the governing body, the Army Council.[13] In other cases, organisation was loose or even non-existent. French anarchists refused to attend the International Anarchists Congress in Amsterdam in 1907 because to them, the very idea of organisation was against anarchist principles.[14]

Movements looking for a leader

Terrorist organisations were rarely founded by a single leader or group of leaders; they either evolved organically or emerges as splinter groups from larger organisations. There are exceptions: Yasir Arafat and a small group of colleagues founded al-Fatah in 1959 and then went out and recruited followers. Al-Fatah was more of a guerrilla resistance organisation than a purely terrorist one, although just as with state terror it can often be hard to tell the difference.

Many terrorist organisations start out as movements looking for a leader; the ideology is there and spreading, but there is not yet a leader to give the movement direction. Theorising about how such ideologies emerge tends to go down one of two tracks: the people involved in terrorism are social deviants or psychopaths, or even insane, or they are the product of poverty and deprivation. In a fascinating piece of research, Nafees Hamid and Claudia Pretus conducted brain scans of young Spanish Muslims who had become radicalised and had expressed an intention and desire to commit terrorist attacks. They found absolutely no sign of brain abnormality; their subjects reasoned just like the rest of the population. Although deprivation played a role, Hamid and Pretus found that the most powerful factor was exclusion, the feeling that decisions were being made about people without their having a say. In other words, they felt powerless, and lashing out through terrorism was a way of reclaiming power.[15]

Emergent organisations often start with people coalescing around an idea, from which leadership gradually emerges. Al-Qaeda emerged out of the Muslim *mujahideen* movement in Afghanistan during the period of military occupation; after the Soviet withdrawal from the country, the mujahideen began to seek out other arenas in which to carry on the struggle against the enemies of the faith. Osama bin Laden gave them guidance and direction, but the ideology behind the movement came from the followers, not himself.[16]

In the southern states in the aftermath of the American Civil War a number of small terrorist organisations emerged, terrorising the black population and killing officials who collaborated with the American government. Many, like the White Man's League and the Knights of the White Camelia, were composed of former soldiers from the disbanded Confederate army. The Ku Klux Klan, the most successful of these organisations, was founded by six ex-soldiers and its ideology spread rapidly with more chapters springing up across the South. There was an attempt to unify the movement through swearing an oath of allegiance and the election of a Grand Wizard, the former general Nathan Bedford Forrest, but in practice Forrest had no control over the organisation and most chapters did as they pleased.[17]

Still in America, in the late 1960s the terrorist group Weather Underground, which carried out a number of bombings of public buildings including the Capitol building in Washington, DC, and the Pentagon, evolved out of a pressure group, Students for a Democratic Society; its leaders, Bill Ayers and Bernardine Dohrn, provided an ideological template for the organisation, but member planned and carried out their own attacks.[18] The Red Brigades in Italy were formed from the merger of several spontaneously emerging hardline communist groups in 1970, and the United Red Army in Japan likewise grew out of a series of communist organisations; the latter soon collapsed, but one of its members, Shigenobu Fusaka, led some of her followers to Palestine where they set up the Japanese Red Army.

She planned and led one of the most violent terrorist attacks in the Middle East, the Lod Airport massacre in 1972.[19]

Splits in organisations can also sometimes produce new terrorist groups. Narodnaya Volya was a breakaway faction from Zemlya i Volya, a more peaceful organisation which preferred talking and debating ideas to direct action.[20] Abu Nidal and his followers left al-Fatah in 1974 in order to pursue a more radical terrorist agenda, setting up the Abu Nidal Organisation; in very similar fashion, Ahmed Jibril and his followers walked away from the PFLP in 1968 to set up PFLP-General Command. In both cases, leaders and followers alike thought the original leaders, Yasir Arafat and George Habash, were not doing enough to take the war to the enemy.[21]

Abraham Stern broke away from the Irgun movement when its leader, Zeev Jabotinsky, decided to collaborate with the British in Palestine during the Second World War; Stern's new group, the Lehi or Stern Gang, disagreed with this policy and wished to carry on the fight. Similarly the Provisional IRA broke away from the Irish Republican Army in order to conduct acts of violence against the British establishment in Northern Ireland.[22] But even these movements can be seen as organic developments, organisations evolving and changing their purpose with new movements breaking away to support those followers who have a different purpose, or wish to go back to the original mission.

Emerging leaders

With rare exceptions, the terrorist leaders that emerged and were chosen by followers were not professionals, having little or no previous leadership or military experience. The Ku Klux Klan is one of those exceptions; many of its members were former Confederate soldiers, and its nominal leader, Forrest, was a well-known general. Given the work of Hamid and Pretus cited earlier, we might expect to find terrorist leaders emerging from poor backgrounds, but this too is rare. Leading figures in French anarchist terrorism did sometimes emerge out of poverty; Octave Garnier, one of the founders of the Bonnot Gang, worked for a butcher as a child and was a petty thief by the age of thirteen, and Émile Henry and François Koenigstein (Ravichol), famous bombers in the 1890s, were born in poverty. Henry is unusual in that he was born into an anarchist family; his father had supported the Paris Commune in 1871.[23] Some of the founders of the Provisional IRA were also from poor backgrounds, including Joe Cahill and Seamus Twomey. This is less surprising, as they came from Catholic communities which had been marginalised and impoverished for centuries.[24]

Otherwise, like revolutionary leaders, terrorist leaders seem to come mostly from the middle classes, and from comfortable backgrounds. George Habash came from a middle-class family and was a choirboy in his local church, before attending medical school at the American University of Beirut where he graduated first in his class; his colleague and sometime friend Wadi Haddad was in the same class. They ran a clinic together in a Palestinian refugee camp before founding the PFLP.[25] Samir

Geagea, who took command of the Lebanese Forces militia in 1986, also trained as a doctor at the same medical school.[26]

Universities and other educational bodies have been important incubators for terrorist leadership. Bernardine Dohrn was a law student at the University of Michigan when she became involved with the Weather Underground; Bill Ayers was just completing a degree in American studies. Both Vera Figner and Sophia Perovskaya both came from noble backgrounds. As women, they were unable to attend university, but both were well educated; Perovskaya was a member of the literary society known as the Circle of Tchaikovsky. Nikolai Morozovsky was a member of the same group and was involved with a scientific magazine; Andrei Zhelyabov was a law student and Lev Tikhomirov was also a student when he first became involved. The Red Brigades in Italy also emerged out of student bodies. Ulrike Meinhof, one of the founders of the Red Army Faction in Germany in the 1970s, had studied philosophy and sociology, and most of the other early members were university educated; Andreas Baader was one of the new who was not.[27] Abu Abbas, the leader of the Palestine Liberation Front who planned the hijacking of the cruise ship *Achille Lauro* in 1985, became involved in radical politics while studying at the University of Damascus.[28]

Why are these particular leaders chosen? We can make one very general observation, namely that leaders who emerge from the lower classes and poverty tend to be more hands-on and more likely to be directly involved in violence; Cahill and Twohey had worked their way up through the ranks in the IRA, and Andreas Baader was generally regarded as the most violent member of the Red Army Faction. Ravichol and Henry were both active bombers, although given French anarchism's rejection of organisation and leadership, it can be questioned whether they were leaders in any conventional since.

The university educated middle class leaders, on the other hand, tended to be planners, organisers and ideologues. This is not to accuse them of holding back from the action, but it says something about what followers want from them. As noted, followers already have their ideology in place. The leaders they choose share this ideology; they must, if they are to be accepted. But they are not themselves marginalised or impoverished, nor do they lack a seat at the table; some came from wealthy families. Bill Ayer's father was chief executive of a large corporation, Perovskaya's was an influential nobleman. They join terrorist causes, not because they feel marginalised, but because they can see that others are, and that stokes their sense of injustice. The largely white members and leaders of the Weather Underground argued that they were fighting for civil rights, among other things, and expressed admiration for militant black groups such as the Black Panthers.[29]

What followers want is someone who can express and communicate their ideology in a way that brings members of the movement together. This is why skilled orators and good writers often make good leaders of movements such as these; they have that power of expression that followers sometimes lack. In terms of sources of power, this is a mixture of authority derived from skill and symbolic-charismatic authority; the most successful terrorist leaders, like Osama bin Laden, become symbols of their movement and their ideology.

Remaining in power

Once that symbolic-charismatic authority is established, it becomes a strong source of power. The ability to communicate now sometimes matters less than simple existence. During his years in hiding, bin Laden was largely unable to communicate with his followers, yet he maintained most of his authority. Rebel groups did break away from al-Qaida, but they would probably have broken away anyway as part of that natural splintering process described earlier.

Bin Laden is an unusual case; most terrorist leaders are much more visible, which of course increases the risk to themselves. Most enjoy only brief careers in power before they are killed or arrested, or their followers desert them for a new leader. Their purpose, once they have become established, is to channel the power of their followers into purposive action. In practical terms, this typically means planning operations and encouraging and supporting groups of followers to carry these out. The success or failure of these operations reflects directly on the leader; terrorist leaders are judged on the results their followers achieve. If operations fail, if terrorists are arrested or killed without being able to strike a blow, then the leader is deemed also to have failed, even if they are not present at the time. Forrest's failure to assert his authority over the Ku Klux Klan led to its temporary disbandment; the United Red Army collapsed after its leader began executing followers who disagreed with him.

As well as channelling the power of followers, terrorist leaders also need to ensure the organisation maintains its moral authority and remind followers to stay true to their purpose. Bin Laden and George Habash did this very well. The leaders of the Weather Underground did not. They failed to win sympathy among the population at large, and after a while followers began to question their own purpose and the movement faded away. The French anarchists similarly failed to retain their moral purpose. Bombing the Chamber of Deputies might win some sympathy, but bombing a restaurant full of innocent people did not. Once that moral purpose erodes, terrorist movements tend to collapse very quickly, with followers either giving up, as most members of the Weather Underground did, or moving on to other causes, like the Russian anarchists in Bulgaria or Shigenobu Fusaka in Palestine.

Leadership as conduit

This concept of leadership as a conduit or channel for the power of followers, enabling followers to express themselves, might be considered a variety of servant leadership. It could be argued that most leaders do this, even if perhaps they are not always aware of it. The conduit can be a force for good, enabling people to fight for causes they believe in or protect those who are in peril. Alternatively it can be a dark force, channelling anger and aggression into horrendous acts of terrorism like the Lod Airport massacre or the bombing of the Restaurant Véry in Paris. The problem is that whether the force is benign or dark depends on the standpoint and ideology of the onlooker.

Whereas terrorists can attempt to claim moral authority, criminal organisations do not always bother to do so. Some occasionally claim to be a positive social force, filling the void left by corrupt or ineffective governments; others deliberately set themselves up as anti-societies, playing by their own rules and creating their own distinct social spaces. We turn our attention next to leadership in organised crime.

Notes

1 Marc Sageman, *Understanding Terror Networks*, Philadelphia: University of Pennsylvania Press, 2004; Ivan Arreguin-Toft, 'Tunnel at the End of the Light: A Critique of U.S. Counter-Terrorist Grand Strategy', *Cambridge Review of International Affairs* 15 (3) (2002): 549–63.
2 Sageman, *Understanding Terror Networks*; Seymour M. Hersh, *The Killing of Osama bin Laden*, New York: Verso, 2016.
3 Lucien van der Walt and Michael Schmidt, *Black Flame: The Revolutionary Class Politics of Anarchism and Syndicalism*, Chico: AK Press, 2009.
4 Colin Smith, *Carlos: Portrait of a Terrorist*, London: Penguin, 2012; Richard Parry, *The Bonnot Gang: The Story of the French Illegalists*, San Francisco: PM Press, 2016; Anna Geifman, *Thou Shalt Kill: Revolutionary Terrorism in Russia, 1894–1917*, Princeton: Princeton University Press, 1993.
5 E.M. Smallwood, *The Jews Under Roman Rule, from Pompey to Diocletian: A Study in Political Relations*, Leiden: Brill, 2001; H.R. Kedward, *In Search of the Maquis*, Oxford: Clarendon, 1993; Wake, *Autobiography*; Marlow, *Suffragettes*.
6 McPhee, *Robespierre*; Schurr, *Fatal Purity*; Bromwich, *The Intellectual Life of Edmund Burke*.
7 Avrich, *Bakunin and Nechayev*; Woodcock, *Anarchism*.
8 David Offord, *The Russian Revolutionary Movement in the 1880s*, Cambridge: Cambridge University Press, 1986; Woodcock, *Anarchism*.
9 Woodcock, *Anarchism*; Sageman, *Understanding Terror Networks*.
10 Offord, *The Russian Revolutionary Movement in the 1880s*; Tim Butcher, *The Trigger: The Hunt for Gavrilo Princip*, London: Vintage, 2015.
11 Vera Broido, *Apostles Into Terrorists: Women and the Revolutionary Movement in the Russia of Alexander II*, London: Viking, 1977; Lynne Ann Hartnett, *The Defiant Life of Vera Figner: Surviving the Russian Revolution*, Bloomington: Indiana University Press, 2014.
12 Barry M. Rubin and Judith Colp Rubin, *Yasir Arafat: A Political Biography*, Oxford: Oxford University Press, 2003.
13 Richard English, *Armed Struggle: A History of the IRA*, London: Macmillan, 2003.
14 Jean Maitron, *Le mouvement anarchiste en France*, Paris: Gallimard, 1975.
15 Hamid and Pretus, 'The Neuro-Science of Terrorism'.
16 Sageman, *Understanding Terror Networks*; Bruce Riedel, *The Search for al-Qaeda: Its Leadership, Ideology, and Future*, Washington, DC: Brookings Institution Press, 2008.
17 George C. Rable, *But There Was No Peace: The Role of Violence in the Politics of Reconstruction*, Athens: University of Georgia Press, 2007; Stanley F. Horn, *Invisible Empire: The Story of the Ku Klux Klan, 1866–1871*, Montclair: Patterson Smith, 1939; Brian Willis, *A Battle From the Start: The Life of Nathan Bedford Forrest*, New York: HarperCollins, 1992.
18 Bryan Burrough, *Days of Rage: America's Radical Underground, the FBI, and the Forgotten Age of Revolutionary Violence*, New York: Penguin, 2015; Arthur M. Eckstein, *Bad Moon Rising: How the Weather Underground Beat the FBI and Lost the Revolution*, New Haven: Yale University Press, 2016.
19 Robert Lumley, *States of Emergency: Cultures of Revolt in Italy From 1968 to 1978*, London: Verso, 1990; Peter Chalk (ed.), *Encyclopedia of Terrorism*, New York: ABC-Clio, 2012.

20 Offord, *The Russian Revolutionary Movement in the 1880s*.

21 Yossi Melman, *The Master Terrorist: The True Story Behind Abu Nidal*, London: Sidgwick & Jackson, 1986; Harold M. Cubert, *The PFLP's Changing Role in the Middle East*, London: Routledge, 1997.

22 Bowyer J. Bell, *Terror Out of Zion: Irgun Zvai Leumi, Lehi, and the Palestine Underground, 1919–1949*, New York: Avon, 1977; English, *Armed Struggle*.

23 Parry, *The Bonnot Gang*; John M. Merriman, *The Dynamite Club: How a Bombing in Fin-de-Siècle Paris Ignited the Age of Modern Terror*, London: Yale University Press, 2016.

24 English, *Armed Struggle*; Peter Taylor, *Provos, the IRA and Sinn Féin*, London: Bloomsbury, 1997.

25 Cubert, *The PFLP's Changing Role in the Middle East*; Bernard Reich, *Political Leaders of the Contemporary Middle East and North Africa: A Biographical Dictionary*, Westport: Greenwood, 1990.

26 A. J. Abraham, *The Lebanon War*, New York: Praeger, 1996.

27 Burrough, *Days of Rage*; Eckstein, *Bad Moon Rising*; Offord, *The Russian Revolutionary Movement in the 1880s*; Broido, *Apostles Into Terrorists*; Lumley, *States of Emergency*; Stefan Aust, *Baader-Meinhof: The Inside Story of the R.A.F.*, trans. Anthea Bell, New York: Oxford University Press, 2009.

28 Michael K. Bohn, *The Achille Lauro Hijacking: Lessons in the Politics and Prejudices of Terrorism*, Washington, DC: Potomac Books, 2004.

29 Burrough, *Days of Rage*; Eckstein, *Bad Moon Rising*.

19

LEADERSHIP IN CRIMINAL ORGANISATIONS

Unlike terrorists organisations, where the ostensible purpose to achieve the goal or die in the attempt, the goal of most criminal organisations – like that of most bureaucracies – is to perpetuate themselves, to survive, grow and extend their power. Few criminal organisations have any guiding ideology beyond the acquisition of power, although some may claim to have one as a means of building relationships with local groups and recruiting more followers.

For example, the Chinese triads evolved out of eighteenth-century secret societies banned for revolutionary activity by the Qing emperors; although some turned into criminal organisations, they continued to have affiliations with revolutionary movements at least until the 1911 Revolution.[1] There are rumours that Pablo Escobar's Medellín drugs cartel in Colombia collaborated with guerrilla organisations such as M-19, although this would seem to be more for economic than political reasons; at other times the drugs cartels also formed paramilitary death squads to fight the guerrillas.[2] The street gangs that ruled much of New York City in the late nineteenth and early twentieth centuries, the Five Points Gang, the Eastman Gang, the Hudson Dusters and others, had connections with Tammany Hall, the Democratic Party political machine that ran New York City from the 1840s to the 1930s. Paul Kelly, the long-time leader of the Five Points Gang, used his connections with Tammany Hall to see off challenges from rival gangs and become the most powerful gang leader in the city for decades. Among the younger gang members he mentored were Al Capone and Charles 'Lucky' Luciano, who went on to be notable organised crime leaders in their own right.[3]

Kelly used the Democratic political machine quite cynically to expand his own power and that of his followers, and Escobar's alliance with the guerrillas would have had the same purpose. There are two reasons why criminal organisations need to grow. The first is that power and greed are the primary motives for leaders and followers; the acquisition of power is an end, not just a means. Second, they are nearly always in a state of conflict, with the legitimate authorities or with each other, or more usually, both. Greater size in terms of numbers of followers, alliances with other groups, wealth and weapons controlled gives them the power to fight, to overcome smaller rivals and to fend off the law enforcement agencies who come after them. Even when defeated, a strong organisation has the resilience to rebuild and revive itself, as the Mafia has shown many times.[4]

Criminal followers

There is not space here to go into the numerous theories on the psychology and sociology of crime, but it is worth briefly considering some of the reasons why people turn to crime. Social deprivation is of course one factor; the gangs of Glasgow in the 1920s and 1930s emerged out of poverty-stricken districts where overcrowding and violence were already rife, and the gangs of New York in the nineteenth century are just one of many other examples.[5]

There is also the notion of *anomie*, first described by sociologist Émile Durkheim as a kind of disconnect between personal and public morals. For whatever reason, some people simply do not feel bound by the moral and ethical standards of the rest of society, and thus feel empowered to act in their own way.[6] This can be coupled with simple greed, the desire for riches and power, without having to work excessively hard to get them. The risks of choosing this path are recognised, but the criminal follower calculates that they are worth the reward. Bartholomew Roberts, one of the most successful pirates of the early eighteenth century, summed up the matter when considering whether to embark on a career in piracy:

> In an honest service there is thin commons, low wages, and hard labour. In this, plenty and satiety, pleasure and ease, liberty and power; and who would not balance creditor on this side, when all the hazard that is run for it, at worst is only a sour look or two at choking? No, a merry life and a short one shall be my motto.[7]

Looking back over time, criminal organisations often appeared at times and places where the rule of law was weak, either because of political upheaval or corruption. Both factors were present in England in the 1320s. The country was still struggling to recover from a famine which had killed a large portion of the population, and the unpopular king Edward II, faced several revolts, with consequent upheaval and breakdown of social order in the countryside. After Edward's overthrow and murder by his own wife, Queen Isabella, in 1327, the situation worsened. Eustace Folville, the younger son of a knight who had no lands or income of his own, seems to have become a sort of 'hit man' for the local gentry in the midlands of England, killing and intimidating people to order. Declared an outlaw along with his brother Richard, he carried on a life of crime including robbery and kidnapping for several years until he finally managed to negotiate a pardon in exchange for military service under the crown.[8]

The first triads arose in China in the tumult surrounding the Manchu invasion and the establishment of the Qing dynasty in the seventeenth century. These secret societies did not at first have criminal leanings, but as political control in China began to crumble under the assault of foreign colonialism and the opium trade, the triads began moving into organised crime. During the 1920s and 1930s one group, the Qing Bang, or Green Gang, controlled all criminal activity in and around Shanghai including opium, gambling, prostitution and people trafficking; among other things, they provided trafficked labour for many of Shanghai's mills and factories. So powerful were they that Chiang Kai-Shek's republican government occasionally used them as a kind of paramilitary force against Mao's communists. The Green Gang's power came from the fact that it could pay and feed its members and their families and offer them some degree of security at a time when China was being torn apart by conflict.[9]

The same is true of the gangs of nineteenth century New York, who provided young men and sometimes women too with a means of subsistence and a possible way out of poverty. In Sicily after the Second World War the Mafia stepped into the institutional void created by the fall of capitalism, taking over large portions of the economy and bribing or terrorising local politicians into supporting them; at the time they had the support of many ordinary Sicilians, who saw them as a stabilising force. The pirates of the Caribbean also found an institutional void, the military weakness of Spain and its inability to protect its empire from determined attackers. Some of the pirates were refugees from political turmoil in Britain, some were impoverished workers, some were runaway slaves; all saw the potential for profit. In the twentieth century the cocaine cartels established themselves in Colombia at a time when the country was in the midst of civil conflict.[10]

The yakuza, the organised crime groups of Japan, originated among peddlers and gamblers, both professions that were seen as social outcasts and so did not regard themselves as bound by the mores of society. The Russian mafia traces its origins back to the days of bandits such as Yemelyan Pugachev in the eighteenth century, who drew their power from outcasts such as runaway serfs, and later to the anarchists and social revolutionaries who took to crime to finance their activities. The modern-day Russian gangs emerged out of Stalin's forced labour camps, where they formed underground organisations to keep themselves alive. When the gulags were abolished, the inmates established transferred their organisations into society and went on to careers of crime.[11]

In all of these cases, political, social and economic disruption uprooted people and plunged them into uncertainty. To money, power and a chance to live a life outside the restrictions of society, we can also add a sense of belongingness and community. In many organised crime organisations, the organisation itself replaces family or whatever social cohort the follower used to belong to. Few go as far as the yakuza, where initiates foreswear allegiance to their own family and pledge themselves entirely to their syndicate, marking the occasion with a formal ritual and pledging of loyalty. But the Mafia refer to themselves as the Cosa Nostra (Our Thing) and groups within the Mafia are known as families; very often their leadership is based around family inheritance. The Caribbean pirates referred to themselves as 'Brethren of the Coast', a term of symbolic loyalty to each other rather than denoting any formal organisation.[12]

Who are the leaders?

In most criminal organisations the leader emerges from below; only in a few cases are leaders imposed through inheritance or other means. Many criminal leaders distinguish themselves through superior skill, intelligence and ruthlessness. Vyacheslav Ivankov, a leading figure in the Russian mafia until his assassination by a rival gang in 2009, was an amateur wrestler who moved into crime after a spell in prison and gradually worked his way up through the ranks until he led Russian mafia activities in the US.[13] Paul Kelly made his living as a boxer and invested his money in saloons and funding illegal gambling rackets.[14] John Dillinger, who led a gang of violent bank robbers in the US in the 1920s, was a petty thief and deserted from the US Navy who turned to robbery to make a living.[15] Pablo Escobar was a low-level criminal who sold counterfeit school diplomas and, allegedly, sanded the names off tombstones for resale to new users before turning to smuggling; another leader of the drug cartels, Griselda Blanco, was a runaway and petty thief who lived on the streets. She went on to lead the operation importing cocaine into Miami for nearly ten years.[16] Benjamin 'Bugsy' Siegel and Meyer Lansky ran a street gang of boys before becoming hitmen for hire during the age of prohibition; they went on to dominate the organised crime scene in the US for many years.[17]

Skill and ruthlessness were not always sufficient, however. Many burgeoning criminal leaders had a patron, someone who trained and mentored them and helped them to become established and accepted among followers. Escobar owed his early success to Alvaro Prieto, a Colombian smuggler who helped Escobar learn the trade and earn enough money to invest in the cocaine market. The pirate captain Bartholomew Roberts was a merchant sailor on a ship captured by the pirate Howell Davis, who pressed him to join his career. Roberts was reluctant at first, but Davis recognised his skills as a navigator and persuaded him. Another important pirate leader, Edward Teach, better known as Blackbeard, owed his elevation to the patronage of Benjamin Horniman, a pirate captain operating out of New Providence in the Bahamas, who recognised Teach's skill and gave him his first command.[18]

As noted, Charles Luciano, who worked with Lansky and Siegel, and Al Capone both learned their trade under the direction of Paul Kelly at the Five Points Gang. Equally spectacular was the career of Gertrude 'Cleo' Lythgoe. Working as a secretary to a bootlegger and smuggler during the Prohibition era in the 1920s, she learned the trade and set up in business for herself, running the rum–running operation between the Bahamas and the USA. Unlike Capone and many of the other gangsters of the day, she was never arrested and died a wealthy woman.[19]

The case of the Green Gang in Shanghai is slightly different. Of its three founders, one, Du Yuesheng, came from a poor family and owed his rise in organised crime to a crime boss patron who came from the same district as himself. Ying

Guixin, on the other hand, was already a wealthy landowner when he helped found the gang; his motives are unclear, but it may have been simple greed, or the desire for excitement. The third, Huang Jinrong, was a detective working for the police force in the French concession in Shanghai, who made contacts in the criminal underworld and ran a string of opium dens before leaving the police to join the Green Gang. As a detective, he was badly paid; like many other police officers over the centuries, he decided there was more money to be made on the other side of the fence.[20]

Inherited leadership in crime gangs, at least in the sense of familial or genetic inheritance, is rare. In 1925, Yamaguchi Noboru inherited the leadership of the Yamaguchi-gumi yakuza gang from this father, but his own successor, Taoka Kazuo, had risen through the ranks and was adopted by Yamaguchi as his heir.[21] The 'snakehead' (people smuggler) Zheng Cuiping, known to the American authorities as Sister Ping, inherited her people-smuggling business from her father; she ran thousands of illegal migrants from China into the US in the 1980s and 1990s, and expanded into fields such as money laundering and kidnapping. However, this is an unusual case, and Ping herself left no heirs.[22]

Although Mafia organisations in both Italy and America are referred to as 'clans' or 'families', this is a misnomer. There were sometimes family connections between gangsters; the three Gallucci brothers established a 'family' in Harlem in the 1890s, dominating the district and, like the Five Points Gang, relying on connections with Tammany Hall to prevent police harassment. All three brothers were eventually killed by rival gangs and the family fell apart.[23] Carlo Gambino appointed his brother-in-law, Paul Castellano, as his heir in the Gambino family in 1976, but Gambino was a special case; he was the most powerful Mafia boss in America, and few would stand up to challenge him. But Castellano's appointment was resented, and rivals quickly gathered to attack him; he was murdered nine years later. More generally, Mafia bosses were chosen by senior members of the family from among their own ranks; in Sicily, it is possible that some were elected directly by the rank and file.[24]

Power and control

The power structures in criminal gangs range from loose and informal to highly formalised. An example of the former is the Hole in the Wall Gang in the American West during the late nineteenth century, a loose coalition of outlaw gangs who shared information and occasionally collaborated but mostly went their own way under their elected leaders. Butch Cassidy was one of the more successful of these leaders, but there were many others.[25] At the other end of the scale are the Japanese yakuza and the American and Sicilian mafia, who have a strong hierarchy with a scale of ranks. Absolute obedience to the boss, the *oyabun* or the *capo*, is demanded, with mutilation or death the frequent punishment for failure.[26]

In practice, it is difficult to know how well these structures really worked. Among the yakuza they seem to have worked reasonably well; there are instances of yakuza rebelling against their *oyabun*, but they are fairly rare. The Sicilian mafia structures seem to have worked relatively well, although rebellions are more common, but the American mafia families have been riven with dissension and revolt. Not many mafia bosses have died of natural causes, and the majority have been killed by their own followers.

In these organisations, and in other less formal ones such as the Russian mafia or the Colombian and Mexican drug cartels, authority is maintained through a mixture of charismatic force and reward. The leader retains power in part by being tougher, harder, braver and more skilful – particularly when it comes to avoiding ambushes – than his or her followers. Ching Shih, the Chinese pirate leader who at the height of her power commanded a fleet of three hundred ships with more than twenty thousand followers, took over the fleet from her husband after his death through a combination of ruthless force and diplomacy, eliminating some rivals and winning over others. Her main rival was Cheung Po, second-in-command of the fleet; Ching won his allegiance by adopting him as her son and heir, so that he would take over the fleet after her death. Later she changed her mind, dissolved that relationship, and married Cheung instead. She proved to be a skilled and ruthless leader who guided her fleet well and made many of its members prosperous. After the death of her second husband she retired and settled in Macao; without her leadership, the fleet slowly lost cohesion and dwindled away.[27]

As noted at the beginning of this chapter, criminal leaders also need to protect and expand their organisations in order to increase the organisation's power and its chance of survival. Carlo Gambino fought off various attempts by powerful rival families, including those of Joseph Bonanno and Joseph Colombo, and expanded his empire until it covered much of the US. After his nephew Emmanuel Gambino was kidnapped and killed by another rival gang, Gambino ordered the leaders of this gang to be killed in retaliation, to demonstrate his power. His family carried on in a position of primacy in the American Mafia even after his death from heart disease, but declined in the late 1980s after the imprisonment of the *capo* John Gotti.[28]

Paul Kelly and the Five Points Gang fought a long war with the Eastman gang, using both force and his influence at Tammany Hall. Eventually Monk Eastman, founder of the Eastman gang, was arrested and imprisoned, and Kelly's men killed his successor, Max 'Kid Twist' Zwerbach, in 2008. After this most of Eastman gang joined the Five Points, who took over the former's territory.[29] In 1929, Al Capone set an ambush for members of the rival North Side gang, rivals for control of organised crime in Chicago. Nine people, mostly members of the North Side gang, were killed in the St Valentine's Day massacre. Capone's power increased, and that of the North Side gang dwindled.[30] Like Kelly and Gambino, Capone established a personal reputation for strength and power which followers found highly attractive and made them more willing to obey orders; the followers believed Capone was a winner, and they wanted to be on his side.

Expansion and growth could also be accomplished through alliances, and here the leader's negotiating skills and personal networks became key assets. Meyer Lansky owed much of his success to his ability to network with not only organised crime groups but also legitimate businesses across the US.[31] Al Capone's alliance with a St Louis crime syndicate, Egan's Rats, gave him the power he needed to dispose of the North Side gang.[32] Pablo Escobar's Medellín Cartel had a long-standing alliance with rival Cali Cartel, dividing up territory and markets between them. Later, when the alliance broke down, the Cali Cartel provided information to police investigators seeking to build a case against Escobar, in hopes that if the Medellín Cartel were to break up, the Cali group could move in and take some of their territory.[33] Some yakuza groups have been known to cooperate with the Japanese police, and as already noted the Green Gang in Shanghai had strong political connections which they used to ensure their complete, unchallenged control of organised crime in the city.[34]

Yet expansion, growth and increasing power brought risks and dangers. The larger and more powerful the organisation, the higher its profile, which meant a greater likelihood that law enforcement agencies would begin to take an interest. Al Capone and Pablo Escobar both became too big and too powerful; the authorities could no longer ignore them. At the same time, other gangs grow jealous of the organisation's power and begin plotting to bring it down, as the Cali Cartel did with Escobar. The Second Mafia War in Sicily in the 1980s began when the Corleonesi family became jealous of their rivals, in particular the Palermo boss Stefano Bontade, and started a war against them. The Second 'Ndrangheta War between organised crime groups in Calabria also began when one of the bosses, Paolo de Stefano, became worried that his rivals were growing too powerful.[35] Internal rivalries also begin to have an impact. Followers in criminal organisation want power and wealth, and the leader's ability to reward them is crucial to securing their loyalty. At the same time, paradoxically, the sense of anomie means the more power and wealth some followers have, the more they want. Many Mafia bosses have been killed by members of their own *families* seeking to seize power from them. Rather than too big to fail, the rule in organised crime appears to be, too big to succeed.

Conclusion

Leaders of organised crime gangs face another paradox. On the one hand they must appear to be strong and have the trappings of power. Some organised crime bosses live deliberately frugal lives, but most prefer the high life. In the American Mafia, palatial houses, fleets of cars, fashionable clothing and friends in show business are all symbols of the leader's power, and these symbols assure followers that the leader really *is* powerful and will reward and protect them. In one sense, there is not much difference between these symbols and the royal barge of the self-proclaimed god-king Shulgi of Ur.

At the same time, though, leaders need to be sensitive to what followers want. The contrast between the processes of collaboration and contest in the social space is particularly vivid in the case of organised crime. Leaders must impose their authority on the organisation – they will not be respected if they do not – and yet at the same time they must act in ways that win the approval of their followers: being strong and forceful, growing the power of the organisation, and rewarding follow-ers by giving them the power and wealth they also desire; knowing while doing so that rewarding followers may, instead of cementing their loyalty, simply make them even more greedy and ambitious. Leadership in this space is a blossom that flowers brilliantly but soon fades. Few organised crime leaders die peacefully as free men or women.

Notes

1 Kingsley Bolton and Christopher Hutton, *Triad Societies: Western Accounts of the History, Sociology and Linguistics of Chinese Secret Societies*, London: Routledge, 2000; Yiu-Kong Chu, *The Triads as Business*, London: Routledge, 2002; Wang Peng, *The Chinese Mafia: Organised Crime, Corruption and Extra-Legal Protection*, Oxford: Oxford University Press, 2017.

2 Roberto Escobar, *Escobar: The Inside Story of Pablo Escobar, the World's Most Powerful Crimi-nal*, London: Hodder, 2010; Steven Dudley, *Walking Ghosts: Murder and Guerrilla Politics in Colombia*, London: Routledge, 2004.

3 Oliver E. Allen, *The Tiger: The Rise and Fall of Tammany Hall*, New York: Da Capo, 1993; Herbert Asbury, *The Gangs of New York: An Informal History of the Underworld*, New York: Dorset, 1989.

4 Henner Hess and Ewald Osers, *Mafia and Mafiosi: Origin, Power and Myth*, London: Hurst, 1998; Diego Gambetta, *The Sicilian Mafia: The Business of Private Protection*, Princeton: Princeton University Press, 1993; Selwyn Raab, *Five Families: The Rise, Decline and Resur-gence of America's Most Powerful Mafia Empires*, New York: Thomas Dunne, 2005; Pino Arlacchi, *Mafia Business: The Mafia Ethic and the Spirit of Capitalism*, trans. Martin Ryle, Oxford: Oxford University Press, 1988.

5 Andrew Davies, *City of Gangs: Glasgow and the Rise of the British Gangster*, London: Hodder & Stoughton, 2013; Asbury, *The Gangs of New York*.

6 Émile Durkheim, *The Division of Labour in Society*, trans. Steven Lukes, Basingstoke: Pal-grave, 2013.

7 Charles Johnson, *A General History of the Robberies and Murders of the Most Notorious Pyrates*, London: Conway, 1998; Cordingly, *Under the Black Flag*.

8 E.L.G. Stones, 'The Folvilles of Ashley Folville, Leicestershire, and Their Associates in Crime, 1326–1347', *Transactions of the Royal Historical Society* 77 (1957): 119–36.

9 Bolton and Hutton, *Triad Societies*; Wang, *The Chinese Mafia*; Brian G. Martin, *The Shanghai Green Gang: Politics and Organized Crime, 1919–37*, Berkeley: University of California Press, 1996.

10 Asbury, *The Gangs of New York*; Gambetta, *The Sicilian Mafia*; Arlacchi, *Mafia Business*; Cordingly, *Under the Black Flag*.

11 Peter B.E. Hill, *The Japanese Mafia: Yakuza, Law and the State*, Oxford: Oxford University Press, 2006; David Kaplan and Alec Dubro, *Yakuza: Japan's Criminal Underworld*, Berkeley: University of California Press, 2012; Federico Varese, *The Russian Mafia: Private Protection in a New Market Economy*, New York: Oxford University Press, 2005; Robert I. Friedman, *Red Mafia: How the Russian Mob Has Infiltrated America*, Boston: Little, Brown, 2000.

12 Hill, *The Japanese Mafia*; Gambetta, *The Sicilian Mafia*; Cordingly, *Under the Black Flag*.

13 Friedman, *Red Mafia*; James O. Fickenauer and Elin J. Waring, *Russian Mafia in America: Immigration, Culture and Crime*, Boston: Northeastern University Press, 1998.

14 Asbury, *The Gangs of New York*; David Critchley, *The Origin of Organized Crime in America: The New York City Mafia, 1891–1931*, New York: Routledge, 2008.

15 John Toland, *The Dillinger Days*, New York: Da Capo, 1995.

16 Escobar, *Escobar*; Richard Smitten, *The Godmother: The True Story of the Hunt for the Most Bloodthirsty Female Criminal of Our Time*, New York: Pocket, 1994.

17 Robert Lacey, *Little Man: Meyer Lansky and the Gangster Life*, Boston: Little, Brown, 1991.

18 Escobar, *Escobar*; Johnson, *A General History*; Cordingly, *Under the Black Flag*.
19 Lythgoe, *The Bahama Queen*.
20 Martin, *The Shanghai Green Gang*.
21 Hill, *The Japanese Mafia*; Kaplan and Dubro, *Yakuza*.
22 Patrick Radden Keefe, *The Snakehead: An Epic Tale of the Chinatown Underworld and the American Dream*, New York: Anchor, 2010.
23 Critchley, *The Origin of Organized Crime in America*.
24 Raab, *Five Families*; Gambetta, *The Sicilian Mafia*; Allan May, *Gangland Gotham: New York's Notorious Mob Bosses*, Westport: Greenwood, 2009.
25 Richard M. Patterson, *Butch Cassidy: A Biography*, Lincoln: University of Nebraska Press, 1998.
26 Hill, *The Japanese Mafia*; Gambetta, *The Sicilian Mafia*; Antonino Calderone and Pino Arlacchi, *Men of Dishonor: Inside the Sicilian Mafia*, trans. Marc Romano, New York: William Morrow, 1993.
27 Antony, *Like Froth Floating on the Sea*; Dian Murray, *Pirates of the South China Coast, 1790–1810*, Stanford: Stanford University Press, 1987.
28 May, *Gangland Gotham*; John H. Davis, *The Rise and Fall of the Gambino Crime Family*, New York: HarperCollins, 1993; Joseph Bonanno, *A Man of Honor: The Autobiography of Joseph Bonanno*, New York: St Martin's, 2003.
29 Asbury, *The Gangs of New York*; Critchley, *The Origin of Organized Crime in America*.
30 Max Allan Collins and A. Brad Schwartz, *Scarface and the Untouchable: Al Capone, Eliot Ness and the Battle for Chicago*, New York: William Morrow, 2018.
31 Lacey, *Little Man*.
32 Collins and Schwartz, *Scarface and the Untouchables*; Daniel Waugh, *Egan's Rats: The Untold Story of the Gang That Ruled Prohibition-Era St Louis*, Nashville: Cumberland House, 2007.
33 Escobar, *Escobar*; Ron Chepesiuk, *The Bullet or the Bribe: Taking Down Colombia's Cali Drug Cartel*, New York: Praeger, 2003.
34 Hill, *The Japanese Mafia*; Martin, *The Shanghai Green Gang*.
35 Gambetta, *The Sicilian Mafia*; Letizia Paoli, *Mafia Brotherhoods: Organized Crime, Italian Style*, Oxford: Oxford University Press, 2003.

20
LEADERSHIP IN CULTS

Crime is one route open for people who reject social norms. Another is membership of cults. Sometimes people are members of cults while carrying on with their 'ordinary' lives, but in other cases, notably some religious cults, they withdraw physically from society and live apart from it in enclosed communities. In either case, they are attempting to fulfil their aspirations, whatever these may be; personal happiness, spiritual fulfilment and seeking knowledge and enlightenment are the most common.

Most religious cults and sects were, and are, benign; that is, they functioned in ways that do no harm to their members or to the rest of society. Some, however, became corrupted, and some were established for dark ends right from the beginning. The often-asked question is, why do people join these movements and why do they remain with them? Why do they follow leaders whose leadership will cause harm to followers, and perhaps even lead them to their death?

Defining what exactly is a cult is not easy.[1] As many observers have noted, the term is an emotionally loaded one, and is often used in a pejorative way; labelling a movement whose philosophy we disagree with as a 'cult' is an easy way belittling or dismissing it and its members.[2] The term is sometimes applied to secular societies such as Rosicrucians or Illuminati, or even the Freemasons, but despite having pseudo-religious and mystical elements to some of their ceremonies, these groups are ultimately secular in nature. There is also the question of the difference between cults and 'organised' or accepted religious faiths. In the west, voodoo (also vodou or vodoun, among other names) was widely believed to be a cult, until research showed that voodoo practices are direct descendants from West African religions.[3] Movements such as theosophy and anthroposophy, and sects such as the Hari Krishna, Baha'i and Falun Gong have all been labelled as cults, usually by people opposed to them.[4]

Without getting into the abstruse literature on the distinction between cults and sects, for the purposes of this book, a cult is a heterodox religious movement either opposed to or outside the boundaries of established religions. Some cults are largely peaceful, like the Adamites of central Europe or the Cathars of southern France in the Middle Ages, and fight only to defend themselves.[5] Others became involved in the politics of their time, like the White Lotus Society, a mixture of Manichaeism and Buddhism that took root in China in the thirteenth century. The Society played an important role in bringing about the liberation of China from the Mongols in the fourteenth century, but three centuries later it launched another revolution against the Qing dynasty, which led to the Society's suppression. Other militant versions of the cult emerged in the nineteenth century.[6] Another fascinating cult is the Red Lanterns Shining, a female cult that emerged in parallel to the Boxer movement in China at the end of the nineteenth century. This was a mystical cult whose members were reputed to have healing powers and the ability to fly.[7] Earlier in this book we mentioned the Diggers and Levellers, Christian cults in sixteenth-century England that, despite having originally had peaceful purposes, got caught up in the politics of the English Civil War.

In this chapter, we are concerned primarily with darker cults, or at least those that have a dark aspect to them. Some of these start off with benign purposes and are gradually corrupted. Although it lacked the organisation typical of cults, the People's Crusade had many of the features of a cult: religious fervour, a sense of mission and purpose, and a charismatic leader. When Pope Urban II preached the First Crusade, he intended that an expedition of European knights and professional soldiers should march to take Jerusalem from the Muslims. However, his message was picked up by a wandering preacher named Peter the Hermit, who began spreading word through the population. Peter urged his followers to go to Jerusalem themselves, arguing that they could overcome the enemy simply by force of faith. In early 1096 around forty thousand people gathered under Peter's command at Köln on the Rhine. Most had no military experience, and many had no weapons. Old people, women and children were among their number.[8]

What was originally intended as a pilgrimage of faith turned into a series of atrocities. The Jewish communities of the Rhineland were attacked and a number of people were killed. As the pilgrims marched east, they attacked the Hungarian town of Zemun and killed most of its inhabitants, and pillaged and burned the city of Belgrade. Crossing the Bosporos, they marched into Asia Minor, where quarrels broke out between senior commanders and Peter the Hermit lost control of his followers. Lacking unity, they were unable to resist attack, and most of the pilgrims were slaughtered at the Battle of Civetot. Only about three thousand managed to escape and find shelter in the Byzantine Empire.[9]

Another version of what Charles Mackay described as collective madness occurred in 1212, when travelling preachers again whipped up fervour and groups of largely unarmed people began making their way towards the Holy Land with a view to 'liberating' Jerusalem.[10] Many were children, followers of a boy preacher from France named Stephen of Cloyes, and it was the presence of these young people that led later historians to dub this the Children's Crusade. The attempt was equally disastrous. The 'crusaders' had no food and subsisted by begging along the

way; thousands died of starvation. At least some of those who arrived at Mediterranean ports to ask for passage to the Holy Land were trafficked instead and ended
up as slaves. None reached Jerusalem.[11]

The flagellants were breakaway groups of Catholics who emerged during the
Black Death in the mid-fourteenth century Europe. They performed public flagellation rituals, flogging themselves to the point of self-harm and even death, arguably
as a form of penitence. Successive popes condemned them and leaders of the cult
were tried for heresy, but the practice continued. Almost inevitably, the flagellants
too their religious zeal too far and began attacking and killing Jews.[12] The Khlysts,
a Russian cult that emerged around 1645, also practiced flagellation and there were
also rumours of unusual sexual practices; an offshoot of the cult, the Skoptsy, practiced self-mutilation including castration and masectomies. In the early twentieth
century the monk Grigori Rasputin adopted many elements of Khlyst philosophy
and practice when setting up his own cult, whose followers included Tsarina Alexandra of Russia.[13]

Unlike earlier cults, the Khlysts were well organised, with cells called *arks* each
led by a male and a female leader. Organisation is one of the features of later
cults. The Oneida Community, founded by John Humphrey Noyes in New York
state, had a complex bureaucracy with twenty-seven standing committees overseeing every aspect of community life, and a detailed ideology. All members were
expected to work to support the community and practiced a carefully managed
form of group marriage whose sole purpose was procreation. However, members
did not always follow the precepts of the founder; accusations of sexual abuse began
to emerge, and Noyes himself was charged with statutory rape and forced to flee
the community.[14] The Church of Scientology, founded by writer L. Ron Hubbard in 1952, started off as a relatively benign organisation dedicated to faith based
on observation and knowledge, but it has engaged in a series of 'black operations'
against its critics, including physical threats and attempts to smear their reputations.
Operation Snow White, carried out by Scientology agents in the 1970s, resulted
in more than a hundred break-ins and thefts of documents from US government
agencies believed to have reports critical of the cult.[15]

Two of the most famous cults of recent times ended in bloody massacres. The
Branch Dravidians, a splinter group from the Dravidians (themselves an offshoot
of the Seventh-Day Adventist church in America), were split between two spiritual
leaders, Vernon Howell and George Roden. Howell eventually drove Roden out,
changing his name to David Koresh and claiming to be a prophet in his own right,
and took over leadership of the sect. When the Branch Dravidians began stockpiling
firearms, US authorities raided their compound near Waco, Texas, and were met with
armed resistance. After a siege, the compound caught fire and burned to the ground.
Koresh and more than eighty of his followers died, some apparently shot by their
fellow cult members when they tried to escape the flames.[16] The People's Temple, a
millenarian sect founded by the Jim Jones in the US in 1956, later moved to Guyana
to escape alleged persecution by the American authorities. After members of the
cult killed US Congressman Leo Ryan, Jones ordered his followers to commit mass

suicide. Hundreds obeyed the order by drinking the flavoured drink Kool-Aid mixed with prussic acid; some who refused were forcibly injected, such as babies, who were too young to drink. In all, 918 people died, including Jones himself.[17]

Finally, there are what is popularly known as 'doomsday cults', where the purpose all along was to commit destruction and cause death. Aum Shinrikyo, founded by Shoko Asahara in 1984 in Japan, brought together elements of Buddhist, Hindu and Christian faiths along with the prophecies of the sixteenth-century French writer, Michel Nostradamus. Asahara claimed to be a prophet and forecast the end of the world in a nuclear holocaust, during which only he and his followers would survive. Those critical of the cult were attacked and sometimes murdered, and followers who tried to leave the cult were killed. The group also began manufacturing nerve agents such as sarin and using these in its attacks. In 1995, for motives that remain unclear, the group attacked several trains on the Tokyo Underground with sarin, killing thirteen people and harming over a thousand.[18] The Order of the Solar Temple, founded in 1984 in Switzerland as an alleged revival of the Knights Templar, claimed that its mission was to unite the Catholic world and destroy Islam in preparation for the second coming of Christ. Its members carried out a number of murders in France and Canada, and several of its cells also committed mass suicide after the fashion of the People's Temple; its founders, Joseph Di Mambro and Luc Jouret, died in one of these mass suicides. So did thirty-nine members of the Heaven's Gate cult in California in an attempt to free their souls so they could travel to a spaceship they believed to be following the comet Hale-Bopp.[19]

Cult leaders

One of the unusual features of cult leadership is that leaders are almost never chosen by followers. Instead, they set themselves up as leaders, and invite followers to join them. Why followers choose to do so will be discussed later in this chapter, but for the moment it is important to look at the defining characteristics of the leaders themselves.

First, the leaders of all the cults we have discussed had a very strong central ideology and view of their own purpose. Often they claimed divine inspiration, thus claiming conferred authority. Peter the Hermit, the child preacher Stephen of Cloyes and Grigori Rasputin all claimed direct contact with God through visions, as did the leaders of the Khlysts. John Humphrey Noyes believed he was carrying out a divinely ordained mission. David Koresh and Shoko Asahara claimed powers of prophecy. Marshall Applewhite and Bonnie Nettles, the founders of Heaven's Gate, formulated their ideas from a variety of religious sources including millenarian prophecies, as did L. Ron Hubbard with Scientology, whereas di Mambro and Jouret pieced together the Solar Temple ideology from sources including Rosicrucianism and other occult writings including the English mystic and satanist Alastair Crowley.[20] How far leaders believed their own words is open to debate, although Applewhite, Jones and the founders of the Solar Temple followed their own precepts to the point of taking their own lives, suggesting they did truly believe at least some of their own ideas.

Second, most of them claimed power over their followers and expected obedience, drawing on their conferred authority to do so. Applewhite and Nettles were unusual in that they did not claim power; they set out a vision and persuaded others to see it. As a boy, Stephen of Cloyes could not command much authority and he too relied on persuasion. Peter the Hermit attempted to establish control over his disorganised followers but did not meet with much success. Grigori Rasputin relied on charisma and as conferred authority, and although he did not give orders as such to Tsarina Alexandra, he could and did expect obedience from his other followers.[21]

Other cult leaders claimed power over their followers, sometimes the power of life and death. Shoko Asahara ordered disobedient followers to be killed; other followers obeyed him willingly.[22] Koresh is presumed to have ordered the killing of followers who tried to escape the fire at the Branch Dravidian compound at Waco, and di Mambro is said to have ordered the murder of a child of one of his followers who he believed as the anti-Christ; and, of course, Jim Jones ordered his followers to take their own lives.[23] Power could be exercised in other ways too, notably through sex. Applewhite again is unusual in that he lived a celibate life, but accusations of sex with underage girls were made against John Humphrey Noyes at Oneida and David Koresh at the Branch Dravidians. Koresh boasted of having children with at least twelve of his female followers, and Jim Jones also had sexual relations with a number of followers at the People's Temple. Grigori Rasputin also used sex, or at least the promise of sex, to gain ascendancy over his female followers. Many of these relationships were physically abusive, and some were with partners under the age of consent.[24]

Conferred authority was reinforced by charisma. Contemporaries noted how Peter the Hermit could hold a crowd spellbound with his sermons and speeches, and Rasputin was also a gifted speaker and a man of mesmerising presence.[25] Early in his career, Jim Jones had been a gifted orator. In addition to preaching in church, he often spoke at civil rights marches, where he supported leaders such as Martin Luther King.[26] Marshall Applewhite and Shoko Asahara were both described as charismatic individuals with excellent communication skills and knew how to purvey their message in terms that their followers would find believable and meaningful.[27] Asahara was also a prolific writer and set out his ideology in great detail, as did John Humphrey Noyes and L. Ron Hubbard.[28]

The combination of conferred and charismatic authority was potent, and with the exceptions already noted, most of these cult leaders controlled a great deal power, much more than any other type of leader we have seen so far in this book. They could order their followers to kill others or take their own lives, secure in the knowledge that most of them would do it. The important question is, why? What attracts followers to leaders like these, and why do they obey these deadly orders?

Cult followers

The most common, and perhaps most controversial, theory is that followers of cults have been brainwashed or programmed, so that they no longer control their own minds and have their decisions made for them by leaders.[29] This view is held by many respected psychologists, but it is refuted by many others. Eileen Barker's lengthy study of the Unification Church, an organisation with cult-like features and has been accused of brainwashing its members, concluded that no brainwashing was involved. She cited as evidence the large number of people who attend Unification Church services or functions once only and never return, and the number of who leave the church voluntarily, having given up on its beliefs. The argument has also been made that if brainwashing was so successful, we would expect cults to have large memberships, whereas most struggle to maintain members and seldom have more than a few hundred followers.[30] Finally, as Charles Mackay remind us, cult movements have been around for centuries, long before modern mental programming techniques were invented.[31]

That is not to say that brainwashing does not occur, but an alternative and entirely plausible explanation is that people join cults for the same reason other people join criminal gangs; in cults, they find personal fulfilment of a kind they cannot experience in everyday society. For some people, cults offer spiritual peace and the promise of salvation. For others, rejected by society, they provide a home, physical and spiritual, and a sense of belonging in the company of like-minded people.[32] Paradoxically, whereas we think of cults as confining and restricting, to these people the cult offers spiritual and mental freedom, and they are willing to surrender a great deal of power over their physical lives in exchange for that freedom.

Followers have expectations of cult leaders just as they do of any other kind of leader. They expect leaders to keep their promises and to lead them to salvation. They expect them also to honour the tenets of the faith they themselves have outlined. Few things can disrupt a cult or cause it to collapse more quickly than the discovery that the leader is a fraud. Chen Hon-Ming, the leader of the Chen Tao cult in America, prophesied that God would appear on television on 31 March 1998. Then God failed to do so, Chen's followers deserted *en masse* and the cult collapsed. When the television evangelist Jim Bakker was accused of fraud and sexual offences, many of his devoted followers became disillusioned and left to follow other evangelists whom they deemed to be more trustworthy.[33]

What defies ordinary belief is why people would be willing to kill or take their own lives. In the former case, the reason often given is the defence of the cult itself. Cult leaders, like all autocrats, will often create an Other, an enemy that the cult must fight against. Sometimes it is defectors from the cult, sometimes it is the political and social establishment and elites who are portrayed as oppressing the cult and threatening it; sometimes it is both. In Japan, Asahara ordered his followers to kill defectors and critics of his cult, and they did so because they believed the cult's existence was threatened. Jim Jones's followers killed Congressman Ryan for the same reason, and Scientologists have often attacked, sometimes violently, people who criticise them.

As for mass suicide, this is often motivated by a genuine belief in life after death, and sometimes suicide is necessary to help the soul make a transition from one world to the next. The Solar Temple and Heaven's Gate members who killed themselves did not in fact believe they were going to die; they were merely setting out on a journey. The same is probably true of the People's Temple suicides, although Jones appears to have ordered this as a spontaneous act and his full motivation is hard to fathom.

This brings up the final and most important point about cult followers; they share the ideology of the leader. I said earlier that the leaders set out their ideology and then persuade people to follow them through charismatic evangelism. The vast majority of people do not respond to this evangelism because they do not agree with the message. The tiny numbers that do agree find something in the message that resonates within themselves. They join the cult because it promises something they have been unable to find in their own lives, and because they believe the leader will provide it for them. The paradox of cult leadership, then, is that leader have great power over their followers, indeed the power of life and death; but only because followers give it to them.

Notes

1 Benjamin Zablocki and Thomas Robbins (eds), *Misunderstanding Cults: The Search for Objectivity in a Controversial Field*, Toronto: University of Toronto Press, 2001; Rodney Stark and William S. Bainbridge, *The Future of Religion: Secularization, Revival and Cult Formation*, Berkeley: University of California Press, 1987; Janja A. Lalich, *Bounded Choice: True Believers and Charismatic Cults*, Berkeley: University of California Press, 2004.

2 Zablock and Robbins, *Misunderstanding Cults*.

3 Wade Davis, *The Serpent and the Rainbow*, New York: Simon & Schuster, 1985; Carolyn Long, *Spiritual Merchants: Magic, Religion and Commerce*, Knoxville: University of Tennessee Press, 2001.

4 Bruce F. Campbell, *Ancient Wisdom Revived: A History of the Theosophical Movement*, Berkeley: University of California Press, 1980; Gary Lachman, *Rudolf Steiner: An Introduction to His Life and Work*, New York: Floris, 2007; Peter Smith, *An Introduction to the Baha'i Faith*, Cambridge: Cambridge University Press, 2008; James Tong, *Revenge of the Forbidden City: The Suppression of the Falungong in China, 1999–2008*, New York: Oxford University Press, 2009.

5 Emmanuel Le Roy Ladurie, *Montaillou: Cathars and Catholics in a French Village*, London: Scolar Press, 1978.

6 B. J. ter Haar, *The White Lotus Teachings in Chinese Religious History*, Honolulu: University of Hawaii Press, 1999.

7 Ono Kazuko, 'The Red Lanterns and the Boxer Rebellion', in Ono Kazuko (ed.), *Chinese Women in a Century of Revolution, 1850–1950*, trans. Joshua A. Fogel, Stanford: Stanford University Press, 1988.

8 Comnena, *The Alexiad*; Frankapan, *The First Crusade*; Tyerman, *God's War*.

9 Ibid.

10 Mackay, *Extraordinary Popular Delusions*.

11 Gary Dickson, *The Children's Crusade: Medieval History, Modern Mythistory*, Basingstoke: Palgrave Macmillan, 2008.

12 Norman Cohn, *The Pursuit of the Millennium: Revolutionary Millenarians and Mystical Anarchists of the Middle Ages*, Oxford: Oxford University Press, 1970.

13 Laura Engelstein, *Castration and the Heavenly Kingdom: A Russian Folktale*, Ithaca: Cornell University Press, 2003; C.L. Sulzberger, *The Fall of Eagles*, London: Hodder & Stoughton, 1977.

14 Robert David Thomas, *The Man Who Would Be Perfect: John Humphrey Noyes and the Utopian Impulse*, Philadelphia: University of Pennsylvania Press, 1977; Spencer Klaw, *Without Sin: The Life and Death of the Oneida Community*, New York: Penguin, 1993.

15 Hugh B. Urban, *The Church of Scientology: A History of a New Religion*, Princeton: Princeton University Press, 2013.
16 Stuart A. Wright (ed.), *Armageddon in Waco: Critical Perspectives on the Branch Dravidian Conflict*, Chicago: University of Chicago Press, 1996.
17 John R. Hall, *Gone From the Promised Land: Jonestown in American Cultural History*, New Brunswick: Transaction, 2004; David Chidester, *Salvation and Suicide: Jim Jones, The People's Temple and Jonestown*, Bloomington: Indiana University Press, 2004.
18 Robert Jay Lifton, *Destroying the World to Save It: Aum Shinrikyo, Apocalyptic Violence and the New Global Terrorism*, London: Picador, 2000.
19 James R. Lewis (ed.), *The Order of the Solar Temple: The Temple of Death*, London: Routledge, 2016; George D. Chryssides (ed.), *Heaven's Gate: Postmodernity and Popular Culture in a Suicide Group*, Aldershot: Ashgate, 2011.
20 Lalich, *Bounded Choice*; Chryssides, *Heaven's Gate*; Lewis, *The Order of the Solar Temple*.
21 Sulzberger, *The Fall of Eagles*; Douglas Smith, *Rasputin: Faith, Power and the Twilight of the Romanovs*, New York: Farrar, Straus and Giroux, 2016.
22 Lifton, *Destroying the World to Save It*.
23 Wright, *Armageddon in Waco*; Lewis, *The Order of the Solar Temple*; Chidester, *Salvation and Suicide*.
24 Klaw, *Without Sin*; Wright, *Armageddon in Waco*; Chidester, *Salvation and Suicide*; Sulzberger, *The Fall of Eagles*.
25 Tyerman, *God's War*; Sulzberger, *The Fall of Eagles*.
26 Chidester, *Salvation and Suicide*.
27 Chryssides, *Heaven's Gate*.
28 Lifton, *Destroying the World to Save It*; Thomas, *The Man Who Would Be Perfect*; Urban, *The Church of Scientology*.
29 Zablocki and Robbins, *Misunderstanding Cults*; Lalich, *Bounded Choice*; Kathleen Taylor, *Brainwashing: The Science of Thought Control*, Oxford: Oxford University Press, 2006.
30 Eileen Barker, *The Making of a Moonie: Choice or Brainwashing?* Oxford: Blackwell, 1986; James A. Beckford and James T. Richardson (eds), *Challenging Religion: Essays in Honour of Eileen Barker*, London: Routledge, 2015.
31 Mackay, *Extraordinary Popular Delusions*.
32 Zablocki and Robbins, *Misunderstanding Cults*; Stark and Bainbridge, *The Future of Religion*.
33 Derek Davis and Barry Hawkins, *New Religious Movements and Religious Liberty in America*, Waco: Baylor University Press, 2003.

21
CONCLUSION

That brings this very incomplete survey of how leadership has been practised to a close. The time has come to reflect on what, if anything, can be learned from it.

The first conclusion, which is not particularly surprising, is that leadership is extremely complex and takes many forms. This should lead us to question whether the current, often quite simple models we use for conceptualising leadership are fit for purpose. Great Man theory, which posits that leaders lead and followers obey, is clearly not fit for purpose and never has been, but there are doubts too about transformational leadership, servant leadership and other concepts which suggest simple relational models, still very often with the emphasis on the leader. These models are often used for training purposes, but do they reflect the reality of leadership? In many cases, the answer must be no.

Focusing on the role of the leader gives us only a partial perspective, because in nearly every case the power of the leader is limited to what followers are willing to concede to them. Even in cases of forced labour or slavery, where consent is given unwillingly, there are still limits on the power of the leader, lines that leaders dare not cross for fear that followers will turn against them. Rebellions and mutinies happen when leaders disregard the risk and cross those lines. But focusing solely on followers is dangerous too. Followers are not homogenous; their attachment to the leader and the cause the leader serves varies according to individual needs, desires and demands. In any organisation, especially one of any size, there will be a rich and varied spectrum of follower motivation, so much so that concepts like 'the organisation' and 'the people' must be open to challenge. The 'people' do not think with a single mind or a single will.

How do leaders connect with this spectrum? Part of the answer, as this book clearly shows, is that leaders don't need to form a positive relationship with every follower, and it is probably pointless to try. Successful leaders know which followers matter and which ones will keep them in power, and even those leaders who are truly dedicated to the organisation and give selfless service need to form coalitions of followers to support them. The power of the leader derives in part from the power of the followers, and leaders need to make sure they have the right followers in the right place.

In part; but not all. Another point that emerges out of this book is that although the consent of followers is necessary to lead, it is not always sufficient. There are other sources of authority, conferred, inherited, inherent and so on, and access to at least some of these sources of authority is necessary to make the leader credible and acceptable to followers. These additional sources of authority are part of what determines whether followers will choose to follow a given leader.

The other part of the recipe is, of course, the promise contained in the contract, implicit or explicit, between leaders and led. Followers follow a leader because they believe the leader will give them something they desire, be it safety, wealth, status, a sense of belonging, self-actualisation or whatever. If they believe the leader is not willing or able to give them these things, then the levels of conflict already present in the social space are likely to ramp up. Again, successful leaders have been the ones who recognise what followers want and are willing to negotiate and collaborate with them, satisfying follower needs in exchange for power.

The twin forces of collaboration and contest that we have followed throughout this book lie at the heart of leadership; indeed, it might not be too much to suggest that they *are* leadership, at least in the sense of leadership being an active force rather than a passive concept. To repeat a point already made, both happen simultaneously, often on several different dimensions at once as leaders compete and collaborate not only with their own leaders but also with other leaders and their followers. Both are essential; it is neither possible nor desirable to do without one or the other.

Contest is omnipresent. Cults are probably the organisations with the lowest level of contest as followers surrender near complete power to leaders, but even here some followers are restless and push back against leadership, looking for power of their own. Sometimes followers want power simply to preserve their own independence; sometimes they want power in order to compel leaders to go in the direction they want, and sometimes they are ambitious and want to seize enough power to supplant the existing leadership and become leaders themselves. Leaders also seek to expand *their* power at the expense of followers, or at least defend the power they have, in order to achieve their own personal and organisational goals.

Yet, as we have said, to get things done leaders are forced to collaborate with followers, and that collaboration often means agreeing to share power. Smart leaders have realised that by giving up a degree of power, they can sometimes achieve more willing collaboration. Without collaboration nothing gets done; an organisation where leadership consists solely of contest will always fail.

It is also important to realise that leadership can be used for malign ends. We do not yet know enough about dark leadership and how it functions, and as a result we are perhaps too ready to believe in leadership as a force for good. It is not. It is a force, pure and simple, a combination of contest and collaboration in the social space, and it can be used for whatever purpose leaders and followers agree: to build great corporations that create wealth and jobs, to find places of spiritual healing and peace, to create great artistic endeavours, to defend people from crime and aggression, or to create repressive regimes and commit mayhem and massacre. Anything is possible, if leaders and followers desire it so and create a contract and a social space to make it happen.

The final point to make is the universality of leadership. Every field of human endeavour has its own special leadership challenges, and we have looked at some of them in passing in this book. But equally, the dialectic and collaborative nature of leadership is the same no matter where it takes place. The sources of power may differ; the levels of collaboration and contest change and shift, but the basic problem of how the leaders and the spectrum of followers meet and engage with each other is the same. Leadership is eternal; it is omnipresent; and it affects almost every aspect of our lives. The task that faces us now is to develop a greater understanding of what leadership is, and stop spending quite so much time dreaming about what we would like it to be. The problems of the real world call for real leadership.

BIBLIOGRAPHY

Abbott, Nadia (1942) *Aisha, the Beloved of Muhammad*, Chicago: University of Chicago Press.

'Abduh, Muhammad (1966) *Risalat al-Tawhid*, trans. Ishaq Musa'ad and Kenneth Cragg, *The Theology of Unity*, London: George Allen & Unwin.

Abraham, A.J. (1996) *The Lebanon War*, New York: Praeger.

Abraham, Richard (1987) *Kerensky: First Love of the Revolution*, New York: Columbia University Press.

'Abu Bakr al-Turtushi's *Siraj al-Muluk: A Masterpiece of Andalusi Political Philosophy*', https:// ballandalus.wordpress.com/2014/12/08/abu-bakr-al-turtushis-siraj-al-muluk-a-masterpiece-of-andalusi-political-philosophy-2/.

Aburish, Said K. (2004) *Nasser: The Last Arab*, New York: St Martin's.

Ackrill, Margaret and Hannah, Leslie (2001) *Barclays: The Business of Banking, 1690–1996*, Cambridge: Cambridge University Press.

Adams, R.J.Q. (2007) *Balfour: The Last Grandee*, London: John Murray.

Adelsteinsson, Jon Hnefill (1998) *A Piece of Horse Liver: Myth, Ritual and Folklore in Old Icelandic Sources*, trans. Terry Gunnell and Joan Turville-Petre, Reykjavik: Iceland University Press.

Agulhon, Maurice (1983) *The Republican Experiment, 1848–1852*, Cambridge: Cambridge University Press.

Ahir, D.C. (1995) *Ashoka the Great*, New Delhi: B.R. Publishing.

Alden, John R. (1996) *George Washington: A Biography*, Baton Rouge: Louisiana State University Press.

Aldred, Cyril (1991) *Akhenaten: King of Egypt*, London: Thames and Hudson.

Alexander, John T. (1969) *Autocratic Politics in a National Crisis: The Imperial Russian Government and Pugachev's Revolt*, Bloomington: Indiana University Press.

'Ali ibn Abi Talib (1978) *Nahjul Balagha* (Peak of Eloquence), trans. S.A. Reza, Elmhurst, NY: Tahrike Tarsile Qu'ran.

Allen, Oliver E. (1993) *The Tiger: The Rise and Fall of Tammany Hall*, New York: Da Capo.

Allfrey, Anthony (1989) *Man of Arms: The Life and Legend of Sir Basil Zaharoff*, London: Weidenfeld & Nicolson.

Alston, Jon P. and Takei, Isao (2005) *Japanese Business Culture and Practices: A Guide to Twenty-First Century Japanese Business*, Bloomington: iUniverse.

Ambler, Tim, Witzel, Morgen and Xi, Chao (2017) *Doing Business in China*, 4th edn, London: Routledge.

Ambrose, Stephen E. (1975) *Crazy Horse and Custer: The Parallel Lives of Two American Warriors*, New York: New American Library.

Ambrose, Stephen E. (1983–4) *Eisenhower*, New York: Simon & Schuster, 2 vols.

Ambrose, Stephen E. (1997) *Band of Brothers*, New York: Simon & Schuster.

Angers, Trent (1999) *The Forgotten Hero of My Lai: The Hugh Thompson Story*, Lafayette: Arcadian House.

Antony, Robert (2003) *Like Froth Floating on the Sea: The World of Pirates and Seafarers in Late Imperial South China*, Berkeley: University of California Press.

Aquinas, St Thomas (1949) *De Regno*, trans. Gerald B. Phelan, Toronto: Pontifical Institute of Medieval Studies.

Arana, Marie (2013) *Bolivar: American Liberator*, New York: Simon & Schuster.

Archdeacon, Thomas (1984) *Becoming American: An Ethnic History*, New York: The Free Press.

Aristotle (2011) *Nicomachean Ethics*, trans. Robert C. Bartlett and Susan D. Collins, Chicago: University of Chicago Press.

Arlacchi, Pino (1988) *Mafia Business: The Mafia Ethic and the Spirit of Capitalism*, trans. Martin Ryle, Oxford: Oxford University Press.

Armand, Émile (2007) 'Anarchist Individualism as a Life and Activity', 1907, www.spaz.org/~dan/individualist-anarchist/library/emile-armand/life-activity.html.

Arreguin-Toft, Ivan (2002) 'Tunnel at the End of the Light: A Critique of U.S. Counter-Terrorist Grand Strategy', *Cambridge Review of International Affairs* 15 (3): 549–63.

Arrian (1971) *The Campaigns of Alexander*, trans. Aubrey de Sélincourt, Harmondsworth: Penguin.

'Arthur Chamberlain', *Grace's Guide to Industrial History*, www.gracesguide.co.uk/Arthur_Chamberlain

Asbury, Herbert (1989) *The Gangs of New York: An Informal History of the Underworld*, New York: Dorset.

Ashcraft, Richard (1987) *Locke's Two Treatises of Government*, Boston: Unwin Hyman.

Asimov, Isaac (2016) *Foundation*, New York: HarperCollins.

Athearn, Robert G. (1956) *William Tecumseh Sherman and the Settlement of the West*, Norman: University of Oklahoma Press.

Attwater, Donald (1939) *St John Chrysostom: The Voice of Gold*, London: Harvill.

Auerbach, Felix (1904) *The Zeiss Works and the Carl-Zeiss Stiftung in Jena*, trans. S.F. Paul and F.J. Cheshire, London: Marshall, Brookes and Chalkley.

Aust, Stefan (2009) *Baader-Meinhof: The Inside Story of the R.A.F.*, trans. Anthea Bell, New York: Oxford University Press.

Avrich, Paul (1974) *Bakunin and Nechayev*, New York: Freedom Press.

Avrich, Paul (1976) *Russian Rebels 1600–1800*, New York: Schocken.

Avrich, Paul (1984) *The Haymarket Tragedy*, Princeton: Princeton University Press.

Axelrod, Alan (2006) *Patton: A Biography*, New York: Palgrave Macmillan.

Axworthy, Roger L. (2004) 'Pulteney, Sir John', in *Oxford Dictionary of National Biography*, Oxford: Oxford University Press.

Ayers, Edward L. (2005) *What Caused the Civil War? Reflections on the South and Southern History*, New York: W.W. Norton.

Ayton, Andrew (1994) 'English Armies in the Fourteenth Century', in Anne Curry and Michael Hughes (eds), *Arms, Armies and Fortifications in the Hundred Years War*, Woodbridge: Boydell.

Babeuf, Gracchus (1964) *The Defence of Gracchus Babeuf Before the High Court of Vendôme*, ed. John Anthony Scott, Yale, CT: Gehenna Press.

Babington, Anthony (1991) *The Devil to Pay: The Mutiny of the Connaught Rangers, India, July, 1920*, London: Pen & Sword.

Bakunin, Mikhail (1871) 'What Is Authority?', www.marxists.org/reference/archive/bakunin/works/various/authrty.htm.

Balasingham, Adele (2003) *The Will to Freedom: An Inside View of Tamil Resistance*, London: Fairmax.

Balserak, John (2014) *Calvin as Sixteenth-Century Prophet*, Oxford: Oxford University Press.

Ban Gu (1983) *The Book of Han*, trans. Homer H. Dubs, *The History of the Former Han Dynasty*, Baltimore: Waverley.

Banat, Gabriel (2006) *The Chevalier de Saint-Georges: Virtuoso of the Sword and the Bow*, Hillsdale: Pendragon Press.

Bandyopadhyay, Sekhar (ed.) (2008) *1857: Essays From Economic and Political Weekly*, Hyderabad: Orient Longman.

Banerji, Rita (2009) *Sex and Power: Defining History, Shaping Societies*, London: Penguin.

Barber, Anthony W. (2009) *Buddhism in the Krishna River Valley of Andhra*, Albany: State University of New York Press.

Barber, Malcolm (2012) *The Trial of the Templars*, Cambridge: Cambridge University Press.

Barber, Richard (1978) *Edward, Prince of Wales and Aquitaine: A Biography of the Black Prince*, London: Allen Lane.

Barczewski, Stephanie (2007) *Antarctic Destinies: Scott, Shackleton and the Changing Face of Heroism*, London: Hambledon Continuum.

Bard, Kathryn A. (ed.) (1999) *Encyclopedia of the Archaeology of Ancient Egypt*, London: Routledge.

Bardin, Pierre (2006) *Joseph de Saint-Georges, le Chevalier Noir*, Paris: Guénégaud.

Barker, Eileen (1986) *The Making of a Moonie: Choice or Brainwashing?* Oxford: Blackwell.

Barnes, Timothy D. (1981) *Constantine and Eusebius*, Cambridge, MA: Harvard University Press.

Barnes, Timothy D. (1982) *The New Empire of Diocletian and Constantine*, Cambridge, MA: Harvard University Press.

Barnouin, Barbara and Yu Changgen (2006) *Zhou Enlai: A Political Life*, Hong Kong: Chinese University of Hong Kong.

Barr, Luke (2018) *Ritz and Escoffier: The Hotelier, the Chef and the Rise of the Leisure Class*, New York: Clarkson Potter.

Barra, Allen (2009) *Yogi Berra: Eternal Yankee*, New York: W.W. Norton.

Barrett, Anthony A. (1989) *Caligula: The Corruption of Power*, London: B.T. Batsford.

Bartlett, W.B. (2007) *The Last Crusade: The Seventh Crusade and the Final Battle for the Holy Land*, London: The History Press.

Bartley, Paula (2002) *Emmeline Pankhurst*, London: Routledge.

Bascomb, Neal (2007) *Red Mutiny: Eleven Fateful Days on the Battleship Potemkin*, Boston: Houghton Mifflin.

Bat'a, Tomás (1992) *Knowledge in Action: The Bata System of Management*, Amsterdam: IOS Press.

Bataille, Gretchen M. (ed.) (1993) *Native American Women: A Biographical Dictionary*, New York: Garland.

Bates, Leonard J. (1963) *The Origins of Teapot Dome*, Urbana: University of Illinois Press.

Bayat, Mangol (1991) *Iran's First Revolution: Sh'ism and the Constitutional Revolution of 1905–1909*, Oxford: Oxford University Press.

Beard, Mary (2016) *SPQR: A History of Ancient Rome*, London: Profile Books.

Beasley, William G. (1995) *The Rise of Modern Japan: Political, Economic and Social Change Since 1850*, New York: St Martin's.

Becker, Peter (1979) *Path of Blood: The Rise and Conquests of Mzilikazi, Founder of the Matabele Tribe of Southern Africa*, London: Penguin.

Beckford, James A. and Richardson, James T. (eds) (2015) *Challenging Religion: Essays in Honour of Eileen Barker*, London: Routledge.

Becraft, Michael (2014) *Bill Gates: A Biography*, Westport: Greenwood.

Beecher, Jonathan and Bienvenu, Richard (eds) (1971) *The Utopian Vision of Charles Fourier: Selected Texts on Work, Love and Passionate Attraction*, Boston: Beacon.

Belknap, Michael R. (2002) *The Vietnam War on Trial: The My Lai Massacre and the Court Martial of Lieutenant Calley*, Lawrence: University Press of Kansas.

Bell, Bowyer J. (1977) *Terror Out of Zion: Irgun Zvai Leumi, Lehi, and the Palestine Underground, 1919–1949*, New York: Avon.

Bell, Madison Smartt (2007) *Toussaint l'Ouverture: A Biography*, New York: Pantheon.

Bennett, Daphne (1990) *Emily Davies and the Liberation of Women*, London: Andre Deutsch.

Bennis, Warren G. and Nanus, Bert (1985) *Leaders: Five Strategies for Taking Charge*, New York: Harper & Row.

Benson, John (2003) *The Working Class in Britain, 1850–1939*, London: I.B. Tauris.

Berle, Adolph A. and Means, Gardiner C. (1932) *The Modern Corporation and Private Property*, New York: Macmillan.

Bernard, J.F. (1973) *Talleyrand: A Biography*, New York: Putnam.

Bernays, Edward (1928) *Propaganda*, London: Routledge.

Bernet, Anne (2005) *Charette*, Paris: Perrin.

Bernier, Olivier (1983) *Lafayette*, New York: E.P. Dutton.

Betzig, Laura (2008) *Despotism and Differential Reproduction: A Darwinian View of History*, Piscataway: Transaction.

Bhopal, Raj (2007) 'The Beautiful Skull and Blumenbach's Errors: The Birth of the Scientific Concept of Race', *British Medical Journal* 335: 1308–9.

Bierbrier, M.L. (1989) *The Tomb-Builders of the Pharaohs*, Cairo: American University in Cairo Press.

Bigongiari, Dino (ed.) (1953) *The Political Ideas of St Thomas Aquinas*, New York: Hafner.

Bilgrami, Muna Haeri (1986) *The Victory of Truth: The Life of Zaynab bint 'Ali*, Karachi: Zahra Publications.

Birchall, Johnston (1997) *The International Co-operative Movement*, Manchester: Manchester University Press.

Birmingham, David (1995) *The Decolonization of Africa*, London: Routledge.

Black Hawk (1916) *Life of Black Hawk*, ed. Milo M. Quaife, Chicago: Lakeside Press.

Blackwell, Richard J. (1991) *Galileo, Bellarmine and the Bible*, Notre Dame: University of Notre Dame Press.

Blickle, Peter (1981) *The German Peasants War of 1525 From a New Perspective*, trans. Thomas A. Brady and H.C. Midelfort, Baltimore: Johns Hopkins University Press.

Bligh, William (1979) *Mutiny on Board the HMS Bounty*, New York: Pendulum.

Blight, David W. (2018) *Frederick Douglass: Prophet of Freedom*, New York: Simon & Schuster.

Bloch, Marc (1961) *Feudal Society*, trans. L.A. Manyon, Chicago: University of Chicago Press.

Bloch, Marc (1973) *The Royal Touch: Sacred Monarchy and Scrofula in England and France*, trans. J.E. Anderson, London: Routledge & Kegan Paul.

Bloxham, Donald (2005) *The Great Game of Genocide: Imperialism, Nationalism and the Destruction of the Ottoman Armenians*, Oxford: Oxford University Press.

Blumenson, Martin (1985) *Patton: The Man Behind the Legend*, New York: William Morrow.

Boeselager, Philipp von (2009) *Valkyrie: The Plot to Kill Hitler*, London: Weidenfeld & Nicolson.

Bogues, Anthony (2003) *Black Heretics, Black Prophets: Radical Political Intellectuals*, London: Routledge.

Bohn, Michael K. (2004) *The Achille Lauro Hijacking: Lessons in the Politics and Prejudices of Terrorism*, Washington, DC: Potomac Books.

Bolden, Richard, Hawkins, Beverly, Gosling, Jonathan and Taylor, Scott (2011) *Exploring Leadership: Individual, Organizational and Societal Perspectives*, Oxford: Oxford University Press.

Bolitho, Hector (1932) *Alfred Mond, First Lord Melchett*, London: Martin Secker.

Bolton, Brenda and Duggan, Anne J. (eds) (2003) *Adrian IV The English Pope (1154–9): Studies and Texts*, London: Routledge.

Bolton, Kingsley and Hutton, Christopher (2000) *Triad Societies: Western Accounts of the History, Sociology and Linguistics of Chinese Secret Societies*, London: Routledge.

Bolton, Timothy (2017) *Cnut the Great*, London: Yale University Press.

Bonnano, Joseph (2003) *A Man of Honor: The Autobiography of Joseph Bonanno*, New York: St Martin's.

Bostridge, Mark (2008) *Florence Nightingale: The Woman and Her Legend*, London: Penguin.

Bosworth, Richard (2002) *Mussolini*, London: Hodder & Stoughton.

Boudreau, Vincent (2004) *Resisting Dictatorship: Repression and Protest in Southeast Asia*, Cambridge: Cambridge University Press.

Bourke, Joanna (2005) *Fear: A Cultural History*, London: Virago.

Bourne, Richard (1974) *Getulio Vargas of Brazil: Sphinx of the Pampas*, London: Knight.

Bourrienne, Louis Antoine (1885) *The Memoirs of Napoleon Bonaparte*, ed. R. W. Phipps, London: Richard Bentley.

Bowle, John (1964) *Henry VIII: A Study of Power in Action*, New York: Little, Brown.

Bowles, Michael (1959) *The Art of Conducting*, New York: Doubleday.

Boyce, Mary (1975) *A History of Zoroastrianism*, Leiden: Brill.

Boycott-Brown, Martin (2001) *The Road to Rivoli: Napoleon's First Campaign*, London: Cassell.

Boyd, Steven R. (ed.) (1985) *The Whiskey Rebellion: Past and Present Perspectives*, Westport: Greenwood Press.

Braddon, Russell (1963) *Woman in Arms: The Story of Nancy Wake*, London: Collins.

Bradford, Sarah (2004) *Lucrezia Borgia: Life, Love and Death in Renaissance Italy*, London: Viking.

Bradley, Keith and Gelb, Alan (1983) *Co-operation at Work: The Mondragón Experience*, London: Heinemann.

Brakke, David (2010) *The Gnostics: Myth, Ritual and Diversity in Early Christianity*, Cambridge, MA: Harvard University Press.

Braudel, Fernand (1982) *Civilization and Capitalism*, trans. Siân Reynolds, London: HarperCollins.

Braun, Harald (2007) *Juan de Mariana and Early Modern Spanish Political Thought*, Aldershot: Ashgate.

Bray, Kingsley M. (2008) *Crazy Horse: A Lakota Life*, Norman: University of Oklahoma Press.

Brearley, Mike (2001) *The Art of Captaincy*, London: Pan Macmillan.

Brendon, Piers (1991) *Thomas Cook: 150 Years of Popular Tourism*, London: Secker & Warburg.

Brickhill, Paul (1954) *Reach for the Sky: The Story of Douglas Bader*, London: Odhams.

Briggs, Charles F. (2009) *Giles of Rome's De Regimine Principum: Reading and Writing Politics at Court and University*, Cambridge: Cambridge University Press.

Brinkley, Douglas (2005) *Rosa Parkes: A Life*, New York: Penguin.

Brinton, Crane (1965) *The Anatomy of Revolution*, New York: Vintage.

Broido, Vera (1977) *Apostles Into Terrorists: Women and the Revolutionary Movement in the Russia of Alexander II*, London: Viking.

Bromwich, David (2014) *The Intellectual Life of Edmund Burke: From the Sublime and the Beautiful to American Independence*, Cambridge, MA: Belknap.

Brown, Dee (1972) *Bury My Heart At Wounded Knee*, New York: Bantam.

Brown, Roger H. (1993) *Redeeming the Republic: Federalists, Taxation and the Origins of the Constitution*, Baltimore: Johns Hopkins University Press.

Bundles, A'Lelia Perry (2008) *Madam C.J. Walker: Entrepreneur*, New York: Chelsea House.

Burnham, James (1941) *The Managerial Revolution: Or, What Is Happening in the World Now*, London: Putnam.

Burns, James MacGregor (1956) *Roosevelt: The Lion and the Fox*, Norwalk, CN: Easton Press.

Burns, Jasper (2006) *Great Women of Imperial Rome: Mothers and Wives of the Caesars*, London: Routledge.

Burns, Michael (1998) *Bader: The Man and His Men*, London: Cassell.

Burrough, Bryan (2015) *Days of Rage: America's Radical Underground, the FBI, and the Forgotten Age of Revolutionary Violence*, New York: Penguin.

Bury, J.B. (1889) *A History of the Later Roman Empire*, London: Macmillan, vol. 2.

Bushman, Richard Lymon (2008) *Mormonism: A Very Short Introduction*, New York: Oxford University Press.

Butcher, Tim (2015) *The Trigger: The Hunt for Gavrilo Princip*, London: Vintage.

Byrn, John D. (1989) *Crime and Punishment in the Royal Navy: Discipline on the Leeward Islands Station, 1784–1812*, Brookfield, VT: Scolar Press.

Byron, George Gordon (Lord) (1814) *The Corsair*, London: John Murray.

Cabell, Craig (2006) *Witchfinder General: The Biography of Matthew Hopkins*, New York: Sutton.

Cadbury, Deborah (2010) *Chocolate Wars: The 150-Year Rivalry Between the World's Greatest Chocolate Makers*, London: HarperCollins.

Cadbury, Edward (1912) *Experiments in Industrial Organization*, London: Longmans, Green & Co.

Calderone, Antonino and Arlacchi, Pino (1993) *Men of Dishonor: Inside the Sicilian Mafia*, trans. Marc Romano, New York: William Morrow.

Campbell, Bruce F. (1980) *Ancient Wisdom Revived: A History of the Theosophical Movement*, Berkeley: University of California Press.

Campbell, John (2003) *Margaret Thatcher: The Iron Lady*, London: Pimilico.

Campbell, Mavis Christine (1990) *The Maroons of Jamaica, 1655–1796: A History of Resistance, Collaboration and Betrayal*, Trenton: Africa World Press.

Canetti, Elias (1973) *Crowds and Power*, Harmondsworth: Penguin.

Canfora, Luciano (2006) *Julius Caesar: The People's Dictator*, Edinburgh: Edinburgh University Press.

Cansiz, Sakine (2015) *Sara: My Whole Life Was a Struggle*, London: Pluto.

Caraman, Philip (1990) *Ignatius Loyola: A Biography of the Founder of the Jesuits*, New York: HarperCollins.

Carlin, John (2008) *Playing the Enemy: Nelson Mandela and the Game That Made a Nation*, New York: Penguin.

Carlyle, Thomas (1841) *On Heroes, Hero-Worship and the Heroic in History*, London: James Fraser.

Carlyle, Thomas (2019) *The French Revolution: A History*, Oxford: Oxford University Press.

Carmona, Michel (1981) *Marie de Médicis*, Paris: Fayard.

Canarina, John (2003) *Pierre Monteux, Maître*, New York: Rowman & Littlefield.

Carpenter, David (1996) *The Reign of Henry III*, London: Hambledon.

Carretta, Vincent (2005) *Equiano, the African: Biography of a Self-Made Man*, Athens: University of Georgia Press.

Cary-Elwes, Charles (1988) *St Benedict and His Rule*, London: Catholic Truth Society.

Cassius Dio (1928) *Roman History*, trans. Earnest Carey, London: Loeb Classical Library.

Castiglione, Baldesar (1959) *The Book of the Courtier*, trans. Charles S. Singleton, New York: Anchor.

Catton, Bruce (1990) *The Army of the Potomac*, New York: Doubleday.

Cavadini, John (ed.) (1995) *Gregory the Great: A Symposium*, Notre Dame: University of Notre Dame Press.

Cazacu, Matei (2007) *Gilles de Rais*, Paris: Tallandier.

Cekota, Anthony (1968) *Entrepreneur Extraordinary: The Biography of Tomas Bata*, Rome: Edizioni Internazionali Soziali.

Chadwick, H.M. (1905) *Studies on Anglo-Saxon Institutions*, Cambridge: Cambridge University Press.

Chadwick, Owen (2003) *A History of the Popes, 1830–1914*, Oxford: Oxford University Press.

Chalk, Peter (ed.) (2012) *Encyclopedia of Terrorism*, New York: ABC-Clio.

Chamberlin, E.R. (1979) *The Sack of Rome*, New York: Dorset.

Chan, A.B. (1996) *Li Ka-shing: Hong Kong's Elusive Billionaire*, Hong Kong: Oxford University Press.

Chan, Wellingon K.K. (1982) 'The Organizational Structure of the Traditional Chinese Firm and its Modern Reform', *Business History Review* 56 (2): 218–35; repr. in R. Ampalavanar Brown (ed.), *Chinese Business Enterprise: Critical Perspectives on Business and Management*, London: Routledge, vol. 1, pp. 216–30.

Chang, Iris (2012) *The Rape of Nanking: The Forgotten Holocaust of World War II*, New York: Basic.

Chandler, David (ed.) (1987) *Napoleon's Marshals*, London: Weidenfeld & Nicolson.

Chandler, David (2002) *Napoleon*, London: Leo Cooper.

Chang, Jung and Halliday, Jon (2005) *Mao: The Unknown Story*, London: Jonathan Cape.

Chang, K.C. (1983) *Art, Myth, and Ritual: The Path to Political Authority in Ancient China*, Cambridge, MA: Harvard University Press.

Chapman, Peter (2010) *The Last of the Imperious Rich: Lehman Brothers, 1844–2008*, London: Penguin.

Chaudhuri, Narayan (2010) *Maharshi Debendranath Tagore*, New Delhi: Sahitya.

Chazan, Robert (1987) *European Jewry and the First Crusade*, Berkeley: University of California Press.

Chenneault, Claire (1949) *Way of a Fighter*, New York: Putnam's.

Chepesiuk, Ron (2003) *The Bullet or the Bribe: Taking Down Colombia's Cali Drug Cartel*, New York: Praeger.

Chernow, Ron (1990) *The House of Morgan: An American Banking Dynasty and the Rise of Modern Finance*, New York: Atlantic Monthly Press.

Chernow, Ron (1999) *Titan: The Life of John D. Rockefeller, Sr.*, New York: Random House.

Cherry-Gerard, Apsley (2010) *The Worst Journey in the World*, London: Vintage.

Chidester, David (2004) *Salvation and Suicide: Jim Jones, The People's Temple and Jonestown*, Bloomington: Indiana University Press.

Christiansen, Erik (1997) *The Northern Crusades*, London: Penguin.

Christianson, Gale (1996) *Isaac Newton and the Scientific Revolution*, Oxford: Oxford University Press.

Chryssides, George D. (ed.) (2011) *Heaven's Gate: Postmodernity and Popular Culture in a Suicide Group*, Aldershot: Ashgate.

Chu, Yiu-Kong (2002) *The Triads as Business*, London: Routledge.

Chung, Jang (2013) *Empress Dowager Cixi: The Concubine Who Launched Modern China*, New York: Knopf.

Church, Stephen D. (2015) *King John: England, Magna Carta and the Making of a Tyrant*, London: Macmillan.

Clark, John Bates (1901) *The Control of the Trusts*, New York: Macmillan.

Clark, Martin (2009) *The Italian Risorgimento*, London: Routledge.

Clauss, Manfred (2001)*The Roman Cult of Mithras: The God and His Mysteries*, London: Routledge.

Cline, Erin M. (2012) *Confucius, Rawls and the Sense of Justice*, New York: Fordham University Press.

Clissold, Stephen (1968) *Bernardo O'Higgins and the Liberation of Chile*, London: Hart-Davis.

Clot, André (1989) *Harun al-Rashid and the World of a Thousand and One Nights*, trans. John Howe, Lanham, MD: Rowman and Littlefield.

Coad, Jonathan (2005) *The Portmouth Block Mills: Bentham, Brunel and the Start of the Royal Navy's Industrial Revolution*, Aldershot: Ashgate.

Cockburn, Patrick (2008) *Muqtada al-Sadr and the Battle for the Future of Iraq*, London: Simon & Schuster.

Cockram, Sarah D.P. (2013) *Isabella d'Este and Francesco Gonzaga: Power Sharing at the Italian Renaissance Court*, London: Routledge.

Coedès, George (1968) *The Indianized States of South-East Asia*, trans. Susan Brown Cowing, Honolulu: University of Hawaii Press.

Cohen, Sheila (2014) *Notoriously Militant: The Story of a Union Branch at Ford Dagenham*, London: The Merlin Press.

Cohn, Norman (1967) *Warrant for Genocide: The Myth of the Jewish World Conspiracy and the Protocols of the Elders of Zion*, London: Eyre & Spottiswood.

Cohn, Norman (1970) *The Pursuit of the Millennium: Revolutionary Millenarians and Mystical Anarchists of the Middle Ages*, Oxford: Oxford University Press.

Cohn, Samuel K. (2004) *Popular Protest in Late Medieval Europe*, Manchester: Manchester University Press.

Cole, G.D.H. (1930) *The Life of Robert Owen*, London: Macmillan.

Collett, Nigel (2006) *The Butcher of Amritsar: General Reginald Dwyer*, London: Continuum.

Collier, Simon (1967) *Ideas and Politics of Chilean Independence, 1808–1833*, Cambridge: Cambridge University Press.

Collins, Amanda L. (2002) *Greater Than Emperor: Cola di Rienzo and the World of Fourteenth-Century Rome*, Ann Arbor: University of Michigan Press.

Collins, Max Allan and Schwartz, A. Brad (2018) *Scarface and the Untouchable: Al Capone, Eliot Ness and the Battle for Chicago*, New York: William Morrow.

Collins, Roger (1989) *The Arab Conquest of Spain, 710–797*, Oxford: Blackwell.

Collins, Roger (1998) *Charlemagne*, Toronto: University of Toronto Press.

Collins, Roger (2000) *Keepers of the Keys: A History of the Papacy*, New York: Basic Books.

Collinson, Patrick (2007) *Elizabeth I*, Oxford: Oxford University Press.

Colman, Penny (1994) *Madam C.J. Walker: Building a Business Empire*, Brookfield, CT: Millbrook.

Comnena, Anna (1969) *The Alexiad*, trans. E.R.A. Sewter, Harmondsworth: Penguin.

Connolly, Owen (1966) *Napoleon's Satellite Kingdoms*, New York: The Free Press.

Connolly, S.J. (ed.) (1998) *The Oxford Companion to Irish History*, Oxford: Oxford University Press.

Connor, Clifford D. (2012) *Marat: Tribune of the French Revolution*, New York: Pluto.

Constable, Pamela and Valenzuela, Arturo (1993) *A Nation of Enemies: Chile Under Pinochet*, New York: W.W. Norton.

Contamine, Philippe (1984) *War in the Middle Ages*, trans. Michael Jones, Oxford: Blackwell.

Coogan, Tim Pat (2002) *Michael Collins: The Man Who Made Ireland*, Basingstoke: Palgrave Macmillan.

Cook, Bernard A. (ed.) (2006) *Women and War: A Historical Encyclopedia From Antiquity to the Present*, Santa Barbara, CA: ABC-CLIO.

Cooper, John M. and Procope, J.F. (1995) *Seneca: Moral and Political Essays*, Cambridge: Cambridge University Press.

Cordingly, David (2006) *Under the Black Flag: The Romance and the Reality of Life Among the Pirates*, London: Random House.

Corley, T.A.B. (2004) 'Palmer, George', in *Oxford Dictionary of National Biography*, Oxford: Oxford University Press.

Cornwall, Julian (1977) *The Revolt of the Peasantry, 1549*, London: Routledge & Kegan Paul.

Cowdray, H.E.J. (1998) *Pope Gregory VII, 1073–1085*, Oxford: Clarendon Press.

Cowen, Ross (2016) *Milvian Bridge AD 312: Constantine's Battle for Empire and Faith*, Oxford: Osprey.

Crassweller, Robert D. (1966) *Trujillo: The Life and Times of a Caribbean Dictator*, New York: Macmillan.

Craton, Michael (1983) *Testing the Chains: Resistance to Slavery in the British West Indies*, Ithaca: Cornell University Press.

Crawford, Harriet (2015) *Ur: City of the Moon God*, London: Bloomsbury.

Crick, Michael (1985) *Scargill and the Miners*, London: Penguin.

Critchley, David (2008) *The Origin of Organized Crime in America: The New York City Mafia, 1891–1931*, New York: Routledge.

Crowley, Jason (2012) *The Psychology of the Athenian Hoplite: The Culture of Combat in Classical Athens*, Cambridge: Cambridge University Press.

Crowley, Roger (2011) *City of Fortune: How Venice Won and Lost a Naval Empire*, London: Faber & Faber.

Cubert, Harold M. (1997) *The PFLP's Changing Role in the Middle East*, London: Routledge.

Cruickshanks, Eveline (2000) *The Glorious Revolution*, Basingstoke: Palgrave Macmillan.

Current, Richard Nelson and Current, Marcia Ewing (1997) *Loie Fuller: Goddess of Light*, Boston: Northeastern University Press.

Curry, Anne (1993) *The Hundred Years War*, Basingstoke: Macmillan.

Cust, Richard (2005) *Charles I: A Political Life*, Harlow: Pearson Education.

Dacey, Karen H. (2009) *The Stanleys of Newton: Yankee Tinkerers in the Gilded Age*, Kingfield, ME: Stanley Museum.

Dadabhoy, Bakhtiar K. (2013) *Barons of Banking: Glimpse of Indian Banking History*, New Delhi: Random House India.

Daddis, Gregory A. (2017) *Withdrawal: Reassessing America's Final Years in Vietnam*, Oxford: Oxford University Press.

Dahl, Robert A. (2000) *On Democracy*, London: Yale University Press.

Dalton, Dennis (1993) *Mahatma Gandhi: Nonviolent Power in Action*, New York: Columbia University Press.

Davies, Andrew (2013) *City of Gangs: Glasgow and the Rise of the British Gangster*, London: Hodder & Stoughton.

Davies, Catherine, Brewster, Claire and Owen, Hilary (2006) *South American Independence: Gender, Politics, Text*, Liverpool: University of Liverpool Press.

Davies, Norman (2005) *God's Playground: A History of Poland*, New York: Columbia University Press.

Davis, Burke (1975) *George Washington and the American Revolution*, New York: Random House.

Davis, Derek and Hawkins, Barry (2003) *New Religious Movements and Religious Liberty in America*, Waco: Baylor University Press.

Davis, John (1905) *Corporations*, New York: G.P. Putnam's Sons.

Davis, John H. (1993) *The Rise and Fall of the Gambino Crime Family*, New York: HarperCollins.

Davis, Wade (1985) *The Serpent and the Rainbow: A Harvard Scientist's Astonishing Journey into the Secret Societies of Haitian Voodoo, Zombies and Magic*, New York: Simon & Schuster.

Dawson, Jane (2015) *John Knox*, London: Yale University Press.

de Roover, Raymond (1955) 'Scholastic Economics: Survival and Lasting Influence from the Sixteenth Century to Adam Smith', *Quarterly Journal of Economics* 69 (2): 161–90.

de Roover, Raymond (1962) *The Rise and Decline of the Medici Bank*, Cambridge, MA: Harvard University Press.

De Neve, Jan-Emmanuel, Mikhalyov, Slava, Dawes, Christopher T., Christakis, Nicholas A. and Fowler, James H. (2013) 'Born to Lead? A Twin Design and Genetic Association Study of Leadership Role Occupancy', *The Leadership Quarterly* 24 (1): 45–60.

Dekmejian, Richard Hrair (1971) *Egypt Under Nasser: A Study in Political Dynamics*, Albany: State University of New York Press.

Delve, Janet (2007) 'Joseph Marie Jacquard: Inventor of the Jacquard Loom', *Annals of the History of Computing* 29 (4): 98–102.

Demarest, David P. (ed.) (1992) *The River Ran Red: Homestead, 1892*, Pittsburgh: University of Pittsburgh Press.

Demoor, Marysa (2017) *Their Fare Share: Women, Power and Criticism in the Athenaeum, From Millicent Garrett Fawcett to Katherine Mansfield, 1870–1920*, London: Routledge.

Derpanopoulos, George, Frantz, Erica, Geddes, Barbara and Wright, Joseph (2016) 'Are Coups Good For Democracy?', *Research and Politics* 3 (1).

Deuchler, Martina (1992) *The Confucian Transformation of Korea: A Study of Society and Ideology*, Boston: Harvard University Asia Center.

Diamond, Jared (1987) 'The Worst Mistake in the History of the Human Race', *Discover*, May, http://discovermagazine.com/1987/may/02-the-worst-mistake-in-the-history-of-the-human-race

Diamond, Jared (1997) *Guns, Germs and Steel: The Fates of Human Societies*, New York: W.W. Norton.

Dickens, A.G. (2005) *The English Reformation*, University Park: Penn State University Press.

Dickson, Gary (2008) *The Children's Crusade: Medieval History, Modern Mythistory*, Basingstoke: Palgrave Macmillan.

Diefendorf, Barbara B. (2008) *The St Bartholomew's Day Massacre: A Brief History With Documents*, New York: St Martin's.

Diemberger, Hildegard (2007) *When a Woman Becomes a Religious Dynasty: The Samding Dorje Phagmo of Tibet*, New York: Columbia University Press.

Dimsdale, Joel E. (1980) *Survivors, Victims and Perpetrators: Essays on the Nazi Holocaust*, London: Taylor & Francis.

Dirlik, Arif (1991) *Anarchism in the Chinese Revolution*, Berkeley: University of California Press.

Dobbins, James C. (1989) *Jodo Shinshu: Shin Buddhism in Medieval Japan*, Bloomington: Indiana University Press.

Dobson, Richard B. (1970) *The Peasants Revolt of 1381*, London: Pitman.

Doi, Takeo (2002) *The Anatomy of Dependence*, Tokyo: Kodansha.

Dolan, Brian (2004) *Josiah Wedgwood: Entrepreneur to the Enlightenment*, New York: Harper.

Donald, David H. (1996) *Lincoln*, New York: Simon & Schuster.

Donnachie, Ian (2000) *Robert Owen: Social Visionary*, Edinburgh: John Donald.

Doran, Susan and Freeman, Thomas S. (eds) (2003) *The Myth of Elizabeth*, Basingstoke: Palgrave.

Doran, Susan and Freedman, Thomas S. (eds) (2011) *Mary Tudor: Old and New Perspectives*, Basingstoke: Palgrave Macmillan.

Dornberg, John (1982) *Munich 1923: The Story of Hitler's First Grab for Power*, New York: Harper & Row.

Dougherty, Carol (2006) *Prometheus*, London: Taylor and Francis.

Douglas, Christopher (2002) *Douglas Jardine: Spartan Cricketer*, London: Methuen.

Douglas, David C. (1964) *William the Conqueror: The Norman Impact Upon England*, Berkeley: University of California Press.

Dowd, Gregory Evans (1992) *A Spirited Resistance: The North American Indian Struggle for Unity, 1745–1815*, Baltimore: Johns Hopkins University Press.

Dower, J.W. (1988) *Empire and Aftermath: Yoshida Shigeru and the Japanese Experience, 1878–1954*, Cambridge, MA: Harvard University Press.

Doyle, William (1989) *The Oxford History of the French Revolution*, Oxford: Clarendon.

Dreiser, Theodore (2010) *An American Tragedy*, New York: Signet.

Drury, Horace B. (1915) *Scientific Management*, New York: Longmans Green.

Dubofsky, Melvyn (1973) *We Shall Be All: A History of the Industrial Workers of the World*, New York: Quadrangle.

Duby, Georges and Perrot, Michelle (eds) (1992–4) *A History of Women in the West*, Cambridge, MA: Harvard University Press, 1992–4.

Dudley, Steven (2004) *Walking Ghosts: Murder and Guerrilla Politics in Colombia*, London: Routledge.

Duffy, Christopher (1986) *The Military Life of Frederick the Great*, New York: Athenaeum.

Duffy, Eamon (2009) *Fires of Faith: Catholic England Under Mary Tudor*, London: Yale University Press.

Dunn, Kevin C. (2003) *Imagining the Congo: The International Relations of Identity*, Basingstoke: Palgrave Macmillan.

Durkheim, Émile (1965) *The Elementary Forms of the Religious Life*, trans. Joseph Swain, New York: The Free Press.

Durkheim, Émile (2013) *The Division of Labour in Society*, trans. Steven Lukes, Basingstoke: Palgrave.

Eccles, Robert G. and Youmans, Tim (2015) 'Materiality in Corporate Governance: The Statement of Significant Audiences and Materiality', Harvard Business School Working Paper.

Eckstein, Arthur M. (2016) *Bad Moon Rising: How the Weather Underground Beat the FBI and Lost the Revolution*, New Haven: Yale University Press.

Edmonds, Walter D. (1948) *The First Hundred Years, 1848–1948*, Oneida: Oneida Ltd.

Edwards, Anne (1992) *The Grimaldis of Monaco*, New York: William Morrow.

Ehrenberg, Richard (1928) *Capital and Finance in the Age of the Renaissance: A Study of the Fuggers and Their Connections*, trans. H.M. Lucas, London: Jonathan Cape.

Eidelberg, Philip Gabriel (1974) *The Great Rumanian Peasant Revolt of 1907: Origins of a Modern Jacquerie*, Leiden: Brill.

Einhard (1969) *Life of Charlemagne*, trans. Lewis Thorpe, *Two Lives of Charlemagne*, Harmondsworth: Penguin.

Eisenberg, John (2009) *That First Season: How Vince Lombardi Took the Worst Team in the NFL and Set It on the Path to Glory*, New York: Houghton Mifflin.

Ely, Richard T. (1900) *Monopolies and Trusts*, New York: Macmillan.

Emerson, Harrington (1909) *Efficiency as a Basis for Operations and Wages*, New York: John R. Dunlap.

Emerson, Ralph Waldo (1850) *Representative Men*, Boston: Phillips, Sampson.

Emmanuel, Steven M. (ed.) (2013) *A Companion to Buddhist Philosophy*, Chichester: Wiley-Blackwell.

Engelstein, Laura (2003) *Castration and the Heavenly Kingdom: A Russian Folktale*, Ithaca: Cornell University Press.

England, Eric Gordon (1928) 'The Eternal Quest', Rowntree Management Conference Paper, 30 September.

Engleman, Dennis Eugene (1995) *Ultimate Things: An Orthodox Christian Perspective on End Times*, Chesterton, IN: Conciliar Press.

English, Richard (2003) *Armed Struggle: A History of the IRA*, London: Macmillan.

Epic of Gilgamesh, trans. N.K. Sandars (1960), Harmondsworth: Penguin.

Epstein, David F. (1984) *The Political Theory of the Federalist*, Chicago: University of Chicago Press.

Equiano, Olaudah (1999) *The Life of Olaudah Equiano, or Gustavus Vassa, the African*, Mineola: Dover.

Escobar, Roberto (2010) *Escobar: The Inside Story of Pablo Escobar, the World's Most Powerful Criminal*, London: Hodder.

Esdaile, Charles J. (2018) *The Wars of the French Revolution*, London: Routledge.

Espoz y Mina, Francisco (1925) *A Short Extract From the Life of General Mina*, London: Taylor & Hussey.

Ettinger, Elzbieta (1988) *Rosa Luxemburg: A Life*, Boston: Beacon.

Evans, G.R. (2000) *Bernard of Clairvaux*, Oxford: Oxford University Press.

Evans, Richard (1993) *Deng Xiaoping and the Making of Modern China*, London: Hamish Hamilton.

Evans, Robert (1979) *The Making of the Habsburg Monarchy, 1500–1700*, Oxford: Clarendon.

Everitt, Anthony (2001) *Cicero: A Turbulent Life*, London: John Murray.

Eze, Emmanuel Chukwudi (1997) *Race and the Enlightenment: A Reader*, Oxford: Blackwell.

Fairbank, John King and Goldman, Merle (2006) *China: A New History*, Cambridge, MA: Belknap.

Falk, Avner (2008) *Anti-Semitism: A History and Psychoanalysis of Contemporary Hatred*, Westport: Praeger.

Falk, Candace (1990) *Love, Anarchy and Emma Goldman*, New Brunswick: Rutgers University Press.

Farmer, Edward L. (1995) *Zhu Yuanzhang and Early Ming Legislation: The Reordering of Chinese Society Following the Era of Mongol Rule*, Leiden: Brill.

Fawcett, Millicent Garrett (1911) *Women's Suffrage: A Short History of a Great Movement*, London: T.C. & E.C. Jack.

Fayol, Henri (1949) *General and Industrial Management*, trans. Constance Storrs, London: Pitman.

Femia, Joseph (2001) *Against the Masses: Varieties of Anti-Democratic Thought Since the French Revolution*, Oxford: Oxford University Press.

Ferguson, Alex and Moritz, Michael (2016) *Leading: Lessons in Leadership From the Legendary Manchester United Manager*, London: Hodder & Stoughton.

Ferling, John E. (2010) *First of Men: A Life of George Washington*, New York: Oxford University Press.

Ferris, William Wayne (1995) *Heavenly Warriors: The Evolution of Japan's Military, 500–1300*, Cambridge, MA: Harvard University Press.

Feuer, A.B. (2002) *America at War: The Philippines, 1898–1913*, Santa Barbara: Greenwood.

Fickenauer, James O. and Waring, Elin J. (1998) *Russian Mafia in America: Immigration, Culture and Crime*, Boston: Northeastern University Press.

Field, Cecil (1947) *The Great Cossack: The Rebellion of Stenka Razin Against Alexis Michaelovitch, Tsar of All the Russias*, London: H. Jenkins.

Filmer, Robert (1991) *Patriarcha and Other Writings*, ed. Johann P. Sommerville, Cambridge: Cambridge University Press.

Finer, Samuel E. (2002) *The Man on Horseback: The Role of the Military in Politics*, London: Routledge.

Fitton, Richard S. (1999) *The Arkwrights: Spinners of Fortune*, Manchester: Manchester University Press.

Fitzgerald, Robert (2007) *Rowntree and the Marketing Revolution*, Cambridge: Cambridge University Press.

Fitzpatrick, Sheila (2017) *The Russian Revolution*, Oxford: Oxford University Press.

Flanagan, Sabina (1989) *Hildegard of Bingen, 1098–1179: A Visionary Life*, London: Routledge.

Fletcher, Richard (1997) *The Conversion of Europe: From Paganism to Christianity, 371–1386 AD*, London: HarperCollins.

Flint, Charles R. (2002) *The Trust, Its Book: Being a Presentation of Several Aspects of the Latest Forms of Industrial Evolution*, New York: Doubleday Page.

Follett, Mary Parker (1924) *Creative Experience*, New York: Longmans, Green.

Follett, Mary Parker (1928) 'Leadership', Rowntree Management Conference Paper, 28 September.

Folsom, Burton W. (2003) *The Myth of the Robber Barons*, New York: Young America.

Foltz, Richard (2013) *Religions of Iran: From Prehistory to the Present*, London: Oneworld.

Forey, Alan (1992) *The Military Orders From the Twelfth to the Early Fourteenth Centuries*, Basingstoke: Macmillan.

Forsyth, D.R. (2013) *Group Dynamics*, New York: Wadsworth.

Fotion, Nicholas (2007) *War and Ethics*, London: Continuum.

Foucault, Michel (1991) *Discipline and Punish: The Birth of the Prison*, trans. Alan Sheridan, London: Penguin.

Fouracre, Paul (2000) *The Age of Charles Martel*, London: Routledge.

Fowler, Will (2007) *Santa Anna of Mexico*, Lincoln: University of Nebraska Press.

Fowler, William W. (2001) *Twenty Years of Inside Life in Wall Street*, Bristol: Thoemmes Press.

Foxley, Rachel (2013) *The Levellers: Radical Political Thought in the English Revolution*, Oxford: Oxford University Press.

Foy, Michael T. and Barton, Brian (2011) *The Easter Rising*, Stroud: The History Press.

Frady, Marshall (2002) *Martin Luther King Jr: A Life*, London: Penguin.

Frankopan, Peter (2011) *The First Crusade: The Call From the East*, London: The Bodley Head.

Fraser, Nicolas and Navarro, Marysa (1980) *Evita: The Real Life of Eva Perón*, New York: W.W. Norton.

French, John R.P. and Raven, Bertram (1959) 'The Bases of Social Power', in Dorwen Cartwright (ed.), *Studies in Social Power*, Ann Arbor: University of Michigan.

Friedman, Milton (1970) 'The Social Responsibility of a Business Is to Increase Its Profits', *New York Times Magazine*, 13 September.

Friedman, Robert I. (2000) *Red Mafia: How the Russian Mob Has Infiltrated America*, Boston: Little, Brown.

Fryde, E.B. (1988) *William de la Pole: Merchant and King's Banker*, London: Hambledon.

Fudge, Thomas A. (1998) *The Magnificent Ride: The First Revolution in Hussite Bohemia*, Aldershot: Ashgate.

Fudge, Thomas A. (2010) *Jan Hus: Religious Reform and Social Revolution in Bohemia*, London: I.B. Tauris.

Furness, Christopher (1908) *Industrial Peace and Industrial Efficiency*, West Hartlepool: Alexander Salton.

Gabriel, Richard A. and Savage, Paul L. (1978) *Crisis in Command: Mismanagement in the Army*, New York: Hill & Wang.

Gage, Beverly (2009) *The Day Wall Street Exploded: The Story of America in Its First Age of Terror*, New York: Oxford University Press.

Galston, Miriam (2002) *Politics and Excellence: The Political Philosophy of al-Farabi*, Princeton: Princeton University Press.

Galton, Francis (1869) *Hereditary Genius*, London: Macmillan.

Gambetta, Diego (1993) *The Sicilian Mafia: The Business of Private Protection*, Princeton: Princeton University Press.

Gambonne, Michael D. (1997) *Eisenhower, Somoza and the Cold War in Nicaragua, 1953–1961*, New York: Praeger.

Gandhi, Rajmohan (2006) *Gandhi: The Man, His People and the Empire*, Berkeley: University of California Press.

Gandt, Robert L. (1995) *Skygods: The Fall of Pan Am*, New York: Morrow.

Gaposchkin, Cecilia M. (2008) *The Making of Saint Louis: Kingship, Sanctity and Crusade in the Later Middle Ages*, Ithaca: Cornell University Press.

Gardiner, A.G. (1923) *Life of George Cadbury*, London: Cassell.

Garland, Lynda (1999) *Byzantine Empresses: Women and Power in Byzantium, AD 527–1204*, London: Routledge.

Garlick, Rhonda K. (2009) *Electric Salome: Loie Fuller's Performance of Modernism*, Princeton: Princeton University Press.

Garner, Paul (2001) *Porfirio Díaz*, Harlow: Pearson.

Garr, Doug (1999) *IBM Redux: Lou Gerstner and the Business Turnaround of the Decade*, New York: Harper Business.

Gaunt, Peter (1996) *Oliver Cromwell*, Oxford: Blackwell.

Gaunt, Peter (2014) *The English Civil War: A Military History*, London: I.B. Tauris.

Geary, Dick (1989) *Labour and Socialist Movements in Europe Before 1914*, Oxford: Berg.

Geifman, Anna (1993) *Thou Shalt Kill: Revolutionary Terrorism in Russia, 1894–1917*, Princeton: Princeton University Press.

Gerstner, Louis V. (2002) *Who Says Elephants Can't Dance?* New York: HarperCollins.

Gibbon, Edward (2010) *The Decline and Fall of the Roman Empire*, London: Everyman.

Gilbert, Martin (1983) *Finest Hour: Winston S. Churchill, 1939–1941*, London: William Heinemann.

Gilbert, Martin (1989) *The Holocaust: The Human Tragedy*, London: HarperCollins.

Gilbreth, Lillian E. (1914) *The Psychology of Management*, London: Sir Isaac Pitman.

Gilby, Thomas (1958) *The Political Thought of Thomas Aquinas*, Chicago: University of Chicago Press.

Gill, Anton (1994) *An Honourable Defeat: A History of the German Resistance to Hitler*, London: Heinemann.

Gill, Conrad (1913) *The Naval Mutinies of 1797*, Manchester: Manchester University Press.

Gillespie, Charles C. (1971) *Lazare Carnot*, Princeton: Princeton University Press.

Gillingham, John (1999) *Richard I*, New Haven: Yale University Press.

Gimbutas, Marija (1971) *The Slavs*, New York: Praeger.

Gimbutas, Marija (1991) *The Civilization of the Goddess: The World of Old Europe*, New York: Harper & Row.

Givins, James B. (2001) *Inquisition and Medieval Society*, Ithaca: Cornell University Press.

Glover, Michael (1968) *Wellington as Military Commander*, London: B.T. Batsford.

Goethe, Johann Wolfgang von (1839) 'Prometheus', in Nathan H. Dole (ed.), *The Works of J.W. von Goethe*, London: Francis Nicholls.

Goffee, Rob and Jones, Gareth (2015) *Why Should Anyone Be Led By You? What it Takes to be an Authentic Leader*, Boston: Harvard Business School Press.

Golan, Daphna (1994) *Inventing Shaka: Using History in the Construction of Zulu Nationalism*, Boulder: Lynne Riener.

Goodwin, Doris Kearns (2009) *Teams of Rivals: The Political Genius of Abraham Lincoln*, New York: Penguin.

Goodwin, Gordon (2004) 'Huntsman, Benjamin', in *Oxford Dictionary of National Biography*, Oxford: Oxford University Press.

Gordon, Andrew (2003) *A Modern History of Japan: From Tokugawa Times to the Present*, Oxford: Oxford University Press.

Gottlieb, Karla Lewis (2000) *The Mother of Us All: A History of Queen Nanny, Leader of the Windward Jamaican Maroons*, Trenton: Africa World Press.

Goudineau, Dominique and Streip, Katherine (1998) *The Women of Paris and Their French Revolution*, Berkeley: University of California Press.

Graham, A.C. (1981) *Chuang-tzu: The Seven Inner Chapters and Other Writings From the Book Chuang-tzu*, London: George Allen & Unwin.

Graicunas, V.A. (1937) 'The Span of Control', in Luther Gulick and Lyndall Urwick (eds), *Papers on the Science of Administration*, New York: Institute of Public Administration.

Greenberg, Kenneth S. (ed.) (2003) *Nat Turner: A Slave Rebellion in History and Memory*, New York: Oxford University Press.

Greene, Julie (1998) *Pure and Simple Politics: The American Federation of Labor and Political Activism, 1881–1917*, New York: Cambridge University Press.

Greenleaf, Ronald K. (1998) *The Power of Servant Leadership*, San Francisco: Barrett-Koehler.

Gregor, James A. (2001) *Giovanni Gentile: Philosopher of Fascism*, Piscatawa: Transaction.

Gregory, Andrew (2001) *Harvey's Heart: The Discovery of Blood Circulation*, Cambridge: Icon.

Gregory, Desmond (2001) *Napoleon's Italy*, New York: AUP.

Greising, David (1998) *I'd Like to Buy the World a Coke: The Life and Leadership of Roberto Goizueta*, New York: Wiley.

Griffin, Roger (1995) *Fascism*, Oxford: Oxford University Press.

Grunberger, Richard (1971) *The Twelve-Year Reich: A Social History of Nazi Germany, 1933–1945*, New York: Holt, Rinehart and Winston.

Guelzo, Allen C. (2012) *Fateful Lightning: A New History of the Civil War and Reconstruction*, New York: Oxford University Press.

Gueniffey, Patrice (2015) *Bonaparte, 1769–1802*, Cambridge, MA: Harvard University Press.

Guilmartin, John (1976) *Gunpowder and Galleys*, Cambridge: Cambridge University Press.

Hadley, Arthur Twining (1896) *Economics: An Account of the Relations Between Private Property and Public Welfare*, New York: Harper & Bros.

Hague, William (2005) *William Pitt the Younger*, London: HarperCollins.

Haigh, Roger M. (1968) *Martin Güemes: Tyrant or Tool? A Study of the Sources of Power of an Argentine Caudillo*, Fort Worth: Texas Christian University Press.

Halecki, Oskar (1961) *A History of Poland*, New York: Roy.

Haley, James L. (2002) *Sam Houston*, Norman: University of Oklahoma Press.

Hall, James (1983) *A History of Ideas and Images in Italian Art*, London: John Murray.

Hall, John R. (2004) *Gone From the Promised Land: Jonestown in American Cultural History*, New Brunswick: Transaction.

Halperin, Samuel (1965) *Germany Tried Democracy: A Political History of the Reich From 1918 to 1933*, New York: W.W. Norton.

Halsall, Guy (2008) *Barbarian Migrations and the Roman West, 376–568*, Cambridge: Cambridge University Press.

Halsted, J.B. (1969) *Alphonse de Lamartine: History of the Revolution of 1848*, Basingstoke: Palgrave Macmillan.

Hamburger, Susan (1999) 'McKnight, William Lester', in J.A. Garraty and M.C. Carnes (eds), *American National Biography*, New York: Oxford University Press, vol. 15, pp. 131–2.

Hamel, Frank (1911) *A Woman of the Revolution: Théroigne de Méricourt*, New York: Brentano.

Hamid, Nafees and Pretus, Clara (2019) 'The Neuroscience of Terrorism: How We Convinced a Group of Radicals to Let Us Scan Their Brains', *The Conversation*, 12 June.

Hamill, Hugh M. (ed.) (1992) *Caudillos: Dictators in Spanish America*, Norman: University of Oklahoma Press.

Hamilton, Alexander, Madison, James and Jay, John (1901) *The Federalist*, ed. Goldwin Smith, New York: The Colonial Press.

Hamilton, James (2002) *Faraday: The Life*, London: HarperCollins.

Handy, Charles (1976) *Understanding Organisations*, London: Penguin.

Hanioglu, M. Sukru (2001) *The Young Turks: Preparation for a Revolution, 1902–1908*, Oxford: Oxford University Press.

Hansen, Mogens Herman (1991) *Athenian Democracy in the Age of Demosthenes*, Oxford: Blackwell.

Harris, Matthew (2010) *The Notion of Papal Monarchy in the Twelfth Century*, Lewiston: Edwin Mellen.

Harrison, Ross (2003) *Hobbes, Locke and Confusion's Empire: An Examination of Seventeenth-Century Political Philosophy*, Cambridge: Cambridge University Press.

Hartnett, Lynne Ann (2014) *The Defiant Life of Vera Figner: Surviving the Russian Revolution*, Bloomington: Indiana University Press.

Haskins, Gay, Thomas, Mike and Johri, Lalit (eds) (2018) *Kindness in Leadership*, London: Routledge.

Hassig, Ross (1998) *Aztec Warfare: Imperial Expansion and Political Control*, Norman: University of Oklahoma Press.

Hattersley, Roy (1999) *Blood and Fire: William and Catherine Booth of the Salvation Army*, New York: Little, Brown.

Hawkins, Hugh (1972) *Between Harvard and America: The Educational Leadership of Charles W. Eliot*, New York: Oxford University Press.

Hawkins, Mike (1997) *Social Darwinism in European and American Thought, 1860–1945*, Cambridge: Cambridge University Press.

Haynes, Sam W. and Saxon, Gerald D. (eds) (2015) *Contested Empire: Rethinking the Texas Revolution*, College Station: Texas A&M University Press.

Head, Constance (1972) *Justinian II of Byzantium*, Madison: University of Wisconsin Press.

Heater, Derek (2006) *Citizenship in Britain: A History*, Edinburgh: Edinburgh University Press.

Hehaka Sapa (1932) *Black Elk Speaks: Being the Life Story of a Holy Man of the Oglala Sioux*, Lincoln: University of Nebraska Press.

Heissig, Walter (2000) *The Religions of Mongolia*, London: Routledge.

Henck, Nick (2007) *Subcomandante Marcos: The Man and the Mask*, Durham: Duke University Press.

Herodotus (2003) *The Histories*, trans. Aubrey de Selincourt, London: Penguin.

Hersh, Seymour M. (2016) *The Killing of Osama bin Laden*, New York: Verso.

Hess, Henner and Osers, Ewald (1998) *Mafia and Mafiosi: Origin, Power and Myth*, London: Hurst.

Hexter, J.H. (1972) 'Fernand Braudel and the *Monde Braudelien*', *Journal of Modern History* 44: 480–539.

Hibbert, Christopher (1975) *The House of Medici: Its Rise and Fall*, New York: Morrow.

Hibbert, Christopher (1980) *The Great Mutiny: India 1857*, London: Allen Lane.

Hibbert, Christpher (2008) *The Borgias and Their Enemies*, New York: Harcourt.

Higham, Charles (2001) *The Civilization of Angkor*, Berkeley: University of California Press.

Hill, Christopher (1972) *The World Turned Upside Down: Radical Political Thought in Seventeenth Century England*, London: Temple Smith.

Hill, Christopher (1996) *Liberty Against the Law: Some Seventeenth-Century Controversies*, London: Allen Lane.

Hill, Peter B.E. (2006) *The Japanese Mafia: Yakuza, Law and the State*, Oxford: Oxford University Press.

Hilton, Rodney (1995) *Bondmen Made Free: Medieval Peasant Movements and the English Rising of 1381*, London: Routledge.

Hirsch, Pamela (1998) *Barbara Leigh Smith Bodichon: Feminist, Artist and Rebel*, London: Chatto & Windus.

Hirschmeier, Johannes (1964) *Origins of Entrepreneurship in Meiji Japan*, Cambridge, MA: Harvard University Press.

Hobsbawm, Eric (1992) *Nations and Nationalism Since 1780: Programme, Myth, Reality*, Cambridge: Cambridge University Press.

Hodgart, Matthew (2009) *Satire: Origins and Principles*, Piscataway: Transaction.

Hoffman, Peter (1988) *German Resistance to Hitler*, Cambridge, MA: Harvard University Press.

Hoffman, Valerie Jon (2012) *The Essentials of Ibadi Islam*, Syracuse: Syracuse University Press.

Hofstede, Geert (2001) *Culture's Consequences: Comparing Values, Behaviors, Institution and Organizations Across Cultures*, 2nd edn, Thousand Oaks, CA: Sage.

Hofstede, Geert and Hofstede, Geert Jan (2005) *Cultures and Organizations: Software of the Mind*, 2nd edn, New York: McGraw-Hill.

Holden, Raymond (2005) *The Virtuoso Conductors*, London: Yale University Press.

Holmes, Richard (2009) *Marlborough: Britain's Greatest General*, London: HarperCollins.

Holt, Edgar (1967) *The Carlist Wars in Spain*, New York: Putnam.

Holt, James C. (2015) *Magna Carta*, Cambridge: Cambridge University Press.

Holyoake, George Jacob (19893) *The History of the Rochdale Pioneers*, London: Swan Sonnenschein.

Homer, *The Iliad*, trans. Herbert Jordan (2008), Norman: University of Oklahoma Press.

Homer, *The Odyssey*, trans. Robert Fitzgerald (1998), New York: Farrar, Strauss and Giroux.

Hommon, Robert J. (2013) *The Ancient Hawaiian State: Origins of a Political Society*, Oxford: Oxford University Press.

Horn, Stanley F. (1939) *Invisible Empire: The Story of the Ku Klux Klan, 1866–1871*, Montclair: Patterson Smith.

Horne, Alastair (1963) *The Price of Glory: Verdun, 1916*, New York: St Martin's Press.

Horne, Alistair (1965) *The Fall of Paris: The Siege and the Commune, 1870–71*, London: Macmillan.

Horne, Alastair (1997) *How Far From Austerlitz? Napoleon 1805–1815*, London: Macmillan.

Horrell, David G. (2006) *An Introduction to the Study of Paul*, London: T&T Clark.

Hosley, William (1996) *Colt: The Making of an American Legend*, Amherst: University of Massachusetts Press.

Houben, Hubert (2002) *Roger II of Sicily: Ruler Between East and West*, Cambridge: Cambridge University Press.

Hough, Richard (1973) *Captain Bligh and Mister Christian: The Men and the Mutiny*, New York: E.P. Dutton.

Hough, Richard (1994) *Captain James Cook*, London: Hodder & Stoughton.

Howard, Michael (1961) *The Franco-Prussian War: The German Invasion of France, 1870–1871*, London: Rupert Hart-Davis.

Howell, Georgina (2006) *Daughter of the Desert: The Remarkable Life of Gertrude Bell*, London: Macmillan.

Hoxie, Robert F. (1915) *Scientific Management and Labor*, New York: D. Appleton.

Hoyt, Edwin P. (1967) *The Guggenheims and the American Dream*, New York: Funk and Wagnalls.

Hoyt, Edwin P. (1993) *The Last Kamikaze: The Story of Matome Ugaki*, Westport: Greenwood.

Huck, Virginia (1955) *Brand of the Tartan: The 3M Story*, New York: Appleton-Centur-Crofts.

Hucker, Charles O. (1977) *China to 1850: A Short History*, Stanford: Stanford University Press.

Hughes-Hallett, Lucy (2014) *Gabriele d'Annunzio: Poet, Seducer and Preacher of War*, New York: Knopf.

Hugo, Victor (2005) *History of a Crime (The Testimony of an Eye-Witness)*, trans. T.H. Joyce and Arthur Lockyer, Paris: Mondial.

Hume, Leslie Parker (1982) *The National Union of Women's Suffrage Societies, 1897–1914*, London: Longman.

Humphreys, R.A. (1969) *Tradition and Revolt in Latin America*, New York: Columbia University Press.

Huntford, Roland (1985) *Shackleton*, London: Hodder & Stoughton.

Huntington, Samuel P. (1957) *The Soldier and the State: The Theory and Politics of Civil-Military Relations*, Cambridge, MA: Belknap Press.

Hurwitz, Marc and Hurwitz, Samantha (2017) *Leadership Is Half the Story: A Fresh Look at Followership, Leadership and Collaboration*, Toronto: University of Toronto Press.

Hutchinson, Robert (2007) *Elizabeth's Spy Master: Sir Francis Walsingham and the Secret War that Saved England*, London: Weidenfeld & Nicolson.

Hutton, Clinton A. et al. (eds) (2013) *Leonard Percival Howell and the Genesis of Rastafari*, Kingston: University of the West Indies Press.

Hutton, Ronald (1985) *The Restoration: A Political and Religious History of England and Wales, 1658–1667*, Oxford: Clarendon.

Hwang, Kwang-kuo (2011) *Foundations of Chinese Psychology: Confucian Social Relations*, New York: Springer.

Hyde, Charles K. (2003) *Riding the Roller Coaster: A History of the Chrysler Corporation*, Chicago: Wayne State University Press.

Hyden, Marc (2017) *Gaius Marius: The Rise and Fall of Rome's Saviour*, London: Pen & Sword.

Iacocca, Lee and Novak, William (1986) *Iacocca: An Autobiography*, New York: Bantam.

Ibarra, Herminia (2015) *Act Like a Leader, Think Like a Leader*, Boston: Harvard Business Review Press.

Icks, Martin (2011) *The Crimes of Elagabalus: The Life and Legacy of Rome's Decadent Boy Emperor*, London: I.B. Tauris.

Inalcik, Halil (2000) *The Ottoman Empire, 1300–1600*, London: Weidenfeld & Nicolson.

Ingham, J.N. and Feldman, L.B. (eds) (1994) *African-American Business Leaders: A Biographical Dictionary*, Westport: Greenwood Press.

Isaacson, Walter (2013) *Steve Jobs: The Exclusive Biography*, New York: Abacus.

Isakhan, Ben and Stockwell, Stephen (eds) (2011) *The Secret History of Democracy*, Basingstoke: Palgrave Macmillan.

Isichei, Elizabeth Allo (1997) *A History of African Societies to 1870*, Cambridge: Cambridge University Press.

Isoaho, Mari (2006) *The Image of Aleksandr Nevsky in Medieval Russia: Warrior and Saint*, Leiden: Brill.

Israel, Jonathan (2011) *Democratic Enlightenment: Philosophy, Revolution and Human Rights, 1750–1790*, Oxford: Oxford University Press.

Ivanhoe, Philip J. (2002) *Ethics in the Confucian Tradition: The Thought of Mencius and Wang Yangming*, Indianapolis: Hackett.

Ivanits, Linda J. (1989) *Russian Folk Belief*, Armonk: M.E. Sharpe.

Iyer, Raghavan N. (1986–7) *The Moral and Political Writings of Gandhi*, Oxford: Oxford University Press.

Jacob, Margaret C. (1997) *Scientific Culture and the Making of the Industrial West*, Oxford: Oxford University Press.

Jacobi, Otto *et al.* (eds) (1986) *Technological Change, Rationalisation and Industrial Relations*, London: Routledge.

Jain, L.C. (1929) *Indigenous Banking in India*, London: Macmillan.

Jalal, Ayesha (1994) *The Sole Spokesman: Jinnah, the Muslim League and the Demand for Pakistan*, Cambridge: Cambridge University Press.

James, Lawrence (1997) *Raj: The Making and Unmaking of British India*, London: Abacus.

Jansen, Marius B. (2000) *The Making of Modern Japan*, Cambridge, MA: Harvard University Press.

Jay, Anthony (1967) *Management and Machiavelli*, London: Hodder & Stoughton.

Jenkins, Romilly (1987) *Byzantium: The Imperial Centuries*, AD 610–1271, Toronto: University of Toronto Press.

Jenkins, Roy (1964) *Asquith: Portait of a Man and His Era*, London: Collins.

Jenkins, Roy (2002) *Churchill: A Biography*, London: Pan.

Jenks, Jeremiah (1900) *The Trust Problem*, New York: Macmillan.

Jenner, W.J.F. (1992) *The Tyranny of History: The Roots of China's Crisis*, London: Penguin.

Jensen, Gary F. (2006) *The Path of the Devil: Early Modern Witch Hunts*, New York: Rowman & Littlefield.

Jepson, Jill (2009) *Women's Concerns: Twelve Women Entrepreneurs of the Eighteenth and Nineteenth Centuries*, New York: Peter Lang.

Jocelyn, Ed and McEwen, Andrew (2006) *The Long March: The True Story Behind the Legendary Journey That Made Mao's China*, London: Constable and Robinson.

John of Salisbury (1927) *Policraticus*, trans. J. Dickinson as *Policraticus: The Statesman's Book*, New York: Knopf.

Johnson, Boris (2015) *The Churchill Factor: How One Man Made History*, London: Hodder.

Johnson, Charles (1998) *A General History of the Robberies and Murders of the Most Notorious Pyrates*, London: Conway.

Johnson, Richard L. (2006) *Gandhi's Experiments With Truth: Essential Writings By And About Mahatma Gandhi*, New York: Lexington Books.

Joinville, Jean de (1963) *The Life of St Louis*, trans. Margaret R.B. Shaw in *Joinville and Villehardouin: Chronicles of the Crusades*, Harmondsworth: Penguin.

Jolly, W.P. (1976) *Lord Leverhulme: A Biography*, London: Constable.

Jones, David Wyn (2009) *The Life of Haydn*, Oxford: Oxford University Press.

Jones, Howard (1987) *Mutiny on the Amistad: The Saga of a Slave Revolt and Its Impact on American Abolition, Law and Diplomacy*, New York: Oxford University Press.

Jones, Peter (2006) *Ove Arup: Master Builder of the Twentieth Century*, London: Yale University Press.

Jones, Stephanie and Gosling, Jonathan (2005) *Nelson's Way: Leadership Lessons From the Great Commander*, London: Nicholas Brealey.

Jones, Whitney R.D. (2005) *Thomas Rainborowe (c.1610–1648): Civil War Seaman, Siegemaster and Radical*, Woodbridge: Boydell.

Jory, Patrick (1998) *Thailand's Theory of Monarchy: The Vessantara Jataka and the Idea of the Perfect Man*, Albany: State University of New York Press.

Josephson, Matthew (1990) *The Robber Barons*, New York: Harcourt Brace Jovanovich.

Judson, Pieter M. (2016) *The Habsburg Empire: A New History*, Cambridge, MA: Harvard University Press.

Jung, Carl (1983) *The Psychology of the Transference*, London: Ark.

Jupp, Peter (1985) *Lord Grenville*, Oxford: Oxford University Press.

Kagan, Donald (1987) *The Fall of the Athenian Empire*, Ithaca: Cornell University Press.

Kai Kaus ibn Iskandar (1951) *A Mirror for Princes*, trans. Reuben Levy, London: The Cresset Press.

Kaiser, Anton (2017) *Joan of Arc: A Study in Charismatic Women's Leadership*, Black Hills: Black Hills Books.

Kalthoff, Otto, Nonaka, Ikujiro and Nueno, Pedro (1997) *The Light and the Shadow: How Breakthrough Innovation Is Shaping European Business*, Oxford: Capstone.

Kamen, Henry (1999) *The Spanish Inquisition: A Historical Revision*, London: Yale University Press.

Kaminsky, Howard (1967) *A History of the Hussite Revolution*, Berkeley: University of California Press.

Kaplan, David and Dubro, Alec (2012) *Yakuza: Japan's Criminal Underworld*, Berkeley: University of California Press.

Karanjia, Burjor Kurshedji (2004) *Vijitatma: Pioneer-Founder Ardeshir Godrej*, Bombay: Penguin.

Karlsson, Gunnar (2000) *A History of Iceland*, Minneapolis: University of Minnesota Press.

Kayloe, Tijo (2017) *The Unfinished Revolution: Sun Yat-sen and the Struggle for Modern China*, Singapore: Marshall Cavendish.

Keaveney, Arthur (2005) *Sulla: The Last Republican*, London: Routledge.

Kedward, H.R. (1993) *In Search of the Maquis*, Oxford: Clarendon.

Keegan, John (1970) *Waffen SS: The Asphalt Soldiers*, London: Pan.

Kellerman, Barbara (2008) *Followership: How Followers Are Creating Change and Changing Leaders*, Boston: Harvard Business Review Press.

Kellerman, Barbara (2012) *The End of Leadership*, New York: HarperCollins.

Kelley, Robert E. (1988) 'In Praise of Followers', *Harvard Business Review*, November: 142–8.

Kelly, Alison (2004) 'Coade, Elizabeth', in *Oxford Dictionary of National Biography*, Oxford: Oxford University Press.

Kelly, Donald R. (1973) *François Hotman: A Revolutionary's Ideal*, Princeton: Princeton University Press.

Kelly, Sean (1993) *America's Tyrant: The CIA and Mobutu of Zaire*, Washington: American Universities Press.

Kelsay, Isabel Thompson (1984) *Joseph Brant, 1743–1807: Man of Two Worlds*, Syracuse: Syracuse University Press.

Kennedy, A.L. (1953) *Salisbury, 1830–1903: Portrait of a Statesman*, London: John Murray.

Kennedy, Hugh N. (2004) *The Prophet and the Age of the Caliphates: The Islamic Near East From the 6th to the 11th Century*, Harlow: Pearson.

Kernan, Ben (2017) *Viet Nam: A History From Earliest Times to the Present*, Oxford: Oxford University Press.

Kershaw, Ian (2008) *Hitler: A Biography*, New York: W.W. Norton.

Khalidi, Rashid (1991) *The Origins of Arab Nationalism*, New York: Columbia University Press.

Khan, Yasmin (2008) *The Great Partition: The Making of India and Pakistan*, London: Yale University Press.

Khlevniuk, Oleg V. (2015) *Stalin: New Biography of a Dictator*, trans. Nora Seligman Favorov, London: Yale University Press.

Kiernan, Ben (2004) *How Pol Pot Came to Power: Colonialism, Nationalism and Communism in Cambodia, 1930–1975*, New Haven: Yale University Press.

King, William Lyon Mackenzie (1918) *Industry and Humanity*, Toronto: University of Toronto Press.

Kipgen, Nehginpao (2016) *Myanmar: A Political History*, New Delhi: Oxford University Press India.

Klaw, Spencer (1993) *Without Sin: The Life and Death of the Oneida Community*, New York: Penguin.

Klinck, Carl and Talman, James J. (1970) *The Journal of Major John Norton, 1816*, Toronto: Champlain Society.

Knight, Roger (2014) *Britain Against Napoleon: The Organization of Victory, 1793–1815*, London: Penguin.

Knoblock, John (1988) *Xunzi: A Translation and Study of the Complete Works*, Stanford: Stanford University Press.

Knoeppel, Charles (1918) *Organization and Administration*, New York: McGraw-Hill.

Kokkonen, Andrej and Sundell, Anders (2012) 'Delivering Stability: Primogeniture and Autocratic Survival in European Monarchies, 1000–1800', QoG Working Paper, University of Gothenburg.

Kopf, David (2015) *The Brahmo Samaj and the Shaping of the Modern Indian Mind*, Princeton: Princeton University Press.

Kotter, John P. (1990) *A Force for Change: How Leadership Differs From Management*, New York: The Free Press.

Kramer, Samuel Noah (1971) *The Sumerians: Their History, Culture and Character*, Chicago: University of Chicago Press.

Kraut, Richard (1992) *Cambridge Companion to Plato*, Cambridge: Cambridge University Press.

Kropotkin, Peter (2015) *The Conquest of Bread*, trans. David Priestland, London: Penguin.

Kujit, Ian (2000) *Life in Neolithic Farming Communities: Social Organization, Identity and Differentiation*, New York: Springer.

Kukral, Michael Andrew (1997) *Prague 1989: Theatre of Revolution*, New York: Columbia University Press.

Kumar, Umesh (1990) *Kautilya's Thought on Public Administration*, New Delhi: National Book Organization.

Künkler, Mirjam and Fazaeli, Roja (2019) 'The Lives of Two Mujtahidahs: Female Religious Authority in Twentieth-Century Iran', in Mirjam Künkler and Devin Stewart (eds), *Female Religious Authority in Shi'i Islam: Past and Present*, Edinburgh: Edinburgh University Press.

Kurth, Peter (2001) *Isadora Duncan: A Sensational Life*, Boston: Little Brown.

Kurtulmuş, Bekir Emre (2018) *The Dark Side of Leadership: An Institutional Perspective*, Basingstoke: Palgrave Macmillan.

Kuykendall, Ralph Simpson (1967) *The Hawaiian Kingdom, 1784–1893*, Honolulu: University of Hawaii Press.

Labarge, Margaret Wade (1962) *Simon de Montfort*, London: Eyre & Spottiswood.

Lacey, Robert (1991) *Little Man: Meyer Lansky and the Gangster Life*, Boston: Little, Brown.

Lachman, Gary (2007) *Rudolf Steiner: An Introduction to His Life and Work*, New York: Floris.

Lacouture, Jean (1968) *Ho Chi Minh: A Political Biography*, New York: Random House.

Ladd, Doris M. (1988) *The Making of a Strike: Mexican Silver Workers' Struggles in the Real del Monte, 1766–1775*, Lincoln: University of Nebraska Press.

Ladurie, Emmanuel Le Roy (1978) *Montaillou: Cathars and Catholics in a French Village*, London: Scolar Press.

Lala, R.M. (1992) *Beyond the Last Blue Mountain: A Life of J.R.D. Tata*, New Delhi: Penguin.

Lala, R.M. (2004) *For the Love of India: The Life and Times of Jamsetji Tata*, New Delhi: Penguin India.

Lalich, Janja A. (2004) *Bounded Choice: True Believers and Charismatic Cults*, Berkeley: University of California Press.

Landon, Robbins H.C. and Jones, David Wyn (1988) *Haydn: His Life and Music*, Bloomington: Indiana University Press.

Lane, Bill (2008) *Jacked Up: The Inside Story of How Jack Welch Talked GE Into Becoming the World's Greatest Company*, New York: McGraw-Hill.

Lane Fox, Robin (1980) *The Search for Alexander*, Boston: Little, Brown.

Large, David Clay (ed.) (2013) *Contending With Hitler: Varieties of German Resistance in the Third Reich*, Cambridge: Cambridge University Press.

Lau, D.C. (1979) *Confucius: The Analects*, Harmondsworth: Penguin.

Laughton, J.K. (2004) 'Norris, Sir John', in *Oxford Dictionary of National Biography*, Oxford: Oxford University Press.

Laughton, J.K. (2004) 'Westcott, George Blagdon', in *Oxford Dictionary of National Biography*, Oxford: Oxford University Press.

Lawday, David (2006) *Napoleon's Master: A Life of Prince Talleyrand*, London: Jonathan Cape.

Lawday, David (2009) *Danton: The Giant of the French Revolution*, London: Jonathan Cape.

Lawrence, C.H. (2001) *Medieval Monasticism*, Harlow: Pearson.

Lawrence, T.E. (1997) *Revolt in the Desert*, London: Wordsworth.

Lawton, Mary (ed.) (1939) *The Paderewski Memoirs*, London: Collins.

le Bon, Gustave (2002) *The Crowd: A Study of the Popular Mind*, New York: Dover.

Le Goff, Jacques (2009) *Saint Louis*, trans. Gareth Gollrad, Notre Dame: University of Notre Dame Press.

Ledeen, Michael (2001) *D'Annunzio: The First Duce*, London: Routledge.

Lee, Lily Xiao Hong and Stefanowska, A.D. (eds) (2007) *Biographical Dictionary of Chinese Women*, vol. 1, Armonk: M.E. Sharpe.

Lee, Peter H. and de Bary, William Theodore (eds) (1997) *Sources of Korean Tradition*, vol. 1, New York: Columbia University Press.

Leepson, Marc (2011) *Lafayette: Lessons in Leadership From the Idealist General*, Basingstoke: Palgrave Macmillan.

Lefebvre, Georges and Soboul, Albert (1962) *The Directory*, London: Routledge and Kegan Paul.

Leighton, Allan (2008) *On Leadership*, London: Random House.

Lenotre, G. (1918) *Georges Cadoudal*, Paris: Editions Transition.

Lepre, George (2011) *Fragging: Why U.S. Soldiers Assaulted Their Officers in Vietnam*, Lubbock: Texas Tech University Press.

Lesher, James H. (2001) *Xenophanes of Colophon: Fragments, a Text and Translation With a Commentary*, Toronto: University of Toronto Press.

Lesko, Leonard H. (ed.) (1994) *Pharaoh's Workers: The Villages of Deir El Medina*, Ithaca, NY: Cornell University Press.

Leuchars, Chris (2002) *To the Bitter End: Paraguay and the War of the Triple Alliance*, Westport: Greenwood Press.

Levick, Barbara (1990) *Claudius*, London: Yale University Press.

Levick, Barbara (1999) *Vespesian*, London: Routledge.

LeVine, Sarah and Gellner, David N. (2006) *Rebuilding Buddhism: The Theravada Movement in Twentieth-Century Nepal*, Cambridge, MA: Harvard University Press.

Levitzion, Nehemia (1973) *Ancient Ghana and Mali*, London: Methuen.

Lewis, James R. (ed.) (2016) *The Order of the Solar Temple: The Temple of Death*, London: Routledge.

Lewis, John Spedan (1954) *Fairer Shares*, London: Staples Press.

Lewis-Williams, David and Pearce, David (2011) *Inside the Neolithic Mind: Consciousness, Cosmos and the Realm of the Gods*, London: Thames and Hudson.

Li Yu-ning (1977) *Shang Yang's Reforms*, Armonk: M.E. Sharpe.

Liebermann, Felix (2005) *The National Assembly in the Anglo-Saxon Period*, New York: Ulan Press.

Lieu, Samuel (1992) *Manicheism in the Later Roman Empire and Medieval China*, Tübingen: Mohr.

Lifton, Robert Jay (2000) *Destroying the World to Save It: Aum Shinrikyo, Apocalyptic Violence and the New Global Terrorism*, London: Picador.

Lili'uokulani (1898) *Hawaii's Story by Hawaii's Queen*, Boston: Lee and Shephard.

Lindsay, Almont (1943) *The Pullman Strike: The Story of a Unique Experiment and a Great Labour Upheaval*, Chicago: University of Chicago Press.

Lipsey, Roger (2016) *Hammarskjöld: A Life*, Ann Arbor: University of Michigan Press.

Liutprand of Cremona (1930) *Relation de Legatione Constantinopolitana*, trans. F.A. Wright, New York: E.P. Dutton.

Livingstone, Marilyn and Witzel, Morgen (2005) *The Road to Crécy: The English Invasion of France, 1346*, Harlow: Longman.

Livingstone, Marilyn and Witzel, Morgen (2018) *The Black Prince and the Capture of a King: Poitiers, 1356*, Oxford: Casemate.

Lloyd, Henry Demarest (1894) *Wealth Against Commonwealth*, New York: Harper & Bros.

Lodge, Tom (2006) *Mandela: A Critical Biography*, Oxford: Oxford University Press.

Loewen, Karin Loewen (2002) 'Okwei of Osomari', in Anne Commire (ed.), *Women in World History: A Biographical Encyclopedia*, New York: Gale.

Long, Carolyn (2001) *Spiritual Merchants: Magic, Religion and Commerce*, Knoxville: University of Tennessee Press.

Long, Michael G. (2002) *Against Us, But For Us: Martin Luther King Jr and the State*, Macon, GA: Mercer University Press.

Lopez, Roberto (1933) *Zaccaria: Genova Marinara nel Duecento*, Milan: Messina.

Lorimer, Michael James (2008) *Sengokujidai: Autonomy, Division and Unity in Later Medieval Japan*, London: Olympia.

Lourie, Arthur (2016) *Serge Koussevitzky and His Epoch*, New York: Andesite Press.

Love, Joseph L. (2012) *The Revolt of the Whip*, Stanford: Stanford University Press.

Lowenthal, Esther (1927) 'The Labour Policy of the Oneida Community Ltd', *Journal of Political Economy* 35: 114–26.

Luckenbill, Daniel D. (trans.) (1931) *The Code of Hammurabi*, ed. Edward Chiera, in J.M. Powis Smith (ed.), *The Origin and History of Hebrew Law*, Chicago: University of Chicago Press.

Lumley, Robert (1990) *States of Emergency: Cultures of Revolt in Italy From 1968 to 1978*, London: Verso.

Lutton, Robert (2006) *Lollardy and Orthodox Religion in Pre-Reformation England*, Woodbridge: Boydell and Brewer.

Luttrell, Barbara (1990) *Mirabeau*, Carbondale: Southern Illinois University Press.

Luxemburg, Rosa (2006) *Reform or Revolution and Other Writings*, Mineola: Dover.

Lynch, John (1981) *Argentine Dictator: Juan Manuel de Rosas, 1829–1852*, Oxford: Oxford University Press.

Lynch, John (1992) *Caudillos in Spanish America, 1800–1850*, Oxford: Oxford University Press.

Lynch, John (2007) *Simón Bolívar: A Life*, New Haven: Yale University Press.

Lynch, John (2009) *San Martín: Argentine Soldier, American Hero*, New Haven: Yale University Press.

Lyons, Malcolm Cameron and Jackson, D.E.P. (1982) *Saladin: The Politics of Holy War*, Cambridge: Cambridge University Press.

Lythgoe, Gertrude (2006) *The Bahama Queen: The Autobiography of Gertrude 'Cleo' Lythgoe*, Mystic, CN: Flat Hammock Press.

Lyttleton, Adrian (2009) *The Seizure of Power: Fascism in Italy, 1919–1929*, London: Routledge.

Ma Yuxin (2010) *Women Journalists and Feminism in China, 1898–1937*, Amherst: Cambria Press.

Machiavelli, Niccolò (1961) *The Prince*, trans. G. Bull, Harmondsworth: Penguin.

Machiavelli, Niccolò (1970) *The Discourses*, ed. B. Crick, trans. L. J. Walker, Harmondsworth: Penguin.

Machiavelli, Niccolò (2001) *The Art of War*, trans. Ellis Farneworth, Cambridge, MA: Da Capo Press.

Mackay, Charles (1841) *Extraordinary Popular Delusions and the Madness of Crowds*, London: Richard Bentley.

Maclean, Fitzroy (1957) *Heretic: The Life and Times of Josip Broz-Tito*, New York: Harper & Bros.

Macmillan, Margaret (2003) *Peacemakers: Six Months That Changed the World*, London: John Murray.

Macoby, Michael (2004) 'Why People Follow the Leader: The Power of Transference', *Harvard Business Review*, September.

Madden, Thomas F. (2003) *Enrico Dandolo and the Rise of Venice*, Baltimore: Johns Hopkins University Press.

Maddicott, John (2010) *The Origins of the English Parliament, 924–1327*, Oxford: Oxford University Press.

Maddicott, John (1996) *Simon de Montfort*, Cambridge: Cambridge University Press.

Maddocks, Fiona (2001) *Hildegard of Bingen: The Woman of Her Age*, New York: Doubleday.

Maier, Pauline (1972) *From Resistance to Revolution: Colonial Radicals and the Development of Opposition to Britain, 1765–1776*, New York: W.W. Norton.

Maitron, Jean (1975) *Le mouvement anarchiste en France*, Paris: Gallimard.

Malcomson, Robert (2003) *A Very Brilliant Affair: The Battle of Queenston Heights, 1812*, Toronto: Robin Brass Studio.

Malcomson, Robert (2008) *Capital in Flames: The American Attack on York, 1813*, Toronto: Robin Brass Studio.

Malinowski, Bronisław (1922) *Argonauts of the Western Pacific: An Account of Native Enterprise and Adventure in the Archipelagoes of Melanesian New Guinea*, London: Routledge and Kegan Paul.

Mallett, Michael (1974) *Mercenaries and Their Masters: Warfare in Renaissance Italy*, New York: Rowman and Littlefield.

Mandel, Bernard (1963) *Samuel Gompers: A Biography*, New York: Penguin.

Manley, Michael (1988) *A History of West Indies Cricket*, London: Andre Deutsch.

Mao Zedong (1937) *On Guerrilla Warfare*, trans. Samuel B. Griffiths, New York: Dover, 2005.

Mao Zedong (1972) *Quotations From Chairman Mao Tse-Tung*, Beijing: Foreign Languages Press.

Maraniss, David (1999) *When Pride Still Mattered: A Life of Vince Lombardi*, New York: Simon & Schuster.

Marbot, Jean-Baptiste de (1892) *The Memoirs of Baron de Marbot*, trans. Arthur John Butler, London: Longmans, Green.

Markopolos, Harry (2010) *No One Would Listen: A True Financial Thriller, the Madoff Whistleblower*, New York: Wiley.

Marlow, Joyce (ed.) (2015) *Suffragettes: The Fight for Votes for Women*, London: Virago.

Marshall, S.L.A. (2000) *Men Against Fire: The Problem of Battle Command*, Norman: University of Oklahoma Press.

Marshall, Tim (2017) *Worth Dying For: The Power and Politics of Flags*, London: Elliott and Thompson.

Marsilius of Padua (2005) *Defensor Pacis*, trans. Annabel Brett, Cambridge: Cambridge University Press.

Martin, Brian G. (1996) *The Shanghai Green Gang: Politics and Organized Crime, 1919–37*, Berkeley: University of California Press.

Marx, Karl (1858) 'Bolivar y Ponte', in *The New American Cyclopedia*, New York: D. Appleton, www.marxists.org/archive/marx/works/1858/01/bolivar.htm

Maslow, Abraham (1954) *Motivation and Personality*, New York: Harper & Bros.

May, Allan (2009) *Gangland Gotham: New York's Notorious Mob Bosses*, Westport: Greenwood.

Mayeur, Jean-Marie and Rebirioux, Madeleine (1988) *The Third Republic From Its Origins to the Great War, 1871–1914*, Cambridge: Cambridge University Press.

Mayo, Elton (1933) *The Human Problems of an Industrial Civilization*, New York: Macmillan.

McBriar, A.M. (1962) *Fabian Socialism and English Politics, 1884–1918*, Cambridge: Cambridge University Press.

McBrien, Richard (1997) *Lives of the Popes: The Pontiffs From St Peter to John Paul II*, New York: Harper & Bros.

McCann, Justin (1937) *Saint Benedict*, London: Sheed & Ward.

McCarthy, Fiona (1962) *Byron: Life and Legend*, London: John Murray, 2002.

McCormick, Blaine and Davenport, David (2003) *Shepherd Leadership: Wisdom for Leaders From Psalm 23*, San Francisco: Jossey-Bass.

McCormick, Donald (1965) *Peddler of Death: The Life and Times of Sir Basil Zaharoff*, New York: Holt, Rinehart and Winston.

McCormick, John P. (1999) *Carl Schmitt's Critique of Liberalism*, Cambridge: Cambridge University Press.

McCrum, Michael (1989) *Thomas Arnold, Headmaster*, Oxford: Oxford University Press.

McElderry, Andrea (1976) *Shanghai Old-Style Banks (Ch'ien-chuang) 1800–1935*, Ann Arbor: Centre for Chinese Studies, University of Michigan.

McElheny, Victor K. (1998) *Insisting on the Impossible: The Life of Edwin Land*, New York: Perseus.

McElligott, Anthony (2009) *Weimar Germany*, Oxford: Oxford University Press.

McEwan, Gordon (2006) *The Incas: New Perspectives*, New York: W.W. Norton.

McFarquhar, Roderick and Schoenhals, Michael (2006) *Mao's Last Revolution*, Cambridge, MA: Harvard University Press.

McIntosh, Gary L. and Rima, Samuel D. (1998) *Overcoming the Dark Side of Leadership: The Paradox of Personal Dysfunction*, Ada: Baker Books.

McKendrick, Neil, Brewer, John and Plumb, J.H. (1982) *The Birth of a Consumer Society: The Commercialization of Eighteenth-Century England*, London: Europa.

McKirahan, Richard D. (1994) *Philosophy Before Socrates*, Indianapolis: Hackett.

McKitterick, Rosamond (1999) *The Frankish Kingdoms Under the Carolingians*, London: Longman.

McLaughlin, Paul (2007) *Anarchism and Authority: A Philosophical Introduction to Classical Anarchism*, Aldershot: Ashgate.

McLean, Iain (2000) *The Legend of Red Clydeside*, Edinburgh: John Donald.

McLynn, Frank (1988) *Charles Edward Stuart: A Tragedy in Many Acts*, London: Routledge.

McLynn, Frank (1998) *Napoleon: A Biography*, London: Pimlico.

McMillan, James F. (1991) *Napoleon III*, London: Routledge.

McMullin, Neil (1984) *Buddhism and the State in Sixteenth-Century Japan*, Princeton: Princeton University Press.

McPhee, Peter (2012) *Robespierre: A Revolutionary Life*, London: Yale University Press.

Meade, Edward S. (1901) 'The Genesis of the United States Steel Corporation', *Quarterly Journal of Economics* 15 (4): 517–50.

Mears, Mike (2009) *Leadership Elements: A Guide to Building Trust*, New York: iUniverse.

Mearsheimer, John J. (2013) *Why Leaders Lie: The Truth About Lying in International Politics*, Oxford: Oxford University Press.

Meierhenrich, Jens and Simons, Oliver (eds) (2017) *The Oxford Handbook of Carl Schmitt*, Oxford: Oxford University Press.

Meisner, Maurice (1999) *Mao's China and After*, New York: Free Press.

Mellet, Paul-Alexis (2006) *Et de sa bouche sortait une glaive; les Monarchomachs au XVIème siècle*, Geneva: Droz.

Melman, Yossi (1986) *The Master Terrorist: The True Story Behind Abu Nidal*, London: Sidgwick & Jackson.

Meltzer, Françoise (2001) *For Fear of the Fire: Joan of Arc and the Limits of Subjectivity*, Chicago: University of Chicago Press.

Melzer, Sara E. and Rabine, Leslie W. (eds) (1992) *Rebel Daughters: Women and the French Revolution*, Oxford: Oxford University Press.

Merriman, John M. (2016) *The Dynamite Club: How a Bombing in Fin-de-Siècle Paris Ignited the Age of Modern Terror*, London: Yale University Press.

Methley, Violet (1915) *Camille Desmoulins: A Biography*, New York: E.P. Dutton.

Mews, Constant J. (2005) *Abelard and Heloise*, Oxford: Oxford University Press.

Meyendorff, John (1983) *Byzantine Theology: Historical Trends and Doctrinal Themes*, New York: Fordham University Press.

Meyendorff, John (1997) *Byzantium and the Rise of Russia: A Study of Byzantino-Russian Relations in the Fourteenth Century*, New York: St Vladimir's Seminary Press.

Michel, Louise (1981) *The Red Virgin: Memoirs of Louise Michel*, trans. Bullitt Lowry and Elizabeth Ellington Gunter, Tuscaloosa: University of Alabama Press.

Miles, Barry (2004) *Frank Zappa*, London: Atlantic Books.

Milkis, Sidney M. and Nelson, Michael (2008) *The American Presidency: Origins and Development*, Washington, DC: CQ Press.

Mill, John Stuart (1985) *The Subjection of Women*, ed. Susan M. Okin, London: Yale University Press.

Mill, John Stuart (2015) *On Liberty, Utilitarianism and Other Essays*, Oxford: Oxford University Press.

Miller, Arthur G. (1986) *The Obedience Experiments: A Case Study of Controversy in Social Science*, New York: Praeger.

Miller, Douglas (2003) *Armies of the German Peasants War 1524–1526*, Oxford: Osprey.

Miller, Michael B. (1994) *The Bon Marché: Bourgeois Culture and the Department Store*, Princeton: Princeton University Press.

Miller, Stuart Creighton (1982) *Benevolent Assimilation: The American Conquest of the Philippines, 1899–1903*, New Haven: Yale University Press.

Miranda, Carlos R. (1990) *The Stroessner Era: Authoritarian Rule in Paraguay*, Boulder: Westview Press.

Mitchell, Allan (1965) *Revolution in Bavaria, 1918–1919: The Eisner Regime and the Soviet Republic*, Princeton: Princeton University Press.

Mitchell, Basil G. (1981) *The Justification of Religious Belief*, New York: Oxford University Press, 1981

Miyamoto Musashi (2005) *The Book of Five Rings: A Classic Text on the Japanese Way of the Sword*, trans. Thomas Cleary, Boston: Shambhala.

Moise, Edwin E. (2008) *Modern China*, 3rd edn, London: Routledge.

Mokyr, Joel (1999) *The Industrial Revolution: An Economic Perspective*, Boulder: Westview.

Mokyr, Joel (2011) *The Enlightened Economy: Britain and the Industrial Revolution, 1700–1850*, London: Penguin.

Montague, C. J. (1904) *Sixty Years in Waifdom, Or, the Ragged School Movement in English History*, London: Charles Murray.

Montgomery, Daniel B. (1991) *Fire in the Lotus: The Dynamic Buddhism of Nichiren*, London: Dai Gohonzon.

Moore, Karl and Lewis, David (2000) *Foundations of Corporate Empire: Is History Repeating Itself?* London: Financial Times-Prentice Hall.

Moorman, John (1968) *A History of the Franciscan Order From Its Origins to the Year 1517*, Oxford: Oxford University Press.

Moosa, Matti (2005) *The Maronites in History*, Piscataway: Gorgias.

More, Thomas (2012) *Utopia*, trans. Dominic Baker-Smith, London: Penguin.

Morgan, Edmund (1989) *Inventing the People: The Rise of Popular Sovereignty in England and America*, New York: W.W. Norton.

Morgan, Gareth (1986) *Images of Organization*, Newbury Park: Sage.

Morgan, Gwyn (2005) *69 AD: The Year of Four Emperors*, Oxford: Oxford University Press.

Morgan, Zachary R. (2014) *Legacy and the Lash: Race and Corporal Punishment in the Brazilian Navy and the Atlantic World*, Bloomington: Indiana University Press.

Morris, Richard (1988) *The Forging of the Union, 1781–1789*, New York: HarperCollins.

Mortier, Roland (1995) *Anacharsis Cloots ou L'utopie foudroyée*, Paris: Stock.

Mortimer, Geoff (2010) *Wallenstein: The Enigma of the Thirty Years War*, New York: Springer.

Mosse, George L. (1964) *The Crisis of German Ideology: Intellectual Origins of the Third Reich*, New York: Grosset & Dunlap.

Mouwad, R. J. (2009) *Les Maronites: Chrétiens du Liban*, Turnhout: Brepols.

Mouffe, Chantal (2000) *The Democratic Paradox*, New York: Verso.

Mousset, Sophie (2014) *Women's Rights and the French Revolution: A Biography of Olympe de Gouges*, London: Transaction.

Mulder, Mauk (1977) *The Daily Power Game*, Leiden: Martinus Nijhoff.

Mullett, Michael A. (2004) *Martin Luther*, London: Routledge.

Mundle, Rob (2010) *Bligh: Master Mariner*, Melbourne: Hachette.

Munoz, Paul Michael (2006) *Early Kingdoms of the Indonesian Archipelago and the Malay Peninsula*, Singapore: Editions Didier Millet.

Murphy, Rhoads (1998) *Ottoman Warfare, 1500–1700*, London: Routledge.

Murray, Dian (1987) *Pirates of the South China Coast, 1790–1810*, Stanford: Stanford University Press.

Nakane, Chie and Oishi, Shinzaburou (1990) *Tokugawa Japan: The Social and Economic Antecedents of Modern Japan*, Tokyo: University of Tokyo Press.

Nederman, Cary J. (1988) 'A Duty to Kill: John of Salisbury's Theory of Tyrannicide', *The Review of Politics* 50 (3): 365–89.

Neeley, Kathryn A. (2001) *Mary Somerville: Science, Illumination and the Human Mind*, Cambridge: Cambridge University Press.

Neil, Stephen (1960) *Anglicanism*, Harmondsworth: Penguin.

Nelson, Siobhan and Rafferty, Anne-Marie (eds) (2010) *Notes on Nightingale: The Influence and Legacy of a Nursing Icon*, Ithaca: Cornell University Press.

Nettlefield, Lara J. and Wagner, Sarah E. (2014) *Srebenica in the Aftermath of Genocide*, Cambridge: Cambridge University Press.

Neville, Peter (2002) *Mussolini*, London: Routledge.

Nevins, Allan (1953) *Study in Power: John D. Rockefeller, Industrialist and Philanthropist*, New York: Charles Scribner's Sons.

Nevins, Allan (1954) *Ford: The Man, The Times, The Company*, New York: Scribners.

Newman, Saul (ed.) (2011) *Max Stirner*, Basingstoke: Palgrave Macmillan.

Nguyen Khac Vien (1999) *Vietnam: A Long History*, Hanoi: The Gioi.

Nicholls, Angus (2006) *Goethe's Concept of the Daemonic: After the Ancients*, London: Camden House.

Nicholson, Helen (2001) *The Knights Templar: A New History*, Stroud: Sutton.

Nietzsche, Friedrich (1961) *Thus Spoke Zarathustra*, trans. R.J. Hollingdale, London: Penguin.

Nietzsche, Friedrich (1968) *The Will to Power*, ed. and trans. Walter Kaufman, London: Vintage.

Nightingale, Florence (1993) *Suggestions for Thought to the Searchers After Truth Among the Artisans of England*, New York: New York University Press.

Nixon, Jon (2018) *Rosa Luxemburg and the Struggle for Democratic Renewal*, Chicago: University of Chicago Press.

Nizam al-Mulk (1960) *The Book of Government or Rules for Kings*, trans. Hubert Darke, London: Routledge and Kegan Paul.

Normandin, Sebastian and Wolfe, Charles T. (eds) (2013) *Vitalism and the Scientific Image in Post-Enlightenment Life Science, 1800–2010*, New York: Springer.

North, Douglass C., Wallis, John Joseph and Weingast, Barry R. (1998) 'Violence and the Rise of Open Access Orders', *Journal of Democracy* 20 (1): 56–68.

Northrup, Linda S. (1998) *From Slave to Sultan: The Career of al-Mansur Qalawun and the Consolidation of Mamluk Rule in Egypt and Syria*, Stuttgart: Franz Steiner Verlag.

Norwich, John Julius (1970) *The Kingdom in the Sun, 1130–1194*, London: Longman.

Nugent, Paul (1996) *Big Men, Small Boys and Politics in Ghana: Power, Ideology and the Burden of History, 1982–1994*, London: Pinter.

O'Callaghan, Joseph F. (1975) *A History of Medieval Spain*, Ithaca: Cornell University Press.

O'Donnell, Pacho (1998) *Juana Azurduy*, Madrid: Planeta.

Offord, David (1986) *The Russian Revolutionary Movement in the 1880s*, Cambridge: Cambridge University Press.

Okey, Robin (2002) *The Habsburg Monarchy, c.1765–1918: From Enlightenment to Eclipse*, Basingstoke: Palgrave Macmillan.

Oliver, Jamie and Goodwin, Tony (2010) *How They Blew It: The CEOs and Entrepreneurs Behind Some of the World's Most Catastrophic Business Failures*, London: Kogan Page.

Olson, Mancur (1971) *The Logic of Collective Action: Public Goods and the Theory of Groups*, Cambridge, MA: Harvard University Press.

Olson, Mancur (2000) *Power and Prosperity: Outgrowing Communist and Capitalist Dictatorships*, Oxford: Oxford University Press.

O'Malley, John W. (1995) *The First Jesuits*, Cambridge, MA: Harvard University Press.

O'Neill, James (2018) *The Nine Years War, 1593–1603: O'Neill, Mountjoy and the Military Revolution*, Dublin: Four Courts Press.

Ono Kazuko (1988) 'The Red Lanterns and the Boxer Rebellion', in Ono Kazuko (ed.), *Chinese Women in a Century of Revolution, 1850–1950*, trans. Joshua A. Fogel, Stanford: Stanford University Press.

Origo, Iris (1957) *The Merchant of Prato*, London: Jonathan Cape.

Orwell, George (2004) *Nineteen Eighty-Four*, London: Penguin.

Osborne, Larry (2018) *Lead Like a Shepherd: The Secret to Leading Well*, Nashville: Thomas Nelson.

Osborne, Richard (2000) *Herbert von Karajan: A Life in Music*, Boston: Northeastern University Press.

Osgood, Josiah (2010) *Claudius Caesar: Image and Power in the Early Roman Empire*, Cambridge: Cambridge University Press.

Ostwald, Martin (2000) *Oligarchia: The Development of a Constitutional Form in Ancient Greece*, Stuttgart: Steiner Verlag.

Otis, Elwell (1878) *The Indian Question*, New York: Sheldon, 1878

Owen, Robert (1815) *Some Observations on the Effect of the Manufacturing System*, London.

Page, Joseph (1983) *Perón: A Biography*, New York: Random House.

Pai, Anant (2004) *J.R.D. Tata: The Quiet Conqueror*, Mumbai: India Book House.

Palenski, Ron (2015) *Rugby: A New Zealand History*, Auckland: Auckland University Press.

Palmer, Dave R. (1994) *1794: America, Its Army and the Birth of a Nation*, Novato: Presidio.

Pankhurst, Christabel (1959) *Unshackled: The Story of How We Won the Vote*, London: Hutchinson.

Pankhurst, Emmeline (1989) *My Own Story*, London: Virago.

Paoli, Letizia (2003) *Mafia Brotherhoods: Organized Crime, Italian Style*, Oxford: Oxford University Press.

Pappas, Nickolas (1995) *Plato and the Republic*, London: Routledge.

Parkes, Rosa and Haskins, James (1992) *Rosa Parkes: My Story*, New York: Scholastic Books.

Parkinson, R.B. (2002) *Poetry and Culture in Middle Kingdom Egypt: A Dark Side to Perfection*, London: Continuum.

Parry, Richard (2016) *The Bonnot Gang: The Story of the French Illegalists*, San Francisco: PM Press.

Pastor, Ludwig von (1902) *The History of the Popes*, London: Kegan Paul.

Patterson, Richard M. (1998) *Butch Cassidy: A Biography*, Lincoln: University of Nebraska Press.

Paxton, Robert (2004) *The Anatomy of Fascism*, New York: Knopf.

Payne, Stanley G. (1995) *A History of Fascism*, London: Routledge.

Payne, Stanley G. (1999) *Fascism in Spain, 1923–1977*, Madison: University of Wisconsin Press.

Payne, Stanley G. (2012) *The Spanish Civil War*, Cambridge: Cambridge University Press.

Pedroncini, Guy (1983) *Les mutineries de 1917*, Paris: Presse Universitaires de France.

Peers, William (1979) *The My Lai Inquiry*, New York: W.W. Norton.

Pendergrast, Mark (2000) *For God, Country and Coca-Cola*, New York: Basic Books.

Pennington, Reina (2003) *Amazons to Fighter Pilots: A Biographical Dictionary of Military Women*, Westport: Greenwood.

Pereira, Anthony (2005) *Political Injustice: Authoritarianism and the Rule of Law in Brazil, Chile and Argentina*, Pittsburgh: University of Pittsburgh Press.

Pernoud, Régine (1982) *Joan of Arc By Herself and Her Witnesses*, trans. Edward Hyams, New York: Scarborough House.

Perry, Elizabeth (2002) *Challenging the Mandate of Heaven: Social Protest and State Power in China*, Armonk: M.E. Sharpe.

Perry, Gina (2013) *Behind the Shock Machine: The Untold Story of the Notorious Milgram Psychology Experiments*, New York: The New Press.

Perry, Laurens B. (1978) *Juárez and Díaz: Machine Politics in Mexico*, DeKalb: Northern Illinois University Press.

Peters, Edward (1988) *Inquisition*, New York: The Free Press.

Peterson, Barbara Bennett (2000) *Notable Women of China: Shang Dynasty to the Early Twentieth Century*, Armonk: M.E. Sharpe.

Peterson, Willard J. (ed.) (2018) *The Cambridge History of China*, vol. 9, Cambridge: Cambridge University Press.

Petroff, Elizabeth Alvida (1994) *Body and Soul: Essays on Medieval Women and Mysticism*, Oxford: Oxford University Press.

Phelan, Craig (2000) *Grand Master Workman: Terence Powderly and the Knights of Labor*, Westport: Greenwich.

Philipp, Thomas and Haarmann, Ulrich (eds) (1998) *The Mamluks in Egyptian Politics and Society*, Cambridge: Cambridge University Press.

Phillips, Donald T. (2001) *Run to Win: Vince Lombardi on Coaching and Leadership*, New York: St Martin's.

Pierce, Michael David (2013) *The Overlord Effect: Emergent Leadership Style at the D-Day Invasion*, London: AuthorHouseUK.

Pietrusza, David (2011) *Rothstein: The Life, Times and Murder of the Criminal Genius Who Fixed the 1919 World Series*, New York: Basic Books.

Pincus, Steven (2009) *1688: The First Modern Revolution*, London: Yale University Press.

Piramal, Gita (1998) *Business Legends*, New Delhi: Penguin India.

Pisan, Christine de (1985) *The Treasure of the City of Ladies*, trans. Sarah Lawson, Harmondsworth: Penguin.

Pisan, Christine de (2008) *The Book of Peace*, University: Pennsylvania State University Press.

Pitkin, Hannah F. (1972) *The Concept of Representation*, Berkeley: University of California Press.

Pitt, Steve (2008) *To Stand and Fight Together: Richard Pierpoint and the Coloured Corps of Upper Canada*, Toronto: Dundurn Press.

Platt, Stephen R. (2012) *Autumn in the Heavenly Kingdom: China, the West and the Epic Story of the Taiping Civil War*, New York: Knopf.

Plokhy, Serhii (2014) *The Last Empire: The Final Days of the Soviet Union*, New York: Oneworld.

Plutarch (1914) *Lives of the Noble Greeks and Romans*, trans. Bernadette Perrin, London: Loeb Classical Library.

Poliakov, Leon (1996) *The Aryan Myth: A History of Racist and Nationalistic Idea in Europe*, New York: Barnes & Noble.

Pollard, Sidney (1965) *The Genesis of Modern Management*, London: Edward Arnold.

Pollard, Sidney (1981) *Peaceful Conquest: The Industrialization of Europe, 1760–1960*, Oxford: Oxford University Press.

Pontuso, James F. (2004) *Václav Havel: Civic Responsibility in the Postmodern Age*, New York: Rowman & Littlefield.

Pope, Dudley (2009) *The Black Ship*, Barnsley, Pen & Sword.

Popham, Peter (2016) *The Lady and the Generals: Aung Sang Suu Kyi and Burma's Struggle for Freedom*, London: Penguin.

Porter, Roy (2001) *The Enlightenment*, Basingstoke: Palgrave Macmillan.

Powell, Anton (2001) *Athens and Sparta: Constructing Greek Social and Political History From 478 BC*, London: Routledge.

Powell, Enoch (1977) *Joseph Chamberlain*, London: Thames & Hudson.

Power, Eileen (2010) *Medieval English Nunneries c. 1275–1525*, Cambridge: Cambridge University Press.

Power, Margaret (2008) *The Egalitarians, Human and Chimpanzee: An Anthropological View of Social Organization*, Cambridge: Cambridge University Press.

Prebble, John (1962) *Culloden*, London: Athenaeum.

Preston, Paul (1993) *Franco: A Biography*, London: HarperCollins.

Price, Alfred (2015) *The Last Year of the Luftwaffe*, London: Greenhill.

Price, Roger (2007) *The French Second Empire: An Anatomy of Political Power*, Cambridge: Cambridge University Press.

Price, S.R.F. (1986) *Rituals and Power: The Roman Imperial Cult in Asia Minor*, Cambridge: Cambridge University Press.

Procopius (1966) *The Secret History*, trans. G.A. Williamson, Harmondsworth: Penguin.

Proudhon, Pierre-Joseph (1923) *The General Idea of the Revolution in the Nineteenth Century*, trans. John Beverley Robinson, London: Freedom Press.

Proudhon, Pierre-Joseph (1994) *What Is Property? An Inquiry into the Principle of Right and Government*, Cambridge: Cambridge University Press.

Psellus, Michael (1979) *Fourteen Byzantine Rulers: The Chronographia of Michael Sellus*, ed. and trans. E.R.A. Sewter, Harmondsworth: Penguin.

Purkiss, Diane (2007) *The English Civil War: A People's History*, London: HarperCollins.

Purvis, June (2002) *Emmeline Pankhurst: A Biography*, London: Routledge.

Quinn, Malcolm (2005) *The Swastika: Constructing the Symbol*, London: Routledge.

Quirk, Robert E. (2009) *Fidel Castro*, New York: W.W. Norton, 1993; Fidel Castro, *My Life*, New York: Charles Scribner.

Raab, Selwyn (2005) *Five Families: The Rise, Decline and Resurgence of America's Most Powerful Mafia Empires*, New York: Thomas Dunne.

Rable, George C. (2007) *But There Was No Peace: The Role of Violence in the Politics of Reconstruction*, Athens: University of Georgia Press.

Radhakrishnan, S. (1993) *The Bhagavad-Gita*, London: HarperCollins.

Radice, Lisanne (1984) *Beatrice and Sidney Webb: Fabian Socialists*, London: Macmillan.

Rai, Raghu and Chawla, Navin (1996) *Faith and Compassion: The Life and Work of Mother Teresa*, Rockport, MA: Element Books.

Railton, George Scott (1912) *The Authoritative Life of General William Booth*, London: George H. Doran.

Ramírez, Sergio (1990) *Sandino: The Testimony of a Nicaraguan Patriot, 1921–34*, trans. Robert E. Conrad, Princeton: Princeton University Press.

Rand, Ayn (1957) *Atlas Shrugged*, New York: New American Library.

Rand, Ayn (1971) *The Fountainhead*, New York: New American Library.

Randal, Jonathan C. (1983) *The Tragedy of Lebanon: Christian Warlords, Israeli Adventurers and American Bunglers*, London: Chatto & Windus.

Ranum, Orest (1993) *The Fronde: A French Revolution, 1648–1652*, New York: W.W. Norton.

Rappaport, Helen (2008) *No Place for Ladies: The Untold Story of Women in the Crimean War*, London: Aurum.

Rasmussen, R. Kent (1977) *Mzilikazi of Ndbele*, London: Heinemann.

Rathenau, Walther (1921) *The New Society*, London: Williams & Norgate.

Ravelhofer, Barbara (2006) *The Early Stuart Masque: Dance, Costume and Music*, Oxford: Oxford University Press.

Ray, Debraj (1997) *Development Economics*, Princeton: Princeton University Press.

Redford, Donald B. (1984) *Akhenaten: The Heretic King*, Princeton: Princeton University Press.

Refuge, Eustache de (2008) *Treatise on the Court*, trans. J. Chris Cooper, Boca Raton, FL: Orgpax Publications.

Reich, Bernard (1990) *Political Leaders of the Contemporary Middle East and North Africa: A Biographical Dictionary*, Westport: Greenwood.

Reid, Charles (1961) *Thomas Beecham: An Independent Biography*, London: Victor Gollancz.

Reid, Robert (1989) *The Peterloo Massacre*, London: William Heinemann.

Reiss, Tom (2013) *The Black Count: Napoleon's Rival and the Real Count of Monte Cristo, General Alexandre Dumas*, London: Vintage.

Rex, Peter (2014) *The English Resistance: The Underground War Against the Normans*, Stroud: Amberley.

Rex, Robert (2002) *The Lollards: Social History in Perspective*, New York: Palgrave Macmillan.

Reyerson, Kathryn L. (2004) *Jacques Coeur: Entrepreneur and King's Bursar*, London: Pearson.

Reynolds, Susan (1994) *Fiefs and Vassals: The Medieval Evidence Reinterpreted*, Oxford: Oxford University Press.

Rhoads, Edward J.M. (2000) *Manchu and Han: Ethnic Relations and Political Power in Late Qing and Early Republican China, 1861–1928*, Seattle: University of Washington Press.

Riall, Lucy (2008) *Garibaldi: Invention of a Hero*, London: Yale University Press.

Riall, Lucy (2009) *Risorgimento: The History of Italy From Napoleon to Nation-State*, Basingstoke: Palgrave Macmillan.

Richardson, Glenn (2014) *The Field of the Cloth of Gold*, London: Yale University Press.

Ridley, Jasper (1976) *Garibaldi*, New York: Viking.

Ridley, Jasper (1983) *Statesman and Saint: Cardinal Wolsey, Sir Thomas More and the Politics of Henry VIII*, London: Viking.

Ridley, Jasper (1994) *Tito: A Biography*, London: Constable.

Riedel, Bruce (2008) *The Search for al-Qaeda: Its Leadership, Ideology, and Future*, Washington, DC: Brookings Institution Press.

Rigby, Nigel and van der Merwe, Pieter (2002) *Captain Cook in the Pacific*, London: National Maritime Museum.

Riggio, Ronald E., Chaleff, Ira and Lipman-Blumen, Jean (eds) (2008) *The Art of Followership: How Great Followers Create Great Leaders and Organizations*, New York: Wiley.

Riley-Smith, Jonathan (1999) *Hospitallers: The History of the Order of St John*, Oxford: Hambledon.

Rinpoche, Khandro (1999) *Blossoms of the Dharma: Living as a Buddhist Nun*, Berkeley: North Atlantic Books.

Ripley, William Z. (ed.) (1905) *Trusts, Pools and Corporations*, Boston: Ginn & Co.

Ripley, William Z. (1926) *From Main Street to Wall Street*, New York: Harper & Bros.

Ritter, E.A. (1978) *Shaka Zulu*, London: Penguin.

Roberts, Andrew (1995) *Eminent Churchillians*, London: Weidenfeld & Nicolson.

Roberts, Andrew (2015) *Napoleon the Great*, London: Penguin.

Robertson, Priscilla (1960) *Revolutions of 1848: A Social History*, New York: Harper & Row.

Robinson, Eric W. (2001) *The First Democracies: Early Popular Government Outside Athens*, Stuttgart: Steiner Verlag.

Robinson, Jane (2004) *Mary Seacole*, London: Constable.

Robinson, Jane (2010) *Bluestockings: The Remarkable Story of the First Women to Fight for Education*, London: Penguin.

Rodger, N.A.M. (1996) *The Wooden World: An Anatomy of the Georgian Navy*, New York: W.W. Norton.

Roe, Mark J. (1994) *Strong Managers, Weak Owners: The Political Roots of American Corporate Finance*, Princeton: Princeton University Press.

Roesch, Joseph E. (2006) *Boudica, Queen of the Iceni*, London: Robert Hale.

Rogel, Carole (1998) *The Breakup of Yugoslavia and the War in Bosnia*, Westport: Greenwood.

Rolland-Boulestreau, Anne (2015) *Les Colonnes Infernales: Violences et Guerres Civiles en Vendée Militaire (1794–1795)*, Paris: Fayard.

Rose, R.B. (1978) *Gracchus Babeuf: The First Revolutionary Communist*, London: Routledge.

Rose, Jonathan (2010) *The Intellectual Life of the British Working Classes*, London: Yale University Press.

Rose, June (1980) *Elizabeth Fry*, Basingstoke: Macmillan.

Ross, Michael (1975) *Banners of the King: The War of the Vendée, 1793–4*, New York: Hippocrene Books.

Rouse, W.H.D. (trans.) (1956) *Great Dialogues of Plato*, New York: Mentor.

Rousseau, Jean-Jacques (1998) *The Social Contract*, London: Wentworth.

Rowe, William L. (1964) *Religious Symbols and God: A Philosophical Study of Paul Tillich's Theology*, Chicago: University of Chicago Press.

Rowell, Stephen C. (1994) *Lithuania Ascending: A Pagan Empire Within Eastern Europe, 1295–1345*, Cambridge: Cambridge University Press.

Rowntree, Benjamin Seebohm (1921) *The Human Factor in Business: Experiments in Industrial Democracy*, London: Longmans Green.

Rowntree, Benjamin Seebohm (1922) 'Opening Address on the Increasing Claims Which Industrial Conditions Make Upon Administration', Rowntree Management Conference Paper, 21 September.

Rubenstein, Joshua (2011) *Leon Trotsky: A Revolutionary's Life*, London: Yale University Press.

Rubin, Barry M. and Rubin, Judith Colp (2003) *Yasir Arafat: A Political Biography*, Oxford: Oxford University Press.

Russell, Bertrand (2009) *Human Society in Ethics and Politics*, London: Routledge.

Ryan, L.V. (1963) *Roger Ascham*, Stanford: Stanford University Press.

Sablinsky, Walter (1976) *The Road to Bloody Sunday: Father Gapon and the St Petersburg Massacre of 1905*, Princeton: Princeton University Press.

Sachs, Harvey (1995) *Toscanini*, New York: Prima Press.

Sachs, Harvey and Solti, George (1997) *Solti on Solti*, London: Chatto and Windus.

Sageman, Marc (2004) *Understanding Terror Networks*, Philadelphia: University of Pennsylvania Press.

Salas, Elizabeth (1990) *Soldaderas in the Mexican Military: Myth and History*, Austin: University of Texas Press.

Salisbury, Harrison E. (1992) *The Last Emperors: China in the Era of Mao and Deng*, Boston: Little, Brown.

Salmond, Anne (2011) *Bligh: William Bligh in the South Seas*, Berkeley: University of California Press.

Salmonson, Jessica Amanda (1991) *The Encylopedia of Amazons*, London: Paragon.

Sampson, Anthony (1974) *The Sovereign State of ITT*, Greenwich: Fawcett Publications.

Sampson, Anthony (2011) *Mandela: The Authorised Biography*, London: HarperCollins.

Sanders, Lionel J. (1987) *Dionysos I of Syracuse and Greek Tyranny*, London: Croom Helm.

Sasaki Tsuneo (2002) 'Toyoda Sakichi', in Morgen Witzel (ed.), *Biographical Dictionary of Management*, Bristol: Thoemmes Press.

Saul, David (2003) *The Indian Mutiny*, London: Penguin.

Saunders, Francis Stonor (2004) *Hawkwood: The Diabolical Englishman*, London: Faber and Faber.

Saxo Grammaticus, *Gesta Danorum*, ed. Hilda Ellis Davidson and trans. Peter Fisher (1979) *The History of the Danes*, Woodbridge: D.S. Brewer.

Scarre, Chris (2012) *Chronicle of the Roman Emperors*, London: Thames and Hudson.

Schama, Simon (1989) *Citizens: A Chronicle of the French Revolution*, New York: Knopf.

Schmitt, Carl (1996) *The Concept of the Political*, trans. George D. Schwab, Chicago: University of Chicago Press.

Schoenberg, Robert J. (1985) *Geneen*, New York: W.W. Norton.

Schurr, Ruth (2006) *Fatal Purity: Robespierre and the French Revolution*, London: Metropolitan Books.

Scott, R.H.F. (1972) *Jean-Baptiste Lully*, London: Peter Owen.

Scott, Robert L. (1943) *God Is My Co-Pilot*, New York: Ballantine.

Schwieger, Peter (2014) *The Dalai Lama and the Emperor of China: A Political History of the Tibetan Institution of Reincarnation*, New York: Columbia University Press.

Scribner, R.W. (1987) *Popular Movements and Popular Culture in Reformation Germany*, London: Continuum.

Sebba, Anne (1997) *Mother Teresa: Beyond the Image*, New York: Doubleday.

Semler, Ricardo (2001) *Maverick! The Success Story Behind the World's Most Unusual Workplace*, New York: Random House.

Sen, Amartya (1983) *Poverty and Famines*, Oxford: Oxford University Press.

Sen, Amiya P. (2013) *Swami Vivekananda*, New Delhi: Oxford University Press.

Service, Robert (2000) *Lenin: A Biography*, London: Macmillan.

Service, Robert (2004) *Stalin: A Biography*, London: Macmillan.

Service, Robert (2009) *The Russian Revolution, 1900–1927*, Basingstoke: Palgrave Macmillan.

Shakapba, Tsepon W.D. (2010) *One Hundred Thousand Moons: An Advanced Political History of Tibet*, Leiden: Brill.

Shamir, Boas, Pillai, Rajnandini, Bligh, Michelle C. and Uhl-Bien, Mary (eds) (2007) *Follower-Centered Perspectives on Leadership*, Greenwich: Information Age Publishing.

Sharman, Lyon (2007) *Sun Yat-sen: His Life and Its Meaning*, Stanford: Stanford University Press.

Sharot, Tali (2012) *The Optimism Bias: A Tour of the Irrationally Positive Brain*, New York: Vintage.

Shastitko, Petr Mikhailovich and Shahani, Savitri (2006) *Nana Sahib: An Account of the People's Revolt in India, 1857–1859*; New Delhi: Shubhada-Saraswat.

Shaw, Christine (1996) *Julius II: The Warrior Pope*, Oxford: Blackwell.

Shaw, George Bernard (ed.) (1931) *Essays in Fabian Socialism*, London: Fabian Society.

Shaw, Ian (2003) *The Oxford History of Ancient Egypt*, Oxford: Oxford University Press.

Shirer, William L. (1960) *The Rise and Fall of the Third Reich*, New York: Simon & Schuster.

Short, Philip (2004) *Pol Pot: The History of a Nightmare*, London: John Murray.

Sillah, Mohammed Bassiru (1984) *African Coup d'Etat and the Revolutionary Mission of the Military: A Case Study of Jerry Rawlings in Ghanian Politics*, Lawrenceville, VA: Brunswick.

Sims, Richard (2001) *Japanese Political History Since the Meiji Renovation, 1869–2000*, New York: Palgrave Macmillan.

Simson, Otto G. von (1987) *Sacred Fortress: Byzantine Art and Statecraft in Ravenna*, Princeton: Princeton University Press.

Sinclair, Upton (2002) *The Jungle*, London: Penguin.

Singer, Charles (1959) *A History of Biology*, London: Abelard.

Singh, Harleen (2014) *The Rani of Jhansi: Gender, History and Fable in India*, Cambridge: Cambridge University Press.

Slowe, Peter (1983) *Manny Shinwell*, London: Pluto Press.

Smallwood, E.M. (2001) *The Jews Under Roman Rule, From Pompey to Diocletian: A Study in Political Relations*, Leiden: Brill.

Smart, Annie (2011) *Citoyennes: Women and the Ideal of Citizenship in Eighteenth-Century France*, Wilmington: University of Delaware Press.

Smiles, Samuel (1859) *Self-Help: With Illustrations of Character and Conduct*, London; repr. Oxford: Oxford University Press, 2002.

Smith, Colin (2012) *Carlos: Portrait of a Terrorist*, London: Penguin.

Smith, Denis Mack (1971) *Victor Emanuel, Cavour and the Risorgimento*, Oxford: Oxford University Press.

Smith, Denis Mack (1996) *Mazzini*, London: Yale University Press.

Smith, Douglas (2016) *Rasputin: Faith, Power and the Twilight of the Romanovs*, New York: Farrar, Straus and Giroux.

Smith, Ed (2012) *Luck: What It Means and Why It Matters*, London: Bloomsbury.

Smith, George David, Seaman, John T. and Witzel, Morgen (2011) *A History of the Firm*, New York: McKinsey.

Smith, Hannah (2006) *Georgian Monarchy: Politics and Culture, 1714–1760*, Cambridge: Cambridge University Press.

Smith, Harold L. (1998) *The British Women's Suffrage Campaign, 1866–1928*, London: Longman.

Smith, Jean Edward (2008) *FDR*, New York: Random House.

Smith, Jean Edward (2012) *Eisenhower in War and Peace*, New York: Random House.

Smith, Peter (2008) *An Introduction to the Baha'i Faith*, Cambridge: Cambridge University Press.

Smitten, Richard (1994) *The Godmother: The True Story of the Hunt for the Most Bloodthirsty Female Criminal of Our Time*, New York: Pocket.

Snow, Edgar (1937) *Red Star Over China*, London: Victor Gollancz.

Snyder, Timothy (2017) *On Tyranny: Twenty Lessons From the Twentieth Century*, New York: Tim Duggan.

Sosis, Richard and Alcorta, Candace (2003) 'Signaling, Solidarity and the Sacred: The Evolution of Religious Behavior', *Evolutionary Anthropology* 12 (6): 264–74.

Southern, Richard W. (1990) *St Anselm: A Portrait in a Landscape*, Cambridge: Cambridge University Press.

Spellberg, Denise (1994) *Politics, Gender and the Islamic Past: The Legend of A'isha bint Abi Bakr*, New York: Columbia University Press.

Spence, Jonathan (1996) *God's Chinese Son: The Taiping Heavenly Kingdom of Hong Xiuquan*, New York: W.W. Norton.

Spence, Jonathan (2013) *The Search for Modern China*, 3rd edn, New York: W.W. Norton.

Spencer, Herbert (2015) *Principles of Psychology*, London: Arkose Press.

Stafford, Pauline (2001) 'Political Women in Mercia, Eighth to Early Tenth Centuries', in Michelle P. Brown and Carol A. Farr (eds), *Mercia: An Anglo-Saxon Kingdom in Europe*, Leicester: Leicester University Press.

Stanton, Shelby L. (2007) *The Rise and Fall of an American Army: U.S. Ground Forces in Vietnam, 1963–1973*, New York: Random House.

Stark, Rodney and Bainbridge, William S. (1987) *The Future of Religion: Secularization, Revival and Cult Formation*, Berkeley: University of California Press.

Starkey, David (2002) *The Reign of Henry VIII: Personalities and Politics*, New York: Random House.

Staunton, Michael (2006) *Thomas Becket and His Biographers*, Woodbridge: Boydell.

Steeples, Douglas and Whitten, David O. (1998) *Democracy in Desperation: The Depression of 1893*, Westport: Greenwood.

Steiner, John Michael (1976) *Power Politics and Social Change in National Socialist Germany: A Process of Escalation Into Mass Destruction*, The Hague: Mouton.

Stellmann, Svenja (2013) *The Impact of Cultural Differences on the Daimler Chrysler Merger*, Munich: Grin Verlag.

Stern, Fritz (1961) *The Politics of Cultural Despair: A Study in the Rise of German Ideology*, Berkeley: University of California Press.

Stevens, John (1995) *The Sword of No-Sword: Life of the Master Warrior Tesshu*, Boston: Shambhala.

Stewart, David O. (2009) *Impeached: The Trial of Andrew Johnson and the Fight for Lincoln's Legacy*, New York: Simon & Schuster.

Stewart, Shirley (2014) *The World of Stephanie St Clair: An Entrepreneur, Race Woman and Outlaw in Early Twentieth Century Harlem*, New York: Peter Lange.

Stone, Rachel and West, Charles (eds) (2015) *Hincmar of Rheims: Life and Work*, Manchester: Manchester University Press.

Stones, E.L.G. (1957) 'The Folvilles of Ashley Folville, Leicestershire, and Their Associates in Crime, 1326–1347', *Transactions of the Royal Historical Society* 77: 119–36.

Strathern, Paul (2007) *Napoleon in Egypt: The Greatest Glory*, London: Jonathan Cape.

Strauss, Barry (2009) *The Spartacus War*, London: Simon & Schuster.

Straw, Carole E. (1988) *Gregory the Great: Perfection in Imperfection*, Berkeley: University of California Press.

Strayer, Joseph (1980) *The Reign of Philip the Fair*, Princeton: Princeton University Press.

Strouse, Jean (2000) *Morgan: American Financier*, New York: Harper Perennial.

Suetonius (1957) *The Twelve Caesars*, trans. Robert Graves, Harmondsworth: Penguin.

Sugawara Makoto (1985) *Lives of Master Swordsmen*, Tokyo: The East Publications.

Sugden, John (1998) *Tecumseh: A Life*, New York: Henry Holt.

Sugden, John (2004) *Nelson: A Dream of Glory*, London: Jonathan Cape.

Sulzberger, C.L. (1977) *The Fall of Eagles*, London: Hodder & Stoughton.

Summers, Mark Wahlgren (1997) *The Gilded Age, Or the Hazards of New Functions*, London: Pearson.

Sumner, William Graham (1883) *What Social Classes Owe to Each Other*, New York: Harper & Bros.

Sumption, Jonathan (1978) *The Albigensian Crusade*, London: Faber and Faber.

Sumption, Jonathan (1990) *The Hundred Years War*, vol. 1, *Trial by Battle*, London: Faber and Faber.

Suny, Ronald Grigor (1993) *Revenge of the Past: Nationalism, Revolution and the Collapse of the Soviet Union*, Stanford: Stanford University Press.

Suny, Ronald Grigor (1994) *The Making of the Georgian Nation*, Bloomington: Indiana University Press.

Sunzi (Sun Tzu) (1963) *The Art of War*, trans. L. Giles, ed. Samuel B. Griffiths, Oxford: Oxford University Press.

Sutherland, Gillian (2004) 'Clough, Anne Jemima', in *Oxford Dictionary of National Biography*, Oxford: Oxford University Press.

Sutton, Anne (2004) 'Whittington, Sir Richard', in *Oxford Dictionary of National Biography*, Oxford: Oxford University Press.

Szatmary, David P. (1980) *Shays's Rebellion: The Making of an Agrarian Insurrection*, Boston: University of Massachusetts Press.

Tacitus, P. Cornelius (1970) *The Agricola and the Germania*, trans. H. Mattingly, Harmondsworth: Penguin.

Tacitus, P. Cornelius (2009) *The Histories*, ed. Rhiannon Ash, trans. Kenneth Wellesley, London: Penguin.

Tai, Hue-Tam Ho (2001) *The Country of Memory: Remaking the Past in Late Socialist Vietnam*, Berkeley: University of California Press.

Taras, Daphne (2003) 'The North American Workplace: From Employee Representation to Employee Involvement', in Bruce E. Kaufman *et al.* (eds), *Industrial Relations to Human Resources and Beyond: The Evolving Process of Employee Relations Management*, Armonk: M.E. Sharpe.

Tarbell, Ida M. (1896) *Madame Roland: A Biographical Study*, New York: Charles Scribner's Sons.

Tarbell, Ida M. (1904) *The History of the Standard Oil Company*, New York: McClure's, 2 vols.

Tarbell, Ida M. (2003) *All in the Day's Work: An Autobiography*, Champaign: University of Illinois Press.

Taylor, Alan (2011) *The Civil War of 1812: American Citizens, British Subjects, Irish Rebels, Indian Allies*, New York: Vintage.

Taylor, Frederick Winslow (1911) *The Principles of Scientific Management*, New York: Harper & Bros.

Taylor, Kathleen (2006) *Brainwashing: The Science of Thought Control*, Oxford: Oxford University Press.

Taylor, Keith Weller (1983) *The Birth of Vietnam*, Berkeley: University of California Press.

Taylor, Larissa Juliet (2009) *The Virgin Warrior: The Life and Death of Joan of Arc*, New Haven: Yale University Press.

Taylor, Steve (2018) *The Fall: The Insanity of the Ego in Human History and the Dawning of a New Era*, London: Iff.

ter Haar, B.J. (1999) *The White Lotus Teachings in Chinese Religious History*, Honolulu: University of Hawaii Press.

Terrill, Ross (1999) *Mao: A Biography*, Stanford: Stanford University Press.

Thapar, Romila (2002) *The Penguin History of Early India From the Origins to* AD *1300*, London: Penguin.

The Chronicle of Novgorod, trans. Robert Mitchell and Nevill Forbes (1914), London: Camden Society.

'The Nigel Farage Story', *BBC News*, 4 July 2016, www.bbc.co.uk/news/uk-politics-36701855

Thomas, Emory M. (1979) *The Confederate Nation, 1861–1865*, New York: Harper & Row.

Thomas, Hugh (2003) *The Spanish Civil War*, London: Penguin.

Thomas, Robert David (1977) *The Man Who Would Be Perfect: John Humphrey Noyes and the Utopian Impulse*, Philadelphia: University of Pennsylvania Press.

Thompson, Augustine (2012) *Francis of Assisi: A New Biography*, Ithaca: Cornell University Press.

Thompson, David J. (1994) *Weavers of Dreams: The Origins of the Modern Cooperative Movement*, Berkeley: University of California Press.

Thompson, Dennis (1970) *The Democratic Citizen: Social Science and Democratic Theory in the Twentieth Century*, Cambridge: Cambridge University Press.

Thompson, Dorothy (1986) *The Chartists: Popular Politics in the Industrial Revolution*, Aldershot: Ashgate.

Thompson, E.P. (1955) *William Morris: Romantic to Revolutionary*, London: Lawrence & Wishart.

Thompson, E.P. (2013) *The Making of the English Working Class*, London: Penguin.

Thompson, Leigh L. (2008) *The Mind and Heart of the Negotiator*, New York: Pearson.

Thompson, Stephen E. (1999) 'Textual Sources, Old Kingdom', in Kathryn A. Bard (ed.), *Encyclopedia of the Archaeology of Ancient Egypt*, London: Routledge, pp. 801–2.

Thorslev, Peter L. (1962) *The Byronic Hero: Types and Prototypes*, Minneapolis: University of Minnesota Press.

Thorsson, Örnólfur (2001) *The Sagas of the Icelanders*, London: Penguin.

Thucydides (1954) *The Peleponnesian War*, trans. Rex Warner, Harmondsworth: Penguin.

Thupten, Jinpa (2013) *Self, Reality and Reason in Tibetan Philosophy: Tsongkhapa's Quest for the Middle Way*, London: Routledge.

Thurston, Robert W. (1998) *Life and Terror in Stalin's Russia, 1934–41*, London: Yale University Press.

Tierney, Brian (1964) *The Crisis of Church and State 1050–1300*, Toronto: University of Toronto Press.

Tilley, Nannie M. (1985) *The R.J. Reynolds Tobacco Company*, Chapel Hill: University of North Carolina Press.

Tillich, Paul (1957) *The Dynamics of Faith*, New York: Harper & Row.

Tillich, Paul (1964) *Theology of Culture*, Oxford: Oxford University Press.

Tillman, Helene (1980) *Pope Innocent III*, New York: Elsevier.

Tobias, Norman (2007) *Basil I, Founder of the Macedonian Dynasty: A Study of the Political and Military History of the Byzantine Empire in the Ninth Century*, Lewiston: Edwin Mellen.

Tocqueville, Alexis de (1964) *Democracy in America*, ed. Andrew Hacker, trans. Henry Reeve, New York: Washington Square Press.

Todd, Jack (2001) *Desertion: In the Time of Vietnam*, Boston: Houghton Mifflin.

Tolstoy, Leo (1957) *War and Peace*, trans. Rosemary Edmonds, London: Penguin.

Tong, James (2009) *Revenge of the Forbidden City: The Suppression of the Falungong in China, 1999–2008*, New York: Oxford University Press.

Tönnies, Ferdinand (2006) *Community and Civil Society*, trans. José Harris, Cambridge: Cambridge University Press.

Tourish, Dennis (2013) *The Dark Side of Transformational Leadership: A Critical Perspective*, London: Routledge.

Townshend, Charles (1996) *Easter 1916: The Irish Rebellion*, London: Penguin.

Trask, Kerry A. (2006) *Black Hawk: The Battle for the Heart of America*, New York: Holt.

Treuherz, Francis (1995) *Homeopathy in the Irish Potato Famine*, London: Samuel Press.

Trotter, Wilfred (1919) *Instincts of the Herd in Peace and War*, New York: Macmillan.

Trow, M. J. (2006) *Spartacus: The Man and the Myth*, Stroud: Sutton.

Tsang, Carol Richmond (2007) *War and Faith: Ikko Ikki in Late Muromachi Japan*, Cambridge, MA: Harvard University Press.

Tsomo, Karma Lekshe (2014) *Eminent Buddhist Women*, Albany: State University of New York Press.

Tsutsui, William M. (2009) *A Companion to Japanese History*, New York: John Wiley.

Tuchman, Barbara (1966) *The Proud Tower*, New York: Macmillan.

Turner, Mary (1982) *Slaves and Missionaries: The Disintegration of Jamaican Slave Society, 1787–1834*, Chiago: University of Illinois Press.

Turner, Michael (2002) *Pitt the Younger: A Life*, London: Continuum.

Turner, Victor (1975) *Dramas, Fields and Metaphors: Symbolic Action in Human Societies*, Ithaca: Cornell University Press.

Tyerman, Christopher (2006) *God's War: A New History of the Crusades*, London: Allen Lane.

Uglow, Jenny (2002) *The Lunar Men: The Friends Who Made the Future*, London: Faber and Faber.

Unger, Harlow (2000) *John Hancock: Merchant King and American Patriot*, Edison: Castle Books.

Unwin, George (1967) *Samuel Oldknow and the Arkwrights: The Industrial Revolution at Stockport and Marple*, Manchester: Manchester Univerity Press.

Urban, Hugh B. (2013) *The Church of Scientology: A History of a New Religion*, Princeton: Princeton University Press.

Urban, William (2000) *The Prussian Crusade*, Chicago: Lithuanian Research and Studies Center.

Ure, Andrew (1835) *Philosophy of Manufactures*, London: H.G. Bohn.

Urwick, Lyndall Fownes (1956) *The Golden Book of Management*, London: Newman Neame.

Urwick, Lyndall Fownes and Brech, E.F.L. (1949) *The Making of Scientific Management*, London: Management Publications Trust.

Utley, Robert M. (1993) *The Lance and the Shield: The Life and Times of Sitting Bull*, New York: Henry Holt.

Vale, Malcolm (1974) *Charles VII*, Berkeley: University of California Press.

van den Boorn, G.P.F. (1988) *The Duties of the Vizier*, London: Kegan Paul International.

van der Walt, Lucien and Schmidt, Michael (2009) *Black Flame: The Revolutionary Class Politics of Anarchism and Syndicalism*, Chico: AK Press.

van Gulik, Robert (2003) *Sexual Life in Ancient China*, Leiden: Brill.

van Henten, Jan Willem and ter Borg, Meerten T. (eds) (2010) *Power: Religion as a Social and Spiritual Force*, New York: Fordham University Press.

Varese, Federico (2005) *The Russian Mafia: Private Protection in a New Market Economy*, New York: Oxford University Press.

Varley, Paul H. (1980) *Jinno Shotoki: A Chronicle of Gods and Sovereigns*, New York: Columbia University Press.

Vasiliev, A.A. (1950) *Justin the First*, Cambridge, MA: Harvard University Press.

Veblen, Thorstein (1899) *The Theory of the Leisure Class: An Economic Study in the Evolution of Institutions*, New York: Macmillan.

Vermaseren, Maarten J. (1970) *Cybele and Attis: The Myth and the Cult*, trans. A.M.H. Lemmers, London: Thames and Hudson.

Vincent, Andrew (2009) *Modern Political Ideologies*, Chichester: John Wiley.

Virgil (2010) *The Aeneid*, trans. Robert Fagles, London: Penguin.

Viroli, Maurizio (2012) *As If God Existed: Religion and Liberty in the History of Italy*, Princeton: Princeton University Press.

Vlasic, Bill and Stertz, Bradley A. (2000) *Taken for a Ride: How Daimler-Benz Drove Off With Chrysler*, New York: John Wiley.

Voltaire (2007) 'The Different Races of Man', in *The Philosophy of History*, New York: Philosophical Library.

Wake, Nancy (1985) *Autobiography of the Woman the Gestapo Called the White Mouse*, Melbourne: Macmillan.

Wakeman, Frederic (1985) *The Great Enterprise: The Manchu Reconstruction of Imperial Order in Seventeenth-Century China*, Berkeley: University of California Press.

Walicki, Andrzej (1998) 'Pëtr Iakovlevich Chaadaev', in Edward Craig (ed.), *Routledge Encyclopedia of Philosophy*, London: Routledge, vol. 2, pp. 270–4.

Walker, Peter (2019) 'UK Poised to Embrace Authoritarianism, Warns Hansard Society', *The Guardian*, 8 April, www.theguardian.com/politics/2019/apr/08/uk-more-willing-embrace-authoritarianism-warn-hansard-audit-political-engagement.

Wallace-Hadrill, J.M. (1996) *The Barbarian West, 400–1000*, Oxford: Blackwell.

Walzer, Michael (2004) *Arguing About War*, London: Yale University Press.

Wang, Peng (2017) *The Chinese Mafia: Organised Crime, Corruption and Extra-Legal Protection*, Oxford: Oxford University Press.

Ward, Geoffrey C. and Burns, Ken (2017) *The Vietnam War: An Intimate History*, New York: Alfred A. Knopf.

Warner, Ezra J. (1964) *Generals in Blue: Lives of the Union Commanders*, Baton Rouge: Louisiana State University Press.

Warner, Marina (1972) *The Dragon Empress: Life and Times of Tz'u-Hsi, 1835–1908*, London: Weidenfeld and Nicolson.

Warnery, Emmanuel von (1798) *Remarks on Cavalry*, London; repr. London: Constable, 1997.

Warren, Kenneth (2001) *Big Steel: The First Century of the United States Steel Corporation, 1901–2001*, Pittsburgh: University of Pittsburgh Press.

Watson, Burton (1958) *Ssu-ma Ch'ien: Grand Historian of China*, New York: Columbia University Press.

Watson, Burton (1968) *The Complete Works of Chuang Tzu*, New York: Columbia University Press.

Watson, Burton (2003) *Han Fei Tzu: Basic Writings*, New York: Columbia University Press.

Watts, Frank (1921) *An Introduction to the Psychological Problems of Industry*, London: George Allen & Unwin.

Watts, Steven (2005) *The People's Tycoon: Henry Ford and the American Century*, New York: Alfred A. Knopf.

Waugh, Daniel (2007) *Egan's Rats: The Untold Story of the Gang That Ruled Prohibition-Era St Louis*, Nashville: Cumberland House.

Waugh, Steve (2005) *Out of My Comfort Zone*, Melbourne: Penguin Australia.

Waugh, William Templeton (1928) *James Wolfe, Man and Soldier*, Montréal: Carrier.

Wayman, Alex and Wayman, Hideko (1990) *The Lion's Roar of Queen Srimala*, New York: Columbia University Press.

Webb, Beatrice and Webb, Sidney (1897) *Industrial Democracy*, London: Longmans, Green.

Webb, Sidney (1917) *The Works Manager To-Day*, London: Longmans, Green & Co.

Webb, Sidney (1920) 'The New Spirit in Industry', Rowntree Management Conference Paper, 16 April, Balliol College, Oxford.

Weber, Max (1968) *The Religion of China: Confucianism and Taoism*, New York: The Free Press.

Weber, Max (2003) *The Protestant Ethic and the Spirit of Capitalism*, New York: Dover.

Weber, Max (2013) *Economy and Society*, Berkeley: University of California Press.

Weber, Max (2015) *Rationalism and Modern Society*, trans. Tony Waters and Dagmar Waters, New York: AIAA.

Wedgewood, C.V. (1963) *The Thirty Years War*, London: Jonathan Cape.

Weinstein, Donald (2011) *Savonarola: The Rise and Fall of a Renaissance Prophet*, New Haven: Yale University Press.

Weissensteiner, Friedrich (2007) *Elisabeth, die rote Erzerhogini*, Vienna: Piper Verlag.

Welch, Jack (2001) *Jack: Straight From the Gut*, New York: Warner Business Books.

Weller, Jac (1962) *Wellington in the Peninsula, 1808–1814*, New York: Modern Literary Editions.

West, Martin L. (ed. and trans.) (1978) *Hesiod: Works and Days*, Oxford: Oxford University Press.

Weston, Mark (1999) *Giants of Japan: The Lives of Japan's Greatest Men and Women*, Tokyo: Kodansha International.

Wetzler, Peter (1998) *Hirohito and War*, Honolulu, University of Hawaii Press.

Whaley, Joachim (2012) *Germany and the Holy Roman Empire*, Oxford: Oxford University Press.

Wheeler-Bennett, Sir John (1958) *King George VI: His Life and Reign*, London: Secker & Warburg.

Whisker, James B. (1999) *The Rise and Decline of the American Militia System*, Selinsgrove, PA: Susquehanna University Press.

White, Theodore H. (1975) *Breach of Faith: The Fall of Richard Nixon*, New York: Atheneum.

Whitehead, Thomas North (1936) *Leadership in a Free Society: A Study in Human Relations Based on an Analysis of Present-Day Industrial Relations*, Cambridge, MA: Harvard University Press.

Whitfield, Eileen (1997) *Pickford: The Woman Who Made Hollywood*, Lexington: University Press of Kentucky.

Whyte, William Foote and Whyte, Kathleen King (1989) *Making Mondragon: The Growth and Dynamics of the Worker Cooperative Complex*, Ithaca: ILR Press.

Wiarda, Howard J. (1968) *Dictatorship and Development: Methods of Control in Trujillo's Dominican Republic*, Gainesville: University Press of Florida.

Wickham, Chris (2015) *Medieval Rome: Stability and Crisis of a City, 900–1150*, Oxford: Oxford University Press.

Wigglesworth, Mark (2018) *The Silent Musician: Why Conducting Matters*, London: Faber and Faber.

Wilkinson, Richard (2017) *Louis XIV*, London: Routledge.

Williams, Charles (2001) *Konrad Adenauer: The Father of the New Germany*, Chichester: Wiley.

Williams, David H. (2003) *The Mythic Meanings of the Second Amendment: Taming Political Violence in a Constitutional Republic*, New Haven: Yale University Press.

Williams, Hettie V. (2010) 'Queen Nzinga (Nijinga Mbande)', in Leslie M. Alexander and Walter D. Rucker (eds), *Encyclopedia of African-American History*, Santa Barbara, CA: ABC-CLIO.

Williams, Stephen and Friell, Gerard (1995) *Theodosius: The Empire at Bay*, London: Yale University Press.

Willis, Brian (1992) *A Battle From the Start: The Life of Nathan Bedford Forrest*, New York: HarperCollins.

Wills, Garry (1999) *A Necessary Evil: A History of American Distrust of Government*, New York: Simon & Schuster.

Willson, David Harris (1963) *King James VI and I*, London: Jonathan Cape.

Wilsher, Peter, McIntyre, Donald and Jones, Michael (eds) (1985) *Strike: Thatcher, Scargill and the Miners*, London: Andre Deutsch.

Wilson, Charles (1954) *The History of Unilever: A Study in Economic Growth and Social Change*, London: Cassell.

Wilson, Derek (2007) *Out of the Storm: The Life and Legacy of Martin Luther*, London: Hutchinson.

Winters, Jeffrey A. (2011) *Oligarchy*, Cambridge: Cambridge University Press.

Winterton, Jonathan and Winterton, Ruth (1989) *Coal, Crisis and Conflict: The 1984–85 Miners' Strike in Yorkshire*, Manchester: Manchester University Press.

Witherington Cornioley, Pearl (2015) *Codename Pauline: Memoirs of a World War II Special Agent*, ed. Kathryn J. Attwood, Chicago: Chicago Review Press.

Witzel, Morgen (2009) *Tata: The Evolution of a Corporate Brand*, New Delhi: Penguin India.

Witzel, Morgen (2012) 'The Leadership Philosophy of Han Fei', *Asia Pacific Business Review* 18 (4): 1–15.

Witzel, Morgen (2015) *Managing for Success*, London: Bloomsbury.

Witzel, Morgen, Bolden, Richard and Linacre, Nigel (eds) (2016) *Leadership Paradoxes*, London: Routledge.

Wolbe, Eugen (1933) *Carmen Sylva: der Lebensweg einer einsamin Königin*, Leipzig: Kochler & Amelang.

Wolf, John B. (1968) *Louis XIV*, New York: W.W. Norton.

Wolf, Naomi (1991) *The Beauty Myth: How Images of Beauty are Used Against Women*, London: Vintage.

Wollstonecraft, Mary (2015) *A Vindication of the Rights of Woman*, London: Vintage.

Womack, John (1968) *Zapata and the Mexican Revolution*, New York: Vintage.

Wood, William (1915) *The Winning of Canada*, Toronto: Glasgow, Brook.

Woodcock, George (1962) *Anarchism: A History of Libertarian Ideas and Movements*, New York: World.

Woods, Frederick Adams (1913) *The Influence of Monarchs: Steps in a New Science of History*, New York: Macmillan.

Woodside, Alexander (1971) *Vietnam and the Chinese Model: A Comparative Study of Vietnamese and Chinese Government in the First Half of the Nineteenth Century*, Cambridge, MA: Harvard University Press.

Wormald, Patrick (1999) *The Making of English Law: King Alfred to the Twelfth Century*, Oxford: Blackwell.

Wright, Robert (1864) *The Life of Major-General James Wolfe*, London: Chapman and Hall.

Wright, Stuart A. (ed.) (1996) *Armageddon in Waco: Critical Perspectives on the Branch Dravidian Conflict*, Chicago: University of Chicago Press.

Wroe, Ann (2004) *Perkin: A Story of Deception*, London: Vintage.

Wu, John C.H. (trans.) (1990) *Tao Teh Ching (Daodejing)*, Boston and London: Shambhala.

X, Malcolm (2007) *Autobiography of Malcolm X*, New York: Penguin.

Xenophon (1914) *Cyropaedia: The Education of Cyrus*, ed. and trans. Walter Miller, London: William Heinemann.

Xenophon (2006) *Hiero the Tyrant and Other Treatises*, trans. Robin A.H. Waterfield, London: Penguin.

Yamamoto Tsunetomo (1979) *Hagakure: The Book of the Samurai*, trans. William Scott Wilson, Tokyo: Kodansha International.

Yorke, Barbara (2001) 'The Origins of Mercia', in Michelle P. Brown and Carol A. Farr (eds), *Mercia: An Anglo-Saxon Kingdom in Europe*, Leicester: Leicester University Press.

Young, Ernest P. (1977) *The Presidency of Yuan Shih-K'ai: Liberalism and Dictatorship in Early Republican China*, Ann Arbor: University of Michigan Press.

Young, Jeffrey S. (1987) *Steve Jobs: The Journey Is the Reward*, Glenview: Scott Foresman.

Zablocki, Benjamin and Robbins, Thomas (eds) (2001) *Misunderstanding Cults: The Search for Objectivity in a Controversial Field*, Toronto: University of Toronto Press.

Zbyněk, Zeman (1997) *The Life of Edvard Beneš*, Oxford: Clarendon.

Zimmermann, Matilde (2000) *Sandinista: Carlos Fonseca and the Nicaraguan Revolution*, Durham: Duke University Press.

Zola, Émile (2001) *Au Bonheur des Dames (The Ladies' Delight)*, London: Penguin.

Zola, Émile (2004) *Germinal*, trans. Roger Pearson, London: Penguin.

Zoroastrian Educational Institute (n.d.) 'The Life and Times of Sir Hormusjee Naorojee Mody, the Napoleon of the Rialto', www.zoroastrian.org.uk/vohuman/Article/Hormusjee%20 Naorojee%20Mody.htm.

Zoroastrian Educational Institute (n.d.) 'The Wadias of India: Then and Now', www.zoroastrian. org.uk/vohuman/Article/The%20Wadias%20of%20India.htm.

Zuckert, Michael P. (2002) *Launching Liberalism: On Lockean Political Philosophy*, Lawrence: University Press of Kansas.

INDEX